Gulf Air War
DEBRIEF

Gulf Air War
DEBRIEF

General Editor: Stan Morse

Aerospace Publishing London
Airtime Publishing USA

Published by
Aerospace Publishing Ltd
179 Dalling Road
London W6 0ES
England

Published under licence in USA and
Canada by
Airtime Publishing Inc.
10 Bay Street
Westport, CT 06880
USA

First published 1991. Reprinted 1992, 1993

Aerospace ISBN: 1 874023 14 X
Airtime ISBN: 1 880588 00 5

General Editor: Stan Morse
Associate Editors: Chris Bishop
                   David Donald
                   Jon Lake
Production Editor:
         Karen Leverington
Picture Researchers and
Editorial Assistants:
         Chris Dorrington
         Tim Senior
Design: Barry Savage
         Robert Hewson
Authors: Dr Alfred Price (Chronology)
         Bob Archer
         Chris Bishop
         David Donald
         Robert F. Dorr
         René J. Francilllon
         David C. Isby
         Paul Jackson
         Peter B. Mersky
         Lindsay Peacock
         Jeff Rankin-Lowe
         Tim Ripley
Artists: Chris Davey
         John Ridyard
         John Weal

Typesetting: SX Composing Ltd
Origination and printing by
   Imago Publishing Ltd
Printed in Singapore

World Air Power Journal is published
quarterly and provides an in-depth
analysis of contemporary military
aircraft and their worldwide operators.
Superbly produced and filled with
extensive colour photography, World
Air Power Journal is available by
subscription from:

UK, Europe and Commonwealth:
Aerospace Publishing Ltd
179 Dalling Road
London W6 0ES
England

USA and Canada:
Airtime Publishing Inc.
Subscription Dept
10 Bay Street
Westport, CT 06880
USA

Acknowledgements

Compiling the *Gulf Air War Debrief* has
been a most enjoyable and enlightening
task. We have been in contact with
hundreds of participating and
supporting service men and women,
and their help has been given most
positively and enthusiastically.

We list below just a few of those who
helped, but we extend our sincere
thanks to all who have contributed to
the project, especially base and unit
commanders and Public Affairs staff
who made it possible for us to
interview their aircrews and
photograph their aircraft.

Dan Abrams
Lt Cdr Gil Bever, USMC
Lt Col Jim Brechwald, USAF
Tom Brewer
Lt Jeff Bright, USNR HCS-5
Rick Burgess
Lt Col William Bryan, US Army
2nd Lt Don Collins, USAF Public Affairs
Maj Keith Coln, USAF
Lt Don Collins, USAF
Capt Jay Creekbaum, USAF
Maj Rick DeChaineau, USMC Public Affairs
Capt Rhory R. Draeger, USAF
Col Roy Duhon, Jr, USAF
Chester O. Falkenhainer, USN
Lt Cdr Mark Fox, USN
Stew Fisher
Michael A. France
Lt Mike Frankel, USAF
Lt Col Michael R. Gannon, USAF Public Affairs
Capt Andrew D. Hall, USMC
Maj Sally Hiatt, ANG
Capt Dan Holzrichter, USMC
Lt Col Barry E. Horne, USAF
Mike Hricko
Lt Devon Jones, USN
Cdr Neil Kinnear, USN
Lt Col Don Kline, USAF
Col Romeo Lalonde, CF
Lt Col Leif Larsen, USMC
John Leenhouts
Col Tom Lennon, USAF
William Lipski
Chris Madden
Capt Charles Magill, USMC
Lt John Marks, USAF
Bob Mehal
Mike Menth
Jerry Merritt
R. J. Mills, Jr
RAdm Riley D. Mixson, USN
Lt Nick Mongillo, USN
Charles Moore
Pat Mulvaney
Maj Dick Naumann, ANG
Lt Cdr David Parsons, USN
Maj Steve Pomeroy, USMC
Art Randolph
Capt Darrel Robertson, USAF
Russ Robison
Brian C. Rogers
Russ Sanborn
Col Lawrence Santerini, ANG
Capt Anthony Schiavi, USAF
Capt Mark Schulte, USMC
Rudy Schwanda
Capt John Sizemore, ANG
Lt Tamara Skipton, USMC
Lt Larry Slade, USN
Joe Small
Lt Col Derle M. Snyder, USAF
Capt Eric Solomonson, USAF
Bill Strandberg
Capt Steve Tate, USAF
Sgt Guy Volb, USAF
Bob Wetzel
Wally van Winkle

CONTENTS

PRELUDE TO CONFLICT

Saddam Hussein rose rapidly through Ba'ath party ranks after the nationalists took power in Iraq in the 1960s, and he ruthlessly used the secret police to eliminate rivals. He achieved complete control of the country before the Iran-Iraq war, and the Gulf war of 1991 can almost solely be blamed on his lust for domination of the Arab world.

Iraq received both Western and Soviet support during the long, bloody war with neighbouring Iran. During the 1980s, Iraq's air force took delivery of large numbers of modern warplanes. These included high-performance Mirage F1s bought from France (right) and small numbers of the Soviet-built MiG-29 'Fulcrum' (below), possibly the most agile fighter in the world.

16 July to 1 August 1990

The causes of the Gulf conflict date from 1961, when the British government formally granted independence to the Sheikdom of Kuwait. The Iraqi government never recognized the new state, and during the next three decades it laid claim to parts of the territory as its own. At the end of the 1980s, with the ending of the war with Iran, the Iraqi government felt strong enough militarily to press its claims for Kuwaiti territory with greater determination than in the past. The Iraqi army had long-standing plans for an invasion of the Sheikdom; these were now updated and the units earmarked for the operation were brought to an increased state of readiness. At the same time, the Iraqi foreign ministry began a diplomatic offensive against Kuwait and other small states along the Persian Gulf.

16 July 1990 Tariq Aziz, the Iraqi foreign minister, accused Kuwait and the United Arab Emirates of 'direct aggression' against Iraq, and complained of encroachment on Iraqi oil supplies. He also complained that excessive oil production by these states was holding down the price of the commodity on the international market, and doing great harm to Iraq.

to page 8

Right: Although Iraq's air force was quoted as being up to 700-aircraft strong in the months leading to war, less than half that number were viable front-line aircraft. Even so, with 350 machines of the capacity of the MiG-29 and Mirage F1, the Iraqi air force was large, outnumbering the air forces of the Gulf co-operation council.

Left: Backbone of the Iraqi air force's tactical strength was its force of Soviet-built MiG-23s, in both fighter and fighter-bomber variants. These were no match for the latest Western designs, but they remained effective warplanes able to deliver chemical weapons.

Above: Iraq had ambitions to control the Middle East, and the Iraqi armed forces were the largest in the region. Iraqi air power was well served with force multipliers like tankers (Ilyushin Il-76 'Midas' shown here) and airborne early warning aircraft in service.

Iraq Air Force

In the West, surprisingly little detailed information is available from published sources on the Iraqi air force. Accounts differ on the numbers of each aircraft type it had purchased, and should be treated with caution.

When the fighting started, the Iraqi air force possessed about 550 fighters, bombers, attack and reconnaissance aircraft in front-line service. That made the Iraqi air force the sixth largest in the world, with about three quarters as many of these aircraft as the Royal Air Force. The air force had a strength of about 40,000 personnel, commanded by Lieutenant General Hamid Sha'aben al Khazraji. Its front-line units were split between two major formations, the Air Defense Command and the Air Support Command.

The Air Defense Command was responsible for the defense of strategic targets and airfields. It controlled all fighter-interceptor units, and those air force personnel manning air surveillance radars and the control and reporting system. The Air Defense Command also controlled those army units equipped with surface-to-air missiles and anti-aircraft artillery assigned to the defense of strategic targets.

When the war started, the Air Defense Command possessed about three Adnan airborne warning and control aircraft, Ilyushin Il-76 'Candid' transports modified by the Iraqis to carry the French Thomson-CSF Tigre radar. The capability of these aircraft is not known, since they played no part at all in the air fighting. It should be borne in mind, however, that a sophisticated technological base is necessary to build an effective AWACS aircraft. There is a lot more to it than simply fitting a long-range radar into a long-range aircraft – witness the problems that dogged the British Nimrod project. One Adnan was severely damaged on the ground, two more flew to Iran. The move undoubtedly saved them from destruction, since these high-priority targets were too large to fit in the hardened aircraft shelters.

Historically, the Iraqi air force has devoted little attention to the difficult problem of sorting friendly from hostile aircraft in confused tactical situations. During the Iran-Iraq war, the Iraqi army set up an AAA and SAM umbrella over its ground forces, and the gunners and missile crews considered all approaching aircraft as hostile. Reportedly, the system worked to such effect that more than three-quarters of Iraqi aircraft losses during that war were hit by 'friendly' forces. Given the almost complete breakdown of the Iraqi command and control system during the recent war, it is almost certain that those Iraqi combat aircraft that did get into the air faced almost continual harassment from both sides until they were back on the ground.

The so-called Air Support Command of the Iraqi air force was responsible for supporting land operations by the army and operations at sea by the navy. This command controlled the operations of all fighter-bomber, bomber and dedicated reconnaissance units within the air force, and of air strikes on enemy shipping.

Some mystery surrounds the most effective type in the Air Support Command inventory, the swing-wing Sukhoi Su-24 'Fencer', which is in the same class as the Panavia Tornado. Had the Iraqi air force attempted to launch an air strike with chemical weapons against Israel or on coalition forces, these were the aircraft most likely to have succeeded. Because of this, airfields thought to operate Su-24s were priority targets, as were those hardened shelters thought likely to house them. According to published sources, at the beginning of the war the Iraqis possessed between 10 and 16 of these aircraft, which it acquired shortly before the declaration of the trade embargo. Only after the end of the war did the Iraqi government reveal that it had sent 24 Su-24s to Iran. Either the allies were singularly unsuccessful in destroying these aircraft on the ground, or else the number of Su-24s purchased by the Iraqis had been underestimated by a factor of about three. It is not known if the Iraqi Su-24 force had its full complement of support equipment and weaponry, or if sufficient crews had completed their conversion training, before the Soviet government stopped further supplies and military assistance.

The Iraqi air force's transport force comprised some 45 aircraft, most of them of Soviet origin. Government-owned aircraft of Iraqi Airways were also available for military use. Its fleet comprised two Boeing 707s, six Boeing 727s, two Boeing 737s and four Boeing 747s, plus about 40 An 12, An 24 and Ilyushin Il-76 ('Candid') freighters.

The units equipped with Scud and other types of surface-to-surface missiles belonged to the Iraqi army, as did all battlefield helicopter units.

The business of keeping serviceable the mixed bag of available aircraft must have presented nightmares for the Iraqi maintenance crews. Combat aircraft had been bought from the USSR, France and China, and it would seem that the size of each purchase depended on how much money was available at the time. The air force operated no fewer than 15 different types of fixed-wing combat aircraft. Except for the Mirage F1, the MiG-21 'Fishbed' and the Sukhoi 'Fitter' (in its Su-7, Su-20 and Su-22 versions), in each case less than 60 examples of each had been procured. In the case of the helicopters, the situation was even worse, and between them the army and the air force operated no fewer than 16 types. No information is available on

Prelude to Conflict

from page 6

18 July The Iraqi government repeated its long-standing claim to part of Kuwaiti territory. It stated that Kuwait had 'stolen' $2.4 billion worth of crude oil from wells in the disputed area, and demanded reparations.

19 July The Kuwaiti foreign minister requested that the Arab League set up a body to arbitrate on the dispute between his country and Iraq.

23 July Saudi Arabia placed its armed forces on alert.

25 July During a meeting with President Saddam Hussein to discuss the disagreement between Kuwait and Iraq, the US ambassador to Iraq, April Glaspie, informed Saddam that the USA had "no opinion" on disputes between Arab nations.

26 July OPEC agreed on production and export quotas for all 13 of its members, at prices below those demanded by Iraq.

27 July Under pressure from Iraq, OPEC raised the target price of oil to $21 per barrel. The US Senate voted to end farm credits to Iraq, and formally prohibited the transfer of military technology.

31 July Western intelligence sources reported signs that Iraqi troops were massing close to the border with Kuwait. Initially, this was regarded merely as a show of force, intended to push the Kuwaiti government into accepting the Iraqi demands.

1 August The Kuwaiti government rejected Iraqi claims to the islands of Bubiyan and Warba at the head of the Gulf, and refused an Iraqi demand that it should write off the $5.5 billion in loans it had made to Iraq during the Iraq-Iran war. The Iraqi representatives walked out of the talks.

to page 10

Above: If Saddam's air force had a major weakness, it lay in the caliber of its pilots. Saddam always feared the possibility of a military coup. In order to forestall such a move he kept a tight rein on the armed forces, which stifled the initiative and skill so vital to air operations.

Below: The Sukhoi Su-20 is a tough, well-proven attack fighter, but it is no match for advanced Western aircraft. Such weakness can be overcome in part by combat-tested pilots, but in spite of a decade of war with Iran the Iraqis offered no opposition to the superbly trained coalition pilots.

used capital punishment to encourage greater enterprise from his air commanders. Following the successful Israeli air attack on the Osirak nuclear reactor in 1981, it is said that he ordered the shooting of all pilots above the rank of captain in the fighter squadron that had been tasked with the defense of the installation.

A total of 148 Iraqi aircraft were flown to Iran during the conflict, including 115 combat aircraft.

Fate decreed that the Iraqi air force should learn, in the most brutal way possible, how far the weaponry and the techniques of air warfare have advanced in the West during the past two decades. Rather like an undertrained flyweight boxer making a challenge for the world heavyweight championship, it was forced into a fight that was far outside its league. Blind faith in one's cause is all very well, but it is no substitute for having technically advanced aircraft and weaponry, and sound training and tactics. The air units opposing Iraq were the best equipped and the best trained from the best of the air forces in the coalition. As is often the case when true professionals tackle a job, they make it seem easy. Certainly the business of knocking out the Iraqi air force was made to look much easier than it would have been had less-capable forces been used. Perhaps the most appropriate epitaph for that unfortunate force was that given by General Tony Peak, Chief of Staff of the US Air Force: "I think they [the Iraqi air force] did rather well under the circumstances. They're a pretty good outfit. They happened to be the second-best air force in the fracas. Having the second-best air force is like having the second-best poker hand – it's often the best strategy to fold early. I think they folded early."

The only option open to the Iraqis was hit-and-run raids using aircraft like the Mirage F1, but allied airborne radar superiority ensured their failure.

serviceability rates in the Iraqi air force, nor is there any hard evidence on the extent to which it was reduced by the international trade embargo. Almost certainly, however, several aircraft of each type had to be cannibalized in order to provide spares for the remainder of the fleet.

According to an unconfirmed report from a press agency in the USSR on 25 January, the commanders of the Iraqi air force

and the Air Defense Command had both been shot for failing to perform their duties with sufficient zeal and determination. No hard news is available on the fate of Lieutenant General Hamid Sha'aben al Khazraji, but it is known that General Mezahim Sa'ib assumed command of the Iraqi air force at about this time. According to another unconfirmed report, on at least one previous occasion President Saddam Hussein had

Dr A.P.

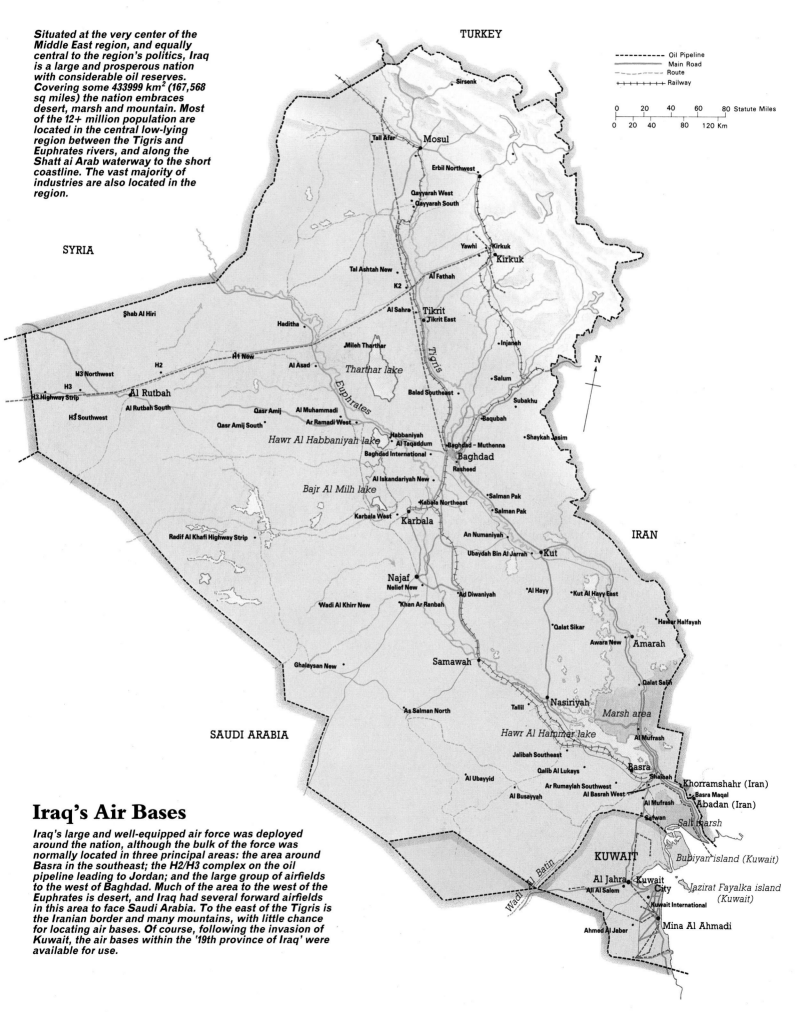

Situated at the very center of the Middle East region, and equally central to the region's politics, Iraq is a large and prosperous nation with considerable oil reserves. Covering some 433999 km² (167,568 sq miles) the nation embraces desert, marsh and mountain. Most of the 12+ million population are located in the central low-lying region between the Tigris and Euphrates rivers, and along the Shatt ai Arab waterway to the short coastline. The vast majority of industries are also located in the region.

Iraq's Air Bases

Iraq's large and well-equipped air force was deployed around the nation, although the bulk of the force was normally located in three principal areas: the area around Basra in the southeast; the H2/H3 complex on the oil pipeline leading to Jordan; and the large group of airfields to the west of Baghdad. Much of the area to the west of the Euphrates is desert, and Iraq had several forward airfields in this area to face Saudi Arabia. To the east of the Tigris is the Iranian border and many mountains, with little chance for locating air bases. Of course, following the invasion of Kuwait, the air bases within the '19th province of Iraq' were available for use.

INVASION

2 August 1990 to 16 January 1991

During the early morning darkness of 2 August, the Iraqi army implemented its long-standing plans for the invasion of Kuwait. The operation was well planned, and particular attention was paid to security and the need to conceal the troop movements from foreign reconnaissance satellites and radio listening services. This attention to detail paid off, and Western intelligence services became aware of the Iraqi intention to invade Kuwait only hours before the leading units crossed the border. Even then, it was thought that the Iraqi troops would do no more than seize the disputed territory and oilfields in the border areas and halt their offensive once these had been secured.

2 August Beginning at 2:00 a.m. local time, troops of the Iraqi Republican Guard crossed the border and advanced rapidly to seize the whole of Kuwait. Isolated pockets of Kuwaiti troops fought the invaders, but they were unable to prevent Iraqi armored units from reaching their objectives. The Emir of Kuwait, Sheikh Jaber Ahmed al-Sabah, and large numbers of his countrymen fled to Saudi Arabia.

Later in the day the United Nations Security Council met in emergency session and passed Resolution 660, which condemned the invasion and demanded an immediate and unconditional withdrawal of Iraqi forces. The Resolution also called for immediate negotiations between the Kuwaiti and Iraqi governments aimed at resolving their differences.

The US government froze Iraqi and Kuwaiti assets and banned trade with the two countries.

At the time of the invasion of Kuwait, the US Navy Middle East Group comprised the command ship USS *La Salle* and a small force of supporting cruisers, destroyers and frigates that had been on exercises in the Persian Gulf. The carrier USS *Independence* and her battle group were just outside the area, in the Gulf of Oman.

6 August King Fahd of Saudi Arabia invited foreign governments to send troops to his country, to safeguard it from possible attack by Iraq. President Bush immediately ordered the implementation of Operation Desert Shield, a large-scale transfer of military forces to the area. Thus began the largest military airlift the world has ever seen, starting with the movement of the 82nd Airborne Division and its equipment to Saudi Arabia.

The Security Council passed Resolution 661, which imposed sweeping sanctions on trade between Iraq and Kuwait and the rest of the world.

In Kuwait, Iraqi troops began to round up nationals from Western nations. President Saddam Hussein announced that his country's occupation of Kuwait was 'irreversible'.

to page 12

A video film smuggled out of occupied Kuwait shows Saladin armored cars of the Kuwaiti army putting up a brief resistance to the invading Iraqis on the morning of 2 August 1991.

Below, main picture: Smoke rises over Kuwait City as Saddam Hussein's army pours in. Few people expected the Iraqi dictator's threats made against Kuwait in preceding weeks to be turned to action, so the events of 2 August came as a shock, especially for those nations to whom Kuwaiti oil was a vital resource.

Below: US President George Bush led the international community's condemnation of the Iraqi invasion, ordering US Central Command to prepare for intervention and offering US protection to Saudi Arabia, whose huge oilfields, the most important in the world, lay just south of Kuwait.

Above: Kuwait's air force was fairly well trained, operating a mix of modern combat aircraft like the Dassault Mirage F1, and older but still effective designs like the McDonnell Douglas A-4 Skyhawk. Without bases, however, the best air force in the world is useless, and Kuwait's airfields were overrun along with the rest of the country. Some pilots managed to escape to Saudi Arabia, where they flew as the Free Kuwait air force.

Left, inset: Iraqi troops in Kuwait move past a poster celebrating Saddam Hussein's triumph in the Iran-Iraq war. The fact that the eight-year struggle had been an ignominious failure was beside the point; the dictator's personality cult allowed no truth but his own. The people of Kuwait were soon to discover the brutal reality behind Saddam's rule.

Below: A Royal Saudi Air Force F-15 patrols the Persian Gulf. The prospect of Saddam Hussein in control of Kuwait's oil was bad enough to the rest of the world; there could be worse to come, however. The massive Iraqi army, the fourth largest in the world, was now on the Saudi Arabian border, within striking distance of the world's largest oil reserves. If Saddam gained control of the Saudi oil fields he could hold the world to ransom. All that stood between the Iraqi dictator and that terrible prospect were the Saudi armed forces: well equipped, well trained, but no match for the Iraqi war machine.

Invasion

from page 10

7 August In a powerful display of the strategic mobility of air power, 48 F-15C/D Eagles of the 1st Tactical Fighter Wing took off from Langley AFB, Virginia, and flew non-stop to Dhahran in Saudi Arabia. It was the longest operational fighter deployment in history, and the flights took between 14 and 17 hours with six or seven in-flight refuelings along the route. In the days to follow more than 20 further squadrons of US combat aircraft would fly direct from their bases in the USA and Europe to airfields in Saudi Arabia.

8 August The Iraqi government announced that it had annexed Kuwait, and that it was now its country's 19th province.

The British government announced its intention to send naval and air force units to the Gulf area.

The aircraft carrier USS *Dwight D. Eisenhower* and her battle group arrived in the Red Sea.

A force of USAF B-52 bombers commenced a deployment to Diego Garcia in the Indian Ocean.

9 August The Security Council passed Resolution 662, which declared Iraq's annexation of Kuwait to be null and void.

The British government announced that it was to dispatch a squadron of Tornado F.Mk 3s and one of Jaguar attack aircraft to the Persian Gulf. The move of British forces into the area was code-named Operation Granby.

10 August President Saddam Hussein called on Moslems all over the world to join in a 'Holy War' against the USA and Israel, should any attempt be made to dislodge his forces from Kuwait. He also ordered the closure of all foreign embassies in Kuwait.

A squadron of Royal Air Force Tornado F.Mk 3 interceptors arrived at Dhahran.

11 August The advance contingent of 500 Egyptian troops landed in Saudi Arabia. A squadron of Royal Air Force Jaguar attack aircraft arrived at Thumrait in Oman. *to page 16*

Top: Following Iraq's invasion of Kuwait, Iraqi ground forces began massing on the border with Saudi Arabia. As a result, air-defense elements very quickly started to maintain combat air patrols with interceptors such as this No. 29 Squadron RSAF Tornado ADV, until such time as reinforcements arrived from the USA and the UK.

Above: Kuwaiti air bases were obvious targets for air strikes by the Iraqi air force during the brief battle to subjugate Kuwait. Nevertheless, a reasonable number of Kuwaiti air force warplanes did escape to Saudi Arabia, assisting eventually in the liberation of their homeland. These are Mirage F1s with 'Free Kuwait' titles.

Below: August 1990 was a particularly anxious time for Saudi Arabia, which could do little but watch and wait as Iraq gathered its forces. These Saudi F-15C Eagle pilots, preparing for an air-defense sortie, can claim some credit for forestalling further Iraqi aggression.

F-15 Eagles Have Landed

Lieutenant Colonel Don Kline, 27th TFS/1st TFW, F-15C Eagle

"I command the oldest fighter squadron in the US Air Force, part of the 1st Tactical Fighter Wing based at Langley, Virginia.

"We saw the Iraqis massing their troops on the Kuwait border at the end of July, and we were brought up to a higher alert state. That's just the standard act that we go through in a crisis. Everybody here thought, 'No, it's not going to happen.' We were told that we might be going to Saudi Arabia in the first week in August. The 71st TFS had been alerted a day or so earlier.

"With the invasion on 2 August it was kind of up and down: Are we going? Are we not going? We started putting three tanks on our jets on Friday 3 August. On the Monday evening, 6 August, we'd headed home for the day when we were recalled. We came back in and they said, 'You're really going, here's the times, push it up.'

"It was all very professional. Nobody ever wants a war, but at the same time the guys were ecstatic. It was, 'Hey, we got a mission, we got a job to do!'

"The 71st was the first to go, on 7 August, with 24 F-15s. We followed on 8 August, with another 24. We flew non-stop from Langley in four cells of six. It took 14, maybe 14½ hours. I think we refueled nine times, which broke the monotony somewhat. We didn't need to, but every time you cross the water you have to stay up on fuel in case you have to divert.

We also had to have fuel on board when we arrived.

"The problem was, we had no idea what to expect. The intelligence we had was very sketchy. We knew a bit about Iraqi air defenses from various sources, but we really didn't know if Saddam was going to push on in to try to roll over Saudi Arabia.

"We had a contingency plan to fight our way in if necessary, landing some of our aircraft and keeping others up in the air until we could get some of the earlier ones turned around. We were fully armed, with four AIM-7s, four AIM-9s, and the gun was loaded out. Our six-aircraft cells were about 30 minutes apart. When we got there, depending on the threat, we could have landed two of four aircraft. When the next group arrived, we would then land the two still flying, and so on until the last cell arrived after about 90 minutes. By that time some of the first ones down would have been ready to get into the air again. In any case, the 71st had been there for a day, so if it was ugly we'd have had some help.

"Fortunately, we didn't have to fight our way in when we arrived at Dhahran. It was a little confused, though. Folks knew we were coming, but we still had to get everybody out of the jets and bedded down. My squadron had one day down on 10 August to recover, and then we were up and operational on 11 August."

Above: Loaded with a full 'bag' of AIM-7 Sparrow and AIM-9 Sidewinder air-to-air missiles, an F-15C Eagle of the 1st Tactical Fighter Wing receives fuel in flight from a Washington ANG KC-135E.

Above: Seen soon after arrival in Saudi Arabia, this 1st TFW F-15C was one of 48 Eagles that moved from Langley AFB, Virginia, in the early days of the crisis as Desert Shield reinforcement moved into top gear. It had still to receive a full armament load but would shortly take its turn to patrol the skies.

Left: Carrying the 1st TFW's 'FF' tail code letters on its fin, an F-15C Eagle roasts in the hot desert sun between combat air patrols. At this time, confidence was high that the diplomats would find a solution but nobody was taking chances, and a full weapons load was always carried when 'CAPping' over Saudi Arabia.

RAF Deployment

Rapid and unequivocal condemnation from the United Kingdom of Iraq's aggression was backed by resolute action in the form of forces dispatched to the Gulf states. This was set in motion on 9 August 1990 when Defence Secretary Tom King announced the forthcoming dispatch of a dozen each of Tornado F.Mk 3 air-defence fighters and Jaguar GR.Mk 1A attack aircraft. The Tornados were already halfway deployed in Cyprus for an armament practice camp, while the Jaguars were kept constantly prepared for short-notice overseas basing – albeit in the slightly less arid climes of Denmark and Norway.

Operation Granby (its uninspiring title chosen for no other reason than that it was next in the list of code names) was placed in the hands of the AOC-in-C RAF Strike Command, ACM Sir Patrick Hine, who effected control from an underground bunker at High Wycombe, 30 miles west of London. In Riyadh, Saudi Arabia, AVM R. A. F. 'Sandy' Wilson was the first Air Commander British Forces Arabian Peninsula, his role passing to AVM W. J. 'Bill' Wratten on 17 November. Initially in charge of all UK forces, the Air Commander became deputy to the army's senior officer when Lieutenant General Sir Peter de la Billière was appointed Commander of British Forces Middle East on 1 November.

The UK build-up at Dhahran, Saudi Arabia, began on 9 August with the arrival of administrative and support personnel by TriStar, the Tornado squadron flying in two days later. As with all other RAF detachments to the Gulf, it comprised aircraft and personnel from more than one unit, so for the sake of convenience was dubbed No. 5 (Composite) Squadron because the senior officer was that unit's CO. As the build-up progressed, the composition of detachments became increasingly complex.

Tornado F.Mk 3s took turns with USAF and RSAF aircraft to mount four-hour combat air patrols of the Saudi border, refueled by VC10 tankers which had arrived at Bahrain on 27 August. VC10s also brought the Jaguar squadron to Thumrait, Oman, on 13 August, then moved to Seeb on 29 August. Oman was some distance from the potential scene of action, so the Jaguars moved up to Bahrain between 7 and 10 October. At Seeb, Oman, a detachment of three Nimrod MR.Mk 2s was installed from 13 August to co-operate with coalition warships in what became a naval blockade of Iraq.

A boost to the offensive force was revealed by the MoD on 23 August when plans for dispatch of a Tornado GR.Mk 1 squadron became known. Leaving Germany on 27 August, the composite unit made for Bahrain, its aircraft wearing the desert pink camouflage first applied to the Jaguars. Tasked with anti-airfield attacks, the Tornado suffered serviceability problems related to heat and sand, although these were eventually overcome. A second squadron, announced on 14 September, left for Bahrain in two elements on 19 and 26 September, but transferred to Tabuk, in the far west of Saudi Arabia, on 8 October.

The Tornado GR.Mk 1 deployment extended to a third squadron shortly before Desert Storm erupted. Following an announcement of 30 December, the new unit was installed at Dhahran between 2 and 4 January. Six more reconnaissance-tasked Tornado GR.Mk 1As were received at Dhahran between 14 and 16 January. Offensive forces then totalled some 50 Tornados and a dozen Jaguars at three bases.

On 1 November, a Hercules detachment formed at Riyadh to function as an in-theater distribution network for the mass of supplies being flown to the Gulf by Hercules, VC10 C.Mk 1s and TriStars. Its complement gradually increased by mid-January to nine aircraft, including two supplied and crewed by the Royal New Zealand Air Force. Hercules were given protective coatings on their undersides for flights into semi-prepared strips – a technique which would be required to evacuate casualties of any land war. Further back, in the United Arab Emirates, five more Hercules were installed for undercover operations.

VC10 K.Mks 2 and 3 tankers were augmented from 14 December when Victor K.Mk 2s began arriving at Bahrain. Six Victors were in place by 16 January, by which time the VC10 force had been concentrated at Riyadh for a month with all nine aircraft in-theater.

Reinforcement of the RAF contingent after the start of hostilities concerned laser-guided bombing capability. A dozen Buccaneer S.Mk 2Bs equipped with Pave Spike laser-designation pods were installed at Bahrain, where the first pair of aircraft arrived on 26 January. While they provided guidance for bombs dropped by the Bahrain and Dhahran Tornados, the Tabuk-based bombers relied on a pair of TIALD pods carried beneath two of five specially equipped Tornado GR.Mk 1s which began arriving on 6 February. In total, therefore, some 62 Tornado GR.Mk 1/1A aircraft took part in Desert Storm, from a total of at least 87 painted in the desert pink camouflage.

P.J.

Below: Tornados of No. 5 Squadron set off on patrol. The RAF's Tornados had little difficulty deploying to the Gulf. Since the Saudis fly the same type of aircraft, a complete support and maintenance infrastructure was already in place.

Left: Tornado F.Mk 3 interceptors from the Royal Air Force's No. 11 Squadron refuel from a No. 216 Squadron TriStar K.Mk 1 tanker on their way to the Gulf. No. 11 Squadron was on its way at the end of August as part of the measured allied response to Iraq's invasion of Kuwait. It was to replace No. 5 Squadron, which had arrived in Saudi Arabia on very short notice on 10 August.

Below: Tornado GR.Mk 1 interdictor strike aircraft of No. 14 Squadron are repainted in desert colors at RAF Brüggen before leaving for the Gulf. Tornado GR.Mk 1 bombers were deployed into the region from the end of August, their presence representing a significant upgrade in Royal Air Force capability from a purely defensive force into one that could hit hard at Iraqi targets.

Above: RAF Jaguars were among the first British attack aircraft to be deployed to the Gulf. They formed part of the initial British response to Iraqi aggression, known as Operation Granby, which was announced on 9 August. The Jaguar force was based at Muharraq, Bahrain, after a period during which it operated from Thumrait, Oman.

Right: A Tornado GR.Mk 1 interdictor/strike aircraft lands at Muharraq after the deployment flight from Europe. Muharraq was one of the major British Gulf war air bases, being the temporary home for Tornado bombers, Jaguar GR.Mk 1A attack aircraft, Buccaneer S.Mk 2B bombers and Victor K.Mk 2 tankers.

Above: Almost as quick as the US to react to the crisis in the Gulf was Great Britain, which code-named its contribution to the reinforcement effort Operation Granby. Initial deployments began moving to the theater in early August, with Tornado F.Mk 3 interceptors among the first RAF warplanes to arrive. Within hours of landing, they had joined US and Saudi interceptors in maintaining a constant combat air patrol.

from page 12

12 August President Saddam Hussein launched his so-called 'peace initiative', in which he offered to consider ending the occupation of Kuwait if Israel and Syria ended the occupation of territories in Palestine and Lebanon, respectively. Although the offer was dismissed out of hand in the West, it would be repeated several times in the months to follow.

The 4th Tactical Fighter Wing, with F-15E Strike Eagle aircraft, began to deploy from Seymour Johnson AFB to Saudi Arabia.

Three Royal Air Force Nimrod maritime patrol aircraft arrived at Seeb in Oman, to assist naval units engaged in the blockade of Iraqi seaborne trade.

13 August Under Operation *Salamandre*, the French aircraft-carrier *Clemenceau* left for Djibouti on the Red Sea carrying 42 anti-tank helicopters of the French Force d'Action Rapide being deployed to the Gulf area. Belgium and the Netherlands also agreed to send naval forces.

15 August In a move aimed at securing his eastern flank, President Saddam Hussein ordered his troops to withdraw from all Iranian territory captured during the 1980-1988 war. At the same time the remaining Iranian prisoners held in his country were repatriated.

The carrier USS *John F. Kennedy* and her battle group left Norfolk, Virginia, to join the US forces deployed for Desert Shield.

17 August In an attempt to deter air attacks on his country by the USA and other nations, President Saddam Hussein announced that Western nationals, including women and children, were to be placed at possible targets as 'human shields'.

The build-up of US forces in Saudi Arabia was now moving ahead rapidly, with an average of about 120 strategic transport aircraft sorties arriving in the area each day.

18 August The Security Council passed Resolution 664, which demanded that the Iraqi government allow all foreign nationals in Iraq and Kuwait to leave these countries. The Resolution also demanded that the Iraqi government rescind its order for the closing of foreign diplomatic missions in Kuwait.

21 August In a glare of publicity, the first of 22 F-117A 'Stealth Fighters' of the 415th TFS, 37th TFW, arrived in Saudi Arabia.

23 August US Defense Secretary Dick Cheney ordered the first of a series of Reserve and National Guard forces to be called to active duty, beginning with three C-141B StarLifter and two C-5A Galaxy squadrons.

to page 30

F-15 in Defense

Lieutenant Colonel Don Kline, 27th TFS, F-15C Eagle

Above: A 1st Tactical Fighter Wing F-15C Eagle gets airborne with the aid of afterburner and heads towards its designated CAP station. USAF, Saudi and British fighters had responsibility for providing air cover throughout the build-up. Missions were generally of two to three hours' duration, with little excitement to relieve the tedium of endless orbits.

Above, inset: Radar-guided Sparrow and infra-red homing Sidewinder air-to-air missiles are readied for loading on an Eagle by a team of USAF munitions specialists.

Below: In addition to airborne CAPs, some Eagles were also held at a high state of readiness on the ground to counter any attempt at incursion by Iraqi warplanes.

Above: Auxiliary fuel tanks were part of the standard 'fit' during Desert Shield and were helpful in allowing the Eagle to remain airborne for up to three hours at a time when 'CAPping'. However, it was still necessary to use inflight refueling, with longer sorties usually involving three visits to the tanker which could be either a KC-135 Stratotanker or a KC-10 Extender.

Right: Saudi and American Boeing E-3 Sentry AWACS (Airborne Warning And Control System) aircraft augmented ground radars and maintained a constant watch on Iraqi skies, directing friendly fighters towards threats during Desert Shield when each side was intent on assessing the opponent's capability.

"Our initial mission was simply to secure the air base at Dhahran, working anything from 40 to 60 miles out. We didn't have to cover a full circle, since any enemy aircraft would be coming from the north. We went up with Saudi AWACS, which were used to working with F-15s, and they showed us the airspace. They'd worked out a good grid structure, where people would know exactly in which area they would have responsibility. The Saudis are very smart with that kind of stuff, and they did an excellent job of initial preparation.

"With two squadrons the 1st Tactical Fighter Wing could keep fighters in the air 24 hours a day, and we did, right up to the outbreak of the war.

"Early on, we played a kind of cat and mouse game with the Iraqis. They were testing us, wanted to see what we had. Obviously, we were kind of interested in what they had, too. They'd come right up to the border, even came south of the line a couple of times before turning and running. We were locking onto them from long distance, their ECM gear was reacting, and I guess convinced them that they weren't going to be able to arrive undetected. A lot of flights made contact, although the closest we got was to within about 17 miles. The couple of times we ran close to the border, we broke off. The Rules of Engagement were strict: don't cross the border, don't go into Kuwait. Our discipline is pretty good, and to my knowledge there was no penetration of Iraqi or Kuwaiti airspace.

"Patrols were usually four-ship missions lasting two or three hours. We'd tank three times. You could make it on two, but that would mean you were low at the end, and you wouldn't have enough gas to commit to combat if it came to that. From about October on we used four ships because that's our fighting entity. Before that the schedulers used to send us up in two ships, but we wanted to fly four-ship patrols. It was difficult for the schedulers, but they managed it, and it paid dividends in combat. Once the war kicked off, you had been flying with these guys so long you knew how they would react in the air, knew you could depend on them.

"In the first weeks, we would mount our CAPs by doing 10-mile racetrack patterns, with left-hand turns. We'd stick to medium altitudes, between 15,000 and 25,000 ft. Everybody got tired of turning left, and doing it so often, so after a while we lengthened them out to about 20 miles, and from there we moved on to do some figure eights and other maneuvers. It was just something to keep your mind occupied while you were up there.

"But there's more to being a fighter pilot than patrolling. Towards the end of September, we finally figured out that we couldn't just keep doing CAPs. Fighter pilot skills are so time perishable that we thought our abilities were being eroded. We began to do continuation training when we weren't on patrol. It was BFM (Basic Fighter Maneuvers). One-on-one, just to hone the skills and get the *g*s back on your body. From there we went into ACT (Air Combat Tactics). If I took a four-ship up it would be two against two, with one pair acting as adversaries. Now we're not going to know the enemy's tactics as well as they are going to know their tactics, so there was a lot of simulation and even guesswork.

"We worked on the old Vietnam trick, where you've got a high leader and a low trailer coming from different azimuths. The high guy will lead you around, and just when you've locked on the low guy comes up and pops you. We also worked a lot at getting the F-15 slowed down enough to ID a low-speed contact, the defector type of thing.

"We were mainly practicing against the Mirage F1, although the F-15's not a good F1 simulator, because we'd heard that their best pilots were in them. Then there was the MiG-29 'Fulcrum', and we knew that they had a lot of MiG-23s and stuff like that, so we would try to work out tactics against those types of aircraft.

"It was a real coalition effort. We would work with different units, F-16s, Tornados, F-15Es, Mirage 2000s and French Mirage F1s. There were some large package exercises which really paid dividends later on. We would concentrate on straight air-to-air combat. Sometimes we'd be the escort. Other times they'd say, 'OK, let's just flip-flop it. F-15s, we'd like you to be the adversaries today.' There'd be a simulated attack by the package on an airfield, and whoever played the adversary would try to mass his forces on the spot. It also gave us a chance to work out some of our own air base defense scenarios, although we never needed them. Of course, when the war started it was a whole different thing."

Kennedy Goes to War

Left: The crest of the USS John F. Kennedy, *the last conventionally-powered aircraft-carrier to be built for the US Navy and one of the first warships to be sent to the Gulf.*

Right, inset: Sparrow, Sidewinder and Phoenix air-to-air missiles are all compatible with the F-14 Tomcat, which is generally thought to be the finest interceptor in the West. Seen on the Kennedy's crowded flight deck, this example is from fighter squadron VF-32.

Left: F-14A Tomcat interceptors are visible in the background as a pilot assigned to the Kennedy's Carrier Air Wing Three walks out to his aircraft for a training mission during the transit from Norfolk, Virginia, to the Red Sea.

Right: Corrosion control is a key aspect of operation at sea, for the salt-laden atmosphere poses many problems. Here, Kennedy deck crew get busy with brushes and water as they clean a Tomcat from VF-32.

By the time Rear Admiral Riley D. Mixson left building T-26 on Friday 10 August 1990, he knew his battle group had a tough time ahead of it. Vice Admiral John K. Ready, Commander, US Naval Air Force, Atlantic Fleet, had told Rear Admiral Mixson to bring his air wing commander and the captain of the carrier USS *John F. Kennedy* (CV-67) to his office. During that meeting, Vice Admiral Ready told his subordinates that they would have five days to put to sea in support of Operation Desert Shield, the huge build-up of allied forces in the Persian Gulf.

It was an incredibly difficult order. The carrier had recently downloaded most of her moveable equipment, ordnance and supplies,

and had also begun deactivating her flight deck catapults and arresting gear in preparation for a yard period.

The squadrons of *Kennedy*'s air wing, CVW-3, were in a fairly relaxed status. Indeed, her two A-7 squadrons, VA-46 and VA-72, were looking forward to beginning the transition to the F/A-18 Hornet and had sent half of their respective aircraft away.

Within that five-day period, however, the entire *Kennedy* battle group, Carrier Group (CARGRU) 2, turned to. While the other support ships and surface combatants went through their own hurry-up preparations, *Kennedy* onloaded ordnance and supplies, and got her cats and arresting gear working again.

Everyone understood the need to push hard, and on Wednesday 15 August, *Kennedy* departed her home port of Norfolk, Virginia. The most pressing need was to requalify the several hundred aircrewmen of CVW-3 in carrier launching and landings, 'CQ' in naval aviation's abbreviated parlance. That afternoon, *Kennedy* began CVW-3's CQ, slowly working her way east towards Gibraltar and the Mediterranean. Rear Admiral Mixson described the first few hectic days of *Kennedy*'s deployment.

"All I had time to do was to get my philosophy on the street. My philosophy about winning, about the things we had to prepare for in short order, and essentially what most battle group commanders would say. I placed importance on being able to talk to each other, to link with each other, to tell it like it is, and on working out all of our weak areas as soon as we can. Rather than just going on a Mediterranean deployment, I felt we would be at war within 20-30

days. As it turned out, we had longer than that. So we had more time to bring everyone together and work them as a team.

"Another aspect of that was the team play. Then, of course, we had to crank out all of these operating orders. My staff did most of that, although I designated some warfare commanders to put out their particular OPTASKs.

"For the air wing, we had to plan not only the usual contingencies for the Med, but also for the Iraqi theater of operations, once we got the targets. It was a very intense time. I don't remember a time in my Navy career that was as intense as the 60 days beginning with that Friday when AIRLANT told us we were going to sea to when we arrived in the Red Sea, and some time after that.

"We left on 15 August, and our schedule was in flux. *Saratoga* had preceded us and had relieved *Eisenhower* in the Red Sea. *Ike* was only in the Red Sea for 19 days. We went over amid discussions about

Invasion

Left: Sailing from Norfolk on 15 August, the Kennedy battle group headed east across the Atlantic and moved hurriedly through the Mediterranean Sea, where it spent about two weeks exercising before receiving orders in September to pass through the Suez Canal.

Below: The ship silhouette on this SH-3H Sea King relates to the naval blockade and records a vessel that was inspected by helicopters from the USS John F. Kennedy.

Left: Deck crew look on as a VF-32 F-14A Tomcat hurtles down the catapult track during flight operations on the USS John F. Kennedy. With a total of four catapults, JFK is able to launch a wave of about 20 aircraft in barely five minutes, with a typical package being made up of a mix of Tomcat fighter and Intruder and Corsair attack aircraft, plus Vikings and Sea Kings for anti-submarine warfare and Prowlers for electronic warfare. Airborne early warning cover is furnished by the Hawkeye.

whether we would stay in the Med for a while for Display Determination – an exercise for which *Saratoga* had really planned in depth as part of her normal peacetime deployment. A lot of schedules were juggled to even out the time in the Red Sea for *Saratoga* and *Kennedy*.

"As it happened, when we got to the Mediterranean and did a few warm-up exercises, we were ordered to go down into the Red Sea and relieve *Saratoga*. So, we were in the Med for about 12-13 days."

For the next half-year, sailing in company with USS *Saratoga* (CV-60) and her battle group, and her air wing, CVW-17, *Kennedy* patrolled the Middle East. She made Alexandria, Egypt, in early September, then went through the Suez Canal to take up station in the Red Sea, which would become her post for the next seven months. During this transit time, the men of the *Kennedy* battle group practiced such things as chemical-warfare defense, ongoing flight operations and CQs. Of course, they also looked after their ships and their complex systems.

Even the flight deck's often overlooked, but important, nonskid surfaces received attention. The rapid deployment had postponed the planned refurbishment of the flight deck's surface. Only when the ship went up to the Mediterranean in November for a few port calls – a short diversion from her Red Sea patrol – did Captain John Warren's flight deck crew get the chance to reapply new anti-skid surface to the huge flight deck. Workers from the Philadelphia Navy Shipyard volunteered to come out to Izmir, Turkey, to help with the resurfacing. At Antalaya, the carrier's ship's company refurbished more of the anti-skid surface. Finally, 30,000 sq ft of the carrier's approximately 177,000-sq-ft flight deck had been renewed; not all, barely one sixth of the total area, but at least the vital areas were reconditioned.

Captain Warren was the Air Boss on *Kennedy*, and thus, was head of the carrier's air department.

"The daily operations, unfortunately, made it hard to maintain the catapults and arresting gear, as well as to keep the flight deck petroleum-free. Without a good nonskid base, the deck became very hazardous. The flight deck and hangar deck crews quickly became experts on how to maneuver aircraft under these conditions, especially during a launch. They kept the planes in a sequence so that we didn't have too many aircraft in the same spot,

allowing room for a plane to slide.

"The pilots also got proficient at knowing when to apply the brakes, as well as how to apply power when needed so they wouldn't slide.

"The environment in the Red Sea was pretty close to optimum. We had practically no pitching decks, but this became a detriment because there was little or no rain to wash the decks. After we washed the deck with a good industrial soap, we rinsed it off with salt water, but we didn't get all the residue off. Rain would have helped, but there is virtually no rain in the Red Sea."

CVW-3 kept practicing and patrolling. While F-14A Tomcats of VF-14 and VF-32 roamed the skies of western and northern Saudi Arabia, their crews familiarizing themselves with the terrain, the A-6s of VA-75 and A-7s from the two recalled light attack squadrons flew strike after practice strike.

Rear Admiral Mixson, a combat-experienced A-7 pilot with more than 250 missions in Vietnam, knew what training his air wing needed and what he needed to get through to most of his young aviators going into combat for the first time.

"A Navy intelligence team came out and gave us a good, in-depth analysis of the Iraqis' organization, including their air force. I think their assessment was pretty doggone accurate. In any assessment, you weigh such things as their hardware, how their pilots are trained, in this case, how Iraq's air force performed in the Iran-Iraq war, as well as their defenses such as SAMs and AAA. That governed our tactics, especially at the start.

"No one could predict, however, that the Iraqi air force would refuse to fly after the first couple of days, and certainly after the first two weeks. We never saw any aggressiveness from their pilots – and this was forecast, by the way. I think if anything, we over-estimated the Iraqi air force in general, and in particular, the pilot in the cockpit.

"I got the few combat-experienced aviators in *Kennedy* and we brainstormed about the smart things we did in Vietnam and the dumb things, too. I put out general guidance to all three air wings in *America*, *Saratoga* and *Kennedy* on things the crews should be aware of as they went into combat. Things like making sure

Above: While in the vicinity of Cyprus, the Kennedy's *two Tomcat squadrons took time out to engage RAF Phantoms in mock air battles as they sought to refine their skills in anticipation of combat. Here, an F-14 of VF-32 flies next to a No. 19 Squadron Phantom after one such session. Air defense cover of Cyprus was shared between the Phantoms of Nos 19 and 92 Sqns.*

Right: A red-vested ordnance specialist prepares heat-seeking AIM-9 Sidewinder missiles aboard the USS John F. Kennedy *while an A-7E Corsair waits to be loaded with conventional iron bombs. The work of the munitions teams is a mixture of hard physical labor and finesse in arming and fuzing these deadly weapons.*

Above: Airborne early warning and control tasks are provided by the Grumman E-2C Hawkeye, and one of these distinctive machines is always airborne during routine flight operations.

Right: Commander John Leenhouts smiles for a self-portrait while flying a VA-72 A-7E Corsair low over the Saudi desert during the intensive training which presaged the opening of Desert Storm.

that all their cockpit switches were set to drop ordnance before going into hostile territory, being aware of the threat as briefed, or section integrity – looking out for each other. We also covered mild jinking from when they entered hostile territory, or ensured that they flew high profiles to stay out of AAA and low-altitude SAM envelopes.

"We had practiced all those things, but the one thing we had emphasized too much in the past was low-altitude, surprise attack. After the first night, after the first bomb hit, the surprise factor was gone. With the intense barrage fire the Iraqis were capable of putting up, and their low-altitude SAMs geared to low-altitude ingress and egress, it was smart to go high. We had to concentrate on that and beat it into the 'system' a little. Of course, after the first night (you saw it on CNN), they didn't need much convincing. The same basic, commonsense things that kept people alive in previous wars certainly applied in this war as well."

P.M.

Below: VA-72's hawk insignia is visible on the fin of this A-7E Corsair as it flashes past an old fort in the Saudi desert. For the long-serving Corsair II, Desert Storm seems certain to mark the end of a combat career that began in the late 1960s in Vietnam. The Kennedy's two light attack squadrons (VA-46 and VA-72) were the only ones operating the A-7E during the Gulf war.

Arab Coalition Air Forces

Karl von Clausewitz declared that, "War is nothing more than the continuation of politics by other means." In Desert Storm, the political aspect could not be forgotten just because war had begun; both factors were equally important. Therefore, one of General Schwarzkopf's most crucial tasks was to keep intact the fragile coalition of nations – many of them Arabs having more in common with Saddam than their Western battle partners. The building of a bridge of mutual trust between very different cultures was a difficult process accomplished with great success. Participation of Arab forces was essential to what may be crudely described as the 'public relations' aspect of Desert Storm.

Naturally, the first Arab coalition air force to do battle was that of Kuwait itself – on 2 August 1990. After a spirited defense against crushing odds, the KAF flew what it could to Saudi Arabia and Bahrain, its main strength being in Mirage F1CK interceptors and A-4KU Skyhawk fighter-bombers, plus a few BAe Hawk Mk 64 armed jet trainers. Squadrons were reformed and re-armed, becoming part of the RSAF for administrative reasons, though wearing the title (in Arabic and English) 'Free Kuwait' on their aircrafts' sides. French technicians assisted with maintenance of the Mirages as well as the Puma, Super Puma and Gazelle helicopters which escaped. Two Hercules were used to support the coalition air transport effort.

Naturally, the Kuwaitis proved to be the most aggressive of the Arab air forces – so much so that there were reports of their temporary hosts depriving them of armament during Desert Shield, lest they started the war of liberation before everyone else was ready. Skyhawks flew combat missions from the first day of hostilities, although Kuwaiti enthusiasm was not always directly translated into bombing results. Helicopters supported the ground war and gained some hits with HOT anti-tank missiles.

Most lavishly armed of the Arab coalition, Saudi Arabia received extra F-15C Eagles from the USAF to augment its interceptor force, which also included Tornado ADVs. RSAF, RAF and USAF fighters flew patrols from Dhahran 24 hours per day from mid-August until victory was achieved. The Saudis gained only two air-to-air victories – from a single engagement which had been carefully stage-managed to guarantee the creation of a local hero.

P.J.

Right: Tactical airlift resources of the Royal Saudi Air Force rest largely with the C-130 Hercules, a type that was also operated by many other members of the coalition. Three RSAF squadrons currently operate the ubiquitous Hercules which, in addition to the primary airlift task, is also used as an aerial tanker and for VIP transport duties. Versions in service are the C-130E, C-130H, KC-130H and VC-130H.

Above: Like many of the oil-rich Gulf states, Bahrain chose the US as a source of military equipment when updating its armed forces. Some single-seat F-5Es and two-seat F-5Fs were the first combat jets to be delivered.

Left: Saudi Arabia's enormous oil revenues enabled it to purchase examples of two of the most advanced Western interceptors. Seen here getting airborne with a full load of Sidewinder and Sky Flash AAMs is a Tornado ADV.

Left, inset: Bahrain's air arm may be smaller than that of Saudi Arabia but it too has its fair share of modern hardware, bought with petro-dollars. The newest and most potent equipment is the F-16C Fighting Falcon.

Left: Although it has received much more potent combat hardware in recent years, Saudi Arabia did acquire a sizeable fleet of F-5 Tiger IIs, many of which were still active when the Gulf crisis arose. Most were F-5Es, but some two-seat F-5Fs remained in use.

Right: Saudi Arabia continues to look to Great Britain as a source of warplanes and was among overseas customers for the British Aerospace Hawk, which it uses mainly as a trainer, although it may also perform light attack and air-defense tasks.

Top: Tornado ADV interceptors of the Royal Saudi Air Force played a worthwhile part alongside their British and American colleagues in patrolling Saudi airspace in the tense period after the Iraqi invasion of Kuwait, when it looked likely that further territorial gains would be sought.

Left: France has achieved a fair degree of success in finding Arab customers for military aircraft and was in fact the only nation to have sold modern warplanes to both sides of the eventual fight. Abu Dhabi was one of the 'good guys' and had only recently taken delivery of the Mirage 2000, a Magic-armed example of which is shown at the moment of take-off.

McDonnell Douglas F-15C Eagle

Saudi Arabia is one of the few nations able to afford the McDonnell Douglas F-15C Eagle. Operating alongside US Air Force F-15s, the Saudi Eagles played their part in defending their country's air space during the Gulf war. This example is a former US Air Force machine, transferred from USAFE to the RSAF before the start of the war. Five squadrons were equipped with Eagles, operating from bases at Dhahran, Khamis Mushait and Taif.

Size
At more than 26 tons take-off weight, the F-15 is a big, powerful fighter, with performance and fighting ability to match.

Sparrow
Main armament in the Gulf was four AIM-7 Sparrow medium-range missiles, carried on the corners of the boxy fuselage.

Right: The United Arab Emirates air force operates a small number of Lockheed Hercules on transport tasks, its fleet including this 'stretched' example of the C-130H derivative.

Below: As part of a modernization program, the RSAF purchased 30 Pilatus PC-9 turboprop trainers, new pilots progressing from PC-9 to Hawk and on to combat types.

Above: Displaying a 'Free Kuwait' inscription on the intake wall, a two-seat TA-4KU Skyhawk sits idly at a Saudi air base following the successful Iraqi invasion. When Desert Shield was supplanted by Desert Storm, Kuwaiti Skyhawks were among the first warplanes to go into action as allied air power began softening up Iraq as a prelude to liberation. Despite its age, the Skyhawk fared quite well and only one was lost in the six weeks that it took to drive Iraqi forces from Kuwait.

Above right: Among other Kuwaiti air force equipment which managed to flee from the oncoming Iraqi army to find sanctuary in Saudi Arabia were several helicopters, including examples of the SA 330H Puma and SA 342K Gazelle.

Right: A brace of US Marine Corps AH-1 SuperCobras clatters off into the desert as a Saudi Navy AS 532 Cougar prepares to launch for an anti-shipping sortie from its home base at Al Jubail. Missions with these helicopters frequently involved surveillance of the Gulf in the ongoing hunt for mines and Iraqi naval craft.

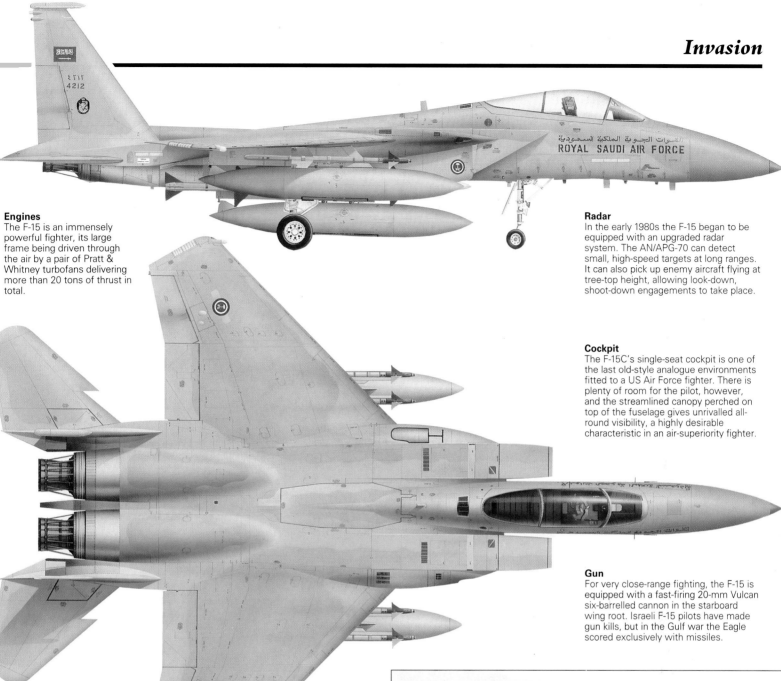

ROYAL SAUDI AIR FORCE

Engines
The F-15 is an immensely powerful fighter, its large frame being driven through the air by a pair of Pratt & Whitney turbofans delivering more than 20 tons of thrust in total.

Radar
In the early 1980s the F-15 began to be equipped with an upgraded radar system. The AN/APG-70 can detect small, high-speed targets at long ranges. It can also pick up enemy aircraft flying at tree-top height, allowing look-down, shoot-down engagements to take place.

Cockpit
The F-15C's single-seat cockpit is one of the last old-style analogue environments fitted to a US Air Force fighter. There is plenty of room for the pilot, however, and the streamlined canopy perched on top of the fuselage gives unrivalled all-round visibility, a highly desirable characteristic in an air-superiority fighter.

Gun
For very close-range fighting, the F-15 is equipped with a fast-firing 20-mm Vulcan six-barrelled cannon in the starboard wing root. Israeli F-15 pilots have made gun kills, but in the Gulf war the Eagle scored exclusively with missiles.

Performance
The F-15 is capable of flying more than twice the speed of sound, but it is its range, acceleration and maneuverability which make it the world's best air-superiority fighter.

Left: Royal Saudi Air Force F-15C Eagles pulled their weight in the round-the-clock CAP effort that was staged during the Desert Shield build-up. Many of these missions required aerial refueling support from KC-135 Stratotankers and KC-10 Extenders of the USAF as well as RSAF KE-3A tankers.

Right: One of the personalities of the war was Saudi Eagle pilot Captain Al-Shamrani, who employed two AIM-9 Sidewinder air-to-air missiles to spectacular effect in shooting down a brace of Iraq air force Mirage F1EQs on 24 January while flying with No. 13 Squadron. His victims were believed to have been attempting an anti-shipping attack with an Exocet missile.

Strategic Airlift

When Saddam Hussein's Iraqi army swept over Kuwait on 2 August 1990, the United States had no forces in the region. Six months later, 525,000 Americans were in the Gulf. Their numbers included the equivalent of nine infantry and armor divisions and two Marine divisions plus a brigade. They had 2,000 main battle tanks, six carrier battle groups, a dozen fighter wings, and a supply line for arms and ammunition which stretched halfway around the world.

The airlift mounted by the US Air Force's Military Airlift Command (MAC) carried people, weapons and equipment of all five US service branches from more than 120 locations to the deserts of the Middle East. Together with the sealift which followed, it made possible the most spectacular build-up of military force in history. But when it began, there were deep-rooted worries.

No matter how it was done, the first units to arrive in Saudi Arabia were going to be lonely – standing by themselves against Iraq's army, the fourth largest in the world.

Below: A Military Airlift Command C-5 Galaxy raises its nose visor and lowers the ramp soon after arrival at a desert base so that the offloading of cargo can begin with the minimum of delay.

Early to mid-August was a time of hard work and innovation, spurred by that serious worrying. The 1st Tactical Fighter Wing from Langley AFB, Virginia, and the 'Ready Brigade' of 2,300 paratroopers from the 82nd Airborne Division, Fort Bragg, North Carolina, moved to Saudi Arabia on 7 August, within 18 hours of the Desert Shield 'execute' order. Even this preliminary move of vanguard forces required dozens of C-141Bs and C-5s, and was far more difficult than it looked, especially since the F-15C Eagles and paratroopers needed to hit the ground ready to fight.

This was just the beginning. MAC's General H. T. Johnson and other planners cobbled together an air bridge which hauled people and equipment on exhausting, 38-hour missions (the round-trip from a US base, to a European location, followed by the round-trip 'down range' to the Saudi deserts). Johnson threw nearly all of his 265 C-141B StarLifters and 85 C-5 Galaxies into the effort and activated elements of the CRAF (Civil Reserve Air Fleet). The size of the effort was stupefying: a C-141B or C-5 landed at Dhahran every seven minutes, around the clock. The tonnage of the 1948 Berlin airlift was exceeded in the first 22 days. Two-hundred-and-twenty-thousand troops and their

equipment were moved by October.

The crews of giant transport aircraft, many of them Reservists who flew on a voluntary basis before being called to active duty on 29 August, kept their aerial supply line moving around the clock, sometimes by pushing themselves to exhaustion. Maintenance people coaxed extra capabilities out of the aircraft. At bases in Europe – Torrejon, Zaragosa, Rhein-Main, Ramstein – transient quarters became so swollen that men and women slept in hallways, in bathrooms, or (at Rhein-Main) in tents. The Torrejon flight line was so choked with C-141Bs and C-5s, a pilot had to be given a map to find his plane.

A typical airlift job was, for example, to haul equipment for the 2nd Marine Division at Camp Pendleton, California. A crew would fly the first leg – for example, from Pendleton to Torrejon. There, another crew in a revolving pool would pick up both the mission and the aircraft, and

continue down range. Routine problems which might delay a departure – cleaning an aircraft, for instance – had to be set aside in the all-compelling effort to keep the aircraft moving, constantly moving. 'The eastbound stage', they called it, evoking memories of stagecoaches which, moving in the opposite direction, had opened up the American West. Down range, there was no place to rest, so the crew would have to bring their C-141B or C-5 *back* to Torrejon before they could sleep.

General Johnson relied heavily on Airlift Control Elements (ALCEs), teams of experts who set up shop at both ends of the air bridge to optimize loading techniques, departures and arrivals. These nerve centers were populated with Air Force logistics officers, themselves C-141B and C-5 pilots,

Below: Dwarfed by a Galaxy's massive bulk, US troops in desert fatigues move away from the newly arrived aircraft to begin the final stage of the long journey from the USA to a base in Saudi Arabia.

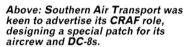

who had trained rigorously in how to achieve mass movements of people and equipment – for decades, their goal had been to move 10 divisions to NATO within 10 days.

The numbers showed that strategic airlift (C-141Bs and C-5s, plus C-130E/Hs and KC-10As when self-deploying) flew 20,500 missions, carried 534,000 passengers, and hauled 542,000 tons of cargo. (A 'mission' was not a sortie, but, rather, the movement of one set of cargo from its origin to its destination, regardless of the number of stops or aircraft changes.) 4.65 billion ton-miles were moved, as compared with 697.5 million during the 65-week Berlin airlift or 136.6 million during Operation Nickel Grass, the airlift to Israel in 1973. To those who participated, there was another way to say what they had done – a bumper sticker, worth saving for the grandchildren, worn by some as a badge of honor: *I Flew the Eastbound Stage.*

R.D.

Above right: Paratroopers of the 82nd Airborne Division jump from an MAC C-141B StarLifter in a rehearsal for a possible airborne assault on Kuwait City. This was one of the options open to General Schwarzkopf in his planning. If it had gone ahead, the paratroopers would have attacked in conjunction with a Marine amphibious assault and a helicopter assault by the 101st Airborne Division.

Right: The magnitude of the airlift task was such that it was beyond the capacity of MAC. As a consequence, KC-10 Extenders from Strategic Air Command were called in to assist with the movement of men and materiel.

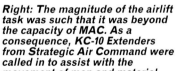

Above: Southern Air Transport was keen to advertise its CRAF role, designing a special patch for its aircrew and DC-8s.

Above: Although it carries Flying Tiger colors, this Boeing 747F of the CRAF was actually operated by Federal Express.

Above: Activation of the US Civil Reserve Air Fleet meant that some unusual commercial aircraft found their way to the Gulf, like this Hawaiian Air DC-8 Srs 62F.

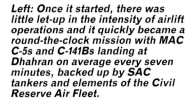

Left: Once it started, there was little let-up in the intensity of airlift operations and it quickly became a round-the-clock mission with MAC C-5s and C-141Bs landing at Dhahran on average every seven minutes, backed up by SAC tankers and elements of the Civil Reserve Air Fleet.

The Marines Arrive

"When our Marine pilots arrived in the Gulf region they had missiles on board their aircraft and their guns were armed," said Lieutenant General Duane A. Wills, Deputy Chief of Staff for Marine Aviation. "We were in a position to fly combat missions in under 24 hours of arriving in-theater, if they had been required."

Rapid deployment has always been one of the main *raisons d'être* of the US Marine Corps and Operation Desert Shield gave them a chance to put their global mobility into action on a massive scale. Within only eight days of President George Bush ordering US forces to Saudi Arabia, on 6 August, the first Marine Corps units arrived in the Middle East and within a month 45,000 Marines were in defensive positions around the Saudi port of Al Jubail to deter further advances by the Iraqi army.

In line with the USMC's Marine Air Ground Task Force (MAGTF) concept, more than 200 aircraft and helicopters were dispatched to support Marine Corps ground element during the first wave of Desert Shield.

A complex deployment plan had been developed by the USMC to ensure it could have a full Marine Expeditionary Force (MEF), of one full division and an air wing, in-theater within 10 days of the 'Go' command being given.

Prepositioned supply ships with war stocks for 30 days arrived in Saudi Arabia from Diego Garcia on 15 August. They were soon followed by two aviation logistic support ships stocked with repair equipment to allow Marine combat aircraft to be maintained in-theater. Marine ground units were flown in by USAF C-141s and C-5s to link up with their equipment at the dockside in Saudi Arabia.

Scores of USMC CH-53s, CH-46s, AH-1s and UH-1Ns of Marine Air Group 16 were stripped down and flown by USAF C-5s to Jubail air base and the King Abdul

Aziz Naval Base south of Al Jubail. The first fixed-wing aircraft to arrive to support I MEF were four squadrons of F/A-18 Hornet multi-role strike aircraft and two squadrons of AV-8B Harrier V/STOL close-support aircraft. These aircraft flew non-stop to Saudi Arabia with the help of air-to-air refueling.

On shore, MAG 13 took on responsibility for close air support with AV-8Bs and OV-10 Bronco observation aircraft based at King Abdul Aziz Naval Base. Other USMC helicopters and AV-8Bs assigned to MAG 40 arrived in the Persian Gulf in September with the 4th Marine Expeditionary Brigade (MEB) aboard the US Navy's Amphibious Group Two. The brigade and its air group carried out in November a large amphibious exercise codenamed Imminent Thunder in eastern Saudi Arabia.

On 8 November 1990 President Bush ordered further large-scale US troop deployments to the Gulf region to boost the coalition's offensive capability. I MEF received significant air reinforcement to bring its strength up to 560 aircraft and helicopters. Thousands of Reservists from the 4th Marine Air Wing were activated and they served in all the air groups of 3 MAW. Most of the reinforcement aircraft were either airlifted or flown directly to Saudi Arabia.

When the coalition air offensive began on 16 January 1991, MAG 11 comprised 84 F/A-18s in six squadrons, two squadrons of A-6E with 20 aircraft, a squadron of 12 EA-6Bs and 15 KC-130s. Some 60 AV-8Bs and 20 OV-10s were ashore with MAG 11. MAG 16 and the newly arrived MAG 26 boasted some 182 helicopters. The 4th and 5th MEBs, along with the 13th Marine Expeditionary Unit (Special Operations Capable), together had some 141 helicopters and 26 AV-8Bs aboard amphibious warfare ships in the Persian Gulf.

T.R.

Above: AV-8B Harrier IIs of Marine Corps attack squadron VMA-331 are ranged along the deck of an amphibious assault ship as they await the start of flight operations while en route to the Gulf. Some Marine air elements were dispatched to the area aboard ship but others made the transit by air with the assistance of inflight refueling.

Hornets Ready for Anything

Major Steve Pomeroy, VMFA-333, F/A-18 Hornet

Above: Reaching Bahrain on 24 August, Major Steve Pomeroy was among the first Marine Corps pilots to be dispatched to the region. With other members of VMFA-333, he was soon hard at work flying combat air patrols in his F/A-18 Hornet, protecting land and naval forces from aerial threats.

"We left Beaufort for the Gulf in late August, transiting through Rota in Spain on to Bahrain, where we were to be based. We arrived on 24 August, and immediately began participation in Operation Desert Shield.

"Marine Corps ground units began to arrive at about the same time. The way the Corps is set up with the Navy means that we always have units afloat in amphibious shipping ready to deploy to trouble spots around the world. I don't know when the decision was made to commit the Marines to go ashore in Saudi Arabia, but I'd guess it was some time in August, coincident with the decision to send Marine air.

"The Marine Corps is geared to short-notice heavy tactical lift, using maritime prepositioning ships (MPSs). These are container vessels, purchased independently from the Navy, located close to potential trouble spots. MPS vessels are permanently on station in the Eastern Mediterranean or in

Below: US Marine Corps resources were drawn from around the world, with VMA-231 'Ace of Spades' AV-8B Harriers deploying from a base in Japan, where they operated as part of the 1st MAW.

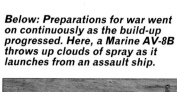

Below: Preparations for war went on continuously as the build-up progressed. Here, a Marine AV-8B throws up clouds of spray as it launches from an assault ship.

Above: Hornet's nest. The scene at Sheikh Isa Air Base on Bahrain was reminiscent of a major Marine Corps air station in the USA with four F/A-18 squadrons in place as well as some A-6E Intruders.

Below: Life at Sheikh Isa lacked some creature comforts and many Marines were forced to live in a tent city adjacent to the flight line, suffering from noise and fumes as well as intense heat.

Right: A CH-53E Super Stallion slows to the hover as it prepares to set down an underslung load at a field for Marine ground forces somewhere in Saudi Arabia.

the Arabian Sea. Each of the ships can support a battalion landing team for 30 days. When equipped with a TAVB (tactical aviation support package) they can also sustain Marine aviation for a similar period. One advantage of the prepositioning system was that when the decision was made to commit the Marines to the Gulf, we were ready to conduct operations from the moment we arrived at Sheikh Isa Air Base on Bahrain.

"In effect, my squadron is a supporting arm for the ground forces. The Marine F/A-18's primary mission is to fly CAS (Close Air Support) for the guys on the ground, but we are also tasked with attaining and maintaining air superiority over the battlefield, as well as deep air strikes. There are two other Marine air missions, but the Hornet doesn't really get involved in electronic warfare and tactical reconnaissance, although we integrate closely with squadrons that do those jobs.

"Our first task was to fly CAPs (Combat Air Patrols) in order to protect the naval and amphibious forces in the Gulf and also to cover the Marines on the ground in eastern Saudi Arabia. The four

Marine Hornet squadrons in the Gulf flew close to 10,000 hours during Desert Shield, supported by Marine KC-130 tankers operating out of Muharraq airport on Bahrain. From the end of August to the beginning of the air war, it was 24 hours a day, seven days a week of continuous barrier CAPs. Two squadrons would work a week on, a week off. Each squadron in turn would work 12 hours on, 12 hours off. There would be a minimum of two aircraft up, with two more either coming or going. I guess each pilot was flying 10 to 15 hours per week.

"It was somewhat monotonous, but there were moments when it appeared that the Iraqis were coming out to threaten surface units. Some of their combat air patrols would head out into the Gulf. As many as 12 aircraft at a time would appear. They could have been setting up a missile strike on our shipping, but as soon as they reached our maximum missile range, they'd turn around. This happened every time. They never got within visual sight, but we know that they were Mirage F1s and MiG-23s and -25s.

"While we were handling the

CAPs, we were also working simulated close air support operations with the ground forces, a lot of whom had come ashore by this time. We conducted amphibious training exercises, the biggest of which was codenamed Imminent Thunder. They made quite a to-do about that in the press, which I guess was the idea, to convince the Iraqis they'd have to face a Marine landing into Kuwait City."

Below: Aerial refueling support of Marine Corps fighter elements was primarily the task of KC-130s operating from Muharraq, Bahrain.

A helicopter door gunner swings his M60 machine gun to cover the sandy banks of the Suez Canal as a US Navy carrier transits from the Eastern Mediterranean to the Red Sea. By the middle of August there were two American carrier battle groups in the region, with more on the way.

from page 16

25 August The Security Council passed Resolution 665, which authorized states to use limited force to ensure compliance with the trade sanctions on Iraq and Kuwait. Ships suspected of attempting to break the blockade could be boarded for the inspection of their cargoes.

By now the carrier USS *Saratoga* and the battleship USS *Wisconsin*, and their supporting warships, were in the Red Sea. With the arrival of *Saratoga*, the *Eisenhower* set sail to return to the USA.

26 August In an operation that would have been unthinkable even a year earlier, a Soviet navy warship requested and received assistance from a Royal Air Force Nimrod to intercept a suspected Iraqi blockade runner.

28 August President Saddam Hussein agreed to the release of all foreign women and children held against their will in Iraq and Kuwait, and within a week all of those who wished to do so had left.

The first squadron of Royal Air Force Tornado GR.Mk 1 bombers arrived in Saudi Arabia.

29 August A C-5A Galaxy cargo plane carrying stores for Saudi Arabia crashed on take-off from Ramstein AFB, Germany, killing all on board. It was the first aircraft loss associated with Desert Shield.

10 September Presidents Bush and Gorbachev met at Helsinki and agreed on the measures they would take against Iraq if that country continued in its refusal to withdraw from Kuwait.

13 September The British government announced that the 7th Armoured Brigade was to move from Germany to Saudi Arabia.

By now the coalition air force units assembled in Saudi Arabia and the neighboring states possessed a greater number of combat aircraft than the Iraqi air force.

14 September Under Operation *Locusta*, the Italian government announced that it was sending a squadron of Tornado attack aircraft to Abu Dhabi.

Four US Air Force Reserve squadrons operating C-141B Star-Lifters were called to active duty.

15 September The French government announced that it would send a contingent of 4,000 troops to Saudi Arabia.

16 September The Security Council passed Resolution 670, which prohibited air traffic to and from airports in Iraq and Kuwait, except in humanitarian circumstances.

At about this time the carrier USS *Midway* left her home port at Yokosuka, Japan, for the Gulf area.

to page 36

French Deployment

As early as 9 August, France concluded that the Iraqi invasion of Kuwait would destabilize the region and decided to reinforce its forces in the Republic of Djibouti, in accordance with treaty obligations with its former colony on the western shores of the Gulf of Aden, and to initiate the deployment of elements of its Force d'action extérieure (FAE, or Rapid Deployment Force), including support and attack helicopters. Accordingly, two days later additional mobile radar and Crotale surface-to-air missiles, as well as tanker-configured C.160NG Transall transports, were sent to Djibouti to beef up Armée de l'air elements – notably the Mirage F1Cs of EC (Escadron de chasse, or Fighter Squadron) 4/30 'Vexin', and the Alouette IIs and C.160s of ETOM 88 which are normally assigned to DA (Détachement air, or Air Detachment) 188. Thereafter, the politico-military situation in the Horn of Africa remained stable, but troubled, and there was no further need for France to increase its military presence in Djibouti. Conversely, the evolving situation in the Arabian peninsula led to a progressive increase in France's military commitments and to its eventual participation in combat operations against Iraq.

Operation *Salamandre*

That commitment, however, took time to congeal as France steadfastly pursued its traditional path of staunch independence in matters of foreign affairs, and as some influential members of its government, notably the Minister of Defense – Jean-Pierre Chevènement, co-founder of a France-Iraq friendship organization – sought to find accommodation with Iraq. Hence, FAE elements and their helicopters wandered apparently aimlessly for seven weeks before settling in and near the King Khalid Military City (KKMC) in northeastern Saudi Arabia. The movements of that force began eight days after the Iraqi invasion of Kuwait when 30 Gazelles and 12 Pumas from the 5ième RHC (Régiment d'hélicoptères de combat, or Combat Helicopter Regiment), one of the components assigned to the Force d'action extérieure of the French army, were loaded aboard the carrier *Clemenceau* (R 98). Leaving ashore its usual complement of Crusader fighters and Super Etendard attack aircraft, but retaining four Alizé ALM anti-submarine warfare aircraft and two AS 365F Dauphin SAR (Search and Rescue) helicopters, *Clemenceau* left Toulon on 13 August as Operation *Salamandre* was initiated with the intent of having forces available in the Gulf should the need have arisen to evacuate French citizens from Kuwait. After transiting through the Suez Canal, the carrier remained in port at Djibouti between 22 and 28 August while the ALAT (Aviation légère de l'Armée de terre) helicopters took part in training exercises ashore. Additional exercises were held with UAE forces as *Clemenceau* made port calls in Fujairah and Abu Dhabi before proceeding to Yanbu, on the Red Sea coast of Saudi Arabia, where the helicopters were to be disembarked for inland movement. Airlift support for that phase of the operation was provided by three C.160F/NGs of ET (Escadre de transport, or Transport Wing) 61 and ET 64 which arrived at Yanbu in late August and moved to the Riyadh IAP in early October.

The first ALAT helicopters to arrive in Saudi Arabia on 9 September, two weeks before *Clemenceau* was unloaded, were two AS 330B Pumas and four SA 342M Gazelles from the 3ième RHC which, along with personnel and support equipment, were airlifted to Yanbu aboard an Air France

The French Armée de l'air combat deployment to the Gulf in October was supported by C-135F(R) tankers of the 93ième Escadre de ravitaillement en vol, or Aerial Refueling Wing.

Above: The French deployment of combat aircraft like this Dassault Mirage F1 was relatively slow, as France tried to use its influence as one of Iraq's main arms suppliers to achieve a diplomatic settlement to the crisis.

Left: French Jaguars of the 11ième Escadre reached Al Ahsa in Saudi Arabia in October. The small Jaguar force had considerable desert experience, with many of its pilots having seen active service in the late 1980s against Libyan-backed rebels in northern Chad.

Above: The Clemenceau ferried helicopters to the Middle East in August, in case French nationals had to be evacuated from the region. Most of its normal air group had been landed, but two search and rescue SA 365F Dauphin helicopters were retained.

Above: Three C.160 Transalls were used by the Armée de l'air for intra-theater transport tasks, distributing supplies shipped to the Gulf over an air bridge from France. Initially based at Yanbu to support the Aviation légère de l'Armée de terre helicopter deployment, the Transalls moved to Riyadh in late October from where they supplied the French combat aircraft at Al Ahsa. In addition to the regular Transalls, the French deployed the EC.160 Gabriel version to Saudi Arabia, which was used for the gathering of signals intelligence.

Left: Aérospatiale AS 531 Pumas of the 5ième Régiment d'hélicoptères de combat land aboard the carrier Clemenceau after exercising ashore in Djibouti. The Pumas were deployed as part of Operation Salamandre, the initial French military response to the Iraqi invasion of Kuwait. Their primary task was to have been the evacuation of French nationals from Kuwait City if that should have been seen to be necessary.

French Deployment

Boeing 747F, and two C-130 Hercules and four C.160Fs of the Armée de l'air. Then, after the Iraqis' forced entry into the French embassy in Kuwait prompted the French government to take more energetic measures, 4,200 men from the 6ième Division légère blindée (Light Armored Divison) departed from Nimes to take position in northeastern Saudi Arabia. *Clemenceau* was unloaded on 22-25 September while logistic support elements, sent by ships, arrived a few days later.

All 48 helicopters were flown to KKMC on 26 September, covering the 1100 km from Yanbu in 10 hours, with three refueling stops, while two C.160s airlifted HOT missiles for the SA 342M Gazelles from Djibouti to KKMC. Four days later, the nine SA 341F/Canon helicopter gunships, nine SA 341F scouts, 32 SA 342M Gazelles/HOT anti-tank helicopters, and 18 AS 330B Pumas were declared operational at KKMC. *Clemenceau* arrived back in Toulon on 5 October and, afterwards, did not sail back in support of either Desert Shield or Desert Storm. Barely had that initial deployment been completed before reinforcement plans were implemented, as 20 SA 342Ms of the 1ier RHC in Phalsbourg and 5ième RHC in Pau, and four AS 330Bs of the 4ième RHCMS (Régiment d'hélicoptères de commandement, de manoeuvre et de soutien, or Command/Transport/Support Helicopter Regiment) in Nancy were flown to Toulon for shipment aboard the *Cap Afrique* and three other merchantmen. A third batch of 40 helicopters, including the experimental Orchidée with surveillance radar, was added at the start of the war.

Right and below: The **Clemenceau** *left Toulon on 13 August, with 30 Gazelles and 12 Puma helicopters from the 5ième Régiment d'hélicoptères de combat in place of her normal air group. She was unloaded at Yanbu on the Red Sea coast on 22 September, after port visits to Djibouti, Fujairah and Abu Dhabi. From Yanbu the helicopters were flown 1100 km to King Khalid Military City in the north of Saudi Arabia.*

Operation *Daguet*

The decision to send combat aircraft to the Gulf was taken by President Mitterand on 14 September 1990 to protest Iraq's forced entry into the French Embassy in Kuwait. The following day Operation *Daguet* was initiated by the Armée de l'air, and aircraft and personnel to be deployed to Saudi Arabia were placed under the command of Général de brigade aérienne (Brigadier General) Gellibert.

By American and British standards, the first phase of *Daguet* was painfully slow as the first eight aircraft (four Mirage 2000Cs from the 5ième Escadre de chasse at BA (Base aérienne, or Air Base) 115 Orange-Caritat and four Mirage F1CRs from the 33ième Escadre de reconnaissance (Tactical Reconnaissance Wing) at BA 124 Strasbourg-Entzheim did not depart until 3 October, delays

being due more to political considerations than to a lack of military preparedness. Quite to the contrary, the Armée de l'air was well prepared for such a deployment; many of its combat pilots were veterans not only of Red Flag exercises but also had flown combat missions in Africa during Operations *Manta* and *Epervier* against Libyan-supported rebels in the desert of northern Chad. Likewise, its tanker and transport crews had gained valuable experience in recent years by supporting deployments to USAF's Nellis air base in Nevada and to trouble spots in various parts of the world.

Taking off from BA 125 Istres-Le Tubé with two C-135FR tankers from the 93ième Escadre de ravitaillement en vol (Air Refueling Wing), the four fighters and four

tactical reconnaissance aircraft were air refueled three times (off Rome, Crete and western Saudi Arabia) to cover the 2400 nm to Al Ahsa Airport, a civilian airport outside Al Hufuf (east of Riyadh, west of Bahrain and 200 nm south of Kuwait). There, the first combat elements of the Armée de l'air were placed under the command of Colonel Jean-Pierre Job (promoted to Brigadier General on 1 December) to report to COMELEF (Commandement des éléments français, or French Command) in Riyadh under Général de corps d'armée Roquejeoffre and his air deputy, Général de brigade aérienne Jean-Pierre Gellibert.

Concurrent with the build-up of ALAT, CAFDA (Commandement 'air' des forces de Défense aérienne, or French Air Defense Command)

and FATac (Force aérienne tactique, or French Tactical Air Command) forces in Saudi Arabia, CoTAM (Commandment du Transport aérien militaire, or French Military Airlift Command) initiated a quasi-scheduled air bridge between France and the Middle East, over which its C.160s, C-130Hs and DC-8-72s were extensively supplemented by chartered commercial transports. CoTAM also set up an intra-theater logistic network, that element evolving from the initial assignment of three Transall tactical transports to Yanbu in early October 1990. Eventually moved to Riyadh's partially-completed Terminal 4, which also became the Saudi destination for military flights from France and the base for the C-135FR tankers deployed by CoFAS (Commandement de Forces

Below: In September, Iraqis forced an entry into the French embassy in Kuwait, which changed France's half-hearted commitment to the military side of the coalition. It was decided to deploy troops and combat aircraft in the Gulf. Four Dassault Mirage 2000C fighters were among the first aircraft to be sent. They arrived at Al Ahsa airport, about 370 km south of Kuwait, on 3 October.

Right: With the increase in France's commitment to the Gulf came a corresponding increase in the size of the intra-theater transport force. The C.160 Transall detachment grew from three to five aircraft, and once the fighting began it more than doubled to 10 Transalls and C-130H Hercules (shown here). Based at Riyadh, the transports were operated by Escadres de transport 61 and 64.

Above: The Mirage 2000Cs based at Al Ahsa mounted their first combat air patrols along the Saudi/Iraqi border in December.

Below: Coalition commanders were unsure if French aircraft like these Jaguars would be under unified command, or whether they would remain independent.

aériennes stratégiques, or French Strategic Air Command) to support the tactical jets, the in-country logistic detachment had grown to five C.160 tactical airlifters before Desert Storm commenced. A Mystère 20 and a Nord 262 were based at Riyadh Military Airport and were operated respectively for command transport and for liaison and ancillary support. After the fighting broke out, the number of C.160s was increased to 10 and two C-130Hs were added to help ferry supplies, food and ammunition to fast-moving ground forces and hard-hitting tactical air units.

Five days after the first combat aircraft had arrived at Al Ahsa, a second batch of four Mirage 2000Cs and four Mirage F1CRs arrived at that base. On 15 and 17 October, they were joined by

Above: Coalition worries about French co-operation in combat proved groundless, as highly professional pilots made their own valuable contribution to the air war.

Right: Coming under the command of Général de corps d'armée Roquejeoffre, French army helicopters operated in support of the Division Daguet, which played such a vital role in the flank maneuver initiating the war's final ground offensive.

French Deployment

two batches of four Jaguars from the 11ième Escadre de chasse from BA 136 Toul-Rosières and in November by two AS 330Ba SAR helicopters of the Escadron d'hélicoptères (Helicopter Squadron) 1/67 'Pyrénées' from BA 120 Cazaux and by a C.160G Gabriel of Escadron électronique (Electronic Squadron) 54 'Dunkerque' from BA 128 Metz-Frescaty. Additional aircraft, equipment and personnel were brought in during the following weeks so that when the United Nations' deadline for the withdrawal of Iraqi forces from Kuwait expired, the Armée de l'air had 51 aircraft (24 Jaguars, 12 Mirage F1CRs, 12 Mirage 2000Cs, two Pumas and one C.160G Gabriel) and anti-aircraft defenses (eight twin 20-mm anti-aircraft gun, a Crotale SAM battery and 10 Mistral short-range SAMs) at Al Ahsa AB. Aircraft in Riyadh included five C-135FR tankers, five C.160s, a Mystère 20 and a Nord 262. In addition, the Armée de l'air had fielded an SDCT (Système de détection et de contrôle tactique) radar protected by Crotale SAMs at KKMC.

Immediately upon arriving at Al Ahsa, tactical aircraft pilots had begun in-theater familiarization flights, and soon after they began flying combat readiness sorties, with C-135FRs providing air refueling when Mirage 2000Cs flew their first CAP sorties on 12 December. During that period, when CENTAF (Central Command Air Forces) was not yet sure that French forces would be authorized by their government to take part in offensive operations after the 15 January deadline, the most significant contribution was made by Mirage F1CRs as their Thomson-CSF Raphael high-resolution SLAR enabled them to gather intelligence deep into Iraq and occupied Kuwait while remaining over Saudi Arabia (in so doing, the F1CRs effectively complemented RF-4Cs of the Alabama ANG which was using its LOROP cameras during flight along the same sectors) and as use of the SARA (Station aérotransportable de reconnaissance aérienne, or Air-Transported Reconnaissance Station) enabled near real-time transmission of data collected with the Super Cyclope infra-red sensor.

R.F.

Above: The Dassault Mirage 2000 is France's premier air defense fighter, and was used to mount combat air patrols over Saudi Arabia, although it saw no action. Armed with Matra Super 530D medium-range, semi-active, radar homing missiles and Matra R550 Magic 2 dogfight missiles, the Mirage 2000 would have been more than a match for most Iraqi air force jets.

Below: A Magic 2 missile on the wingtip station of a Dassault Mirage F1CR reconnaissance jet of 33ième Escadre de reconnaissance is armed. Iraq's large and well-equipped air force was considered a serious threat to allied forces, at least in the early stages of the operation to protect Saudi Arabia, so most coalition front-line machines carried some form of self-defense missile.

Dassault Mirage 2000C

France deployed a total of 12 Mirage 2000Cs to Saudi Arabia. Operating out of Al Ahsa, their task was to assist in the protection of Saudi air space.

Radar
The Mirage 2000 is equipped with a Thompson-CSF RDM multi-mode radar with an operating range of over 100 km (62 miles). It can be used for surveillance and target acquisition, and also provides guidance for the fighter's Matra Super 530 medium-range missiles.

Super 530
The Matra Super 530D is a semi-active radar-homing missile, with a range of 40 km. It is capable of both snap-up and snap-down operation.

Powerplant
The Mirage 2000 is powered by a SNECMA M53-P2 turbofan which can deliver 95.1 kN (21,385 lb) of thrust. This can drive the aircraft from the ground to Mach 2 at an altitude of 15000 m in four minutes.

Matra R550 Magic
First developed in the 1960s, the Matra Magic short-range heat-seeking missile is comparable to the American AIM-9 Sidewinder. The Magic 2 has a range of five km.

Performance
The Mirage 2000 has a maximum speed of Mach 2.2, and with a 1700-liter drop tank has a range of more than 1500 km (925 miles).

Color scheme
Most of the Mirage 2000s deployed to the Gulf retained their European color scheme in various shades of gray, but a few of the aircraft were repainted in the desert color scheme depicted.

Right: A Mirage F1CR lifts off from Al Ahsa airport. The F1CRs were one of the coalition's most capable battlefield reconnaissance assets, each being equipped with a Thompson-CSF Raphael high-resolution side-looking airborne radar (SLAR) set. This enabled the Mirages to look deep into Iraq and occupied Kuwait from their patrol areas on the Saudi side of the border, gathering vital intelligence on Iraqi troop movements in the weeks leading up to the outbreak of war.

Above: Fearing that it too would be invaded by Iraqi forces, Turkey used NATO channels to request reinforcement in December 1990. In response, Allied Command Europe's Mobile Force sent 42 aircraft which included six Italian RF-104G Starfighters, seen here at Erhac.

from page 30

21 September President Saddam Hussein's Revolutionary Command Council issued a statement that there was "not a single chance of any retreat" from Kuwait, and that any attempt to eject the Iraqi forces from the country would lead to "the mother of all battles".

7 October Under Operation Scimitar, 12 CF-18 Hornet fighters of No. 409 Sqn of the Canadian Forces flew from Germany to Qatar to join the coalition forces in the Gulf area.

8 October An RF-4C of the Alabama Air National Guard crashed near Abu Dhabi, killing both crewmen. Two US Marine Corps UH-1N Huey helicopters crashed in the North Arabian Sea, killing all eight men on board.

10 October An F-111F aircraft of the 48th TFW crashed in the Arabian Desert, killing both crewmen.

Following a spate of flying accidents the USAF halted all Desert Shield flying in Saudi Arabia except for the continuous standing patrols by E-3 AWACS aircraft, for an urgent review of flight safety procedures. When flying was resumed a few days later, there was a marked reduction in accidents.

8 November President Saddam Hussein dismissed the Chief of Staff of the Iraqi armed forces, and announced that Lieutenant General Hussein Rashid had been appointed to succeed him.

President Bush announced that the US government was to send a further 100,000 troops to Saudi Arabia. Between now and mid-January, the strength of the US Air Force units in the theater would double. Although the purpose of the move was not publicized at the time, its effect would be to shift the coalition forces from a defensive posture to one where they had sufficient strength to expel the Iraqi forces from Kuwait.

During this period allied F-14, F-15, F/A-18 and Tornado fighters carried out high-speed probing flights towards Iraq, turning away just short of the border. RC-135 electronic reconnaissance aircraft and E-3 AWACS aircraft observed the Iraqi fighter and missile re-action to these missions, to gain vitally important information on the operation of their air-defense system. Following several such flights the Iraqi High Command realized what was happening and decided to ignore the provocations. To prevent the allies collecting such information, most of the air-defense radars were left off and interceptors were not vectored onto the potential intruders. This policy would remain in force until the air war began in earnest.

19 November The Iraqi government announced that it was sending a further 250,000 troops to strengthen the defense of Kuwait.

22 November The British government announced that it would send a further 14,000 troops to Saudi Arabia.

to page 40

RC-135 Rivet Joint

The aircraft, systems, operations and tactics of the electronic air war in the Gulf may have lacked drama and media attention, but they made the success of the entire war effort possible. In particular, the electronic intelligence (Elint) effort allowed the allies to look deep into the Iraqi operational and strategic depths. The RC-135s – their crews' skills honed by experience listening to the Soviets – and the other allied Elint aircraft in the Gulf war have not attracted the same attention as the radar-equipped Boeing E-3 AWACS and E-8 Joint STARS aircraft, but were key to the victory.

The RC-135's business – Elint – is collecting and analyzing electronic emissions. The allies directed an extensive Elint effort against Iraq, yielding an effective and comprehensive intelligence picture. Whenever the Iraqis used a radio or radar, they had to assume that this would reveal its type and location, and probably the content, to the allies.

The number of RC-135s in the Gulf varied. The first, diverting from a planned detachment to RAF Mildenhall, UK, was among the earliest USAF aircraft to arrive in Saudi Arabia in August 1990, after the invasion of Kuwait. Others remained in the Gulf 10 weeks after the cease-fire and are likely to be in the Gulf for years to come.

For most of Operation Desert Shield, however, there were three USAF RC-135s based at Riyadh in Saudi Arabia (at least two of which were RC-135V or RC-135W Rivet Joint-configured aircraft) detached from the Strategic Air Command's 55th Strategic Reconnaissance Wing at Offutt AFB, Nebraska. Other RC-135s may have been detached and it is likely some operated along the Turkey-Iraq border. More than half of SAC's strategic reconnaissance aircraft – RC-135s, U-2s and TR-1s – were committed to the Gulf war.

The Rivet Joints' main line of work is Comint (Communications intelligence). They are configured – and each aircraft has an antenna array, often unique, that suggests its purpose – for their primary mission: to monitor and record enemy communications. While this information is usually brought back for post-mission analysis, since at least the mid-1980s they have also had some capability for inflight transmission and analysis.

The value of the RC-135's Elint was increased because they could provide their information to the field commanders in a timely fashion, which was not the case with much other – especially imagery – intelligence. While the RC-135s lacked a full forward-deployed exploitation system or the ability of some U-2Rs to relay intercept data directly to the US in real time through a wideband satellite link, improved connectivity between processing facilities and theater headquarters paid dividends throughout the war. These resulted from efforts under the Constant Source and TENCAP (Tactical Exploitation of National CAPabilities) programs instituted in the mid-1980s to expedite this intelligence flow, and which were probably expanded to include RC-135s as well as national technical means after the importance of communications intercepts was demonstrated in the Korean Airlines 747 shootdown.

During the months of Operation Desert Shield, the 55th SRW found the tempo of round-the-clock Elint operations to be a challenge to sustain. Crews had to be shuttled between Riyadh and Offutt; 12- to 14-plus-hour missions were considered milk runs, and most were about 24 hours in length. This soon put the aircrews above the Air Force's allowable monthly flying hour totals. The aircraft also shuttled back to Offutt as they required servicing, as it was not possible to forward deploy much of the maintenance required for the RC-135's unique and sophisticated electronics. Despite this, the mission-capable rate reportedly remained 'in excess of 90 per cent', a remarkable achievement for a complex yet ageing system subject to near-constant use.

None of the RC-135s are new: "all old enough to vote", in the words of one officer. The 55th had been ordered to retire its six oldest RC-135V Rivet Joints, their airframes dating from the early 1960s, but this move was postponed by the Gulf commitment. SAC was soon concerned about the effect of the greatly increased operational tempo on airframe life of even the 'newer' RC-135Ws.

The 55th SRW's crews flew a variety of mission profiles to collect Iraqi Elint during the months of Operation Desert Shield. Perhaps the most dramatic were when they would stand off while numbers of fighters assembled over Saudi Arabia and moved at high speed towards Kuwait or Iraq, only turning away at the last minute before crossing

The coalition had an immense advantage over the Iraqis, especially in the highly secret world of Sigint. Electronic reconnaissance aircraft like the RC-135W (above), the RC-135V (left) and RAF Nimrod R.Mk 1 (below) sucked in and analyzed Iraqi radar, and communications transmissions, giving war planners a good picture of enemy activity.

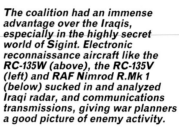

Above: Most secret of Gulf air war participants was the RAF's Nimrod R.Mk 1 electronic reconnaissance aircraft, probably based at Seeb in Oman.

Left: Normally resident at Metz, one of the French air force's few EC.160 Gabriels was dispatched to the Gulf, where it assisted in the allied electronic intelligence-gathering effort, working closely with a DC-8 and two Pumas.

the border. This is a time-honored technique to force the enemy to use their radios to pass warning messages and to light up their radars against a possible preemptive strike. But, collecting against Iraqi communications was difficult. During Operation Desert Shield the Iraqis minimized the use of their radios and air-defense radars, reducing both Elint available to the allies and equipment failures.

The Rivet Joint force may have been reinforced before the opening of Operation Desert Storm. Then, in the words of a USAF general, "we had a Rivet Joint in the air 24 hours a day." There have been widespread reports that the allies were able to monitor Iraqi communications throughout the conflict, and that this provided

much valuable intelligence.

While, in peacetime, the RC-135s normally work in isolation around the borders of potential threats, in Desert Storm they were integrated with not only other Elint assets – air, land and sea – but also with offensive EW and hard-kill weapons throughout the war.

"We systematically attacked every [C³I center] we could find," according to USAF General Glenn Profitt, chief of electronic combat forces for Central Command. It required the Rivet Joints and other allied Comint aircraft to locate these targets and determine which were important and which could be ignored.

Other allied actions made the Rivet Joints' job easier. For example, the Iraqis had put down extensive landline communications

– including using fiber-optic technology – to provide secure communications, with extensive back-up systems, including buried telephone lines and troposcatter radios. These lines became a target for allied special operations forces, forcing the Iraqis to resort to radio links that would be subject to intercept by the Rivet Joints or other allied Comint. Once they were detected, analyzed and located, they would be prioritized and probably put on the target list for hard-kill weapons carried by tactical aircraft, or by jamming, such as from EC-130H Compass Call aircraft.

It is likely that the Rivet Joints may have branched out into monitoring Iraqi air-defense radars as well as communications. While SAC is reluctant to discuss the

specifics of any hardware changes made to the Rivet Joints as a result of the Gulf war, one possible Rivet Joint radar-collection target was the lower-frequency Iraqi early-warning radars that may have had the potential to detect F-117A stealth aircraft. Certainly, effective allied Elint against these radars enabled them to be put near the top of the targeting list, which resulted in their destruction in the opening hours of Operation Desert Storm.

Regardless of which emitters they were listening to, Rivet Joints allowed allied commanders to electronically watch the Iraqi air defenses in action. According to USAF Colonel George Muellner, assistant deputy chief of staff for requirements for TAC, it was Rivet Joint-produced information that showed that Iraqi air-defense radars would shut down as soon as they detected F-4G 'Wild Weasels' switching on their fire-control radars – providing proof of the power of the 'Weasel'.

"The Elint nets worked well . . . there was no problem with the Elint nets," was how one USAF officer summarized the results of the Gulf war. The Rivet Joints were only part of a massive allied Elint operation, carried out in the months of Operation Desert Shield as well as during the fighting. US Navy EP-3Es and EA-3Bs were also reportedly committed to the Gulf. USAF TR-1As were also used for Comint and radar surveillance, supplemented by US Army ESM aircraft, both fixed wing (including RC-12s and RV-1D Quick Looks) and helicopters (including EH-60A Quick Fix IIBs), which provided intelligence vital to the rapid outflanking movements of the ground campaign. At least one USAF-USMC Senior Warrior C-130 was also in action. EW combat aircraft such as the US Navy's EA-6B and the USAF's F-4G, EF-111A and possibly RF-4Cs were used to help refine the electronic order of battle prior to hostilities. The British contributed one or more RAF Nimrod R.Mk 1s, and the French deployed one DC-8 Sarigue, one EC.160 Gabriel and two modified SA 330 Puma helicopters. It is known that there were other airborne Elint platforms – both US and allied – whose work is likely to remain secret for years to come.

The ESM problems seen in earlier conflicts – adapting systems and threat libraries of electronic signatures originally designed against Soviet-designed threats to include Western-designed threats – did not recur.

D.I.

US Army Aviation in Saudi

"There were just row after row of AH-64A Apaches, they stretched all along the ramp at Dhahran. I didn't know we had that many helicopters!" said a US Army soldier in August 1990.

From 8 August a constant stream of USAF C-5 transport planes was arriving at the Saudi Arabian air base to deliver hundreds of US Army helicopters. Eventually, some 1,000 helicopters would be operating in support of US Army units throughout the Middle East.

Ever since the Vietnam War the US Army has invested heavily in rotary-wing hardware, and has developed a concept of operations – AirLand Battle – to integrate helicopters closely with ground units. AirLand Battle calls for units, from battalions up to armies, to penetrate deep into the enemy's rear, to surround and eventually destroy his main forces. Helicopters are to be used to lift troops behind enemy lines, move supplies forward to advancing ground units and to destroy enemy armor with surprise missile attacks. Terrain, night or bad weather does not provide the enemy with shelter or a safe haven thanks to the use of night-vision equipment and electronic surveillance.

By 1990 each US Army division had been provided with a combat aviation brigade to enable it to put AirLand Battle into practice. Army corps have their own aviation brigades, which include two battalions of Apaches, to give corps commanders the capability to strike deep at enemy second-echelon units. The US Army also has a unique air-mobile unit, the 101st Airborne Division (Air Assault), which has been developed for strategic helicopter operations deep behind enemy lines.

During August and September 1990 six complete aviation brigades and numerous small support-helicopter units were deployed to Saudi Arabia. First to arrive on USAF C-5s were the Special Operations Command MH-6s and MH-60 Pave Hawks of the 160th Special Operations Aviation Brigade. In the early days of Desert Shield US commanders were very concerned with the Iraqi armor superiority, and top priority was given to getting anti-armor forces to Saudi Arabia. So the 82nd Aviation Brigade, of the 82nd Airborne Division, with its 18 AH-6As, 12 AH-1F Cobras, 31 OH-58 Kiowa scouts and 41 UH-60 Black Hawks, was flown to Dhahran in the first days of the Desert Shield deployment. To further bolster the anti-armor capability of the XVIII Airborne Corps, the 12th Combat Aviation Brigade, with 36 AH-64As and 40

support helicopters, was flown into Dhahran from its bases in Germany during late August. Transport helicopters were provided by the CH-47 Chinooks, UH-60s and UH-1 Hueys of the 18th Aviation Brigade.

In mid-September, US Navy fast transport ships started to arrive in the Middle East with hundreds of helicopters on board for the aviation brigades of the 101st Division, the 1st Cavalry Division and 24th Infantry Division (Mechanized). The 101st boasted some 36 Apaches, 21 AH-1Fs, 122 UH-60s, 91 OH-58s and 32 CH-47Ds. In the aviation brigades of the other two divisions of XVIII Corps were 18 Apaches, 15 UH-60s and 25 OH-58s.

After arriving in Saudi Arabia the US Army helicopter units deployed to remote airstrips to practice operating in the harsh desert conditions. The featureless terrain made it difficult for aircrews to use their night-vision equipment, and during the early months of Desert Shield there were a number of crashes. Eventually the helicopter crews mastered desert flying, thanks to intensive training and electronic aids.

Prior to its deployment to Saudi Arabia the Apache had developed a notorious reputation for unreliability. This, however, was due to a shortage of spares in the US and the AH-64 units that moved to the Middle East were provided with extensive spares support. Soon Saudi-based units were reporting availability levels in excess of those attained in peacetime; in some cases, rates of over 90 per cent were attained.

To give the US ground forces an offensive capability, President Bush ordered the US VII Corps to Saudi Arabia from Germany in November 1990. The armor-heavy formation took a formidable force of more than 300 helicopters with it.

Each of its three divisions' aviation brigades was equipped as those in the armored divisions of XVIII Corps. The 11th Combat Aviation Brigade was assigned as a corps-level unit, with 36 Apaches of the 4th/229th Attack Helicopter Regiment and 2nd/6th Cavalry Regiment. CH-47Ds, UH-60s, OH-58s and UH-1Hs were attached to the brigade to move forward supplies and for observation duties.

T.R.

Above: Dehydration and dust are an ever-present hazard in the heat of a Saudi desert and became a problem to men and machines alike. But the usual field innovations kept everything at a high rate of readiness.

Above: A clutch of Sikorsky UH-60 Black Hawks rests during a lull in the almost continuous grind of assault exercises that allowed coalition forces to bring combat skills to the highest pitch as they readied themselves for war.

Below: Wearing full NBC kit, Army ground support personnel conduct a decontamination exercise using a Kiowa armed scout helicopter. In the event, Iraq did not employ chemical weaponry but the allied forces were well prepared.

Above: An OH-58 Kiowa scout leads AH-1 HueyCobra and AH-64A Apache gunships during an exercise.

Below: Ancient and modern methods of transportation meet as a UH-60 Black Hawk overflies camels.

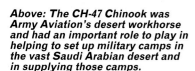

Above: The CH-47 Chinook was Army Aviation's desert workhorse and had an important role to play in helping to set up military camps in the vast Saudi Arabian desert and in supplying those camps.

Right: The obligatory sunglasses and flying helmet are modelled by an Army Apache pilot from the 101st Airborne Division.

Apache on the Warpath

Lieutenant Colonel William Bryan, 2nd Battalion, 229th Aviation Regiment, AH-64 Apache

"We'd had rumblings for some days that we were to be sent to the desert. We were alerted on 7 August, given seven days' notice to move. Most of the battalion's wheeled vehicles, the support and sustainment pieces, were sent to Jacksonville for shipment by sea. The fighting end of the battalion, 34 aircraft together with a few wheeled vehicles and essential pieces of equipment, moved from our base at Fort Rucker to Fort Benning in Georgia on 15 August.

"The battalion was moved out to Saudi Arabia over the next eight days, in 10 C-5 Galaxy sorties and 10 C-141 StarLifter sorties. Once in-theater, the helicopters were reassembled. Every aircraft was ready to go within 72 hours. It was almost like a peacetime exercise; some tasks took us even less time than it would have done back in the States.

"An Apache battalion has 18 AH-64s, together with 13 OH-58 scout helicopters. There are three UH-60 Black Hawks, used to haul things like ammunition and water, as command and control platforms, and for search and rescue.

"We were attached to the 101st Airborne Division. It's the only air assault division in the world, and it has the largest aviation brigade. There are 10 battalions, including two Apache battalions, one battalion of CH-47 heavy lift

helicopters, one AH-1 Cobra attack battalion, one Cavalry squadron with AH-1s and OH-58s, one command and control battalion flying UH-1 Hueys, and one air traffic control battalion.

"Our first base was about 50 km west of Dhahran, 100 km south of the Kuwait border. We were there to block the Iraqi armored forces massed on the border. The only assets present in-country were aviation assets, so we were up there as a deterrent. About 80 per cent of the division's equipment was coming by sea, so for the first month or so we were simply buying time, deterring an Iraqi attack on Saudi Arabia. Once the rest of the division and its equipment arrived, we were a real defense.

"Up until the beginning of December, we were strictly on the defensive. However, once the heavily armored VIIth US Corps began to occupy our sector, we began the transition to an offensive plan. The XVIIIth Airborne Corps of which we were part moved much further west. We were to be part of a deep strike through lightly defended areas of Iraq."

Above right and right: Orders to move to the Gulf were quickly set in motion by Army Aviation units. Armed helicopters like the Apache and HueyCobra were airlifted out by MAC, with less essential heavy equipment following courtesy of Military Sealift Command.

from page 36

29 November The Security Council passed Resolution 678, which authorized member states to use 'all necessary means' against Iraq, unless that country withdrew its military forces from Kuwait by 15 January 1991. In effect, the Resolution was a countdown to war.

6 December Following a long period of intensive diplomatic activity, President Saddam Hussein agreed to allow all foreign nationals to leave Iraq and Kuwait, thereby abandoning his previous policy of using them as 'human shields' at possible targets. Within a few days all of those who wished to leave had done so.

13 December The US government announced that it now had the following forces deployed in Saudi Arabia: 750 main battle tanks, 90 air superiority fighters (F-14s and F-15s), 335 attack aircraft (A-6s, AV-8Bs, A-10s, F-111Fs and F-117As) and 220 dual-role aircraft (F-15Es, F-16s and F/A-18s). In addition, there were F-4G 'Wild Weasel' and EF-111A electronic support aircraft, large numbers of KC-10 and KC-135 tankers, and several hundred helicopters and transport aircraft.

24 December President Saddam Hussein declared that if war broke out, Israel would be his first target for attack.

28 December The carriers USS *America* and USS *Theodore Roosevelt* left the USA to join the US forces assigned to Desert Shield.

2 January 1991 NATO announced that it would deploy 42 combat aircraft of the Allied Mobile Force to bases in southern Turkey, to strengthen the defenses in that area and deter a possible attack on that country by Iraq. The force comprised 18 AlphaJets from Germany, 18 Mirage 5s from Belgium and six RF-104 Starfighters from Italy.

6 January In a bellicose speech to the Iraqi nation, President Saddam Hussein stated that his armed forces were fully mobilized and ready to fight in order to maintain the hold on Kuwait.

9 January US Secretary of State Baker met the Iraqi Foreign Minister Tariq Aziz in Geneva, in a bid to arrive at a settlement to the Gulf crisis that would be acceptable to both sides. The talks broke down after a few hours, without agreement.

15 January The Security Council deadline passed without military action, to obvious sighs of relief in Baghdad. Perhaps, as the Iraqi President had assured his people all along, the Americans and the other coalition forces simply had no stomach for a fight?

to page 48

Above: Other elements of Allied Command Europe's Mobile Force that were deployed in reply to the Turkish request for assistance included a total of 18 Luftwaffe AlphaJet light attack aircraft.

Radar Reconnaissance

A most important facet of operations during Desert Storm was the provision of timely intelligence, particularly concerning the movements of Iraqi ground forces. Standard tactical reconnaissance aircraft such as the McDonnell Douglas RF-4C and Grumman F-14/TARPS were widely used for target and battle damage assessment, but the crucial task of providing the 'big picture' fell largely to aircraft carrying stand-off radars. Not that these did not undertake reconnaissance of a more intimate nature, being used for individual targetting requirements, but their ability to monitor large areas of the battlezone made them invaluable to theater commanders.

Two USAF types were heavily used, the Lockheed U-2R/TR-1A and Grumman/Boeing E-8A. Drawing aircraft from both the 9th Strategic Reconnaissance Wing at Beale AFB, California, and the 17th Reconnaissance Wing at RAF Alconbury, UK, the 1704th Reconnaissance Squadron (Provisional) was established at Taif in Saudi Arabia with both U-2R and TR-1A aircraft to provide high-altitude surveillance. Dozens of missions were flown before, during and after the conflict, the TR-1As using the ASARS-2 nose-mounted radar to peer deep inside Iraq and Kuwait from their lofty perch.

ASARS-2 is a synthetic aperture radar which gives high-resolution imagery at long slant ranges, detecting armor and truck concentrations. Allied to ASARS-2, the U-2R/TR-1As carry a full Comint (Communications intelligence) suite, allowing them to eavesdrop on Iraqi military communications. The gathered intelligence is data linked to ground stations for 'filtering', whereby intelligence personnel sort the raw data into what is trivial and what is

Top and above: In helping provide senior allied commanders with the 'big picture', the TR-1A and U-2R employed radar and other sensors to obtain top-grade intelligence on Iraqi dispositions and, with the aid of Comint equipment, on Iraqi intentions. Details of the full extent of TR-1A operations are sketchy but mission symbols on one aircraft provide clues as to the number of sorties flown.

crucial. At least two of the 'C-Span III' U-2Rs were deployed to Taif, featuring a large satellite communications 'data-shunt' on its back. This allows the real-time transmission of gathered intelligence across very large distances.

U-2Rs and TR-1As were also used in the traditional photo-reconnaissance role, but they were hampered in these operations for some of the time due to the unusually bad weather early in the war, and smoke from oil fires later. Naturally the operations of the 1704th RS(P) are surrounded by secrecy, yet it can be assumed that the U-2Rs and TR-1As played a crucial role in providing the Riyadh command with excellent intelligence about the intentions of and forces available to their opposite numbers in Baghdad.

In military terms, the TR-1A is regarded as an intelligence gatherer, whereas the E-8A Joint STARS is considered more as a battlefield control platform. Still firmly in the development stage, the two J-STARS prototypes were rushed to the Gulf to bolster the coalition surveillance effort. Flying with the hastily-established 4411th Joint STARS Squadron at Riyadh, the two aircraft amassed more than 600 hours flying time during 54 combat missions.

Joint STARS is intended to achieve for the land war what the E-3 Sentry does for the air war, namely, to provide a complete picture of vehicles in a given area. A giant Norden side-looking radar is mounted underneath a Boeing 707 airframe, with operator stations inside the cabin. In SAR (Synthetic Aperture Radar) mode it can detect and locate stationary objects such as parked armor. By alternating the SAR mode with a Doppler moving target mode, the radar can accurately plot slow-moving objects and display an overall tactical picture on a screen.

J-STARS became a victim of its own success in the Gulf, as everyone wanted its intelligence. With only two systems available, the 4411th had a hectic time trying to fulfill as many requests as possible. However, its intelligence was astonishing, and its prowess forced the Iraqis to abandon convoys as a means of moving vehicles *en masse*, having to move them in twos or threes to try to defeat the ever-vigilant eyes of the J-STARS operators.

In addition to its basic surveillance operation, the J-STARS also acted as a control and targetting platform for tactical aircraft. Its most notable use in this role was when hunting 'Scud' missiles with F-15E aircraft. The radar was used to spot 'Scuds' in the western Iraqi desert, target information being passed to the F-15Es. The two aircraft types proved exceptionally compatible, as the type of SAR imagery generated by J-STARS and the APG-70 radar of the F-15E are very similar. The E-8s were used to direct many other allied aircraft types onto targets such as vehicle/armor groups.

Both E-8As performed uncomplainingly in Desert Storm, but prioritizing their missions rapidly became a problem as J-STARS's capabilities became manifest. Intelligence officers wanted long loiters to produce complete positional data on Iraqi ground units, while air force targetters wanted the E-8 to guide tactical aircraft onto individual targets. However, the Joint STARS emerged as one of the many success stories of the war.

Radar reconnaissance of a more local nature was provided by a third stand-off radar platform, the Grumman OV-1D Mohawk. Deployed alongside Grumman RV-1D Elint and Beech RU-21/RC-12D Comint platforms, the often overlooked Mohawk was mainly used at corps level to provide battlefield commanders with radar intelligence of their opponents. However, in certain circumstances the Mohawk was required to turn its side-looking radar to intelligence-gathering of a wider nature, particularly while J-STARS was not airborne and when TR-1s could not launch from Taif due to excessive crosswinds.

For stand-off reconnaissance, the OV-1D is fitted with an APS-94D side-looking radar in a large fairing under the starboard forward fuselage. This sensor has moving target capability and presents a picture of vehicles within a specified area similar to, though much more limited than, those of the other platforms. The type also gathers more conventional reconnaissance using cameras, and can be reconfigured from SLAR-carrier to infra-red reconnaissance platform at field level in a brief time.

Together, the U-2/TR-1, E-8 and OV-1 gave coalition commanders the ability to monitor the precise movements of Iraqi army units throughout the war, allowing theater and field commanders to make their tactical decisions with great confidence. More specifically, the success of the E-8 has gone a long way towards ensuring that it remains within the defense budget over the coming years. **D.D.**

Above: Mission-related sensors on the U-2R and TR-1A are located in the nose section and in the bulky superpods which mar the otherwise clean lines of the type's massive plank-like wing structure.

Right: In addition to the mission symbols depicted on the previous page, some TR-1As and U-2Rs that operated with the 1704th RS(P) in the Gulf acquired tail artwork.

Below: Hurriedly called into use even though still very much under development, the E-8 J-STARS accumulated over 600 hours while making a valuable contribution to allied success. Its job was to provide overall control of the battle field, combining reconnaissance and command in real time.

Strike Force

Since the early days of August 1990, military power had been pouring into Saudi Arabia, the Gulf states and Turkey so that on 16 January 1991, the day before Desert Storm broke, a total of 600,000 troops, 4,000 tanks and 150 major warships were on hand. Combined with the huge amount of air assets assembled in the theater, the combat force at General Schwarzkopf's command was the most powerful ever gathered in modern times.

Leading the air assets were the precision strike aircraft, which would shoulder the brunt of the campaign during the opening days. F-117s, F-15Es, F-111s, A-6s and Tornados would provide the main thrust of attack as the coalition sought to break down the Iraqi defense infrastructure. Enabling these sophisticated jets to perform their task was a huge supporting cast, consisting of tankers, escort fighters, defence suppression platforms, reconnaissance aircraft, special forces and rescue assets.

Other air assets assembled in the Gulf region were primarily concerned with the ground war which would inevitably follow the initial air assaults, but these too could undertake their fair share of attack missions to soften up the Iraqi defenses before the main land thrust. Principal among these types were attack helicopters, AV-8Bs, F/A-18s, F-16s, A-10s, Jaguars and B-52 bombers, the latter to fly from as far away as Diego Garcia, England and Spain to deliver their enormous loads of destruction.

Finally a huge armada of transports and helicopters was involved to ensure that every coalition serviceman had the supplies and equipment necessary to perform at the peak of his capabilities when the call finally came to go to war.

Above: Twelve RAF Jaguar and over 40 Tornado strike aircraft were sent to air bases in Bahrain and Saudi Arabia under Operation Granby. On the outbreak of war, they flew bombing, defense-suppression and reconnaissance duties.

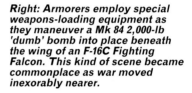

Right: Armorers employ special weapons-loading equipment as they maneuver a Mk 84 2,000-lb 'dumb' bomb into place beneath the wing of an F-16C Fighting Falcon. This kind of scene became commonplace as war moved inexorably nearer.

Left: Although it is no slouch in air-to-air combat, the Fighting Falcon functioned primarily as a strike fighter throughout Desert Storm. Close to 200 USAF F-16Cs were eventually deployed to Gulf airfields during the build-up.

Left: In addition to the large force that was assembled to the south of Kuwait and Iraq, further US air power concentrations could be found at Incirlik, Turkey, with F-111Es of the 20th TFW available for interdiction/strike missions.

Left: Almost certainly making its combat swan song, the Phantom was assigned in modest quantities for specialist missions like defense suppression and reconnaissance. A gaggle of F-4G 'Wild Weasels' is depicted here.

Right and above right: Tactical Air Command's much-vaunted F-117A stealth fighter made its way overseas for the very first time in August 1990 when elements from Tonopah's 37th TFW were deployed to the Khamis Mushait Air Base in Saudi Arabia, this being a brand-new facility with extensive hardened shelter accommodation.

Strike Force

Left: With Iraq possessing a huge force of tanks and other armored fighting vehicles, 'tank-busting' potential was a prerequisite of the allied air armada. There are few machines that are more effective in dealing with armor than the A-10 Thunderbolt II.

Above: Resplendent in a coat of freshly applied 'desert pink', an RAF Tornado GR.Mk 1 streaks across inhospitable terrain at low level during one of many training trips. Bereft of visual cues, low flying was hazardous; two RAF aircraft were lost on such sorties.

Above: Still in the process of being introduced to operational service when Desert Shield got under way, the F-15E Strike Eagle was hurriedly sent to the Gulf.

Left: F-16 Fighting Falcons were drawn from a variety of regular and Air National Guard outfits. These included a batch from the 388th TFW, which is normally resident at Hill, Utah.

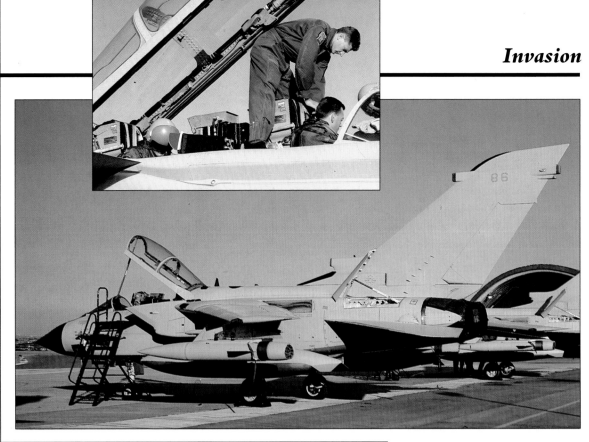

Above and inset: In addition to RAF and Saudi Arabian Tornados, a modest contingent of Italian air force personnel was assigned to the coalition and these also flew the Tornado, employing a desert camouflage scheme similar to that of the RAF machines.

Below: Canadian military hardware in the Gulf included warships as well as one CF-18 squadron, which undertook strike/attack duties on the outbreak of war.

RAF Tornados and Jaguars were used to give warships some practice in dealing with air threats, and often simulated anti-ship missiles during the months of the build-up to war.

Right: France's contribution to the air power that was amassed in the Gulf was spearheaded by the Jaguar, but the Armée de l'air did also send Mirage 2000 interceptor fighters and Mirage F1CRs for tactical reconnaissance.

Above: For more than three decades, the massive strike power of the Boeing B-52 has been available to American commanders. The giant bombers were poised to strike at Iraq from bases as far apart as Great Britain and Diego Garcia in the Indian Ocean.

Below: Red-shirted 'ordies' – ordnance technicians – on a carrier load an AIM-9 Sidewinder missile onto a US Navy F-14. Fighters like the Tomcat had been flying defensive CAPs since the start of the crisis, but were now about to go on the offensive.

Above: A pair of EF-111A electronic warfare aircraft skim low over the desert. The 'Sparkvark' is a highly sophisticated jamming aircraft, and would be essential to the success of any attacks against the extensive and apparently effective Iraqi air defenses around Baghdad.

A Grumman F-14 Tomcat stands by, ready for launch on one of the waist catapults of an American supercarrier in the Red Sea. The six carriers the US Navy deployed to the Middle East made a huge contribution to the air power available to the coalition.

Coalition Air Power Dispositions on the Eve of Operation Desert Storm

This map depicts the main air bases of both Iraq and the coalition forces on the eve of war, together with the principal combat units assembled under Desert Shield at each of their respective bases. The inset area provides detail of the central Gulf region, where the majority of allied air power was concentrated. Triangles denote the principal cities.

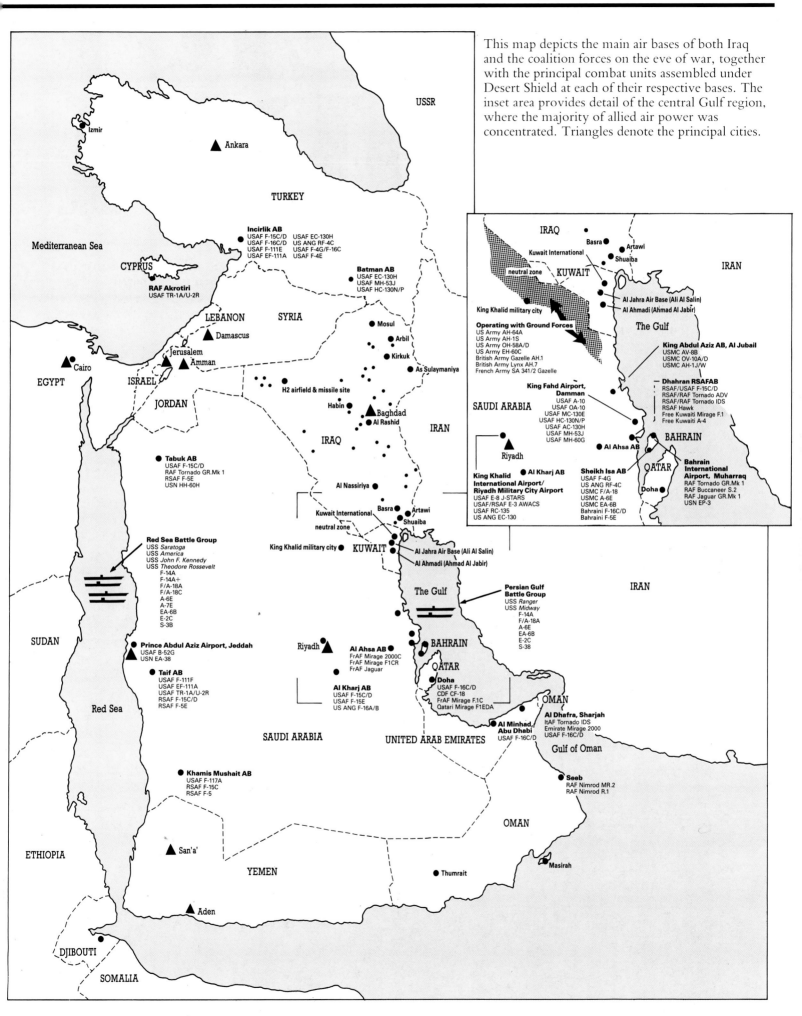

USSR

Izmir

▲ Ankara

TURKEY

Mediterranean Sea

Incirlik AB
USAF F-15C/D   USAF EC-130H
USAF F-16C/D   US ANG RF-4C
USAF F-111E   USAF F-4G/F-16C
USAF EF-111A   USAF F-4E

CYPRUS

RAF Akrotiri
USAF TR-1A/U-2R

LEBANON

▲ Damascus

SYRIA

Batman AB
USAF EC-130H
USAF MH-53J
USAF HC-130N/P

▲ Mosul

● Arbil

● Kirkuk

● As Sulaymaniya

Jerusalem ▲

▲ Cairo   ▲ Amman

EGYPT   ISRAEL

JORDAN   H2 airfield & missile site

Habin   ▲ Baghdad
Al Rashid   IRAN

● Al Rashid

IRAQ

Tabuk AB
USAF F-15C/D
RAF Tornado GR.Mk 1
RSAF F-5E
USN HH-60H

● Al Nassiriya

Kuwait International

neutral zone

Basra ● Artawi
Shuaiba

Red Sea Battle Group
USS *Saratoga*
USS *America*
USS *John F. Kennedy*
USS *Theodore Roosevelt*
F-14A
F-14A+
F/A-18A
F/A-18C
A-6E
A-7E
EA-6B
E-2C
S-3B

King Khalid military city ● KUWAIT

Al Jahra Air Base (Ali Al Salin)
Al Ahmadi (Ahmad Al Jabir)

SUDAN

The Gulf

IRAN

Prince Abdul Aziz Airport, Jeddah
USAF B-52G
USN EA-38

Riyadh ▲

Persian Gulf Battle Group
USS *Ranger*
USS *Midway*
F-14A
F/A-18A
A-6E
EA-6B
E-2C
S-38

Al Ahsa AB
FrAF Mirage 2000C
FrAF Mirage F1CR
FrAF Jaguar

Taif AB
USAF F-111F
USAF EF-111A
USAF TR-1A/U-2R
RSAF F-15C/D
RSAF F-5E

BAHRAIN

QATAR

● Doha

Red Sea

Al Kharj AB
USAF F-15C/D
USAF F-15E
US ANG F-16A/B

Doha
USAF F-16C/D
CDF CF-18
FrAF Mirage F1C
Qatari Mirage F1EDA

SAUDI ARABIA

UNITED ARAB EMIRATES

OMAN

Al Minhad, Abu Dhabi
USAF F-16C/D

Al Dhafra, Sharjah
ItAF Tornado IDS
Emirate Mirage 2000
USAF F-16C/D

Gulf of Oman

Khamis Mushait AB
USAF F-117A
RSAF F-15C
RSAF F-5

● Seeb
RAF Nimrod MR.2
RAF Nimrod R.1

▲ San'a'

YEMEN

OMAN

ETHIOPIA

● Thumrait

▲ Aden

● Masirah

DJIBOUTI

SOMALIA

Inset (central Gulf region)

IRAQ

● Basra   ● Artawi
● Shuaiba

Kuwait International

neutral zone   KUWAIT   IRAN

King Khalid military city

Al Jahra Air Base (Ali Al Salin)
Al Ahmadi (Ahmad Al Jabir)

The Gulf

Operating with Ground Forces
US Army AH-64A
US Army AH-1S
US Army OH-58A/D
US Army EH-60C
British Army Gazelle AH.1
British Army Lynx AH.7
French Army SA 341/2 Gazelle

King Abdul Aziz AB, Al Jubail
USMC AV-8B
USMC OV-10A/D
USMC AH-1J/W

King Fahd Airport, Damman
USAF A-10
USAF OA-10
USAF MC-130E
USAF HC-130N/P
USAF AC-130H
USAF MH-53J
USAF MH-60G

Dhahran RSAFAB
RSAF/USAF F-15C/D
RSAF/RAF Tornado ADV
RSAF/RAF Tornado IDS
RSAF Hawk
Free Kuwaiti Mirage F.1
Free Kuwaiti A-4

SAUDI ARABIA

▲ Riyadh

BAHRAIN

● Al Ahsa AB   QATAR

● Doha

Bahrain International Airport, Muharraq
RAF Tornado GR.Mk 1
RAF Buccaneer S.2
RAF Jaguar GR.Mk 1
USN EP-3

King Khalid International Airport/Riyadh Military City Airport
USAF E-8 J-STARS
USAF/RSAF E-3 AWACS
USAF RC-135
US ANG EC-130

● Al Kharj AB

Sheikh Isa AB
USAF F-4G
US ANG RF-4C
USMC F/A-18
USMC A-6E
USMC EA-6B
Bahraini F-16C/D
Bahraini F-5E

DESERT STORM

17 to 25 January 1991

Following 5½ months which had seen the largest military build-up since 1945, and culminating in intensive diplomatic preparations to secure agreement for military action from each of the states involved, the US-led coalition was now ready to go into action. The time for talking was over. Now military might alone would decide whether Kuwait would ever be allowed to resume its existence as an independent state, or if it would forever remain a province of Iraq.

17 January, Thursday As they had been throughout every minute of the previous 5½ months, E-2 Hawkeye and E-3 Sentry AWACS aircraft were airborne in positions to track the movements of friendly and Iraqi aircraft. As the deadline passed these planes continued operating as before, giving no sign that anything was in the offing.

The first coalition aircraft to take off specifically for the initial attack on Iraq (soon after dark on the evening of 16 January) belonged to Task Force 'Normandy', a force of eight AH-64 Apache helicopters belonging to the US Army's 101st Airborne Division with a CH-53 mother ship to assist with navigation. In addition to its load of Hellfire laser-guided missiles and 70-mm rockets, each attack helicopter carried a 230-gal external fuel tank. The task force's mission was to destroy two Iraqi air-defense radars to the west of Baghdad and some 380 nm (700 km) inside Iraqi territory, to open a corridor through which attack forces of high-speed jets could pass unseen. The helicopter attack was timed to begin shortly before the main air strike forces entered the radars' areas of cover. The operation was to be flown by helicopters rather than fixed-wing aircraft because of the

importance of the targets, the need to achieve surprise, and the requirement to get an immediate assessment of the results of the attack. In the words of Colonel Dave Carothers of the US Army Aviation Division, "They wanted to ensure that they had eyeballs on the target, and that they had in fact taken the sites out."

Next to take off, at about 1:00 a.m. on 17 January, were the heavily-laden tanker planes which were to supply fuel to the shorter-range aircraft penetrating into Iraq. Some 60 tankers, US Air Force KC-135s and KC10s, US Navy KA-6Ds and Royal Air Force Victors and VC10s, provided refueling support for the initial wave of attacks. In the areas used by the AWACS and tanker aircraft, US Air Force F-15s, US Navy F-14s, Canadian CF-18s and Royal Air Force Tornado F.Mk 3s flew combat air patrols in readiness for any attempt by the Iraqis to deliver a riposte.

At around midnight, F-117A 'Stealth Fighters' of the 415th TFS, 37th TFW, began taking off from Khamis Mushait in the extreme south of Saudi Arabia and heading north to rendezvous with their assigned tankers. Aircraft of other waves of the initial attack soon

to page 49 **(17 January continued)**

Above: The skies above Baghdad are lit with an awesome display of wasted firepower. Cruise missiles and F-117A 'Stealth Fighters' strike with impunity at some of the most heavily defended targets in the world, as the fury of the Iraqi gunners comes to nothing.

Left: Even as the first attacks struck stunningly at the heart of Baghdad, the peaceful desert night was shattered all over the Arabian peninsula by the sound of jet engines. Thousands of warplanes added their own contributions to the pinpoint destruction raining down on Iraq.

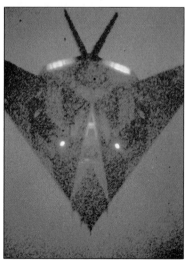

Spearheading the attack were America's most advanced aircraft. The Lockheed F-117A 'Stealth Fighter' (above) struck silently out of the night, while the F-15E fighter bomber (left) carried more ordnance than a World War II heavy bomber, and delivered it with far greater accuracy.

Left: The waiting is over. The most skillful pilots in the world, their abilities sharpened by months of preparation, have been given the go-ahead to unleash the most concentrated aerial campaign of modern times.

Below: War in the Gulf was dominated by technology. Coalition aircraft made their attacks by day or night. Whatever the visibility they were able to hit their targets with an accuracy measured in inches.

from page 48 (**17 January continued**)

lowed them into the air.

Next in order of launching were the Tomahawk surface-to-surface cruise missiles which, at measured intervals, roared like so many flaming fingers into the night sky from the battleships *Wisconsin* and *Missouri* and the cruiser *San Jacinto* from positions near the head of the Persian Gulf. In all, a total of 52 of these weapons would be fired from the warships during the first day of the conflict.

The Tomahawk missiles led the attack on the Iraqi capital, and the first independent confirmation that the war had begun came with a CNN news report at 2:37 a.m. Television pictures showed tracer rounds arcing over Baghdad, punctuated by a succession of explosions as the Tomahawks found their targets.

Meanwhile, the Apache helicopters of Task Force 'Normandy' had arrived in the area of their targets and split into two teams of four, one assigned to each radar site. Commencing at 2:38 a.m., the helicopter crews delivered their attacks from ranges between 3 and 1½ nm (from 6 to 3 km), using their infra-red night vision equipment to aim their weapons with devastating accuracy. First they directed their fire at the electrical generators at each site, then at the communications facilities, and finally at the radars themselves. In less than two minutes the Apaches fired 27 Hellfire laser-guided missiles, about 100 70-mm rockets and some 4,000 rounds of 30-mm ammunition. In that short time, both of the radar stations were reduced to smoking ruins. Their task completed, the helicopters turned round and headed for friendly territory.

Also at about this time, F-117As commenced their attack on Iraqi air-defense installations to the west of Baghdad, to prepare the path for other attack forces. The first attack by a manned aircraft on Baghdad itself took place at 3:00 a.m., when one of the 'Stealth Fighters' hit a communications center. That night F-117As of the 415th and 416 TFSs attacked 34 targets, all of them associated with the Iraqi air-defense system, of which 13 were in the area in and around Baghdad. Each 'Stealth Fighter' carried a 4,000-lb load of laser-guided bombs made up of 2,000-lb GBU-10s, or the stronger-cased GBU-27s designed for use against concrete-protected targets, or the 500-lb GBU-12s.

As the follow-up raiding forces headed for their various targets, the degree of disruption of the air-defense control system caused by the earlier attacks meant that often the defenders had little warning of their approach before the forces hit their targets. F-15Es used their new LANTIRN navigation pods to assist in night attacks on 'Scud' missile launching sites, missile storage bunkers and other targets.

to page 50 (**17 January continued**)

Desert Storm

from page 49 **(17 January continued)**

F-111s attacked precision targets with laser-guided bombs, and airfields with Durandel runway-cratering bombs.

Royal Air Force Tornados hit three airfields that night. During one of these attacks, eight Tornados from the Muharraq squadron carrying JP 233 airfield denial weapons hit the airfield at Tallil.

Royal Air Force Tornados were the only aircraft equipped with the specialized JP 233 runway-denial weapon. This dispenses hundreds of sub-munitions to crater and mine runways and taxiways, keeping the enemy from taking off or landing.

Fighter support for the attacking forces was provided by F-15 and F-14 fighters, and defense-suppression support was provided by F-4Gs and US Navy A-7s and F/A-18s carrying HARM anti-radar missiles, and RAF Tornados carrying the new ALARM defense-suppression missile. Electronic-jamming support came from EF-111A Ravens, EA-6B Prowlers, EC-130 Compass Call aircraft and (according to some reports) a number of electronic decoy drones.

It is believed that the first coalition aircraft to brush with an Iraqi fighter was an unarmed EF-111A Raven aircraft engaged in a medium-altitude stand-off jamming mission over western Iraq. A Mirage F1 rolled in behind the Raven and launched a missile at it. The American pilot, Captain Jim Denton, put his aircraft into a high-speed diving turn to avoid the missile, and released chaff and fired infra-red decoy flares. The missile passed safely clear of the Raven, which pulled out of the dive a few hundred feet above the ground and entered a tight turn to the right. The Mirage pilot did not quite manage to follow this maneuver, however. Captain Brent Brandon, the Raven's Electronic Warfare Officer, recalled, "We got so low, he couldn't hack it and smeared into the ground behind us." The EF-111A's crew observed a sudden flash, then a fireball behind them as the Mirage smashed itself to pieces. It was the first Iraqi aircraft destroyed during the conflict.

For the initial wave of air strikes, the 48th Tactical Fighter Wing launched 53 F-111Fs in forces of between four and six aircraft. These attacked a dozen separate targets, including the major airfields at Balad and Jalibah in Iraq, and those at Ali Al Salem and Ahmed al-Jaber in Kuwait where the hardened aircraft shelters were thought to contain 'Scud' missiles; the F-111Fs also attacked chemical weapons storage bunkers at H-3 airfield, Salman Pak and Ad Diwaniyah. Although they had fighter and SEAD (Suppression of Enemy Air Defenses) support packages operating in target areas, the F-111Fs operated independently as single-aircraft units flying in trail with a 1-1½ minute spacing. During the ingress for their first attacks, many of the crews were struck by the general air of unreality of it all. Lieutenant Dave Giachetti, WSO in one of the planes, remembered, "I thought it was kinda eerie, because outside everything was so calm and so quiet. We went in at low level on TFR. In the built-up areas

to page 51 **(17 January continued)**

Above: General Dynamics F-111Fs have been in service for many years, but they remain some of the most effective all-weather strike aircraft available. F-111Fs based at Taif were used to make pinpoint attacks on high-value Iraqi targets on the first night of Desert Storm.

Below: Coalition plans called for an unprecedented air campaign against Iraq and the invasion forces in Kuwait. Thousands of sorties required hundreds of thousands of bombs, like these 2,000-pounders being readied for an F-16 squadron.

Above: The F-4G 'Wild Weasel' defense-suppression aircraft used its specialized electronics and HARM missiles to wreak havoc on Iraq's air-defense radars.

Left: Ground crew cheer as a General Dynamics F-16 Fighting Falcon sets off into the early morning light of Day One of Operation Desert Storm. Without the advanced electronics of larger types, the F-16 was relegated to simple iron bombing, but it was the most numerous type in the coalition inventory and it dropped a lot of bombs.

from page 50 **(17 January continued)**

everyone had their lights on, the street lights were on. On the way in we flew parallel to a road for some time, there were cars moving with their lights on. We were flying at 400 ft at 540 kt towards our target and I thought, 'Man, they don't even know we're coming!'"

Six of the unit's F-111Fs hit Balad, two launching GBU-15 electro-optical guided bombs at the maintenance complex while the other four dropped CBU-89 cluster weapons with area-denial mines at each end of the runways and among the aircraft shelters. At about the same time, 240 nm to the west, another six F-111Fs attacked the chemical weapons storage bunkers at H-3 airfield with LGBs. As they pulled away from the target, four Royal Saudi Air Force Tornados attacked the runways. Supporting that attack was a Navy defense-suppression force from USS *Kennedy* in the Red Sea comprising three EA-6B jamming aircraft, 10 A-7s carrying HARMs (High-speed Anti-Radiation Missiles), and four F-14 fighters. Captain Mike Buck, leading the F-111F attack, recalled, "We didn't do very well that time, most of the bombs missed because of the threat reactions. There were [Iraqi] fighters up, some of the guys got tapped [had radars lock onto them], a couple of guys got missiles shot at them. I got tapped a couple of times, I didn't see anything

to page 52 **(17 January continued)**

First Kill

Captain Steve Tate, 71st TFS/1st TFW, F-15C Eagle

Left: Captain Steve Tate is seen in the cockpit of the fighter in which he scored the coalition's first kill of the war.

Captain Tate entered the history books in the early morning of 17 January when he scored the first kill of the Gulf war. He also was the only Langley-based pilot to get a kill in the war. Captain Tate took off with three other F-15C pilots at 0130 on the first strike of the war. He flew his regularly assigned Eagle, serial number 83-0017. Given the importance of this first combat mission of the war, every squadron tried to put pilots and aircrews in 'their' planes, the ones that carried their names below the canopies.

"We flew for one hour toward the central Saudi Arabia-Iraq border, joined on a tanker and got gas. Then we headed north, straight to Baghdad. AWACS initially called out a few bandits, which apparently turned around

and landed.

"Our target area was 'clean' (no airborne threats). We were escorting the strike force which included F-4G 'Wild Weasels', F-15Es, F-111s, EF-111s and B-52s. F-117s were also involved. The entire sortie was at night and we flew with our lights off.

"I split my four-ship into two counter-rotating CAPs oriented toward two different threat axes. My wingman, Bo Merlack, and I were low, and Daman Harp and Mark Atwell in numbers three and four were high above us. Initially, I headed southeast on a contact which turned out to be an F-111. Bo and I jettisoned our external wing gas tanks.

"As I turned back to the right, toward the northeast, AWACS called out a possible bogey heading

toward Daman and Mark – and the strike package. At that time, 0320, I locked up the bogey, a Mirage F1 heading west at 8,000 ft. I confirmed he was a bandit and shot a Fox one (AIM-7 Sparrow, radar-guided missile) at 12 nm. The missile hit the Mirage at four nm off my nose. We saw the huge fireball and immediately headed south to our CAP station. We stayed there for another five minutes, but no other Iraqi planes came up. The fireball from my kill was incredible. It completely lit up the sky and I could see the airplane break up or explode into millions of pieces, burning all the way to the ground. It kept burning on the ground, too.

"There was AAA everywhere, SAMs were being shot and friendly

airplanes filled the dark skies. Bombs were dropping everywhere, and the 'Wild Weasels' were shooting their HARMs at all the SAM sites. Needless to say, it was very stressful. It was a long haul back to the tanker to get gas and return to Dhahran."

The 1st Tactical Fighter Wing, normally based at Langley, Virginia, is the oldest fighter unit in the US Air Force. The wing's two squadrons were the first American forces into Saudi Arabia after Iraq's August invasion of Kuwait, and its F-15Cs were extensively used on escorts and CAPs. After Captain Tate's kill, however, luck was to desert the wing, and it was hardly to get a sniff of air-to-air combat for the rest of the war.

from page 51 (**17 January continued**)

come my way but I reacted to the threat. The AWACS was calling the threats, so I had to honor the calls."

Other F-111Fs attacked the aircraft shelters at Jalibah airfield. Captain Brett Plentl remembered, "We crossed the border at low level, listening to AWACS calls on where the Iraqis were. We had planned to go attack either medium or low altitude, depending on where the fighters were – the fighters were our biggest concern on the first night. Once AWACS said, 'Picture Clear', we decided to release our bombs from altitudes around 10,000 ft. It was a poorly defended target so we could go in at medium altitude. Right after we were done, a four-ship of Royal Air Force Tornados came in with JP 233 to hit the runways."

Elsewhere, coalition fighters had their first encounters with enemy aircraft. Shortly after 3:00 a.m. Captain Steve Tate of the 71st TFS, 1st TFW, was leading a flight of four F-15Cs providing cover for strike groups of F-15Es and F-111s, supported by F-4Gs and EF-111As, that were attacking targets in the Baghdad area. Far to the southwest a patrolling E-3 Sentry reported an enemy aircraft, later identified as a Mirage F1, apparently closing on the No. 3 aircraft in Tate's flight. Tate later recalled, "My No. 3 had just turned south, and I was heading northeast on a different pattern. I don't know if the bogey [unidentified aircraft] was chasing him, but I locked him up, confirmed he was hostile and fired a missile." Tate launched an AIM-7 Sparrow at the rapidly closing Iraqi plane from a range of 12 miles, and shortly afterwards he saw a fireball about four miles in front of him as the weapon impacted. "When the airplane blew up, the whole sky lit up. It continued to burn all the way to the ground and then blew up into 1,000 pieces." It was the first air combat victory of the war.

There were several other fleeting contacts between opposing fighters, but all of them ended inconclusively. According to one unconfirmed report, during the night the confusion on the Iraqi side was so great that one MiG-29 became separated from its wing aircraft and, when the latter moved in front of it, shot it down.

No coalition aircraft was lost in the initial wave of air strikes, which comprised 671 sorties.

During their return flight the Apache helicopters that had delivered the initial attack landed in a remote area of Iraq to take on fuel brought in by a CH-47 Chinook 'Fat Cow'. When the refueling operation was complete the force took off and headed for home, but on the way the Chinook came under attack from a ground-launched missile. Despite the helicopter's low-flying evasive maneuver and the use of electronic countermeasures, the missile exploded close to it and blew away its aft landing gear. Nevertheless, the Chinook and all of the other helicopters engaged in the mission returned to friendly territory, having suffered no casualties. The 950-nm (1750-km) round trip had taken more than 15 hours.

Also during the night US Army helicopters inserted several special forces teams into points in Iraq and Kuwait.

At 4:00 a.m. the first of the daylight attack-force packages began taking off, timed to complete their refueling and to cross the Iraqi border at first light so they could hit their targets at sunrise.

Soon after dawn, 12 French air force Jaguars, operating from Al Ahsa in Saudi Arabia, attacked Ahmed al-Jaber airfield in Kuwait with 550-lb bombs and Belouga cluster bombs. The targets were heavily defended and four of the Jaguars suffered damage, in one case after taking a direct hit from an SA-7 shoulder-launched missile. One of the pilots suffered a head wound when a rifle-calibre round struck his cockpit. All of the Jaguars landed safely in Saudi Arabia, though two were forced to put down at Al Jubail. Royal Air Force Jaguars were also in action over Kuwait that morning.

Shortly after dawn, four Royal Air Force Tornados from the Muharraq squadron delivered a low-altitude toss-bombing attack with 1,000-lb bombs against Shaibah airfield. One of the aircraft caught fire after being hit by ground fire; both crewmen ejected and were taken prisoner.

to page 62 (**17 January continued**)

Black Jet over Baghdad

Above: 'Stealth Fighters' always struck at night. They were the only warplanes to fly missions against the heavily defended targets of downtown Baghdad and were assigned 31 per cent of targets in the first 24 hours of the war. Despite being assigned the most dangerous targets, not one aircraft was damaged during the entire war. The aircraft often flew two missions per night, although the pilots only flew once.

Below: Average F-117A missions were 5.4 hours long, and a number of inflight refuelings were essential. Take-off, transmitting and refueling were always conducted in pairs, but attacks were usually made singly, even though up to six aircraft may have been simultaneously dropping bombs on a single target.

Spearheading the attack on Iraq by coalition air forces was the Lockheed F-117A, deployed from its secret base at Tonopah Test Range, Nevada, to Khamis Mushait in the south of Saudi Arabia. Its much-vaunted 'stealth' properties allowed the 'Black Jet' to operate undetected over Iraq, while its dual infra-red weapons system and laser-guided bombs gave it the ability to attack targets with the utmost precision.

Aircraft from the 37th TFW's 415th TFS, commanded by Lieutenant Colonel Ralph W. Getchell, were the first deployed, on 19 August 1990, followed later by the 416th TFS in December and a handful of aircraft and instructors from the 417th TFTS in January. By 16 January a force of around 45 machines was in-theater to begin combat operations, with around 60 combat-qualified pilots. The

F-117As deployed to Saudi Arabia with just one stop. After a night's rest at Langley AFB, Virginia, the aircraft continued to Khamis Mushait in a single 14-hour-plus hop, graphically illustrating their global deployment capability.

During the first night's activity, the F-117As were primarily tasked against key nodes in the Iraqi air-defense network, notably command centers and communications sites. This 'roll-back' of the defenses was highly effective, making operations for other aircraft easier and forcing the Iraqis into a position from which they could not recover. As the campaign progressed, a wealth of strategic targets fell under bombs from the 'Black Jet', including chemical and nuclear facilities, bridges, key centers in Baghdad and airfields. F-117As are credited with the destruction at Al Taqaddum of Tu-16/H-6 bombers being prepared for a chemical bombing raid.

F-117As flew 1,271 combat missions during Desert Storm, of which around one third were flown over Baghdad, where the 'Black Jets' penetrated the massed defenses of an estimated 3,000 AAA pieces and 60 SAM sites. No hits were recorded on any of the aircraft. Over 2,000 bombs were dropped, all believed to be 2,000-lb laser-guided weapons. The GBU-27 Paveway III was the standard weapon, available with Mk 84 HE or BLU-109 penetrator warheads. Alternatively, the GBU-10 was used, with the Paveway II seeker head. F-117A pilots averaged 21 missions, the high-time flier recording 23. These figures are low in comparison with other types, but the complexity of the F-117A mission required long hours of planning and debriefing either side

of the flight itself.

Average mission length was a tiring 5½ hours, all flown at night. At 6,800 ft, the elevation of the runway at Khamis Mushait ate considerably into the take-off performance of a fully-loaded jet, so a top-up refueling was required to allow the F-117A to take off with less than a full fuel load. The aircraft then stayed with the tanker for about 90 minutes, receiving additional fuel prior to the drop-off point at the Saudi-Iraq border. The 'Black Jet' then continued on its own into Iraqi territory.

For missions against Baghdad, the F-117A was in Iraqi airspace for about 30 minutes: for those going up north to targets near Tikrit and Mosul, the duration was more like 45 minutes. Accurate INS navigation took the F-117A to the target area (the F-117A uses the same system as the B-52). The pilot then used the forward-looking infra-red system to locate and positively identify the target, followed by tracking, bomb release and laser designation using the downward-looking infra-red/laser turret. Such were the characteristics of many of the F-117A's targets that it had to use its low-observable properties to the full as it orbited while the pilot ascertained the exact aim-point (which was often small and well-concealed). Conventional aircraft would not have been survivable enough to pinpoint the required target in some of these cases.

For the most part, defenses only reacted to F-117A attacks after the first bombs struck. However, on

the first night some EF-111A jammers, which were escorting F-15Es attacking H2 and H3 airfields, arrived at their 'jam on' point some one or two minutes before the F-117As entered their own target area, sparking off intense fire. This did have its advantages, for the USAF quickly learned the lessons of creative jamming, using the EF-111As to initiate a massive AAA barrage some time before attack aircraft struck, by which time the AAA sites were unable to put up much fire due to hot barrels and low ammunition stocks at the guns.

All missions were flown completely radio-silent. As with other aircraft, the F-117As used procedural deconfliction, the main drawback being that their progress could not be monitored by radar. Missions were consistently flown over differing routes at varied altitudes to keep the Iraqis guessing. As Lieutenant Colonel Getchell emphasized, "all mission planning was proactive, not reactive."

No information has been released as to whether the F-117A was ever detected by the Iraqis, but the complete lack of any battle damage lends considerable weight to the opinion that the defenses had no idea where the F-117As were. Infra-red sensors may have detected the aircraft, but the ceramic tile 'platypus' exhausts present a vastly-reduced heat signature compared to conventional aircraft. The paint scheme was highly effective at night, even to friendly tanker

As important assets, the F-117s had to be protected from possible Iraqi chemical or even nuclear strikes, so they were based far away from the 'Scud' and air threats. Khamis Mushait in southern Saudi Arabia is a brand new base, obviously designed to operate high-value aircraft. Off the runways, the heavy concrete revetments, taxiways and parking aprons all have the additional blast protection of being dug in below ground level. Two F-117As were housed in each of Khamis Mushait's hardened aircraft shelters, each of which was fitted with blast doors and an air purification and filtration system. About 40-45 aircraft from the 37th TFW were assigned to Saudi Arabia and flew 1,271 combat sorties. Their base was approximately 650 miles from the Iraq border and 900 nm from Baghdad.

Black Jet over Baghdad

crews. As Lieutenant Colonel Getchell explained, "We're talking to them on the radio, coming in on the boom. They have these floodlights on the tanker's fin, and they still can't see us as we approach. They're straining into the dark and all of a sudden a 'Black Jet' appears out of nowhere, right under the boom!"

On leaving Iraqi airspace, the F-117A picked up a post-strike refueling prior to the long haul back to 'Tonopah East', as Khamis Mushait was quickly named (on account of its high elevation and arid, mountainous terrain, which closely resembled those characteristics of the F-117A's Stateside base). Now was the time many pilots felt the fatigue of combat flying. Not only had they been flying for about three hours, but the adrenalin was subsiding after threading their aircraft silently through some of the heaviest defenses in the world.

Pilots aimed to arrive at Khamis Mushait with around 40 minutes fuel for orbiting, plus enough for a divert. This gave the jets extra time to wait for any fog to burn off or bad weather to clear. Without conventional flaps, the F-117A lands hot, around 175 kt plus or minus several knots depending on aircraft weight and other factors. A long debrief faced the pilot, followed by a well-earned day's rest.

After leading his squadron into battle, Lieutenant Colonel Getchell summed up the feelings of the F-117A pilots. "We felt well-trained and confident, but ever since the first time we threw rocks at each other, anyone going into battle has the same thought – 'Can I do it?'. We were going in to do it and we just hoped we'd get it right. As far as the overall effort went, Desert Storm demonstrated three important things: (**1**) the effect of technology; (**2**) the organizational skill of the allied forces; and (**3**) the will of the US people. We hoped we played our part in all that."

D.D.

Stealth Goes to War

Lieutenant Colonel Barry E. Horne, 415th Tactical Fighter Squadron, F-117A

Below: Because of its stealth characteristics, pilots were able to loiter over their targets, ensuring that their weapons hit home. They scored 80-85 per cent bomb hit rates (compared to 30-35 per cent typical in Vietnam), often against targets as small as windows or ventilation shafts.

Colonel Barry E. Horne became part of an aerial warfare revolution when his F-117A attacked Iraq.

"We flew 18 aircraft of the 415th TFS to Langley AFB in Virginia, and staged from there non-stop to Khamis Mushait AB in Saudi Arabia. As I was airborne mission commander, I flew in one of the accompanying tankers. We tanked several times from March AFB KC-10As. We don't strictly have dedicated tanker crews, though back in the 'black' days there were dedicated tanker crews out of Beale who refueled us, but that was for security reasons, not because of any special problems in refueling the F-117A. In fact, stories about the 'Wobblin Goblin' aside, it is just about the easiest airplane I have ever refueled in. So although we don't have our own tanker support, the importance of our mission meant that whenever we wanted tankers we had them."

During the Gulf war, the 'Black Jet' was able to operate with impunity over Iraq, being the only machine allowed into the heavily defended skies over downtown Baghdad. More than 40 F-117As were deployed to Saudi Arabia, and they dropped the first bombs of the war, hitting the central communications building of the Iraqi military machine. Later, it was footage from their imaging infra-red weapons system which showed the world the amazing accuracy of modern precision-guided weapons.

"F-117As flew 1,271 combat sorties, which was around 7,000 combat hours. Our guiding principle was that we concentrated on high-value, heavily defended targets, which lent themselves to the use of precision-guided munitions. That means we went after aircraft hangars, command and control bunkers, telecommunications, power plants in the early stages, line-of-communication targets like bridges. Bridges were something new for us. We had not trained to do them, but they asked us if we could and we said, 'Yeah, we'll try to do bridges.'

"There were lots of communications targets. We wanted to cut Baghdad's communications, because we were certain in our own minds that that was where Saddam Hussein was running his war from. We logged a lot of transmitter towers, and communications centers.

"We also did a lot of airfield work. Along with the F-15Es, Tornados and F-111s, we drove their air force out of Iraq and into Iran. They couldn't hide them, they couldn't protect them in those barns, and if they flew the F-15s shot them down. It took them a couple of weeks to figure that one out, and that's when they ran. Our preferred weapons for most of these missions were laser-guided 2,000-lb bombs, mostly GBU-10s and GBU-27s. We launched them from a range of altitudes.

"Combat missions could last up to six hours. It would start the day before, getting the tasking mid- to late-evening. Mission planning people would look at the task, co-ordinating with other agencies, like air defense, but most importantly with the tankers. That took quite a time, working out times and locations that we would need refueling, and just how much fuel we'd need.

"Early in the afternoon of the following day, we'd bring in the pilots who were to fly the mission. The mission planners would stand up and brief us. We'd take our mission packages, go and sit down in a private little corner to study the mission for the next hour or so. It really wasn't much different from what you'd see in a World War II movie.

"We'd plan to launch in daylight, late afternoon, wanting to use as much of the night over the target as possible. We might fly two or three waves a night, depending on how far away the targets were. Some targets were close together, and we'd go in a package, while others were widely spread.

"Being the aircraft it is, the F-117 needed far less support on strikes. Occasionally we had EF-111s and F-4Gs, but the whole point about the 'Black Jet' is its ability to work in the face of the EW threats those aircraft are designed to counter. So our mission did not depend on them."

Lockheed F-117A 'Stealth Fighter'

Designed, built and entering service under conditions of total secrecy, the Lockheed F-117A 'Stealth Fighter' is unique in the number of advanced technologies successfully introduced on a single, highly unusual airframe.

Structure
The F-117A is constructed from aluminium and composites, with RAM (Radar Absorbing Material) sprayed onto the surface and onto key points like leading edges and the joins of each facet of the fuselage.

Sensors
All air data for the F-117A's instruments come from four facetted plastic and metal pitot sensor probes in the nose. These presented enormous problems in reducing their radar signature. They also require heating to prevent them icing up in flight.

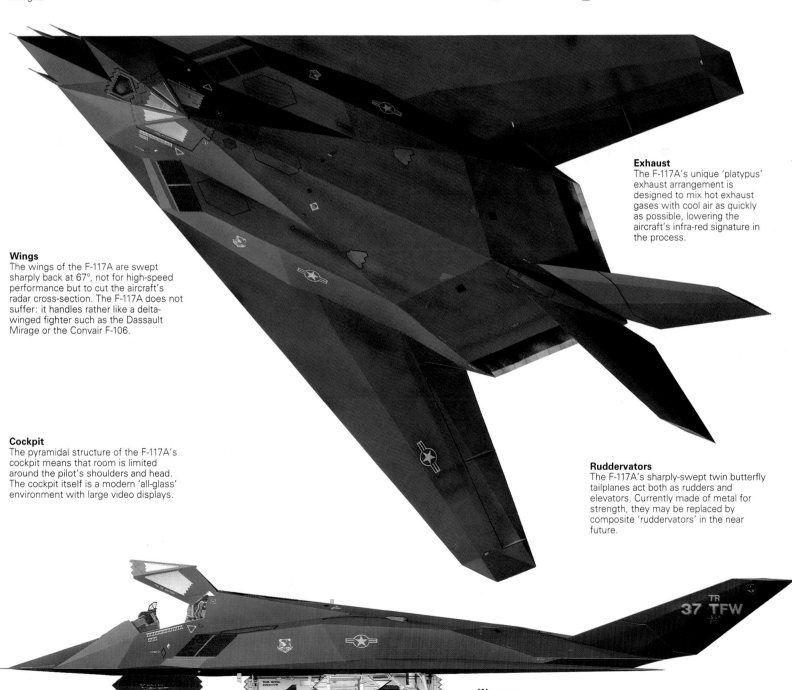

Exhaust
The F-117A's unique 'platypus' exhaust arrangement is designed to mix hot exhaust gases with cool air as quickly as possible, lowering the aircraft's infra-red signature in the process.

Wings
The wings of the F-117A are swept sharply back at 67°, not for high-speed performance but to cut the aircraft's radar cross-section. The F-117A does not suffer: it handles rather like a delta-winged fighter such as the Dassault Mirage or the Convair F-106.

Cockpit
The pyramidal structure of the F-117A's cockpit means that room is limited around the pilot's shoulders and head. The cockpit itself is a modern 'all-glass' environment with large video displays.

Ruddervators
The F-117A's sharply-swept twin butterfly tailplanes act both as rudders and elevators. Currently made of metal for strength, they may be replaced by composite 'ruddervators' in the near future.

Weapons
The F-117A carries its weapons internally to cut radar reflection. It has been cleared to carry most of the US Air Force's tactical air-to-ground inventory, though in the Gulf the F-117A was armed almost exclusively with laser-guided 2,000-lb bombs.

RAF Tornados: Day One

"At this point, you would remove all personal items from your flying clothing and place them in the bag provided." Up to now, it had seemed like a war exercise: intelligence data, route planning, preflight briefing, donning of clothing and safety equipment – routines practiced an untold number of times prior to a training sortie over the green fields of Europe. 'Sanitization' before walking to the aircraft was always taken as read. "The first time it sank in that I was *really* going to war was when I put my wallet and wedding ring into that little plastic bag," said one Tornado crewman.

Only the day before, 16 January, had aircrew been briefed on the war plan, and heard the name 'Desert Storm' for the first time. At Tabuk, Dhahran and Muharraq, a force of RAF Tornados stood ready for action, waiting for H-Hour and not yet knowing that Saddam had been granted just one day of grace following expiry of the UN ultimatum. After 0012 hours GMT on 17 February, the words 'Iraq' and 'enemy' became synonymous.

It was about 2230 GMT on 16 January (0130 local time the following day) that the first RAF combat missions were launched. Weighed down by a pair of JP 233 airfield-denial dispensers and extra-large drop tanks, aircraft dragged themselves off the ground at an unaccustomed weight of 30.5 tonnes and turned towards their Iraqi targets. In the east of the war theater, Wing Commander Jerry Witts of No. 31 Squadron led four aircraft from Dhahran and Wing Commander John Broadbent eight from Bahrain, all of them heading for Tallil airfield in southeast Iraq.

The Tornados' appointment with the airfield defenses was to be a lonely one, but they were far from being without friends as they cast off from the tanker and began descending to 200 ft (61 m) as enemy airspace was entered. Keeping watch over the war theater were three E-3 Sentries, which would warn the attacking force of any air threats. Closely collaborating with this airborne eye were fighter CAPs of USAF or Saudi F-15 Eagles, or RAF or Saudi Tornado F.Mk 3s. Flying in advance was a fighter sweep, perhaps of F-16 Fighting Falcons, while to keep defense radars off the air, F-4G 'Wild Weasel' Phantoms were on constant patrol. Ground radio communications with Iraqi fighters were jammed by USAF EF-111A Ravens and their carrier-based equivalents, the EA-6B Prowler.

Hurtling over Tallil at a height of 180 ft on the radar altimeter, Tornados scattered two JP 233s per aircraft over the sprawling base's parallel runways and associated taxiways, making their escape without loss. One of the navigators, Flight Lieutenant Jerry Gegg, recalled soon after landing, "It's absolutely terrifying. There's no other word for it. You're frightened of failure; you're frightened of dying. You're flying as low as you dare but high enough to get the weapons off. You put it as low as you can over the target – just to get away as fast as you can."

Having feared heavy losses, crews were exuberant at their success and good fortune in spite of fearsome flak. Those in the second wave of the night were not so lucky, however. Four Muharraq Tornados were tasked against Shaibah, close to the city of Basrah, for post-dawn lofting of 1,000-lb (454-kg) bombs. One of ZD791's Sidewinders was hit by flak and exploded, seriously

damaging the aircraft and forcing Flight Lieutenants Adrian 'John' Nicholl and John Peters of No. XV Squadron to eject. "We had a bit of a laugh together," Nicholl later recalled. "We sat in the desert for a while and had a discussion." Attempts to rescue the pair from enemy territory were unsuccessful, the crew being captured, mistreated and then paraded on Iraqi TV in a counter-productive propaganda stunt.

Tornado eye view of a large Iraqi target airfield. These huge bases were hellish to put out of business. With multiple long runways, taxiways and prepared desert from which aircraft could operate, effective attacks were a statistical nightmare.

Far right: A flight of Tornados equipped with JP 233 anti-runway munitions tanks up prior to an airfield attack.

Above: Strain shows on the faces of a returning Tornado crew after a first-night strike. There was little gloating in the coalition camp as the success of the first day's air raids became clear. To the pilots braving Iraq's low-level air defenses, there was just relief that the first mission was over and they had made it back safely. The Tornado pilots were under particular strain, as theirs were among the most dangerous missions of the war; they were losing aircraft and crews at the rate of one per day.

Left: Ground crewmen at Dhahran prepare a Tornado GR.Mk 1 for the night's sortie. Tornados flew from three bases, Dhahran and Tabuk in Saudi Arabia and Muharraq on Bahrain, and attacked strategic targets throughout southern Iraq and Kuwait. Their early ordnance included JP 233 runway-denial weapons, ALARM anti-radiation missiles and lofted 1,000-lb bombs.

Above: A navigator's-eye view of the stark Saudi landscape shows just how low RAF Tornado crews flew. Although equipped with terrain-following radar, pilots most often flew manually in order to keep emissions down.

The western contingent of Tornados, at Tabuk, also mounted two waves in the first few hours. Wing Commander Travers Smith, CO of No. 16 Squadron, was first away at 0210 local time on 17 January, leading three more Tornados towards Al Asad airfield. Leaving an hour later were two additional Tornados, each carrying three ALARM anti-radar missiles and transiting direct because of their lighter weight. Their role was to strike the defences at 0350: five minutes before the JP 233 aircraft. One bomber returned early with technical trouble, but the others successfully hit their target. A second wave of four visited Al Taqaddum airfield shortly after 0400 the same night, three of them dropping JP 233s successfully in spite of having no ALARM support.

As darkness fell on the first day of Desert Storm, the third wave of Tornados prepared for action. Muharraq sent four aircraft to Shaibah and four more to Ubaydah bin al Jarrah, all of them with JP 233s. The Jarrah formation took off at midnight, local time, and the Shaibah wave two hours later, their shorter journey requiring only one pre-attack refueling from a VC10. Approaching Shaibah at 550 kt (1019 km/h) with terrain-following radar switched off, crews relied on the radar altimeter to keep them 200 ft (61 m) above the (hopefully) flat desert. To distract the attention of the defenders as attackers swept in, US forces laid on a diversion. Just 20 seconds before time-on-target, F-111F laser designators and Navy A-6E Intruders bombed an oil refinery a mere mile north of the Tornados' track. By all accounts, the resultant explosion considerably exceeded expectations, and had the unwelcome effect of skylining the aircraft as they approached. Instead of aimlessly hosing flak to all points of the compass, Iraqi gunners were now learning to direct it at low level along the aircraft's path, increasing both its psychological and actual effect. All weapons were released satisfactorily, but three minutes later ZA392, flown by Wing Commander Nigel Elsdon, CO of No. 27 Squadron, was seen to crash into the ground, killing both the pilot and the navigator, Flight Lieutenant Max Collier. The remaining three aircraft landed back at base after 1 hour 55 minutes in the air.

Jarrah's attackers received an equally hostile reception. Having taken on fuel at above 10,000 ft (3050 m), the Tornados dropped to 300 ft (91 m), crossed the Iraqi border and steadily descended to 200 ft (61 m) during a black and uneventful low-level flight of 30 minutes over the desert. The target was sighted in a blaze of anti-aircraft activity a full five minutes out, the softening-up force clearly having stirred up a hornets' nest. Flying parallel to the runway, the formation was in 'card four', the leading pair two miles apart, the trailing pair 30 seconds' flying time behind them. Turning now towards the airfield, the spacing was closed up to one mile and the interval to 15 seconds, then further tightened to 10.

With one minute to go, Flying Officer Ingle and Flight Lieutenant McKernan in ZD744 felt a bump and thought they had been hit, but the aircraft continued to fly, albeit reluctantly. At 550 kt (1019 km/h) the Tornados swept over the runway, Nos 1 and 2 dropping their JP 233s at one-fifth and three-fifths along its length, the others at the two-fifths and four-fifths points. After turning for home, Ingle was having difficulty flying his aircraft and could not keep control above 350 kt (649 km/h). Eventually finding the tanker, he could only maintain formation by adopting the unusual (for refueling) wing angle of 45°, but managed to complete the journey to Muharraq without further incident. Inspection then showed that a birdstrike had removed a large section of the port wing's leading edge.

At Tabuk, meanwhile, Wing Commander Mike Heath of No. 20 Squadron was leading eight JP 233-equipped Tornados to Al Asad, which six struck successfully shortly after 2300 local time. At the same time, four ALARM Tornados from the same base were hitting the defenses at H-3 airfield in preparation for an attack due early on 18 January. Eight more JP 233 sorties were flown from Dhahran, only four of them successfully, one aircraft having to make an emergency landing with double generator failure.

So ended the Tornado GR.Mk 1's first 24 hours of Desert Storm, during which some 60 sorties were flown, including 44 with JP 233s. The aircraft, the ALARM missile and the JP 233 had all seen their combat debuts, but at the cost of two Tornados. Attrition of 3.3 per cent was well below the double figures sustained at Bomber Command's darkest times, but aircrew would not need a calculator to conclude that they could not survive a 'tour' of 30 missions, were that World War II system to be reintroduced. Fortunately, however, Day 1 was for the Tornado both the moment of supreme triumph and extreme tragedy. Those who said it could only get better were, for a change, right.

P.J.

Kennedy at War

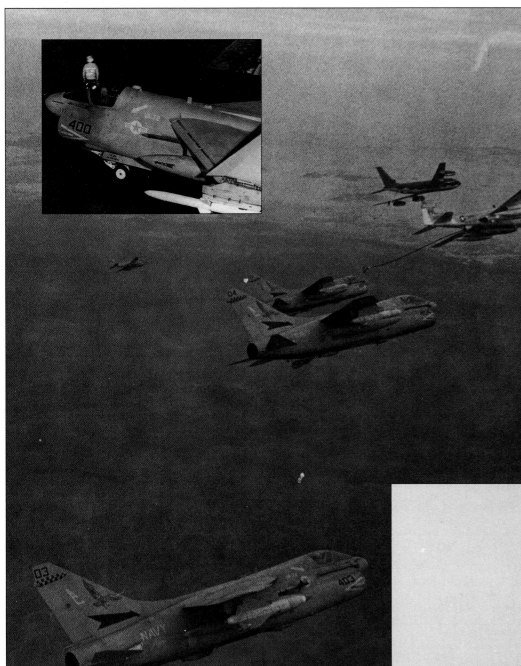

especially now that his ship would be in combat around the clock. A former A-7 pilot, too, he watched with pride as the Navy's last two fleet Corsair squadrons maneuvered on *Kennedy*'s flight deck in the early-morning darkness of 17 January, preparing to participate in the first strikes against Iraq. Of all the aircraft that

"The day we got the execute orders to go to war really stands out in my mind," relates Rear Admiral Riley Mixson. "*America* had just steamed into the Red Sea and we had all three flags, CAGs and the COs of the major ships together on *Kennedy*. We were briefing how we would fight the war and, suddenly, the execute order came in to begin launching strikes at 0120 that night, including Tomahawks. There was a lot of anxiety, and excitement, a little fear. The casualties were predicted to be much higher, and our aircraft losses were supposed to be much higher.

"I was very concerned that we would lose more pilots than we

actually did. It was hard not to walk the flight line, which I did, to talk to the crews. The greatest joy was when the *Kennedy*'s air wing checked in after the strike and were all accounted for."

With a third carrier, USS *America* (CV-66), in the Red Sea, and as the senior battle group commander, Rear Admiral Mixson became commander of Task Force 155, working with the other two rear admirals, Doug Katz of *America*'s battle group, and Nick Gee, who had *Saratoga*'s battle group.

Captain Warren in *Kennedy* had more localized considerations. As the Air Boss, his job was one of the most important in any carrier, but actually flew in combat, these A-7s did not receive any battle damage.

"I really enjoyed watching the A-7s get out there and participate in what would be their last war. It was a pleasure having them on the deck because they were so agile and so consistently up and ready. When we had done all our practice missions, the A-7s would generally go off in a sequential order. They were always ready and easier to get to the catapults than larger aircraft.

"It was good to see them have as good a success rate as they did. We launched *18* loaded A-7s in one launch, nine per squadron. (They had 12 planes per squadron.) It was incredible! Two major strikes per day on the average.

"The A-6s did well, too. In fact, once the war started, all the squadrons did well. They had an amazing FMC (Fully Mission Capable) rate. Our launches of 36-40 airplanes were very high, with a commensurate sortie-completion rate. I felt really proud watching the A-7s go out. Their discipline was outstanding (like the rest of the squadrons) around the ship. VA-46 and VA-72 did their community proud in their last hurrah.

"The first strike was truly one of the best launches of the whole cruise. That afternoon we got the word about the execute order. Everyone got prepared with a calm professionalism. We went up on the roof to get the aircraft ready. All the ordnance was loaded. The decision was made in plenty of time and the entire sequence was well planned. There was not one push-back, not one suspend, no aircraft problems. Everything went like clockwork.

"After the launch, of course, we were on pins and needles wondering what was happening. Were we going to get all our aircraft back? About four to five hours later, Captain John Gay, the carrier's CO, called over the IMC that all aircraft had checked in off target and they were all coming back."

For the next six weeks, with very little rest, the men, aircrews and planes of *Kennedy* and its air wing flew round-the-clock strikes against Iraq. Coming from their position in the Red Sea, the aircrews faced long flights to and from their targets deep into enemy

A carrier deck crewman directs a bomb-laden A-6E towards a catapult. Intruders took the Navy's war directly to the Iraqis and ran the gauntlet of intense air defense, losing four aircraft to enemy fire.

Above: A red-vested ordnanceman aboard the Kennedy moves past weapon trollies carrying bombs and AIM-9 Sidewinder air-to-air missiles.

Left: CAP cover for Navy strike missions was primarily entrusted to F-14 Tomcats like this VF-32 machine being hurled down Kennedy's catapult track. Tomcats did not score but they secured the airspace around the Navy's ships and strike packages.

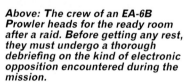

Above: The crew of an EA-6B Prowler heads for the ready room after a raid. Before getting any rest, they must undergo a thorough debriefing on the kind of electronic opposition encountered during the mission.

territory. Missions of four to five hours' duration were the norm and, occasionally, especially in the cases of the F-14s standing long and, ultimately, relatively quiet, CAP duty, six to seven hours. These lengthy missions required several inflight refuelings. Air Force KC-135s orbited on established tracks for hours while a strike was in progress, although the carrier also used her so-called 'organic' tanking assets, KA-6Ds.

By the time a cease-fire was announced on 28 February, CVW-3 had flown more than 11,000 sorties, including 2,895 combat sorties. *Kennedy* aircraft had delivered 3.7 million lb of ordnance on Iraqi targets, both in Iraq and Kuwait, while participating in 114 air strikes. Incredibly, CVW-3 suffered no aircraft or aircrew losses in combat. CVW-3 planes had launched 12,300 times from their carrier and accomplished some 10,500 arrested landings.

USS *John F. Kennedy* and USS *Saratoga* returned home in late March. While *Sara* headed for its home port of Mayport, near Jacksonville, Florida, *Kennedy* steamed north towards Norfolk. On 28 March, the huge carrier nudged into Pier 12 of the naval base, its seven-and-a-half-month combat deployment finally completed. The day before, planes of CVW-3 and CVW-17 roared over NAS Oceana and NAS Norfolk in the largest return fly-in ever seen in the Hampton Roads area. Thousands of people, family, friends, interested onlookers and the ever-present press, cheered and waved American flags as the aircrews taxied in, the crews' smiles and raised eyebrows proof of their incredulity at the size of the welcome. It was a fitting end to this most intense deployment since Vietnam.

P.M.

Left: US Navy Tomcats and Prowlers take on fuel from a Royal Air Force VC10 tanker, using the probe-and-drogue technique familiar to them.

Above: Armed and ready to fight, an F-14A from VF-32 mounts a combat air patrol high above the Kennedy battle group as it cruises the Red Sea.

Left: With its bomb racks empty, an A-7E Corsair 'traps' aboard the Kennedy at the end of a bombing mission over Iraq. The Sidewinder missiles are carried for self-protection against enemy fighters.

Above: Airborne early warning and control at sea are provided by the distinctive E-2C Hawkeye. Each carrier has at least four birds, Kennedy's E-2 detachment coming from VAW-126.

Bottom: Bombs erupt as a Navy strike package hits one of the large Iraqi airfield complexes. This is the H-2 field in the western desert.

Carrier Air Wing Three's reach and power are symbolized on the unit's shield device.

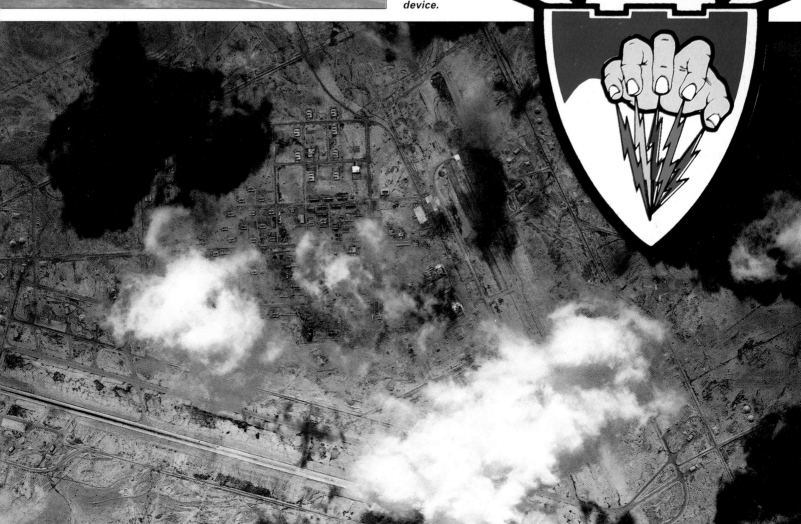

from page 52 **(17 January continued)**

Flying as part of one of the early-morning strikes, a section of four F/A-18C Hornets from VFA-81, from USS *Saratoga* in the Red Sea, was heading for a ground target in western Iraq. The AWACS aircraft providing surveillance of the area and a Grumman E-2C Hawkeye from VAW-125 detected two Iraqi fighters closing on the force. Lieutenant Commander Mark Fox and Lieutenant Nick Mongillo were vectored into attack positions and shot down the enemy planes using AIM-7 and AIM-9 missiles. After the engagement the F/A-18s reformed, and continued with their briefed mission against the ground target.

That afternoon a pair of MiG-29s attempted to intercept a force package comprising 24 F-16s with supporting aircraft – F-15Cs, EF-111s and F-4G 'Wild Weasels'. Warned of the Iraqis' approach by an E-3 AWACS aircraft, several F-15Cs of the 58th TFS, 33rd TFW, moved into position to engage the enemy fighters. Captain Charles Magill (a US Marine Corps officer on exchange) and Captain Rhory Draeger each destroyed one of the MiGs using AIM-7 missiles.

When the F-16s reached the target area they came under attack from AAA and SAMs, but due to the electronic jamming and attacks on the enemy radars by the F-4G 'Wild Weasel' aircraft, the ground fire was generally inaccurate. "The F-4Gs were launching their anti-radiation missiles over our heads to attack enemy radars that stayed up while we were in the target area," one of the F-16 pilots later commented. "Tremendous explosions were going off at all our assigned target locations and the sky was filling with 37-mm AAA's white puffy airbursts. By the time [the] last aircraft pulled off the target . . . you could have gotten out and walked on the layer of flak left by the AAA."

During the first day of the war, in addition to those mentioned above, F-15Cs of the 58th TFS, 33rd TFW, claimed the destruction of three more enemy fighters, two Mirage F1s by Captain Robert Graeter and a MiG-29 by Captain Jon Kelk, in each case with AIM-7 missiles.

Throughout the day, F-14 Tomcat fighters fitted with TARPS (Tactical Air Reconnaissance Pod System), TR-1 and RF-4C reconnaissance aircraft photographed the targets that had been hit to provide information for bomb-damage assessment.

After dark on 17 January one of the targets for the 48th TFW was President Saddam Hussein's summer palace at Tikrit, to the northwest of Baghdad. Four F-111Fs ran in at low altitude, supported by two EF-111s at medium altitude. On the way in a MiG-29 attempted to engage the force. Lieutenant Bradley Seipel, WSO in the leading F-111F, recalled, "The four F-111Fs were flying in trail, about one minute apart, down at 400 ft at 540 kt. Then the AWACS came up and said there was a MiG vectoring on us. He said, 'Redskin 51 [Seipel's callsign], you have a MiG vectoring on you!' So we went down to 200 ft and pushed on full military power to give us 600 kt. We went scooting along low and fast, and shortly thereafter the MiG pilot realized he couldn't make the corner and he came off of us. Then the AWACS came up and said, 'OK, now he's not on you, Redskin 51, he's on you, Redskin 52.' The MiG pilot actually ended up nibbling down the line, and he finally did a good conversion on the last guy in the trail. That ended up in a high-speed chase of about 70 miles to the southwest." In the end the F-111F was able to shake off its pursuer, but its crew was forced to abandon the attack (it was one of the few occasions where an Iraqi fighter was able to prevent a coalition aircraft reaching its target). The other three F-111Fs continued with the mission, and carried out a devastatingly precise attack with GBU-15s on the President's palace.

Elsewhere that night, F-111Fs of the 48th TFW began precision attacks on the hardened aircraft shelters at Iraqi airfields. Using LGBs, they scored hits on 23 of the shelters. During the nights to follow the unit would take a steadily mounting toll of these shelters.

As part of the Royal Air Force effort that night, four Tornados

to page 64 **(17 January continued)**

Splash One 'Fulcrum'!

Captain Charles Magill, USMC, 58th TFS/33rd TFW, F-15C Eagle

"**I** was leading eight F-15s on our first day-strike mission at about three o'clock in the afternoon. We were marshalling south of the Iraq border on the tanker. The AWACS came up and said they had a couple of 'Fulcrums' CAPping south of the target area, Al Taqaddum airfield.

"We pushed out in front of the strike package and as we got close enough to the bandits that they became a threat to our strike package, I took one of my four-ships toward them. The other four F-15s continued sweeping the area, looking for other bandits."

"As we approached the intercept, AWACS assured us they were the only two bandits in the area. We had four good radar, and we sanitized the area to confirm that there was no other threat around.

"The Iraqis had a pretty sophisticated air-defense system. They fired a few SAMs at us as we headed toward the MiGs. We jettisoned some external tanks so we could be more maneuverable and descended a bit. We were a little nervous about AAA and the shoulder-launched SAMs. We pushed up the speed and got past the initial surface-to-air threat. Our RHAW scopes were clean. We pressed on towards the MiGs, which were in a sort of hot-cold CAP south of the target.

"The two blue MiGs turned north at a bad time, so we accelerated. When they turned back into us at low altitude, we were at a medium altitude and we let them have it. My No. 3, Captain Rhory Draeger, fired one Sparrow; I fired two. There was no sign of ejection."

Captain Draeger scored another kill – a MiG-23 – on 26 January, in F-15C 85-0119, one of the eight USAF pilots who scored two kills during the war.

Captain Magill credits his wingman, First Lieutenant Mark Arriola, with sanitizing the area while the two shooters concentrated on engaging the MiGs. First Lieutenant Arriola flew with Captain Magill throughout the war, accumulating 50 missions.

"'He sanitized the area,' Captain Magill said, 'called the breaks and did a tremendous job. There were SAMs and flak coming up and it took great presence of mind and concentration to perform his duties.'"

Captain Draeger's wingman was Captain Tony Schiavi, who would

Captain Charles ('Sly') Magill, on exchange duty with the USAF's 58th TFS 'Gorillas', was the only Marine Corps officer to get a MiG kill.

get a kill, too, on 26 January, against a MiG-23, on the same flight that Draeger got his second kill.

Captain Magill credits training and preparation for allowing him to get his once-in-a-lifetime opportunity.

"Prior preparation is the key. Everything was very hectic. We had SAMs. The first time in combat, those really get your blood boiling. Then, when I jettisoned my wing tanks, I shorte[d] out one of the 'pig tails' – the fuel sensors – and my fuel gauge went to zero, even though I knew I had gas. We were over enemy territory, 'bitchin' Betty' – the audio alarm – was screaming 'Bingo! Bingo!', the fuel gauge read almost zero, and we were just about to throw our ordnance against the enemy. The first time was pretty hairy. There were a lot of things going through my mind. I had to prioritize everything. When you get down to the bottom line, everything was incredibly basic. Weapons system set up just right, shoot your ordnance at the first opportune moment, watch the MiGs blow up and get the hell out.

"The kills were extremely clean, no ejection. Now, as we flew out, we were low on gas, and we had t[o]

Below: The 58th TFS 'Gorillas' is one of three squadrons in the 33rd TFW at Eglin AFB, Florida, and provided most of the people and F-15C aircraft which deployed to Tabuk.

egress without conflicting with the strike package. Everything was channellized out. We ended up going the quickest direction home, which would take us toward the strikers. I didn't want to get in their way and I certainly didn't want any fragging, where they shot *us*.

"I got my four aircraft climbing back to a descent altitude, with a pretty good airspeed since we were still a couple of hundred miles north of the border. The Iraqis fired a few SAMs – maybe SA-2s or SA-3s – at us. I couldn't be sure. We jettisoned our last tanks and got down to the low-altitude regime again. We used chaff, all of our decoys. After the kill, there was no time to relax because that's when something can really bite you."

Captain Magill flew 50 missions during Desert Shield and Desert Storm, accumulating 400 hours in seven months, including 105 in January and 138 in February.

His squadron, the 58th TFS, received the 1990 Hughes Achievement Award as the Air Force's outstanding air-to-air combat squadron, in recognition of the 58th's leading tally of Iraqi aircraft shot down. The squadron roster of shooters is as follows:

Above and below: F-15C Eagles were the first warplanes to arrive during Desert Shield and were the premier air-to-air killers of Desert Storm. Typical load, seen here, is four AIM-7M Sparrows and four AIM-9M Sidewinders. Late in the war, more than 1,000 combat hours were flown with the AIM-120 AMRAAM (Advanced Medium-Range Air-to-Air Missile), though none was ever fired at an Iraqi aircraft. F-15C pilots from Eglin AFB, Florida, claimed 17 of the war's 41 aerial kills.

Capt. Jon Kelk	17 Jan.	MiG-29
Capt. Robert Graeter	17 Jan.	F1 (2)
Capt. Charles Magill	17 Jan.	MiG-29
Capt. Rhory Draeger	17 Jan.	MiG-29
	26 Jan.	MiG-23
Capt. Lawrence Pitts	19 Jan.	MiG-25
Capt. Richard Tollini	19 Jan.	MiG-25
Capt. Craig Underhill	19 Jan.	MiG-29
Capt. Cesar Rodriguez	19 Jan.	MiG-29
	26 Jan.	MiG-23
Capt. Anthony Schiavi	26 Jan.	MiG-23
Capt. David Rose	29 Jan.	MiG-23
Capt. Anthony Murphy	7 Feb.	Su-17 (2)
Col. Rick Parsons	7 Feb.	Su-17 (2)

from page 62 **(17 January continued)**

from the Muharraq squadron carried out a low-altitude attack on the runways at Ubaydah Bin Al Jarrah airfield with JP 233s. During the final part of the attack run, flying at high speed at low altitude, one of the Tornados suffered a bird strike as one or possibly two large herons struck the port wing just inboard of the tip. The aircraft lurched to one side and the crew thought it had been hit by enemy fire, but the pilot, Flag Officer Nigel Ingle, realigned the Tornado on the target and completed his attack run with JP 233s. With the wings jammed in the 45° swept position, he returned to base and made a safe landing. With a replacement leading-edge slat, the aircraft would again be ready for action the following night.

Also that evening, Shaibah airfield near Basrah, ironically a one-time Royal Air Force base, claimed a second Tornado from the Muharraq squadron. Wing Commander Nigel Elsdon, the unit commander who was leading the four-aircraft attack, had completed his bombing run with JP 233s and was moving clear of the defended area around the target when his aircraft crashed into the ground. None of the other crews in the force saw the aircraft being engaged by the enemy before it impacted, and the reason for the loss is not clear. Both crewmen were killed. Elsdon would be the most senior coalition officer killed during the campaign. Despite press reports claiming that the ultra-low-level attacks with the JP 233 weapons system was the reason for the relatively high losses suffered by the Tornados, in fact, this would be the only loss of an aircraft in the course of a JP 233 sortie.

During that evening an attack force of Italian air force Tornados ran into difficulties on its way to attack a target in Iraq. Eight aircraft had taken off from Abu Dhabi in the United Arab Emirates, but one suffered a technical failure soon after take-off and had to abort the mission. The other seven made their rendezvous with USAF KC-135 tankers, but due to turbulence in the area six of them were unable to take on fuel and had to return to base with their weapons. The seventh Tornado took on fuel and continued alone with the mission, but it was shot down and both crewmen were captured.

After dark the Iraqi army fired a 'Scud' surface-to-surface missile at Dhahran, but the weapon was intercepted and destroyed in flight by a Patriot surface-to-air missile – the first-ever occasion of an operational shoot-down of a ballistic missile.

Up to midnight on 17 January, coalition aircraft flew a total of 2,107 sorties. In contrast, during the same period allied intelligence sources estimated the Iraqi air force flew 24 combat sorties and lost eight aircraft in air-to-air combat: three MiG-29s, three Mirage F1s

to page 75 **(17 January continued)**

A Lockheed F-117A 'Stealth Fighter' comes in to land at Khamis Mushait. The 'Black Jet' led the massive allied air assault on Iraq, hitting targets in Baghdad with deadly accuracy.

Aardvark at War

Colonel Jim Brechwald, 48th Tactical Fighter Wing (Provisional), F-111F

"August to 17 January we used basically to plan the first two days of the war. We executed those plans and from then on we got taskings from headquarters. On the first night my assignment was to lead a mission against a very important target northwest of Baghdad. Very, very deep into the heart of the country. I used two GBU-15 aircraft and two with GBU-24. The route was flown hi-lo-hi. You'd go in high to do a multi-ship night tanker refueling and then take off from the tanker and join your low-level route as single ships.

"So after the tanker you'd let down and ensure your jamming pod is set properly and your lights are turned off so nobody can see you. We have EF-111 jamming support and an F-15 CAP to ward off the air threat. One of the GBU-15 aircraft has a maintenance problem and we're down to three aircraft. Even though I'm flight lead the remaining GBU-15 aircraft goes in first. There's a lot of triple-A and several SAMs, and a MiG-29 intercept attempt, but he gets in and delivers his bomb on target: direct hit. I follow him in and we get intercepted by the MiG but we don't go off course as we're low and fast on the TF. We shake him off but the same MiG intercepts the No. 3. The AWACS gives him egress vectors but it takes 60 miles to shake him off, and he never makes it to the target.

"That was one of the smaller packages, most of them were eight to 20 aircraft so we could saturate the defenses – blow in and blow out, multi-directions to make it real hard for the defenses to pick up our aircraft, because initially we didn't know how effective they would be.

"We used the GBU-15 first to soften up the target so that the penetrating bombs could be delivered deep in the bowels of the target. We learned as we progressed how to employ these munitions better. For some of the hardened targets we used two or four at a time, depending on how hard or important the target was. It was like a piledriver effect. They were set up for the first to go in, the second to go right in the same hole, the third and fourth following, so that you get deeper and deeper into the target.

"The GBU-15 was good to kill easily identifiable targets at night using infra-red. These were soft targets as we did not

Above: The 48th Tactical Fighter Wing is one of the US Air Force's most important Europe-based formations, and it was flown to the Gulf in August. As with many other units, the wing produced its own Gulf patch.

Right: The heaviest weapon carried by the F-111F was the 5,000-lb GBU-28/B. Basically an eight-in artillery barrel bored out and filled with explosive, it was used as a ground penetrator and bunker buster in the last days of the war.

Above: An F-111F lands at Taif, in western Saudi Arabia. With more than 60 aircraft from the 48th TFW (Lakenheath, England) supported by a squadron of EF-111A 'Sparkvarks', (from Upper Heyford), the Taif wing was one of the most powerful in the whole region.

have the penetrator version. The weapon has good stand-off capability, more so than the laser-guided bombs. It requires special training, and not everyone was qualified to deliver it. The pumping station which was on TV was a perfect target. The GBU-10s and -24s were very accurate, and they both came in penetrator versions which were widely used against the hard targets.

"Initially we didn't know what was our biggest threat; we had to sort that out at the start. As you

Left: With its heavy bombload, long range, good dash speed, and above all its highly effective Pave Tack target acquisition and designation system, the veteran F-111F proved to be one of the most important coalition combat types, especially at night.

Right: The Aardvarks were deployed to Saudi Arabia in such a hurry that there were no weapons available for them to use. Each of the 32 bombers in the first two waves carried four 2,000-lb laser-guided bombs, so at least they'd have something to drop.

where it's exploding and you can change to miss that. But again, you're flying through lead, airborne lead, and your job is to minimize the danger.

"We were expecting the air threat to be effective and lethal, but we were hoping that they were not as well-trained as the coalition forces, and that proved to be the case. They proved effective on the first night because they caused one of my aircraft to not make the target. They may not have made any actual kills, but their mission is complete if they cause anyone to drop their bombs before they get to the target.

"We did a mission against an airfield just west of Baghdad, with 12 aircraft. We tried a new concept, delivering GBU-24 penetrator bombs against hardened aircraft shelters at different altitudes, and it was a multi-ship, multi-axis attack, and we had great success that night. We destroyed well over 12 shelters, using a re-attack concept. Normally we would go in and do one pass and leave the area and go home. This night we went back again. I personally killed two large shelters, with secondary explosions indicating that there were aircraft inside. It was a mission that was very well planned, using time compression and varying altitudes which really saturated the target. There was a lot of AAA in the area that night, and a few SAM threats.

"A secret to our success was the ability to know when to go offensive. Before you take off you study your threats, and you have confidence in the jamming pod, the 'Wild Weasel' support, the F-15 support and the EF-111 support. When you get to the target area and experience a threat, you have to make a decision to go offensive some time in your profile before you get to the target. The people who did best in this war were the people who were able to sort out the threats and counteract them and then at a certain point approaching the IP, they concentrated all their energies on killing the target.

"If you were in defensive mode all the time, the chances of you hitting the target were consistently a lot lower than the guys that decided to go offensive some time in their attack profile. If you go too early, you may never get to the target at all because a threat may get you, but you have to weigh both, and not really focus totally on one or the other. You just had to keep your situational awareness up about what was happening around you, and as mission commander this not only meant for yourself but for all the other aircraft in your mission package, which could number over 40!"

can see from looking at the other types of aircraft that were shot down, triple-A was the biggest threat for every aircraft system. Airfields and high-value sites around Baghdad had more triple-A sites. The Iraqis were unable to use their acquisitioned radar effectively because of the EF-111 jammers, so most of the firing was just barrage, in the hope of being lucky. Once in a while they would be brave enough to turn their radar on but we also had 'Wild Weasels' in the area, so that as soon as radars were

turned on, they would jam a HARM down on them.

"It was sporadic fire and in some cases very heavy, aiming at the aircraft noise. When we highlighted ourselves, either using afterburner or flying through a lightning storm, the barrage changed to aimed fire, but when you flew on a bit or came out of 'burner, it went back to barrage. We took triple-A hits in one of our jets the first night, so we were very lucky, but we were also meticulous in our planning and assessment of

the threats. We picked routes both in and out to avoid the majority of threats. A lot of time was spent planning missions, and I think that was a big contributor to us not losing any of our jets.

"Barrage AAA is unpredictable by its nature, but sometimes there's a pattern you can see. Sometimes there are areas that are less intense than others, and at night you can see what to avoid. You maneuver the aircraft to avoid not only lateral intensity but the vertical intensity. Sometimes you'll see a certain level

F-111 Wing Commander

Colonel Tom Lennon, 48th Tactical Fighter Wing (Provisional), F-111F

"Somewhere in mid-August I was notified to deploy 18 aircraft with precision-guided munitions capability, and a short while later I was notified to add another 14. Eight of those aircraft had to be GBU-15 capable, and all the crews PGM-trained. Because there were no in-place munitions, we were also tasked to deploy with our bombs, so we had four 2,000-lb PGMs on all 32 aircraft that deployed in the first two flights.

"We went into Taif in southwestern Saudi Arabia and they really didn't know we were coming. They were surprised at the numbers we took and how fast we moved in down there. We set up housekeeping and started training, acquainting our people and the aircraft with the desert. We also had to set up a one-hour alert with two aircraft with PGMs. In late November I was tasked with another 32 aircraft, and what with depot maintenance requirements, I ended up with 66 aircraft deployed when the war started.

"Initially we were tasked against the strategic targets, because of the size of the threat. You have to consider that this was the fourth largest army in the world. Airfields, command and control centers, chemical storage sites: all these had to be kept under control. We worked the strategic targets for about the first 30 days of the war and then shifted over to softening up the battlefield, going against tanks and artillery.

"Because of the capabilities we had with the F-111 we operated mostly as our own strike package. All -111s, not mixed in with other people because we have a high dash speed and can carry a heavy payload a long way. It's easier for us to operate by ourselves from that aspect. But with a large package of strike aircraft, probably somewhere between 16 and 24 aircraft depending what the target was, we would then add EF-111 jammers, F-4G HARM shooters and some F-15 CAPs to go along with us. Occasionally we had some coalition integration with Tornados, who did the suppression of an airfield just prior to us coming in for shelter take-down.

"For me it was the first time I'd got to lead an F-111 strike package of that size. On the first night we were planning on 54 aircraft leaving Taif, with about six EF-111s as EW support. The target I selected was a large airfield north of Baghdad. I'd planned to go about half way to Baghdad at medium altitude because of fuel before dropping down, but about 30 miles inside Iraq we started getting a lot of indications that people were looking at us and locking onto us so we were forced to descend a lot earlier than we planned. Going across the Euphrates you could see all the lights on, and the blink-blink of people shooting at us. About abeam of Baghdad we saw an aircraft, but it looked like he couldn't do a conversion on us. We were running at about 650 kt on the TF at 200 ft, and we just accelerated on out.

"We swung north around Baghdad, heading west, going into our target area, and you could see triple-A over on the left side, you could see missiles being shot, I've never seen any defenses like it. The sky was red with triple-A. I was the first one in and my initial attack was to drop a GBU-15 on a hangar. We came to release point, hit the pickle button and for some reason the bomb didn't come off. We went into our turn and came back for a re-attack but the triple-A, even though it was barrage for the most part, tended to follow me – they were using the sound of the jet. We had three missiles launched at us just as we

Desert Storm

General Dynamics F-111F

The F-111 first saw combat in Vietnam in 1968. For its time, it was an extremely advanced combat aircraft. Initial teething problems were soon overcome and by 1972 it had matured into the most effective all-weather strike aircraft in the world. Continual updating over the years means that it remains one of the most potent fighter bombers in the world today. Although overshadowed in the Gulf by the F-117A and the F-15E Strike Eagle, it could be argued that the 'Aardvark' was the most successful allied bomber of the war.

Performance
The F-111F used its long range, good weapons load and high dash speed to make slashing attacks on important Iraqi targets. The F-111F is powered by a pair of Pratt & Whitney TF30-P-100 engines, each delivering more than 25,000 lb of thrust.

Radar
The F-111F is fitted with a multimode General Electric AN/APQ-144 radar and a Hughes AN/APQ-146 terrain-following radar which enable it to carry out low-level operations in all weathers, whatever the visibility.

Cockpit
The F-111F's two-man crew sits side by side. The seating arrangement means that the weapons systems operators, who are normally called GIBs or 'Guys In Back', in F-111Fs are YOTs, or 'You Over There'.

Pave Tack
The F-111F carries the Pave Tack pod in its weapons bay and under the fuselage. Pave Tack has a stabilized turret containing an infra-red sensor and a laser designator. This makes it possible to make smart weapon attacks without the need for third-party designation.

Paveway
The F-111F was almost exclusively used to drop laser-guided weapons in the Gulf, mostly Paveway IIs or the Paveway III depicted here. These consist of a standard bomb, in this case a BLU-109 steel-jacketed bunker buster, to which a laser guidance system has been added.

Left: The F-111Fs of the 48th Tactical Fighter Wing are normally based at RAF Lakenheath, UK, and during the Gulf war the wing's official headquarters remained in England. This is why the unit based at Taif in Saudi Arabia was known as the 48th TFW (Provisional).

Left: Colonel Tom Lennon (second from the right) discusses a mission with ground crew and staff officers. Colonel Lennon took great professional satisfaction from leading 50-aircraft strikes against some of Iraq's most heavily defended targets.

released the second weapon, which had to be negated.

"We ended up dropping back down to 200 ft on the TF, running out, hitting a tanker and coming back to our field, only to find it just like the UK, socked-in with fog! Tankers were scrambled and we stayed around until the sun opened up a little hole and we could start landing. Out of 53 aircraft launching that night, 26 of them got into Taif, the others having to divert to other bases for fuel. We turned those, got them home and still launched 40 aircraft that night in the second night wave of the war.

"Two other missions stand out

for me. One was where we had absolutely no defenses against us, and we took a five-ship in with four bombs each. We took out 20 aircraft shelters that night. The other one was when I was involved in the concept validation of dropping PGMs against tanks and armored vehicles, which we did the last 12 days of the war and at which we ended up being very, very successful – something like 920 tanks and armored vehicles.

"We used 500-lb GBU-12 laser-guided munitions against the tanks, but for other targets it was mostly 2,000-lb munitions. We also dropped a lot of land mines, CBU-89s that were dropped to

keep people out of areas at, for instance, chemical storage areas or airfields. We did a little bit of 'Scud' hunting and were partially successful. It was very difficult to find the mobile launchers, and with the F-111F and the Pave Tack, it's much better against fixed targets. If we could preplan our mission we'd have very high success rates: if it was a catch-can, we were not as successful.

"I was awful proud of everyone. Not just everyone who went down to Taif, but those back at Lakenheath. My wing was activating contingency hospitals back at base. In hindsight I'm not sure if anything could have gone

better. It was a colossal show by everyone from the lowest-ranking guy in the US Air Force to the Brits up the road from me, to the generals who were running the show. We were allowed by the national command authorities to conduct the war the way the war was supposed to be conducted. Also, our realistic peacetime training made a difference when we had to go to war. I'm honored and proud to have been allowed to have been a commander of a large flying wing in this war, which will probably end up being one of the greatest, if not *the* greatest, air campaigns in history."

D.D.

Laser-guided Weapons

An infra-red image of a building, shelter or bridge; cross hairs neatly aligned over the target; a black dot enters the screen at the bottom and darts towards the cross hairs; a large explosion and the target is hit. This was the abiding image of the air war against Iraq, provided courtesy of the infra-red systems of the A-6, F-111 or F-117. The key element in the aerial campaign before the land battle began was the use of PGMs (Precision-Guided Munitions), most of which were aimed using laser designation.

All laser-guided weapons work on the same principles. The designation system provides an image (either daylight or IR) on a cockpit screen, allowing the weapons system officer to align cross hairs over the design impact point. When this position is locked into the system, the infra-red sensor and its boresighted laser designator will remain pointing at the designated point. Bombs are released into the general vicinity of the target, and a few seconds from impact the designator fires a coded beam of energy at the impact point. The weapon has a seeker in the nose which detects the reflected laser energy from the designated point ('sparkle') and then aims itself towards the point by the use of controllable fins. It will only follow the energy with the right preprogrammed code.

Several laser-guided weapons were employed during Desert Storm, encompassing all three generations of Texas Instruments Paveway laser-guided bombs. Paveway I and Paveway II bombs have a gimballed seeker head on the tip of the weapon, behind which are small canard fins. The Paveway I family has fixed rear fins, whereas the Paveway II has rectangular fins which pop out on release to provide additional lift and therefore greater stand-off range. Two-thousand-lb GBU-10A/B Paveway Is were dropped by Grumman A-6E/TRAMs, while the equivalent weight GBU-10C/B Paveway IIs were launched from A-6s, F-15E Eagles, Pave Tack-equipped F-111Fs and F-117s.

Unique to the US Navy during Desert Storm was the GBU-16/B 1,000-lb Paveway II bomb, and the AGM-123A Skipper II. The latter is essentially a GBU-16 with a Shrike missile motor attached to the rear to provide greater stand-off range. French Jaguars were also equipped with a laser-guided missile, the Aérospatiale AS 30L, for which designation was provided by the ATLIS pod. Another 1,000-lb weapon was the RAF's standard laser-guided bomb, comprising the Paveway II guidance system allied

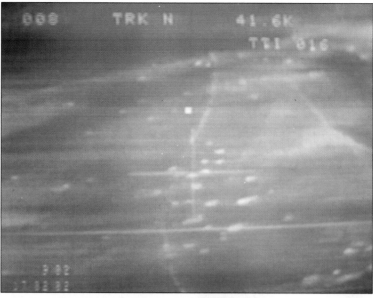

Above: Central to the devastating coalition success was the ability to detect targets by day or night. Infra-red sensors allowed allied aircraft to pick up their targets in complete darkness, the view coming up on the pilot's or weapons system operator's screen as a television picture. Setting cross-hairs on the target meant that a laser 'sparkle' was generated at that point, on which the bombs would home.

to a British Ordnance warhead. Another Paveway II weapon was the GBU-12B/B 500-lb bomb, used by a variety of aircraft (notably F-15E and F-111) for 'tank plinking' operations against the Republican Guard.

An important laser-guided weapon was the GBU-10I, which was a 2,000-lb bomb with Paveway II guidance but featuring the BLU-109 warhead. This warhead is a cylindrical unit (as opposed to the extended teardrop shape of standard bombs), encased in steel for maximum penetration effect and very useful against hard structures such as bunkers and

aircraft shelters.

Paveway III bombs were restricted to use by the F-111F and F-117. This family has a new seeker head and canard group, dispensing with the gimballed seeker in favor of an internally mounted unit giving a cleaner profile to the nose of the weapon. The canards are much larger, while full Paveway III bombs also have much larger area rear fins. These were used in five versions, the 2,000-lb GBU-24/B and GBU-24A/B (BLU-109 warhead) for use by F-111Fs, the 2,000-lb GBU-27/B and GBU-27A/B for use by the F-117, and the 5,000-lb F-111-dropped

Above and above inset: The F-111F could carry four precision-guided munitions, the example above being armed with two GBU-24A/B 2000-pounders used to take out individual Iraqi tanks. Guidance was provided by the aircraft's own stabilized Pave Tack turret (inset) which had both infra-red sensors and laser target markers.

Left above and left: Iraqi bunkers and hardened aircraft shelters were prime targets for coalition laser-guided bombs. The weapons of choice were 2,000-pounders, those like the GBU-10I with hardened steel casings being able to penetrate the thick concrete with ease.

Above right: American laser-guided bombs were seen with two kinds of guidance system. Paveway I and II seekers are gimbal mounted at the nose of the weapon, while the updated Paveway III has a longer, fixed nose with the seeker behind a window at the very tip.

Right: The GBU-27 was tailored to the F-117A. This is the version with the BLU-109 (I2000) steel-cased penetrator warhead.

GBU-28/B 'bunker buster'.

GBU-27 bombs were reportedly coated in radar-absorbent material for stealth considerations so as not to give away the position of the F-117 when it opened its bay doors and released the weapons. In order to fit the F-117's internal weapons bays, the GBU-27 variants featured the smaller Paveway II-style rear fin group, but due to the aircraft's stealth capabilities, the corresponding drop in range as compared to that of the GBU-24 was not important. Similarly, the GBU-28 'Deep Throat' weapon featured Paveway II-style fins allied to the upgraded seeker and canards.

Laser-guided Bombs

Laser-guided bombs are 10 times more expensive than normal bombs, but they are more than 100 times as accurate.

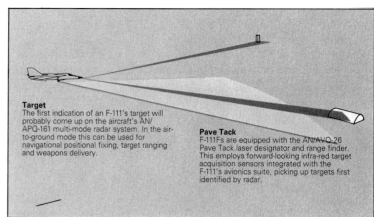

Target
The first indication of an F-111's target will probably come up on the aircraft's AN/APQ-161 multi-mode radar system. In the air-to-ground mode this can be used for navigational positional fixing, target ranging and weapons delivery.

Pave Tack
F-111Fs are equipped with the AN/AVQ-26 Pave Tack laser designator and range finder. This employs forward-looking infra-red target acquisition sensors integrated with the F-111's avionics suite, picking up targets first identified by radar.

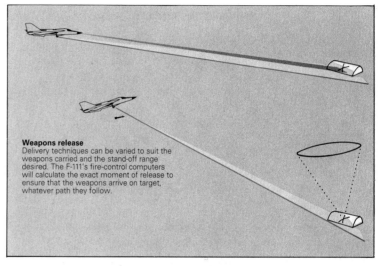

Weapons release
Delivery techniques can be varied to suit the weapons carried and the stand-off range desired. The F-111's fire-control computers will calculate the exact moment of release to ensure that the weapons arrive on target, whatever path they follow.

Weapons flight
Guided munitions can be released in a dive, lofted or released in level flight. They should arrive in a 'basket' over the target, which gives them a chance to pick up the reflections of the laser designator.

Attack profile
The position of the Pave Tack turret under the aircraft allows the crew almost total freedom of choice of flight path into and out of the target area. No matter what the plane does, the Pave Tack turret will remain fixed on the target.

Laser
The Pave Tack's laser designator does not illuminate the target until the last seconds of the attack. As the weapons enter the guidance basket, their sensors pick up the laser 'splash' and home in for the kill. Pave Tack's FLIR supplies imagery to a cockpit CRT display and videotape recorder for bomb-damage assessment.

Paveway IIIs with large rear fins had been developed to give a low-level delivery capability, the bomb being released in a toss maneuver and the large rear fins giving it an excellent stand-off range. In Desert Storm the low-level release profile was not required, and LGBs were largely released from medium altitude. In the case of the A-6E/TRAM, F-111F, F-117 and F-15E fitted with both pods of the LANTIRN system, designation of the target was achieved autonomously, but for other LGB carriers the 'buddy-lase' system was used. F-15Es notably worked as pairs, with one aircraft carrying the laser targetting pod to 'lase' for both itself and its wingman.

Royal Air Force laser-bombers used 'buddy-lasing' to great effect, flying Pave Spike-equipped Buccaneers to designate targets for Tornado. However, the Pave Spike pod is only daylight-capable, so the hasty introduction of two TIALD infra-red designation pods for carriage by Tornados greatly expanded the RAF's capabilities to strike targets. The 1,000-lb bombs had to be used in twos or threes to knock out shelters, and the RAF would have received 2,000-lb GBU-10 weapons in due course if the war had been prolonged.

D.D.

F/A-18Cs Score the US Navy's First Air-to-Air Kills in the Gulf War

Lieutenant Commander Mark Fox and Lieutenant Nick Mongillo, VFA-81, F/A-18 Hornet

Lieutenant Commander Mark Fox in the cockpit of a VFA-81 F/A-18C. Note the other aircraft of CVW-17 on Saratoga's flight deck.

Above: Lieutenant Nick Mongillo is seen beside AA 410, in which he scored the second Navy kill of the war. Lieutenant Mongillo had only recently arrived in the squadron, having previously served as a flight instructor before joining the 'Sunliners'.

Right: Lieutenant Commander Fox flies AA 401 during a combat mission in February. He scored his kill in this aircraft a few weeks before.

On 17 January Lieutenant Commander Mark Fox and Lieutenant Nick Mongillo launched with five other VFA-81 Hornets as part of a CVW-17 strike. In reality, Lieutenant Commander Fox was an airborne spare and was not scheduled to cross the beach. However, three of the scheduled strikers aborted for various reasons, such as loss of cabin pressurization, loss of radios and a failure to transfer fuel from the centerline drop tank. Lieutenant Commander Fox joined the three remaining aircraft as they headed inland.

CVW-17 in USS *Saratoga* (CV-60) flew the strike together with aircraft from CVW-3 from USS *John F. Kennedy* (CV-67). It was the first daylight strike of the Gulf war. The previous night had seen an intense first-strike effort by hundreds of allied aircraft against Iraqi facilities, especially around Baghdad and the major airfields in western Iraq, codenamed H-2 and H-3.

Although the enemy defenses had got everyone's attention – there had been heavy concentrations of AAA and SAMs, and a few Iraqi interceptors had taken off – the planners had scheduled an ongoing series of around-the-clock strikes. Planes had been lost during the first strikes, all to flak and SAMs. The MiGs and Mirages had been in the air, but none had been flown aggressively. The threat was there, however, and not to be taken lightly.

The USAF had had fairly good hunting over Baghdad and other target areas, and its F-15Cs had downed three Mirage F1s and three MiG-29s. Now it was the Navy's turn.

The four Sunliner F/A-18Cs each carried four Mk 84 2,000-lb bombs, a hefty load for a single-seat aircraft. They approached their target, H-3 airfield in western Iraq, in a 'wall', lined abreast. The other two Hornet pilots were Commander Bill McKee, VFA-81's Executive Officer, and Lieutenant Commander 'Chuck' Osborne.

High overhead, the ever-present AWACS and an E-2C from *Saratoga*'s VAW-125 monitored the strike. Although they were under visual ID (VID) Rules of Engagement, the Hornet pilots knew the E-2 could make the difference. The Hawkeye used various geographic reference points for its calls.

As he ran in on his target, Lieutenant Commander Fox was confident of himself, his aircraft and the rest of his flight.

"I didn't leave thinking I wasn't going to come back later. During the few hours before we entered Iraqi airspace, I thought about a lot of practical things. I made sure everything was set up, switches were in the right position, and that I kept the other three planes in sight. There wasn't time to think about anything but the mission."

As they ran in from the south, the radio was alive with calls from other portions of the strike group. *Kennedy*'s package had run into a few MiG-29s that had tailed the strikers as they exited the target area after delivering their ordnance.

The 'Fulcrums' stalked the CVW-3 planes as two F-15Cs from the USAF's 33rd TFW, based at Eglin AFB, Florida, dropped from their CAP station. The F-14 escort watched as the F-15s streaked past and fired missiles at the MiGs. Two MiG-29s failed to return to their base.

When Lieutenant Commander Fox and his flight were about 30 miles from their target, their systems set up for the bomb delivery they would soon make, the E-2 called a bandit alert as MiGs seemed to head for the VFA-81 Hornets soon after the *Kennedy* group had left the area. The Hornets flew on.

Then, Lieutenant John Joyce, the E-2's Air Control Officer (ACO) – one of the three Naval Flight Officers (NFOs) in the back of an E-2 – made another call, this time with a real sense of urgency.

"Hornets, bandits on your nose, 15 miles!"

That was it. Lieutenant Commander Fox and Lieutenant Mongillo each thumbed the knurled knob on the control stick that selected the missiles and changed their systems to the air-to-air mode. Their hands tightened on the stick-mounted trigger that fired their missiles.

As the flight flew on, Fox, in F/A-18C AA 401 (BuNo 163508) and Mongillo in AA 410 (BuNo 163502) looked for the oncoming MiGs. Fox got a lock-on at 10 miles – two MiG-21s in a left

AA 401, the aircraft in which Lieutenant Commander Fox scored his MiG kill, is actually the squadron commander's aircraft, although the plane is flown by whatever pilot is scheduled. Toting four 2,000-lb iron bombs, Sidewinders and Sparrows – the same load it carried during its 17 January MiG-killing mission – 401 formates with a Saratoga F-14A+ and a Wisconsin ANG KC-135.

echelon, a standard Soviet formation. Commander McKee and Lieutenant Commander Osborne had also locked up the lead MiG.

"It all happened very quickly. I switched back to air-to-air and got a lock on one of them. I had the MiG on the right while the second Hornet in our formation – Lieutenant Mongillo – took the MiG on the left. The other two Hornets had also acquired radar locks.

"The MiGs approached us, nose on, supersonic at Mach 1.2. Our relative rate of closure was more than 1,200 kt. They weren't maneuvering.

"I shot a Sidewinder first. It was a smokeless missile and I thought, at first, that I had wasted it because I couldn't see it tracking toward the MiG. I fired a Sparrow. The Sidewinder hit, though, followed by the Sparrow. The first missile actually did the job, and the Sparrow flew into the fireball. The whole event, from the E-2's call to missile impact, took less than 40 seconds."

Lieutenant Mongillo fired a single Sparrow which took out the second MiG-21.

"The Iraqi pilot knew what he was getting into when he climbed into that jet and took off after us.

That's how I view this whole thing. I haven't had any haunting second thoughts that I probably killed the guy. Given the opportunity he would have been glad to do the same to me.

"I don't consider myself a steely-eyed killer, but in a war, to beat the enemy, you have to kill him – and this was war."

Following their two kills, the two new shooters rejoined their flight and continued with their bomb delivery. Throughout their engagement with the MiGs, they had kept their bombs, all 8,000 lb of them. As the four F/A-18s came off target and headed south, they could see the two columns of black smoke rising up from the desert where the two MiGs had crashed – in the same relative formation as when they were shot down.

Fox credits his squadron maintenance department for keeping the aircraft up and ready for just such a mission as the MiG-killing flight of 17 January. He is also grateful for the E-2 crew's timely call.

"We are well trained. We fly an utterly reliable airplane. It's a real confidence builder to successfully complete a mission (he eventually flew 18 missions in the war) and then go back and do it again. I went back that same night.

"I didn't take the Iraqi threat lightly. My mouth still went dry and my heart beat faster when I went north of the border."

Talking about the strike-fighter concept that the F/A-18 represents, he has a definite opinion.

"This is the first time to my knowledge that an airplane scored a kill while carrying four 2,000-lb bombs, then continued on to hit its target. If the MiGs had got behind us, we would have had no choice but to honor their threat. You can't do that with 8,000 lb of bombs. We

would have had to jettison our ordnance to face them, and that would have served their purpose in stopping our strike. They failed; we succeeded.

"The idea of a plane having both air-to-air and air-to-ground missions is viable. American industry has produced the technology needed to build such a plane with outstanding performance in both missions."

These two kills were the Navy's only confirmed air-to-air kills of Iraqi fixed-wing aircraft.

The CAG-bird E-2C of VAW-124 wears two MiG-21 silhouettes to indicate the squadron's role in the downing of the Iraqi fighters by VFA-81. AA 600 was not, however, the Hawkeye on that mission.

Tanker War

One of the least publicized aspects of Desert Storm concerns the part played by inflight refueling in allowing allied air power to achieve its objectives. Had it not been for the presence of a substantial tanker force, it seems certain that the air offensive which presaged the ground war would have lasted even longer and might well have been significantly more costly in terms of losses.

As it transpired, in the all-important early stages when the allies sought to gain air supremacy by knocking out key Iraqi air bases and command and control centers, the tanker undoubtedly made a major contribution by permitting coalition strike packages to carry a greater payload of ordnance and, in so doing, to inflict a greater degree of damage. At the same time, it fully justified its claims to be a 'force multiplier' by making it possible for the size of the various packages to be reduced, thus allowing the allied air command to spread its resources much more effectively and engage many more targets.

Since it made the biggest contribution to the coalition, it follows that the United States assembled the largest tanker task force in the Gulf, but the size of that force might well come as a surprise. Statistics released by the Pentagon after the war reveal that no fewer than 256 KC-135 Stratotankers and 46 KC-10A Extenders were deployed to the region during Operations Desert Shield and Desert Storm, and a

high proportion of those would have been present throughout the war, when 15,434 sorties were recorded. During those sorties, a total of 110 million gallons of fuel was supplied to just under 46,000 receivers.

As single manager of the Air Force tanker fleet, Strategic Air Command was obviously heavily committed, but the scale of the operation was such that it entailed mobilization of Air National Guard and Air Force Reserve tanker outfits. This process began as early as 22 August 1990 and eventually encompassed all second-line units.

To facilitate operational control of SAC bomber and tanker assets in the Gulf, the 17th Air Division was organized in Saudi Arabia. This in turn directed the activities of a number of temporary units such as the 1702nd Air Refueling Wing (Provisional) at Seeb, Oman,

and the 1703rd ARW (Prov) at King Khalid International Airport, Saudi Arabia. Other airfields which hosted tankers included Jeddah and Dhahran in Saudi Arabia; Cairo West in Egypt; and Al Dhafra and Dubai in the United Arab Emirates. Moving farther from the war zone, tankers also operated from bases in Europe in support of SAC B-52Gs engaged on long-range bombing missions from Fairford, England, and Moron, Spain.

Additional US tanker resources were furnished by the Marine Corps, which stationed a number of KC-130 Hercules at Bahrain, from where they were mostly used to support attack and fighter-attack forces. The US Navy had its own carrier-borne KA-6D Intruders at sea and probably also made use of 'buddy' refueling packs fitted to aircraft like the F/A-18 Hornet and

Upper left: The tanker's 'basket' dominates the view that a Tornado navigator sees during refueling from an RAF Victor K.Mk 2. The work of the tanker force went largely unrecognized, but their presence was a vital factor in permitting the allies to achieve almost all their objectives before the start of the ground war. Warplanes would top up after launch within allied airspace, but tankers also supported strikes within enemy territory.

Left: The KC-135 Stratotanker was numerically most important of the USAF tanker types. Over 200 aircraft served in-theater for Desert Shield or Desert Storm. Variants in use included the KC-135A, KC-135E, KC-135Q and KC-135R.

RAF Jaguars top off their tanks during a post-strike rendezvous with one of the VC10 tankers deployed to Gulf. This operation was repeated on countless occasions.

Left: Unofficially referred to as 'Pinky' and 'Perky', two TriStars from No. 216 Squadron were painted in desert camouflage. They were used to refuel Tornado F.Mk 3 interceptors of the RAF which undertook combat air patrols during the course of Desert Storm.

Above: An RAF Tornado F.Mk 3 closes on the 'basket' deployed by a Victor K.Mk 2 of No. 55 Squadron. During the seven weeks of war, Victor tankers from this Muharraq-based unit racked up an impressive tally of 299 combat sorties.

Left: The US Navy warplanes used their own tankers, but they also made use of KC-135 Stratotankers of the Air Force. VA-72 A-7E Corsair IIs are seen here as they prepare to receive fuel from a KA-6 Intruder and a KC-135. In the distance, a pair of EA-6B Prowlers wait their turn before moving in for a welcome 'drink' in very busy airspace.

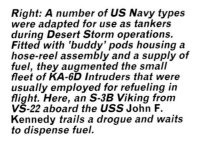

Right: A number of US Navy types were adapted for use as tankers during Desert Storm operations. Fitted with 'buddy' pods housing a hose-reel assembly and a supply of fuel, they augmented the small fleet of KA-6D Intruders that were usually employed for refueling in flight. Here, an S-3B Viking from VS-22 aboard the USS John F. Kennedy trails a drogue and waits to dispense fuel.

Tanker War

the A-7E Corsair.

Several other members of the coalition also routinely used aerial refueling. Most notable among these was the United Kingdom, which dispatched almost its entire tanker fleet to the Gulf region, stationing a maximum of nine VC10 K.Mk 2/3s of No. 101 Squadron at King Khalid Airport and seven Victors of No. 55 Squadron at Bahrain. Between them, they accumulated 680 sorties during the 43-day war, this tally being increased still further by two No. 216 Squadron TriStar K.Mk 1s which flew from King Khalid. Receivers were predominantly RAF Jaguars, Tornados and Buccaneers, but fuel was also furnished to Canadian CF-18s, French Mirage 2000s and a variety of US Navy and Marine Corps warplanes.

Both France and Italy were also in the refueling business, the former with a small number of C-135FRs at King Khalid, and the latter using 'buddy'-configured Tornados after an inauspicious start to combat operations. On the occasion in question, heavy turbulence prevented six out of the seven Italian aircraft from getting pre-strike fuel from a SAC KC-135 and they duly aborted, leaving the singleton to press on alone to the target where it was shot down with the loss of one crew member. After that, the Italian contingent forgot all about 'force multipliers' and instead chose to adopt a sort of 'force divider' policy, whereby it used half of its Tornado force as tankers and half as bombers.

L.P.

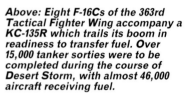

Left: The imposing bulk of a SAC KC-10A Extender almost fills the boomer's field of view as it tops off its own tanks. Almost 75 per cent of SAC's Extender fleet was used for support of operations in the Gulf at one time or another during the build-up and the war.

Above: Eight F-16Cs of the 363rd Tactical Fighter Wing accompany a KC-135R which trails its boom in readiness to transfer fuel. Over 15,000 tanker sorties were to be completed during the course of Desert Storm, with almost 46,000 aircraft receiving fuel.

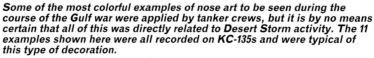

Some of the most colorful examples of nose art to be seen during the course of the Gulf war were applied by tanker crews, but it is by no means certain that all of this was directly related to Desert Storm activity. The 11 examples shown here were all recorded on KC-135s and were typical of this type of decoration.

from page 64 **(17 January continued)**

and two unidentified fighters, a debilitating and unsustainable 33-per cent loss rate. Also during the first day, 18 transport aircraft, most of them airliners belonging to Iraqi Airways, flew to airfields in Iran to escape destruction.

Coalition losses during the first day were an F/A-18 of VFA-81 from USS *Saratoga* (pilot killed in action), a Kuwaiti Air Force A-4 (pilot taken prisoner), an A-6E Intruder of VA-35 from USS *Saratoga* (both crewmen taken prisoner), and two Royal Air Force and one Italian Tornados (two crewmen killed, four crewmen taken prisoner). In each case the aircraft was lost in combat.

Under the initial plan for the coalition air attack, devised the previous September, the air war was to be split into four separate phases. During Phase I, covering the first week or 10 days of hostilities, coalition air operations were to have had three main objectives: first, to gain air superiority over Iraq and Kuwait; secondly, to destroy Iraq's strategic attack capability, her nuclear, chemical and biological production facilities and the 'Scud' missile launching and storage sites; and thirdly, to disrupt the Iraqi command and control structure. Phase II, lasting about three days, was aimed at suppressing the air defenses of the Iraqi forces deployed in and around Kuwait. During Phase III, which was to last from the end of Phase II until the beginning of the ground offensive, the aircraft were to continue attacking Phase I and Phase II targets as required, while shifting the main weight of the attack to Iraqi army units in the Kuwait theater of operations. Phase IV was to be the air support for ground operations, should these become necessary.

As a result of the doubling of the coalition air strength between November 1990 and the start of hostilities, the commander had sufficient planes to run Phases I, II and III concurrently. Thus, from the first day of the war, Iraqi troop positions in the Kuwait theater of operations came under air attack.

18 January, Friday Shortly after dawn seven 'Scud' missiles, almost certainly the Al-Hussein version fitted with a 330-lb warhead and with a maximum range of about 375 miles, struck Haifa (two) and Tel Aviv (three) in Israel, causing several casualties. The two other missiles fell harmlessly clear of populated areas. One 'Scud' fired at Dhahran in Saudi Arabia was intercepted and shot down by a Patriot missile.

Systematic attacks continued against airfields and air-force related targets in Iraq, and the Iraqi air force continued to offer only minimal resistance.

B-52 bombers and A-10 attack planes were reported in action against targets in the Kuwait area. Attempts were made to hit the Iraqi tanks and armored vehicles, but these proved difficult targets. To protect them, the Iraqis had bulldozed 10-ft-deep trenches wide enough to take the vehicle. The vehicle was then driven in, and sand was piled around it to provide camouflage and protection. That produced a very small target, and one that was difficult to attack effectively from any direction other than directly above.

French Jaguars attacked a munitions storage facility at Ras Al Qulayah on the east coast of Kuwait. Four of the Jaguars carried the AS 30L laser-guided missile, fired from about 4,000 ft in a dive from about 7,000 ft. A video from one of the attacking aircraft showed an AS 30L smashing through the door of a large hangar-like building used for munitions storage. The other eight Jaguars attacked the facilities with 550-lb bombs.

F-111Es of the 20th TFW based at Incirlik in Turkey, with fighter escorts and SEAD aircraft, began attacking targets in Iraq, thus opening up a second line of approach against Iraq.

During the day the total number of Tomahawk cruise missiles fired to date reached 196.

After dark there was considerable air activity over western and southern Iraq in an effort to prevent the missile launches against Israel

and Saudi Arabia. 'The Great 'Scud' Hunt' had begun. F-15Es of the 4th TFW flew armed reconnaissance missions over roads in the areas where the mobile launchers were thought to be operating. The aircraft flew in pairs, the leader carrying four 2,000-lb GBU-10 laser-guided bombs and the wingman carrying either six CBU-87 cluster-bombs or 12 Mk 82 iron bombs. The F-15Es patrolled the roads at altitudes of around 15,000 ft, searching with their LANTIRN night-vision equipment for the 'Scud' mobile launchers and their support vehicles. When one of the target vehicles was located, the leader attacked first, and if the target had not been hit the wingman followed. In a move aimed at confining the 'Scud' launching and support vehicles to roads, other aircraft dropped large numbers of area-denial mines on areas of flat ground over which the vehicles might otherwise have passed.

During the day two Iraqi fighters were shot down in air-to-air combat, and three Tupolev Tu-16 'Badger' bombers were destroyed on the ground during an attack on Al Taqaddum airfield.

US Navy A-6Es from VA-75 operating from the USS *John F. Kennedy* in the Red Sea launched three AGM-84 SLAM (Stand-off Land Attack Missile) weapons at a power station in Iraq. After launch the missiles were taken under control and guided to the target by an A-7E of VA-72.

Coalition aircraft losses: one US Navy A-6E Intruder of VA-35, USS *Saratoga* (both crewmen killed in action), a USAF F-15E of the 4th TFW (both crewmen killed in action), and a US Marine Corps OV-10A Bronco of VMO-2 (both crewmen taken prisoner). All of the above were combat losses.

19 January, Saturday Air attacks continued against targets in Iraq, and French Jaguars carried out a further attack on the Ras Al Qulayah munitions storage facility.

The 33rd TFW had another good day and its F-15Cs claimed four Iraqi fighters in air-to-air combat. Two MiG-25s were shot down by Captains Lawrence Pitts and Richard Tollini, in each case with AIM-7s. Captain Craig Underhill shot down a MiG-29 with an AIM-7. Another MiG-29 crashed into the ground during maneuvering combat with Captain Cesar Rodriguez, and the latter claimed it. Elsewhere, the F-15Cs of the 525th TFS, 36th TFW, shot down two

to page 76 **(19 January continued)**

A Grumman F-14 Tomcat dispenses flares as it swoops low over heavily defended hostile territory. The flares are designed to decoy heat-seeking missiles away from the fighter. Most coalition combat aircraft carried countermeasures of this sort.

from page 75 (**19 January continued**)

Mirage F1s with AIM-7 missiles.

Royal Air Force Tornado GR.Mk 1A reconnaissance aircraft flew their first operational mission. These aircraft were equipped with infra-red sensors feeding video recorders, and the system was optimized for night low-level operations. One GR.Mk 1A hunting for 'Scud' launchers located a missile and launcher, which were later attacked by other aircraft.

Four 'Scud' missiles were fired at Israel. Two struck Tel Aviv soon after dawn and injured 17 people, the other two fell on unpopulated areas. Under strong political pressure from the US government, the Israeli government agreed not to retaliate against Iraq for these attacks.

In a series of small-scale actions off the Kuwait coast, US and British naval forces seized nine oil platforms and took 12 Iraqi prisoners.

During the day the nuclear-powered submarine USS *Louisville* in the Red Sea fired a Tomahawk missile at a target in Iraq.

The Iraqi air force flew its greatest number of combat sorties during a single 24-hour period during the conflict, about 55. As mentioned above, six, possibly seven, Iraqi fighters were shot down in air-to-air combat.

One USAF F-46 'Wild Weasel' was lost to ground fire. The F-4G, returning low on fuel after one of its tanks had been punctured by enemy fire, ran out of fuel as its crew attempted to put down at an emergency landing ground in Saudi Arabia; both crewmen ejected safely. A Royal Saudi Air Force Tornado was lost in a non-combat-related incident.

20 January, Sunday Two 'Scud' missiles were fired at targets in Saudi Arabia, both being shot down by Patriot missiles.

The Iraqi army also fired three 'Frog' short-range surface-to-surface missiles against a target in Saudi Arabia. All fell harmlessly in the desert and there were no casualties.

Air attacks continued against targets in Iraq and Kuwait, but bad weather over targets forced several aircraft to return with their bombs.

That night the 48th TFW sent a striking force of 20 F-111Fs against Balad airfield. Flying at altitudes between 12,000 and 20,000 ft, the aircraft attacked the runways, taxiways and hardened shelters with laser-guided bombs. The AAA fire was so severe that several aircraft attacking from the lower altitudes were forced to abandon their bombs to take evasive action. Iraqi fighters were also active in the area, and one F-111F crew discovered that this was still a threat to be reckoned with. Weapons System Officer Captain Jerry Hanna recalled, "We had attacked the taxiway intersection from about 18,000 ft, and were egressing the target heading northeast. We were the tail-end Charlie, the 20th aircraft to attack out of 20. We aimed our GBU-10s into the taxiway intersections from about 18,000 ft, and started to egress the target heading northeast. Then on the RHWR we heard a MiG-29 'Fulcrum' close in and lock-on his radar. We immediately initiated a high-speed combat descent, the pilot got the wings back and we went screaming downhill. Puking chaff, we went from 19,000 to about 4,000 ft in a heartbeat! The adrenalin was really pumping, Jim [the pilot] was busy trying get the plane close to the ground, I was on the radio hollering at the AWACS that we had been jumped by a MiG and to get the F-18s coming back in our direction. I got the TF (Terrain-Following) radar on so that it would take over when we got close to the ground. That guy had us locked-up on his radar for 35 seconds; it felt like five years!" Finally, the RHWR fell silent, but by then Hanna was getting close to the ground and he could see AAA coming towards the plane from the right, so the crew pulled back up to medium altitude. The rest of the egress was without incident.

to page 78 (**20 January continued**)

Intruder's First Strike
Lieutenant Commander Gil Bever, VA-35, A-6 Intruder

As the 15 January 1991 deadline for Iraqi forces to withdraw from Kuwait came and went, USS *Saratoga* prepared for what looked to be a protracted and intense conflict. Lieutenant Commander Gil Bever and his commanding officer, Commander J. B. Andersen, a member of one of the five crews of VA-35's complement on the 1983 Lebanon strike, were two of the few aviators with post-Vietnam combat experience. Bever tried to tell other crews what their first missions might be like.

"The deputy CAG had not been in combat either, and he came to the seminar I held. I relived some of my experiences, some things people could look for.

"'You'll be *so* busy,' I told them. 'If you're planning on reading a checklist when you're going across the beach, forget it. You'll have your head outside the cockpit looking for bullets and SAMs. You need to memorize critical information like attack heading, TOTs (Time on Targets), your egress heading, and where the threats are. Memorize combat-checklist items like ECM gear, chaff programs, and set it all up before you go into combat. Once the bullets start flying, you won't have time to say, 'OK, now, time to turn the Master Arm on . . .'"

When the execute order came on the afternoon of 16 January, Lieutenant Commander Bever and his squadron mates were ready. He talked about the first strike, in the early hours of the next day.

"That was confusing, since it had been planned for so long and we had practiced it. The target was west of Baghdad. We launched and picked up the tanker tracks. All the strike axes centered around Baghdad. We even had BQM-74 drones that went downtown. Those were the 'cruise missiles' the Iraqis claimed to have shot down. Our fighters won't have a lot of drones to shoot for a long time; they all went to Baghdad. They tooled around, sucking up bullets and SAMs.

"We had a huge support package going in with us. We had planes dropping decoys, shooting

A bomb-laden A-6E Intruder from VA-35 'Panthers' replenishes its fuel tanks from a KC-135E of the Kansas Air National Guard.

Right: This VA-35 Intruder was hit by ground fire during an airfield attack on day two of the war. The crew got back safely, but the aircraft was later scrapped.

Above left: *Lieutenant Commander Bever saw combat action when attached to A-6E Intruder squadron* **VA-35,** *flying from the* **USS** *Saratoga.*

Above: *An A-6 Intruder of* **VA-35** *sits on the deck of the* **USS** *Saratoga, as it waits its turn for launch. Although the A-6 is getting old, it remains a capable all-weather bomber.*

Right: *Two* **VA-75** *Intruders overfly the Kennedy, while the rest of the squadron launches from the carrier's bow catapults. Intruders are equipped with a* **TRAM** *turret under the nose that combines forward-looking infra-red detection with laser designation and range finding. However, despite the fancy kit, bombing runs have to be conducted in vulnerable stable flying altitudes.*

Right: *Saudi Arabia is a stark country, as is clear from this A-6 right-seater's view from an Intruder skimming inverted over a ridge. After the first couple of days, few missions were flown at such low level, most A-6 attacks being at medium altitude, well clear of Iraqi anti-aircraft fire.*

MY 🐾 IS BACK

HARMs, as well as fighters for escort during this two-stage attack on this airfield, a primary field for MiG-29s.

"Timing is paramount for everything here. We started splitting off, then we'd press on towards the target. We all had TOTs, so we knew when we had to leave the tanker, and checking our time, distance and headings, we'd co-ordinate everything to be on time. There'd be four A-6s, a minute apart between all their bombs, from the first to the last, then there'd be Hornets shooting HARMs, taking out radars so they wouldn't be shooting at *us*. Then there'd be EA-6s jamming, staying with the strike package to protect us in case anything (radar, missiles, AAA) came up.

"We rolled in from 25,000 ft, and released at 15,000, high altitude. We decided later that wasn't high enough because there was still too much stuff going *over* us. Each of our four A-6s carried four 2,000-lb bombs, one on each wing station for that first strike. That was a pretty good load for us, although we had other loads depending on our missions. Other loads included 10 Mk 83s (1,000-lb bombs), LGBs, Rockeyes – up to 20 – although when we carried a big load, we lost a lot of maneuverability and speed, naturally.

"We went in, and there was stuff flying around. Then we heard that there was a MiG-25 in the air. We couldn't get clearance to fire, either. He launched against us, and everyone was maneuvering around. That night, the first airplane that was shot down was a Hornet from our air wing (Lieutenant Commander Michael S. Speicher, VFA-81, in an F/A-18C, BuNo 163484). He was shooting HARMs against the field, and somewhere got knocked down.

"We came up to the north, right along the river, and followed it to the target, made a left turn, and egressed, right down on the deck, low, almost the way we came in. It was busy, like the Fourth of July."

from page 76 **(20 January continued)**

The Royal Air Force lost a Tornado, following a technical failure shortly after take-off for a combat mission. The crew ejected safely.

Seven Tornados from the Muharraq squadron attacked Tallil airfield that evening, four of the aircraft loaded with 1,000-lb airburst fuzed bombs which they aimed at the air-defense positions, and three with JP 233 runway cratering munitions. As one of the aircraft pulled up to toss-launch its 1,000-pounders at the target it was shot down by a Roland missile. Both of the crew ejected and were taken prisoner.

US Marine Corps AH-1W Cobra helicopters went into action against ground targets in Kuwait.

During the 24-hour period the Iraqi air force flew about 25 sorties, without loss.

Allied losses: the US Navy lost an A-6E which landed on its carrier with battle damage and had to take the barrier; it was judged to be damaged beyond repair. Three USAF aircraft, two F-16s (one pilot taken pirsoner) and one F-15E of the 4th TFW (both crewmen taken prisoner), were lost to ground fire. The Royal Air Force lost one Tornado in combat and one to non-combat causes. Two US Army helicopters, a UH-60 and an AH-64, were destroyed (non-combat losses).

At a press conference that afternoon, British Defence Secretary Tom King stated that so far the Royal Air Force had mounted attacks on 12 airfields in western and southern Iraq.

The Iraqi government claimed the destruction of 170 aircraft and cruise missiles during the conflict so far (compared with 14 aircraft admitted lost by the coalition). It is likely that several of the aircraft claimed destroyed were in fact decoys.

Coalition armorers and ordnance technicians had plenty of opportunity to exercise their wit in the traditional manner. Bombs have carried messages like these for as long as they have been dropped by aircraft.

21 January, Monday Seven 'Scud' missiles were fired at Dhahran and Riyadh, all destroyed by Patriot missiles or falling clear of their targets. There were no casualties.

The aerial bombardment of Iraq and Kuwait continued, though again poor weather prevented many attacks, forcing aircraft to return with their bombs.

A US Navy F-14A+ of VF-103 from USS *Saratoga*, flying on an escort mission, was shot down over Iraq. The pilot was rescued by helicopters escorted by two A-10s, but they failed to find the RIO and he was later taken prisoner.

22 January, Tuesday A 'Scud' missile hit a built-up area of Tel Aviv and caused three deaths. Seven 'Scuds' were fired at Saudi Arabia, but all were shot down by Patriot missiles or landed clear of their targets. There were no casualties.

to page 80 **(22 January continued)**

AWACS

When the first strikes went into Baghdad, Iraqi fighters blocking the way were pinpointed by AWACS. When a Saudi pilot shot down two Iraqi Mirages in an air-to-air engagement, the entire kill scenario was choreographed by AWACS. When the Iraqi air force decided to bolt and began taking its warplanes towards refuge in Iran, American F-15C Eagles were directed to pick them off, by AWACS.

AWACS (Airborne Warning And Control System) was all-seeing, all-knowing. It was the allies' uncelebrated hidden weapon which kept tabs on enemy air, gave direction to friendly warplanes, and maintained a continuous radar picture of the battle zone, from the Red Sea to the Arabian Sea.

To most allied airmen at the start of Desert Shield in August 1990, the Persian Gulf region was as alien as the red spot on the planet Jupiter. But Saudi Arabia was familiar to the men and women who 'ran' the air war from this flying radar station. AWACS, a lumbering, omnipresent offspring of the Boeing 707-320, was made to appear distinctive by its Westinghouse AN/APY-2 ODR (Overland Downlock Radar) mounted on pylons in a revolving, black, saucer-like disk, or rotodome, atop its fuselage.

E-3 Sentry AWACS crews of the 552nd Airborne Command & Control Wing under Colonel Gary Voellger had been rotating in and out of Saudi Arabia for a decade. They knew the turf. Their maintenance people had long since learned to cope with heat, sand, fog and the Arabic language. They also knew their Iraqi adversary: in addition to years of experience hanging around Riyadh, E-3 crews benefitted from an 'all source' intelligence center at the allies' air headquarters, known in slang as The Black Hole. E-3 personnel had a complete Order of Battle of Iraqi forces in hand when they set forth to serve as flying radar platforms for the Desert Storm war effort.

To fix things so that "Saddam Hussein won't be able to sneeze without us knowing it," as one crew member described it, the Desert Storm battle plan called for maintaining four E-3B/C Sentry AWACS platforms in the sky at all times. Three were assigned the western, central and eastern sectors of the theater of operations, using callsigns COUGAR, BUCKEYE and BOSTON respectively, and protected by F-15C Eagles flying HAV (High Asset Value) combat

Above: Facing aft in the work bay of an E-3B Sentry AWACS. With a mission controller overseeing their efforts, AWACS crew members spot Iraqi aircraft, track them and provide vectors to enable allied fighters to intercept.

Right: The Boeing 707-320 airframe and disk-shaped rotodome are the distinctive features of the E-3B/C AWACS 'flying radar station', seen here ready to depart on a mission from Riyadh Military Airport.

Right, below: AWACS crews routinely flew some of the very longest combat support missions of the war. Refueling in flight and 14- to 16-hour sorties made it possible to mount a 24-hour radar watch on the Iraqis.

air patrols. A fourth served as an airborne spare and stayed ready for contingencies. The 552nd, normally home-based at Tinker AFB, Oklahoma, had enough E-3s in-theater that maintenance people were able to support this commitment. The Royal Saudi Air Force also flew AWACS missions with its own E-3A Sentry airplanes.

A walk-through of one of Colonel Voellger's aircraft would reveal, first, an airline-style flight deck housing pilot and co-pilot. Positions for navigator, flight engineer and crew chief are not usually occupied now that E-3B/C models have global positioning navigation.

Above: AWACS personnel were familiar with Saudi conditions, unlike most coalition personnel, since they had been operating in the country for years. Surveillance had to be 24 hours a day and along the entire border area, constantly orchestrating raids – to keep the enemy under maximum pressure.

a thickening of the aircraft walls) are another galley, three bunks and three rows of aft-facing, passenger-style seats. On a typical mission – those in Desert Storm lasted 16-18 hours – an AWACS aircraft carried at least two full crews.

From 16 January until the cease-fire, AWACS flew four continuous orbits (including the spare) to control more than 3,000 combat sorties per day, while maintaining a mission capable rate of 98 per cent – nine per cent higher than in peacetime.

R.F.D.

Behind the flight deck, the AWACS mission officer is located in the cabin, just aft of communications equipment and the main computer (both on the left). Behind this position are three sets of display consoles, each with three operators – the first row facing aft, the next forward and the final set of three facing again to the rear. These nine positions are manned by enlisted men and women trained in radar surveillance and intercept duties.

Further aft, past a galley and ahead of the rotodome supports, a radar maintenance crewman faces aft on the left. Behind the rotodome supports (seen as merely

The ability of commanders to maintain real-time control of the air battle was key to the success of Desert Storm, as was maintaining integrity of allied air space, and AWACs was key to those tasks. Had Iraqi fighters been able to penetrate allied airspace and get among high-value targets, the course of the war could have altered significantly.

from page 78 (**22 January continued**)

The bombardment of targets in Iraq and the Kuwait theater of operations continued. Four Iraqi ships were attacked, and two left dead in the water. French air force Jaguars attacked a naval base in Kuwait, launching six AS 30L laser-guided bombs at three Iraqi ships.

The systematic attack began on the hardened aircraft shelters at Iraqi airfields. US aircraft employed the GBU-27 2,000-lb laser-guided bomb, which was fitted with a delayed action fuze to enable the weapon to penetrate the roof of the shelter before exploding.

In the course of a toss-bombing attack with 1,000-pounders on an Iraqi radar site, a Royal Air Force Tornado was shot down. Both of the crew were killed.

Aerial photographs showed several fires in the Al Wafra oilfield in Kuwait; later reports suggested that these might have been caused by tests of the fire trenches that formed part of the Iraqi defensive line.

Five captured coalition airmen were forced to appear on Iraqi television and made to denounce the war. The move raised an international outcry on the misuse of prisoners, and it was not repeated.

Three Iraqi transport planes flew to Iran.

One Royal Air Force Tornado was lost in combat, and a US Marine Corps AV-8B Harrier was lost to non-combat causes. A US Army AH-1 Cobra was destroyed (non-combat loss).

23 January, Wednesday Four 'Scud' missiles were launched against Saudi Arabia; all were engaged by Patriot missiles and there were no casualties. One 'Scud' was launched against Israel but there were no casualties there either.

Over Kuwait the low cloud lifted, allowing coalition aircraft to employ their full force in attacks on Iraqi ground forces. French Jaguars attacked artillery concentrations, and Kuwaiti and Italian aircraft were also in action.

US Navy A-6s attacked and sank the armed Iraqi tanker *Almutanabi* off the coast of Kuwait.

That night, poor weather caused several attacks to be aborted. In one of these, Colonel T. Lennon lead a force of 20 F-111Fs of the 48th TFW to attack Tallil airfield. He attempted a laser-guided bomb attack from low altitude, but the cloud base was so low that he was forced to abandon the mission and ordered his aircraft to abort the attack and return to base with their bombs.

During the day, eight more Iraqi transport planes flew to Iran.

At a news conference, General Colin Powell stated the coalition air forces had now achieved air superiority. As a result, the majority of coalition missions could now be flown at altitudes between 8,000 and 20,000 ft. As one USAF officer put it, "That has always been our strategy, to suppress the SAMs and get up out of the weeds."

Of the 66 Iraqi main and dispersal airfields, only five (four of them in the vicinity of Baghdad) were reported still able to operate aircraft. Of the 30 main Iraqi operating bases, 25 had been damaged by air attack.

24 January, Thursday Clear skies allowed coalition aircraft to go into action against targets in Iraq and Kuwait in full force.

Off Kuwait, the Lynx helicopter from HMS *Cardiff* located an Iraqi minesweeper, a landing craft and a patrol boat. US Navy A-6s were directed in to attack the craft and all three were sunk. Allied naval forces captured the small island of Qaruh off the coast of Kuwait.

French Jaguar fighter-bombers attacked artillery positions in the south of Iraq.

Vectored into a firing position from 80 miles away by an E-3 Sentry aircraft, Captain Ayehid Salah al-Shamrani, flying an F-15C of No. 13 Sqn Royal Saudi Air Force, shot down two Mirage F1 fighters with AIM-9 missiles. It appears the aircraft were escorting one or more Mirage F1s attempting to deliver an Exocet attack on allied warships in the Gulf. The other Mirage(s) escaped. These were the first Iraqi planes to be shot down for five days.

to page 82 (**24 January continued**)

Special Operations

General H. Norman Schwarzkopf was deep into the planning of Operation Desert Storm when he called for Air Force Colonel George A. Gray III. Gray was asked whether the MH-53E helicopters from his 1st Special Operations Wing could guarantee the success of a vital mission. Schwarzkopf was reassured by the Air Force man's response, and reportedly said, "Okay, Colonel, you get to start the war."

In the early morning of 17 January, two pairs of USAF MH-53J Pave Low helicopters took off from a Saudi airfield, each pair in company with four AH-64 Apache attack helicopters of the US Army's 1st Battalion, 101st Aviation Brigade. Their task was to simultaneously attack and destroy two air-defense radar sites, 22 and 37 km inside Iraq. By knocking out the overlapping coverage from the two sites, the raid was to create a 'radar black' corridor in Iraq's air defenses, through which coalition air power would pour in an overwhelming assault on Iraq's command and control infrastructure.

The Sikorsky-built Pave Lows had been designed for covert penetration missions, and their sophisticated long-range navigation equipment ensured that the Apache teams could reach the radar sites within 30 seconds of each other.

At 0238 that morning, the attack went in, the Apaches successfully using Hellfire missiles, 2.75-in rockets, and 30-mm gunfire to create the required hole in the Iraqi defenses. All aircraft returned safely, but not before the big Sikorskys had used flares to decoy heat-seeking shoulder-fired surface-to-air missiles away from the force. The vital contribution that the Pave Lows made to the success of the mission was virtually ignored in the explosion of postwar publicity, but that is about par for the course where Special Operations are concerned.

The 1st Special Operations Wing forms part of the US Air Force's Special Operations Command, headquartered at Hurlburt Field in Florida. The Wing was deployed to the Gulf in force. Among the units under Colonel Gray's command were the 8th Special Operations Squadron with its MC-130E Combat Talons; the 9th Special Operations Squadron supporting the rest of the Wing with its HC-130H Combat Shadow tankers; the 16th Special Operations Squadron equipped with AC-130H

Above: A Combat Talon MC-130E of the 7th SOS refuels. Operating out of Batman in Turkey, these covert operations aircraft were involved in a behind-the-lines rescue attempt in northern Iraq, but delay in getting permission to overfly Syria meant that the mission failed and the downed airmen were captured.

Spectre gunships; the 20th Special Operations Squadron and its MH-53J Pave Low helicopters; and the 55th Special Operations Squadron, flying MH-60 Pave Hawk helicopters.

Little has been released about the Wing's operations in the Gulf, nor of the US European Command's 39th Special Operations Wing which operated out of Turkey during the war. That is how Special Operations personnel like it, since one normally only hears about them when things go wrong. On this occasion, nearly everything went right, although there was one tragedy when an AC-130 with 14

Above: US Army AH-64A Apache helicopters played a key role in knocking out two Iraqi air-defense radars well behind enemy lines.

Right: The Sikorsky MH-60J Pave Hawk of the USAF Special Operations Command made its combat debut when being used for combat rescue and covert infil/exfil missions behind enemy lines.

Left: MH-53J Pave Low helicopters can be seen in various types of camouflage at a gathering of Special Operations helicopters. Two of these powerful machines got Desert Storm underway by acting as pathfinders in the very first strike at Iraq's air defenses.

Above: Minigun-armed HH-60H helicopters of the US Navy were based at Al Jouf, from where they were used for covert operations, although with greater emphasis on combat rescue than the USAF Special Operations helicopters.

crew members on board was shot down during the battle to retake the Saudi town of Khafji.

The specialists of the 1st Special Operations Wing undertook a wide range of operations. The four Combat Talon MC-130s of the 8th Special Operations Squadron won the nickname '8th Bomb Squadron' when they began to drop massive 15,000-lb BLU-82 'Daisy Cutter' bombs. Flying at 17,000 ft or more, they managed to get the bombs to within 50 ft of the aim points. As a BLU-82 contains over five tonnes of high explosive, that is as good as a direct hit.

Initially used to blast through Iraqi border defenses, the huge bombs had a dramatic effect. One British SAS team, observing an explosion from many miles away, thought that a tactical nuclear device had been detonated. On another occasion an advancing infantry unit found that every Iraqi within three miles of the blast had been killed. The Combat Talons also dropped more than 17 million leaflets in the course of 40 sorties into hostile territory.

MC-130s also flew tanker missions for the MH-53J Pave Low helicopters of the 20th Special Operations Squadron. After taking part in the first official mission of the war, the 20th went on to fly more than 60 missions behind enemy lines. The squadron's MH-53Js were heavily involved in the campaign to find and neutralize Iraqi 'Scud' missiles, using their night-vision systems to seek out mobile 'Scud' launchers while inserting and extracting Special Forces ground teams. One such team found 29 'Scuds' ready to fire at Israel less than two days before the end of the war. The site was blasted by Air Force A-10As.

Special Operations forces were also responsible for combat rescue operations in the Gulf. In this they took the place of the Air Force's Air Rescue Service, which was not deployed, although numbers of ARS personnel did serve in the Kuwait theater of operations. The Special Operations helicopters managed a few rescues, the first being performed by the 20th SOS, an MH-53 from which picked up a downed Navy F-14 pilot. The Tomcat's RIO had already been captured and the pilot was dodging a pair of Iraqi trucks, which were closing in when the Pave Low arrived on the scene. The Iraqi trucks were taken out by the helicopter before it successfully plucked the pilot to safety.

C.B.

from page 80 (**24 January continued**)

Press reports stated that during the first week of the war nearly all Iraqi air-defense radars had been destroyed or damaged, though 20 per cent of them were later put back into action. Other reports stated that Iraq's capability to develop and produce nuclear weapons had been destroyed, as had about half of the country's chemical and biological weapon manufacturing capability.

The Royal Air Force announced that half a squadron of Buccaneer aircraft had been ordered to Saudi Arabia, to act as laser designator aircraft for the Tornados.

During the day, coalition air forces flew more than 3,000 sorties.

Two more Iraqi transport planes flew to Iran. A US spokesman announced that to date, at least 15 Iraqi aircraft had been destroyed on the ground during attacks on airfields.

An F-16 was shot down and its pilot rescued by helicopter. One US Navy F/A-18 was lost (non-combat loss).

25 January, Friday After a pause the previous day, eight 'Scud' missiles were launched against Israel. All were hit by Patriot missiles, but the warhead of one of them fell on a house in Tel Aviv, killing two people and injuring 69. Two more 'Scuds' were fired at Saudi Arabia but caused no casualties.

Cloud cover again restricted air operations over the Gulf area.

US Navy A-6 aircraft attacked the Iraqi naval base at Umm Qasr and left four ships burning.

Meanwhile, in Kuwait itself, Iraqi troops began pumping oil into the sea to cause a massive oil slick off the coast, intended to hamper allied naval operations in the Gulf.

to page 84

The Iraqi occupiers of Kuwait pumped crude oil directly into the sea from offshore terminals, in a cynical attempt to wage ecological war against Saudi Arabia.

Iron Bomb Intruder

Right: Bombing missions into Iraq and Kuwait involved a package of different aircraft. The Intruders and Hornets doing the attacking were usually escorted by fighters, by HARM-equipped defense-suppression aircraft, and by electronic warfare aircraft whose task it was to jam enemy radars. The primary Marine jamming platforms were the EA-6B 'Prowlers' of VMAQ-2, based at Sheikh Isa AB on Bahrain.

Left: Lieutenant Colonel Leif Larsen of VMA(AW)-533 'Hawks' stands in front of his A-6E Intruder, which is festooned with mission markers and has the aircraft side number enclosed in bomb silhouettes.

Lieutenant Colonel Leif Larsen, VMA(AW)-533, A-6 Intruder

"The first night of the war we saturated the Iraqi defenses. The air campaign was going to go on 24 hours a day, seven days a week, for as long as it took. Everybody was involved: Air Force, Navy, Marines, allies.

"Our first mission was against a railroad yard south-southeast of Basra. It was mainly a Marine package. We're trained as part of a Marine Air Ground Task Force, working to support our troops on the ground. We train together, so we work more effectively in combat together. Occasionally we had a bit of help. We used Air Force tankers occasionally, but most of the time it was Marine KC-130s.

"That first package had about 48 airplanes, going against four separate targets. USMC F/A-18s hit a power plant maybe a couple of miles from the railyard, others went after an airfield. We had the railyard, and more A-6s targeted a bridge maybe 20 miles north. There were six EA-6Bs, 12 A-6s, maybe 22 F/A-18s. Eight of the Hornets would have been in the fighter escort role, eight more dropping bombs, and six were HARM shooters, although those might have been dual-role. We also had eight F-4G 'Wild Weasels' shooting HARM, the only Air Force guys that we really worked closely with. Their task was SEAD (Suppression of Enemy Air Defenses).

"Take-off was under EMCON – no communications. We followed a taxi and take-off plan, then followed our assigned corridors north. With so many people in the air, deconfliction was important: we held at specific points at assigned altitudes until it was time to go.

"The weather was pretty clear. Thirty miles from the coast we could already see triple-A and missiles going up. I guess they just thought, 'they're coming, they're coming'. It looked like unaimed barrage fire. They were shooting SAMs ballistically, without lock-on.

"As we reached land, the AAA in particular would be going on all around us. In those conditions, time seems to stand still a little. You wish you were getting there faster, and your airplane doesn't seem to be going fast enough.

"Crossing the coast inbound, we had F/A-18s shooting HARMs over our heads, missiles coming up from the ground and a lot of triple-A. Most of the gunfire was well below our altitude, but there was some big stuff, probably 100-mm, bursting around us every 15 or 20 seconds. I saw seven or eight SAMs come up in the 15-20 minutes we were over land, though none was coming at me. The visibility had to be 50 miles. Sometimes that's even worse than bad visibility, because you can see everything coming up at you.

"Then there isn't time to worry. You're concentrating on getting to the point where you start your bomb run. The bombardier/navigator in the right-hand seat is concentrating on trying to pick up the target on radar, and then getting a clear FLIR picture of the target area.

Left, sequence: At Sheikh Isa, Marine armorers begin loading an A-6E Intruder of VMA(AW)-533. The flight line is packed with people, vehicles and aircraft. While the pilot does a 'walk-around' check (middle), an armorer makes a last check of the bombs, which Marines have painted to brighten Saddam Hussein's day. Checked out, unchocked and ready to go (bottom), the bomb-laden A-6E Intruder taxies out.

Above: Imitating actor Slim Pickens in the movie 'Dr. Strangelove', a Marine armorer shows some spirit amid graffiti-covered bombs.

"We pushed into a 30° dive about eight or nine miles from the target that night. Coming down from 24,000 ft meant that we were going to release our weapons with a lot of energy. The bombardier/navigator had a good FLIR picture by this time, and could break out the target.

"The computer takes the target data from the systems, calculates the weapons release point. It doesn't matter if we're in a 20° dive or 40° dive, or if we're doing 400 kt or 500 kt, the computer solves the problem. All we have to do is center steering on the screen, step the system into attack and commit, so that the computer can let the bombs fly when we reach the correct point. I have readouts that tell me how far I am from the target, and from preflight planning I know that the bombs should be dropping off about two-and-a-half miles from the target for this type of attack profile.

"Our goal was for the bombs to drop at 15,000 ft. You can feel the bombs come off, but you also back the computer by pickling manually just to be sure they're all off. You know the stick (time it takes all the bombs to be released) takes about a second and a half, so once the first one drops you say 'one potato, two potato', and then you're ready to pull off. The aim was to have pulled out of the dive by 12,000 ft. At that altitude, you're in the envelope of some of the lighter triple-A, like 57-mm and even 23-mm, but it's only for 20 or 30 seconds, and then you're passing through 15,000 ft again in the climb.

"We could see the bombs going off, but there was a light cloud layer so from certain angles you couldn't see the ground well enough to see where they were hitting. Bomb damage assessment we got later showed that five out of the six airplanes in my division were in the general target area, successfully cutting most of the tracks in that railyard.

"Once the bombs are off, the A-6 flies a lot better. You don't have the drag of 12 Mk 82 500-pounders, so you have a more maneuverable airplane that can get you home a little faster. For the last minute or so you've been concentrating on weapons delivery parameters, but now you're watching your radar-warning equipment and the sky around you for missiles coming at you.

"We turned 180° to get on our egress heading as we pulled back up to altitude away from the bulk of the triple-A. We didn't form up; just went for our assigned egress altitude. If we could see our lead or wingman and it was easy to join up, we did, but otherwise we came back individually. Once out of the target area, we put our lights back on. Remember, there were 48 aircraft up there and we wanted to see and be seen. We'd planned the return to base carefully, aiming to reach a holding point at a set time, then reaching another point about 30 miles from the base a fixed time later, from where we'd descend to the field. The whole package flowed nicely, and all the aircraft got back safely.

"I felt relieved that everybody had made it through. I also had a really good feeling about the success of my first combat mission."

AIR OFFENSIVE SOUTH

26 January to 10 February 1991

During the first 11 days of Desert Storm, the main attack by coalition aircraft and cruise missiles had concentrated on striking at airfields, air-defense radars, military command and control facilities, government and Ba'ath party administrative buildings, electricity generating plants, and factories involved in the development and production of nuclear, chemical and biological weapons. In the course of these operations 18 Iraqi planes had been destroyed in air-to-air combat and several more on the ground, while the coalition air forces lost 17 aircraft to ground fire.

Having taken the measure of the Iraqi air force, and in the process gained a high degree of air superiority over it, the F-16 and the F/A-18 dual-purpose fighters were now used almost exclusively in the attack role against ground targets. The areas designated for air-to-air refueling could be moved progressively further into Iraqi territory, enabling the short-range aircraft to spend more time over enemy territory.

Now the coalition air forces began to shift the weight of their attack against targets in Kuwait and the surrounding area, including military storage facilities and supply routes, as part of the preparation for the forthcoming land battle. It must be stressed, however, that the shift was one of emphasis rather than an entirely new phase in the offensive. Prior to this date battlefield targets had come under heavy attack from the air, and afterwards targets deep in Iraq would continue to be hit.

---

26 January, Saturday Four 'Scud' missiles were launched at Israel and two at Saudi Arabia, causing no casualties.

For the allies the attacks on the hardened shelters at Iraqi airfields brought an unforeseen bonus. The Iraqi High Command saw that the policy of keeping its best combat aircraft on the ground in the shelters would not save them for long, and it was decided to evacuate the most modern planes to Iran. During the day, 27 combat planes and two transports flew to airfields in Iran. The move was a complete surprise to the Iranian government, which had received no advance warning. As a result Iranian air-defense units went into action against the incoming combat planes, shooting down one and damaging two.

Royal Air Force Tornado and Jaguar aircraft attacked 'Silkworm' surface-to-surface missile launching sites in Kuwait.

With the establishment of coalition air supremacy, the French air force Mirage F1 reconnaissance aircraft were allowed to begin operations (previously these had stayed out of the combat area, for fear that they might be taken for Iraqi aircraft of the same type and mistakenly engaged).

During the day three MiG-23s were shot down by F-15Cs of the 58th TFS, 33rd TFW, in each case with AIM-7 missiles. The successful pilots were Captains Anthony Schiavi, Rhory Draeger (second victory) and Cesar Rodriguez (second victory). At least three more Iraqi aircraft were destroyed on the ground during attacks on airfields.

27 January, Sunday The day saw the largest Iraqi losses during a single engagement. During a daylight patrol south of Baghdad, two F-15Cs of the 53rd TFS, 36th TFW, were advised by the E-3 AWACS aircraft controlling them that a force of hostile aircraft was airborne to the southeast of them. The section leader was Captain Jay Denney, his wingman Captain Benjamin Powell. Initially the F-15s were at altitudes of around 30,000 ft to keep outside the reach of Iraqi SAM batteries in the area, and the Iraqi aircraft were at about 5,000 ft. The F-15s turned to close on the enemy planes almost head-on. When the two forces were 40 miles apart the Iraqi aircraft turned away, but it was too late to save them. The F-15s accelerated and closed rapidly to within firing range, and Denney launched an AIM-7 which sped after the trailing aircraft, a

MiG-23, and exploded nearby. The MiG appeared undamaged, so the F-15 pilot closed the range and fired an AIM-9 Sidewinder. This time the missile scored a direct hit and the enemy plane disintegrated.

Meanwhile, Powell had fired an AIM-7 at another of the enemy aircraft, but it too failed to hit. The No. 2 continued closing rapidly on the low-flying enemy aircraft until they were beneath the nose of the F-15, then rolled his aircraft on its back to engage. As Powell pulled down the nose he caught sight of the enemy planes: a MiG-23 in close formation with a Mirage F1. The American pilot launched two AIM-7 Sparrow missiles in rapid succession and watched them

to page 85 **(27 January continued)**

Below: Once the coalition switched to attacks on Iraq's army, huge raids by tactical aircraft like these F-16s hammered at Iraqi troops in Kuwait and southern Iraq.

Inset: Ordnancemen on a US carrier wait to arm an A-6 Intruder. Although the Iraqi army was now being attacked, the strategic campaign continued.

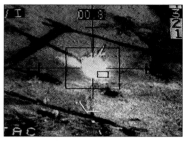

French air force Jaguars (left) scored some notable successes using **AS 30** laser-guided missiles. Typically, the Jaguar would carry a missile under the right wing, an Atlis laser designator pod under the fuselage, and a fuel tank under the left wing. The **TV** pictures are from the tape record of a successful **AS 30** attack on an Iraqi ammunition store just outside Kuwait City. Some 60 **AS 30**s were fired, 80 per cent hitting their targets.

Above: Iraq protected its facilities with the best European expertise, but the precision-guided weapons used by the allies could usually find a weak spot, and specialist concrete piercers smashed their way through. Once inside, the concrete structure of bunkers or hardened aircraft shelters contained the explosion, with devastating effect to anything or anyone within.

from page 84 **(27 January continued)**

streak towards their prey. There was a huge fireball as the left-hand aircraft, the Mirage, exploded and crashed into the desert. Shortly afterwards, the second missile exploded close to the MiG-23 and it too went down. As this was happening, Denney was in hot pursuit of the remaining enemy plane, a MiG-23, which was turning away to the left. The American pilot launched a single AIM-9, which exploded against the MiG and sent it tumbling to the ground.

The bombing of targets in Iraq and Kuwait continued. Due to poor weather during several of the past 10 days, however, aircraft failed to hit their primary targets on 40 per cent of the missions and either attacked secondary targets or returned with their bombs. This, in combination with the aircraft diverted from other missions to take part in 'The Great 'Scud' Hunt', led to some slippage in the timing of the coalition bombing offensive.

To halt the outflow of oil being pumped into the Persian Gulf by Iraqi troops, that night three F-111Fs of the 48th TFW delivered a precision attack with GBU-15s on the two pumping stations involved. In each case the targets were situated close to built-up areas that were heavily defended, and the attacks had to be carefully planned and executed. The bombs were tossed from F-111Fs flying supersonic at 20,000 ft over the sea, the aircraft then turning round and diving to low altitude to avoid enemy fire. Another F-111F, flying parallel with the coast about 50 miles out to sea, guided the missiles onto the targets. Both pumping stations were hit and the flow of oil ceased.

During the day 20 Iraqi combat planes flew to Iraq and, as stated above, four more were destroyed in air-to-air combat.

28 January, Monday One 'Scud' missile was launched at a target in Saudi Arabia, but was shot down by a Patriot. Another 'Scud' was launched at Israel, but it fell on an uninhabited area and caused no casualties.

US Navy A-6s attacked the Iraqi naval base at Umm Qasr. Royal Air Force Tornados attacked an oil refinery in southern Iraq.

One Iraqi fighter was shot down in air-to-air combat. A further eight combat aircraft flew to Iran, bringing the total number of aircraft sent there to around 100. Following considerable diplomatic activity and speculation on whether the aircraft would be allowed to take any further part in the fighting, the Iranian government

to page 100 **(28 January continued)**

The Hornet's Sting

Major Steve Pomeroy,
VMFA-333, F/A-18 Hornet

"**O**ur squadron's first mission actually took off before the first bombs hit Baghdad. That was a high-speed defense-suppression run, using HARMs in support of a strike package going into Iraq. My own first mission was the same thing in support of a Navy carrier strike at Basra. I don't know the specific targets the Navy was going after, though being Basra the chances were that they were after petro-chemical complexes, airfields, air-defense sites or possibly bridges. We stood off from the target area before the strike package arrived, trying to locate and neutralize all of the radar-guided SAMs that we knew were there. I guess we were successful. Nobody was shot down. I don't know how successful the strike itself was, since the bad weather at the time precluded a lot of bomb damage assessment.

"Our mission was not quite the same as the Air Force's 'Wild Weasels'. They went out to hunt SAMs. It didn't matter if they were accompanying a strike or they were preparing for one to come later. They considered a mission successful when they removed the radar. We'd actually be escorting a strike, and we went out with the intention of destroying an air-defense site. In the second phase of the war we'd use HARMs to make sure that the missile radar was down and then go in with bombs to physically destroy the radar and missiles. The mission was known as a SEAD (Suppression of Enemy Air Defense) roll-back. Either the enemy air-defense system in Kuwait or southern Iraq would be destroyed or they would be moved back to safety, allowing us free rein in the theater of operations to go after significant military targets like artillery positions, infantry concentrations and armor.

"A typical strike would involve more than 12 aircraft, with HARM shooters, jamming aircraft, bombers and maybe refueling support depending on how far you were going. If you are going to this effort to shut off a site, you might as well make sure you're going to destroy it. I saw as many as eight bombers used to take out a single site.

"At night you could see the SAMs and AAA really well. I didn't see any SAMs fired during the day, but the folks who did told me that the ignition signature was really intense. They'd see the smoke on the ground and pick up the missile in time to take evasive action. The shoulder-launched

Above: The entire 'tailhook Marine Corps', including numerous F/A-18 Hornet squadrons, gathered at Sheikh Isa Air Base, Bahrain, which inevitably became 'Shakey's Pizza' in Marine parlance. F/A-18As of VMFA-314 'Black Knights' are shown receiving attention.

missiles were fairly easy to see. They'd look like the bottle rockets you'd fire on the Fourth of July, and were relatively simple to evade. Some of the later versions didn't leave much of a trail, but any F-18s that were hit were not so seriously damaged that they couldn't get back. The Hornet could, and did, take some pretty serious hits and still get 200 miles or more back to base.

"Missiles could be defeated by a combination of onboard expendables like flares or chaff, onboard jamming and by hard maneuvering. Any missile that stays in the same relative position to you is locked on. If you put a move on it, a sharp turn, and it doesn't follow, then you know that

it either has broken lock, didn't have a lock in the first place, or is aimed at someone else. It could get scary, particularly going out at night. Low on the horizon you see a rocket launched against you. You turn to defeat it yet it stays in the same relative position and on what

you presume to be decreasing range. You turn back and look again, and it is still there. By now your heart's racing, but then you notice that it hasn't moved relative to the horizon, and you realize it's a bright star, or Venus. I know that happened to more than one pilot.

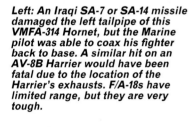

Left: An Iraqi SA-7 or SA-14 missile damaged the left tailpipe of this VMFA-314 Hornet, but the Marine pilot was able to coax his fighter back to base. A similar hit on an AV-8B Harrier would have been fatal due to the location of the Harrier's exhausts. F/A-18s have limited range, but they are very tough.

"My most memorable mission was a big strike. I'm a striker rather than one of the SEAD escort. My particular target was a railroad yard. Lousy weather, pitch black, low overcast so you can see all of the AAA and surface-to-air missiles coming up through it, but you can't physically see the target. We can acquire the target based on radar predictions. You're looking through the head-up display, showing slant range, elevation. You've told the computer where the target is, and weapons are released based on that information.

"We are a four-plane mission, which is part of a much larger package of 30 or more aircraft all going to targets in the same vicinity. The guys shooting HARMs and the guys providing the jamming are doing it for the whole package. Take off, get fuel from tankers in real bad visibility, climb back to altitude, in and out of clouds all the way. Approaching the coast the weather clears out some, except for the low overcast layer. As we get closer to the target I can see tracers from the AAA coming through the clouds. They are densely packed, although only

Hornet Strike

Marine Corps air power is largely a self-contained entity. Strikes are carried out by F/A-18 Hornets and A-6 Intruders, escorted by Hornets in the fighter role and with suppression of enemy air defenses provided by HARM-shooting Hornets and EA-6 Prowler jamming aircraft. A large strike is very carefully planned, to ensure that the attacking aircraft have the maximum of support when they are at their most vulnerable, on their bombing runs within the range of enemy anti-aircraft artillery and short-range surface-to-air missiles.

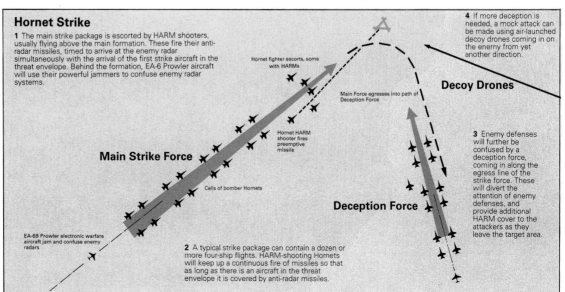

Hornet Strike

1 The main strike package is escorted by HARM shooters, usually flying above the main formation. These fire their anti-radar missiles, timed to arrive at the enemy radar simultaneously with the arrival of the first strike aircraft in the threat envelope. Behind the formation, EA-6 Prowler aircraft will use their powerful jammers to confuse enemy radar systems.

2 A typical strike package can contain a dozen or more four-ship flights. HARM-shooting Hornets will keep up a continuous fire of missiles so that as long as there is an aircraft in the threat envelope it is covered by anti-radar missiles.

3 Enemy defenses will further be confused by a deception force, coming in along the egress line of the strike force. These will divert the attention of enemy defenses, and provide additional HARM cover to the attackers as they leave the target area.

4 If more deception is needed, a mock attack can be made using air-launched decoy drones coming in on the enemy from yet another direction.

Hornet fighter escorts, some with HARMs

Decoy Drones

Main Force egresses into path of Deception Force

Main Strike Force

Hornet HARM shooter fires preemptive missile

Cells of bomber Hornets

EA-6B Prowler electronic warfare aircraft jam and confuse enemy radars

Deception Force

one in five rounds fired is a tracer. There are a lot of shells in the air. I see four or five missile launches coming up through the overcast; a brief flash from the launch lighting up the underside of the cloud layer, then the missile itself climbing through. We all see SAMs detonate in the distance or burn out and fall away; at least they are not coming for me. The AAA is still going off above the canopy as I dive in to release my bombs, and it's there all the way to the coast on the way out.

"We released bombs in a fairly steep dive. Delayed fuzes were used to ensure penetration of hardened targets. We didn't hit everything we aimed at, but in general if an average F-18 pilot could see the target he could hit it. Something as small as a tank might not be destroyed by a single bomb, but it would almost certainly be rendered inoperable. Most of the time we used 1,000-lb bombs, although some targets called for 2,000-lb bombs and others only needed 500-lb bombs. One-thousand-lb weapons were best. We normally carried five, although the aircraft could handle much more, but flying long distances we also carried wing tanks.

"Ninety-nine per cent of our targets were hard, where you either had to put a bomb through something like a bunker wall or hit something hard, like a tank. I won't say we weren't trying to kill people, because we were, but it was predominantly equipment or ground facilities that we were going for."

Above: An F/A-18 Hornet approaching a tanker with refueling probe out carries a typical SEAD warload of three 'bags', and two each of HARM, AIM-7M Sparrow and (not seen) wingtip AIM-9M Sidewinders.

Below: A VMFA-232 'Red Devils' Hornet taxies towards the runway as a second ship begins its take-off roll. The 'Devils' deployed to Bahrain from Kaneohe Bay, Hawaii.

HARM Shoot

HARM – High-speed Anti-Radiation Missile – is a system designed to suppress enemy air defenses. In the Gulf, HARMs were fired in large numbers to ensure that for as long as an attack aircraft was within range of enemy air defenses, those defenses would be under attack. HARMs can be fired *preemptively* so that they kill enemy radars just as the strike force enters the missile's lethal zone, or *intimately* from shorter range while the raid is under way.

HARM shoot

2 HARM shooters have to work out when the enemy is going to detect an attack, and when that attack comes within range of enemy missiles.

1 Radar waves can be detected by attackers long before their reflections are returned to the enemy. HARM shooters can fire their missiles before the enemy knows that they are there.

4 HARM missiles zoom to high altitude after launch, which is why HARM shooters often flew above and behind the main strike package.

A

HARM shooter preemptively launches missiles

Main strike force prepares to attack

Intimate HARM shooters accompany strike

3 The timing of HARM launches (A) is such that the first missiles arrive over the target (B) just before the first attack aircraft get within range of the defenses.

HARM missile homes on enemy radar

B

McDonnell Douglas F/A-18 Hornet

Two-seat F/A-18D Hornets from VMFA(AW)-121, the 'Green Knights', operated out of Sheikh Isa Air Base on Bahrain in the 'Fast FAC' role. Their task was to use their advanced avionics, developed to enable them to make night attacks, to find and mark targets for other coalition aircraft.

Gun
The Hornet's 20-mm cannon is mounted on the centerline above the radar, firing through a port just in front of the pilot. Fast FAC Hornets could use their guns to engage ground targets, or as a self-defense measure along with Sidewinder missiles in the event of attacks by Iraqi fighters.

Cockpit
The Fast FAC versions of the F/A-18D dispense with dual controls in the rear cockpit, the flight officer having three CRT displays and independent weapons controls. The night-attack variant is equipped with a Hughes AN/AAR-50 FLIR thermal image navigation set, which gives TV-like pictures in all weathers.

Armament
Apart from guns and AIM-9 Sidewinder missiles, Fast FAC Hornets were armed with two LAU-97 rocket pods, each of which carried four five-in, folding-finned aircraft rockets. These were used to mark targets for other attack aircraft.

Radar
The Hornet's AN/APG-65 multi-mode radar can function in a variety of air-to-air and air-to-ground modes. It can track 10 targets simultaneously, displaying eight to the pilot or flight officer. The aircraft's fire-control system can use radar data to target ordnance, guns or missiles.

Avionics
Hornets are equipped with comprehensive communications equipment, including data links which can pass target information directly to other aircraft. Radar warning receivers are matched with chaff dispensers, self-protection jammers and ECM equipment.

Performance
The F/A-18 is powered by a pair of General Electric F404 low-bypass-ratio turbofans. Capable of more than Mach 1.8, the only major fault with the Hornet is its lack of endurance.

Below: The Marines brought their own air-refueling assets to Desert Storm. The hard-laboring KC-130 Hercules was indispensable to the Hornets' success.

Right: 'Fast FAC', callsign COMBAT, is a two-seat night-attack F/A-18D Hornet of VMFA(AW)-121 'Green Knights', which operated from Bahrain.

Eagle at War

Colonel Joseph R. (Roy) Duhon, Jr, 33rd TFW, F-15C Eagle

"As you know, by looking at a map, that Saudi Arabian peninsula is huge – 1,500 miles by 1,500 miles, basically. We were on the western side [at Tabuk]. Which gave us some unique logistical support problems."

Colonel Duhon is DCM (Deputy Commander for Maintenance) of the 33rd Tactical Fighter Wing, Eglin AFB, Florida, which scored 17 aerial victories in the Persian Gulf. During the war, Duhon was the 'number two' of the wing under Colonel Rick Parsons and used the term LWC (Logistics Wing Commander, based on Saudi terminology) of Parsons' 33rd TFW (Provisional) at Tabuk. Colonel Duhon flew C-7 Caribous in South Vietnam and later flew B-52 Stratofortresses during the Linebacker II campaign against North Vietnam in December 1972. He is also a former FB-111A pilot. He is widely credited with the support and maintenance successes which enabled the Tabuk-based Eglin F-15s to succeed in Operation Desert Storm.

"Some of these problems were solved a month and a half into Desert Shield by providing a C-5 out of Charleston. We sent the parts up [from Eglin] to Charleston. The Desert Express flew out of Charleston to Dhahran, landed at Dhahran, and then we had C-130s that fanned out from there. The C-5s and C-130s were dedicated to Desert Express only and not used for other parts of the routine airlift. They were dedicated for both strategic and tactical, or for both inter- and intra-theater lift. Other C-130s would ride the whole route, the whole gamut, hauling supplies around in a 1,500-mile country, but our dedicated, Desert Express C-130 would come straight out from Dhahran with the critical logistics we needed to keep our F-15s up and fighting.

"We had to police ourselves by making sure [we didn't abuse the process] of assigning a priority to parts we needed right away to keep our F-15s flying. So we used that system only when we really needed a critical part. This war will go down in history as an unbelievable success story from the logistics standpoint – just getting the people over there as fast as we did is a hell of an undertaking, and then you supply those folks and all that equipment for five months before you ever start shooting: *that* is an achievement.

"Remember, the way we deploy, we deploy with 30 days [of supplies]. And we were out there for months.

"In the F-15 world, the 1st Tactical Fighter Wing arrived [on 7 August 1990 at Dhahran, the first unit in Desert Shield] and immediately started flying its wartime mission. Only difference is, they weren't shooting. When we arrived [in September], we pulled some of their mission because they were really overtaxed – and that hurt them later on because they got themselves behind, but they fixed that. We pulled some of the load off them and then we started flying our wartime mission.

"We started doing things a little differently in the wartime-mission thought process, in contrast to the type of war we had always thought we would fight. We'd always thought we would fight in the F-15, load missiles, tanks, launch, punch the tanks off, fight, shoot the missiles, and come back and land two-and-a-half hours later, three hours at the most. Even on CAPs [Combat Air Patrols] in the European scenario when all these great massive air furballs were going to occur over the FEBA [Forward Edge of Battle Area], that's the kind of war we always thought we were going to fight.

"But in the Persian Gulf war we were flying five-, six-, nine-hour sorties. So when you change your war process – we were launching sorties, lots of sorties, but we were launching long sorties – now, that really demands a lot from you. It requires your maintenance folks to sit on their hands for a long time and then run like a son of a gun when that airplane hits the ramp.

"Now, the good news is, of course, you've got folks who are motivated, doing their job, beating each other over the head to do their job.

"We were *all* well trained. If you put one of our pilots in one of our airplanes, and I'm talking about the American F-15 against one Iraqi pilot in one of his airplanes, MiG-29, F1, you'll find our pilots with their training, with their capability in the airplane, will normally come out on top. About 99 per cent of the time.

"Why did we get 17 kills when the other F-15 wing only got one? I think two reasons: the first is location. He [Saddam Hussein] was, in fact, moving his airplanes around, trying to save them. The second was, we could not shoot anybody down if we weren't in the air. We, the maintenance folks, provided our pilot with the airplane every time he asked for it. We accepted sorties when other people had to turn them down because they didn't have airplane availability. When we did that, when we put the pilot in the air, with the missiles, with the systems working – we didn't launch an airplane that didn't have all of its

Captain Rhory Draeger shot down two Iraqi fighters during Desert Storm. Draeger was a member of the 59th TFS 'Golden Pride', which, because of solid experience, was 'shanghaied' to serve with the 58th TFS 'Gorillas'.

Eagle Kill

Captain Rhory R. Draeger, 58th TFS/33rd TFW, F-15C Eagle

Captain Draeger's first kill of the Gulf war came on 17 January, against a MiG-29.

"We were sweeping out in front of a strike package. We were a four-ship. The strike package consisted of F-16s, F-4G 'Wild Weasels', EF-111s, and other F-15s, some of which were with us and some of which were with the strike package.

"It was a morning mission. The actual strike was around noon. It was our first combat mission. We had taken off from our air base [at Tabuk], tanked, and heard AWACS calling MiGs airborne while we were on the tanker. 'UNION Flight, bandits southwest, Baghdad, medium altitude.'

"The actual strike package was going to an airfield just west of Baghdad. As we head up there, the

Above and right: AIM-9M Sidewinders (above), which home on heat sources, have been standard on USAF fighters for years. The F-15C Eagle (right) can also carry AIM-7M Sparrows beneath the fuselage and AIM-120 AMRAAM missiles on the wing stations, as shown. All were carried in the Gulf, though AMRAAMs were never fired.

Left: The F-15C Eagle was rarely seen with bright colors or flashy markings during the Desert Shield and Desert Storm operations, but as 'plain' as it appeared the Eagle spoke for itself. Some missions, including HAVCAPs (e.g., protecting AWACS), lasted many hours and, as shown here, the F-15C frequently returned to the tanker to 'top off'.

Right: A pair of Eglin's F-15C Eagles, deployed to Tabuk, formate on a Royal Saudi Air Force F-5 immediately before the start of the war on 17 January. Tabuk was a true coalition base, playing host not only to Saudi F-5s and USAF Eagles, but also to a squadron of Royal Air Force Tornado bombers.

systems working – he could go out there and make his mission happen. So he's out there, airborne, with more exposure time and therefore gets luckier.

"A sidelight to this issue is, if you look at our kills, from an aircraft standpoint and from a pilot's standpoint, we had 36 pilots in-theater with 24 airplanes. We got 12 pilots and 12 airplanes with kills. That's a quantum leap from the Southeast Asia scenario where, when they wanted to go up and shoot somebody – they thought they had a good chance of the MiGs being up – they selected those crews that were going to shoot and kill, and they would select those airplanes from past performance records, and they would hand-massage those guys into the right place at the right time, so to speak. And everybody

else herded. That was how they thought of it. They would literally say at the briefing, 'Steve Ritchie, you're lead. DeBel goes in the back seat. Feinstein and Madden, you're here. All of you guys who get the kills, you're here.' And these guys would get the best airplanes – 247, 463, and so on. 'That's our line-up,' they'd say. 'All you other guys take these other airplanes and go fly.' Well, they didn't really plan on the other guys in the herd doing any shooting.

"We didn't do that. Every one of our pilots had to be a shooter. Because of the demands we had on our airplanes, because of the time requirements – if we'd have flown 48 sorties per day (which we did better than) with 24 airplanes with a three- or four-hour mission, then we could have done a bit more hand-selection of pilots – but

---

bandits are still there. They end up being MiG-29s. They're in a CAP just southwest of Baghdad, around that southern lake – there's three lakes on the west side of Baghdad, and right just southwest of that southern lake is where they're CAPping.

"We initially start out at about 13,000 ft, doing a couple of turns. During that time period, we'll close the distance from about 80 miles down to 40, when they're coming back hot. As they turn back cold one more time, now, we're thinking that they're out of gas because they've been airborne so long, so we're kind of saying, 'Oh, man, they're heading back towards their airfield now.'"

While UNION Flight pressed in on the MiGs, the F-15s came under heavy surface-to-air missile and gun fire, made evasive maneuvers, jettisoned wing tanks (while retaining centerline tanks), and dove to lower altitude.

"We dumped our tanks off at about halfway in on the intercept. We were closer than we wanted to

be to a SAM site. We got indications that they were launching on us.

"They get just west of their airfield now and it looks like they're turning back into it, but in reality they turn back towards us. During this time period, we close it from 40 down to 17 miles. And so, when they make their turn back in, at about 17 miles, I'll lock up the western man and shoot him with one AIM-7.

"Sly Magill will lock one up and shoot him with two AIM-7s." Captain Charles J. ('Sly') Magill, a Marine Corps exchange officer with the 58th TFS, was leader of UNION Flight with First Lieutenant Mark J. Arriola as his wingman. Captain Draeger was in the number three position accompanied by his wingman, Captain Tony Schiavi.

"These were AIM-7Ms. I see the missiles from the time they leave the aircraft until the time they hit. That's unusual. You normally don't see that because the rocket motor will burn out.

"Because of the environmental conditions, I see it all – even though we didn't have them visually when we first fired. Very shortly after firing, I pick them up. They descended. They were at 13,000. Now they're at 500 ft. When I actually shoot I don't see them, but at about 12 miles or so I start to pick them up. They're at low altitude, flying in echelon formation about a mile between them. And I see the missiles go right into impact. I call, 'Splash two.'

"This means, we got two fireballs out there and the two MiGs are dead that we were going after. There were no Iraqi shoots. Our missiles hit them head-on and they just dropped out of the sky. Real small fireballs because they were real low on gas.

"From what we could tell, they never locked us up. They might have been attempting to, but we didn't get any indications that they had.

"From what I could see, the MiG-29s had a camouflaged paint

scheme. It was kind of in shadows so it was hard to tell.

"When we get done with our mission and we're claiming a kill, we fill out paperwork that says, 'This is what happened.' Each guy in the flight fills out the paperwork. Even if they didn't shoot, they verify it, so you've got witnesses. A wingman will say, 'We did see a fireball,' or, 'We did see his missiles track to the target,' and that's used to try to verify the kill. There are other means too. The paperwork is sent up to headquarters and a board meets. It's decided at a higher level than just a captain. They go through all the data and say either, 'Yes, it was a kill,' or, 'No, it wasn't.' Both of my kills were pretty straightforward and there wasn't any doubt about who was shooting at what, or what happened."

Captain Draeger was flying F-15C Eagle 85-0119 when he downed the MiG-29 as described above. His second kill was a MiG-23 on 26 January.

because we were flying six-, seven-, and nine-hour missions . . . the airplane is *gone!* When they say they want airplanes for a mission and we're performing maintenance miracles to provide them, we expect that every pilot will be as good as every other pilot.

"When they say, 'I want four airplanes,' you might have five on the ramp. So you give them the best four and away they go. And you can't pick the best four from historical records because, the way we were doing it, we didn't have any historical records. So any airplane is capable of shooting down. We'd send a four-ship up and everybody came back and did a victory roll.

"That tells you the way the pilots did their tactics. Nobody was told, 'You protect, I'll shoot.' They got in there, they fought together. They divided up the enemy and they figured out how they were going to shoot, and they got in there and shot 'em. The game plan was, if a guy got a shot, he took it. The pilots will tell you, that was a big bonus – not having to worry, when they pushed that button, whether the missile would come off or not come off. It would go and hit its target.

"We also developed some pretty ingenious ways to turn aircraft around in-theater. We were at a Saudi base [Tabuk]. The Saudis in the northwest part of the country were not really of the belief that they were going to be attacked or be part of the war.

"We started looking over the ramp and we talked to the Saudis – who were excellent, overall. It took time and tact to work with them but pretty soon they were [co-operating].

"We were on one side of the runway. There were two runways – military and civil. They gave us a dispersal area that had hardened shelters, made for F-5s. The F-15 would go into them very gently, very carefully.

"We had two alert bird shelters. Those had an open door and were easier to get in and out of – and those were on five-minute alert. We did not use any of the other shelters to actually launch airplanes out of, because you had to tow the airplane anyway – you had to be very careful towing them in and out. We did put airplanes in the shelters to protect them and, also, when we had an airplane broken, of course, we would push it into a shelter.

"We had three key areas on [Tabuk] airfield:

"Death Valley: We took the end-of-runway location where you do your 'last chance' check and put six airplanes there, after discarding the idea of putting planes at both ends

when we ran into rock damage. The troops named it Death Valley. That was our quick-turn area. If the airplane came down Code One★ – whether it had missiles gone, tanks gone, guns fired, whatever – if it could quick-turn, we put it in that spot. And we put all the resources in that area to turn the F-15 fast – but not any heavy maintenance stuff.

"Disneyland: Then we had a heavier maintenance area – which was also our alert area. And we also had places there where you could do an ICT [Integrated Combat Turn(around)] or quick turn. We could do everything at once – load, gas, wipe the windshield, send the airplane out. But Disneyland was primarily a place where you could take care of Code Two★ breaks that were not too hard to fix.

"Center Stage: We felt that the main ramp was a hell of a target. If we were ever going to get attacked, that was the place for it. If we were ever going to be attacked by aircraft, the main ramp had a big hangar on it which was kind of like a beacon. We thought, 'This is the place they're going to attack.'

"But Center Stage also had all the shops. The heavy shops. All our avionics shops, supply, warehousing. So this was where we planned to take Code Three★

Above: An Eagle takes fuel in flight. Though many credit hi-tech weaponry with winning the war, the victory was actually achieved because of many years of rigorous training, practice and exercises, including deployments of F-15Cs like this one to trouble spots around the world. A joint command, headquartered in the allies' 'Black Hole' in Riyadh, drew on experience to guide aircraft as dissimilar as the F-15C and KC-10A on their missions.

Above: AWACS early-warning platforms, with evocative callsigns like COUGAR and BUCKEYE, maintained 24-hour surveillance of Saddam Hussein's air force and told F-15C Eagle pilots when and where to engage. The E-3B Sentry crews could spot an Iraqi fighter the moment it lifted off.

Above: Eagles were meant to fly, and this F-15C is soaring nicely. Much of its success was due to the high sortie rate coming from maintenance techniques improvised on the spot at Tabuk's three principal arming areas, known in airmen's slang as Center Stage, Disneyland and Death Valley. The crews maintaining the F-15Cs at these spots achieved very quick turnarounds.

airplanes. If the airplanes were hard broken – aircraft battle damage, for instance, although we didn't actually have any; an engine change – we had the resources there to do it quickly.

"Our supply system: We went in. We were a tenant wing. We were somewhat constrained. The base commander didn't want a tent city so we never built one, we lived in hard barracks, three to a room. I took one of my young officers, Captain Dave Underwood, who had been a munitions supply officer, and I said, 'You're my chief of supply.' He set up a supply system built from the ground up. He's a super guy. He started with nine supply folks, plus our asset folks out on the ramp who work in our AGS [Aircraft Generation Squadron].

"We took everything we needed to fight the war. We divided it up. Engines – we put 'em out in the dispersal area in Disneyland. We put MREs [Meals, Ready to Eat] there. We put water there. Bottled water, so that if we got chemicalled we would have water. We had munitions, everything we needed – so that if one area took a hit, we could still fight. We put parts. We had two shelters set up like a mini-warehouse with parts. We had a supply person in each of those who knew what was in them. In every shelter, there was an individual – a supply person, or in some cases an aircraft maintenance person – who knew exactly what was in that shelter, 24-hours-a-day. You'd punch his belly button and say, 'Give me this.'

"We had some special ways to make sure we never ran out of critical parts. We were flying six- and seven-hour sorties, even before the war started. During those sorties, we were tasking the F-15 radar system to its maximum. A lot of guys will tell you, even 1.5 hours with seven or eight *g*s is real demanding on the radar. However, what the pilots were asking that radar to do, in almost every mission, was – at some time or other, they had every mode actuated, looking, trying to figure out, 'Are you bad?', 'Are you good?' – both sides had Mirage F1s, lots of stuff like that, so you had to be very careful when you started going after somebody. So radar parts were very critical.

"We had two kinds of radar on the base, APG-63 and APG-70. The APG-70 is kind of a Baby Strike Eagle. Both had O-25 black boxes, and we were repairing black boxes over there – bits and pieces, circuit card, we would repair. We would open it up, clean it, reseat it, put the circuit cards right back, and get it working – because there was a dust problem.

Above: Pilots did not always fly the airplanes bearing their names, so it is not certain that this F-15C Eagle close-up depicts Captain Cesar A. ('Rico') Rodriguez, although this is unquestionably 'his' jet. Rodriguez claimed a MiG-29 'Fulcrum' and a MiG-23 'Flogger' in Gulf air combat.

Left: 85-0104 was the F-15C flown by Captain Anthony E. ('Tony') Schiavi when he claimed a MiG-23 on 26 January, using AIM-7M Sparrow missiles. Though it appears to be marked as the wing commander's aircraft, Colonel Rick Parsons actually flew 85-0102, nicknamed 'Gulf Spirit'. Parsons got one kill but was awarded two on official orders because of a typographical error.

"We had a dust problem while Dhahran had a wet sand problem; we didn't have the humidity that Dhahran had. You'd open up your boxes, open up the panels of the airplane, let the airplane sit still for awhile, and any surface that had oil or hydraulic fluid on it was now coated with dust. So dust was another enemy we had to defeat in order to kill MiGs."

★Code One: an aircraft reported by its pilot, when returning from a mission, to be in perfect operating condition. Code Two is a pilot report of a minor 'write-up'. Code Three is a pilot report of an aircraft with a mechanical problem too serious for further operation.

Left: Captain Anthony Schiavi of the 58th Tactical Fighter Squadron, 33rd Tactical Fighter Wing, shot down a MiG-23 on the same flight that Captain Rhory Draeger and Captain Cesar Martinez scored their second kills, each shooting down one of the same aircraft type.

MiG Killer

Captain Anthony Schiavi, 58th TFS/33rd TFW, F-15C Eagle

"The mission we were on was protection – a 'high asset value' (HAV) combat air patrol, which we called a HAVCAP (in this case protecting an E-3B/C Sentry AWACS aircraft). By this time in the war, we were doing so well in the air-to-air portion that we had a lot of flexibility. This was unlike earlier when, if you were tied to HAV, you were doing [only] HAVCAP. If you were doing a sweep, you did *only* that. Things were more stringent because the threat was much higher.

"We had an eastern AWACS, a central AWACS and a western AWACS, and they all just covered their own ground. 'COUGAR' and 'BUCKEYE' were the callsigns for the western and central AWACS.

"But at this point, we're into the war about nine days and we're doing well. Maybe you're on a HAVCAP mission but they'll call up and say, 'Hey, there's a strike package of x number F-111s, how would you like to do a pre-strike sweep for them? Or a CAP between a threat area and a target airfield?' So you could go up on a routine HAV mission and have something good happen.

"We'd been up on CAP for about an hour and-a-half. We'd just gone down to the tanker to get our first air refueling. We were 80 to 90 miles southeast of H2 and H3 airfields, near the Jordanian border. We were a four-ship on the tanker. My two-ship was the second to fuel up. As we were coming off the tanker, AWACS called and said, 'Hey, we've got bandits taking off from H2, a whole group of them, heading northeast.' At that point in time, [CHEVRON] our flight lead, Captain [Rhory] Draeger, asked for permission to commit on them. AWACS said, 'Go get 'em.'

"We started to commit northeast to get an intercept vector on these guys, a cut-off vector. We had our other two-ship head south. In the F-15, firepower is awesome. When you get four F-15s running in a wall toward somebody, there's no way you're not going to come out victorious. So our game plan at all times, when we can do it, is to keep the four-ship together, to use that firepower. They were a little bit lower on gas, just because they'd been on CAP while we were down at the tanker. They were instructed to come with us, as long as they could, as long as they had gas, and we'd go in as a four-ship against these guys.

"These guys [Iraqis] take off from H2 in a big gaggle. We're coming at them. They're heading northeast and we're trying to cut them off. They were not heading for Iran, which was too far from H2, but were just moving, the way they were doing all the time.

"About 100 miles away from them, we're going as fast as we can with three bags of gas. Initially, I'm thinking, 'There's no way we're going to catch these guys. They're 100 miles away and with our vector we're slowly starting to cut them off, but it's going to take a long time and a lot of gas.' We close it to about 80 miles and we're probably just about at the point where we need to turn back, getting too far up there, into an area where they have ground threats. So right at this point, just as we're saying, 'We're not going to be able to get these guys,' four *more* take off right behind them from H2 – and we're *in there*, we're in a perfect geometry for these new guys.

"Do they know about us? My conjecture is, the first group of Iraqis called back and said, 'We're gone, we're out of here. Now you can launch the next bunch.' Or, maybe the first group is saying, 'Here's our chance to drag four Eagles and sandbag the sons of bitches.' That was one of the things we had to think about as we started this turn into this intercept: What happens if these guys, the first group, do a 180 [180° turn, so that we're caught between two groups of bogies]. They could get us in a pincers. And we were obviously thinking about it. Captain Draeger was thinking about it.

"Of course, AWACS can see quite a ways, so we'll have warning if they try to box us in. So we don't *know* if they're aware of us – but we always think worst case.

"AWACS eventually loses the first group because they're so far away. At this time, we still don't know what type of aircraft are in either group, although in fact they're MiG-23 'Floggers'. So that's something else you have to think about – what airplane am I going up against? And you have to think worst case. You don't know. But of course when you're intercepting and chasing the guy by the tail you're not worried quite as much because he's not going to shoot you while he's flying away from you.

"So we're running our intercept against the second group of MiG-23s to take off from H2. They're at low altitude. They're below 1,000 ft. Our radar, as awesome as it is, at 80 miles we're painting these guys and we can see them at low altitude.

"For reasons unknown, one of these guys suddenly turns around, goes back, and lands. Maybe an aircraft problem.

"Now we're 40 miles and with this guy going back, we don't know if they're running some new tactic on us or what they're doing. But the other three continue and we're watching them on the scope. They're coming on our radar scope in the kind of Soviet-type formation, what we call a 'Bic' formation, that we've talked about all the time.

"It's so funny. Here, war is happening. And it's just like training. There's three blips on

Left: Iraqi targets. The French-built Mirage F1 can be a good fighting machine in the right hands, but Iraqi pilots were not up to taking on Eagles. Captain Robert Graeter proved that, downing two F1s on the first day of the war.

Above: At least five of Iraq's potent MiG-29 'Fulcrum' fighters were shot down by F-15Cs. It appears that Iraqi 'Fulcrum' pilots had less experience than those who flew Mirages, and far less than their USAF and Saudi opponents.

your screen. They're in the standard 'Bic' formation.

"We're coming in about 30 miles from the merge. We punch our wingtanks off, but keep the centreline tank on. Okay, so we have better maneuverability now if we get in an engagement in this thing. If the man decides to engage us and our missiles don't work or whatever, we'll be able to turn more tightly without those tanks.

"We're descending out of the mid-twenties [20,000 ft] doing about Mach 1.1 or 1.2. The weather was overcast. We couldn't see the ground. We're also thinking, 'We may never see these guys.' We can shoot at them, obviously, but once the missiles go through the clouds, at best we'll see a glow.

"The critical decision as you get within 20 miles is, 'Okay, who's going to target who?'

"That's Captain Draeger's job as Number One to decide. So he does that. He says, 'Okay' – his philosophy is that, hey, I'm going to take the map-reader first, and that's usually the guy out front; if you kill the guy that's leading the thing, everybody else will go, 'Oh, shit, what do we do now?' – so he targets the leader, or the map-reader as he calls him.

"He targets me as Number Two on the northwestern trailer. Draeger and I are One and Two. Now there's only one [Iraqi] left so he says, 'Okay, Three and Four, both of you take the southernmost guy.' [The HUD 'box' is used to identify bogies, relative to each other, by geographic direction].

"We acknowledge. I say, 'CHEVRON 2, sorted. 270. 25

miles.' It's just like William Tell. If they were closer together, it might be necessary to refer to them by using a BRA call, meaning bearing, range and altitude – but that's not necessary.

"The other two pilots were Captain [Cesar] Rodriguez as Number Three – he's the guy who got the maneuver kill earlier, the Iraqi who flew into the ground – and Captain Bruce Till was the last guy.

"So we're coming in and the other thing we're looking at is, are we spiked or not spiked [locked up by the other guy]? That's our other indication of whether they know we're there, our RWR scope. At this point, there's no indication – but you can never be sure your system is working accurately.

"So the flight lead has called the target plan and now all we have to do is lock the guy we're supposed to lock, and shoot. Like I said, we got an early 'bandit, bandit' call on these guys at about 35 or 40 miles so we know these guys are bad, which takes a lot of the guesswork out.

"We take our shots. Captain Draeger shoots first. We're now well inside 20 miles. He shoots. His missile comes off. I see it [guiding]. I shoot next. Just a couple seconds after him. Because Bruce and Rico are offset from us, they have to wait a little longer before they get in range so it's probably several more seconds before you hear Rico fire.

"As the missiles start flying off, we pick up the first tally-hos [visual sightings] about 10 miles from the merge. We can see the

'Floggers' running across the desert, fast. A lot of times you can see the missile, you can keep a tally-ho on that missile.

"I mentioned the weather before. At about 10 or 12 miles, there's a sucker hole that just opens up. So we go diving through. So now we're in a visual environment, versus shooting through the clouds. For some reason it's just opened up, which is perfect for us.

"Captain Draeger's missile hits his man, hits him right in the back – the old 'Flogger' running across the ground, there – and he's flying so low you can see the dust kick up around it. He calls, 'Splash'. Then he looks again. The airplane flies right through the fireball and comes out the other side. It hit him but didn't just knock him out of the sky. He's burning but not down. Captain Draeger goes to a heater [prepares to fire a Sidewinder heat-seeking missile], to put some heat on this big fire. But before he can do this, the fire reaches the wing root and it suddenly explodes in a huge fireball. I'm so busy watching this, watching this guy blow up – so amazed by the damage the warhead did, that I've almost forgotten my own missile.

"[Draeger] comes off. He says, 'Let's come off north.' First thing you do when you start blowing guys up is, you think about getting the hell out of here, fast. Once people see fireballs, that gets their attention and you don't want to be around. So he says, 'Let's come off north.'

"Right about then, my missile [hits] my guy. I call a second,

'Splash.' There's another big fireball. After the first guy blows up, the other two guys do a hard, right-hand turn, right into us. Whether they picked up a late visual on us, and saw us, and were coming down through the clouds, or what, I don't know – but what they were doing was too late and my missile hit him.

"As for what the MiG-23s looked like, they were camo'd and they were two-and-a-half to three miles in front of us when they actually blew up, so we saw them pretty well. Number Four's missiles were maybe two seconds late, so Number Three, Captain Rodriguez, got the kill.

"There was a road right underneath them. I think they were navigating following the road. The first guy blows up and the other two blow up on the other side of the road – three fireballs right in a row. My guy blows up, zoom, and a moment later I hear Rodriguez call the third 'Splash.'

"So as we come off, our big concern now is – it's called a 'Bitchin' Betty' on the airplane – we're worried about Bingo fuel. We still have our centerline tank, but as we start to egress Captain Draeger and I punch off our centerline tanks also so that we can get some speed up and get away from any ground threat (we're fairly low in here), and now our big concern is to get back.

"We call AWACS and tell them that we've splashed three fireballs. AWACS says, 'Say type,' and that's when we say, 'Floggers.' We didn't use any code word. We just said, 'Floggers'."

Down in Iraq, Part I: Survival in the Desert

Lieutenant Devon Jones, VF-103, F-14A(Plus) Tomcat

Flying from USS Saratoga, VF-103 is based at Oceana, Virginia.

Lieutenant Devon Jones flew nearly 30 missions after his dramatic rescue by MH-53Js in the Iraqi desert.

Lieutenant Devon Jones (pilot) and Lieutenant Larry Slade (RIO) manned their F-14A(Plus), AA 212 (BuNo 161430), for an early morning escort mission on 21 January 1991. Although it was the fourth day of the Gulf war, neither man had yet crossed the beach – actually gone on a strike. Today they were scheduled to escort an EA-6B Prowler of VAQ-132 near the big Iraqi airfield at Al Asad. The Prowler would shoot one HARM and turn for home. Lieutenant Jones described the mission.

"We had an early-morning strike, 0610, 50 miles into central Iraq, with A-6s dropping DSTs (Destructors – a form of delayed-reaction bomb) on the airfield at Al Asad. Our particular mission was to escort a single EA-6B with HARMs. Our Prowler was to go to 45 miles and take a prebriefed HARM shot, pressing in from a west-to-east axis. At 30 miles, on the same axis, he would look for a target-of-opportunity shot. If there wasn't anything there, we'd turn around and egress. So, it wasn't a CAP.

"Things went pretty smoothly for the first part. Tanking was a little rough because of the turbulence and the night. (Sunrise at that time wasn't until around 0730.) Coincidentally, my RIO and I briefed that if we went down, the night cover wouldn't be there for long, maybe an hour. And, unfortunately, that proved to be true.

"We escorted the EA-6B in. The time and altitude were changed for weather. We had a lot of weather to contend with but I felt comfortable above the clouds. We

got under 45 miles and he took his HARM shot. We pressed in to 30 miles. (The Prowlers generally carried two HARMs, for target-of-opportunity shots. If nothing came up, they would just jam whatever they could, like GCI, depending on the threat surrounding the targets, which varied.)

"We were working between 26,000 and 30,000 ft. There was no chance for a second shot so we turned left to egress. I tallied a SAM coming up through the clouds. My RIO saw it, too. It turned out to be an old SA-2, like the ones used in Vietnam. The SA-6 was the SAM we worried the most about, but in the early stages, most of the weapons that brought planes down – not the CAS (Close Air Support) guys, but the people on standard strikes – was the old stuff, SA-2s and SA-3s, tried and proven. In the CAS arena, we lost A-10s, F-16s and Harriers to shoulder-fired weapons – SA-7s, Rolands. The SA-6 and IHAWK were never players, although we couldn't figure out why.

"I added power, rolled into the SAM as briefed, to give the missile tracking problems. As we rolled down, almost inverted, the SAM tracked us, came up toward our tail and detonated with a bright, white flash. The F-14 shuddered and kept rolling right.

"The impact ripped my mask off, which was a big distraction and very frustrating because now we were going down and the mask was flopping all around. Lot of eyeball-out negative *g*. I had my mask on, tightly, but the missile explosion ripped the bayonet fittings out of my helmet.

"Now, the plane was starting to go into a flat spin and I was getting thrown around, helpless. I couldn't talk to my RIO or see my instruments – altitude, airspeed. He was trying to get me on the ICS while I was trying to recover the airplane. The only thing I could sense was dark or light. It was light in the clouds, dark when we were outside.

"It was obvious that I was not going to recover the aircraft, so I pulled the handle just as my RIO was starting to go for the handle himself. Later, when we got back together, he asked me, 'Who pulled the handle?' and I told him I was pretty sure I did because my hands were charred black from the rocket motor. Nothing serious, though.

"What a great feeling, jumping out of an airplane on your first combat mission. Unfortunately, this was par for the course; we didn't change too many statistics from Vietnam. Most of the guys that went down did so on one of their first combat hops. After your first five missions, your survivability goes up something like three-fold. The learning curve is steep, intelligence gets better and the enemy is just not throwing up as much stuff at you.

"We bailed out at around 14,000 ft. I wasn't in a very good seat position but the seat worked like a charm. I expected to get hurt since I was slumped over trying to get the handle. It took me a while to find the handle because I was

getting tossed around and was hunched over. I was conscious through the entire ejection because I remember the blast and opening shock. We didn't have a lot of airspeed. The plane was spiralling down, giving pretty good eyeball-out *g*.

"The EA-6 saw us go down. They saw the smoke around our airplane and made a call. The strike leader made a call, and my RIO made a mayday call in the chute. He had a different radio, a PRC-112, from my PRC-90. The -112 is a newer radio with a direction-finding capability, but there was just one PRC-112 for each aircrew.

"As we came down, we were in and out of clouds. I don't fly with gloves, and at that altitude, my hands were so cold that my fingers were starting to get numb. Even though my radio was tied to my gear, I didn't trust that. I started to take my radio out but since I was afraid of dropping and losing it, I put it back in. I didn't see how I could survive without my radio.

"Once I collected myself, I used the four-line release. I looked over about 500 ft to the left, and I saw my RIO in his chute. Stupidly, I yelled something to him but he was way out of range, especially

Three EA-6Bs of VAQ-132 take up a formation over Saudi Arabia during Desert Shield in October 1990. Lieutenants Jones and Slade were escorting one of these aircraft when their F-14A+ was shot down.

A VF-103 F-14A+ flies a low-level training mission on 4 September 1990, only 500 ft above the ground. This photo gives a good idea of the fantastic terrain in Saudi Arabia, but the Iraqi desert was open and exposed.

with his helmet on, in the dark. It was quite a change from being in the plane with all its violent movement and ICS comm, to being in the chute where it was so quiet. We lost sight of each other as we disappeared through the clouds.

"In Saudi Arabia, where we had been tanking, the cloud layers ranged from 8,000 ft, so I expected to come out at that altitude. Actually, the ceiling was only 150 ft. As I came out of the cloud, everything got dark, so I knew I was underneath the layer. I thought I had another 8,000 ft to go. But, the ground came up and hit me very hard. It was just too dark to see the ground.

"My RIO did see the ground and prepared for the landing; he hurt his tailbone. I didn't see it coming and was OK. Sometimes, ignorance *is* bliss, I suppose. It was like a quarterback being blindsided; he's loose, so he's not going to get hurt as much. I wasn't braced so I just fell over."

After the trauma of ejecting and the uncertainty of where he would come down, Lieutenant Jones took stock of his situation.

"Now reality finally hit me, in a big way. I was down on the ground, inside Iraq. I could see my Tomcat's crash site and the ball of flames. I estimate that I came down five to eight miles north of the crash site. That was in my favor, but . . . The first thing I became aware of after I landed was how heavy my seat pan was. I'd forgotten since water survival training.

"'Boy,' I said, 'this thing's heavy.' I stood up to get rid of it.

"There's an initial shock that goes through you that has nothing to do with SAR. I thought, 'Geez, I'm going to be a POW. My family's going to go nuts. They'll probably rip my finger nails out and shoot me!'

"After that, though, some SERE School training started seeping through. First, I had the green seat

pan and a big orange-and-white parachute spread out on the ground. I started looking for a bush or tree to hide this stuff under, but there was nothing. Just a big dirt – hard dirt, not sand – parking lot. So, I wadded up my chute into a small ball and put it under the seat pan. I thought that if the Iraqis were flying around, looking for me in a helo, they might not see the green seat pan.

"I made a radio transmission. I said I was on the ground, OK, and heading west – as I walked *east*. I'd like to say I did that to fool the Iraqis, but it was really out of confusion. (It was the first time I'd been shot down, after all.) Obviously, looking for terrain, looking for my RIO, trying to get him on the radio, in the dark, was confusing. I decided, finally, that it was time to move and I tried to get my bearings.

"I looked at the smoke at the crash site. All the winds had been out of the west, so I tried to use the way the smoke was blowing. Unfortunately, the winds were from the east. The horizon was only just starting to glow and I couldn't see the sun yet. I began walking toward what I thought was the west. All the briefs told us to walk southwest for SAR, towards the Saudi border. I thought I was moving west, away from Al Asad. As the sun came up, however, I realized my mistake.

"My helmet had reflective tape so I took the helmet off. I couldn't bury anything because the ground was so hard. My primary objective was to get as far away from my plane as I could. With the sun coming up, I wasn't thinking rescue, only evasion.

"I used my helmet to 'canoe' out some dirt, then hid my helmet by putting the dirt around it, ripping the visor off since it would glint in the sun. I knew the Iraqis would find me if they made an effort, but I thought hiding my helmet might buy a little time.

"I was also very aware that I was leaving footprints everywhere because of the soft layer of dust over the main hard-packed earth. I could also see fresh human and animal footprints and tire tracks, residue from campfires and debris. I kept looking for places to stop, but there was nothing, no mounds, no hills.

"Finally, I came to a little vegetation, small bushes, really, and a few small mounds. I thought the only chance I had was to try to dig into one of those mounds and hide. I walked for 2½ hours before I decided that there was nothing that would help me. I had expected helos to be in the air looking for me, at least at first light, but I hadn't seen or heard anything. I thought there'd be a full-scale effort to get us. I'd been making calls all along, but got no reply. Later, after I got back, I learned that a helicopter had been up for three hours looking for us. But they had been given a bad cut, wrong directions, and were looking for us 30 miles farther south.

"About 0900, I saw something blue and cylindrical, two miles away, like a parked car. As I approached it, I realized it was some sort of tank, maybe 20 ft long. It was time to stop and do something, so I went to a little wadi area, found a little mound and started digging with my hands. I took out my survival knife. The dirt was neither hard or soft, and I started digging a hole with my knife. I dug for an hour and ended up with a hole 4 ft long and 3 ft deep. My hands were blistered and bloodied but it was a pretty good-sized hole, about 1,000 ft east of that blue, metallic tank.

"As I looked at the tank, I thought it might be a fuel tank, which wasn't good. There'd be a

lot of traffic. I took off my life-preserver to hide anything that was shiny and kept digging. I kept sizing the hole, trying it out. I still hadn't seen or heard anything or anyone. The weather was broken to overcast, and the sun was in and out. A little chilly and bright, not hot.

"I probably finished the hole around 1000, but I'd done some dumb things. I had dug up a tremendous amount of dirt in an untouched area. All this upturned dirt would probably draw attention from the air. I decided to put dirt back into the hole and *slide* under it, like a blanket. Of course, that didn't work and I had to take it all out.

"Then, I sprinkled light, sandy dirt on the darker earth. I got into the hole, took off as much gear as I could and scrunched down. I took off my harness and my leg restraints, which were toast anyway from the ejection. I kept my *g*-suit. I had a little mound between me and the road. I laid my radio on the edge of the hole and tried to get comfortable.

"About 1030, I guess, I heard the first sound. Actually I had heard two single jets high overhead before. I thought they were Iraqis on a training flight.

"'I hope they shoot them down,' I mumbled to myself. It turned out later that they were probably F-15s, part of a RESCAP for *me*.

"Anyway, I was down in my hole, pretty well covered, when I heard a truck. Of course, I'd heard a lot of things that weren't there, but it was definitely there. I was facing west. The truck came rumbling up to the tank. My heart was pounding. It was a blue, stakebed truck, obviously a farmer's truck.

"I felt I was pretty well hidden and I started thinking about using a

AA 210, an F-14A+ of VF-103. The 'Sluggers' and their sister squadron, VF-74, were the only two squadrons to fly the upgraded F-14A+ during the war. The remaining Tomcat squadrons in the other four carriers (Midway is too small to operate the Tomcat) flew the F-14A.

vehicle to escape. I had my .38 pistol, but it was covered with mud. Two guys got out, just working for Allah. Three minutes later, they went back. I thought the tank probably wasn't fuel, but water. That was a little perk, thinking I had water available. I had gone through most of the water in my survival gear.

"I had worked so hard digging this hole. I had put myself on a water ration, but I wasn't going to die of dehydration like some guys in Vietnam, even though they had water in their bottles.

"Although I hadn't located anyone, I kept making radio calls. I had also found a few bushes and sticks to put on top of me for camouflage. I was pretty busy. I was fairly comfortable using the radio. I didn't expect a day recovery, so I wasn't thinking rescue at this time.

"A funny, kind of scary, thing happened. Everyone likes this part. I was sitting in my hole, trying to push the sun across the horizon, shivering a little, either out of cold or fear. Suddenly, I caught a movement near my left shoulder. There was a black scorpion in there with me. Not a big one, but still a scorpion. He was trying to climb up the side of the hole, which was pretty steep.

"Stupid bugs. They get to the top of something and they fall down again. I was rooting him on. 'Come on, buddy.' But there wasn't a whole lot of room in there for him and me. Sure enough, he got to the top and landed on my arm. Immediately, my survival instinct took over. I flicked him off and flew out of my hole, my cover blown, but I went one versus one with him and killed him. My hole never felt the same, though. He did his job if he was sent by the bad guys."

At a little after 1200, Lieutenant Jones tried again to raise someone with his radio.

"By now it was 1205. I had got out to dig some more. I turned on my radio just to listen. There

wasn't any reason to say anything as far as I could tell. We had a 10-minute block, on the hour, so I figured I'd listen to the last five minutes. I was still trying to contact my RIO, but I didn't know that he had already been captured.

"Suddenly, I heard American voices! I was on 2828, the SAR frequency.

"'Slate 46, how do you read?'

"To my surprise someone came back with my callsign. That was the first time that I knew anyone even knew my callsign, or that there had been an ongoing SAR effort. I started thinking real fast.

"Whenever I thought about the big picture, where I was, it would mortify me. As long as I kept taking it one step at a time, I was OK. It's like a combat mission or flying the ball. If you think about the big picture, if you're scared about getting a no-grade or a wave-off, you're not thinking about the mission or what you need to be doing. Anyway, someone started talking to me. I was having reception trouble, mainly range, I guess.

"'Let me come a little closer so I can talk to you,' he said.

"That was a real boost, but, I wondered, who was this guy? Did we have Pave Low-equipped helos out here? Were the SEALs out here?

"He got DF cuts on me, using voice counts. I thought he was in the air, but I didn't know what type of airplane or where he was. Suddenly, I heard him.

"'OK,' he said, 'I'll pickle a flare.' He asked me where I was relative to my plane's crash site. Of course, this was after we'd gone through our authentication procedures. Everyone asks me if I cross-authenticated him. No! I dare anyone else to have enough presence of mind to do that. What would I say? 'No, don't come and get me! I'd rather sit out here and starve to death, or maybe become a POW.'

"He was basically coming north. 'Look to your south,' he told me. 'I'll pickle a flare.'

These A-10s seen at Al Jouf are aircraft from the Sandy squadron that rescued Lieutenant Jones. Other rescue assets at Al Jouf included the HH-60 helicopters of Navy Reserve Squadrons HCS-4 and HCS-5.

"I tried to find out what type of plane he was.

"'I'm at 18,000 ft,' he said.

"'Who would be way up there?' I thought. He pickled the flare but I couldn't see him. He passed me, heading north, and shot off another flare. This time I saw it.

"'OK, now, I'll come down to where you can see me,' he said. Lo and behold, he was an A-10, a 'Sandy', like those guys in Vietnam, trained in combat SAR. He was 'Sandy' 57. I brought him in with standard aviator talk. He didn't see me, but he flew right over me at 50-100 ft and dropped a waypoint in his INS.

"'I've got to get some gas,' he called. 'Minimize your transmissions and come back up in 30 minutes.' He headed south to the tanker track just south of the border. I found out later that he was also talking to the helicopters. They had been up from 0600-0900 looking for us, but had given up because it was getting too bright. They had recovered at Ar'ar, an airfield just inside the Saudi border.

"The 'Sandy' pilot gave the helos a good cut toward me and they began heading for me. I also found out that the A-10 had a wingman. As the helos started out they heard MiGs being vectored toward them;

so did the F-15 RESCAP just inside the Iraqi border. As soon as the F-15s got their vectors, the MiGs ran away. After they got their gas, the A-10s returned, caught up with the helos and brought them in.

"In the meantime, I had seen another farmer's truck coming up the same road toward the blue tank. Now, this guy left in my direction, right at me. He hadn't seen me, but my heart didn't know that. They drove right past me, about 30-40 yd away, but didn't see me. They would have had to have been actually looking for someone.

"As the truck went over the horizon, I heard the A-10s talking to the helicopters, telling them they had another 30 miles to my position. The helos were actually on the ground, waiting for the 'Sandys' to clear the way for them.

"They asked me to shine my signal mirror south, which I did, but they didn't see it. Then one of the A-10s told me to start looking for a helo about 15 miles out. As I looked south at standard helo altitudes – maybe 500 ft – I couldn't see them. But I did get a tally on the A-10s flying in a circle. I talked them in.

"I had made a mistake earlier when I first contacted the 'Sandys'. They asked me where I was

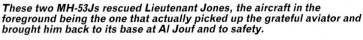

These two MH-53Js rescued Lieutenant Jones, the aircraft in the foreground being the one that actually picked up the grateful aviator and brought him back to its base at Al Jouf and to safety.

relative to my plane's crash site.

"'About eight to 10 miles north,' I replied. 'About 1,000 yd due east of a blue tank.' The Iraqis must have been listening to our transmissions, and, of course, they must have known where the tank was.

"As the planes came in, everything seemed to be heading to a big crescendo. About half a mile down the south road, I spotted a truck, an army truck, with the canvas covers – a grunt truck. I think we all saw it at the same time because the A-10 called, 'We've got a fast mover on the dirt road.' This guy was boresighting right at me, down in my hole. I saw a lot of dust and I thought I had actually seen two trucks. We'll have to figure that out later.

"I had a moment of panic there. But, hey! the A-10s have those huge cannons, and the helos must have .50-cal. Within three to four seconds, the 'Sandies' set up a squirrel cage and rolled in on the truck, maybe 100 ft AGL, 200 ft slant range. They opened up with their 30-mike-mike. By the time they each finished two runs there was nothing out there, just flames and dust, *about 100 yd from me.* I guess the Iraqis had finally figured out where I was through all our radio talk.

"For the first time, I looked to the east and saw the Pave Low, about five ft off the ground, watching the A-10s. I started talking to him. I had never seen such a beautiful sight as that big, brown American H-53. [The helicopter was an MH-53J of the 1st SOW from Hurlburt Field, Florida. These special forces aircraft carry Pave-Low III Enhanced Capabilities, and had also seen combat service in Panama, in December 1989.]

"He got about 50 yd away from me and I popped out of my hole for the first time. I grabbed my kneeboard cards and gear as he landed about 20 yd away. One of

the special forces guys jumped out and waved me on. I jumped in and off we went, 140 miles to go at 140 kt, at 20 ft! Pretty impressive machine. Just what you'd expect from these special forces people with lots of guns hanging off them. As I looked out the back for the first time, 20–30 miles to the south, I saw the second helo. They had been flying cover for each other. Big spines on these guys, I'll tell you, being 150 miles into enemy territory during the day, in a helicopter.

"They got me to Al Jouf. Believe me, I had a map out, watching the lat-long on their INS. I knew *exactly* when we were over the border. I had been on the ground exactly eight hours. The A-10s had been airborne eight hours for that mission, and the helos had been up three hours.

"Everyone took care of me. They were living under pretty harsh conditions. Carrier living looked pretty good compared to their situation, eating only MREs, one shower . . . but they had

nurses.

"We had a big photo session on the tarmac. I don't know who was happier, me or everyone else. It's got to be a great feeling, picking someone up. I found out that the two 'Sandy' pilots were Captain Paul Johnson and Captain Randy Goff of the 354th TFW, Myrtle Beach AFB, South Carolina. They were on TV a few days later. I hope they at least get DFCs. They can have the Medal of Honor as far as I'm concerned. My CO wrote to their skipper, as well."

USAF Captains Randy Goff (left) and Paul Johnson (right) of the 354th TFW were the A-10 'Sandy' pilots who located Lieutenant Jones and guided the helicopters to him. Captain Johnson received the Air Force Cross and Captain Goff the Distinguished Flying Cross.

A Vought A-7 Corsair loaded with CBUs launches for a raid on enemy ground forces from USS John F. Kennedy.

from page 85 (**28 January continued**)

announced that it would not release the Iraqi aircraft until the war ended.

A large ammunition storage area was hit in southern Iraq, causing an enormous explosion. Describing it later, General Schwarzkopf said, "Let me give you a reference. If, on a scale of one to 10, the eruption of a volcano registered 10, and the recent explosion at the Soviet rocket-propellant plant would register nine, the explosion . . . registered 12. We now have confirmation that we destroyed over 125 storage revetments."

A US Marine Corps AV-8B Harrier was shot down, the first allied aircraft to fall in combat for three days. The pilot was taken prisoner.

29 January, Tuesday Attacks on Iraqi troop positions continued. Coalition warplanes caught an Iraqi column of 24 vehicles, including some tanks, in transit in Kuwait and scored hits on all of them. Ground attack missions in the area were co-ordinated from an EC-130E airborne command and control center.

During the afternoon, Lynx helicopters from HMS *Brazen* and *Gloucester* observed several contacts on their radar off the coast of Kuwait. These turned out to be a force of about 17 small patrol boats, thought to be carrying troops. The craft were attacked with Sea Skua missiles. Other helicopters in the area joined in the action, including a US Marine Corps AH-1W Sea Cobra helicopter gunship and Royal Saudi Navy Dauphin helicopters. Five boats were claimed sunk, others were damaged and several were later seen beached.

The attacks on the Iraqi airfields continued, and included one by a force of 10 Royal Air Force Tornados, two armed with ALARM missiles and eight with 1,000-lb bombs, on Al Taqaddum airfield west of Baghdad. In separate attacks, Royal Air Force Tornados destroyed a fuel storage site at Ad Diwaniyah and hit Ubaydah Bin Al Jarrah airfield.

That night, F-111Fs of the 48th TFW began their sustained campaign against bridges on the Iraqi supply routes when they carried out an attack with laser-guided bombs on the five-mile long causeway and bridges carrying the main supply road over Hawr Al Hammar Lake to the northwest of Basrah. This target would be attacked several times during the weeks to follow.

The exodus of aircraft to Iran continued, and 15 Iraqi aircraft took off to fly there. Over northern Iraq one of them, a MiG-23 'Flogger', was intercepted and shot down by an F-15C piloted by Captain David Rose of the 58th TFS, 33rd TFW.

Intelligence information indicated that Tuz Khurmatu airfield, 30 miles south of Kirkuk, was being used as a staging post for Iraqi aircraft flying to Iran, and that several of these aircraft were on the

to page 102 (**29 January continued**)

Down in Iraq, Part II: POW

Lieutenant Larry Slade, VF-103, F-14A(Plus) Tomcat

Lieutenant Larry Slade (left) and Lieutenant Devon Jones (right) enjoy a moment at NAS Oceana shortly after Lieutenant Slade was released from six weeks of suffering as a POW.

While Lieutenant Jones struggled to survive in the desert, his RIO, Lieutenant Slade, had already been picked up. By nightfall, the young aviator was in Iraqi hands. Six weeks as a POW is not anywhere as long as the six years many American crewmen spent in North Vietnamese prisons, but to Larry Slade, each week must have seemed like a year.

"The airplane had departed controlled flight pretty violently and entered a flat spin. At 24,000 or 26,000 ft I reached for the secondary ejection handle with my right hand. I couldn't talk to my pilot since his oxygen mask had come off. I couldn't tell whether he was trying to get the plane under control and I told myself I would give him until 15,000 ft before ejecting us.

"I held on to the handle, but I was also bent out of position, though not as much as he was. I looked at my altimeter and the last thing I saw was 10,200 ft. I began to pull the handle as the canopy blew off. I felt the seat go up the rails. I recall everything clearly, especially deciding to pull the handle. I don't remember actually

pulling it, though.

"The ejection was fairly easy, but the air was very cold. I felt the seat fall off and my chute deploy. I saw Devon's parachute, and I could see it was fully deployed. I pulled out my radio and called the AWACS.

"'Mayday, mayday! Slate 46 is down!'

"I thought I heard them reply but it was tough to tell with my helmet on. I restowed the radio. I lost sight of my pilot quickly as we went into the clouds, but I saw the explosion as our plane hit the ground. Our descent took five to 10 minutes so we floated for quite a while. The wind was quite strong.

"The fire from our plane helped me guess how far it was to the ground, and I began preparing for my landing. I had used my four-line release to steer away from the crash site. I got ready to make my best eight-point roll, but I hit too fast and sat on my rear – hard.

"I gathered up my parachute – which had different colored panels, orange, white, brown, green – and wrapped it under the light brown panel. The wreck burned all morning. I never saw my pilot. I made another call on the radio. This time, I *know* I didn't get a reply, because I took my helmet off.

"I placed the wreck to my rear and struck out. I needed to get as far away from the crash site as possible. I estimated I landed five to 10 miles away from the plane, because of the winds. I walked for 2½ hours, using my radio every hour, without a reply. The terrain was very dry and flat, and I came to a small, round knoll. Dawn was breaking and I needed to find some place to hide. I tried to use my survival knife to dig in but the land was too hard, too rocky. So, I just dusted myself up to try to blend in a little.

"At one point, I thought I heard a beacon when I turned on my radio. It might have been my pilot's, but I couldn't communicate with him.

"At about 1030, a white Datsun pickup truck came around the knoll. It was probably bad luck because I don't think they were looking for me; they were just driving by. Two men stopped and got out. One had a 12-gauge shotgun, the other, an AK-47. The man with the AK-47 was in a very shabby uniform, like he had gotten it from an army surplus store. No insignia. The other man was a Bedouin in a black covering, not in the service. Maybe they were just friends driving around.

"They approached me, but it never crossed my mind to pull out my pistol. I was obviously had. They made me strip off all my gear. It was very cold and I was shivering and shaking by this time.

"They bound my hands, but were very polite. They put me between them in the pickup and took me to their *tent* – where they *fed* me. That was a surprise. It was a very leisurely lunch. They didn't seem to be in any hurry to go anywhere.

"When we finished, we got in the truck again and drove to Baghdad, about 3½ hours away. I didn't know we were going to Baghdad. Through sign language and pidgin English, they asked me if I wanted to go to either Saudi Arabia or Baghdad. Of course, I told them Saudi Arabia, choosing the northern-most town I could recall.

"The Bedouin indicated he understood and that they would take me to the town in Saudi Arabia. I thought, 'perhaps, perhaps'. I tried not to get my hopes up and watched how much time it took. If it took three hours, it would be Baghdad; eight, Saudi Arabia. Sure enough, 3½ hours later, we pulled into an army camp, and I knew it wasn't Saudi Arabia. Since I didn't let myself believe that I'd end up in Saudi Arabia, I wasn't too disappointed; only one half of my heart sank.

"For the rest of the day, I was shuttled to six different camps, blindfolded and handcuffed. I never saw them. My captors would throw me in the truck and drive me to the different places, usually 45 minutes apart. They'd take me out and ask me questions, very haphazardly, nothing very organized. It was clear these were not real interrogations. I was obviously a subject of interest and was probably working my way up to the main camp.

"People came out to see me, take pictures of me and poke at my gear. There was a lot of animosity, especially from the bystanders. They'd pick on me, kick me, and if they spoke English they'd say things like, 'You kill our children.' I did have a core of people and they didn't let things get out of control.

"I spent that night in Baghdad, beginning three days of hardcore interrogation. Then I was shuttled off to a prison, the first one, actually. At that point, they took my blindfold off, after three days. I was in a cell by myself, but I could communicate with other prisoners.

"In retrospect, I was shot down on the fourth day of the war and they had already had a few prisoners – a couple of Tornado crews, an A-6 crew and a Marine OV-10 crew. They already had an idea about how they wanted the prisoners to flow to the upper echelon, basically a bounty setup. The government would pay captors money when they brought a prisoner in, quickly, and relatively unharmed, although the captors could hit us a little.

"We POWs compared stories. Everyone was taken to this interrogation center eventually, after the first series of interrogations."

What had gone through Lieutenant Slade's mind after he landed? What were his chances of evading?

"I made a decision. It was better to be captured than to die in the desert from thirst. We had water bottles, of course, but we had also been told not to try to navigate in the desert, especially that far in-country.

"I relied heavily on my SERE training. At one point, they asked me if I wanted to go to the bathroom, which was the first time they had asked me, instead of my asking them. They took me outside the building – which I thought was odd since there were bathrooms inside. I was still blindfolded. As I started to urinate, it sounded strange, like on cloth. I thought I had an American flag under me and that I could also hear the hum of a camera. That's a type of situation we hear about in SERE training. I wanted to slap myself for being that dumb. I had visions of that picture on a *Newsweek* cover. I stopped. I could never tell if that is what had happened. No one could tell me. Frankly, I'm glad not to know for sure."

Lieutenant Slade and his fellow POWs were on the receiving end of allied bombing raids. They had front-row seats.

"I know for sure I was in Baghdad, in different prisons. The first prison was going to be permanent, but 11 days after my capture, all the allied prisoners were turned over to – and this is pure conjecture – the Ba'ath party, instead of the Iraqi army. Our jailers were dressed in civilian clothes. On the night of 23 January, our prison was bombed and we were moved to a civilian jail.

"We stayed in the jail until the end of February, then moved to another army prison. Our care was much better there. The bombing had stopped by then, and we began to think that maybe we could see the end of it all.

"The vast majority of the POWs were together by 23 February, at this one prison. During one raid, there were four separate, immense explosions. I'm guessing 2,000-lb bombs. I'm a fighter guy, of course. The explosions took down two entire wings of the four-storey building. That really angered the guards.

"The first bomb hit and the guards took off, headed for the basement. That was an incredible night. I really thought it was over. After they were sure the raid was over, the guards came back upstairs. They had no intention of pulling us out of our cells to shelter us. If we died by our own bombs, so what."

During one raid, Lieutenant Jeff Zaun, an A-6 BN from VA-35 who, together with his pilot, Lieutenant Robert Wetzel, had been shot down on the second night of the war, found himself free.

"His window was blown out and he climbed outside the building. He got back in, though, and came down our corridor. The building was in shambles, but miraculously, none of the allied prisoners was hurt. All the tiles, the ceiling and windows were blown out.

"Just as he re-entered the building, so did the Iraqis, and they were angry about the bombing. They showed up with other army guys with AK-47s and rifles. I heard Jeff (Lieutenant Zaun) screaming, 'Prisoner, prisoner, prisoner!' I heard the AK-47s' breeches being cocked, and I thought, 'Oh, boy!' But they just took him away, as they did all of us."

Lieutenant Slade discusses the interrogations he experienced at the hands of his Iraqi jailers.

"I had a total of six interrogations, some of what we called soft-sell where they just asked me questions, or took an I'm-a-pilot-too tack. I had no idea if he was, although he sounded like he might have been.

"Then there were the hard-sells, where they pounded on me. For the most part they didn't use any classic torture methods. They just beat me up, tied my hands behind my back and double-blindfolded me to the point where I couldn't even blink.

"They beat us even when we answered their questions. It was confusing. I held out as long as I could until I said, 'OK, here's the answer.' Then, they beat me anyway.

"After a hard-sell session, the next interrogation would probably be a soft-sell. 'If you have a problem answering this question, remember your *last* session.' Of course, we could remember very well.

"I answered questions just to make the beatings stop, even though the answers were complete garbage. Some I didn't know the answer to, and I'd tell them, then I'd make up something. I could hear them writing it down. I thought, 'You idiots!' It was an exercise in patience for me, taking things one day at a time. Some time toward the end of February, they banged me up against the wall and broke my seventh vertebra."

Lieutenant Slade was blindfolded and never saw his interrogators, probably so that he could not identify them later, or perhaps because the Iraqis understand how terrifying it is to lose one's sight.

"February was tough. I played lots of mental games. The days were *extremely* long. I went over calculus problems and engineering. Or I'd think about my hobbies, my motorcycle, or building the ideal house. Whatever it took to get through.

"I thought about my family a lot. I felt that if I was reduced to counting the bricks in the cell, I would have lost control."

from page 100 **(29 January continued)**

ground. At short notice, that night the 48th TFW launched an eight-aircraft striking force against the airfield. The F-111Fs arrived to find only one transport plane in the open, which they destroyed. The raiders then attacked the hardened shelters with laser-guided bombs and hit eight of them, producing secondary explosions in two (indicating that they contained aircraft or munitions).

A US Army OH-58 Kiowa helicopter crashed in Saudi Arabia (non-combat loss).

30 January, Wednesday During the early-morning darkness Iraqi troops launched five short thrusts into Saudi Arabia. One was observed in its initial stages by the cameras of a patrolling Pioneer remotely piloted aircraft. Following attacks by AH-1 Cobra gunships and AV-8B Harriers, the thrust was brought to a halt, with the loss of 22 tanks destroyed or damaged. Three more of the thrusts were halted soon after they crossed the Saudi border, but the remaining thrust, with about 50 tanks, was able to force its way down the coast road as far as the abandoned town of Khafji, where it established itself. During the action to dislodge the enemy US Marines suffered their first ground casualties. A-10s and AH-1 Cobra helicopters went into action against the force and claimed the destruction of about 14 Iraqi tanks.

Off the coast, Lynx helicopters from the Royal Navy warships *Cardiff, Gloucester* and *Brazen*, and US Navy A-6s and F/A-18s, took part in a multinational action against a flotilla of Iraqi fast patrol boats, some of them equipped with Exocet surface-to-surface missiles, which appeared to be moving to support the thrust on Khafji. Eight Iraqi boats were claimed sunk. Royal Air Force Jaguars, attacking with CRV7 high-velocity rockets, sank three Iraqi landing craft.

In separate actions, US Navy A-6s attacked three landing craft in the Shatt-el-Arab Channel, two of which were left dead in the water. Elsewhere, an A-6 attacked a patrol boat and set it ablaze. Other A-6s attacked patrol boats at the Umm Qasr naval base, sinking one and damaging two.

Attacks on Iraqi troop positions in and around Kuwait continued. Eight Royal Air Force Jaguars attacked a howitzer battery north of Kuwait City, and five more hit a command post.

Press reports stated that Iraqi ground forces in the Kuwait area were showing considerable skill in the improvisation of decoy tanks and other vehicles, using paraffin stoves to give them a thermal signature and metal foil to give a radar signature.

Following several days during which there was minimal enemy air activity, General Horner, the US air commander, declared that the coalition air forces had now achieved air supremacy over the Iraqi air force.

During the day, 15 Iraqi planes flew to Iran.

to page 106 **(30 January continued)**

The EF-111A 'Sparkvark' was one of the most important aircraft of the war, using its powerful and sophisticated avionics to jam and bewilder Iraqi electronic defenses.

The Spikes of Al Jouf
Commander Neil Kinnear, HCS-4, HH-60H

As the Desert Shield build-up continued, and planners probably realized they would have to force the Iraqis from Kuwait, they also realized that they needed forward-based SAR (Search and Rescue) assets. The Naval Air Reserve Helicopter Combat Support Special (HCS) squadrons were a natural choice. Of course, Reservists always know they can be called up and train for such an event. When they were mobilized for Desert Shield, both squadrons – HCS-4 and HCS-5 – were just beginning to get to know their new aircraft, the Navy's new SAR helo, a version of Sikorsky's H-60. The HH-60 used chaff and flare dispensers, and infra-red jamming to confuse enemy heat-seeking missiles.

By late December 1990, Det 1 of HCS-4 and Det 1 of HCS-5 were in-theater under the combined name of 'Spike'. Initially, the Spikes set up camp at Tabuk on 10 December and worked out of a tent city next to the hangar that housed 4th Flight, the Royal Saudi air force's SAR squadron flying the UH-1N. As the deadline for Iraqi withdrawal from Kuwait came and went, the Spikes received orders on 16 January to move to Al Jouf, northeast of Tabuk. When Desert Shield gave way to Desert Storm on the early morning of 17 January, the reserve SAR combined unit was in place.

Commander Neil T. Kinnear, the commanding officer of HCS-4, describes the call-up, initial site selection, deployment and missions.

"In August 1990, Commander Craig Tomlinson, who transferred from HC-9, and I visited COMCRUDESGRU-8 to talk with Rear Admiral Nick Gee and his staff. We briefed them on our squadron's capabilities and those of our HH-60H.

"The planners said they needed two two-plane HCS dets immediately. We were transitioning to the HH-60H, having turned in our HH-1K Hueys the year before. HCS-5 had gone operational with their new helos, with two aircraft, in June 1990. HCS-4 was not scheduled to be operational until October 1990. So, we had only one det ready to go.

"HCS-5's second det was in training; my first det was in training. Between those two dets, we had enough trained people to make one det. We sent our people to California and formed a combined det that gave the Navy

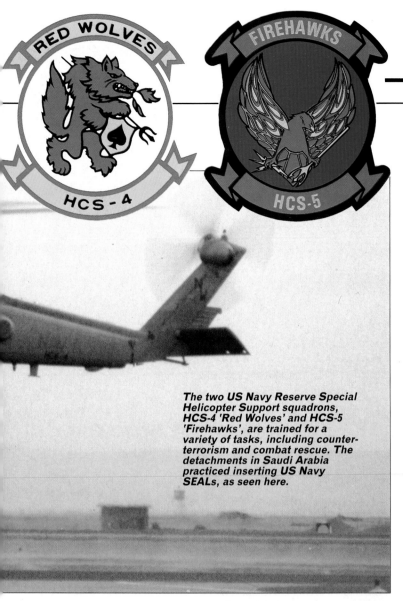

The two US Navy Reserve Special Helicopter Support squadrons, HCS-4 'Red Wolves' and HCS-5 'Firehawks', are trained for a variety of tasks, including counter-terrorism and combat rescue. The detachments in Saudi Arabia practiced inserting US Navy SEALs, as seen here.

speed was 110 kt. That arrangement worked out well politically.

"We worked out a deal with Admiral Mixson (Rear Admiral Riley Mixson, CTF-155) that when hostilities began, we needed to give tactical control to SOCCENT, more specifically to AFSOC, Air Force Special Ops Command. The Air Force had its people at King Fahd airfield, and they developed the plan that to cover the western sector they would go to Al Jouf, and forward deploy daily to Ar'ar.

"Mission tasking was a problem. The way it was supposed to work was that if someone was shot down, he or his wingman would call on the radio. The AWACS would pick it up and call the Joint Rescue Co-ordination Center at Riyadh. Riyadh would call SOCCENT, which would go to AFSOC for available assets. AFSOC would then call us and give us the data, and we'd launch. CSAR (Combat Search and Rescue) mission tasking was somewhat cumbersome."

The Spikes first mission of Desert Storm was scrubbed; the back-up mission was to put a two-plane det into Ar'ar from Al Jouf by 0300 on 17 January.

"This was probably the scariest night of the war, and probably the most confusing for everyone concerned. We launched, the Air

Force Pave Hawks (MH-60Gs) and Pave Lows (MH-53Js) launched, there were a couple of C-130s tooling around, and everyone was flying low-level. No one was talking to anyone. It was one of the darkest nights I've ever seen in my life. I worked the hardest I have ever worked to get from Al Jouf to Ar'ar.

"In the coming days, we flew 3,000 sorties each day, although we spread them over 24 hours.

"Our living conditions took some getting used to. We lived in tents, filled lots of sandbags, and lived on MREs (Meals, Ready to Eat). It was a month before we could get a shower built.

"We put a package into Ar'ar every day. We covered it for 24 hours a day, seven days a week with a ready 15. We briefed with the USAF 'Sandies'. We knew where the strike routes were. The flight environment was somewhat hostile, not only from the enemy point of view but also from the environment. The sand, how dark it was, the lack of lighting.

"Our combined group got the callsign 'Spike'. HCS-4 was the 'Redwolves', while HCS-5 was the 'Firehawks'. Out in the sands of Al Jouf, we became the 'Spike Det'."

Commander Kinnear talked about some of the Spikes' missions.

"The VF-103 shoot-down on 21 January. We were on deck. The USAF 53s had launched and had to return for fuel. The second time they were going to give it to us, but the 'Sandies' called back to say they had located Lieutenant Devon Jones, the F-14 pilot.

"On 13 February, a Saudi F-5 went in. We launched from Ar'ar. We spent all afternoon looking for him, but couldn't find him.

"On 14 February there was an F-111 coming off a raid at H-2. He thought he was under fire and dove for the deck. Unfortunately, he levelled off a *little* bit too low. It was a classic crash pattern with a long streak on the ground and the engines at the far end.

"An RAF Tornado from Tabuk crashed at night. Its hydraulics locked up after take-off, and it crashed 20 miles north of the field. The Saudis were going to wait until day, but one of our crewmen was there, AMS2 Dan High. He went with them, and using his NVGs, they found him. The Saudis got the credit but we helped.

"We flew 461 sorties. HCS-4 flew 234, HCS-5 flew 227. We flew more than 264 hours and HCS-5 110 NVG hours, HCS-4 flew 154. Mission hours: HCS-4 400, HCS-5 350, for a total of 750. HCS-4 had a 94-per cent mission capable rate, while HCS-5 had 85 per cent."

the required two-plane dets. The combined det was put on alert on 10 August, and was ready to deploy, although no one knew when or where they were going, or how.

"In western Saudi Arabia, there was one four-plane Huey squadron at the Royal Saudi airfield at Tabuk – the 4th Flight – with UH-1Ns. They were only day, VFR only, and would not fly at night. Their radius of action was 125 nm. When we showed up, we advertised 250 nm, although we knocked that back to 210 because when you start going into bad-guy country, you can't always go in a straight line.

"The reason we were initially sent to Tabuk was because of a hole in the western sector where a lot of training exercises were being conducted in August through November. If someone had gone down, it would have taken a day or two before anyone could have gotten to them. We told them, 'We can provide you with 24-hour coverage.' We worked a deal with the Saudis that they would work during the day, from sunrise, and we would take over at sunset. If they got a call during the day and it was more than 125 miles, we would cover the Saudis. If we have to we can cruise at 150 kt; their best

Above: Combat rescue is a risky business, and crews must be ready to go in under fire, make their pick-up and get out. The HH-60s that were used in the Gulf were armed with M60 7.62-mm door-guns, which was considerably less firepower than other special operations helicopters in-theater could call on.

Below: Spike crews stand on 'alert 15' – ready to be in the air within 15 minutes of a call – during Desert Storm. Most of these men are part-time warriors. The war with Iraq saw the largest call-up of Reservists since Korea, with these citizen-sailors finding themselves in action halfway round the world.

Defense Suppression

A jamming pod and an AGM-88A HARM missile are visible beneath the wing of this EA-6B Prowler as it moves towards the catapult of a US Navy carrier. Prowler missions included stand-off 'white snow' jamming and strike escort.

Above: Developed from the General Dynamics F-111 fighter bomber, the EF-111A is the most sophisticated electronic warfare aircraft in the world, with state-of-the-art receivers and jammers.

Right: Iraq's electronic eyes and ears were quickly reduced to near ineffectiveness by the skill of a defense-suppression force using weaponry and jamming to clear the skies for allied air power.

Left: A veteran of many previous wars, the F-4 Phantom still played an important role in the Gulf. One variant that was crucial was the F-4G 'Wild Weasel', which used HARM missiles to suppress enemy defenses.

Inset above: EF-111A emitters are housed in the ventral 'canoe', while the receivers are located in a bulged fin-top fairing in similar fashion to the Navy's EA-6B Prowler. Note the many mission marks.

A key factor to the overall success of Desert Storm was the effectiveness of the coalition electronic warfare assets. Both jamming aircraft and defense-suppression aircraft were widely used to minimize the threat posed by Iraqi surface-to-air missile sites and heavy radar-guided AAA. So important were the jammers and HARM shooters that few strikes were mounted without their support. Apart from the Tornado GR.Mk 1 carrying BAe ALARM anti-radar missiles, all of the dedicated defense-suppression aircraft were fielded by the United States.

For jamming support, the USAF relied on the Grumman/General Dynamics EF-111A Raven, and the US Navy/Marine Corps on the Grumman EA-6B Prowler, although the Lockheed EC-130H 'Compass Call' was used to jam Iraqi communications. Both EF-111A and EA-6B were aimed at the radars which supported the Iraqi air-defense network, especially those used to guide SAMs. Each aircraft has a series of receivers in a fin-top 'football' aerial, which detects, locates and classifies hostile radars. This information is passed to an onboard computer, which then initiates electronic countermeasures.

On the EF-111A, the ALQ-99E system is more automated than that on the EA-6B, and the aircraft is flown by a crew of two (pilot and Electronic Warfare Officer), whereas the EA-6B requires four crew (pilot and three ECM Officers) to fly the aircraft and operate the ALQ-99 Tactical Jamming System. The EF-111A carries its jammers in a long canoe fairing under the fuselage, whereas the Prowler has pods under the wings or centerline, three being a usual number.

Both aircraft operated in different modes to satisfy the requirements of the mission. Stand-off jamming saturated the Iraqi defenses before and during attacks, while aircraft also accompanied strikes in the escort mode. The Raven was particularly

Above: F-16C Fighting Falcons of the USAF can also carry and fire the AGM-88A, especially when employed in the 'killer' role alongside F-4G 'Wild Weasels'.

Above: Tornado strike aircraft of the RAF were also involved in suppressing the Iraq defensive radar network. Armament for this role was the relatively new and unproven ALARM missile (seen here under the fuselage), which although rushed into service performed as intended. A total of 121 ALARMs was expended.

Below: Another type extensively used in the suppression of enemy air defenses was the F/A-18 Hornet of the US Navy. This HARM-armed Marine Hornet is being readied at the Sheikh Isa Air Base on Bahrain for a defense-suppression sortie. A typical Marine strike always had some HARM 'shooters' in its line-up.

successful in this role as its high speed at low level allowed it to penetrate deep within Iraq. EF-111As from the 390th ECS were based at Taif as part of the 48th TFW(P) alongside F-111Fs, while those from the 42nd ECS were mainly based at Incirlik, Turkey, with the 7440th Composite Wing. Prowlers served on board all six of the US Navy's carriers, and with Marine squadron VMAQ-2 at Sheikh Isa, Bahrain.

Prowlers were also used to fire AGM-88 HARM anti-radar missiles at those air-defense radars that still operated after the barrage of jamming. This role was extremely important to the safety of the coalition air forces, and kept a large fleet of aircraft busy. The USAF's HARM shooting was performed by the elderly F-4G 'Wild Weasel', which flew from Sheikh Isa and Turkey on strike package support missions. For the Navy and Marine Corps, the F/A-18 Hornet was the principal HARM platform, backed-up by the EA-6B and A-7E. In all, over 1,000 HARMs were fired during the war, and the missile proved extremely lethal to any Iraqi radar that was fool enough to switch on when defense-suppression aircraft were in the area, whether it guided SAM or anti-aircraft gun.

HARM basically homes on the radar energy being emitted, but it is so advanced that even if the radar shuts down quickly, the HARM memorizes its position and kills it anyway. Demonstrating another HARM capability, missiles were often fired preemptively moments before a strike package entered the target area, waiting to detect a radar being switched on and attacking it if it did so. Certainly the preemptive HARM was a very effective way to suppress defenses, for the launch command over the radio was usually sufficient to keep radars silent.

Where the F-4G scored over most other HARM platforms was in its APR-47 Radar Homing and Warning System, which detects, analyzes and locates radars across a wide area. Data is displayed on a large screen in the Electronic Warfare Officer's cockpit, allowing him to prioritize the threats and attack them accordingly. The Prowler had this capability, but was also saddled with the jamming mission. F/A-18 Hornets used their standard radar-warning receivers and information from jammers in order to launch HARMs.

HARM shooters and jammers played an enormous part in the suppression of one of the world's most dense air-defense systems. Just as Eagles, Tomcats and Tornados kept the skies clean of Iraqi fighters, so the EF-111As, EA-6Bs, F-4Gs and F/A-18s kept the radars at bay. Further efforts were made by attack helicopters and Fairchild A-10s which took out battlefield air defense radars with precision missiles. The overall effectiveness of defense suppression can be seen in the remarkably short coalition loss list, which reflects the fact that after the fighters and SAM/AAA radars had largely been negated, the major threat remaining was unguided AAA, for which there is little solution other than to fly round the densest concentrations or to destroy the guns.

D.D.

An immense variety of munitions was used by the coalition. These ground crewmen are wheeling a TMD (Tactical Munitions Dispenser) towards a Torrejon-homebased F-16. The TMD dispenses a mix of anti-personnel and anti-armor mines.

from page 102 **(30 January continued)**

During a press briefing held that afternoon in Riyadh, General Norman Schwarzkopf gave details of the results of the first two weeks of the air attack on Iraq. He said that 75 per cent of the Iraqi's command, control and communications facilities had been hit, and one-third of those were completely destroyed or rendered inoperative. Attacks had been made on the air-defense nerve system, striking at 29 such targets. As a result, the Iraqis had abandoned the centralized control of their air defenses in Iraq and Kuwait.

To date, 38 airfields used by the Iraqis had come under attack. Coalition aircraft had flown a total of 1,300 sorties against them, and some had been hit with as many as four separate attacks. At least nine of the airfields were non-operational. To date, more than 70 hardened aircraft shelters had been destroyed at the airfields (out of 597).

There had been 535 sorties against 31 Iraqi weapons plants and munitions storage areas. The Pentagon claimed that all three plants involved in the development of nuclear weapons, and all major Iraqi factories engaged in the production of missiles, had been destroyed.

Power stations had come under systematic attack, and it was estimated that about one-quarter of the Iraqi electrical generation capacity had been destroyed and about one-half of it had been damaged.

The attacks on bridges, carried out mainly by the F-111Fs of the 48th TFW using laser- and TV-guided bombs, continued. To date, of the 36 road and rail bridges that had been initially targeted, 33 had already been attacked in air operations involving 790 sorties. In several cases bridges had spans dropped and were unusable.

A total of about 1,500 sorties had been flown to counter the Iraqi 'Scud' missile attacks, and 30 launchers had been destroyed.

31 January, Thursday A 'Scud' missile came down on Israel but it caused no casualties.

Bombing raids on the Iraqi troop positions continued. Arab coalition forces, supported by US Marines, completed the capture of Khafji. Five US Marines were killed when their armored personnel carrier was hit in error by a Maverick missile launched from an A-10, during a close air support mission at night.

Off the coast of Kuwait, the Lynx helicopter from HMS *Gloucester* scored a hit with a Sea Skua missile on a 'Polnochny'-class landing craft, leaving the ship stopped. Later the vessel was finished off by A-6s and Jaguars, which left it on fire and abandoned.

Three more Iraqi aircraft were reported destroyed on the ground at their airfields.

An AC-130 Hercules gunship was shot down over Kuwait and crashed into shallow water off the coast. It is believed that the aircraft was hit by a hand-held SAM-7 missile. The aircraft had been tasked for a night combat mission, but in responding to a call for help from US Marines it remained in the area after first light, which led to its loss. All 14 men on board the aircraft were killed.

to page 108

The Saga of the Iraqi Aircraft Flown to Iran

Late in April the Iraqi government revealed that a total of 148 aircraft had flown to Iran during the conflict, 11 more than previously listed in US official accounts. Of these, 115 were combat aircraft, as follows: 24 Mirage F1s; 24 Sukhoi Su-24 'Fencers'; 40 Su-22 'Fitters'; four Su-20 'Fitters'; seven Su-25 'Frogfoots'; four MiG-29 'Fulcrums'; 12 MiG-23 'Floggers'. Thirty-three Iraqi transport aircraft were flown to Iran, most of them civil aircraft belonging to Iraqi Airways or seized from Kuwait Airways: one Boeing 707; one Boeing 727; two Boeing 737s; two Boeing 747s; 15 Ilyushin Il-76s (that figure probably includes one or more Adnan AWACS aircraft); five Dassault Falcon 20s and 50s; one Lockheed Jetstar; one Airbus A300 (Kuwait Airways aircraft); five Airbus A310As (Kuwait Airways aircraft).

In a further twist to the story, the Iranian Foreign Minister Ali Akbar Velyati stated that only 22 Iraqi aircraft reached his country and that the others 'must have been shot down' by coalition aircraft. In a move that would seem to indicate that the Iranians intend to incorporate the best of the aircraft – and almost certainly the Sukhoi Su-24 'Fencer' attack aircraft – into their own air force, there are reports that at least 15 of the Iraqi aircraft held at Tabriz airfield in northwest Iran have been repainted in Iranian markings. Most probably the aircraft are being held in lieu of the reparation payments demanded by the Iranian government for losses suffered in the Iran/Iraq war.

Iran was not the only state to receive Iraqi aircraft. Immediately before or immediately after the start of the war, two Iraqi Airways Boeing 707s flew to Nouakchott, Mauretania, and two Boeing 747s and two Boeing 727s flew to Tunis. **Dr A.P.**

Pictures taken by a Japanese TV crew were the first unclassified confirmation of the flight of Iraq's air force. Many Iraqi pilots considered internment by old enemies in Iran a better option than death in their home skies, or at the hands of Saddam's executioners.

Saddam's Earache: The EC-130H Compass Call

US General John Galvin, Supreme Allied Commander Europe, expressed it best: "Schwarzkopf was able to dismantle the electromagnetic spectrum [so that] he effectively closed Saddam's eyes and ears. He therefore made Saddam less mobile, less able to react, less able to gain intelligence – basically, less able to orchestrate and put the air, land and sea [elements] together." No aircraft did more to close Saddam's ears than the US Air Force's seven to nine (approximately) Lockheed EC-130H Compass Call communications-jamming aircraft that took part in the Gulf war.

The Compass Call force – split in peacetime between the 41st Electronic Combat Squadron at Davis-Monthan AFB, Arizona, and the 43rd Electronic Combat Squadron at Sembach AFB, Germany – started to arrive in the Gulf as the allied build-up gained momentum during Operation Desert Shield. At least two were at Incirlik AFB in Turkey. Others were deployed to Saudi Arabia, operating alongside EC-130Es from Riyadh International Airport.

The Compass Call is one of the most sophisticated C-130 versions. Its 'main armament' is a battery of communications jammers. The C-130's size and power supply allow for enough jammers to be packed in to permit either barrage or spot jamming over a large number of frequencies.

While opportunities for using the Compass Call's communications-jamming capabilities during training are extremely limited, due to the potential damage to civilian communications and transportation, experience in the Green Flag exercises at Nellis AFB had shown just how effective the Compass Call could be, and both Central Command and its crews went to the Gulf with high expectations. They were not, it appears, to be disappointed.

The Rivet Fire program in the mid-1980s installed computerized scanning capability on the Compass Calls, using data acquired by Elint aircraft to search for enemy radio communications. Once acquired – and prioritized – by the computer, the electronic warfare operator, sitting in the back of the Compass Call, will then either record the intercepted radio traffic for intelligence analysis or, more likely, initiate one of a number of jamming programs, using computer power management techniques. In one of

the most common techniques, Iraqis using voice communications would find their earphones full of a wailing described as bagpipes played back at high speed. If the Iraqis were to then switch to a pre-arranged alternative frequency, they would often find that the bagpipes – directed by the Compass Call's computer – had beaten them to it.

The jammers are not the Compass Call's only weapon. They also have a capability for 'spoofing', invading enemy voice communications nets with trained operators, to pass misleading orders and force the enemy into time-consuming authentication procedures. When the Gulf deployment started, the Compass Call force was not set up for spoofing Iraqi communications; most of the emphasis had gone into preparing against Soviet or Warsaw Pact opponents. No one wants to let the Iraqis know whether the Compass Calls were using their spoofing capability during the war.

Compass Call also has capabilities for beaconing enemy aircraft and unspecified ways of affecting enemy IFF. Together, this made them a formidable weapon against Iraqi air defenses. The Compass Call also carried self-defense systems. Because they could possibly be located in flight by the Iraqis triangulating the source of the jamming, Compass Calls carried one or more jamming pods, usually ALQ-101s, ALQ-119s, or Block I ALQ-131s. They also had chaff and flare dispensers.

The effectiveness of the Compass Call depended on the Comint (Communications intelligence) work being carried out by allied aircraft. Before the war, a land, sea and air Elint effort had aimed to develop an accurate picture of Iraqi emitters, both radars and radios, and how they fitted into their overall war-fighting capability.

Airborne communications jamming "was used and it seemed to work quite well . . . Compass Call was our primary drill," according to USAF Major General John Corder, director of operations for Central Command Air Forces. "They jammed the hell out of communications," according to retired Admiral Julian Lake, former head of Navy EW programs.

Jamming helped drive Iraqi emitters from the electromagnetic spectrum. According to one US official, "The Iraqis were judged to be very good in controlling the radar emissions from their missile

Above: EC-130H Compass Call can refuel in flight for long-duration missions. The aircraft loiters near hostile air space, jamming enemy communications.

Below: USAF Electronic Security Command airmen aboard EC-130H Compass Calls are rigorously trained, and were used to both jam and confuse Iraqi radios.

sites until the last moment." The opening of Operation Desert Storm resulted in the Iraqi air-defense radars 'lighting up' until they were again silenced, this time by allied action and what General Colin Powell suspected were "clever operational security techniques on their part": by 23 January there was a 95 per cent reduction in activity from that seen on 17 January. But later events proved, in the words of Frank Kendall, US Under Secretary of Defense for tactical warfare programs, "the willingness to turn on your radars and fight didn't seem to be there."

The Iraqis had first- and second-generation secure radios with ECM capability, but these were not used effectively in the face of allied EW efforts. They provided the Comint

aircraft with much valuable intelligence and were vulnerable to Compass Call jamming. "Anytime the Iraqis came on the radio, they were jammed," said USAF Colonel Richard Atchison, who worked in intelligence at Central Command headquarters. Communications jamming aircraft, especially the Compass Calls, also forced air-defense radars – not receiving target information – to light up and search, making them vulnerable to HARM-missile-armed defense-suppression aircraft. The severance of communication was so complete that the captured diary of one Iraqi air-defense battery commander revealed that he had not heard from his superiors for the last three weeks of the war!

D.I.

Lines of smoke fill the desert sky as another fully loaded B-52 flight departs from Riyadh en route to Iraqi army positions.

from page 106

1 February, Friday Little air activity over the battle area, due to poor weather.

An announcement on Spanish radio stated that B-52s operating from the airfield at Moron de la Frontera near Seville were taking part in attacks on Iraqi positions.

That night, Royal Air Force Tornados attacked the airfields at Habbaniyah and Al Taqaddum.

2 February, Saturday One 'Scud' missile was fired at Israel, causing no casualties.

Attacks on Iraqi troop positions resumed.

A USAF A-10 (pilot taken prisoner) and a US Navy A-6 (both crewmen killed) were shot down by ground fire over Kuwait. One US Army AH-1 was lost over Saudi Arabia (non-combat loss).

3 February, Sunday One 'Scud' missile was launched against Israel, another at Saudi Arabia, causing no casualties.

Attacks on Iraqi troop positions continued. Royal Air Force Jaguars attacked gun emplacements on the island of Faylaka, 10 miles north of Kuwait City.

Royal Air Force Tornados carried out a daylight attack on an oil pumping station in Iraq.

A US spokesman announced that since 24 January, at least 13 Iraqi aircraft had been destroyed during attacks on airfields.

Returning from an attack on Iraqi troop positions, a B-52 suffered a progressive failure of the electrical system and crashed into the Indian Ocean about 15 miles out on the approach to Diego Garcia; this incident was officially listed by the US Air Force as a 'non-combat loss'. Over Saudi Arabia, the US Army lost a UH-1 helicopter (non-combat loss).

4 February, Monday USS *Missouri* engaged ground targets in Kuwait with her 16-in guns.

Near to the Iraq-Kuwait border, US Marine Corps AV-8B Harriers caught a force of tanks and other vehicles in the open and brought it under attack, claiming the destruction of 25 of them with Rockeye cluster-bombs.

That afternoon a US spokesman announced that to date, 27 of the 35 bridges on the initial allied 'hit list' had been damaged so seriously as to render them unusable.

5 February, Tuesday Attacks continued on Iraqi troop positions, concentrating on Republican Guard units. According to one report, the Tarrakalna Division had lost about 150, or more than a third, of its tanks. The other two Republican Guard armored divisions, the Medina and the Hammurabi, had also been hit hard.

On the night of 5/6 February, Colonel Tom Lennon, commander

to page 116 **(5 February continued)**

Electro-optical Guided Weapons

While laser-guided bombs accounted for the majority of PGMs (Precision-Guided Munitions) dropped during Desert Storm, a significant number of EO (Electro-Optical) guided weapons was launched. These involved tried and trusted ordnance such as the Maverick, and combat debutantes such as SLAM.

The AGM-65 Maverick missile was widely used against armor and other small, hard targets, chiefly from Fairchild A-10As but also from McDonnell Douglas/BAe AV-8B Harrier IIs. This missile was available with either a daylight or infra-red seeker head. The image from the seeker is displayed on a screen in the aircraft's cockpit, which the pilot uses to acquire the target. When this has been achieved he directs cross hairs on the screen to lie over the desired impact point of the missile, and locks in the position. The missile is then fired. Using a contrast auto-tracker, the missile flies towards this image, and is devastatingly accurate, although with only a short range: A shaped-charge warhead punches a hole through armor or concrete, filling the inside of the tank or bunker with molten metal.

Of much greater punch were the other three types of EO-guided weapon used in Desert Storm. US Navy A-6Es were the launch platform for over 100 AGM-62 ER/DL (Extended Range/Data Link) Walleye II missiles. This weapon is a large guided missile with a 500-lb warhead. It has a TV seeker in the nose and a small motor in the back, allowing it to be used from greater distances than the Maverick, and with a much greater kill capability. A data link sends back the seeker's image to the launch aircraft, which needs a pod to receive these signals, and the Bombardier/Navigator of the A-6 can return flight directions to the missile. In this way the Walleye II can be 'flown' towards its target.

AGM-84E SLAM (Stand-off Land Attack Missile) operates in a similar fashion, but over much greater ranges. Based on the 500-lb warhead and body of the AGM-84 Harpoon anti-ship missile, SLAM replaces the active-radar seeker of the Harpoon with an infra-red seeker as used in Maverick. Launched from a great distance, it uses GPS (Global Positioning System) navigation to follow a preprogrammed low-level course towards the target. As it nears the target, approximately a minute's flight-time away, it switches on the seeker whose image is relayed to an AWW-9 Walleye data link pod carried on a directing aircraft. The pilot then 'flies' the SLAM towards the target using the relayed image on a cockpit screen.

Seven SLAMs were fired during Desert Storm, of which four hit their targets. Launches were from A-6E Intruders and F/A-18 Hornets. The first combat use of the weapon provided some of the most dramatic footage to emerge from the war. Two SLAMs were launched from A-6 Intruders against an Iraqi hydro-electric plant. The first was seen to hit the side wall of the building, creating a large hole. Following some two minutes behind, the second SLAM could be seen being 'flown' straight through the aperture to explode deep within the building, destroying the equipment inside. Control for both weapons had been effected by a pilot in a Vought A-7E many miles away.

Equally impressive footage was released after one of the 100 launches of the GBU-15 'glide bomb'. Once again GBU-15 is a devastatingly accurate weapon which can be 'flown' by the Weapon Systems Officer of the launch or directing aircraft. Again a Maverick-style seeker head is used, grafted onto the front of a 2,000-lb warhead. The BLU-109 hard-target warhead was not ready for GBU-15 use during Desert Storm, and it is not believed that the cluster-bomb warhead was used either.

GBU-15 has large wings fore and aft to give it an outstanding range when launched from high speed and high altitude. A data link sends back the seeker image to an AXQ-14 data link pod, which presents the seeker's image on the cockpit screen. Control inputs made by the WSO are returned by the AXQ-14 to the bomb's control fins. The bomb can either be 'flown' all the way to impact, or an image can be locked into the bomb's control system in much the same way as Maverick.

During Desert Storm the GBU-15 was employed by the F-111Fs of the 48th TFW(P), although the F-15Es of the 4th TFW(P) also have GBU-15 capability. Most were the older GBU-15(V)1/B bomb with large trapezoidal wings, although a few of the newer GBU-15(V)2/B weapons may have been used,

SLAM Attack

Harpoon is one of the most capable missiles currently in the inventory of the US Navy, but its radar seeker head is only effective in detecting ship-sized targets in open water. SLAM (Stand-off Land Attack Missile) is an attempt to exploit the 100-km range of the missile and its powerful 225-kg high-explosive blast warhead in the land attack role.

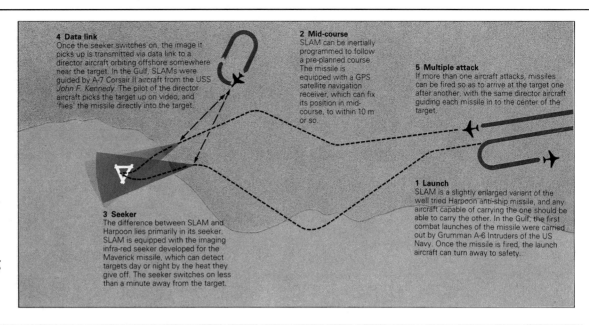

4 Data link
Once the seeker switches on, the image it picks up is transmitted via data link to a director aircraft orbiting offshore somewhere near the target. In the Gulf, SLAMs were guided by A-7 Corsair II aircraft from the USS *John F. Kennedy*. The pilot of the director aircraft picks the target up on video, and 'flies' the missile directly into the target.

2 Mid-course
SLAM can be inertially programmed to follow a pre-planned course. The missile is equipped with a GPS satellite navigation receiver, which can fix its position in mid-course, to within 10 m or so.

5 Multiple attack
If more than one aircraft attacks, missiles can be fired so as to arrive at the target one after another, with the same director aircraft guiding each missile in to the center of the target.

3 Seeker
The difference between SLAM and Harpoon lies primarily in its seeker. SLAM is equipped with the imaging infra-red seeker developed for the Maverick missile, which can detect targets day or night by the heat they give off. The seeker switches on less than a minute away from the target.

1 Launch
SLAM is a slightly enlarged variant of the well tried Harpoon anti-ship missile, and any aircraft capable of carrying the one should be able to carry the other. In the Gulf, the first combat launches of the missile were carried out by Grumman A-6 Intruders of the US Navy. Once the missile is fired, the launch aircraft can turn away to safety.

Above: The F-111Fs of the 48th TFW based at Taif were the only aircraft to drop the devastatingly effective GBU-15 glide bomb. Launched at speed and altitude, the GBU-15 has an effective glide range of 80 km. In hostile environments, it is normally launched indirectly, the operator picking up the target after launch. The operator can then lock the weapon onto the target. There are two kinds of seeker – television for daylight use, and imaging infra-red for use at night.

these featuring square wings. The AGM-130 rocket-boosted version was not used, however. The impressive footage mentioned earlier concerned the use of GBU-15s dropped from an F-111F against the oil facility that was creating the large slick in the Gulf. The bomb was clearly seen being 'flown' into the pump manifold group which was controlling the flow of oil into the sea. The dead hit immediately staunched the flow, ending Iraq's attempt to pollute the water beyond hope.

D.D.

Above: A pair of AGM-62 ER/DL Walleye II-armed A-7Es of VA-46 'Clansmen' takes on fuel from a KA-6D. The Walleye II is a developed version of the electro-optical guided glide bomb first used in Vietnam. Walleye can be flown into the target either by the launch aircraft or by any other aircraft fitted with a guidance pod.

Right: Maverick was the smallest EO-guided weapon used in the Gulf. Most Mavericks in use were clear-weather television-guided missiles. Maverick is ideal for taking out armor from beyond the range of short-range air-defense systems such as self-propelled anti-aircraft guns or shoulder-launched SAMs.

France in Combat

On 15 January 1991, when the French government realized that its last minute diplomatic efforts were not going to convince Saddam Hussein to withdraw his forces from Kuwait, COMELEF ground and air components were placed under CENTCOM (Central Command). However, with the pro-Iraqi Defense Minister still yielding some influence in Paris, CENTCOM was notified that French forces were not to be uzed inside Iraq (a restriction soon lifted). Accordingly, targets initially assigned to Jaguars were all inside occupied Kuwait, while Mirage 2000Cs flew defensive CAPs over Saudi Arabia and provided escort to strike aircraft operating over Kuwait. Moreover, and notwithstanding an acute shortage of tactical reconnaissance aircraft, CENTAF elected not to avail itself of the F1CRs as the coalition partners feared that the French Mirages would too easily be confused with Iraqi Mirages.

The first French combat mission saw 12 Jaguars take off at 0530 on 17 January, and after being refueled by four C-135FRs, these tactical fighters made a low-level strike against a 'Scud' missile depot and communications facilities at the Ahmed Al Jaber AB. The targets were hit accurately with 250-kg bombs and Belouga bomblet dispensers, but two Jaguars were forced to divert to Jubail after one was hit by an SA-7 missile which set fire to its engines and another was hit in one engine by a shell; the pilot of a third landed safely back at Al Ahsa even though a bullet had gone through his Crouzet flight helmet. Quickly learning their lessons, French pilots flew their next mission – a strike against a munitions storage facility at Ras Al Qulayah, flown at a higher altitude

with four Jaguars firing AS 30L laser-guided missiles in a dive from an altitude of 4,000 ft and at a 10-km stand-off range to blast a storage hangar, while eight others dropped bombs. Only minor damage was sustained by Jaguars in this attack but a repeat attack had to be flown the next day as pilots, lacking prior training with live AS 30L missiles, had missed their target. That repeat mission was highly successful, but bad weather forced the cancellation of the 20 and 21 January missions. By then, reinforcements had either arrived (four Jaguars reaching Al Ahsa on 18 January to bring the number of French strike fighters to 28) or were scheduled to be deployed, with two Mirage 2000Cs arriving on 6 February, to bring the total to 14. The fifth and sixth F1CRs

arrived on 7 February.

These early missions proved some of the tactics developed in peacetime to be faulty, notably those favoring very low-level attacks as employed during Red Flag exercises in which surface-to-air missiles and enemy aircraft are effectively replicated but dense conventional air-to-ground fire, such as encountered over occupied Kuwait and Iraq, are missing. However, these missions confirmed other lessons, such as the importance of carrying an ample supply of chaffs and flares and of using electronic countermeasures (ECM). Hence, Jaguars normally operated from Al Ahsa with a 56-cartridge Alkan 5020 conformal chaff/flare launcher beneath each wing root, an ESD Barax ECM pod on the port

external pylon and, when not carrying a Magic 550 air combat missile, a Philips/Matra Phimat chaff launcher pod (or Boz chaff/flare launcher) on the starboard external pylon. Occasionally, an 18-cartridge Lacroix flare launcher was carried in place of the drag chute. Typical offensive loads comprised either a pair of 250-kg bombs on the internal pylon beneath each wing and a 1200-liter tank beneath the fuselage; a ventral tank and a Belouga bomblet dispenser beneath each wing; or an AS 30L laser-guided missile beneath the starboard internal pylon, a 1200-liter tank on the port internal pylon, and a Thomson/CSF Atlis designator on the centerline.

Following the replacement of Defense Minister Chevènement with Pierre Joxe, the level and scope of Jaguar operations were expanded, two daily missions being flown beginning on 23 January and, much to the satisfaction of French pilots, targets inside Iraq being struck from 24 January, the first target being mechanized units of the Iraqi Republican Guard. Thereafter, weather permitting, Jaguars kept up the pressure and attacked a variety of targets including the airfields at Tallil, Shaiba and Jalibah. By the time the cease-fire was declared on 28 February, Jaguars had flown 615 sorties without a single loss, a rather gratifying achievement for the pilots and support personnel of an

Left: Carrying both Matra Super 530 and Magic missiles, a Mirage 2000 of the French air force's EC 5 is about to depart on a combat air patrol from a base at Al Ahsa, Saudi Arabia.

Left and inset left: Bombs fall free from a French Jaguar during a medium-altitude strike mission somewhere over the Kuwait theater of operations, while a pilot back from a sortie gives the universal signal of success before he quits his aircraft.

Above: French warplanes committed to the war effort included Mirage F1CRs for reconnaissance, although these were often used as bombers alongside the Jaguars, serving as 'pathfinders' by virtue of their more comprehensive navigation and attack equipment.

aircraft considered by many to be obsolete.

The most modern fighters in service with the Armée de l'air, the Mirage 2000Cs of the 5ième Escadre de chasse, were selected for Operation *Daguet* in preference to those of the 2ième Escadre de chasse as they were equipped with RDI (Radar Doppler et Impulsions) radar instead of the less capable RDM (Radar Doppler Multi-fonction) fitted to early production 2000Cs. Moreover, prior to being deployed or shortly after arriving at Al Ahsa, these aircraft had their RDI radar upgraded to the latest S4-1 and S4-2 standard and additional self-protection systems were installed (including a chaff/flare dispenser scabbed beneath the rear fuselage). Armed with four BVR Super 530D missiles and a pair of Magic 2 dogfight missiles, these fighters would have been a fair match for most Iraqi fighters, possibly even the much vaunted but somewhat disappointing MiG-29s. Unfortunately for their pilots, Mirage 2000Cs were kept over Saudi Arabia and Kuwait in the early days of Desert Storm when Iraqi fighters were still active further north and later, when Iraqi fighters attempted fleeing to Iran, they were not sent to join F-15Cs blocking escape routes. Consequently, in spite of flying 508 sorties on defensive air patrols and to escort Jaguars and Mirage F1CRs, the 2000Cs remained unblooded.

Even though they were grounded during the first days of Desert Storm, dual-role Mirage F1CRs were eventually blooded as, beginning on 26 January, they joined Jaguars on bombing sorties over Kuwait and southern Iraq. From 5 February, Mirage F1CRs were again uzed in the reconnaissance role as the 'Scud' hunt diverted an excessive share of limited USAF tactical reconnaissance assets, missions being flown by a pair of aircraft to ensure completion even if the primary aircraft was forced to abort or suffered an equipment failure. Whether operating in the strike or reconnaissance roles, the swept-wing Mirages and their precise SNAR (Système de Navigation d'Attaque et de Reconnaissance, or Strike and Reconnaissance Navigation System) nav system performed well and reliably.

First supporting the deployment of FATac's single-seaters to Saudi Arabia and Qatar, CoFAS' tankers were based at Riyadh IAP to provide air-refueling support for aircraft based in Saudi Arabia. Prior to taking part in refueling operations under combat conditions, the C-135FRs were fitted with chaff/flare dispensers and Dassault Electronique Adèle

Above: With its twin afterburners blazing brightly, a French Jaguar gets airborne for another attack mission. Like their counterparts from the Royal Air Force, French Jaguar pilots completed well over 600 combat sorties during the war to liberate Kuwait. They sustained some injury but no combat losses.

Left: Returning Jaguars head for the flight line at Al Ahsa after completing a mission. In addition to conventional bombs, Jaguars were used to drop the Belouga bomblet dispenser and to launch laser-guided AS 30L air-to-surface missiles. There is no doubt that the French pilots performed well.

radar-warning receivers. At peak strength, six C-135FRs, more than half the meager force of French jet tankers, were in Saudi Arabia, and during Desert Storm they flew 220 refueling sorties.

In support of Desert Shield and Desert Storm, CoTAM aircraft flew 1,340 sorties on the France-Gulf route, transporting 10500 tonnes of freight and 21,000 military passengers; in addition, CoTAM aircraft performed 1,020 intra-theater sorties, carrying 12,400 passengers and 5500 tonnes of freight. While both C.160s and C-130Hs proved effective and reliable in the táctical airlift role, France's participation in the Gulf air war highlighted the Armée de l'air's shortfall in the strategic airlift arena. Conversely, CoTAM SAR helicopters proved equal to the task as the two night-capable Pumas sent to Al Ahsa were credited with rescuing three allied airmen, the first being a pilot from the 138th TFS, New York ANG, which ejected from his crippled F-16A during a training sortie over Saudi Arabia on 13 January 1991. No details have been released on operations by the more discreet C.160G Elint aircraft, one of which was bazed at Al Ahsa, and by the DC-8-55 'Sarique', the latter being known to have made at least one short-term deployment to the theater of operations.

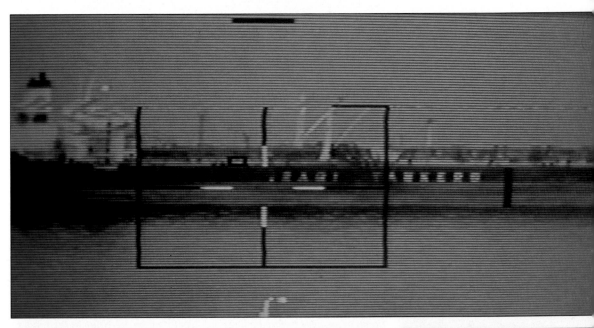

The Armée de l'air in the Gulf War
Flight Hours and Number of Sorties

Aircraft	Desert Shield Hours/Sorties	Desert Storm Hours/Sorties
Jaguar	1,258/775	1,088/615
Mirage 2000	1,163/702	1,416/508
Mirage F1C	545/637	130/150
Mirage F1CR	731/442	264/114
C-135FR	914/123	913/220
C.160	796/205	1,176/272
TOTALS	5,407 hours 2,884 sorties	4,987 hours 1,879 sorties

Operations *Artimon, Busiris, Libage, Méteil, Ramure* and others

Although dominated by *Daguet* and *Salamandre*, France's direct participation in the Gulf air war was not limited to operations by tactical aircraft, tankers, transports and helicopters in Saudi Arabia. As part of Operation *Artimon*, the guided-missile destroyers *Dupleix* (D 641) and *Montcalm* (D 642), each embarking a pair of Lynx helicopters from Flotille 31F, joined the naval blockade in October 1990. Operations *Busiris* and *Méteil* were undertaken to strengthen the defense of the United Arab Emirates, with a squadron of Crotale SAMs being deployed to Abu Dhabi and eight Mirage F1Cs from the 12ième Escadre de chasse being flown from Solenzara to Doha, Qatar, on 17 October 1990 (pilots for these

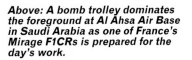
Above: A bomb trolley dominates the foreground at Al Ahsa Air Base in Saudi Arabia as one of France's Mirage F1CRs is prepared for the day's work.

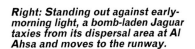
Right: Standing out against early-morning light, a bomb-laden Jaguar taxies from its dispersal area at Al Ahsa and moves to the runway.

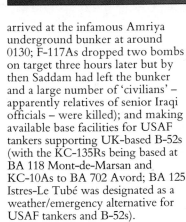

aircraft initially came from EC 1/12 'Cambrésis', later from EC 3/12 'Cornouailles'). Furthermore, some 50 maintenance personnel from the 30ième Escadre de chasse deployed to Saudi Arabia on October 1990 to help maintain free Kuwait Mirage F1s. Initially kept at Taif, to avoid possible misidentification with Iraqi Mirages, the Kuwaiti-flown, French-maintained Mirage F1CK-2s were moved to Dhahran AB when the virtual elimination of the Iraqi air force made it unlikely that friendly Mirages would be mistaken for enemy aircraft. The Armée de l'air also sent personnel to Abu Dhabi to

help the United Arab Emirates air force achieve operational status with its Mirage 2000s.

Other French wartime contributions were less direct but no less effective. They included providing Mirage F1s for dissimilar aircraft combat training; furnishing detailed information and specifications on French-supplied equipment of the Iraq forces and assessment of Iraqi pilots' training and capabilities; contributing human intelligence (such as during the night of 12-13 February when a French agent notified the coalition forces that Saddam Hussein had

arrived at the infamous Amriya underground bunker at around 0130; F-117As dropped two bombs on target three hours later but by then Saddam had left the bunker and a large number of 'civilians' – apparently relatives of senior Iraqi officials – were killed); and making available base facilities for USAF tankers supporting UK-based B-52s (with the KC-135Rs being based at BA 118 Mont-de-Marsan and KC-10As to BA 702 Avord; BA 125 Istres-Le Tubé was designated as a weather/emergency alternative for USAF tankers and B-52s).

Barely one week after the cease-

Left: This is the view through the head-up display imagery during an AS 30L attack on an Iraqi oil tanker moored alongside a jetty. Like other allied air units, the French relied heavily on 'smart' laser-guided weapons in precision attacks against hard targets.

Right: A pre-dawn scene at Al Ahsa as a 5ième Escadre Mirage 2000C is 'prepped' for an early CAP mission over Saudi Arabia. French CAPs, like those of the British, produced no air-to-air combat successes, since no Iraqi aircraft were encountered.

Below: Although no losses befell France's Jaguar force, ultra low-level operations resulted in some battle damage being sustained by several aircraft. This was one of the worst instances and resulted in severe damage to an engine.

Right: This Jaguar took a single bullet round through the main canopy, happily without dire consequences for the pilot, although the bullet passed through his helmet.

Right, center: A key element in precision attacks was the Atlis designator pod, which marked targets for AS 30 missile attacks. It was normally carried on the centerline stores pylon of the Jaguar.

Right, bottom: Distinctive mottled markings on the casing of the weapon shown here identify it as a Belouga bomblet dispenser. Used extensively against 'soft' targets like troops and trucks, it was found to be particularly effective.

Below: Normally employed to fuel France's small strategic nuclear force, the C-135FR Stratotanker was deployed in support of French aircraft in the Gulf. At the height of the war, six of the 11 aircraft on charge were based at Riyadh, and they finally clocked up 220 refueling sorties during Desert Storm operations.

fire was declared, tactical aircraft began returning to France as four Jaguars arrived at Toul-Rosières on 5 March. On 18 March, the first Mirage 2000Cs reached Orange-Caritat. However, for the Armée de l'air and other coalition forces the cease-fire did not end the need to serve, as Saddam Hussein turned his ire towards his Shi'ite and Kurd opponents. Thus, beginning on 8 April, CoTAM sent five C.160s to Incirlik AB in Turkey to airlift and air-drop supplies to Kurdish refugees. Similar duties befell a C-130H which was sent to Tabriz AB in Iran on 16 April.

R.F.

Operation Friction: Canada in the War

Canadian military involvement in the Middle East began on 10 August 1990, when Prime Minister Brian Mulroney announced that Canada would send two destroyers and a supply ship. Their mission was to support a multinational effort in the Gulf region.

The following two weeks saw the two destroyers, HMCS *Athabaskan* and HMCS *Terra Nova*, and the supply ship, HMCS *Protecteur*, undergo extensive refits and upgrades. These improvements enabled them to work more effectively in the interdiction mission called for by the UN Security Council. Some of the equipment fitted had already been procured for installation on the new frigates for Maritime Command, which are not yet in service. Six CH-124A Sea Kings were modified, changing from an ASW-dedicated role to one better suited for its new tasks. Personnel from the Royal Canadian Artillery, equipped with Blowpipe and Javelin anti-aircraft missiles, also joined the ships.

The three ships, now designated as Canadian Task Group (CTG) 302.3, sailed from Halifax on 24 August. The deployment was officially named Operation Friction, and which would eventually be expanded to cover the entire Canadian effort in the region. The inevitable T-shirts prepared by the Sea King crews renamed the mission as the 'Persian Excursion'.

The Prime Minister announced in mid-September that a squadron of CF-18s would be sent to the Gulf to provide air cover for the Canadian ships and augment the multinational forces already in place. The work of the Air Task Group was co-ordinated primarily with the United States Navy and Marine Corps to ensure 24-hour-a-day protection of the combined fleets.

No. 409 Tactical Fighter Squadron, from CFB Baden-Soellingen, began its deployment on 4 October, with the first CF-18s leaving two days later. They arrived, via RAF Akrotiri, Cyprus, on 7 October, flew familiarization missions on 8 October, and their first CAPs on 9 October. Designated as the Canadian Air Task Group Middle East (CATGME), it established itself near the city of Doha, the base soon becoming known as 'Canada Dry One'. Security was provided by 'Mike' Company of 3rd Battalion, The Royal Canadian Regiment, also from Baden-Soellingen. The base was shared with resident Qatari Emirate air force F-1s and AlphaJets, French air force F1s and USAFE F-16Cs of the 614th TFS, 401st TFW.

The initial deployment consisted of 18 CF-18s, 36 pilots and 255 ground crew. This was later adjusted to 28 and 235, respectively.

Typically, 18 CF-18 sorties were flown each day: 10 CAPs and eight training flights. Most CAPs were without scheduled tanker support, although 'tanking by opportunity' with USMC KC-130s, USAF KC-10s and RAF VC10s took place frequently.

Unlike most of the American units, Canada instituted a rotation for its personnel. 409 Squadron was replaced by 439 Tactical Fighter Squadron, also from CFB Baden-Soellingen, in mid-December. Security for 'Canada Dry One' was also transferred to 'Charlie' Company, 1st Battalion, Royal 22 Regiment, which arrived from CFB Lahr, Germany. Included as part of 439 was 416 Tactical Fighter Squadron, integrated into 439, rather than the two operating as a wing or group. In fact, more personnel were from 416 than from 439. CFB Cold Lake-based 416 is known as 'Lynx' Squadron and 439 as 'Tiger', so the name 'Desert Cats' was a natural choice. It should be noted that pilots came from other CAF squadrons, too. The 'Desert Cats' had personnel from 409, 410, 421 and 441 Squadrons supplementing 439 and 416.

On 11 January 1991, an additional six CF-18s deployed to Qatar. These were from 441 Tactical Fighter Squadron at CFB Cold Lake and brought the total number of operational aircraft to 24. A CC-137 (Boeing 707) also deployed to Qatar to provide aerial refueling to Canadian and allied aircraft. Later, two other CF-18s would be sent to enable the force to be kept at 24 aircraft while maintenance was carried out.

Temperatures in Qatar frequently reached 40°C during the later months of 1990, but the hot, dry, dusty conditions did not adversely affect the Canadian CF-18s. Quite the contrary, in fact, as it turned out that the engines had never worked better. The fine dust in the air acted as a compressor wash and peaked up engine performance, according to Colonel Romeo Lalonde, commander of Canadian Air Task Group Middle East, who adds that the "electric jet just loved the dry, hot climate. Consequently, there were no modifications required to prepare the CF-18s for operations in that part of the world."

The word went out to all coalition fighter forces on 12 January to arm up with all available resources. Within 12 hours, all CF-18s were fully armed with three

AIM-7M Sparrows and four AIM-9M Sidewinders. The Canadians were congratulated by General Horner, COMCENTAF, for being the first wing in the Middle East to achieve 100 per cent operational weapons readiness status.

Colonel Lalonde was informed that the codeword from General Schwarzkopf to commence wartime plans would be 'Wolfpack'. On the morning of 16 January, Lieutenant Colonel Don Matthews, CO of the 'Desert Cats', selected six pilots to receive additional information concerning the commencement of hostilities. They were to become the first Canadian flying officers at war, with Canadian resources, since World War II.

Colonel Lalonde takes up the story: "At 0200 [local time] 17 January, in the moonlit darkness of the Persian Gulf, the first series of Tomahawk missiles lifted off the USS *Wisconsin* – the callsign 'Wolfpack' was issued by General

Schwarzkopf. The aircraft-carrier flagship USS *Midway* had onboard Major Joce Clouthier as our liaison officer to co-ordinate operational missions with the USN. He was, in fact, on duty, sitting beside Admiral Marsh in the flag room of the USS *Midway* when the order to execute came in and he received the call. Upon confirming the order with Admiral Marsh, he initiated the alarms to put the US Seventh Fleet on battle stations. If anybody asks, you can tell them that a Canadian fighter pilot started the Gulf war."

The primary role of Canada's CF-18s was that of combat air patrol in the central Gulf, providing air cover for the Canadian Naval Task Group. On 17 January, the Chief of the Defence Staff, General John de Chastelain, announced that the fighters' role had been expanded to include sweep and escort duties in support of other elements of allied air forces.

Sweep missions and escort

Left and inset left: The CF-18 Hornet is the most potent aircraft in the inventory of the Canadian Forces, so naturally it was the weapon of choice in the Canadian deployment to the Gulf. The first wave of aircraft and pilots were sent from No. 409 Tactical Fighter Squadron, based at Canadian Forces Base Baden-Soellingen in Germany.

Right: Canadian CF-18s were based at Doha, in Qatar, on a base shared with the Mirage F1s of the Qatari air force. The first task of the Canadian fighters was to provide cover for the Canadian warships which were in the Gulf.

Left: Being given CAP tasks meant that the primary weapons for Canadian CF-18s were AIM-7 Sparrow medium-range missiles and the smaller AIM-9 Sidewinder short-range missiles.

Below: The Canadian Hornet force numbered 24 aircraft by the time the shooting started, and the 'Desert Cats' maintained a 24-hour watch over about a fifth of the coalition fleet.

Above: Canadian pilots are highly trained, but the Gulf war was their first combat in four decades.

missions are similar. The former required the CF-18s to clear or 'sweep' a section of airspace to allow a bombing strike package to arrive at, attack, and depart from a target unscathed. Escort differed slightly in that the CF-18s flew ahead of the package and then followed it out after the attack was completed. Both types of mission involved four CF-18s at a time. No Canadian aircraft encountered Iraqi aircraft. They "never did come up to fight," as Colonel Lalonde put it. Sweep and escort missions began by comprising about 20 per cent of Canadian assignments, primarily escorting the 401st TFW, co-located at Doha, Qatar. They developed into escorting F-4G 'Wild Weasels', Buccaneer laser target designators, and RAF Tornados deep into Iraqi territory.

About 1.5 hours into a two-hour CAP mission, Captain Steve 'Hillbilly' Hill and Major Dave 'DW' Kendall were asked by Papa Bravo (the ship controlling their CAP) if they would "like to strafe

a boat". Several A-6 Intruders had disabled two other Iraqi boats in the area, but were unable to attack the vessel because they were 'winchester' (out of ammunition). Another A-6 was on its way and the Canadians were asked to hit the boat so that the *en-route* Intruder could finish it off. After being cleared in to attack by an E-2C, both CF-18s strafed the boat until they, too, were 'winchester'. Each aircraft made another pass, attempting to obtain a lock for a shot with an AIM-9M Sidewinder, but the heat signature of the boat was insufficient for missile guidance. The Canadians made a further pass each, this time trying to get a lock with an AIM-7M Sparrow. The wingman's missile failed to lock, but the lead's did and the missile was launched. However, it impacted the water about 50 ft to the right of the boat. The CF-18s were now at 'Bingo' fuel and the attacks were discontinued.

On 20 February, an air-to-

ground role was authorized for Canadian CF-18s. Combat air patrols to protect allied shipping continued. CAPs ranged between 12 and 24 hours per day, with both 15-minute and one-hour alerts maintained. Fully 20 per cent of all coalition fleet defense missions were flown by the 'Desert Cats'.

The authorization of air-to-ground missions meant that Canada was about to become involved in actual bombing missions for the first time in almost four decades. Half of the CF-18s were quickly reconfigured with the appropriate munitions airlifted to Qatar from Germany. During those three days, pilots who had completed the Fighter Weapons Instructors course worked with the others to refresh their skills for an orderly transition to the air-to-ground role. CF-18 pilots are dual-qualified, so the change was accomplished quickly.

The ground war began at 0400 on 24 February and the first Canadian time on target was met at

0900 that day. Because the coalition forces had established total air superiority, high altitude 'Vietnam-type' tactics were used. Attacks were carried out by rolling in from 30,000 ft to avoid anti-aircraft artillery and SAMs, and releasing the bombs above 15,000 ft in high-angle dives. This required VFR conditions, but clouds and smoke did not stop the attacks. In those circumstances, bombs were dropped from straight and level flight at 30,000 ft using the CF-18s' sophisticated systems. Radar acquisition and designation of targets enabled the mission computers to calculate the parameters and to automatically 'pickle' the bombs at the precise moment, "effectively turning dumb bombs into smart bombs," according to Colonel Lalonde.

Air-to-ground missions required a lengthy transit from Qatar to a refueling track southwest of Kuwait. Before crossing the border, they received updated information on the primary targets. It was not unusual for these to have already been overrun by coalition ground forces, resulting in reassignment to other targets, deeper in enemy territory.

CF-18s on air-to-ground missions still carried four air-to-air missiles and 500 rounds of 20-mm ammunition for self-protection. The bombing missions were typically flown in four-, eight-, or 12-ship packages and required no dedicated air-to-air escorts. Overall mission profiles were similar to the sweep missions, except that the CF-18s were dropping the bombs themselves. During 56 sorties over the course of three-and-a-half days, more than 100 tons of bombs were dropped by the 'Desert Cats'. Targets included artillery positions in southern Kuwait, Republican Guard positions, and vehicles and equipment retreating north from Kuwait City towards Al Basrah.

At 0200 on 30 January 1991, 'Hornet 13' flight was tasked to attack an Iraqi patrol boat. Designated as a TNC-45, the boat was capable of launching the Exocet missile. It also carried anti-aircraft guns.

The TNC-45 had been one of four Iraqi ships, three of which were attacked by A-6E Intruders until all ordnance was expended. The request was then made for a CAP aircraft to search for the fourth boat until another A-6 attack could be mounted. Soon after the CF-18s broke off their attacks, the Intruders returned. A 'seaworthiness kill' was awarded to the A-6s with an assist to the CF-18s. A suitable silhouette was painted on a CF-18.

J.R.-L.

from page 108 **(5 February continued)**

of the 48th TFW, led an experimental attack by a pair of F-111Fs on tanks and armored vehicles of the Republican Guard dug into the desert north of Kuwait. Examining Pave Tack videos taken from planes flying over these areas, officers in the wing's planning cell had noted that the disturbed areas of sand produced a distinctive infra-red signature and could easily be picked out. For the test each aircraft carried four GBU-12 500-lb laser-guided bombs, and the crews were to see if these weapons could be guided accurately enough onto the tanks to destroy them. On arriving over the enemy positions the pair began their task of destruction. Cruising at 14,000 ft, safely outside the reach of the AAA, the two crews delivered a series of deliberate attacks on the stationary targets. The mission was a complete success: seven tanks destroyed for an expenditure of eight GBU-12s. Video film, showing secondary explosions as fuel and ammunition in the vehicles exploded, testified to the accuracy of the claim. In the days to follow, the 48th was to shift almost the entire weight of its attack against this type of target.

The first B-52s arrived at Fairford, England, in preparation for attacks on Iraqi troop positions.

During the day a further 23 Iraqi combat aircraft flew into Iran. A US spokesman reported that 59 Iraqi aircraft had been destroyed on the ground during attacks on airfields, in addition to those previously claimed.

Coalition losses: one US Navy F/A-18 in action (pilot killed), and one US Army AH-1 Cobra (non-combat loss).

6 February, Wednesday The Iraqi government announced that it was severing diplomatic relations with the USA, Great Britain, France, Italy, Egypt and Saudi Arabia.

Poor weather restricted attacks in the battle area, but did not prevent B-52s from attacking Iraqi troop positions.

During a night attack, an F-117A demolished one span of the important Jumouriyah Bridge in the center of Baghdad. That brought the number of bridges dropped so far to 42.

Lieutenant Bill Hehemann, flying an F-15C of the 53rd TFS, 36th TFW, intercepted and shot down two Su-25 'Frogfoot' attack aircraft making for Iran, in each case using an AIM-9 missile. Another F-15C pilot of the same unit, Captain Thomas Dietz, shot down two MiG-21s that were also trying to escape to Iran.

In the afternoon Captain Bob Swain, flying an A-10 of the 706th TFS, 926th TFW, had dropped his bombs and fired his two Maverick missiles at Iraqi tanks. Then, as he later recounted, "As I was leaving the target, I noticed two black dots running across the desert that looked really different than anything I had seen before. They weren't putting up any dust and yet they were moving fast across the desert." They were helicopters, which Swain reported to the observation aircraft directing attacks in the area. The latter fired two smoke rounds into the desert to mark their location. Swain tried to engage one of the helicopters with an AIM-9 missile, but when it failed to acquire he attacked with his 30-mm gun. "Some of the bullets ran through him, but we weren't sure if it was stopped completely. So I came back with the final pass, hit it, and it fell apart. It was just in a bunch of little pieces."

Also on that day, an F-14A of VF-1 flown by Lieutenant Stuart Broce and the squadron commander Commander Ron McElraft, operating from USS *Ranger* in the Persian Gulf, shot down an Mi-8 'Hip' helicopter using an AIM-9 missile.

Elsewhere, an Alouette was destroyed on the ground, to bring the total of Iraqi aircraft destroyed during the day to four fighters and three helicopters.

By now the Iraqi air force had virtually abandoned any attempt to fly combat missions in defense of its homeland or against the coalition forces massing on its borders, and its surviving fixed-winged aircraft would play no further part in Desert Storm.

to page 120 **(6 February continued)**

Strike Eagle Missions
Captain Darrel Robertson and Captain Jay Greenbaum, 336th TFS, F-15E Strike Eagle

"In the beginning, the first four days of the war, I simply could not envision anybody having so much triple-A. I got real bad jitters, because I figured I might have had a 50/50 chance of surviving if this kept up. However, the absence of any air threat, and the countering of the Iraqi missile defenses, meant that we could move from low-level attacks to medium-level. When I planned my first passes, I pretty much pooh-poohed radar-guided AA. But when you go in there, the first thing that comes home is that it doesn't need to be aimed. If there's enough of it, and you have to fly through it, some of it is bound to connect. That first night, after the bombs went off, there was a solid wall about half a mile north of us, just cascading over the jet and underneath us. You're watching, mesmerized, you can't believe you're still there.

"There was one mission where I wasn't even over the Iraqi border when we began to see the triple-A. The target was 160 miles away, and it was non-stop all the way in, while we were dropping our bombs, and all the way out as far as the border. Of course it wasn't always like that. On pre-planned targets, you'd see us snaking in individually, maybe one or two tracers would come up from alert or nervous gunners. Then the airburst, and they'd all open fire. You'd get a pretty good feel for what was dangerous, like the light stuff that looked spectacular but couldn't get up to our altitude.

"There were three distinct missions for the F-15E. Strategic missions into Iraq, 'Scud'-busting in the west, or going into the Kuwait theater of operations to do the Republican Guard, its tanks and its artillery. Because of our FLIR and LANTIRN targeting pod, we could work in the dark as well as in daylight, so nine out of 10 of our missions were at night. Fatigue could have been a problem, operating against your natural biorhythms like that, but once you get used to it you function pretty normally.

"Because the F-15E has the most advanced systems in the Air Force, we ended up being catch-alls for different kinds of short-notice missions. If something came up that needed to be handled in a hurry, they preferred to give it to us. We've got a two-seat jet, we can set up or change the navigation or attack systems real easy, and we're accurate.

Right: Although there were two squadrons of F-15Es in the Gulf at the start of the war, there were only five laser-targetting pods available, so most of the Eagle force was restricted to 'dumb' bombs. Since the F-15E's most important task was 'Scud' hunting, laser targetting was unimportant, as the best way to deal with a 'Scud' launch unit is to drop a series of cluster-bombs around it.

"The 'Scud' missions were flown like that. We'd be up there hanging around, when AWACS would come up and say that they needed someone to go to this place right now. It got to be kind of frustrating. You'd be loitering over western Iraq, 'Scuds' were becoming harder and harder to find, and you didn't get a lot of feedback. You kind of wondered why nobody else was doing it. Of course, it was because no other jet could have been given a target in the air and have had any chance of finding it. Naturally, we had back-up targets in case we couldn't find the 'Scuds'.

Below: F-15E Eagles of the 4th TFW cover the ramp at Al Kharj. The F-15E is the most modern strike aircraft in the world, and the 48 aircraft of the 335th and 336th Tactical Fighter Squadrons made a major contribution to coalition strike power.

Above: The F-15E was developed from the superb F-15 fighter, and it retains all of the performance which made the Eagle the world's most effective air-superiority aircraft. To that has been added the ability to carry a phenomenal weapons load, which it can deliver day or night with pinpoint accuracy.

Below: Iraqi ammunition bunkers bear witness to the accuracy and effect of the F-15E's weapons. The attack Eagle's advanced navigation systems and multi-mode air-to-ground radar mean that it can make accurate blind attacks, and that's before considering that the aircraft also has FLIR sensors and can be equipped with LANTIRN all-weather navigation and targetting pods.

There was always something we could drop bombs on.

"We carried a bunch of different ordnance. In the beginning, when we thought the air-to-air threat was going to be higher, we carried two AIM-7s and six Rockeye cluster munitions or CBUs. Later it would be 12 CBUs or 12 Mk 82 500-pounders, or occasionally Mk 84 2,000-pounders, depending upon the target. It wasn't until later in the war that we got hold of laser targeting pods and could transition to GBU-12 laser-guided bombs. Up until then we'd have maybe five crews with pods, and we'd buddy-lase, with the designator marking targets for other aircraft. And it made you think. When you're trading one bomb for one target, and you see 14 tanks destroyed with 14 hits, you know that without a doubt you are seriously kicking some butt.

"I only flew two daylight missions, but I got shot at by a heat-seeking SAM during one of them. We had flown over it, and he fired as we turned. I looked back and could see this thing coming up at me, smoking like crazy, and I could see the red of the exhaust. The smoke trail started from right on the ground, so I could see exactly where it had come from. As I turned, it turned with me. I remember thinking, 'Ah, there's a missile, it's coming up at me, I guess I'd better do something.' So I did, automatically like I'd been trained to do. My wing tanks came off, although I don't remember punching the button. I turned into the missile, and we punched out chaff and flares. The missile passed beneath us and exploded about 1,000 ft away. That was kind of interesting."

Above: When a supply of targetting pods arrived late in the war, the F-15E's took part in the most precise of bombing raids: dropping Iraqi bridges.

Proven Force

At 1:50 a.m. on 18 January 1991, 28 USAF F-111Es, F-16Cs and F-15C aircraft disappeared into the night sky above Incirlik Air Base. The Turkish Foreign Ministry at first announced that the aircraft were on a 'night training mission', but when they returned three hours later with their bomb racks empty the world knew the USAF had opened its 'second front' against Saddam Hussein.

Over the next 42 days the 120 USAF aircraft based at Incirlik were to fly some 4,600 sorties, inflicting heavy damage on key targets in northern Iraq. 'Proven Force', as the deployment of US Air Forces in Europe (USAFE) assets to Turkey was codenamed, enabled the anti-Iraq coalition forces to strike at targets out of range of aircraft based in Saudi Arabia, and denied Saddam a safe sanctuary for his forces in the northern third of Iraq.

Planning for the 'second front' began a few days after the Iraqi invasion of Kuwait in August 1990, with USAFE staff officers at Spangdahlem Air Base, in Germany, starting top-secret studies to lay the ground for the movement of over 100 combat aircraft to Turkey from bases in Germany, Britain, Holland and Spain.

By chance, a detachment of around 20 F-111Es from the 77th Tactical Fighter Squadron (TFS), 20th Tactical Fighter Wing (TFW) was taking part in a routine weapons training at Incirlik when the Gulf crisis erupted. The Upper Heyford strike aircraft remained in Turkey and were soon reinforced by 24 F-16 Fighting Falcons of the 612th TFS from the 401st TFW at Torrejon, Spain. Incirlik had been constructed as a NATO reinforcement base during the height of the Cold War, with hardened aircraft shelters, ammunition bunkers, fuel tanks and command facilities. It also has a fuel pipeline to the nearby port of Iskindern. While Incirlik was nominally under Turkish command, the USAF's 39th Tactical Group administered the base and ran its infrastructure.

By early January USAFE's plans were at an advanced stage and US Secretary of State James Baker visited Turkish President Turgut Ozal to get final approval for US air strikes to be launched from Incirlik. Ozal gave his permission but it was not until the Turkish parliament gave its President war powers on 17 January that 'Desert Storm North' could begin in earnest.

When the first air strike took off from Incirlik in the early hours of 18 January the number of aircraft at the base had more than doubled from the 40 or so that had been present five months earlier. Some 30 F-15C Eagles from the 525th TFS, 36th TFW, and the 32nd Tactical Fighter Group (TFG) flew in from Bitburg, Germany, and Soesterberg, Holland, respectively. Five EF-111A Ravens from Upper Heyford's 42nd Electronic Countermeasures Squadron (ECS), three E-3B/Cs AWACS of the 552nd Airborne Command & Control Wing and a similiar number of EC-130H Compass Call jamming aircraft of the 43rd ECS from Sembach, Germany, provided comprehensive electronic warfare support. Two dozen F-16C 'Wild Weasel' and F-4G Phantom IIs from the 52nd TFW at Spangdahlem were also deployed, along with a handful of 26th Tactical Reconnaissance Wing RF-4Cs from Zweibrücken for photo recon work. A dozen KC-135A tankers from the 96th Bomb Wing completed the USAF contingent at Incirlik. Accommodation for the extra ground and air crews was provided in a giant tent city, called Tornado Town, built from scratch by a USAF 'Prime Beef' civil engineering team.

To provide combat search and rescue, five MH-53Js of the 21st Special Operations Squadron (SOS) and four HC-130P/Ns of the 67th SOS, both home-based at Woodbridge, Suffolk, took up residence at Batman Air Base, 150 miles from the Turkish/Iraqi border. Anti-aircraft and anti-ballistic missile defense at Incirlik was provided by US Army Patriot missiles from the 4th Battalion, 7th Air Defense Artillery. Other US Army Patriots were based at Batman and Royal Netherlands Air Force Patriot batteries were temporarily deployed to protect Diyarbakir Air Base. Early warning information on Iraqi 'Scud' launches was provided by the US-manned radar station at Pirinclik, near Diyarbakir. At the request of the Turkish government, air elements of NATO's ACE Mobile Force were dispatched to eastern Turkey in January. The German, Belgian and Italian aircraft involved in this deployment played no part in the US air offensive against Iraq.

USAFE's Inspector General, Brigadier General Lee A. Downer, was appointed commander of US air forces in Turkey for the duration of the Gulf war. To fully integrate the different types of aircraft at Incirlik into one command structure, the 7440th Composite Wing (Provisional) was formed at the base. Although still in the US European Command's Area of Responsibility (AOR) the wing received its orders from Central Command in Saudi Arabia,

F-16 Fighting Falcons taxi out of Incirlik's hardened shelters and move towards the active runway, as an F-15C from Bitburg's 36th TFW returns after completing a combat air patrol sortie from this major air base in Turkey.

Above: Patriot missiles are ready for action near a camouflaged control facility at Incirlik air base, as an F-16C Fighting Falcon lands. US aircraft attached to the 7440th Composite Wing mounted some 4,600 sorties from Incirlik during the war, hitting numerous targets in northern Iraq that lay out of reach of Saudi-based aircraft.

Left: Like Saudi-based units, those that flew from Incirlik in Turkey needed inflight-refueling support in order to complete their missions. Here, a boom operator aboard a KC-135A Stratotanker lies recumbent as he 'flies' the boom into the receptacle of a receiving aircraft.

Above: With an AGM-88A HARM under its wing, an F-4G 'Wild Weasel' Phantom tops off its tanks from a KC-135 Stratotanker before moving into hostile airspace and taking on Iraq's SAM radar sites. SEAD was of vital importance if coalition air losses were to be minimized.

and was fully integrated into its daily air tasking order. The benefits of combining the 120 aircraft, 450 aircrews and 2,000 ground crew deployed to Incirlik into a single wing were demonstrated even before the first air strike was launched from the base.

General Downer only received final clearance for the first attack just two hours before the strike aircraft were due to lift off. He summoned his aircrew to the base briefing room and told them they were going to war. "Things became quiet, people focused, sensing the tension of potential

combat," he said. "I told them they had more training than any troops for previous wars and they were ready."

For the next 42 days and nights strike packages were launched from Incirlik against a wide range of targets in the northern third of Iraq, southward to around the city of Tikrit. Airfields, command posts, chemical weapons sites, nuclear facilities, surface-to-air missile and anti-aircraft artillery positions, troop concentrations and communications posts were all visited by the 7440th's aircraft. Its RF-4Cs, E-3 AWACS and

EC-130Hs also scoured northern Iraq for 'Scud' missile launchers but none were found. The Compass Call Hercs used their electronic countermeasures equipment to try to detect the weather radars associated with 'Scud' missiles.

During daylight hours two strike packages were launched from Incirlik and one night raid was mounted. Around 55 aircraft were grouped into a typical day-strike package under the control of an E-3 AWACS. The main bomber component was made up of 20 F-16s armed with 500-lb or 1,000-lb bombs. Eight F-4G 'Wild Weasels'

were attached to take out Iraqi radars with AGM-88 HARM or AGM-45A Shrike missiles and a similar number of F-15s flew top cover. Three EF-111As and EC-130Hs also accompanied the strike packages to jam radars. Smaller-sized strike packages were launched at night – usually about 40 aircraft – with 12 F-111Es as the main attack component. Eight F-16Cs reconfigured as 'Wild Weasels' with HARMs or Shrikes joined these nocturnal forays instead of the F-4Gs.

On the first night of the war F-111Es made their attacks from only 200 ft, but intense AAA soon forced them up to 25,000 ft. Upper Heyford's Aardvarks lacked the Pave Tack laser-guidance system of the F-111F so the 20th TFW pilots at Incirlik had to rely on radar for accurate night bombing. F-111E pilots, however, joked that the Iraqi AAA was so bright that they could almost read their maps by it.

The Iraqi air force put up no resistance to the 7440th's strike packages and any enemy aircraft that took to the air during the American forays into Iraqi airspace were soon dealt with by high-flying Eagles. AWACS support enabled Iraqi planes to be tracked as soon as they took off and F-15 combat air patrols to be vectored to intercept them. A total of three Iraqi fixed-wing aircraft and two helicopters were shot down by the 7440th's Eagles. Two Mirage F1s were claimed by the 36th TFW on 19 January, a MiG-23 fell to the 32nd TFG on 29 January and the two helicopters were hit by the 36th TFW on 11 February. All kills were made with AIM-7 Sparrows.

During the second week of the war, the Iraqi fighters at Kirkuk fled to Iran in line with their air force's policy of getting out of harm's way. Unfortunately, Proven Force did not have enough aircraft to mount continous CAPs along the Iran/Iraq border so the Kirkuk aircraft were able to escape unmolested.

None of the 7440th's aircraft was lost over Iraq during the war, although an F-16C of the 401st had to make an emergency diversion to Diyarbakir. On the final approach the Falcon suffered an engine failure but the pilot successfully ejected.

With no USAF aircraft being shot down over northern Iraq the Special Operations units at Batman were not called upon to perform in this role, but some reports suggest their MH-53Js and MC-130s were used to insert British and American special forces troops into northern Iraq to encourage Kurdish rebels and to collect intelligence on Iraqi forces.

T.R.

from page 116 (**6 February continued**)

One US Army UH-1 Huey helicopter was lost (non-combat loss). The Commander of French Forces stated that the allied air strikes had reduced the effectiveness of the Republican Guard units in the Kuwait area by 30 per cent.

7 February, Thursday In the battle area, poor weather again restricted air attacks.

Royal Air Force Tornados, operating with Buccaneers to provide laser designation of targets, attacked Iraqi bridges.

Two F-15Cs of the 58th TFS, 33rd TFW, shot down three Iraqi aircraft, thought to be Sukhoi Su-22 'Fitters', attempting to fly to Iran. The successful pilots were Colonel Rick Parsons and Captain Anthony Murphy, and in each case the aircraft were shot down using AIM-7 missiles. These were to be the last Iraqi fixed-wing aircraft to be shot down in air-to-air combat before the cease-fire three weeks later. Also on that day, an F-15C of the 36th TFW destroyed an Iraqi helicopter with an AIM-7 missile. A further seven Iraqi aircraft flew to Iran.

8 February, Friday One 'Scud' missile was fired at Saudi Arabia, causing no casualties.

Attacks by coalition aircraft continued, concentrating on Iraqi troop positions in the Kuwait theater of operations, and against bridges and hardened aircraft shelters at airfields. As part of these operations, Royal Air Force Tornados, supported by laser marking Buccaneers, attacked three bridges and an oil refinery.

US Navy A-6s and a Royal Navy Lynx helicopter took part in a combined engagement which led to the destruction of two Iraqi patrol boats.

A British government spokesman announced that the half-squadron of Buccaneer laser-designator aircraft already in Saudi Arabia had been increased to a full squadron. Also, two Tornados had arrived at Tabuk fitted with TIALD (Thermal Imaging And Laser Designation), equipment still at the experimental stage which would provide a night laser-designation capability for the RAF bombers.

9 February, Saturday One 'Scud' missile was fired at Israel, causing no casualties.

The air attacks on Iraqi troop positions and supply lines continued. B-52s went into action for the first time from the airfield at Fairford in Gloucestershire, UK.

Three more Iraqi planes flew to Iran.

A Marine AV-8B of VMA-231 was lost over Kuwait, the first allied aircraft shot down for four days. The pilot was taken prisoner.

to page 123

A Royal Air Force Hercules C.Mk 3P trucks around the clock at Bahrain.

RAF Transport Effort

Often overlooked in any war, the transport elements of the coalition air arms played an enormous part in keeping the wheels of war greased smoothly. The air bridge between the Gulf and the West was manned by a huge fleet of large transports bringing men and matériel into the war zone to key points such as Riyadh and Dhahran. In order to move the loads from there to where they were needed, the allies established a classic 'hub and spoke' operation.

British and French tactical transports were moved in-theater to support this operation, both forces being based at King Khalid International Airport at Riyadh. The Royal Air Force formed its Air Transport Detachment at the base on 30 October 1990, with three aircraft and personnel from the Lyneham Transport Wing. Its force was augmented by two Royal New Zealand Air Force C-130Hs (with three crew) on 23 December, these aircraft coming from No. 40 Squadron at Whenupai. More RAF Hercs arrived to swell the force to nine aircraft in total, in preparation for the land war.

A task which was envisaged for the ATD was casualty evacuation, but in the event there was thankfully little need for this operation. Instead, the Hercules were used to move warloads into and out of the war zone, often using desert strips to support the British troops as they moved forward. Loads arrived from the United Kingdom or Germany on the RAF's strategic transport force of VC10s and TriStars, and in Lyneham-based Hercules. The ATD was then tasked to take it to its destination, allowing the other transports to depart home for more. Apart from the desert strips, the Hercules were regular visitors at the RAF's bases at Tabuk, Muharraq, Dhahran and Seeb.

Flying into desert strips precluded the use of the stretched Hercules C.Mk 3, the rear fuselage not providing enough ground clearance for rough-field operations. In deference to the rough strips, the ATD aircraft were flown in 'strip preparation' configuration, which entailed low tire pressures, pumped-up oleos and black rubber underseal protection for the bottom of the fuselage and the aerials. Internally the holds were stripped of most seating so that the Hercules could accommodate any load at very short notice.

After the liberation of Kuwait

Right: With its landing gear down and locked, the RAF's only desert-pink camouflaged Hercules banks gently to port as it approaches a landing strip somewhere in the wastes of the desert. This aircraft, from No. 47 Squadron, supplied outlying British units deep in the war zone.

Above: Score marks on the desert reveal that this strip has been a scene of considerable activity by allied airlifters. Such terrain is hard on aircraft: all RAF Hercules were fitted with black rubber underseals to protect them from stone chip damage.

City, the RAF Hercules began operations into the International Airport, and when the cease-fire came into effect the whole 'hub and spoke' operation began in reverse, ferrying men and equipment back to Riyadh where other transports took them back home. The New Zealanders went home in the beginning of April, and Riyadh operations closed down on 14 April. The ATD moved to Bahrain International Airport, from where it continued to operate scheduled services to the major British enclaves in the area: Dubai, Riyadh, Seeb, Al Jubail and Kuwait. By late April, the detachment was down to just two aircraft, although the use of proper airfields allowed a C.Mk 3 to be used.

The Royal Air Force Air Transport Detachment operation was closely mirrored by that established by the French. Also

Above: New Zealand's contribution to the anti-Saddam coalition was a detachment of No. 40 Sqn C-130H Hercules. Operating out of King Khalid International Airport, they flew regular shuttle missions between Saudi Arabia and RAF Lyneham, UK.

Right: The Lockheed TriStar was a particularly useful type for the RAF airlift task. Its impressive load-carrying ability was put to the best possible use, with mixed load operation being a feature of both the build-up and withdrawal phases of Gulf activity.

Above: VC10s from No. 10 Squadron bore much of the burden of maintaining the air bridge to and from bases in the Gulf region, and scarcely a day went by without Brize Norton witnessing several movements. Minimal turnaround times and high utilization taxed the RAF's modest airlift fleet close to the breaking point at times.

based at King Khalid IAP, Riyadh, the French employed seven Transall C.160s from Escadre de transport 61 at Orléans and ET 64 at Evreux to ferry loads that had arrived from France aboard Hercules, DC-8s and other transports. Once again these aircraft supported French troops in the field, as well as the main air base at Al Ahsa.

The intra-theater support network set up by the Americans was huge, but it too used the same principle, using the redoubtable Hercules to move on cargo that had arrived in-theater on Lockheed C-141 StarLifters and C-5 Galaxies, or in civilian aircraft. Together, the efforts of the in-theater transport units meant that the land, sea and air forces were probably the best-equipped and best-supplied army to have ever gone to war.

D.D.

Right: A permanent detachment of RAF Hercules transport aircraft was a vital feature of in-theater operations, these performing 'hub and spoke' services from the main terminals like Riyadh to outlying facilities such as those located at Tabuk and Seeb. Since it was sometimes necessary to fly close to the front line, a fair amount of time was spent at low level in order to minimize the threat from enemy air and ground forces, which might have been operating in the areas through which the Hercules most commonly passed.

PREPARING THE BATTLEFIELD

10 to 23 February 1991

By now the systematic and destructive attacks on Iraqi forward positions, supply depots and routes used to carry supplies to the front line were at an advanced stage and were continuing.

A major fear for coalition military commanders at this time was that when the ground offensive began, the Iraqi air force might launch its remaining aircraft in one huge kamikaze-style attack on allied troop positions, with some of the aircraft loaded with chemical weapons. To reduce the chances of such an attack succeeding, coalition aircraft resumed the attack on the runways at airfields in the east of Iraq, using LGBs dropped from medium altitude to crater them.

Meanwhile, unobserved by Iraqi reconnaissance aircraft, the huge force of US, British and French armored units that were to carry through the powerful outflanking movement around the west of the Iraqi defensive line began their move to jumping-off positions in remote areas of desert well to the west of the Saudi-Kuwait border.

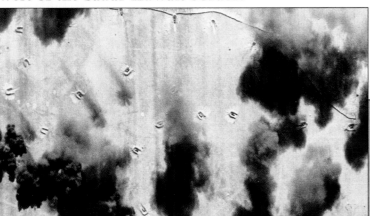

Left: Explosions erupt around the dug-in units of Iraq's Republican Guard as they come under air attack. The Guard were Saddam's most trustworthy and best-equipped troops, which made them primary targets for coalition air power.

Below left, inset: General Colin Powell, Chairman of the US Joint Chiefs of Staff, explains the roots of coalition strategy. It was a simple plan: "We're going to cut them off, and then we're going to kill them."

10 February, Sunday Air attacks on Iraqi troop positions and supply lines continued, with 2,800 sorties flown over Iraq and Kuwait.

That night, Royal Air Force Tornados went into action for the first time with TIALD, the new laser-designator equipment, to mark an armament factory in Iraq for attack by other Tornados. Tornados also attacked hardened aircraft shelters at airfields, and four bridges (two of them pontoon bridges built to reopen supply routes to Kuwait).

French fighter-bombers attacked bridges in Iraq and artillery batteries in Kuwait.

11 February, Monday A 'Scud' missile was launched at Saudi Arabia, and another against Israel, causing no casualties. US Air Force F-15Es destroyed four mobile 'Scud' launchers, three in the west used to attack Israel and one in the south used to attack Saudi Arabia.

Early that morning the Lynx helicopter from HMS *Cardiff* located and attacked an Iraqi patrol craft off Faylaka Island, and damaged it using Sea Skua missiles. Later the vessel was finished off by US Navy A-6 aircraft.

F-15Cs of the 36th TFW destroyed two Iraqi helicopters, in each case with AIM-7 missiles.

12 February, Tuesday During the 24-hour period, some 900 sorties were flown by coalition aircraft, mainly against Iraqi ground forces in the Kuwait area and against bridges in the rear areas. The F-111Fs continued their systematic attack with LGBs on dug-in tanks and armored vehicles.

Royal Air Force Jaguars and Tornados attacked Iraqi pontoon bridges erected to replace bridges on important supply routes.

13 February, Wednesday During a night attack by F-117As on targets in Baghdad, two laser-guided bombs penetrated the roof of a large concrete bunker which was thought to be a command facility, and exploded inside. Whatever its military uses, the structure also served as a shelter and that night it housed a large number of civilians. More than 300 people were killed or wounded, which caused an international outcry as television pictures were shown of dead women and children being removed from the building.

The attacks on Iraqi troop positions and supply routes continued.

During the day a force of Royal Air Force Tornados, with Buccaneers to provide laser marking for the LGBs, attacked the road and rail bridges over the River Euphrates at Fallujah and caused spans to drop. One bomb failed to guide properly, however, and it came down near the center of the city, causing several civilian casualties. Following an Iraqi government outcry that the city had been deliberately targeted, a Royal Air Force spokesman admitted the error.

During attacks on airfields in Iraq and Kuwait, four transport aircraft and a Super Frelon helicopter were destroyed on the ground.

The F-111Fs of the 48th TFW continued their attack on Iraqi vehicles dug in and dispersed over wide areas of desert in the battle areas, and achieved their greatest success of the war. In the course of a full wing operation with 46 aircraft each laden with four GBU-12 laser-guided bombs, they scored hits on a total of 132 tanks and armored vehicles. It was a remarkable demonstration of the effectiveness of LGBs in action, representing a 71-per cent hit rate under operational conditions. The wing was the most successful single coalition unit against dug-in tanks and armored vehicles, and by the end of the conflict it would be credited with the destruction of 920 (about one in seven of the tanks and armored vehicles destroyed by all arms of the coalition).

In a typical airfield attack of this period, shortly before midnight four Royal Air Force Tornados of the Tabuk Detachment dropped 1,000-lb LGBs on the aircraft shelters at Al Taqaddum, from altitudes of around 23,000 ft. Two TIALD Tornados provided laser marking for the bombs. Supporting the attack were two Tornados carrying ALARM, two F-15s and three EF-111As.

A Royal Saudi Air Force F-5E fighter failed to return from a bombing raid on Iraq.

14 February, Thursday Four 'Scud' missiles were launched against Saudi Arabia. According to press reports these were of the Al Abbas type, an Iraqi modified version of the 'Scud B' with larger propellant tanks to give a maximum range of about 485 nm (900 km). It is believed the missiles were fired from a point near Fallujah, in central Iraq. The missiles all landed on desert areas of Saudi Arabia, where they caused no casualties or damage.

US Marine AV-8Bs began dropping 500-lb napalm bombs to ignite the oil trench barriers that formed part of the Iraqi fortification system.

During a medium-altitude daylight attack on Al Taqaddum airfield, by Tornado GR.Mk 1s with Buccaneers providing laser marking, one of the GR.Mk 1s was shot down by a SAM. It was the first Tornado loss for more than three weeks. The aircraft was engaged by two SA-2s, believed to have been guided optically. Flight Lieutenant Rupert Clark, the pilot, later stated, "The first one got us as we were trying to evade and then the second one also hit. The whole cockpit was shattered, wrecked. The instruments were gone, as were both

Main picture: A Boeing B-52 claws into the air from the snowy runway of RAF Fairford, in England. B-52s hammered the Republican Guard, shattering morale as much as destroying men and equipment.

Inset: Although many coalition aircraft were switched to softening up the Iraqi army, hardened targets like aircraft shelters and command bunkers continued to be hit hard.

to page 148 **(14 February continued)**

Falcons on Guard

Left: F-16A Fighting Falcons from Air National Guard units in South Carolina and New York were flown to Saudi Arabia barely two weeks before Desert Storm hostilities got under way. Despite flying the oldest version of the F-16, they drew some tough missions and more than justified their presence.

Major Keith 'Kubla' Coln, Captain John 'Smiley' Sizemore and Major Dick 'Disco' Naumann, 157th TFS, SC ANG, F-16 Falcon

Left, above left and above: South Carolina's 157th Tactical Fighter Squadron reckoned it had a good claim to go to Saudi Arabia, since it was the first ANG unit to pick up the F-16 and had done well in USAF competitions and exercises. The outfit got its wish, moving to the Gulf just a couple of days before the end of 1990. It was among the first units in battle when Desert Storm kicked off in earnest in mid-January 1991.

"It wasn't but a couple of weeks after the Iraqi invasion that the President started talking about using the Reserves and the Guard. We began to politic a bit, because we didn't want any other Guard squadron involved unless we were. We were the first Guard or Reserve squadron to get the F-16, we won the Gunsmoke competition in 1989, so we're the reigning world's champions. Plus, the guys in the squadron are always very patriotic and very motivated, so we really wanted to be involved.

"It worked. We kind of knew we were going, but there was some kind of tension in home life, a kind of emotional roller coaster. It was a relief once we knew for certain. We were activated on Christmas Day, and we left McEntire on 29 December.

"Anybody tells you they weren't just a little bit frightened is lying, because you don't take off on something like this, fly for 13½ hours, knowing you're going somewhere strange and possibly hostile, without feeling some concern.

"We left around 3:30 in the afternoon of 29 December, and arrived in Saudi Arabia about 13½ hours later. Or 15½ hours if you were in Sparky's cell. Their tanker broke, and they could only get a little bit of gas at a time. They got a spare tanker launched out of Spain, so they didn't have to abort, but it took them about 15½ hours. It's a long time to be in a single-seat aircraft.

"We were deployed to a base near Al Kharj. The wing was the 4th TFW (Provisional), and included our squadron, the New York ANG, two squadrons of Strike Eagles, a squadron of F-15Cs from Bitburg, and some C-130s.

"Everything was temporary, all tents. Every night it seemed like something new was going up. They're building the early warning HQ for the Saudi air force there so it had a long concrete runway and plenty of concrete ramps, but not much else.

"When we got there it was a little bit surprising to learn that the wing commander was not expecting us for another couple of days. But there we were. It took a while for us to get our gear together down on the flight line. We were trucked up to a bunch of 10-man tents. We walked inside, and there was absolutely nothing inside except for a stack of boxed furniture. We cut open the boxes and started assembling it with our Swiss Army knives, because they were the beds we were going to sleep on that night.

"The next day we finished assembling our living quarters, doing a little scrounging around

the base to pick up supplies. Our master carpenter was stolen first thing in the morning. They took him down the flight line to build the squadron. It was the same thing, a big tent with no insides. Our man went to work building the place from the ground up. We joined him the day after. We put in the floor, built all of the briefing rooms, life support, operations area, duty desk, intelligence. We covered walkways, we built the whole thing. We didn't know how long we were going to be there, so we made it as comfortable as possible with what we had."

Bombing with the F-16

"They divided the whole of the theater into kill boxes. Each was 30 by 30 miles, and each box was given a designator. They'd give you a target in that kill box. If you couldn't find it or if it had already been hit, you'd be clear to drop on any other target within the box.

"That's the way we started working after our defense-suppression missions, right up until the start of the ground war. The basic tactics involved bombing from high altitude. The biggest problem was finding the targets. We were flying the oldest F-16s out there, and our inertial navigation system is not all that accurate. In the 'A' model you're doing well if you get to within two miles of a given set of co-ordinates.

"You couldn't pinpoint the aim point exactly. Once you got there, you'd look around. You'd see something, and ask yourself, 'Is it this one? Is it that one?' You didn't want to sit up there and orbit, at least in the early days, so you made a snap decision and dropped your ordnance and hoped that it was right. As the war went on and the threat began to drop, we'd go down to lower altitudes and in many cases make multiple passes.

"You can imagine the difficulty. From 20,000 ft, looking down the track to find an individual vehicle with the unaided eyeball is almost impossible. Every now and then you'd catch a reflection off a windshield, and you'd try to lock on to that because you'd be 99 per cent certain that that was a good target. They were usually

Above: Saudi Arabia is about as far removed from McEntire ANGB as it's possible to get, but Guard pilots made the 14-hour deployment without much difficulty, refueling several times on the way.

camouflaged: anything obvious was likely to be a dummy. Sometimes we'd bomb those, depending on what else we saw. There were many, many targets up there. Some looked empty, but after you'd dropped bombs on them you'd see this big column of black smoke and there would be secondary explosions. Others you'd drop bombs on and get nothing.

"About a week before the ground war started we began to work with fast Forward Air Controllers, Pointer FACs we called them, from their 'Pointer' call sign. These were basically a pair of F-16s which would orbit over a kill box, one looking for targets with binoculars while the other kind of cleared his path.

"Once they found the targets, they'd brief us on the locations. They'd give us the target, and we'd go up there. The FAC would go in, marking the target with cluster-bombs or six Mk 82 500-pounders, then we'd go in to find the target he'd marked. Four out of five times we'd be carrying Mk 84 2,000-pounders. For a while, early in the war, we carried CBU-87 Tactical Munition Dispensers, which were highly effective, but all of a sudden they took them away from us and gave us some older CBUs left over from the Vietnam era. The Mk 82s and Mk 84s were our best bombs, but the old CBUs didn't work too well.

"One day, a Pointer called us in on an ammo dump. He was going to mark for us, then called up and said he didn't have to, because he'd had a flight in there before, and secondaries were already going off. There were 20 bunkers burning when we arrived, so we just rolled in and started hitting those.

"The best things to blow up were the oil stores. Big white storage tanks. I was bombing some Republican Guard positions close to an airfield, and seeing those big white storage tanks I remember thinking, 'Boy, that sure would be a good target.' I came back the next day, but they were already burning. Somebody had got to them before we did.

"On another occasion, a Pointer called us in to hit some triple-A sites above a disused storage compound. He marked it with a CBU. When the cluster-bomb went off, there were little speckles everywhere. At first I figured the CBU had gone haywire, because these speckles started lighting up all down the road, along a regular housing neighbourhood maybe five miles long and about a mile wide. What we were actually seeing was the Iraqis firing at us. Normally

Above: A bomb-laden F-16C of the 363rd Tactical Fighter Wing waits with engine running for the order to move out towards the runway. The crew chief stands in the pilot's line of sight, ready to direct his aircraft from its parking spot.

Left: Shark-mouth graffiti adorns a 2,000-lb bomb suspended beneath the wing of an F-16 as it awaits the call to battle.

Falcons on Guard

you don't see triple-A during the daytime, but this was about five in the evening, the sun was going down behind some cloud, and it was kind of dark on the ground. They had anti-aircraft guns on the flat roofs of the houses, and the whole place was lit up.

"That was the day we were going for the bridge. One of the spans had been damaged by an LGB in an earlier raid. The FAC asked us what kind of ordnance we had. We told him we had Mk 84s. He told us to come up and give the bridge a shot. Well, we hit it, but I think the bombs went off on the superstructure, knocking a hole in it without dropping the span. Five or six vehicles crossing were destroyed. It hammered home the realities of war, seeing those vehicles turn into balls of flame in front of your eyes.

"All in all, I thought we did very well in the Gulf. Obviously there are some limitations when you're operating F-16s. It would have been nice to have had the precision-guided munitions available to the Strike Eagles, because from 20,000 ft or more it is just hard to see targets when the only sensor you've got is the human eye. We

didn't do too badly though. The problem was damage assessment. The only record you have in the F-16A is your HUD camera, and that's designed for air-to-air use. There is no way of proving that you have killed the target that you've just dropped on. Not like the F-15Es and F-117s, which have those targetting pods that keep onto the target until the bomb hits.

"We could claim we hit what we aimed at, but the kill was not confirmed unless there was a picture of a burning tank or a wrecked convoy. You'd come back and report what target you went against, and how effective you think you were. Pilots might exaggerate their success, since that's human nature, but intelligence people think that all fighter pilots lie. If we claimed eight tanks destroyed, they would cut that to five and pass it up channels, where the figure would be cut more, and the pilot's original report would get lost.

"That's why, as far as the Air Force was concerned, we were not too effective. But there were 300 F-16s over there, more than any other type. I guess we must have done something right."

Above: Munitions specialists show no sign of nerves as they clamber over a trailer-load of bombs that are destined for delivery against targets in Iraq and Kuwait. With the A-10A Thunderbolt, the F-16 was the most numerous of the allied warplanes in the Gulf; it also suffered more losses than most other types, five falling to combat-related causes during the 42 days of war.

Below: Two New York ANG Fighting Falcons lead a four-ship formation out of a dispersal area towards the runway at the start of another bombing raid. The New York F-16As were equipped with the belly-mounted GPU-5/A Pave Claw 30-mm cannon, but mixed results due to software problems meant that they only used it in combat for one day.

Above: The F-16 is the most numerous aircraft type in the USAF's inventory, so it is natural that Falcons in the Gulf should have come from a variety of units. These cluster-munition-armed F-16Cs are Tactical Air Command aircraft, from the 388th TFW at Hill AFB, Utah.

Right: A ground crewman gets busy with a brace as the magazine of a M61A1 Vulcan 20-mm gun is hastily replenished between sorties. Many pilots squeezed off a 20-mm cannon burst as they pulled off a target after bomb release.

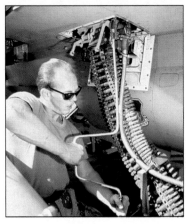

Falcon Art

F-16 nose art varied in quality from the sublime to the downright bizarre, as this small selection shows. Sadly, much of the artwork was deleted before units returned to the USA and it seems very unlikely that all of it was recorded on film for posterity.

Falcon versus SAM

"We went up to CENTAF, the Central Airforces HQ in Riyadh. We were trying to find out what our first mission was going to be. It was a very fancy place, the headquarters for the Saudi Arabian air force. Marble entrance, marble columns, lush gardens, very ornate. I thought that these guys had it pretty good. They got to live up here in the city, eating hamburgers and everything. Then, when we found them, they were down in the basement, with exposed wiring and leaky pipes all over the place. They'd just come in from four months in tents, so maybe they didn't have it so good after all.

"We found the gentleman who was planning our mission in an area called the 'Black Hole'. This was where they did all the targetting. We were a little concerned; the area they had us going into was one of the most heavily defended pieces of real estate in the whole theater. They used little colored stick pins denoting SAM sites and artillery sites. Well, that first-day target had so many pins in it that you couldn't have gotten another one onto the map. We had been tasked with taking out five SAM sites with 16 airplanes. We wanted four ships per site, so we asked if we could fly 20, which was OK.

"Our task was SEAD (Suppression of Enemy Air Defenses). We were supposed to suppress these SAM sites for a follow-on package 20 minutes behind us – F-16s, British Tornados and French Jaguars. The SAM sites were arrayed around Kuwait City, El Salimiyah airfield, Kuwait International and Al Ahmedi Al Jabbar.

"The next day, back in our tents at Al Kharj, we got the word that the war was to start that night. At the same time CENTAF called and doubled the number of SAM sites we were assigned from five to 10. This spread our force pretty thin, but we said we'd do it. In any case, most of the sites were due to be hit by 'Wild Weasels' and cruise missiles that night, and the guy from CENTAF said that we might well find our targets were just smoking holes in the ground when we got there.

"We planned the mission late into the night, getting to our tents for some sleep at about 11:00 p.m. We were woken an hour later as two squadrons of Strike Eagles took off. We'd heard them before, of course, but this time was different, because we knew that they were going to war.

"Up early, and down to the squadron for the latest intelligence briefing. We were into our aircraft, engines running, at first light, so we could be over the target at about 0800 local. Our IP was over the southwest corner of Kuwait, about an hour's easy cruise away. From that point, we split into our attack elements to head for individual targets.

"As we came across the border, everything seemed quiet. We were carrying 2,000-lb Mk 84s, equipped with radar fuzes designed to detonate the ordnance about 15 ft off the ground. It spreads frags out in all directions, and deals real well with SAM sites. We couldn't see a whole lot, since we were above the clouds. There were holes every now and then, but you couldn't really make out what was down there. I thought that maybe the planning guys were right.

"Right about the time I was thinking that, all hell broke loose. We started getting triple-A fire and many, many SAM launch indications, both visually and on sensors. Everybody was talking on the radio at once, but we proceeded to our targets. Some guys couldn't get to theirs, because of the cloud cover or the SAM defenses: they came back and dropped on El Salimiyah.

"We had one pilot up at Kuwait City who dodged one SAM, and as he rolled back to acquire his flight leader he saw another flash by close enough for him to see that the wings were camouflaged. Fortunately it was clear above his airplane before it exploded.

"Everyone delivered their ordnance, then headed back to the IP. Counting heads over the radio, we had all made it, which seemed a miracle because the SAM fire was so thick. Looking back to where we had just been the sky was like spaghetti from the smoke trails of all the missiles.

"I feel pretty relaxed about it now, and in the thick of it you didn't have time to be scared, but when I got back to the ground alive I guess it was one of the two happiest days of my life. Our squadron commander parked his airplane next to mine, then came over and shook hands. He told me that he'd ranked the mission as one of the five most exciting he'd ever flown, and this from a guy who'd been on maybe 240 combat missions in Southeast Asia.

"We were supposed to have been the third people to visit this area, but looking at the way they threw things at us we were the first airplanes into that sector of sky since the war started. We'd convinced ourselves it would be like a walk in the park. What we didn't know was that it was going to be a walk in Central Park at midnight.

"After debriefing and looking at all of our HUD films, we reckoned that we'd seen about 50 SAMs visually, and we'd had electronic indication of twice that many launches. There was some triple-A, but since we were ingressing at 25,000 ft and bottoming out of our bomb delivery dive at 15,000 ft, we were way above the envelope of the light stuff, we didn't pay much attention to it. Of course, at low level, that would have been different.

"At CENTAF, we'd met some of the French Jaguar pilots who followed us. They'd told us they were going to go in at low level. We didn't figure that was such a good idea, as the area was heavily defended with triple-A. They just said that that was how they'd trained and that was how they'd do it. They went in with eight airplanes. They all got back, but one pilot was badly wounded, and five out of the eight ships were so badly damaged that they never flew them again.

"I guess it was a combination of things that helped us to survive unscathed. Certainly our equipment and tactics and training worked. ECM, chaff and the like worked well. I guess the chaplain and some prayers helped, too.

"Later that afternoon I talked with a captain I knew who'd also been into Kuwait. He asked me where we'd been, so I told him SAM Town, which is what we'd renamed Kuwait City. He thought it was kind of strange, because his package had followed us into exactly the same piece of sky only 15 minutes later, and nobody had spotted a single SAM. I guess they'd fired them all at us."

'BUFFs' at War

Though it has long since qualified for veteran status, Boeing's B-52 Stratofortress was quickly introduced to combat action when Desert Shield evolved into Desert Storm and the various elements of the coalition set about driving Iraqi forces out of Kuwait on 17 January 1991. In a war that was largely won by air power, the elderly 'BUFF' may well have been long on years, but it had few peers when it came to the sheer weight of ordnance that it could deliver on a single sortie. The contribution made by the B-52 to the successful outcome of Desert Storm should not be underestimated.

In view of its ability as a 'bomb carrier', it was hardly surprising that the B-52 figured prominently in the reinforcement effort that went by the code name Desert Shield, but the initial cadre only numbered about 20 aircraft. By happy coincidence, these had been engaged on a Giant Warrior exercise at Andersen AFB, Guam, at the time of the Iraqi invasion in August 1990, and were very quickly moved to the island base at Diego Garcia so as to be closer to the theater of operations should Iraq have been tempted to move against Saudi Arabia. Subsequently, as the negotiations dragged on and the probability of war steadily increased, more B-52s were dispatched to the region. Some were to be based in-theater, at King Abdul Aziz airport in Jeddah, Saudi Arabia, while Cairo West airport in Egypt was also used as a bomber base.

Finally, with Desert Storm a reality, two other airfields hosted SAC's heavyweight, but these were much further from the battlefield. In Spain, B-52s began gathering at Moron in late January, the number here eventually rising to around the two-dozen mark. RAF Fairford in England received eight on 5-6 February, launching its first combat sorties just a few days later, on 9 February. At the peak of Stratofortress operations, therefore, the total number in use exceeded 80.

In assembling this collection, SAC cast its net fleet-wide, drawing aircraft from all six of the Bomb Wings (the 2nd, 42nd, 93rd, 97th, 379th and 416th) that operated the B-52G version. These units also provided the bulk of the human resources that were necessary to conduct effective combat operations, but they were to some degree augmented by personnel from SAC's four B-52H units (the 5th, 7th, 92nd and 410th Bomb Wings). Once in-theater, men and machines were assigned to provisional bomb wing organizations that were created especially for Desert Storm. Thus,

by way of illustration, Diego Garcia hosted the 4300th Bomb Wing (Provisional), while Fairford had the 806th BW (Prov).

As already noted, it was the B-52G which was dispatched to the war zone. It is this variant that now bears the brunt of SAC's operations in the conventional warfare arena. Even though it is capable of operating with air-to-surface missiles and can execute pinpoint attacks against hard targets, that option seems to have been overlooked during Desert Storm. Instead, the 'BUFF' concentrated on saturation bombing of soft targets, with particular attention being paid to the Republican Guard. Touted in the popular press as an elite body, Republican Guard elements for the most part failed to live up to their reputation, but may well have been badly demoralized by around-the-clock bombing. There can be little doubt that the B-52 played an influential part in rendering them (and many other Iraqi soldiers) very close to being *hors de combat* before the ground war even started.

In conducting saturation attacks, the preferred weapon seems to have been the 750-lb M-117 'iron' bomb. This was the only ordnance expended by the B-52Gs from Fairford, and it is highly probable that all the other specially-formed provisional units were similarly armed. Maximum payload comprised no fewer than 51 bombs, with 27 housed internally and the balance distributed equally between two underwing racks.

A single B-52G is thus clearly able to inflict considerable damage over a wide area but, as was the case in Vietnam, the Stratofortress usually operated in cells of three aircraft. In the Vietnam conflict, the cell concept was employed for mutual electronic countermeasures protection against the surface-to-air missile threat. However, the B-52's offensive avionics equipment has since been updated, and it is feasible that retention of the cell method was driven more by the desire to maximize destructive potential than by a need for self-protection

Whatever the reason, in a three-ship strike, co-ordinated weapons release of no fewer than 153 bombs typically resulted in a 1.5-mile long by 1-mile wide swath of destruction. Since it was usual to bomb from high-altitude – out of sight and beyond earshot – the weapons would arrive with little or no warning, adding greatly to the terror and confusion of those in the target areas. While they may be hard to quantify, it would be unwise to ignore psychological aspects when assessing B-52

Above: Eight J57 turbojet engines working at full stretch produce a lot of power. All of that power is needed as the engines impel a B-52G laden with 51 750-lb bombs skywards from the RAF base at Fairford, England, at the start of a Desert Storm mission to Iraq.

Below: Flight-line scenes such as these were everyday sights at RAF Fairford, which had eight 'BUFFs' in residence, four of which were usually launched daily on bombing raids against targets in distant Iraq and Kuwait.

Inset left: Even though it only existed for a few weeks, the bomb wing at Fairford designed its own unique emblem, which was worn by flight crews stationed there.

Above: Long-range bombing mission support aircraft included KC-135 Stratotankers, which also ferried crews and supplies to Fairford for the resident 806th Bomb Wing.

Right: Although it relies mainly on electronic means for defense against threats such as missiles and fighters, the B-52G is fitted with four radar-directed .50-caliber machine guns in the tail cone. Here, a member of the support team at RAF Fairford exposes the mechanism of the turret to confirm it is fully loaded and ready for action, just in case Iraqi fighters attempt to disrupt its attack.

Left: Old it may be, but the B-52G made a significant contribution to the allied cause during seven weeks of war. Operating from air bases in the Gulf, Spain and the United Kingdom, the mighty 'BUFF' delivered almost half the ordnance expended by the allies, inflicting massive damage on the Iraqi war machine in the process.

operations, for exposure to repeated attacks would undoubtedly have affected the morale of the Iraqi soldiers and might well have been influential in persuading many to surrender when the ground offensive began in earnest on 24 February.

Although they represented only a small proportion of the air armada at the allies' disposal, the B-52s are estimated to have been responsible for almost half of the 55,000 tons of ordnance that rained down on targets in Kuwait and Iraq during just six weeks of war. That extraordinary figure was reached with little cost in terms of men and aircraft, for just one B-52G was lost. Even that unfortunate incident was not attributable to enemy action, the aircraft concerned apparently suffering a crippling technical problem which eventually led to it crashing into the Indian Ocean

while returning to Diego Garcia. Three of the six-man crew died in this accident.

Apart from that, there was evidently one instance of battle damage, but even that was an 'own goal', for the aircraft involved (also from Diego Garcia) was understood to have been struck by an AGM-88 HARM anti-radar missile launched by a friendly fighter. Damage was confined to the area around the tail, with the quad .50-caliber machine gun package being blown away. Official comment on this incident has been guarded, but there is speculation that the HARM actually homed on the radar associated with the defensive armament. Embarrassing it may have been, but the 'BUFF' involved recovered safely and will presumably be repaired.

L.P.

Jaguar: The Desert Cat

First RAF attack aircraft to be sent to the Gulf following Iraq's invasion of Kuwait, the SEPECAT Jaguar GR.Mk 1A served throughout Desert Storm. Smaller and less sophisticated than the Tornado, it nevertheless worked hard during the conflict and suffered not one single loss to enemy action.

All three squadrons from RAF Coltishall, Nos 6, 41 and 54, plus No. 226 OCU from Lossiemouth, provided a total of 12 aircraft and a peak of 22 pilots for the JagDet at Muharraq, Bahrain. Among several special modifications, the aircraft were fitted with overwing rails for a pair of self-defense AIM-9L Sidewinder AAMs, complementing a Westinghouse AN/ALQ-101(V)-10 jamming pod on the port outer pylon, a Philips-Matra Phimat chaff pod opposite and two Tracor AN/ALE-40 flare dispensers under the rear fuselage. Two 264-Imp gal (1200-liter) fuel tanks on the inboard wing pylons at first limited the weapons load to a pair of 1,000-lb (454-kg) retarded bombs or 582-lb (264-kg) Hunting

BL755 cluster-bomb weapons under the fuselage, although two internal 30-mm ADEN cannon had 150 rounds each.

Led by Wing Commander Bill Pixton, the JagDet was assigned to day operations only and was further constrained by poor weather. While working-up at first involved practice of low-level missions over the desert, as a direct extension of European tactics, the *modus operandum* was changed before combat began. It was concluded – quite correctly, as the Tornado force painfully discovered – that medium-level missions, supported by a fighter and 'Wild Weasel'/jamming package, would offer the best prospect of safety.

Accordingly, the bombs' retarding tails were replaced by free-fall fins and the low-level BL755 was replaced by the Bristol Aerospace (Canada) CRV-7 rocket, 19 of which were contained in a LAU-5003B/A pod, for a total weight of 530 lb (240 kg). Because of its high speed (Mach 4), CRV-7 is accurate over ranges of 6000 m.

Crews were organized to

Above: Group Captain David Henderson, Officer Commanding the RAF contingent that operated from Muharraq International Airport, Bahrain, poses with one of his charges. The Jaguar carried a pair of overwing AIM-9L Sidewinders and four 1,000-lb HE bombs mounted in tandem pairs underwing.

provide two eight-ship missions per day, but only four Jaguars participated in the first operation, flown on the opening day of the war: 17 January. Squadron Leader Mike Gordon led Flight Lieutenant Steve Thomas, Flight Lieutenant Roger Crowder and Flying Officer Mal Rainier against an Iraqi army barracks in Kuwait, each aircraft carrying two bombs. It was not long into the war before a single fuel tank was attached under the fuselage and twin carriers fitted to the inner pylons to allow the weapons load to be doubled. Most bombing missions were flown thus, the weapons fuzed for air burst, impact or delayed action.

CRV-7 was used from the

Above: There are fighters, and there are targets. This Iraqi T-55 tank happened to be on the wrong end of an attack by rocket-armed 'Desert Cats'.

Below: Two HE bomb-laden Jaguars get airborne in close formation. Weapons carried in the Gulf included 1,000-lb bombs, cluster munitions and air-to-ground rockets.

Above: Four Jaguars fly in tight formation as they leave Bahrain on their way to a target in Kuwait. Overwing Sidewinder missiles were always carried for self-defense, but the Jaguars went about their business unopposed, never once being challenged by Iraqi fighters.

Below: Ground crew cluster around a Jaguar as its pilot prepares to climb in before an attack mission. During seven weeks of war, Jaguars logged more than 600 sorties, during which they dropped and fired an impressive amount of ordnance. In spite of a number of low-level operations, only two or three minor instances of battle damage occurred.

Below: Cruising over the desert, a Jaguar displays its full battle rig, with overwing AIM-9L Sidewinder air-to-air missiles, an ALQ-101 jamming pod, a Phimat chaff dispenser and Rockeye CBUs.

Jaguar: The Desert Cat

outset, aircraft carrying two pods per mission. Unfortunately, hasty integration with the Jaguar's weapons-aiming computer resulted in inaccurate deliveries and its temporary withdrawal from the inventory. Rewritten software was provided by Ferranti in the commendably short time of two weeks, and CRV-7 returned to the Jaguar's armory with satisfying results.

In the interim, a replacement was obtained in the form of the American CBU-87 Rockeye II cluster-bomb, which – unlike BL755 – could be released from the new operating height of above 10,000 ft (2626 m). CBU-87 was first carried on 28 January, rapidly gaining the RAF's respect. It was soon used widely against a variety of targets, but the normal aircraft load was only two per sortie. "It's proved to be unbelievably effective – a nasty piece of equipment, really quite vicious," reported Flight Lieutenant Max Emtage. "It is excellent against troops; excellent against soft-skinned vehicles; ammo storages if they are not hardened; petrol stores and that sort of thing. Not pleasant at all. I would not like to be anywhere near it when it went off."

Main 'trade' for the JagDet was in the area of Kuwait south of the capital, although several forays were made to the Republican Guard encampments further north and to a few targets in Iraq itself – the first of these on 18 January. Not until 19 January was the weather good enough to permit a full day of operations, with 19 sorties flown against SAM and artillery sites, but thunderstorms two days later wiped out the entire flying

program. Fuel and ammunition dumps and command centers featured on the target lists, and despite the high concentration of defenses in the area of operations, only three Jaguars received bullet holes in the first 10 days.

Beginning on 26 January, SY-1 'Silkworm' coastal-defense missile batteries were attacked in Kuwait as part of preparations for an amphibious landing. Although the much-publicized potential Marine Corps assault was a deception, it would have been mounted had the coalition's ground thrust deep into Iraq misfired. There were some interesting sea interludes associated with the secondary task of providing 'cab rank'-type CAPs for the Support Combat Air Patrol (SuCAP) and Combat SAR (CSAR) roles, refueled sortie lengths being up to four hours for the two aircraft thus detailed. These ended on 5 February, after 48 sorties (23 missions), due to a scarcity of naval targets, but not before two Jaguars had destroyed a 1120-tonne Polnocheny-C landing craft on 30 January.

Wing Commander Pixton's description of the attack illustrates the curious tactical situation in which the coalition air forces found themselves. "The AWACS was telling us that the picture was clear, so there were no enemy fighters in the area. We almost set up an academic range pattern on the ship. It will sound terrible, and my professional counterparts at home will probably have a fit, but we did two passes [CRV-7] rockets and four passes [30-mm ADEN] guns each, when normally we would never consider re-attacking in a high-threat environment."

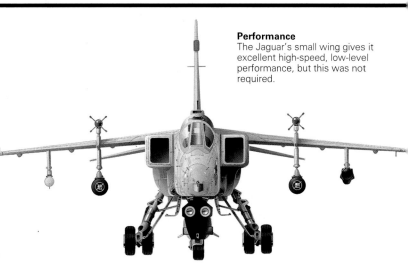

Performance
The Jaguar's small wing gives it excellent high-speed, low-level performance, but this was not required.

Camouflage
RAF Jaguars, like the Tornado bombers and Buccaneers, were painted desert pink for protection on the expected low-level missions over the desert.

Below: A Sky Guardian RWR (Radar Warning Receiver) display dominates the right-hand side of the cockpit in this pilot's view of the 'front office' of a Jaguar on its way into battle.

Having dropped its load of BL755 CBUs on Iraqi positions, these Jaguars make a safe return to base. Jaguars also dropped CBU 87 Rockeyes supplied by US forces in Saudi to allow them to attack from greater height, and fired Canadian-built CRV7 rockets.

SEPECAT Jaguar GR.Mk 1A

XZ3641Q *'Sadman'* was one of the Coltishall Wing aircraft flying out of Muharraq. It was one of two RAF Jaguars that flew 47 missions in the Gulf.

Cockpit
As a strike aircraft, the Jaguar's single-seat cockpit does not require the all-round visibility of an air superiority fighter. Internally, the cockpit is old fashioned, having been designed long before the modern 'all-glass' control panels became possible.

'Wedge' nose
The characteristic wedge shape of the Jaguar's nose is caused by the windows of the aircraft's Ferranti laser rangefinder and marked target seeker.

Countermeasures
Electronic defense of the Jaguar was provided by an American-built ALQ-101 radar-jamming pod beneath the port wing and a French-built Philips-Matra Phimat chaff-dispensing pod under the starboard wing.

Guns
The Jaguar is armed with a pair of hard-hitting 30-mm ADEN cannon, and carries 150 rounds per gun. Jaguars made highly successful cannon attacks on Iraqi naval patrol craft, which were trying to flee to internment and safety in Iran.

Weapons
Jaguars can carry up to eight 1,000-lb bombs, but a normal load in the Gulf was four weapons. The other weapon stations were used for ECM pods, chaff pods and fuel tanks.

Self-defense
In the early days of the war, the Iraqi air force was expected to be a threat, so Jaguars carried a pair of AIM-9L Sidewinders on overwing pylons

---

On 3 February, bombs were used against six gun emplacements on Faylakah Island, 10 miles (16 km) off the Kuwaiti coast, paving the way for its symbolic re-capture.

Bombing of the Republican Guard intensified during the second week of February, while on 12 February the campaign against Iraqi communications was supported by a mission against a pontoon bridge constructed to replace one knocked down by LGBs a few days before. Also on 30 January, the hitherto little-used reconnaissance capability of the Jaguar came into its own. Although four standard BAe-built centreline recce pods had been taken to the Gulf, only two aircraft were configured for the role, of which just one was fitted with the BAe unit – its vertical linescanner replaced by an F126 survey camera. For the other Jaguar, a Vinten VICON long-range optical pod was purchased. Sometimes operating as a pair, and often flying

with an attack force for extra protection, the aircraft gathered data on the approach routes to future targets as a supplement to satellite imagery, completing 31 sorties in 21 separate missions.

The final phase of the Jaguar's war brought individual artillery pieces into the target lists, an early success being destruction of five Astros multi-ramp rocket-launchers on 13 February. Once the land war began on 24 February, Jaguars operated exclusively north of Kuwait City for the remaining three days of war. Sorties of all types flown in combat totalled 611 in 920 hours 15 minutes. Of these, 532, representing 114 missions, were offensive sorties which resulted in the release of 750 bombs of 1,000 lb (454 kg), 385 CBU-87s, 32 LAU-5003 pods (608 CRV-7 rockets), eight BL755 CBUs, 9,600 rounds of 30-mm ammunition and three (accidentally launched) AIM-9L Sidewinders.

P.J.

Flying low and fast over the almost featureless desert terrain of southern Iraq, an RAF Jaguar GR.Mk 1A based at Muharraq on Bahrain 'pops' an infra-red decoy flare, a counter to heat-seeking missiles.

Tomcat in Action

Lieutenant Commander David Parsons, VF-32, F-14 Tomcat

A Tomcat from VF-102 – the 'Diamondbacks' – gets ready for a night launch from USS America (CV-66) during Desert Storm.

"Naturally, the Navy fighter crews wanted a piece of the diminishing air-to-air action. It was becoming obvious that the Iraqis were not going to use their large air force, and that envisioned aerial dogfights would be few.

"Finally, as the Iraqi threat diminished, we paired the fighters off by twos. It was obvious that the Iraqis definitely didn't want to fight and were running from us, or we were shooting them out of the sky. They wouldn't go anywhere near an AWG-9 of the F-14. That's a big part of the reason why the F-14s didn't get any kills.

"Another reason was the way the Air Force set themselves up for on-station CAP. They were there all the time. If anything got airborne, the Air Force got vectors to it. We asked for those CAPs but they wouldn't give them to us.

"There was an F-15 squadron at Tabuk which was very close to Iraq, and it was easy to cycle them on and off those missions. We were anxious to show what the long-range Phoenix could do. But it didn't happen. On my first day mission, there were a lot of Iraqi airplanes airborne over targets. As soon as we pointed our AWG-9s – our powerful radar – at them, they ran. They skedaddled in every direction. We recreated the missions based on the calls we recorded.

"We were frustrated, but the attack guys loved what the AWG-9 did. They asked us, 'Is there a pod

Desert Storm is under way, and Lieutenant Commander David Parsons and Lieutenant Jim Kuhn of VF-32 wear camouflaged helmet covers. The velcro patches on their flying suits indicate where insignia have been discarded for security reasons, although Parsons wears his VF-32 patch for the photo. Kuhn's fingerless gloves give him a better feel of his controls.

we can carry that will transmit the AWG-9's frequency?' They were serious.

"The Iraqis were very familiar with F-14s, having fought them during the war with Iran. I don't know if they knew the F-15's radar frequency, but they wouldn't react when an F-15 got close. But when a Tomcat put his nose out there, they were gone.

"Our radar was so powerful that it could saturate their warning gear and would not give them a definite location of the F-14, only an indication that he was out there . . . somewhere. It must have been a weird, unsettling feeling knowing we were out there, stalking them.

"It was very frustrating for us not to get kills, but we were too disciplined to strip off and go after the MiGs. That wasn't our job. We were supposed to stay with our attack guys. We won the attack crews' respect, and a new camaraderie with them that we had never experienced before.

"They'd tell us they wanted us all around them, 'one on the right, one on the left, one in front, and one behind.' These were the same guys who told us, during exercises,

'We don't need you. You guys do your thing, but we're going to go this way *without you.*'

"One A-6 crew got chased by a 'Foxbat' which had locked them up when the Intruder went off on its own. They saw the MiG's afterburners go over their plane as he began his break turn. The A-6 guys came back yelling for fighters.

"So, we couldn't even have done TARPS if we'd wanted. Everyone wanted fighters. Early on, we were putting four F-14s on a fighter sweep. 'Shoot, they're running from us,' we said, 'We could probably put one F-14 out there.' Our basic unit is two, so we used two Tomcats on the sweep.

"As we headed for the target, like the H-2 airfield in western Iraq, the MiGs would run from us until we made our turn for home. Then they'd come after us. I was on the tail end of a strike – two F-14s guarding two Prowlers – and

here come these MiG-29s running us down from behind. Our AWG-9s weren't pointing at them.

"We decided to let them come close enough so we could turn, and point our radars at them. Then we could shoot them before they could run away. As we waited, some F-15s blew right by us. That was their job. All the discipline we learned from Top Gun . . . that's how it went down. We had 'commit' criteria. We wouldn't run after an airplane unless inside so many miles. The criteria changed according to the particular mission.

"Usually, though, however we approached or exited the target

A Kennedy Tomcat is guided towards the catapult by a member of the carrier's deck crew.

area, there'd be F-15s stationed all around us. There were even tankers in-country. They were serious about quickly winning air superiority. They pretty much got it. Air traffic control became more of a concern. You'd see things on your radar and get all psyched up, then we'd discover they'd be friendlies. Tornados, Saudi F-5s . . .

"There were a lot of aircraft out there, especially when 'Scuds' became such a priority. Whenever information on 'Scuds' came through, a strike package would go after the missiles. There'd be attack planes ready to go. It was incredible what you'd run into. We had an F-117A fly right by us at night. He popped up and went whipping right by us, coming out of Baghdad. We ran into A-10As

deep into western Iraq, just daring anything to move.

"*Roosevelt* had already gone east, but *America* stayed with us until the first week in February when it left for the Gulf to help out around Kuwait.

"The Marines were still calling for recce assets. We were told to give a TARPS pod to VF-102 in *America*, so we gave them an extra pod. We now were down to two pods. We also got new tasking to look for 'Scuds' every day with our TARPS jets.

"We were working very long hours. We briefed for two to three hours, flew the long missions, debriefed for another two to three hours, then went back to planning the next mission, and in between tried to eat and grab some sleep. The more senior you were in the

planning hierarchy determined how much work you had to do. The real junior guys only had to come to the briefs but everyone pitched in to help out. Our planning teams of four or five people would be running around trying to get the latest intelligence, scan the ATO, and co-ordinate with the other squadrons in the wing.

"While the threat of Iraqi interceptors quickly retreated, the allied aircrews still were concerned about the formidable AAA and SAM defenses. The enemy had used this vast system to fairly good effect, and everyone treated the thickets of flak guns and SAM sites with respect. The 'Scud' campaign – a surprise to most of the allied planners – also required immediate, intense attention.

"It was hard for intelligence to keep up because there was so much information coming in, such as where the enemy missile sites were. They were moving their SAMs around on us.

"Of course, we didn't want to fly in the SAM envelopes, but when the VF-103 F-14A(Plus) was bagged, everyone was electrified. If those guys got shot down with the better RHAW gear and greater thrust, then we were certainly at risk in our regular F-14As. That really worried us.

"We plunged into 'Scud' TARPS. Requirements would come out every day on the ATO telling us where to look in 'the 'Scud' Box'. These concentrations were usually along the main

highways, like in the northwestern portion of Iraq that paralleled the border with Saudi Arabia. The Iraqis hid mobile 'Scud' launchers everywhere, under highway bridges and in trenches. Originally, we thought they didn't have many mobile launchers, but it turned out that they had more than 300. They were like roaches and could easily hide in the underpasses. We had 'friendlies' on the ground looking for the launchers. There was just so much territory to cover. They dug trenches, drove the launchers into the trenches, then covered them over with tarps.

"Every day a section of Tomcats from the *Sara* or *JFK* launched to look for 'Scuds'. That solved our BDA problem. I constantly visited the strike cell and looked at all the tasking we had for targets, which was usually posted two days ahead. I'd look to see if we had already hit the targets with TARPS, or if it was within the big 550-mile 'Scud' TARPS mission parameters. If the targets were anywhere in there, we'd just divert a little and try to get pre-strike BDA.

"If the strike we're at night, we'd get the post-strike photography from previous missions. I kept a running data base of what we had already hit and what we *would* hit so that we could provide strike leaders with current pictures.

"We had a dedicated USAF tanker, right up at the border. Those tankers would even cross the border. We'd always ask them to head north from the tanker track so

Afterburners blazing, a VF-14 Tomcat blasts down the No. 1 catapult on the Kennedy's flight deck. Kennedy was part of the Red Sea Battle Group, which also included USS America (CV-66), Saratoga (CV-60), and the nuclear-powered Theodore Roosevelt (CVN-71).

Left: Looking over an F-14 pilot's shoulder during a carrier approach. The Tomcat RIO's visibility from the rear cockpit is excellent, unlike that from the old F-4 Phantom.

Below: F-14s from Kennedy's two fighter squadrons, VF-14 and VF-32, generate contrails over Saudi Arabia during a Desert Storm mission.

we would be topped off as we crossed into Iraq.

"One day, I asked, 'Can you go north with us?', meaning north of his tanker track.

"'Stand by,' the tanker said. Then he came back, 'Yeah, how far in-country do you want to go?'

"'No,' I said, 'just to the border.'

"'We'll go in-country,' he replied enthusiastically.

"I just needed him to take us to the border, because we'd accelerate to 480 kt when we crossed the border and be unable to tank.

"'Well, we'd like to go in-country,' the -135 pilot said.

"'I'll tell you what,' I offered jokingly – we're doing this all on secure-comm channels – 'You can meet us on the way out and if we have gas, we'll take you on a tour.'

"'Oh, okay,' he laughed. That was pretty funny, especially when my pilot, who thought we were serious, said, 'We're taking them on a tour?'

"We had seen tankers over the border. We joked that they were just looking for some excitement, or trying to accumulate points for an Air Medal. It was one point for a mission in-theater, and two points if you crossed the border. Most of the tanker missions were as boring as all get-out. As we egressed, we'd join up on either side of a tanker's cockpit and wait

until the crew had their cameras ready. Then we'd light the burners and climb or roll away. They loved it.

"The tanker guys were great. We really loved them. Everyone we worked with – Brits, USAF – came out to the ship during Desert Shield so we could meet them face-to-face. We resolved a lot of confusion. We kept telling them they were flying too fast. We couldn't refuel at higher weights and altitude without tapping burner.

"'We're just following what our book says,' they told us. They had some manual that told them the speed at which F-14s tanked. Of course, it was wrong. We tank at 250. They quickly understood, and were very accommodating.

"The TARPS missions geared up, just after the F-14 got shot down on 21 January, near Al Asad, a very heavily fortified base, a megabase. One day, we were going to hit an airfield near there. A flag staffer – someone on the admiral's staff – came down and told us, 'We want you to take pictures of Al Asad.' Well, that got our attention.

"'Wait a minute, isn't that where the A(Plus) got bagged?'

"'Yeah, we need to get pictures.'

"This was soon after we started using I-2000s on the bunkers – the laser-guided, steel-nosed bunker

busters – that could penetrate the bunkers. The Iraqis were pulling their planes out of the bunkers, and hiding them all over the place. They had thought that their NATO-standard, Belgian-designed bunkers were impervious, but the I-2000 was one of the little surprises we had for them. That's when they started flying to Iran.

"With all this activity and information, intelligence thought they were hiding airplanes around the field and wanted pictures so we could hit it.

"'You're asking us to go into an SA-2 and SA-6 field,' we told them. 'Plus a lot of low-altitude stuff.'

"'They said F-14s would never go over the beach,' we said, 'then they told us we'd never go near the SAM envelope.'

"'Well, what do you need?'

"'We want a jammer (EA-6B) and a HARM shooter.'

"'OK, we'll put it on the strike ops scheduling board.' That's when we knew we were going.

"We tied into the main strike group so the Iraqis wouldn't know we were heading to Al Asad. The strike was going right by it. At the last second, the three F-14s and the EA-6B would split off. We had two F-14s from VF-32 – the TARPS bird (Lieutenant Jim Kuhn and me) and our escort – plus an F-14 from VF-14, our sister squadron, escorting the EA-6B jammer/HARM shooter, from VAQ-137.

"As we started approaching the time when we knew the SA-2 would fire – when we would be vulnerable – that's when the HARM would already be in the air. We had a codeword for when the HARM was launched. We had several words, like 'Downtown' and 'Get Some!' One pilot even used, 'Eat Me!' We planned for the preemptive HARM to be shot, followed by another if necessary.

"We raced up to the field, Mach 1.2. We went blowing through,

and the Prowler shot the HARM just as he planned, broadcasting 'Downtown'. Then we heard it again.

"'Damn!' we said, 'their radars are up!' Obviously, more than one radar was radiating, probably an SA-2 or an SA-6.

"Time really compressed as we looked out for SAMs. My biggest worry was to have a missile come unseen right up beneath us, so we kept jinking. My pilot, Lieutenant Kuhn – his callsign is 'Dog' – wanted to keep jinking, even when we were over the target, so I had to tell him to hold it steady to take the pictures. It took a lot of discipline during these TARPS missions to fly straight and level over the target. It was hard to force myself to look inside the cockpit to make sure the cameras were running. All we wanted to do was look out for SAMs.

"I thought about the VF-103 crew who had been downed. At that point we thought the RIO was dead since we had not heard anything and he hadn't appeared on the Iraqi 'TV shows'. The pilot had been rescued. I looked down at the bright, yellow sand and kept thinking how desolate the place was.

"'If I go down there, those people definitely don't like me,' I thought as I contemplated my reception after a bail-out.

"We raced out of there. Nothing had been shot at us, although we knew they had tried. Later, the Prowler crew said that the SA-2 had come up and tried to shoot, but they thought that their HARMs had taken out the radar.

"So, we got the pictures and the ISs looked at them. We sent the photos over to the Tornados because they were going in there. Right after that, we were tasked to go to Al Qaim, a super phosphate plant up in the extreme northwest corner. It was the most heavily defended target outside Baghdad. They had four SA-3 batteries and

The end of a busy day or, perhaps, the beginning of a busy night. Desert Storm called for a round-the-clock effort from coalition forces, an effort that was to last for more than six weeks of intense air activity.

Above: Hundreds of craters pockmark the surface of Iraq's Al Qaim superphosphate fertilizer plant, one of the most heavily defended targets of the war.

Below: Grumman EA-6B Prowlers did yeoman service throughout the war, providing jamming capabilities on every strike. The Gulf war also gave the Prowler the chance to demonstrate its ability as a HARM shooter.

two SA-2s, plus all the AAA and low-altitude SAMs. That's where the F-15E Strike Eagle went down. We didn't feel good about going there, either. If they could bag the F-15E, they could easily get us.

"Al Qaim reminded me of the Thanh Hoa Bridge in Vietnam. Everyone tried to get it. We sent B-52s up there and they couldn't get it. The B-52s had problems because they bombed from such a high altitude. We had a jet stream of about 116 kt. The winds changed considerably down on the deck and

made bomb-impact prediction difficult.

"The plant was important because it produced uranium for the Iraqis' nuclear bomb project. One of the by-products of producing the phosphate is this really rough yellowcake. We had fired SLAMs at the facility, but, although we knew the SLAMs had hit it, the picture stops as soon as the missile hits, so we didn't know how badly we had damaged the building.

"It was a huge place and we tried

to destroy it. Some crews had gone up there the preceding day but turned back because of the intense SAM activity. No one faulted them; it was just a hornet's nest with all the sites up. You could go in and get bracketed. As you tried to avoid one site, another would get you.

"We decided to come in at high altitude and come screaming down to 10,000 ft at Mach 1.2. I remember seeing the blue settlement ponds far away. It all seemed so serene. No real flak, nothing like what they talk about over Germany in World War II. We hardly ever saw flak, except minor AAA, because we were up so high.

"I had trouble believing this was this horrible target everyone talked about, like when everyone talked about going to Berlin in World War II. We started calling it 'Big Al'. 'We're going to Big Al's place.'

"The Air Force said they'd send in the Strike Eagles and take out the SAM sites. Then they got bagged! They did have some success, however.

"As we closed on Big Al, I kept saying to Dog, 'Faster! Faster!' I knew the airplane was going as fast as it could but I couldn't help it.

We had an A-7 off our wing with four HARMs, plus an EA-6B. We knew the A-7 would preemptively fire one HARM, but anything after that meant that more SAM sites were up. Our callsign for a HARM shoot was 'Downtown', after Colonel Broughton's book on going downtown to Hanoi during Vietnam.

"We heard, 'Downtown!' Then, 'Downtown, downtown . . . !' There was no delay. That really got our hearts beating fast. There were three SAM sites up. We were looking.

"We had an Expanded Chaff Adapter (ECA) on the airplane with 120 rounds of chaff. I yelled at Dog, 'Chaff, chaff, chaff!' We were continuously pumping chaff out. I watched the TID to make sure the chaff was firing.

"Before the mission, I must have talked to the Prowler crew for two hours, saying, 'Which angle do we want to go in, which sites do you think are active, is this the right angle?'

"They were confident. 'Yeah, we'll be able to protect you.'

"After the brief, I asked, rhetorically, 'You guys are going to keep us safe, right?'

"'We think we can.'

"'Wait a minute,' I said, 'You didn't say you *thought* you could last night!'

"'Well, we'll try our best.'

"'Don't say that!' I said. 'Say you're gonna do it. Make me feel good.'

"After we got back, one of our pilots came up to us. 'I really didn't think I would see you back.'

"Both missions were 'super-real' moments for me. I checked out my nine-mm pistol and loaded it. Normally, I didn't chamber a round, but I did this time, and put the safety on. Because if I came down, I wasn't going to make it easy for them to get me. This was a place we had really hit hard and the Iraqis wouldn't be happy to see me.

"Normally, Dog and I talk a lot during a hop, but on our way to Al Qaim, we didn't talk for 45 minutes.

"Finally, I called him. 'Do you feel like talking?'

"'No.' I knew he was really serious.

When we came up to our tanker, I looked up, and written on the KC-135's belly in big, orange letters, was 'Kick Ass!' I started laughing.

"'Hey, Dog.'

"'What!'

"'Just look up at the belly of the tanker.'

"Shortly after, the airplane started shaking, and I knew he was laughing and having a hard time holding the stick steady."

Tac Recon

A key factor in the successful outcome of any conflict is good intelligence. There can be little doubt that the allied forces were well-served in this area during the Gulf war, being able to draw upon a variety of sources and sensors in determining Iraqi dispositions as well as strengths and weaknesses. Much of the information on which they based their successful campaign would have come from the 'high frontier' of space, courtesy of reconnaissance satellites. Still more would have originated from electronic surveillance, and some would have been provided by special forces operating deep inside Iraq at great personal risk. All of those contributions were perhaps of greatest value in formulating the 'big picture', but commanders in the field were no less dependent upon timely intelligence if they were to achieve their objectives successfully.

In view of that, it is perhaps surprising to note that dedicated tactical reconnaissance aircraft resources were limited, to say the least, and made up only a very small proportion of total allied air power. The oldest but most numerous type was the long-serving RF-4C Phantom, which was flown from Sheikh Isa Air Base on Bahrain. Even then, only

some 18 aircraft were involved, but Tactical Air Command's apparent near-abdication of its responsibilities for reconnaissance meant that it was necessary to turn to the Nevada Air National Guard for these machines and also, to a large extent, for crews to man and service them, as well as to process and interpret the imagery they obtained.

Other land-based assets were provided by other members of the coalition. France's contribution consisted of half-a-dozen Mirage F1CRs at Al Ahsa, Saudi Arabia, but these were by no means solely concerned with reconnaissance, for about half of their war missions were flown as bombers in conjunction with French Jaguars, which they frequently led to the target area. British resources were marginally more numerous and comprised six Tornado GR.Mk 1As at Dhahran and, during about the last two weeks of the war, a brace of Jaguar GR.Mk 1As at Bahrain. Finally, Saudi Arabian RF-5E Tigereyes might also have played some part in the overall reconnaissance effort, as did a small number of carrier-borne US Navy F-14A Tomcats fitted with the Tactical Air Reconnaissance Pod System (TARPS).

L.P.

Above: The Mirage F1CR was hardly the safest airplane to fly in the Middle East, since Iraq also had Mirages in service. France's Escadre de reconnaissance 33 flew the type on photo missions.

Left: These F-14A Tomcats of VF-32 'Swordsmen' were configured for the high-altitude TARPS mission, with TARPS pod, AN/ALQ-167 jammer, and an ECA (Expanded Chaff Adapter).

Below: 'Smooth Character' was one of the Alabama Air National Guard RF-4Cs flown on LOROP missions by Reno crews. RF-4Cs flew daylight missions only, but nevertheless had a key role in 'Scud' hunting.

Left: A shark-toothed RF-4C Phantom of the Alabama Air National Guard launches from Sheikh Isa Air Base. The Birmingham-based squadron had the only LOROP (LOng-Range Oblique Photography) RF-4Cs in-theater. The crews were replaced after December 1990 by Guardsmen from Reno, Nevada.

Right: A desert-pink Jaguar heads into harm's way equipped with a centerline recce-pod. Fortunately, Saddam Hussein had no tactical reconnaissance assets, while the coalition could call on RF-4Cs, F-14A TARPS and Tornado GR.Mk 1As, in addition to Jaguars.

Tornado GR.Mk 1A – Searching for 'Scuds'

The specialized reconnaissance Tornado GR.Mk 1A was unblooded and unproven when fighting began, and gave its crews some harrowing experiences before acquitting itself nicely. The GR.Mk 1A's near real-time observable infra-red linescan proved valuable in the hunt for Iraqi 'Scud' missiles.

Among the first in the RAF to know that their presence would be required in the Gulf, the reconnaissance crews of Nos II and 13 Squadrons were last to arrive before hostilities began. No tardiness on their part was responsible, for the Tornado GR.Mk 1A reconnaissance aircraft had only recently entered service and was suffering problems with the quality of its imagery. Fortunately, a hastily-developed 'fix' applied to six aircraft, together with exemplary work from interpreters in the associated Reconnaissance Intelligence Centre, turned the aircraft into a valuable weapon in the coalition armory.

Representing a new generation in data acquisition, the GR.Mk 1A records its pictorial information on videotape instead of traditional film. Beneath its forward fuselage is the aperture for a Vinten 4000 horizon-to-horizon infra-red linescan, while on each side, ahead of the air intakes, are BAe side-facing infra-red sensors to provide a less-distorted view of the middle distance. Linescan can operate at night without need of photo-flashes, and so it was that all Desert Storm missions were flown under the cloak of darkness.

Six aircraft and nine crews eventually arrived at Dhahran between 14 and 16 January, but were not given any viable tasks on the first day of the conflict. Suggestions that they might undertake damage-assessment of air bases hit in JP 233 raids were firmly rejected as near-suicidal. Procedure was for the coalition recce cell at Riyadh to sift the requests for coverage at an early evening meeting and then assign them to the most appropriate asset. Accordingly, while the bombing Tornados received 24 hours' notice

of missions, their reconnaissance compatriots learned where they were going a mere two or three hours before take-off.

Fortunately, an urgent and most worthwhile task was not long in arriving: the first three missions for the Tornado GR.Mk 1A were all to be ''Scud' hunts' against the elusive mobile missile launchers which were attacking Saudi Arabia and threatening to bring Israel into the conflict as an embarrassing ally.

Wing Commander Al Threadgould (commander of No. II Squadron) and navigator Flight Lieutenant Tim Robinson were first away from Dhahran on the evening of 18 January, flying ZA397. Because no tanker aircraft was available for their short-notice mission, the Tornado carried a pair of 495-Imp gal (2250-liter) drop tanks under the wings and two 330-Imp gal (1500-liter) tanks beneath the fuselage, more than doubling its internal fuel capacity

of 1,400 Imp gal (6364 liters).

A fuel feed problem just before reaching the search area forced an urgent return to friendly territory, so the cause was taken up by Squadron Leaders Dick Garwood and Jon Hill flying ZA400, and a No. 13 Squadron crew, Flight Lieutenants Brian Robinson and Gordon Walker, in ZA371. The pair brought back images of a 'Scud' launcher in firing position, and secured media headlines for the Tornado GR.Mk 1A on its first night of operations. Unfortunately, however, bad weather prevented attack aircraft from catching the launcher before it was driven away.

Garwood recalled on landing, "It was a very, very black night; probably one of the darkest I have flown on. Once you get out over the desert, especially over Iraq, there are no lights on the ground. You are flying very low. We saw the odd Bedouin encampment flash by on the left-hand side of the

wing." On arrival at Dhahran, the aircraft was found to have a single flak hole in the top of the rudder.

Usual operating altitude was 200 ft (61 m) with 'hard' ride selected on the terrain-following radar, and at speeds between 540 and 580 kt (1000-1075 km/h). Most sorties were of 2½ to 3 hours' duration, involving 20 to 60 minutes over Iraq. The longest, of 4 hours 25 minutes, was a 'Scud' hunt flown on 24 January by Flight Lieutenants Rick Halley and Angus Hogg of No. II Squadron, in ZA371. A normal sortie – invariably unaccompanied – might involve three or four line-searches of a strip of road or a section of river, the routes between which had to be planned to avoid known defended areas. Pinpoint targets were visited for pre- or post-attack examination, and searches flown ahead of infiltration routes of Special Forces.

P.J.

British Helicopters

Helicopters of all three UK armed services were involved in Operation Granby, transporting troops and equipment as well as taking an offensive role at sea. Even as Iraqi troops were invading Kuwait, Lynx HAS.Mk 3s of the Royal Navy were in the Gulf aboard frigates of the Armilla Patrol. As the coalition build-up progressed during the closing months of 1990, Lynx were a key element in the blockade of Iraq's seaborne trade, carrying boarding parties to search suspect vessels.

With the transition to war, elimination of the Iraqi navy became of paramount concern. In close collaboration with US Navy helicopters and warships, Lynx undertook regular searches of the northern Gulf, looking particularly for TNC45 patrol boats armed with Exocet anti-ship missiles – a weapon that the UK had good cause to remember from the Falklands war nine years earlier. Another missile which had proved its potential in that conflict was the air-launched Sea Skua arming the Lynx.

Thus, with greater firepower than its USN counterparts, the Lynx became the main coalition anti-ship helicopter. In the first successful Sea Skua operation, HMS *Cardiff*'s Lynx was supported by another Lynx from HMS *London* and an RAF Nimrod, when it sank a Zhuk patrol boat. The eventual tally was 15 Iraqi ships, including five TNC45s.

Navy Sea Kings included the two HAS.Mk 5 used for mine patrols and troop-carrying HC.Mk 4 versions of the same helicopter. The casualty-clearing ship, RFA *Argus*, had its own Sea King flight for medical evacuation, each helicopter able to carry nine stretchers, but the majority of those deployed went into the desert to assist the RAF rotary-wing element. Wearing sand filters and the ubiquitous desert pink camouflage, the main force of HAS.Mk 4 Sea Kings arrived by sea in Saudi Arabia on 6 January and was immediately set to work on the mundane but essential task of hauling men and supplies.

On 24 October it had been announced that the RAF was preparing to dispatch a support helicopter unit to assist the increased army contingent in Saudi Arabia. First on the scene, 7 Brigade had relied on US helicopters, but when 4 Brigade was also dispatched, RAF back-up was required for the 30,000 troops of the thus-formed 1 (British) Armoured Division.

Deliveries of the first 15 Puma HC.Mk 1s were undertaken to Jubail as airfreight inside USAF

C-5 Galaxies from 2 November onward, while an advanced guard of three Chinook HC.Mk 1Bs was similarly flown out on 24 November, backed by others arriving by sea on 6 January. These two types of RAF aircraft joined with the RN Sea Kings to form Support Helicopter Force Middle East, but some of the Chinooks – including the initial deliveries – were assigned to special forces for missions into Iraq and Kuwait.

Pumas and Sea Kings remained close to the troops, leaving Jubail for King Khalid Military City (KKMC) on 22 January and then proceeding westward as General Schwarzkopf's 'left-hook' thrust

into Iraq was prepared. Night-vision goggles were regularly used and the uprated inertial navigation equipment proved a godsend in the featureless terrain. Also near KKMC, the Chinook squadron concentrated on logistics resupply for the division, carrying seven-ton ICO containers, reloads for the Multiple Launch Rocket System, other ammunition and even unserviceable Pumas and Sea Kings. Most satisfying for the Chinooks was the mass airlift of 3,000 prisoners of war as the conflict drew to a close, and re-occupation of the British embassy in Kuwait City.

Impending departure of lighter

helicopters of the Army Air Corps was announced on 22 November, the Lynx AH.Mk 7s and Gazelle AH.Mk 1s arriving at Jubail, Saudi Arabia, from Germany during December. They moved to a forward base north of KKMC in January after training in the very new desert environment. Armed with TOW missiles, the anti-tank Lynx were without the trees and hills which they used for cover in Europe, while the target-scouting and artillery-spotting Gazelles felt even more naked in the face of their enemies. Issue of night-vision goggles and a hastily-installed infra-red sighting system for the Lynx allowed the cloak of night to

Above: *The Royal Navy Lynx, like this example from HMS London, played a major part in the destruction of Iraq's small navy. Lynxes claimed a total of 15 ships destroyed, including five Exocet-capable TNC45-class fast-attack craft that the Iraqis had captured with the fall of Kuwait. Sea Skua anti-ship missiles were the Lynx's primary weapons.*

Left: *Sea King HC.4s of the Fleet Air Arm were painted desert pink when they were used to support British Army and Royal Marine reconnaissance units operating close to enemy positions.*

Top: *Carrying a clutch of Hughes TOW anti-tank missiles, this pink-painted Westland Lynx of Britain's Army Air Corps is representative of the AH.Mk 7s that were dispatched to the Gulf during December 1990. Aided by Gazelle scouts, the Lynx managed to destroy a respectable number of Iraqi tanks and other AFVs during the brief but intense ground war in late February.*

Above: *British Chinook HC.Mk 1s were formed into a composite squadron from No. 7 and No. 18 Sqn based in Germany and Odiham during peacetime. They were all painted in desert pink, although some received an additional dappled paint job to tone down their presence at night.*

redress the balance.

The coalition advance in the land war beginning 24 February was so swift that ground-refueling and re-arming parties had difficulty in keeping up with the helicopters as they accompanied the leading elements of UK forces deep into Iraq. With conflict at an end, the entire helicopter force had little time for rest, as there were numerous peacetime tasks to be performed, including mine-clearance and preparing for withdrawal. Communications were assisted by the sole Army Air Corps fixed-wing aircraft in the Gulf, an Islander AL.Mk 1.

P.J.

Above: *Looking very weather-beaten after months in the desert, five invasion-striped Sea King HC.Mk 4s go back to sea for a while at the end of the war. They were soon to be back at work, however, participating in Operation Safe Haven in Turkey and northern Iraq.*

Right: *British Army Gazelles served as scout helicopters for TOW-equipped Lynx 'tank busters' in the Gulf, while the RAF Pumas supported ground forces of the coalition by moving men and supplies.*

Tanker Conflict

Lieutenant Commander Gil Bever, VA-35, A-6 Intruder

An A-6 crew's view of the business end of a KC-135 from the Maine Air National Guard. The -135's relatively short hose can cause problems for inexperienced Navy crews. Normally, the Stratotanker uses its rigid boom when refueling Air Force aircraft; however, the hose and basket are required when tanking Navy and Marine planes, which use an inflight-refueling probe.

As the war evolved, one of Lieutenant Commander Gil Bever's concerns became the regular, potentially dangerous crowded area around the USAF tankers' booms.

"There'd be a gaggle every night around the tankers, before and after a strike. We'd have 20 airplanes joining up on four tankers going up, and 20 planes joining on four tankers coming back. There were three different tanker tracks that were used the most. That was just *our* air wing. The *Kennedy* air wing would be doing the same thing on another tanker. All these things happened on a regular basis.

"Crews would get disoriented because they joined up so far away. Even though most of the missions were at night, we flew day missions, too. We were working a 12-on, 12-off cycle. Actually, we'd be on for 16 hours. The first launch would be on for 1000, last recovery at 0200. There'd be a big day strike, followed by a big night strike, and the deck would be respotted in between. Every time we went required a massive logistics push. That's where the Air Force did very well.

"They had those tankers up there most of the time, with lots of prior co-ordination because of the long distances involved. We had to come from the Red Sea with so much ordnance that everyone needed gas. That was just to get to the target, then we needed more gas to get back to the ship without being low state on the ball, not being emergency fuel. Tanking was critical.

"We couldn't have carried some of the loads on our A-6s without the tanking we had available. For the strike packages we flew, the tanking worked out as time-control – making our TOTs after getting gas and waiting at a certain point. The tanking gave us the time to wait for everyone so that we could form up and hit the target in a co-ordinated attack.

"We had guys get 'ugly' in their rendezvous, with four of our five guys on a tanker every night. As you'd plug in, you'd get nervous because of the closure rate of someone else, screaming underneath you, and you might be on the middle tanker, with other planes below you. There weren't too many places to run to.

"Fortunately, that happened more at the beginning, and smoothed out as we got more proficient. Before the war, we practiced with the Air Force, complete with an air wing launch, joined up, made our timing, and then hit simulated targets in Saudi Arabia.

"Everyone in our wing eventually got comfortable.

However, squadrons from other ships that arrived just as, or right after, the war began, didn't have that luxury. We had one A-6 from *America* onboard our ship one night because he had ripped off his refuelling probe. When he came back to his ship, they weren't ready to recover him, but *Saratoga* was. He trapped, and our guys repaired his probe, gassed him up, and launched him to make his scheduled recovery onboard *America*.

"We never ripped a probe off one of our airplanes, although we bent a few. We put 500-mph tape on them after we'd pulled out the wrong way. The basket's made out of 'kryptonite'! We had to use a lot of caution getting in and out.

"I tanked more from a KC-135 during this cruise than I ever thought I would in my whole career. I once ferried a plane from Norfolk, Virginia, to Rota, Spain, and tanked from a KC-135. It was supposed to be a night-qualification flight, but it became much more. There was no time to train, and I ended up squeezing the black juice out of my control stick.

"Before this cruise, I had plugged a KC-135 only 10 times, total. It only took one week to equal that during the war. I flew 17 strikes during the war. That's 34 plugs, going and coming. Plus, I flew eight support missions, like KA-6D tankers and decoy (Tactical Air-Launched Decoy – TALD) missions. I also plugged KC-135s during the rest of the cruise, when they were over the Red Sea, during extended recoveries. The Red Sea was a great area to operate in; we had KC-135s all the time. We got plenty of practice."

Head-on rendezvous were one of the most potentially dangerous problems.

"One thing that the Air Force didn't understand about our A-6s was that we didn't have an air-to-air radar. We have to *see* them all the time. The weather was, for the most part, nice, but occasionally it would get bad. We'd get these little puffy clouds. Once, as we were joining up, I had the tanker in sight. Suddenly, he disappeared. He went into the clouds while he was in his tanker circle.

"Now, the F/A-18s have radar, so they pressed on. We can't do that, jumping through a cloud looking for a tanker. We'd be asking for a fireball. We had to break off our rendezvous, and wait for the tanker to come out of the clouds, while he kept giving us updates on where he was.

"When the KC-135 reappeared, we found ourselves in opposite circles with him. He was right in front of us. It doesn't take much to get offset, and end up going head-on with him.

Two VA-35 A-6Es tank from a USAF KC-135 from the Kansas Air National Guard at the start of a daylight mission during Desert Storm. The Intruders carry Mk 83 1,000-lb iron bombs, a favorite weapon during the war.

"Sometimes I saw pilots get disoriented, thinking the tanker was going the other way, away from them. Their lights weren't that helpful. You had to get up close to tell which direction the tanker was moving.

"I kept telling the pilots to enter the pattern tangentially. I never put the lights on my nose. In left turns, always put the lights off your left wing; push them to your nine o'clock. Now you can see where he is and you just bend it around, chase him down and get on the bearing line. Guys kept pressing on, and it turned out that the tanker was coming right at them. They were in trouble.

"The KC-135 is a big airplane, and it can get confusing. You don't have a reference point to use to rendezvous, not like being over a carrier. Normally, you make sure you stay tangential to the carrier, going in circles until you pick up the lights and join in. If you stayed pointed too long at the tanker, you'd end up in a big whifferdill, making left-hand circles. Doing this at night, of course, carried an extra thrill.

"There were other airplanes that you had to watch out for; you didn't have to worry just about yourself. Maintain your altitude, and watch above and below.

"The Hornets had air-to-air radar and they could put the tanker on the nose. The radar tells them that he's getting closer and they can make their cut-away. But we A-6 crews had to rely on our eyes."

A few times, Lieutenant Commander Bever was cut out of the tanker pattern.

"I was already joined up, and again this is from a head-on, the cut-out would happen because another plane pressed it too long. Although I was already on the bearing line, the other pilot lost sight of me. He ended up increasing his turn. Fortunately, this was after the strike and he didn't have any bombs or he would have departed. He turned right over me, forcing me to unload, step down, and watch him come over me trying to rendezvous. He made the turn, got sucked behind the tanker, and I stepped down. I told my BN to keep him in sight behind me.

"An added problem was that the KC-135s did not all have the same lights. They never had the same configuration twice. One night, I was single-generator and couldn't turn on my probe light. I found a -135 with one, red twirlie. He had no runway lights underneath. Normally, they were well lit, but this guy had nothing.

"When the A-6 is single-generator, we have minimum outside lighting. I left my anti-smash on. A Hornet came toward us. I thought he probably hadn't seen me, and probably hadn't seen the tanker, either. On top of that, my BN used both our flashlights – his and mine – to light up the basket. I couldn't see the basket! We kept calling the tanker to turn his lights on . . . nothing. Many times what the Air Force had for frequencies was not the list we had. We'd end up having to call them on guard. They were trying to be professional, but someone wasn't getting the word.

"In the meantime, the Hornet finally saw our flashlights and realized we were there. Then, he called to ask me to turn my anti-smash off. The light must have bothered him.

"'Negative,' I replied, 'we're single-generator.' I had my hands full, anyway. I was trying to get into the basket and he wanted me to change my lights. I needed my anti-collision light for self-defense, especially with minimum exterior lighting. I didn't have a probe light to see the basket, just my BN holding our flashlights.

"Well, we got in, got our gas, and got out of there. Boy, was I glad! It seemed that one out of

every three missions, the KC-135s were not on our frequencies, and we never got it straightened out. When we'd finally get them on another frequency, they'd say, 'Uh, no, we're supposed to be up canary 3!' We were supposed to be up canary seven, or red four.

"A couple of times, our own guys were on the wrong frequency. One pilot was low state, needs gas, and he's calling, 'This is Meat! (fake callsign) I need some gas now! Can anyone hear me?'

"Someone else answered, 'Yeah, I hear you!' Turns out that both those guys were on the wrong frequency. Then the first guy wondered why no one would let him in ahead of them. No one heard him, except for the second pilot on the same, wrong frequency.

"It was a very comm-intensive war. Normally, we would do this without a word. Everything is prebriefed; everyone's got the plan. You launch and do it, with a minimum of calls. Maybe an abort call. But there was a lot of chatter during tanking and when we talked to the AWACS. There were so many airplanes in-country, that to keep us from shooting each other, we required an incredible amount of communication."

Desert Pirates

Vortex generator
The small vertical strakes behind the wing leading edge excite the boundary layer, improving the Buccaneer's low-speed handling.

Self-defense
Buccaneers carried a single AIM-9L Sidewinder for self-defense, but did not need to fire them in the Gulf.

O f all the RAF elements in Desert Storm, the Buccaneer force proved the most vital and the fastest to respond. Without the help of a 30-year-old bomber – more at home skimming the cold waters between the UK and Iceland than at medium altitude over Iraq's arid wastes – Tornados would have spent the war scattering 1,000-lb (454-kg) bombs only slightly more accurately than did Lancasters in World War II.

On the morning of 23 January, following the Tornados' abandonment of JP 233 attacks and the safe return to their bases after medium-level 'dumb' bombing raids, RAF Lossiemouth received an urgent call. Having been previously advised that Buccaneer S.Mk 2Bs would under no circumstances be needed in the Gulf in their secondary role as laser-designators, the resident squadrons were required to recall personnel and aircraft from other duties and dispatch an initial six aircraft to Muharraq with all haste. Three days later, after aircraft had been camouflaged, fitted with Have Quick II secure radios and Mk XII Mode 4 IFF, the first pair was dispatched to the Gulf. Back at base, qualification trials of the aircraft's AN/ALE-40 chaff/flare dispenser system were only carried out on 27 January, while, once in-theater, AIM-9L Sidewinders were issued for self-defense, replacing -9Gs assigned in Europe.

Buccaneers allowed the Tornado force to regain the accuracy of attack lost when missions were transferred above 20,000 ft (6096 m) to evade most of the light SAMs and AAA surrounding targets. Each was fitted with a Westinghouse AN/ASQ-153 Pave Spike target-designating system, externally indicated by an AN/AVQ-23E laser pod on the port inner (No. 1) underwing pylon. A Westinghouse AN/ALQ-101(V)-10 jamming pod was attached on the starboard outer position (No. 4), balanced by the Sidewinder to port (No. 3), the remaining position being left empty. The weapons bay was used for fuel, so Buccaneers usually had to undertake aerial tanking only once (when outbound), compared with two or three times for the Tornados.

At Muharraq, Wing Commander Bill Cope and his crews from Nos 12 and 208 Squadrons, plus No. 237 OCU, had a short and intensive training period with Tornado crews which had never dropped Laser-Guided Bombs (LGBs) before. Their first mission took off shortly after dawn on 2 February, bound for the road bridge across the Euphrates at As Samawah, and comprised two

Buccaneers and four Tornados from Muharraq. Each of the latter carried three LGBs, a cell of two Tornados and a Buccaneer being assigned to each end of the bridge. Flight Lieutenant Glen Mason and Squadron Leader Norman Brown flew the Buccaneer (XW547) leading the first cell.

In this and subsequent missions, the second cell was flying between 45 and 120 seconds behind. The minimum of 45 seconds equated to the bomb fall time, as to designate both ends of the bridge simultaneously would almost certainly result in some bombs being lured from one target to the other. As Pave Spike is a daylight, black-and-white TV system, location of targets at a slant angle from medium altitude through humidity and dust was sometimes difficult. The practice was therefore

adopted of boresighting the Pave Spike (locking it dead ahead) and diving to around 15,000 ft (4572 m) while acquiring the target in the pilot's HUD. Once the navigator had sight of the target on his TV screen, the pod's rotating head would be unlocked and the aircraft would climb, perhaps to above the altitude of the two Tornados flying level and in close formation.

The As Samawah raid was entirely successful, Wing Commander Cope and Flight Lieutenant Carl Wilson (in XX899) being responsible for designating the opposite end for their two Tornados. The six aircraft returned to Muharraq after 3 hours 40 minutes in the air, although in later missions the Buccaneers would fly home independently of the bombers. This was done at altitudes as high as 37,000 ft

(11278 m) – well above the Tornado's comfortable cruising altitude.

From 5 February onwards, Dhahran's Tornado squadron also participated in the Pave Spike/LGB attacks, which continued to concentrate on bridges until the last was attacked on 13 February. During that mission, against the Fallujah road bridge, three bombs failed to guide, one of which landed in the town market place and caused unintended civilian casualties. By a fluke, another 'wild' bomb actually hit a nearby bridge but, of course, was insufficient to destroy it. In this part of the coalition campaign to sever Saddam's communications and supply lines to Kuwait, the Buccaneers directed 169 LGBs to destroy or render completely unusable 24 bridges. Target

Below: Engineers conduct a ground run of a Buccaneer at Muharraq as they prepare the aircraft for combat. The Pave Spike laser pod is below the port wing.

Above and right: 'Sky Pirates' Buccaneer aircraft and aircrew joined the conflict on 2 February and greatly enhanced the accuracy of the Tornado strike force, which henceforth used precision-guided munitions.

BAe Buccaneer S.Mk 2B

The Buccaneer has been in service for nearly 30 years, but still had a vital part to play in the Gulf war. It flew in initially to support the Tornado force as a target designator, but also later dropped LGBs in its brief campaign. Like many aircraft in the war, the aged Buccaneer was probably fighting its last campaign.

ECM
The Buccaneer carries a Westinghouse AN/ALQ-101 ECM pod on its starboard outerwing pylon. Developed for the F-4 Phantom, this provides powerful radar jamming capability over a broad band of frequencies.

Refueling probe
The Buccaneer's refueling probe is removable, but is almost always carried. It is offset to the right to avoid obscuring the pilot's forward view.

Radar warning
The large bullet fairing in the center of the Buccaneer's 'T' tail contains forward- and rearward-looking radar-warning receivers, which generate visual warnings on a cockpit CRT as well as sounding audible warnings.

Pave Spike
The AN/AVQ-23E Pave Spike pod carried on the Buccaneer's port inner wing station is a daylight-only laser-designation unit originally developed to arm the USAF's F-4D and F-4E Phantoms. In the Gulf, one Buccaneer would guide LGBs for two RAF Tornados.

Performance
The Buccaneer is an aircraft of the 1950s, and lacks the supersonic performance of later designs, but it is still an immensely strong aircraft able to carry heavy loads at high subsonic speeds.

Nose art
The 12 Buccaneers deployed to the Gulf from Lossiemouth in northeast Scotland, and took as their names some of the famous whiskies distilled in the region. They also acquired additional, less formal names, this example being both '*Glenfiddich*' and '*Jaws*'.

Airbrake
The Buccaneer's tail fairing splits into a pair of large, hydraulically actuated port and starboard airbrakes. They are infinitely variable, and can be used at any speed.

locations (some with more than one bridge) were Al Amarah, Ataq, Al Busalih, Fallujah, Al Khidr, Kifl, Al Kut, Maftul Waddam, Al Medinah, An Nasiriyah, Qal'at Salih, Ar Ramadi and As Samawah.

Said one crewman flying second in a Tornado cell, "We come in close to get concentration of bombs on target – within about 100 yd of the other [Tornado]. We just sit there for 30-40 seconds in close formation and wait for the bombs to come off the lead aircraft, which is the cue to drop our bombs. It boosts morale a lot, because the boys can now come back and say, 'We did the job,' whereas at night you might see secondary explosions, but you don't know where or what it is. But when you see a bridge going up, you know you have hit it. It's a wonderful feeling."

By way of a diversion, POL installations at Ad Diwaniyah and Bayji were attacked on 9 February, while airfield raids began on 12 February with a mission to Wadi al Khirr. Initially, hardened aircraft shelters were the prime targets, this switching, as the campaign developed, towards taxiways/ runways (beginning 16 February), command bunkers and ammunition storage.

Since 8 February, 12 Buccaneers and 18 crews had been based at Muharraq, expanding the designation service which was now taken on every Tornado raid from Dhahran and Muharraq. The first attempt at a 'double mission' with four Buccaneers and eight Tornados was made on 14 February against Al Taqaddum. One Tornado in the final cell was shot down by two SA-2 SAMs while the crew was preoccupied with

lining up on the target. Such large raids were immediately abandoned as too complex and unwieldy.

Poor weather, which had begun on 10 February, began taking its toll on missions – which were normally flown, just in case of a chance break in cloud over the target. On 20 February, all five missions were aborted for this reason. The next morning, Sidewinders were relinquished as unnecessary, Buccaneers instead carrying two LGBs on the Nos 2 and 3 positions to add to the effect of their raids. Tactics were for the aircraft to bomb after the Tornados, diving from 25,000 ft (7620 m) at an angle of 40° so that their bombs would fall into the laser 'basket' produced by their own AVQ-23 pod. First recipient of this own-designation technique was the taxiway at Qal'at Salih.

It was in such a style that the

Buccaneer ended its war. Having designated for Tornados over Shayka Mayhar on the afternoon of 27 February, the Buccaneers went round again. The first removed a wing from a parked Antonov An-12 'Cub' transport despite its bombs failing to explode, whilst Cope and Wilson blew up another 'Cub' with a successful brace of bombs. Buccaneers dropped 48 of their own LGBs during the campaign, the final part of which involved attacks on airfields at Amara (New), Al Asad, Habbaniyah, Jalibah (Southwest), Kut Al Hayy (East), Qal'at Salih, Qal'at Sikar, Ar Rumaylah, As Salman (East), Shaibah, Shayka Mayhar, Tallil, Ubaydah bin al Jarrah and Wadi al Khirr. Operational sorties flown totalled 216, for 678.5 airborne hours.

P.J.

A-7's Last Cruise

People always compared Vought's pugnacious little A-7 Corsair II to a squashed F-8 Crusader, but it was really a new design when it flew for the first time in September 1965. The Corsair was a result of a competition to replace the Douglas A-4 Skyhawk. After joining the fleet in 1966, the A-7A flew its first combat missions in Vietnam with VA-147 on USS *Ranger* (CV-61) in December 1967.

Corsairs flew throughout Vietnam in Navy gray and Air Force green-and-brown. They carried the war to the North Vietnamese during Linebacker in 1972, and patrolled the oceans and trouble spots of the world afterwards.

A-7s were ready to rattle the windows in Iran during the aborted rescue of the US hostages in April 1980, and three years later, VA-15 and VA-87 flew strikes in Grenada and Lebanon.

The Middle East became the Corsair's favorite hunting ground. In March and April 1986, it showed Khadaffi's navy what the 'Line of Death' was really all about. When Iran flexed its muscles in the Persian Gulf in April 1988, A-7s of the 'Mighty Shrikes' of VA-94 and the 'Fighting Redcocks' of VA-22 'discussed' the matter with the Ayatollah's minions.

By early 1990, several light

attack squadrons had either decommissioned or transitioned to the capable McDonnell Douglas F/A-18 Hornet. Things seemed generally quiet around the world and it was time to say good-bye to the faithful little Corsair. But, Iraq's Maximum Leader had plans.

Suddenly, President Bush and his planners were asking the old question, "Where are the carriers?", and the A-7 was called back into action one more time. Halfway through their pre-transition to the F/A-18 (they had sent half their people and planes away), VA-46 and VA-72 rushed out to meet USS *John F. Kennedy* (CV-67) as the huge carrier left Norfolk, Virginia, on 15 August and headed east.

Desert Storm became the Corsair's finest hour, and together with newer, more technologically advanced aircraft, *JFK*'s two light attack squadrons frequently put up their entire complement to fly strikes with iron bombs or to defend other strikes in SEAD (Suppression of Enemy Air Defense) missions with HARMs.

Kennedy's Air Boss, Captain John W. Warren, a former A-7 pilot himself, commented on the success of VA-46 and VA-72.

"I really enjoyed watching the A-7s get out there and participate in their last war. It was a pleasure having them on the deck because

Almost engulfed by steam venting from a catapult track, this A-7E Corsair II is readied for launch from the USS John F. Kennedy. The aircraft's outer stores stations are fitted with triple ejection racks (TERs), carrying conventional iron bombs, while self-defensive AIM-9 Sidewinders are mounted on fuselage rails. The 1990-91 deployment seems certain to be the A-7's last combat cruise in US Navy hands.

Left: Sidewinders and bombs arm this A-7E Corsair II as it heads across the Arabian peninsula on the way to attack Iraqi targets. Only two Navy light attack units, both based on the USS John F. Kennedy, used Corsairs during the war.

Right: A trio of VA-72 A-7Es armed with CBUs (Cluster Bomb Units) sets off to attack Iraqi military targets in Kuwait. Widely used by coalition forces in the desert, the CBU is highly effective against 'soft' targets like trucks and troop formations.

Left: A member of the Kennedy's deck crew verifies that the nose tow link on an A-7E Corsair II of VA-72 has correctly engaged the catapult shuttle. In a few moments, the catapult will be tensioned, and the A-7's engine wound up to full military power, before aircraft and pilot are hurled aloft.

Right: An A-7E from VA-72 comes in tight against another machine from the 'Blue Hawks' over the unforgiving Saudi landscape.

they were so agile and so consistently up. . . They were always ready and easier to get to the catapults than larger aircraft. . . We launched *18* loaded A-7s in one cycle, nine per squadron. It was incredible! Two major strikes per day on average.''

From 0100 on 17 January 1991, and the next 42 days of Desert Storm, the two A-7 squadrons flew 731 sorties and more than 3,100 hours.

After their return from the Gulf, however, the 'Clansmen' of VA-46 and the 'Bluehawks' of VA-72 were ordered to stand-down and decommission. In a situation that can only be chalked up to the fortunes of war, the two units, which had been originally scheduled to transition to Hornets, would be no more, while the two former A-7 squadrons who were slated for decommissioning, VA-37 and VA-105, would change to the F/A-18s, even as their former mounts were flying their last combat sorties.

P.M.

Right: Mission marks show how busy the Corsair was in the Gulf war. The top aircraft is the VA-72 'CAG-bird' sporting a special desert camouflage.

from page 123 (**14 February continued**)

engines. We tried to glide for a minute or two but the controls froze up and then I ejected." Clark landed safely and was taken prisoner. His navigator, Flight Lieutenant Stephen Hicks, was killed.

An EF-111A Raven radar-jamming aircraft returning from a combat mission crashed just inside Saudi Arabia; both of the crew were killed.

A US official spokesman stated that to date, coalition air attacks had destroyed about 1,300 Iraqi tanks, 800 armored personnel carriers and 1,100 artillery pieces; that was about a third of the total deployed in the Kuwait area.

15 February, Friday An announcement made early that morning on Baghdad Radio, on behalf of the Iraqi Revolutionary Command Council, stated that the Iraqis were prepared to withdraw from Kuwait. Initially, there was euphoria in the coalition camp that the crisis might be solved without any need to resort to a major ground offensive. But when the full details of the offer became known it was found to be couched in vague language and hedged with many conditions. It fell far short of the various United Nations Security Council Resolutions, and the coalition governments judged that it did not form a basis for a settlement. The fighting was to continue.

To clear paths through the Iraqi minefields, C-130 Hercules transport planes began dropping BLU-82/B 'Big Blue' weapons, each weighing 15,000 lb and filled with fuel-air explosive to give an extremely powerful blast effect. For the same purpose, helicopters dropped CBU-55B cluster-bombs, each containing three bomblets filled with fuel-air explosive.

An F-15E of the 336th TFS, 4th TFW, on an anti-'Scud' patrol over Kuwait, used a laser-guided bomb to destroy an Iraqi Hughes 500 helicopter while the latter was in the hover. Also on that day an A-10A of the 711th TFS, 10th TFW, piloted by Captain Todd Sheehy, destroyed an Iraqi Mi-8 with cannon fire.

Off the coast, a Lynx helicopter from HMS *Manchester* sank an Iraqi naval salvage vessel with Sea Skua missiles.

Two USAF A-10s of the 354th TFW were shot down while attacking Iraqi tanks in northwestern Kuwait (one pilot was killed, one taken prisoner). Also, a US Navy A-6E was lost to non-combat causes.

It was announced that to date, the coalition air forces had flown a total of 67,000 sorties.

16 February, Saturday Iraqi forces fired four 'Scud' missiles at Israel, claiming to have hit the Israeli nuclear facility at Dimona. The Israelis denied this and reported there had been no casualties. One 'Scud' was fired at Saudi Arabia, again without causing casualties.

Attacks on Iraqi army positions continued.

One US Army UH-1 Huey helicopter and a USAF F-16C were lost (non-combat loss).

17 February, Sunday US Army AH-64 Apache attack helicopters engaged an Iraqi force, and took 20 prisoners.

Two US soldiers were killed when their armored vehicle was struck in error by a Hellfire missile fired from a US helicopter.

Allied heavy artillery commenced the bombardment of Iraqi positions in the battle area.

Attacks on hardened shelters at Iraqi airfields continued. Reportedly, more than half of the 594 shelters, and the aircraft inside them, had now been destroyed.

A USAF F-16C of the 363rd TFW was shot down and its pilot, Captain Scott Thomas, ejected and came down by parachute 40 miles inside Iraqi-held territory, and was rescued by US helicopters.

18 February, Monday On this and the next three days, thick cloud hindered operations in the Kuwait theater of operations.

US Navy A-6s claimed the destruction of five Iraqi aircraft on the

to page 150 (**18 February continued**)

EC-130 PsyWar Broadcaster

Crew of EC-130(RR), 193rd Special Operations Group, Saudi Arabia

"The 193rd Special Operations Group is unique. We have two missions that are not flown by any active components of the Air Force, let alone Reserve or Air National Guard units. The unit participated from the outset of Desert Shield, and was very successful. Like most people in the Guard, we're civilians. We live in the everyday world, and we're not used to being soldiers all the time. But once we got over there, we were totally committed."

Propaganda has always played a big part in warfare, but with the growth of the broadcast media in the 20th century its importance has grown dramatically. Lord Haw Haw and Tokyo Rose were famous figures during World War II, and they had their equivalent in Baghdad Betty, broadcasting to the troops of the anti-Saddam coalition in the Gulf. The Iraqis overdid their propaganda effort, however, when they included the cartoon character Bart Simpson in the list of Hollywood stars who were having their wicked way with the wives American GIs had left behind.

The coalition psychological warfare effort was much more subtle, and vastly more successful. Central to that effort were the EC-130E(RR) Hercules of the 193rd Special Operations Group, part of the Pennsylvania National Guard. These aircraft were flying broadcast stations of great sophistication and complexity, and by the end of the war they were beaming their special PsyWar programs at the Iraqi troops 24 hours a day.

"We demoralized the Iraqis, we told them the truth. Our broadcasts had a lot to do with the annihilation of enemy morale. If we said that they were going to be bombed, they were bombed. Those people learned to trust us more than they trusted their own leadership. It's probably true to say that psychological operations were a major factor in the surrenders of thousands of Iraqi troops, and we had a big part to play in that.

"We're a stand-off platform, so we didn't have to fly into bad guy territory, at least while it was still considered bad guy territory. Operating from altitude, our broadcast system had a big advantage over ground-based transmitters. We were a high-value asset, so we didn't get to anywhere where the ground threat counted. We were always escorted by fighters, and AWACS kept us under close observation. Missions averaged between eight and 10 hours. Because we were forward deployed we could be in our orbit area in a relatively short time, so we didn't have to spend much time in transit.

"Although our most important missions to date have been flown during Operation Desert Shield and Operation Desert Storm, we have operational experience from when the local broadcast facilities had been blown away, and for 30 days we were a flying radio station. We were also involved in Operation Just Cause in Panama.

"We have eight assigned EC-130Es, four of which are 'Comfy Levi' configured for the 'Senior Scout' mission we perform on behalf of the US Air Force Electronic Security Command. This is basically a standard C-130E into which the palletized mission systems are fitted.

"'Senior Scout' is highly classified, so I can't say much about it. I can say more about our other main mission, however. Originally designated 'Coronet Solo' but now known as 'Volant Solo', it arose after the Dominican crisis in 1965. A Navy admiral who had been in charge of the whole operation said that it would have been nice to have been able to broadcast over the local news networks as well as to break into the military nets. This unit was at the time flying C-121 Super Constellations in the medevac role. The role was changed, and by 1967 the aircraft were in business as large radio and television broadcasting platforms. In 1978 the unit began converting to the EC-130E, and by 1982 when I joined we had just got rid of the last Super Constellation.

"Our primary mission is defined as conducting psychological operations using electromagnetic transmissions, covering commercial AM and FM radio bands, VHF and UHF television bands, and military VHF, HF and FM frequencies. There's nothing really cosmic about the equipment we use. It's not the kind of gear you could buy from the Radio Shack in your local mall, but it is pretty much the kind of stuff you could order off the shelf if you were setting up a small state-of-

Above: The unique EC-130Es of the 193rd Special Operations Group perform two sensitive missions – the 'Senior Scout' intercept of enemy communications and 'Volant Solo' psychological warfare broadcasts. As a high-value asset with very powerful broadcast capabilities, the EC-130s did not generally fly over 'bad-guy' territory, but they followed the front line as it moved into Iraq and Kuwait.

Right: The 193rd Special Operations Squadron, Pennsylvania Air National Guard, has a unique 'special ops' role using electronic airwaves both to intercept enemy communications and to broadcast propaganda. The EC-130E does both jobs.

Below: When Arabic-speaking linguists aboard 'Volant Solo' EC-130Es told the Iraqis it was time to surrender, they believed it. So many of Saddam Hussein's troops gave up that the allies were hard-pressed to accommodate them.

Above, inset: In March 1990, the US Air Force created its Special Operations Command to cover 'black' missions supporting SEALs and Green Berets. The winged dagger borrowed from the British SAS is the universal motif of special forces.

the-art commercial TV or radio station. The system is fully palletized, so if you want more of one capability over another, you can pull transmitters off and replace them with ease. The first time I saw the equipment in back, there was one very sophisticated-looking piece, looked kind of like a microwave, but I figured it must be a spectrum analyzer or other such piece of high-tech wizardry. I looked at it, and looked at it, and finally I asked one of the guys what this thing that looked like a microwave was. 'Well', he said, 'it's a microwave. The crew use it for cooking up their flight meals!'

"The flight crew of five includes two pilots, a navigator, a flight engineer and a loadmaster. We might augment the crew for long missions: the C-130 can fly for 10 or more hours on internal fuel, and with air-to-air refueling flights can go on indefinitely. If we're on a long mission we'll trade off some back-end crew seats for additional air crew, and we'd carry another pilot, and possibly an extra navigator and flight engineer.

"The basic mission crew of six includes an electronic warfare officer and five electronic communications system operators. These are the ones who have the most fun. They're the program directors, or 'disc jockeys'. Modulation sources include cassette tape, reel-to-reel tape, video

playback, and there are eight aircrew broadcast mikes for live transmissions. Program materials include prerecorded audio and video and live broadcasts using linguists as required. We can also rebroadcast ground station signals.

"The squadron has no linguists, and our back-end personnel are not trained as professional broadcasters, although they will sometimes act in the role. Generally speaking, it is the customer who provides the specialists, the customer usually being the US Army. It's the Army which is primarily responsible for psychological operations within the Department of Defense. It has a trained cadre of linguists and broadcasters who generally fly with us.

"In the Gulf, the Army provided Arab linguists; normally, Arabic speakers are pretty hard to come by. We had at least two with us every time we flew. The Army also provided the training for some of the Kuwaitis who flew with us, people who had been here in the US at the time of the invasion. The fellow assigned to me had been an electrical engineering student at Arizona State. He spoke excellent English, but more to the point he was a native speaker [of Arabic]. It is always better for psychological reasons to have a native speaker broadcasting than someone who has learned the language."

from page 148 (**18 February continued**)

ground in 'protected positions'.

Coalition warships continued to mount shows of force off the coast of Kuwait, with the intention of strengthening Iraqi fears of a large-scale seaborne invasion attempt. In separate incidents on that day, two US Navy warships, the helicopter-carrier USS *Tripoli* with 2,000 Marines on board, and the guided-missile cruiser *Princeton*, suffered damage when they detonated mines during operations in shallow waters off Kuwait. Seven members of the two ships' companies suffered minor injuries, and both vessels were able to continue their assigned tasks.

19 February, Tuesday One 'Scud' missile was fired at Israel, but there were no reports of damage or casualties. F-15Es were in the area at the time of the launch but low cloud prevented them from finding the launcher. During that 24-hour period, coalition aircraft flew 100 'Scud'-hunting sorties.

AH-64 Apache helicopters and A-10s continued their attacks on Iraqi tanks and vehicles. During one of these actions they attacked a force of some 300 Iraqi tanks and combat vehicles that had been located north of the Saudi border. Twenty-eight tanks, 26 other vehicles and three artillery pieces were claimed destroyed.

One OA-10A of the 23rd TASS was shot down, and the pilot captured.

20 February, Wednesday In an operational test carried out that day, two AH-64 Apache and two OH-58 Kiowa helicopters attacked a bunker complex housing Iraqi troops some distance behind the front line. The Kiowas provided laser-target marking for Hellfire missiles launched by the Apaches. Following the attack a loudspeaker-fitted UH-60 helicopter offered Iraqi troops inside the bunkers the chance to surrender, and more than 400 did so. CH-47 Chinook helicopters were sent to collect the prisoners and take them to Saudi territory. This combination of Apache and Kiowa helicopters to attack bunkers would be employed several times during the days to follow.

One US Army OH-58 Kiowa was lost during a night action, and both of the crew were killed. In non-combat-related incidents a USAF F-16, a US Marine Corps CH-46E Sea Knight and an Army UH-60 Black Hawk were destroyed.

21 February, Thursday President Saddam Hussein delivered a bellicose speech on the war, threatening his enemies with terrible losses if they attempted to launch a ground offensive. This at the very time his foreign minister was in Moscow to discuss his terms for bringing peace to the area. With the coalition ground offensive expected to begin almost any day, there was considerable diplomatic activity aimed at settling the conflict in a manner that would be satisfactory to both sides.

Three 'Scud' missiles were launched at Saudi Arabia, but they caused no casualties.

One US Navy CH-46E was lost in a non-combat-related incident.

22 February, Friday Three 'Scud' missiles were launched at Saudi Arabia, but no casualties were caused.

Air attacks on battlefield targets and the Iraqi lines of communication continued, and for the first time there were daylight attacks on targets near Baghdad.

President Bush issued the ultimatum that unless the Iraqi forces began an unconditional withdrawal from Kuwait by noon, Washington time, on 23 February (8:00 p.m. Baghdad time), and completed their withdrawal within seven days, they would be ejected from the country by force.

Allied reconnaissance aircraft and satellites gave the first evidence that Iraqi troops had begun to ignite the oil wells in Kuwait.

One US Navy SH-60B was lost (non-combat loss).

23 February, Saturday Two 'Scud' missiles were launched at Saudi Arabia and one at Israel, but no casualties were caused.

Allied bombing attacks on targets in the battle area continued. During the afternoon, A-10s began attacks with Maverick missiles to destroy the valves on pipes carrying oil to fire trenches the Iraqis had built as part of their system of fortifications.

Coalition aerial reconnaissance revealed that more than 300 oil wells were now ablaze in Kuwait.

There was considerable diplomatic activity up to and past President Bush's deadline of 8:00 p.m., and the deadline was marked by attacks by F-117As on targets in Baghdad itself.

A US spokesman claimed that in the course of the air attacks to date, a total of 1,685 tanks, 925 armored personnel carriers and 1,485 artillery pieces had been destroyed.

to page 158

A Mirage 2000 fighter of the French air force taxies past US Air Force KC-135 tankers before setting off on a combat air patrol over the Saudi/Kuwait border. French C-135F(R) tankers were also used in the Gulf to support the French deployment.

French Helicopters at War

On 17 January 1991, with France fully committed to operations against Sadam Hussein's regime, the Division Daguet (known to most coalition partners as the 6th French Division) began a 300-km westward movement from King Khalid Military City towards Rhafsa to take up position across from the Iraq border. There, reinforced with elements of the US 82nd Airborne Brigade, it prepared for its assigned task in the ground phase of the air-land battle, a quick jab north-northeast, on both sides of a paved highway linking the border with Al Salman Air Base and the town of As Samawah along the main highway linking Baghdad with Basrah. When that move began, on 22 February, helicopters assigned to the Division Daguet were divided into eight escadrilles (flights), the first with Gazelle gunships, the second with Gazelle scouts, the third through sixth with Gazelle/HOT for anti-armor operations, and the seventh and eighth with Pumas. Effectively supporting the fast-moving Division Daguet, Gazelles blasted resistance points while Pumas ferried troops and supplies, thus helping reach the goals set for that phase of the operation, i.e., the capture of Al Salman Air Base on the morning of 26 February and the establishment of a 'sanitary' zone shielding the bulk of the allied ground forces from possible attacks by Iraqi reinforcements that might have come from Baghdad.

R.F.

Left: The white stripes that were applied to all allied helicopters as an identification aid prior to the ground battle are visible on this French army Puma as it flies low and fast over the southern Iraq desert. French and British Pumas were kept busy moving troops and supplies during the swift ground advance that completed the Iraqi collapse.

Above: In addition to their anti-armor tasks, Gazelle helicopters of the French army also fulfilled a variety of other functions. These included liaison and communications for components of the Division Daguet as it moved more deeply into Iraq in a bold operation designed to isolate the Iraqi army in Kuwait, breaking its will to continue fighting.

Above: One task that was due to be performed by helicopters like the Puma entailed the evacuation of wounded personnel for medical treatment. As it turned out, only light casualties were sustained and few 'casevacs' were flown.

Left: A HOT anti-armor missile streaks away from a French army Gazelle during the ground war. In concert with rotary-winged craft from other allied units, Gazelles helped to destroy much of Iraq's substantial armored capability.

Tornado in a Desert Storm

For the RAF's Panavia Tornado GR.Mk 1s, 'Gulf war' was an appropriate name: there was a sizeable gulf between the war the aircraft was designed to fight at 200 ft (61 m) over Europe against ferocious Warsaw Pact opposition and the conflict in which it found itself, 20,000 ft (6096 m) over the Iraqi desert with the enemy's fighter aircraft on vacation in the country next door. Adjustment to these unaccustomed surroundings took some time – and some losses – but the Tornado quickly found its niche in the coalition war effort and contributed much to the successful outcome.

Three reinforced squadrons, averaging 15 aircraft and 24 crews each, were based at Tabuk and Dhahran in Saudi Arabia and Muharraq on Bahrain. Crew shifts were organized to provide two waves of eight aircraft per base per night. Some of the Tabuk aircraft initially operated in the defense-suppression role with BAe ALARM anti-radar missiles, while Dhahran had an extra six Tornado GR.Mk 1As for reconnaissance.

Later, five aircraft with provision for TIALD designator pods were added to the Tabuk strength, while all losses in action were speedily replaced by aircraft and crews which had been standing by in Europe. In all, over 60 individual Tornados (out of at least 84 modified and painted for Middle East service) took part in the bombing and recce campaign.

Being unprepared for the almost immediate collapse of the Iraqi air force, the coalition formulated a sustained program of airfield-denial with the Tornado GR.Mk 1 and its purpose-designed Hunting JP 233 bomblet dispenser as a key element. Produced a generation before the stand-off dispensers now in the trials stage, and optimized for use in heavily defended airspace, JP 233 required its carrier to fly at 200 ft (61 m) over some of the most strongly defended real estate in the Middle East in order to deliver its runway-cratering charges.

During the first three nights of the war (16/17 to 18/19 January), 63 Tornado sorties delivered JP 233s to their assigned targets at Al Asad,

H-2, H-3, Shaibah, Tallil, Al Taqaddum and Ubaydah bin al Jarrah, accompanying aircraft providing defense suppression by firing ALARM or by lofting 1,000-lb (454-kg) free-fall bombs which exploded at 15 ft (4.5 m) above the airfield defenses. Three aircraft were lost during this phase, of which two – with bombs, rather than JP 233 – appear to have been hit by Euromissile Roland short-range SAMs. The fourth loss, during another lofting attack, this time on Ar Rutbah radar station, was sustained in the early hours of 22 January.

While senior officers maintained that JP 233 would be used again if the situation so demanded, the Tornado force undertook no further raids of this type after the third night. With a few exceptions, attacks then moved up to medium altitude – above 20,000 ft (6096 m) – where only the larger SAMs and 100-mm AAA could reach. The former danger was greatly diminished by the activities of the HARM-equipped USAF F-4G 'Wild Weasel' Phantoms and RAF Tornados carrying ALARMs –

although stocks of the latter were expended well before the war's end.

Despite Tornado losses – which were (as the Chief of Air Staff disclosed after the conflict) a fraction of what had been feared – the JP 233 raids had been most effective. Now, aircraft were dropping eight 1,000-lb (454-kg) bombs each, but doing so with aiming equipment designed to cope only with the minimal atmospheric changes between 0 and 200 ft (61 m). Given (for example) a 100-kt (185-km/h) easterly wind at dropping altitude, but a light southerly breeze on the ground, the weapon-aiming computer was unable to make appropriate corrections.

This ineffective form of attack, begun on 20 January, was further weakened after three or four days, when the bomb load on many missions was reduced to five. The Tornado's engines were also optimized for low level, with the result that aircraft were having difficulty getting above 20,000 ft with large fuel tanks (borrowed from the Tornado F.Mk 3

Adorned with Schultz's well-known cartoon character, two Tornados from Bahrain's 'Snoopy Airways' head back to base after another bombing mission during the seven-week war against Iraq. The Tornado force lost proportionately more aircraft than any other allied unit.

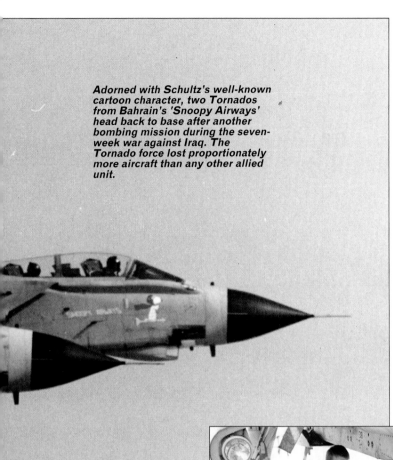

Above: Wing Commander Mike Heath of No. 20 Squadron had a short war, ejecting from a Tornado GR.Mk 1 with control problems on 20 January. Both he and his pilot, Squadron Leader Peter Battson, escaped, but were invalided back to the UK.

Below: RAF armorers check that a clutch of conventional free-fall bombs has been correctly loaded. Other ordnance that was employed by RAF Tornados included the JP 233 sub-munitions dispenser, laser-guided bombs and British Aerospace's new ALARM anti-radiation missile. One Tornado was lost when its bombs exploded on release.

interceptor) and 8,000 lb (3629 kg) of weapons. Outbound aerial tanking brackets were reduced in altitude as a consequence.

Until early in February, free-fall bombing was undertaken on airfields, petrochemical plants and storage, barracks, radar/communications sites and the Rufhah Fuwad 'Scud' test base. There was the occasional spectacular success, such as a large fire at the Al Azzizyah oil refinery on 1/2 February, but crews rarely saw the effect of their efforts. That changed after 2 February, when total air supremacy allowed regular daylight raids to augment those formerly flown at night or at dawn and dusk.

As a means of improving accuracy, dive-bombing was tried. Starting from 24,000 ft (7320 m), the Tornado was rolled onto its back (to maintain positive *g*) and dived at 30° while the pilot acquired the target on his HUD. Pull-out was achieved at about 16,000 ft (4880 m) – still above SA-8 SAMs and most of the light flak – the aircraft's computer determining the correct moment of

weapons release. In this free-fall part of the campaign, only one Tornado was lost (on 23 January) when one of its bombs exploded immediately on release.

Revised tactics had reduced both losses and accuracy. Precision returned with the arrival of laser designators, initially in the form of Pave Spike-equipped Buccaneers serving Muharraq (from 2 February) and Dhahran (5 February). These two bases immediately switched to bombing the road and rail bridges linking Baghdad with its garrison in Kuwait, and thereby played a major part in this important stage of the coalition master plan. Tabuk, meanwhile, carpet-bombed (with minimal effect) ammunition storage dumps at Al Iskandariyah, Karbala and Qubaysah, and attacked fuel refineries, pumping stations and stores at Bayji, H-2, Al Habbaniyah, Al Hadithan and Al Hillah, as well as the power station at Al Musayib.

Arrival of TIALD-equipped Tornados allowed Tabuk to switch to precision missions on 10 February, and from then until the end of Desert Storm few free-fall bombing missions were flown by the three Tornado bases. The anti-bridge campaign ended on 13 February after a small contribution by Tabuk, efforts now being directed towards Hardened Aircraft Shelters (HAS) on Iraq's major airfields. One Tornado carrying two LGBs was sufficient for a HAS, compared with four aircraft and 12 LGBs per bridge.

On 16/17 February, by which time the coalition had destroyed some 350 of Iraq's 594 HASs, the target of airfield attacks was changed to command bunkers, fuel/ammunition storage and runways/taxiways. The latter were singled out for particular attention just prior to the opening of the land offensive on 24 February, in case Iraq planned to launch a mass chemical-bombing raid on the

Left: Wreckage of the Tornado flown by Battson and Heath, which was abandoned after leaving Tabuk, was scattered over a large expanse of the Saudi desert.

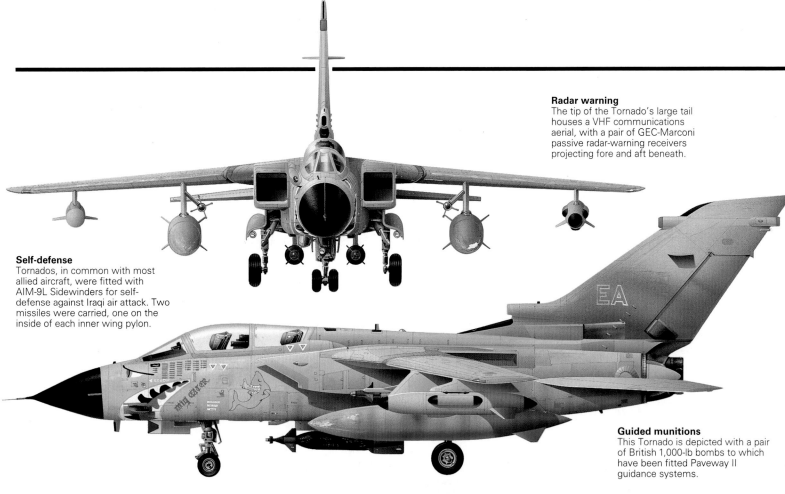

Radar warning
The tip of the Tornado's large tail houses a VHF communications aerial, with a pair of GEC-Marconi passive radar-warning receivers projecting fore and aft beneath.

Self-defense
Tornados, in common with most allied aircraft, were fitted with AIM-9L Sidewinders for self-defense against Iraqi air attack. Two missiles were carried, one on the inside of each inner wing pylon.

Guided munitions
This Tornado is depicted with a pair of British 1,000-lb bombs to which have been fitted Paveway II guidance systems.

advancing troops. Throughout the laser-bombing phase only one Tornado was shot down (on 14 February) by a pair of SA-2 SAMs at medium altitude.

In all, six Tornados were lost in enemy territory, for a total of five aircrew killed and seven held prisoner until ultimately released. The Tornado force flew some 1,600 bombing sorties, during which it delivered over 100 JP 233s and around 4,250 free-fall bombs and 950 LGBs. Many sorties were abandoned in the air over the target due to a combination of weather and political constraints prohibiting blind bombing. Even so, stocks of bombs had become depleted to the extent that Muharraq Tornados had planned to begin using US-supplied CBU-87 cluster-bombs on 28 February, while American Mk 84 2,000-lb (907-kg) bombs would have been introduced a week later, had the war continued.

P.J.

ALARM: Ravaging the Radars

Several weapons saw their first combat use in Desert Storm, but few arrived in the war theater before their operations manual had been written. One exception was the BAe ALARM (Air-Launched Anti-Radar Missile), which had only completed manufacturer's firing trials in October 1990. The need for suppression of Iraq's vast network of air-defense radars was such that ALARM was sent to the Middle East having only once been tested in an over-simplified trial of its homing capabilities.

While BAe personnel at Lostock worked with urgency to build up stocks of ALARM, Tornado GR.Mk 1 crews of Laarbruch's No. 20 Squadron were given one week to familiarize themselves with the missile's complex programming system and two weeks to fly simulated attack patterns before transferring to Tabuk late in November. There they flew a further series of trials in company with other Tornado squadrons, practicing attack missions over the desert and accumulating sufficient experience to write the Standard Operating Procedures, or 'bible', for ALARM.

At first, ALARM could only be carried on the inner wing pylons, displacing the 330-Imp gal (1500-liter) drop tanks to their alternative position beneath the fuselage. By early January, however, aircraft had been modified to take up to three ALARMs on launch rails attached to the belly, whilst 495-Imp gal (2250-liter) tanks went on the inner wing positions. External equipment was completed by the usual BOZ-107 chaff/flare pod, Sky Shadow jammer and two AIM-9L

Panavia Tornado GR.Mk 1

'*MiG Eater*' was one of the most heavily used of the RAF's Tornado bombers. Based at Tabuk, in northwestern Saudi Arabia, it flew some 40 missions into hostile territory. The Tabuk force was led by No. 16 Squadron, but included elements of Nos 2, 9, 13, 14, 20 and 617 Squadrons.

Performance
The Tornado's small, variable-geometry wing gives its two-man crew a very comfortable ride in most flight regimes, especially during high-speed, low-level missions.

Radar
The Tornado's multi-mode, terrain-following, ground-mapping radar is its primary attack/navigation system. A chin-mounted sensor contains the windows for a Ferranti laser-rangefinder/marked target seeker, which enables the Tornado to drop LGBs onto designated targets.

Left: ALARM anti-radiation missiles can be seen beneath the belly of this Tornado GR.Mk 1. Making its combat debut, ALARM was one of a number of weapons used to suppress Iraqi anti-aircraft defenses.

Sky Shadow
The ARI 23246/1 Sky Shadow electronic countermeasures system is an autonomous ECM pod which incorporates both active and passive electronic warfare systems, using an integral transmitter/receiver and a powerful signal processor.

Weapons
With all wing pylons occupied by pods or fuel tanks, the Tornado's offensive weaponry was carried almost exclusively under the fuselage. Weapons carried included bombs, JP 233 airfield denial weapons, and ALARM missiles.

Sidewinders. Tabuk eventually received eight specialist crews plus nine ALARM-capable Tornados, the latter having been modified with a MIL-STD 1553B digital databus. When not on their defense-suppression missions, aircraft were capable of normal bombing sorties.

ALARM is designed to provide several possible modes of attack but, unlike its US equivalent, the AGM-88 HARM, it is not only a point-and-shoot weapon. It is intended to provide bombers with either a safe corridor through a defended area or to suppress the defenses of a target under attack – in each case providing this security for up to 10 minutes. It does so by being able to climb after launch to about 70,000 ft (21336 m), where the rocket motor temporarily is stopped and a parachute deployed. While slowly descending, ALARM searches for radar transmissions and compares them with a pre-loaded library of signals. Those of interest are then sorted according to a list of priorities, which may be changed up to the moment of launch.

On picking up its assigned target, ALARM jettisons the parachute and dives on the radar. If no signal is heard, the missile will float to the ground on its parachute

and explode harmlessly – but this will mean that the defenders have been intimidated into keeping their equipment switched off while the attacking force has passed through.

Defense-suppression missions with ALARM are carefully planned from data supplied by Elint aircraft. A large amount of such information was gathered by No. 51 Squadron Nimrod R.MK 1Ps and similar US aircraft during the closing months of 1990. Attackers were thus able to plan their moves knowing the position of most defensive radars in the vicinity of the airfields which would be first

Left: A handful of RAF Tornados was used for laser-designation, but only two development examples of the TIALD (Thermal Imaging And Laser Designating) pod were available. One designator aircraft normally accompanied two bombers.

Below: Three 1,000-lb laser-guided bombs are visible below the belly of a Tornado as it departs for a combat mission with three similar aircraft.

ALARM: Ravaging the Radars

on coalition hit-lists. Because of ALARM's potential for precise pre-programming in position as well as signal discrimination, a missile could be 'hung' above each SAM site five minutes before the bomber force attacked, primed to react as soon as a designated type of enemy radar switched on.

ALARM was in use from the first night of war. At 2310 GMT on 16 January (0210 local time, 17 January), two Tornados took off from Tabuk to support four of their companions that had left an hour earlier to attack Al Asad airfield with JP 233s. Flight Lieutenants Roche and Bellamy in ZD810 and Flight Lieutenants Williams and Goddard in ZD850 had three ALARMs under each Tornado and, being far lighter than the bombers, could take off later and omit a tanker rendezvous.

Skimming the desert at 200 ft (61 m) with 'hard' ride selected on their terrain-following radar, the ALARM aircraft approached the target from a slightly different direction to the bombers and launched their missiles at 0350 local time: five minutes before the force of three Tornados was due. All came home safely, while eight bombers which returned to the airfield that evening were similarly unscathed despite having no ALARM escorts. At almost the same time, four ALARM aircraft left for H-3 airfield and launched 10 missiles successfully in a softening-up procedure. A few hours later, a second four-ship supported an attack by three bombers from Tabuk on H-3, but despite good ALARM launches the optically-directed flak was severe

enough for the JP 233 attack to be cancelled.

Only twice was ALARM used to support allied forces. Four Tornados were tasked on the evening of 21 January to accompany a USAF F-15E Strike Eagle raid on a 'Scud' storage depot at Al Qaim. Each carried three missiles, of which 10 were successful. Two more ALARM aircraft teamed up with the F-15s to attack the same site on the evening of 23 January. Plans for a Saudi Tornado bomber raid to be backed up by ALARM were called off because of vague mission planning by the RSAF. Unable to provide a precise time-on-target or details of direction of approach, the Saudis suggested that in the interests of avoiding a collision the RAF should fly around the target with navigation lights switched on until the bombers decided to arrive. The rejoinder from Tabuk does not bear repetition.

From 22 January, Tabuk's Tornado bombers switched to medium-level missions to avoid the heavy AAA lower down, but the missile launchers stayed at 200 ft (61 m) for a little longer. Their first daylight mission was flown against Qubaysah ammunition dump in the early afternoon of 22 January, but these forays did not become a regular feature until a week later.

Beginning with a two-ship, with three missiles each, against a barracks at H-3 on 24 January, the defense-suppression force began flying with the main formation at 20,000-24,000 ft (6100-7320 m). The following day, allocation of ALARMs was cut to two per aircraft to conserve dwindling

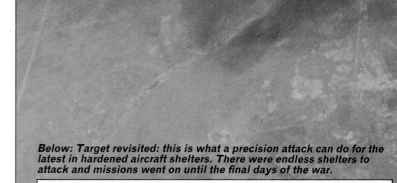

Below: Target revisited: this is what a precision attack can do for the latest in hardened aircraft shelters. There were endless shelters to attack and missions went on until the final days of the war.

With wings swept forward, a Tornado waits for the rest of its flight to air refuel from a tanker before heading to target. It was the first war the aircraft had experienced and things did not initially run smoothly. But, enhanced weapons and avionics were rushed through and the superbly trained aircrews adapted and innovated to make a significant contribution to the strike war. Targets included bridges, fuel dumps, airfields, 'Scud' production facilities, air-defense centers, power stations and ammunition dumps. They were certainly among the busiest of allied warplanes, clocking up 1,600 bombing sorties.

Smoke erupts from an industrial plant after a medium-level bombing raid by Tornados. In the late stages of the war, Tornado missions were more often against infrastructure targets rather than airfields.

Above: The forward field of view of a Tornado navigator is limited, although during a bombing mission his attention is mainly concentrated on finding the target on radar. At other times he's checking his 'six' for bandits.

Below: A brace of 1,000-lb laser-guided bombs nestles beneath this Tornado GR.Mk 1 as it receives fuel from an RAF VC10 tanker. 'Palm tree' mission symbols show it to be a Dhahran-based machine.

stocks. Nevertheless, the final mission in which missiles were launched was flown on the late afternoon of 13 February when ZD748 and ZD851 supported a TIALD/laser-guided bombing raid to Al Taqaddum air base, carrying a pair of ALARMs each. On 26 February, ZD746 and ZD851, similarly equipped, took off shortly after dawn to escort a mission against Habbaniyah air base, but this was aborted because of the weather.

By then, 24 ALARM missions had been flown, totalling 52 sorties (including four aborted after take-off), during which 123 rounds were fired. Lead aircraft was ZD746 with 12 successful and two aborted missions, for a total of 31 missiles launched. Targets attacked included the airfields at Al Asad, H-2, H-3, Habbanniyah and Al Taqaddum; ammunition dumps Al Iskandariyah and Qubaysah; a POL dump at H-3; the Al Musayib Power Station; Bayji oil refinery; and the communications station at

Right: Laser-designation support of Tornados flying from Muharraq on Bahrain was furnished by the Buccaneer, which was fitted with the Pave Spike laser-designation pod. In the first days of their deployment, these veteran aircraft only operated as designators, but they later began carrying two precision-guided weapons, using them in attacks on airfields.

Al Kufah.

USAF 'Wild Weasels' continued to harass Iraqi radars whenever possible, but the operators had become extremely reluctant to use their equipment. Many SAMs were guided visually until radar was turned on at the last moment in the remote hope that the target could be locked onto for homing. The occasional lucky hits achieved in this way were but a fraction of the losses the coalition might have suffered from a fully-functioning radar network.

P.J.

THE GROUND WAR

24 to 28 February 1991

By now, the US, British and French armored formations were established at their jumping-off positions in readiness to launch a series of powerful thrusts aimed at outflanking the Iraqi lines of defense in Kuwait. Remarkably, the huge forces of troops and equipment, accompanied by an enormous logistics tail, had moved into position without Iraqi air force interference, or even with it gaining an inkling of what was taking place. A single high-speed, low-altitude run by an Iraqi fighter over the coalition troop assembly areas, which could then have broadcast its findings by radio, might have been sufficient to compromise the allied plans. But no such flight took place. The surviving Iraqi combat aircraft, whether at their home airfields or those in Iran, were all confined to the ground.

24 February, Sunday At 4:00 a.m. coalition troops with strong air and artillery support launched a series of ground thrusts into Kuwait and southern Iraq. Armored forces crossed the Saudi frontier at several points, penetrated the defensive line and advanced rapidly.

In the largest helicopter assault operation ever launched, a force of some 2,000 men of the US 101st Airborne Division seized a position some 50 miles inside Iraq and set up an airhead at a point codenamed 'Cobra'. The force was transported by more than 100 UH-60 Black Hawk and CH-47 Chinook transport helicopters operating in relays, with AH-64 Apache, AH-1F Huey Cobra and AH-58 Kiowa helicopters flying as escorts. Later in the day, a further 2,000 men of the same division reached the airhead with a column of some 700 trucks. As well as serving as a supply base for the advance into Iraq, the air-

head would be used by Apache helicopters attacking targets in the Iraqi rear areas.

Meanwhile, off the Kuwaiti coast, there were several feint landing operations and displays of force intended to strengthen the Iraqi impression that a large-scale amphibious operation was about to be launched.

Iraqi forces began demolishing public buildings in Kuwait.

Three 'Scud' missiles were launched at Saudi Arabia, but they caused no casualties.

Two more Iraqi aircraft flew to Iran.

Some 5,500 Iraqi prisoners were taken during the first 10 hours of the offensive.

to page 162

Above: Allied troops were aware that Iraq had a chemical warfare capability, and prepared for the eventuality of it being used. Well trained in dealing with chemical attacks, the troops were even able to joke about it.

Right: After weeks of aerial pounding, allied commanders expected plenty of Iraqi prisoners, and plenty of prisoners was what they got.

Lieutenant General Sir Peter de la Billière commanded Britain's forces in the Gulf. A highly decorated former commander of the SAS, he had served for long periods in the Gulf and his command of Arabic stood him in good stead in the multi-national coalition.

Right: A Royal Air Force Puma lands in a swirl of sand. Such was the pace of the allied advance that helicopters were often the only way to keep leading units supplied.

Below: The wasteland that is Kuwait is testimony to the Iraqi army's disregard for normal civilized conduct. Their use of oil as a weapon might well be classed as ecological terrorism, and the effects will be felt for decades.

Left: Burning oilwells combine with the setting sun to create a scene from Dante's 'Inferno'. Iraqi forces blew up nearly 700 Kuwait well heads before fleeing from the advancing coalition forces.

Below: Close-support and anti-tank aircraft like the McDonnell Douglas AH-64A Apache came into their own with the commencement of the ground war, ripping through Iraqi armor.

Apache to the Fore

Lieutenant Colonel William Bryan, 2nd Battalion/229th Aviation Regiment, AH-64 Apache

"Ten days prior to G Day, the allied offensive on 24 February, the 101st's Apache battalions began flying armed reconnaissance missions into Iraq. On occasion we went as deep as 150 km into hostile territory. We even began to take prisoners, the first attack helicopter unit ever to do so. About 100 km into Iraq, we found an infantry battalion astride a road that the 101st were to use on G Day. We went in at first light, and began to work the position, using 30-mm cannon and 2.75-in dual-purpose rockets. The Air Force worked in some air strikes. After we had been engaged for about five hours, we got a leaflet team to drop some leaflets, and an Arabic speaker told them over a PA set that if they surrendered they would be given safe passage and would not be harmed. Once some surrendered, the rest began to follow. There were 476 of them! We alerted the brigade Chinook battalion, brought in eight CH-47s to haul them back to captivity.

"We knew that on G Day, the division was going to establish an airhead very deep inside Iraq, so in the week before that my mission was reconnaissance, to check the route into the country, destroy fortifications and clear the zone of enemy forces. The 101st's sector was 50 km wide and 200 km deep. On G Day, the division moved along preselected air routes to an operating base 150 km into Iraq. We had troops on the ground and the forward base up and running within eight hours.

"The sector we were in was far to the west of the main Iraqi troop concentrations. It was lightly defended and lightly populated. We reached the Euphrates, about 50 km north of the division's forward base, that first day. The Iraqis we did see realized that they were about to be bypassed, and they tried to run to the north. Once they saw the armed helicopters appear they would get out of their vehicles and take cover. We engaged the vehicles, destroyed them.

"We did not use the OH-58s as air scouts. In the desert, there is no problem with target acquisition. The human eyeball can see for 20 or 30 km, especially with the dust signatures that helicopters and vehicles throw up. The traditional scout role, which is acquiring targets, is not needed. In any case, the OH-58 does not have the kind of navigation system we do. No Doppler, no inertial, no global-positioning system. I used them as command and control assets. The Apaches did their own scouting and attacking, with the OH-58s following up behind, providing air defense with their Stinger heat-seeking missiles and co-ordinating with artillery and air strikes.

"When we came across a convoy, I would attack with one of the battalion's three companies. As the attack progressed I had one company attacking, one about 30 km back in a holding area, and one 50 km back at the FARP (Forward Area Refueling Point) at the division's forward operating base. That way there was one company conducting the engagement, one company at the holding area about five or 10 minutes' flight time away and the third company refueling and re-arming. There might only have been a third of the people up there, but the enemy was being engaged continuously. If you really want to pile them all in you can, but then there's going to be a break in the action when everybody goes back to re-arm and refuel.

"Companies normally operate in two teams. The light team of two Apaches will usually be the first to engage, covered by the heavy team of three or four helicopters. Then the heavy team will take up the fight. In Europe we're taught to mask, to use the terrain as cover from behind which we launch attacks. In the desert, you couldn't hide. It should have been extremely dangerous, since some of their anti-aircraft missile systems outranged us, but the Iraqis showed little or no desire to fight. They had the equipment, but they didn't have the resolve.

"Had the Iraqis been an armored force we would have made stand-off attacks, but in this case we shot them with 30-mm cannon fire to get them stopped and the people dismounted. Then we fired three Hellfires, which took out the three lead vehicles. From that point on we were able to finish them off with 30-mm and 2.75-in rockets.

"Hellfire is for point targets, something hard that has to be engaged with a precision munition with a lot of penetration. It is laser guided, fired by the gunner in the front seat. You acquire the target, illuminate it with a laser, and fire the missile. The missile will hit the point illuminated by the laser, and will do it at ranges of more than five km. How much further, I'm not allowed to say. The 2.75 is a good area weapon if you have a lot of vehicles or personnel in a small area, and can strike from a good stand-off distance, about eight or nine km. Each rocket has got nine sub-munitions, which were effective against light armor and personnel and in this case were extremely effective against trucks.

The Chain Gun is in between. It is officially an area weapon, but it is extremely accurate and will penetrate light armor if you are within two km.

"Our greatest concerns were the Iraqi shoulder-fired air-defense weapons. We could get around the sophisticated long-range systems by flying at low altitude and letting the ground clutter mask our signature. But with the man-pack SAMs one person in a hole in the ground can take you out. We also knew that the enemy had over 5,000 armored vehicles, each of which mounted a heavy anti-aircraft machine gun, and he had large numbers of 23-mm and 57-mm cannon. But as long as we stayed three km away we were generally out of range, and in any case we were flying at 25 ft or less.

"We flew a number of joint attack teams with Air Force A-10s and F-16s. Normally we'd also be using artillery, but we were so far ahead that most of the time we were out of range. It was a spontaneous thing, not planned, as would happen in Germany. If we found a target we would contact the Air Liaison Officer – the ALO – to tell him where we were and where the target was. As fighters arrived on station they would report to the ALO. He would assign fighters to missions, giving the Air Force guy our frequency. He'd come on and talk to us direct, getting a briefing on where to attack and from what direction. Sometimes we'd use our lasers to designate for his weapons, and sometimes we'd shoot white phosphorus rockets to give him something to aim at. He'd come in, make two or three passes, wait for our damage assessment and then head for home."

Above: The CH-47D Chinook was used by the 101st Airborne Division for everything from hauling fuel to transporting Iraqi prisoners. CH-47D pilot Major Marie T. Rossi was the highest-ranking American killed in the war.

Below: 'Dustoff', a US Army UH-60V Black Hawk helicopter, prepares to evacuate casualties from the battlefield. Together with UH-60A and UH-60L general-purpose ships, the 'medevac' was indispensable to Army ground operations.

Apache Attack

Attacks on Iraqi armor were primarily preemptive strikes to sanitize a corridor through which following allied armor could move. Reconnaissance from satellites, J-STARS, aircraft and helicopters, or special forces usually identified the enemy and, if they were within the corridor, they were engaged and neutralized by the Apache force. Operating from secured sites well ahead of allied armor, Apaches were able to set up fire and maneuver attacks, constantly changing aircraft to keep the enemy under fire and the momentum of the advance under way.

Above: An AH-64 Apache prowls the desert by day – not a typical view since the Apache, and allied forces generally, were at their greatest advantage over the Iraqis in combat at night.

Above: The OH-58D Kiowa Warrior with mast-mounted sight was developed to work in co-ordination with the Apache. But, because of the sparse Iraqi air defenses, Apaches often operated without the scouts.

Above: Like the Indian warriors after which they are named, these Apaches lay in wait at a FARP (Forward Area Refueling Point). From here they await the call to move up to the battle front.

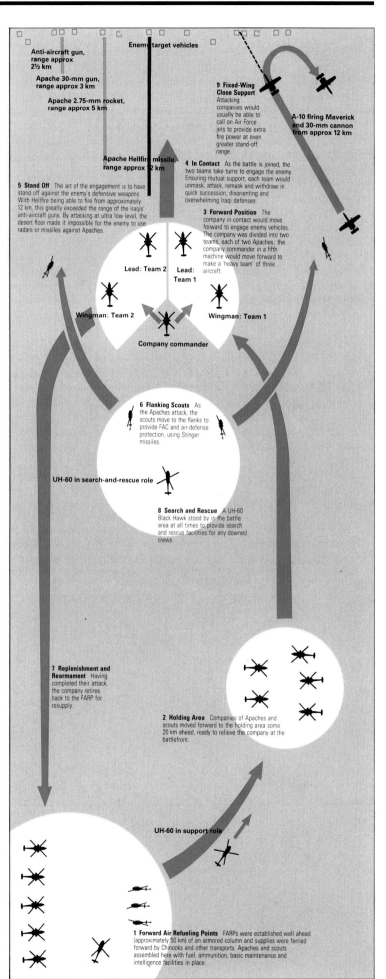

Anti-aircraft gun, range approx 2½ km

Apache 30-mm gun, range approx 3 km

Apache 2.75-mm rocket, range approx 5 km

Apache Hellfire missile, range approx 2 km

Enemy target vehicles

9 Fixed-Wing Close Support Attacking companies would usually be able to call on Air Force jets to provide extra fire power at even greater stand-off range.

A-10 firing Maverick and 30-mm cannon from approx 12 km

5 Stand Off The art of the engagement is to have stand off against the enemy's defensive weapons. With Hellfire being able to fire from approximately 12 km, this greatly exceeded the range of the Iraqis' anti-aircraft guns. By attacking at ultra low level, the desert floor made it impossible for the enemy to use radars or missiles against Apaches.

4 In Contact As the battle is joined, the two teams take turns to engage the enemy. Ensuring mutual support, each team would unmask, attack, remask and withdraw in quick succession, disorienting and overwhelming Iraqi defenses.

3 Forward Position The company in contact would move forward to engage enemy vehicles. The company was divided into two teams, each of two Apaches; the company commander in a fifth machine would move forward to make a 'heavy team' of three aircraft.

Lead: Team 2

Lead: Team 1

Wingman: Team 2

Wingman: Team 1

Company commander

6 Flanking Scouts As the Apaches attack, the scouts move to the flanks to provide FAC and air-defense protection, using Stinger missiles.

UH-60 in search-and-rescue role

8 Search and Rescue A UH-60 Black Hawk stood by in the battle area at all times to provide search and rescue facilities for any downed crews.

7 Replenishment and Rearmament Having completed their attack, the company retires back to the FARP for resupply.

2 Holding Area Companies of Apaches and scouts moved forward to the holding area some 20 km ahead, ready to relieve the company at the battlefront.

UH-60 in support role

1 Forward Air Refueling Points FARPs were established well ahead (approximately 50 km) of an armored column and supplies were ferried forward by Chinooks and other transports. Apaches and scouts assembled here with fuel, ammunition, basic maintenance and intelligence facilities in place.

Harrier: Marine Close Air Support

from page 158

25 February, Monday US, British and French armored columns thrust deep into Iraq, meeting little resistance.

Iraqi Republican Guard armored units started to move forward to counterattack the advancing coalition forces, but when the vehicles came out into the open they immediately came under heavy attack from the air. During these operations, Captain Eric Solomonson and Lieutenant John Marks, A-10 pilots of the 76th TFS/23rd TFW, claimed the destruction of a total of 23 enemy tanks in a single day. Their squadron had located an Iraqi armored column on the move, and brought it to a halt by destroying the tanks at the front and the rear of the column. On their first mission of the day the pilots each destroyed four enemy tanks, and during subsequent missions Marks claimed eight more and Solomonson seven.

Two 'Silkworm' surface-to-surface missiles, Chinese-built copies of the obsolete Soviet 'Styx', were launched against coalition warships operating off Kuwait. One of the missiles was shot down in flight by a Sea Dart surface-to-air missile from the HMS *Gloucester*, and the other crashed harmlessly into the sea.

From the US forward helicopter base in Iraq, AH-64 Apache and AH-1 Cobra helicopters attacked enemy forces along the valley of the River Euphrates.

In Kuwait itself more than 500 oil wells were now on fire, producing a pall of smoke that restricted visibility over large areas of the country and out to sea. As a further part of their 'scorched earth' policy, Iraqi troops continued to blow up public buildings in Kuwait City. One US pilot returning from a mission over Kuwait reported of the scene on the ground, "It looks like I imagine hell would look."

A total of 270 Iraqi tanks were claimed destroyed during the day's fighting.

That evening a 'Scud' missile was fired at Riyadh, but it was intercepted and shot down by a Patriot. Later that evening a Scud aimed at Dhahran fell on a building at nearby Khobar used to billet US troops, killing 28 and wounding 89. It was later announced that the missile

to page 172 **(25 February continued)**

Captain Andrew Hall, VMA-231, AV-8B Harrier II

A Marine Corps CH-53E Super Stallion passes the USS Raleigh (LPD-1) as the amphibious force in the northern Gulf prepares for a landing on the coast of Kuwait, a threat that diverted Iraqi defenses from inland.

"It was pretty much a trans-world flight that got us to the Gulf. We were in Japan for a normal six-month deployment when the crisis began. We figured that we were going to be extended there, then at the end of November they called us and gave about three weeks notice to get to the Gulf. For logistic reasons it was easier for us to go eastward, using inflight refueling. We started from Japan to Wake Island, from Wake to Hawaii, from Hawaii to Yuma in Arizona, Yuma to Cherry Point in North Carolina, from Cherry Point to Rota in Spain, and from Rota to the King Abdul Aziz Air Base near Al Jubail in Saudi Arabia. It took us a couple of weeks, and we arrived on 22 December.

"By the time we got to Saudi we were not too worried about the Iraqi air-to-air threat, so in spite of our location, which was about 70 miles north of Dhahran and 100 miles south of the Kuwaiti border, we didn't fly CAPs, since the F-15s were on CAP 24 hours a day. We were initially told that we would only get involved once the ground war started, flying close air support for Marines pushing through Kuwait or making an amphibious landing.

"It turned out that we were in action from the first day of the war. Some Marine units in the Khafji area were taking artillery fire, so the Harriers were called. The guys flying that mission came in over the water, and attacked on the instructions of a FAC (Forward Air Controller) in an OV-10. They knocked out the artillery pieces, much to the pleasure of the Marines on the receiving end of the Iraqi artillery fire.

"Once the command decided they were going to fly us, we were mostly assigned to daylight battlefield air interdiction. You would be assigned a sector of a 'kill box', about 30 miles by 30 miles. Your sector would be a quarter of the box. You'd be given a primary target within that area, and a secondary target. If you couldn't find either, then you'd hunt for something of military significance. It could be artillery, or vehicles on the move, or revetments, or infantry positions, or command posts.

"We flew in fairly high, at 15,000 ft or more. This was to keep the effects of triple-A and hand-held SAMs to a minimum. Obviously, they also had longer-range radar-guided SAMs, but with the number of HARM shooters that were around at any given time, we felt a lot better.

"From that height, troops on the ground were difficult to see, but you could see trucks moving along a road, or artillery in revetments. We'd have intelligence before the mission, and reconnaissance photos, and we'd have the targets plotted on a map. Once we were in the right area, we'd roll in on our attack, usually seeing whatever we were trying to hit by the time we passed through 10,000 ft. If you couldn't find it, you and your wingman would go on to the secondary target, and if you couldn't find that you'd fly along roads looking for something. It was unbelievable, the number of targets that were available.

"There are six pylons on the Harrier, which gives you widely varied options on how to load them. Initially, for maybe a week and a half, we carried one Sidewinder for self-defense. Our normal bomb load was four

Below: As one Marine put it when he composed a barracks-humor ditty, "We do a good job of killing tanks, but we didn't come here to yank and bank." Press reports of an air-to-air kill by an AV-8B Harrier proved erroneous, but one Marine pilot did get an adrenaline 'high' from an unwanted encounter with an Iraqi fighter. In 'operations' in Saudi Arabia, pilots re-enact the meeting with a MiG.

Left: Captain Andrew Hall was among the pilots of Marine Attack Squadron VMA-231 'Aces'. They were uprooted from Japan and deployed to the Gulf, arriving just before Christmas.

Above: Captain Bill Delaney at the controls of SHANK 03, alias AV-8B Harrier 163673, makes the long deployment from Iwakuni, Japan, via the USA to King Abdul Aziz Air Base at Al Jubail in Saudi Arabia.

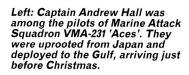

Left: SHANK 01, the personal aircraft of VMA-231 skipper Lieutenant Colonel 'Venom' Jones, prepares to fire up at Rota, Spain. The squadron is seen just before setting off on the last of five long stages from Japan to Saudi Arabia, where it formed part of the Desert Shield force.

Below: Captain Hall's AV-8B is ready to go, with CBU-58 cluster bombs and AIM-9M Sidewinder on port wingtip only. Harriers did little close support, being used more for battlefield interdiction, killing many tanks in the path of the advancing Marine ground force.

Below: The AV-8B Harrier, with exhausts near the center of its fuselage, was undeniably vulnerable to infra-red guided missiles. Nevertheless, it was successful in combat, with 85 per cent mission availability and only four aircraft lost.

AV-8B Harrier II

bombs, 500- or 1,000-pounders, or Rockeye cluster munitions. We can carry smart weapons, like Laser Maverick, but I guess not more than half a dozen were fired the whole war. We can also drop PGMs (Precision-Guided Munitions), but in the Gulf we left them to the Marine A-6 crews. We basically dropped unguided bombs. Later in the war, we usually carried six bombs each sortie, and I would say that cluster munitions made up the majority of our ordnance drop.

"Theoretically, we could have dropped iron bombs in level flight from 15,000 ft. But the steeper you are diving, the more accurate you are. Once, I got too close to the target before rolling in, and I had to push over to 63° to get in parameters. I felt like I was standing on the rudder pedals, as 45° is the steepest we really use.

"In a typical mission, carrying the Mk 20 Rockeye, there are two aircraft at 15,000 ft or more, attacking from different directions. I roll my aircraft into a 45° dive, popping chaff if there is any threat of radar-guided SAMs, and accelerate 500 kt true. Bombing symbology comes up on the head-up display as I pass through 10,000 ft, and I'm aiming for a 6,000-ft release. I guide the CCIP (Constantly Computed Impact Point) cross at the target, press the pickle button, then pull four or five gs away from the target.

"At the same time, I'm releasing decoy flares and jinking, to counter hand-held heat-seeking SAMs and AAA, until I'm back up to altitude. For maybe 30 seconds or so, I am in the envelope of medium/heavy triple-A and hand-held SAMs. Not a long time, but longer than any of us like. By co-ordinating the pull-up with my wingman, we can get back together with minimum wasted time. Once together we take up a combat spread – about 1½ mile separation.

"Each Rockeye carries up to 247 anti-armor bomblets. The bombing pattern would be about 200 ft wide by 300 ft long. Typically each AV-8B would drop two in a pass, leader and wingman overlapping to cover the entire target.

"When Rockeye hits, you can see the really dark little puffs of black smoke as the bomblets go off. The pattern starts at the point closest to your aircraft, and you can see it spread. You can tell when something is hit because there is a secondary explosion. Tanks, armored vehicles, artillery shells: anything explosive, and Rockeye will set it off."

Bombload
Harriers in the Gulf carried a variety of weaponry on their six wing pylons. With triple ejector racks, the AV-8B can carry three bombs on each of the inner pylons, but this was rarely seen after the early days. Four or six bombs, one to a pylon, were more common.

Below: Harrier pilots were never to forget the stark sights beneath them as they flew combat sorties. Smoke from burning enemy convoys and from the infamous oilwell fires combined with low-hanging clouds to create difficult flying conditions for ground attack aircraft.

Above: Conditions were never luxurious at King Abdul Aziz Naval Base or at the Tanajob FOL (Forward Operating Location). Marines lived in tents, and bombs baked in the hot desert sun.

Below: Flags of the United States and of the Marine Corps adorn a group portrait of VMA-231 pilots. In the front row is a vacant slot for Captain Russell Sanborn, shot down 9 February and still a prisoner when this photograph was taken.

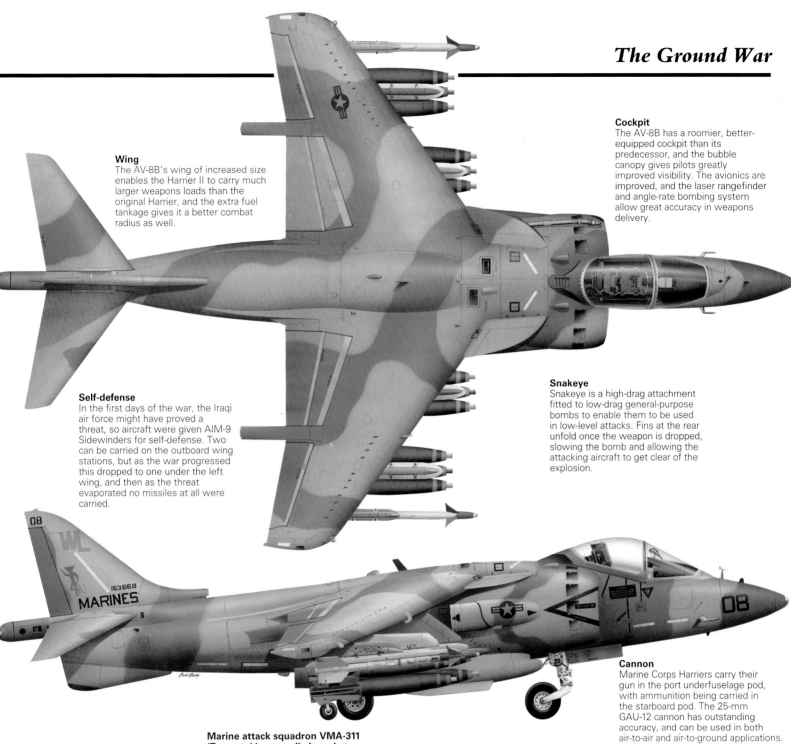

Wing
The AV-8B's wing of increased size enables the Harrier II to carry much larger weapons loads than the original Harrier, and the extra fuel tankage gives it a better combat radius as well.

Cockpit
The AV-8B has a roomier, better-equipped cockpit than its predecessor, and the bubble canopy gives pilots greatly improved visibility. The avionics are improved, and the laser rangefinder and angle-rate bombing system allow great accuracy in weapons delivery.

Self-defense
In the first days of the war, the Iraqi air force might have proved a threat, so aircraft were given AIM-9 Sidewinders for self-defense. Two can be carried on the outboard wing stations, but as the war progressed this dropped to one under the left wing, and then as the threat evaporated no missiles at all were carried.

Snakeye
Snakeye is a high-drag attachment fitted to low-drag general-purpose bombs to enable them to be used in low-level attacks. Fins at the rear unfold once the weapon is dropped, slowing the bomb and allowing the attacking aircraft to get clear of the explosion.

Cannon
Marine Corps Harriers carry their gun in the port underfuselage pod, with ammunition being carried in the starboard pod. The 25-mm GAU-12 cannon has outstanding accuracy, and can be used in both air-to-air and air-to-ground applications.

Marine attack squadron VMA-311 'Tomcats' is normally based at Yuma MCAS in Arizona, but during the Gulf war it was one of four Marine Corps AV-8B squadrons flying from the King Abdul Aziz air base.

Left: USS Nassau (LHA-4) became the first general-purpose assault ship to launch American warplanes in combat when it hosted AV-8Bs from VMA-331 'Bumblebees' and AH-1W Cobras from HMLA-269. One Nassau Harrier was lost in combat on 27 February. Mounting combat missions from a deck was a new experience for many sailors and Marines aboard the Nassau. Space was at a premium, and bombs were everywhere. Men routinely worked 16- to 18-hour days keeping the AV-8Bs of VMA-331 in combat.

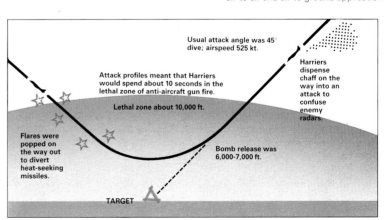

Usual attack angle was 45° dive; airspeed 525 kt.

Harriers dispense chaff on the way into an attack to confuse enemy radars.

Attack profiles meant that Harriers would spend about 10 seconds in the lethal zone of anti-aircraft gun fire.

Lethal zone about 10,000 ft.

Flares were popped on the way out to divert heat-seeking missiles.

Bomb release was 6,000-7,000 ft.

TARGET

Attacking with the Harrier
Bombing with the Harrier was a dangerous mission and took the aircraft well within the lethal zone of enemy anti-aircraft fire. Usually the missions would be carried out in two-ship formations, with five-second separation to confuse defenders. Attacks would be made using the Angle Rate Bombing System, which calculates the precise moment to release bombs when in the dive.

Intra-theater Transport

L argely overlooked is the story of the intra-theater, or tactical, airlift within the Persian Gulf region. C-130E/H Hercules and C-21A Learjet transports fanned out like the spokes of a wheel from hubs at Dhahran and Riyadh. They flew 52,300 sorties, carrying 514,600 passengers and 245,200 tons of cargo.

MAC's chief, General Johnson, explained, "There has been very little publicity about our C-130 force – and for good reasons. We did not want to tip off the Iraqis about the preparations for General Schwarzkopf's 'Hail Mary' pass [the end run to the west during the ground assault].

"Our C-130 squadrons played a crucial role in the preparation and conduct of the ground war. Between the beginning of the air war and the commencement of the ground war, our crews were flying around the clock, moving troops, equipment and supplies to forward staging areas.

"These crews saved the day after the ground war began. The worst weather in 15 years turned much of the desert into a swamp. When the Army's truck convoys became bogged down, our C-130s airdropped tons of ammunition and supplies to our forces deep in enemy territory. Without them, there would have been no 100-hour victory."

C-21A Learjets carried follow-up copies of the daily ATO from the 'Black Hole' in Riyadh to USAF fighter units in the field. C-21As also carried the photographic results of reconnaissance sorties to Riyadh from bases such as Sheikh Isa, where RF-4C Phantoms were sleuthing on the Iraqis.

Johnson devised a shortcut to get high-priority items to the war zone when needed. Called the 'Desert Express', this effort matched up priority items – for example, targeting pods needed by F-15E Eagles – with the needs of the outfit employing them. Routine methods of scheduling and planning were thrown by the boards: if it was needed, a special-category 'Desert Express' message was sent and the item was found and delivered.

Following hostilities, the airlift continued during Operation Provide Comfort as MAC supplied US forces dealing with the aftermath of war and with the Kurdish refugee problem in western Iraq. The strategic portion of Provide Comfort included 1,004 missions moving 10,840 passengers and 35,560 tons of cargo between 7 April and 19 June 1991. Intra-theater operations included 497 fixed-wing airdrop missions, parachuting supplies to refugees, as well as 1,627 non-MAC helicopter airdrops.

R.F.D.

Above: Military Airlift Command C-130 Hercules tactical transports gather at a desert strip in readiness to move material and men before the ground war begins.

Left: Deserts are pretty featureless, so tactical airlift crews, such as this C-130 pilot, needed accurate navigation to effectively support the ground forces operating over thousands of square miles of territory.

Above: During the build-up to war, Air National Guard Boeing C-22s were occasionally seen at various airports and air bases in Saudi Arabia. They were carrying senior ANG officers to the region to monitor Guard fighter units mobilized for Desert Shield.

Below: VIP-configured transports, such as this Boeing VC-135, were a commonplace sight at Saudi airfields as the US war machine geared itself for battle. In most cases, they were used to fly in senior commanders and staff from the Pentagon in Washington.

Nose art is traditionally linked with fighter and bomber aircraft, but Desert Storm saw this form of decoration being applied to some less usual types. Many military Airlift Command C-130 aircrew jumped on the bandwagon and added artwork to their aircraft. In part, this decoration was traditional in nature, but much of it stemmed from modern culture with 'Teenage Mutant Ninja Turtles' and 'Roger Rabbit' well to the fore when it came to representation.

Above: Moving personnel, mail and urgently needed equipment between carriers at sea and the shore bases was the task of the US Navy's C-2A Greyhound. With six carriers gathered in the region, working days were long for aircraft like this VRC-50 Greyhound, seen here taxiing on arrival at Bahrain.

In addition to the heavier metal like the Hercules, effective conduct of modern warfare is helped by the availability of communications and liaison aircraft. These were much in evidence in the Persian Gulf during Operations Desert Shield and Desert Storm. Types that were to be seen were many and varied and included US Army Beech C-12s (above left), US Air Force C-21A Learjets (above right), and C-20 Gulfstreams (below). The US Navy also dispatched a number of Beech UC-12 utility aircraft to the area for use in support tasks.

Left: A Military Airlift Command C-130E arrives at a Saudi base. Smoke from the hard-pressed brakes shows that the aircraft is heavily laden with supplies. Over 50,000 intra-theater airlift sorties were flown by MAC during the course of Desert Shield and Desert Storm.

Marine Helos

"When the 'Whiskey' Cobras came in it was a slaughter. They were taking out tanks and BTRs all over the area – the Iraqi counterattack got nowhere", was how one USMC helicopter pilot described an attack by Hellfire-armed AH-1W Cobra gunships during the 1st Marine Division's advance into Kuwait City.

The Cobra's intervention saved the lightly defended headquarters from being overrun by a surprise Iraqi counterattack from the burning Burqan oil field on the first day of the ground war. This attack was only one of many helicopter operations that ensured the success of I Marine Expeditionary Force's (I MEF) offensive to free Kuwait City.

As well as anti-armor tasks, the 323 USMC helicopters deployed to the Middle East for Desert Storm flew close air support, escort, recon, troop transport, supply, casevac and deception missions. Many of them were carried out at night by flight crews using night-vision goggles. Operating from forward airstrips in support of the 1st and 2nd Marine Divisions were 39 AH-1s, 30 UH-1 Hueys, 60 CH-46 Sea

Knights and 53 CH-53 Sea Stallions of Marine Air Groups 16 and 26. Afloat in the Persian Gulf with the 4th and 5th Marine Expeditionary Brigades (MEB) and the 13th Marine Expeditionary Unit (Special Operations Capable) (MEU (SOC)) were 39 AH-1s, 20 UH-1s, 60 CH-46 and 22 CH-53s.

The surprise Iraqi raid on the Saudi Arabian border town of Khafji on 29 January gave the USMC the chance to show what their AH-1W ('Whiskey' Cobras, in Marine Corps parlance) could do. After Saudi Marines fled from the town, the Cobras were called in to soften up the occupying Iraqi troops to allow Saudi National Guard and Qatari troops to retake it. Hellfire and TOW guided missiles were used with devastating effect by the 'Whiskey' Cobras to take out Iraqi observation posts in a tower.

The Marine gunships also teamed up with USAF AC-130 Spectres and A-10As to hit follow-on Iraqi armored units trying to support their comrades trapped in Khafji. On the same night that Khafji was occupied, two other Iraqi armored units attempted to make incursions into Saudi Arabia further inland, but

Above: A US Navy phibron, or amphibious squadron, forms the backdrop as the imposing bulk of a Marine Corps CH-53E descends to alight on a landing platform. For a time, it seemed as if the coalition planned a major landing on the coasts of Kuwait. It was no mere feint; had it been needed, such a landing would have gone in hard.

Left: General purpose amphibious assault ships like the USS Saipan (LHA-2) were an important part of the large coalition naval force that assembled in the Gulf. Docking wells allow such vessels to handle landing craft, and a carrier-sized deck CH-53E and CH-46E transport helicopters, AH-1W gunships, and Harrier II close support fighters.

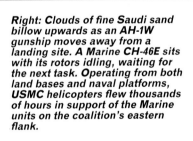

Above: Gray and desert camouflage paint adorns *USMC CH-53Es* at a Saudi base. They have gathered to airlift ground troops from the rear echelons to fresh positions nearer to the front line during the closing stages of *Operation Desert Shield.*

Above left, inset: *T*ightly holding on to their weapons, an apprehensive group of Marines wears ear mufflers as they fly into action in the noisy cabin of a *CH-46E.*

Below: *A Marine Corps CH-46E* crew chief checks ahead of the aircraft as the pilots await permission to take off on a mission. The *CH-46* is the primary Marine Corps transport and assault helicopter, and 60 were deployed to the Gulf.

Right: *Clouds of fine Saudi sand billow upwards as an AH-1W gunship moves away from a landing site. A Marine CH-46E sits with its rotors idling, waiting for the next task. Operating from both land bases and naval platforms, USMC helicopters flew thousands of hours in support of the Marine units on the coalition's eastern flank.*

Below: *Inflight refueling of US Marine Corps CH-53Es allowed them to undertake long-range missions in support of fast-moving allied forces once the ground war began. Marine aircraft almost invariably used their own KC-130 'flying gas stations'. Operating out of Sheikh Isa Air Base on Bahrain, these were equipped with a pod-mounted hose and drogue to transfer fuel.*

they were successfully repulsed by USMC units backed up by more 'Whiskey' Cobras.

When I MEF ground units crossed into Kuwait at the start of the coalition ground offensive on 24 February, USMC CH-46s and CH-53s played a key role in airlifting supplies and troops forward. Helicopters from the MAG 26 flew TOW-armed jeeps and Humvees deep into Kuwait on the first day of the war to reinforce the Marine infantry of Task Force Toro, which had infiltrated through Iraqi minefields on foot. The Sea Knight and Sea Stallion pilots had to fly their machines through thick smoke from burning oil fields to reach their landing zone, but still put their vital cargoes down on time.

Three days later MAG 26 carried out another deep penetration air assault to deliver a security force onto the eastern edge of Kuwait International Airport in support of USMC tank units fighting Iraqi armor nearby. AH-1J/T Cobras flew escort for the transports after being replaced in the anti-armor role by the more capable 'Whiskey' Cobras.

While the 1st Marine Division was advancing past the Ahmed Al Jaber airfield its LAV-25 battalion detected an Iraqi armored force approaching the divisional command post. The scout vehicles initially engaged the Iraqi armor with their 25-mm cannon and then marked targets with laser designators for Hellfire-armed AH-1Ws. More than 60 Iraqi tanks were destroyed in this engagement. During the final stages of the advance into Kuwait City the Marine Cobras were operating at extreme range and were often refueled from mobile fuel trucks or CH-53s just behind the front line. Marine Corps helicopters also made use of Task Force 160 refueling trucks, which were forward supporting US Army Special Operations Command helicopters.

Out in the Persian Gulf helicopters deployed with Marine amphibious warfare forces were kept busy supporting raids and deception missions along the Kuwait coast. On 29 January the 13th MEU(SOC) captured Umm al Maradin island, and on 25 February a major deception operation was carried out against R'as as Sabiyah by the 4th MEB. More than 60 helicopters flew dummy approach and strike missions against the Kuwaiti peninsula, while USMC AV-8B Harriers flew in support from USS *Nassau*. A number of Iraqi divisions were subsequently moved into this area in response to the USMC feint.

T.R.

Above: Potential landing sites abound in the desert terrain over which much of the ground war was fought. This helped rotary-winged craft to play a major part in the battle. Prepositioning of fuel and munitions enabled the attack helicopter forces to fan out and engage Iraqi troops and armor from all points of the compass.

Top: A Marine servicing team runs towards an AH-1W Cobra, which keeps its rotors turning as it lands to re-arm with a fresh load of TOW anti-armor missiles. In a matter of minutes, the Cobra will be on the move again, flying low over the desert as it returns to inflict still more damage on Iraq's badly battered army.

Bell AH-1W Super Cobra

Originally developed during the Vietnam War, the Bell AH-1 was the world's first dedicated gunship helicopter. The Marine Corps was to adopt the type, suitably upgraded for overwater operations, as one of their primary close-support machines.

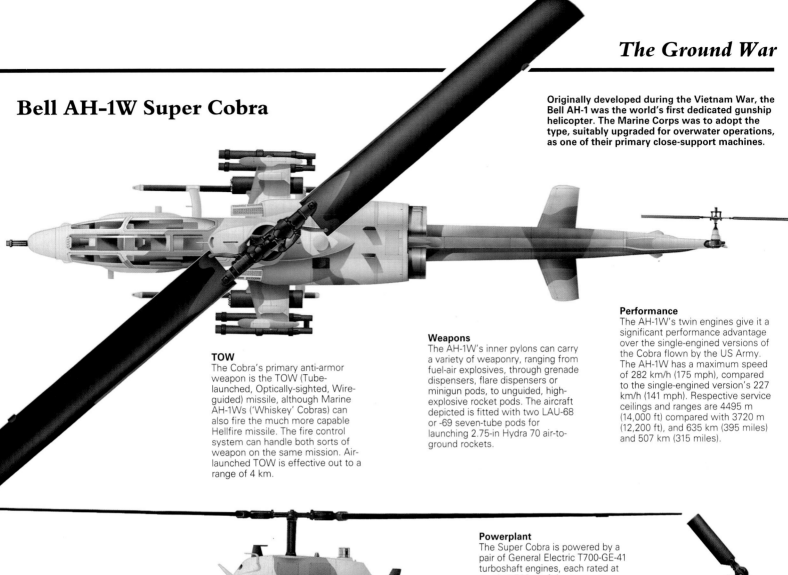

TOW
The Cobra's primary anti-armor weapon is the TOW (Tube-launched, Optically-sighted, Wire-guided) missile, although Marine AH-1Ws ('Whiskey' Cobras) can also fire the much more capable Hellfire missile. The fire control system can handle both sorts of weapon on the same mission. Air-launched TOW is effective out to a range of 4 km.

Weapons
The AH-1W's inner pylons can carry a variety of weaponry, ranging from fuel-air explosives, through grenade dispensers, flare dispensers or minigun pods, to unguided, high-explosive rocket pods. The aircraft depicted is fitted with two LAU-68 or -69 seven-tube pods for launching 2.75-in Hydra 70 air-to-ground rockets.

Performance
The AH-1W's twin engines give it a significant performance advantage over the single-engined versions of the Cobra flown by the US Army. The AH-1W has a maximum speed of 282 km/h (175 mph), compared to the single-engined version's 227 km/h (141 mph). Respective service ceilings and ranges are 4495 m (14,000 ft) compared with 3720 m (12,200 ft), and 635 km (395 miles) and 507 km (315 miles).

Powerplant
The Super Cobra is powered by a pair of General Electric T700-GE-41 turboshaft engines, each rated at nearly 1,700 shaft horsepower. Twin engines are an important safety feature for the overwater missions Marine Cobras fly.

Cannon
The AH-1W is armed with a General Electric undernose turret which mounts an M197 three-barrelled 20-mm cannon. It has a rate of fire of 690 rounds per minute, but a 16-round burst limiter is incorporated into the firing switch.

Left: Marine helicopters dot a forward operating location, as they resupply and await new orders before rejoining the battle. The two AH-IWs are being refueled from the CH-53 deep in the war zone. At times, the push into Kuwait and Iraq forged ahead so fast that allied leaders were hard-pressed to stay abreast of events.

Right: A Marine Corps Cobra pilot and gunner settle into their AH-1 as they prepare to depart on another sortie. Their task was simple: to search for fresh targets for their gun and missiles. Along with the US Army's AH-64 Apaches, the AH-1s of the Marine Corps inflicted terrible suffering on an Iraqi army already demoralized by weeks of intense bombardment from the air.

The only Coast Guard aircraft to participate in the war were the HU-25B Guardians based on Bahrain. Optimized for search, rescue and maritime surveillance, they were primarily used in monitoring the huge oil slick that the Iraqis had pumped into the Persian Gulf.

from page 162 **(25 February continued)**

had not been engaged by Patriot batteries because it had been calculated that the trajectory of the 'Scud' would take it clear of the area the batteries were assigned to protect (in fact the building hit was on the edge of the protected area).

The number of Iraqi prisoners taken by coalition forces now topped 14,000.

Coalition combat losses: one US Marine Corps AV-8B Harrier of VMA-542 (pilot rescued by helicopter), an Army AH-64 helicopter (crew uninjured) and an OV-10A Bronco spotter plane (one crewman taken prisoner, one killed).

26 February, Tuesday At 1:00 a.m. Baghdad radio announced that President Saddam Hussein had ordered his troops to withdraw from Kuwait. After the ambiguities of his previous 'peace offer' there was considerable speculation on the significance of the statement.

Meanwhile, US and British armored units continued their sweeping movement intended to outflank and cut off the whole of the Iraqi ground force in Kuwait. Helicopter-borne troops reached points on the River Euphrates, cutting the road between Baghdad and Basra. Tallil airfield was captured and three MiG fighters, three helicopters and a transport aircraft were destroyed on the ground.

British troops engaged in a night clash with an Iraqi armored division, during which they knocked out some 40 tanks. British Army Lynx helicopters, in action with TOW missiles, destroyed four enemy tanks and several tracked vehicles. During the action nine British soldiers were killed when two of their armored personnel carriers were attacked in error by an A-10.

Later that morning President Saddam Hussein appeared on Baghdad radio, stating that Kuwait was no longer part of Iraq and confirming that his forces would have left the Emirate 'by the end of the day'. Coalition governments quickly pointed out that the broadcast, by itself, fell short of the requirements of the various United Nations Security Council Resolutions and formed no basis for a cease-fire.

During the morning came indications that the Iraqi troops were indeed pulling out of Kuwait, and by the late afternoon Kuwait City had been abandoned and was in the hands of resistance fighters.

From the south, Arab coalition forces and US Marines advanced rapidly on Kuwait City. At Kuwait International Airport the

to page 180 **(26 February continued)**

Battlefield Bronco
Captain Mark Schulte, VMO-1, OV-10 Bronco

Above: Captain Mark Schulte and his observer, Captain Dan Holzrichken, from US Marine Corps observation squadron VMO-1, pose with one of the unit's desert-camouflaged Broncos.

Above: A trio of Broncos accompanies a tanker over the desert. The OV-10s had crossed the Atlantic aboard US Navy carriers, before flying the length of the Mediterranean to their operating base at Al Jubail.

"The second day of the ground war, we found an Iraqi tank brigade. The fog had moved in real good that morning, and we had clouds everywhere. The guys on the ground, part of the 1st Marine Division, thought that they had enemy movement to the northeast.

"We got on station at about 0900, and started looking. We could see our troops, but just to the north of them the clouds were still there, the fog was still there. We'd head out for a mile, make a lazy turn back to our troops. Then we'd go another mile out a little further along, repeating the maneuver all round their front. If we didn't see anything, we'd start again, maybe two miles out, and so on.

"You don't want to go too high or too low. If you're high, you're pretty much clear of the threat envelope. But, and I don't care what anyone else says, you can't see very well, especially an enemy that's dug-in well. If you are down low, you can see real well of course, but you are right in the middle of the threat envelope, and if you get yourself shot down you're not doing anybody any good. You've got to find a happy medium. During the air war I stayed high and away from the threat. During the ground war we came down to about 5,000 ft. That's high enough that you are unlikely to be hit by triple-A or

Above: TOW-armed Sea Cobras of the Marine Corps prepare to do battle with Iraqi armor. Information on enemy concentrations was regularly provided by forward air controllers flying in OV-10 Broncos.

infantry weapons, and low enough that you can tell the difference between a live dug-in tank and one that had been knocked out two weeks before.

"We finally found the Iraqi tank brigade, maybe 40 tanks. The first thing we did was to ensure our friendly forces knew from where the enemy was coming so that they could set up defenses. We immediately started calling for bombers. Being Marines, the AV-8 was the aircraft of choice for us. The clouds were clearing up nicely, so anyone we called in would see these guys coming.

"Initially, the Iraqis were coming in column, which is tactically pretty stupid. I guess they were trying to pass themselves off as surrendering. We circled over them, realizing that that might not have been too smart either, but we just had to know. Eventually, we determined in our own minds that they were not surrendering. We advised 1st Marine Division that these people were probably going to attack, and they should be prepared.

"At about that time, the tanks started spreading out into an attack formation. Finally, they sent a round down range, which pretty much started the engagement. Since I was in contact with the ground at the time, I asked the ground-based forward air controller whether he knew of any airs on station. He replied that there was a division of Cobras at a check point, and could I get them? So we flew over to the Cobras and escorted them back to attack the southern flank of the Iraqi brigade.

"The four Cobras used TOW missiles. They took out at least eight tanks. After they'd expended their TOWs they went back behind friendly troops. We flew high over our own line and started calling up air support. As soon as we got the jets in we'd fly back out there and take out the rear elements. We got a pair of Harriers each time, and each Harrier would make two runs. As they finished, we'd fly back and try to call up some more. We did that three times.

"After about two-and-a-half hours, the engagement was just about over. The guys on the ground took out a lot of tanks themselves, and they also designated targets for Hellfire-armed Cobras. Marine Cobras can carry Hellfire, like the Army Apaches.

"The Iraqis were very brave. They didn't all just up and surrender. These guys mounting the counterattack just kept coming, even when our tanks and air just overpowered them.

Above: V/STOL AV-8B Harrier IIs were among the 'customers' which relied on Bronco FACs for targets. Here, an AV-8B meets a KC-130 for fuel before rejoining the battle.

"In addition to controlling air assets, we could also give advice to the guys on the ground. Since we're up in the air, and since we're in close contact, we can tell them, 'Hey, you're going the wrong way, you want to come further over here.' We're also useful for clearing up confusion: towards the end of this engagement somebody from another battalion close by thought that they were being overrun by Iraqi tanks. We went to search them out and found that they were American tanks."

Above and left: Variations in camouflage pattern are evident on these two Marine Corps Bronco FAC aircraft. Two basic versions were used in Desert Storm and both are shown here, the sand-and-tan colored machine being an OV-10A. The other aircraft is an OV-10D, which can operate at night using the FLIR turret under the nose. Up to four special forces commandos can be carried in the rear fuselage.

Helicopter Air Assault

In dry language, 24 February 1991 was the day the allies launched their ground assault on Iraqi forces in Iraq and Kuwait. More descriptively, it was the day the sky filled with bugs.

The sky itself was hard to see, for the desert lay beneath scudding clouds – and, in the east, fog. But anyone looking up would have seen so many helicopters, with so many rotors thrashing, that it looked as if the Middle East had been invaded by a plague of hyperactive insects.

At least 550 helicopters were in-theater. Two-thirds of them flew in the air assault. Sikorsky, builder of UH-60A/L Black Hawks (and of specialized models, among them the UH-60V 'Dustoff' medevac helicopter), claimed to have more of its airframes in Desert Storm than any other aircraft manufacturer. But much of the movement of soldiers and marines was achieved with CH-47D Chinooks and CH-46E Sea Knights.

To the west, more than 2,000 US air assault troops plunged 50 miles (80 km) into Iraq at first light in the largest helicopter operation in history. This thrust was the final movement in what became known as the 'left hook' or, in General H. Norman Schwarzkopf's analogy with American football, the 'Hail Mary' play. With poor C^3I (Command, Control, Communications and Intelligence), Iraq overlooked obvious signs that the left hook was coming.

To the east, US Navy SEALs landed on the beach in very small numbers (some put there by MH-53J Pave Low helicopters) to make noise, show movement and fake a 13th Marine Expeditionary Unit invasion of the Kuwaiti coast. Some CH-46Es lifted off from assault ships in the Gulf, acting busy to convince any surviving Iraqi radar operators that a Marine assault was coming. Marines remained poised to hit the beach – and to be inserted by helicopter deeper inland – but the invasion was deceit. It was never intended.

The massive assault by the US Army to the west – avoiding a head-on attack against fortifications and, instead, striking the enemy where he was not defended – vindicated the US's AirLand battle doctrine, which stressed mobility, flexibility and the use of aviation to shift ground forces quickly. It was not so much Schwarzkopf's brainchild as that of a small cadre of lieutenant colonels, nicknamed the 'Jedi Knights', who had struggled for years to make highly mobile warfare a part of US Army doctrine. All favored helicopter insertion to put troops in the right places at the right time. In a world

of shoulder-mounted IR (Infra-Red) missiles, this decidedly did *not* mean setting down in a 'hot' LZ (Landing Zone) under direct fire, as had been done in Vietnam. Speed, surprise and deception could, and did, get friendly troops *behind* the enemy.

General Colin Powell, Chairman of the Joint Chiefs of Staff, had even broadcast to Saddam Hussein a message Saddam failed to hear – "We're going to cut them off and then we're going to kill them."

In the helicopter assault to the west, 2,000 men of the 101st Airborne seized Salman airfield 50 miles (80 km) inside Iraq. More than a hundred CH-47D Chinooks and UH-60A/L Black Hawks brought these troopers to their objective, flanked and guarded by AH-64 Apaches.

It was the largest attack by helicopter-borne troops in history. One pilot who shuttled back and forth with men and equipment was Major Marie T. Rossi, 32, deployed as part of Company B, 2nd Battalion, 159th Aviation Regiment, 24th Infantry Division (Mechanized), from Fort Stewart, Georgia.

The 'Shithook', soldiers inevitably called the Chinook. The US Army's only medium-lift helicopter, intended to operate at low level and at night hauling supplies, combat support equipment and troops to the battlefield, the twin-turbine CH-47D is powered by two T55-L-11A turboshaft engines rated at 3,750 shp each and carries 33 soldiers. Under a $1.7-billion, five-year contract of 1985, Boeing converted 240 A, B and C model Chinooks into CH-47D models; an order for 197 more followed in 1989. The CH-47D was deemed 'twice as productive' as Vietnam-era versions and able to carry 26,000 lb of cargo (11794 kg) on its triple-cargo-hook system, and grossed 50,000 lb (22680 kg) on a typical mission. The CH-47D model incorporates revised electrical systems, glass-fiber rotor blades, modular hydraulic systems and single-point pressure refuelling.

The US Army felt it had solved problems which had caused Congress to ask whether the CH-47D "[was] a reliable workhorse or an accident waiting to happen" – troubled by a faulty combiner transmission, a fire danger to aluminum flight control rods and hairline cracks in the shaft structure.

In the Gulf, Chinooks flew as low as 40 ft, passing over an ancient lake bed into the area being secured and expanded by the 101st Airborne and the 24th Mechanized. Rossi's was just one of column

after column of Chinooks reinforcing the Americans in Iraq with field artillery, trucks, boxes of ammunition and fuel. Rossi was asked whether low-level flying unnerved her. She admitted that piloting a helicopter at low level entailed risk.

The 101st Airborne set up at Salman as a key location to fuel and supply troop-carrying helicopters for assaults into the strategic Euphrates River valley to cut off the main highway between Basra and Baghdad.

The Marine Corps, which had some of the most difficult fighting

in its head-on assaults on Iraqi positions in eastern Kuwait, generally gives credit to the CH-46E Sea Knight for doing a good job. Production of the H-46 series had ended in 1971. Powered by two 1,650-shp T58-GE-16 engines, the CH-46E upgraded version carried 25 troops or 7,000 lb (3175 kg) of cargo. Its range with a full payload was less than 100 miles (161 km), the Sea Knight never having been intended for long-distance operations across vast deserts.

Because of the CH-46E's short 'legs', during earlier skirmishes

US Army Black Hawks and Apaches are seen on the move as the ground war begins to intensify. In the initial wave of the land battle, over 2,000 airborne infantrymen were ferried 50 miles into Iraqi territory, in one of largest heliborne assaults ever mounted.

Above: The UH-60V variant of the versatile Sikorsky Black Hawk is the US Army's principal 'medevac' helicopter. Airlifting casualties to rear-echelon treatment centers and prompt tending of wounds and injuries saves many lives. During Desert Storm, however, the overwhelming coalition attack suffered few casualties, and the 'Dustoff' evacuation units generally found little to do.

Below and bottom: The CH-47 Chinook was one of the most versatile helicopters in the Gulf. Much in demand for support tasks, the medium-lift Chinook can carry underslung and internal loads with equal ease. The current model in US Army service is the CH-47D, which is considerably more capable than earlier versions, with a 10-tonne load-carrying capacity. The CH-47's main task was to airlift heavy equipment around the battlefield. The Royal Air Force also used the CH-47 in the Gulf.

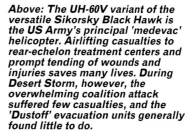

Left: A CH-53 comes to a hover as it delivers an underslung load. Helicopters ranged far and wide during the ground war, but the demand for their services placed great strains on both the machines and the crews manning them.

Above: The Bell UH-1 Iroquois has been largely superseded in combat formations by the UH-60, but it remains in widespread use. It saw service in the Gulf, nearly 30 years after its combat debut in Southeast Asia.

around Khafji the Marines had set up an FOL (Forward Operating Location), known as Lonesome Dove, which enabled Sea Knights and their AH-1W Cobra escorts to be replenished and to fly missions from within a couple of miles of the ground fighting. A field maintenance facility, airlifted into Lonesome Dove, provided 'full service', with considerable improvisation, and kept the Marines' aging fleet in the air. More than a few Marines, however, wished their service's plans to acquire the tilt-rotor MV-22 Osprey had materialized.

"I love it like my mother," said CH-46E plane captain Sergeant Arnold Grove, "but she's old and so is it."

The assault against Iraq, spearheaded by Chinooks and Sea Knights, ended in the liberation of Kuwait within 100 hours. On 1 March, just a short time after the cease-fire which followed the victory, Major Marie T. Rossi's CH-47 flew into a microwave tower on a low-level mission. All aboard were killed. Rossi was the highest-ranking American to die in Desert Storm.

R.F.D.

'Warthog' War

Above: The Fairchild A-10 was in the twilight of its career when it was called to arms for the first time. It was always considered vulnerable in its NATO environment, and in the desert it was expected to stick out like a sore thumb. However, the A-10 became one of the stars of the war, causing immense damage to Iraqi vehicles while being able to accept and survive enemy fire. This is one of the OA-10A FAC aircraft of the 23rd TASS.

Left: Shark mouths are a traditionally aggressive method of marking combat aircraft, but on few aircraft can it be seen to such effect as the A-10s of the 23rd TFW.

Left: At the heart of the A-10's power is its gun, and the huge 30-mm cannon projectiles which it fires. Made of depleted (non-radioactive) uranium, the milk bottle-sized 30-mm cannon shells ripped through the armor of Saddam's army.

Below: 'Warthogs' from the 511th Tactical Fighter Squadron, 10th Tactical Fighter Wing, stand ready at Al Jouf, for a 'Sandy' combat rescue mission.

Second only to the F-16 Fighting Falcon in terms of quantity deployed to the Gulf region during Desert Shield, Fairchild Republic's A-10A Thunderbolt II received little publicity once the fighting started in earnest, with most of the glory going to the 'sexier' hardware such as the F-117A and the F-15E Strike Eagle. Had it not been for the presence of around 200 much-maligned 'Warthogs', however, it seems certain that the ground forces would have paid a far higher cost in terms of loss of life when battle was joined on the ground.

Like other USAF warplanes, the A-10A was quick to deploy eastwards as Desert Shield moved into top gear. Eventually, most of the 23rd TFW and the 354th TFW were shifted to Saudi Arabia. Other units that dispatched A-10As to the area between August 1990 and January 1991 included the UK-based 10th TFW and an Air Force Reserve outfit from New Orleans, Louisiana.

Within days of the air war starting, the Thunderbolt II was heavily committed to softening up the Iraqi defenses in Kuwait. Once the ground war kicked off it worked in close co-operation with US Army helicopter gunships, ranging ahead of the troops and 'sanitizing' areas through which they would have to pass. In both tasks, the A-10A proved itself to be highly adept at 'busting' tanks, and exacted a heavy toll of Iraqi armor with its GAU-8/A Avenger 30-mm cannon and AGM-65

Maverick air-to-surface missiles. Combat activity was by no means confined solely to anti-armor operations, for the A-10A also engaged known troop concentrations with more conventional forms of ordnance such as the Rockeye cluster-bomb unit. Other weaponry that was routinely carried included at least one AIM-9 Sidewinder infra-red missile for self-defense purposes.

As it transpired, Iraqi attempts to disrupt coalition air power were few and far between, and there is no evidence of any Sidewinder being fired from an A-10A. Even though aerial threats were to all intents and purposes nonexistent, the A-10A's operating envelope did place it at considerable risk to ground fire, with inevitable consequences; a total of five 'Warthogs' was lost in combat.

Some idea of its undoubted worth can be gleaned from the performance of just two 'Warthog' pilots. In a single day (25 February), Captain Eric Solomonson and First Lieutenant John Marks of the 23rd TFW accounted for 23 tanks between them as the allied troops steamrollered their way over the opposition. Other A-10A pilots no doubt proved themselves almost as

'Warthogs' Kill 23 Tanks in One Day

As the ground war slipped into its second day, with allied tanks and troops rolling across the desert sands, the venerable A-10A 'Warthog' continued to prove its low-tech mettle against Iraqi armor. There were dozens of anti-tank sorties on the morning of 25 February, but one which stood out was flown by a pair of A-10A pilots who set a record of sorts. A large column of Iraqi tanks was rolling south from areas occupied by the Republican Guard. Captain Eric Solomonson and Lieutenant John Marks of the 76th TFS/23rd TFW scrambled to engage them.

Solomonson arrived over Iraq at sunrise. Solomonson and Marks, after considerable action already, were surprised to see no anti-aircraft fire coming at them. The way was paved by a FAC (Forward Air Controller) in an OA-10, who confirmed that no friendlies were in the area. "You guys can just go in there and start shooting."

A haze shrouded the target area where some Iraqi tanks were smoldering from earlier A-10A attacks. Others had scattered. Some were pulling off both sides of the road, while others tried to hide in prepositioned revetments. Marks came up with the idea of straightening out the confusion by following the tracks where they had churned up the sand. "At the end of the tracks there was the hot spot – a tank."

The A-10A pilots, carrying infrared AGM-65 Maverick missiles and 30-mm ammunition (1,174 rounds), swooped through the haze and attacked the tanks. The Maverick missiles, which detect and home on heat sources, had unusually rich targets with the tank engines

Left: A burned-out Iraqi T-55 main battle tank stands mute testimony to the tank-killing power of the 'Warthog'. Since the A-10's 30-mm gun/Maverick missile combination is capable of destroying even the latest laminated-armor fighting vehicles, 30-year-old designs like the T-54s and T-55s, which made up the bulk of Iraq's armored inventory, stood no chance.

Below: Armorers suffer under the fierce desert heat as they prepare to load Mk 20 Rockeye II cluster-bombs onto an A-10 from the 23rd Tactical Fighter Wing, normally based at England AFB in Louisiana. Rockeye cluster-bombs were widely used in the Gulf. Primarily a weapon used against soft-skinned and lightly armored vehicles, each Rockeye consists of a Mk 7 CBU (Cluster Bomb Unit) loaded with 247 Mk 118 anti-tank bomblets.

Above: 'Warthog' warpaint was most often displayed in the ladder access door. This machine is from the 353rd Tactical Fighter Squadron, the 'Panthers', part of the 354th Tactical Fighter Wing which is normally based at Myrtle Beach, South Carolina.

proficient in taking on enemy armor, but perhaps the most extraordinary incidents were those in which two A-10As flown by AFRes personnel managed to account for a couple of enemy helicopters with the 30-mm gun. These engagements occurred on 6 February and 15 February and were, in fact, unique, being the only aerial encounters of Desert Storm in which this type of weapon was employed.

L.P.

Fairchild A-10 Thunderbolt II

A-10s from the 23rd TFW deployed from England AFB in Louisiana to Saudi Arabia for the whole of Operations Desert Shield and Desert Storm. 80-186, or *'Tiger 1'*, was the wing commander's aircraft.

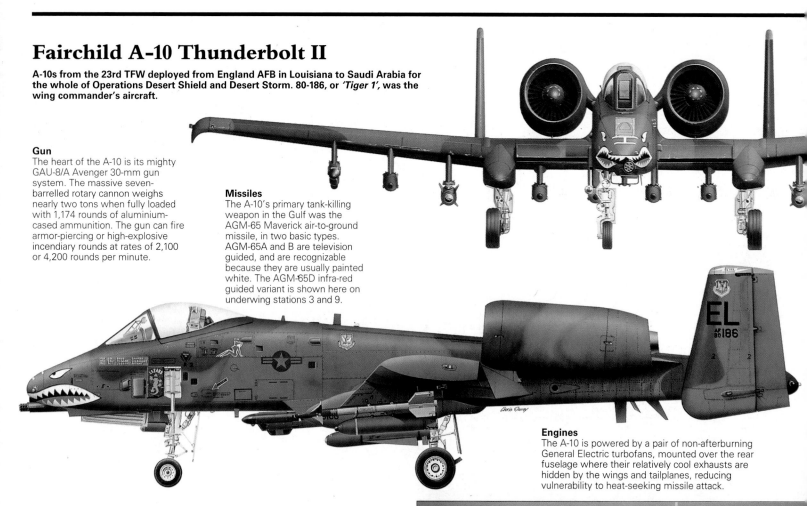

Gun
The heart of the A-10 is its mighty GAU-8/A Avenger 30-mm gun system. The massive seven-barrelled rotary cannon weighs nearly two tons when fully loaded with 1,174 rounds of aluminium-cased ammunition. The gun can fire armor-piercing or high-explosive incendiary rounds at rates of 2,100 or 4,200 rounds per minute.

Missiles
The A-10's primary tank-killing weapon in the Gulf was the AGM-65 Maverick air-to-ground missile, in two basic types. AGM-65A and B are television guided, and are recognizable because they are usually painted white. The AGM-65D infra-red guided variant is shown here on underwing stations 3 and 9.

Engines
The A-10 is powered by a pair of non-afterburning General Electric turbofans, mounted over the rear fuselage where their relatively cool exhausts are hidden by the wings and tailplanes, reducing vulnerability to heat-seeking missile attack.

Below: Armorers examine the shattered wing and undercarriage of a battle-damaged A-10. The tough A-10 was the aircraft best able to go into the envelope of Iraqi short-range air defenses and survive. Although two A-10s and two OA-10 FACs were lost during the war, they formed a tiny percentage of losses compared to missions flown and damage inflicted.

Right: Although the A-10 was thought to be coming to the end of its career, 194 A-10s accounted for over 1,000 tanks, nearly 2,000 APCs and artillery pieces, 1,400 other vehicles, 190 radar sites and nearly 100 surface-to-surface missile sites. 'Night Penetration' was a 355th TFS aircraft, credited with destroying one 'Scud' and 22 tanks, artillery pieces and armored vehicles.

running and extremely hot. It took 10 minutes for the pair to kill six tanks with Mavericks. Two more fell beneath the driving force of the A-10's 30-mm GAU-8/A seven-barrelled cannon. The gun is the most powerful (in terms of muzzle velocity) ever mounted in an aircraft, firing uranium-depleted rounds the size of a milk bottle, which can penetrate the steel hull of a tank, or even the 'reactive armor' employed by some Soviet tanks, at distances up to 7,000 yd (6200 m).

Throughout the day, the A-10A pilots were to see T-62s and at least one T-72 – the principal tracked vehicles of Iraq's armory.

No one in uniform likes war, but as he pulled off and looked back at eight tanks burning and exploding, ammunition cooking off and creating a furious spray behind him, Solomonson thought, "For an A-10 pilot it just doesn't get any better than this."

Rather than return to their original base, the 'Warthogs' set down at a FOL (Forward Operating Location) where they refueled and re-armed. At first, the pilots thought they would be instructed to shut down and simply sit alert. Instead, an operations officer found Solomonson and

Ordnance
A-10s have four weapons stations under each wing and three under the fuselage, numbered from 1 to 11 from the port wingtip. Weapons used in the Gulf included Mk 20 Rockeye II anti-armor cluster-bombs (depicted here) and a variety of bombs, cluster munitions and air-to-ground rocket pods.

Self-defense
Stations 1 and 11 were used for self-defense systems. Station 1 usually carried a pair of AIM-9 Sidewinder air-to-air missiles, while station 11 was reserved for an electronic countermeasures pod, in this case the AN/ALQ-119.

Above: It is not surprising that the A-10's powerful armament should figure largely in the nose art of the USAF's Warthog squadrons.

Top: The starboard nose art of 'Tiger 1' depicted above.

Above: The Air Force accountants would not be amused if this enemy bicycle cost a Maverick.

Performance
The A-10 is a slow machine, and the USAF has been looking to replace it with a faster jet. This ignores the facts that the Warthog is highly agile, carries a large weapons load which it can deliver extremely accurately, and is very strongly built. Any replacement is unlikely to be able to do the same job as well.

shouted, "Get saddled up again! Go!" Marines needed help just southwest of Kuwait City. Solomonson and Marks were told to get there, fast.

The duo's second mission was more intense than the first – more like what had been predicted for a high-intensity conflict. A Marine F/A-18 Hornet flying 'Fast FAC' told the approaching A-10A pilots that two AV-8B Harriers had already been hit. One was down and the other was leaving the area on fire, the pilot preparing to eject.

The Marine pilots had had a real ordeal. The second Harrier pilot apparently succeeded in getting back to safety without having to eject. In the first AV-8B, Captain Scott Walsh of squadron VMFA-542 ejected, making a shaky but safe parachute landing. He was eventually rescued by a Navy SH-60B helicopter – only the third combat rescue of the war.

Before the SH-60B appeared, Solomonson and Marks got on the air with an offer to help out in the search and rescue for Walsh, but the FAC told them to continue on because he had enemy tanks on the ground and the Americans on the ground needed help immediately.

Arriving on the scene, Marks

was surprised that American ground forces had pushed so far forward. "The targets were parked in revetments on both sides of a major road running west out of Kuwait City."

In a fast and furious engagement, Solomonson and Marks took out eight more tanks, six with Mavericks and two with cannon fire.

Their long day was not finished.

The pilots returned to their main base, re-armed, and launched again to support Marines who were now probing at the outskirts of Kuwait City. The A-10A pilots were told to remain on station while Saudi artillery fired into the target area. Then, the A-10As moved in and set seven more tanks afire.

Says Marks, "We called in our bomb damage assessment to the wing operations center and they

said we'd set an all-time record for Maverick and bullet [cannon] kills."

As Solomonson explained the success of the A-10, "We're impressing a lot of people. We're coming in with more confirmed bomb damage than any other jet. No kidding, see the targets and know they are destroyed. We also only report the stuff we see blowing up or on fire. There are other jets that fly a lot faster, a lot higher, but don't drop nearly as much stuff, nor can they hang out in the target area as long as we can."

R.F.D.

from page 172 **(26 February continued)**

Marines fought a fierce battle with Iraqi troops who appeared not to have received the order to withdraw.

The Iraqi withdrawal from Kuwait quickly turned into a fighting retreat. The columns of vehicles streaming out of Kuwait City on the three available routes showed up clearly on the display of the E-8 J-STARS radar aircraft monitoring the battlefield, and large numbers of aircraft were brought in to bomb and strafe them. One of the columns was attacked by US Marine Corps aircraft, which waited until the leading vehicles were some distance from Kuwait City and then dropped mines across the road to bring them to a halt. Attacking aircraft were assigned to killing zones, with eight fresh aircraft entering the area every 15 minutes to keep up the momentum of the attack. In the words of Major General Royal Moore, Commander of Marine Air Wing 3, "It was a turkey shoot for several hours, then the weather turned sour."

By the end of the day, 21 Iraqi divisions were claimed destroyed or rendered ineffective, amounting to about half of the force that had occupied Kuwait. In some areas of the country pockets of resistance held out, where the disruption of communications prevented troops from receiving their President's withdrawal order. Coalition forces had taken some 30,000 prisoners.

General Neal, the official US spokesman in Riyadh, listed the options open to the Iraqi troops: "If they try to go back to Basra, the Air Force will kill them. If they go to the other side of the Tigris, the bridges are down. If they try to move south into Kuwait, they will run into coalition forces and the US Marines."

A 'Scud' missile was launched against Saudi Arabia, the final one to be fired during the conflict. It caused no casualties.

to page 182

As the ground war got into full swing, aircraft like the F/A-18 Hornet made the final switch from strategic to battlefield tasks, with Marine Corps Hornets getting involved in close air support missions.

Apache Rampage

Lieutenant Colonel William Bryan, 2nd Battalion/229th Aviation Regiment, AH-64 Apache

"We never got into a real tank battle. On the fourth day of the ground war we did do a classic deep attack, moving about 300 km towards Basra and intercepting one of the Republican Guard divisions as it attempted to withdraw north across the Euphrates. We used the same movement technique, attacking in three companies, but each company attacked in line, five abreast rather than as two teams. By that time there were so many oil well fires, and so many vehicles burning, that it was almost dark even though it was mid-afternoon. We had to use our FLIR (Forward-Looking Infra-Red sensors) to see the targets, and even that was blanked out by smoke at 3000 m. We called it 'hell's half-acre'. You could only see about 300 m with the naked eye.

"There were hundreds of vehicles in the column. This time we were fired on; we were engaged by several heat-seeking missiles, and we think some radar-guided SAM-6s were fired. It was like an inferno: there were so many fires and so much smoke that none of the enemy systems could acquire us. Most of what we fired at we hit, however. Visually, you could just see the flash of the explosions going off in the tunnel-like darkness, but through the FLIR the intense heat created by burning vehicles was easily visible.

"I was extremely excited when the time came to engage my first target, and that in spite of the fact that I was one of only three guys in the battalion who had seen action, in Vietnam 20 years ago. It all happened very quickly: at the same time, you are so focussed and keyed up that it seemed to take forever for the Hellfire to get to the target, although it was only a few seconds. The first couple of engagements were really touch and go, because we didn't know if we

The Apache's PIC (Pilot In Command) and gunner are players in a real-life, hi-tech video game. Able to operate in any weather, Apache gunners can acquire multiple targets and ripple-fire their full range of weapons. A pair of Apaches could rip through a convoy in minutes.

Below: A great black blotch in the night, the OH-58D Kiowa Warrior spells trouble for nocturnal Iraqis. Although 'Deltas' can carry weapons, they generally worked with Army Apaches and Marine AH-1W 'Whiskey' Cobras as scouts and FACs during the desert war. However, they also served on board Navy ships, providing night reconnaissance. During that tasking the OH-58Ds took out air-defense sites on oil rigs using Hellfires and rockets, and captured over 50 Iraqis during an assault on a Kuwaiti island.

Left: Like giant bugs, AH-64 Apaches roam the desert, each lugging two rocket pods, eight AGM-114 Hellfires and a full load of 1,200 rounds of 30-mm Chain Gun ammunition. The 229th Aviation Regiment used the AH-64 in harsh conditions, and it performed well.

were going to be engaged. There's no place to mask in the desert, and you feel completely vulnerable.

"There has been a lot of controversy about the Apache. We lived with that aircraft through sandstorms, moisture (we had 10 in of rain in January) and extreme heat, yet the aircraft continued to operate with more than 90 per cent serviceability. There was no other platform in the Gulf that could fly so low, or could enagage such an array of targets with pinpoint accuracy, whatever the weather or the time of day or night. It was one of the few pieces of equipment that could move 300 km in a matter of hours, engage a major enemy force and return. Most important, however, it was manned and maintained by highly motivated and proud people. We've come a long way in the 20 years since Vietnam, and the caliber of the American soldier is probably the best we've ever had. If you take these type of people and give them this type of high-technology equipment, you're practically unbeatable."

Right: Silhouetted by the setting sun, an AH-64 Apache scours the desert terrain. Visible ahead of the main landing wheels is the helicopter's powerful 30-mm Chain Gun. Critics said that the AH-64 would need skids to operate in the desert, but the wheeled undercarriage caused few problems.

The Ground War

from page 180

27 February, Wednesday Coalition forces were now in position astride the routes of Iraqi forces trying to escape from Kuwait into Iraq. The latter were now under heavy attack from the ground and from the air, and large numbers of vehicles caught in traffic jams on the roads out of Kuwait City had been destroyed.

Saudi and Kuwaiti troops were now in full possession of Kuwait City.

In a speech at the United Nations, the Iraqi ambassador stated that his government was now ready to implement every one of the Security Council Resolutions concerning his country, if a cease-fire were ordered. President Bush stated that further assurances would be needed from the Iraqi leader in person, before he would order such a cease-fire.

Meanwhile, a large-scale tank battle was in progress between US armored units and Iraqi Republican Guard units to the north of Kuwait.

By the evening, General Schwarzkopf claimed that 3,000 of the estimated 4,300 Iraqi tanks in the Kuwait theater of operations had been destroyed, as had 2,140 of the estimated 3,110 artillery pieces and 1,856 of some 2,870 armored personnel carriers.

During the night, coalition aircraft attacked targets in and around Baghdad for the last time. In a final attempt to knock out Iraq's top military leadership, two F-111Fs of the 48th TFW each dropped a single GBU-28 'bunker-buster' bomb on the important underground command center at Al Taji airfield to the north of Baghdad. Hastily developed under a crash program, this weapon weighed 4,700 lb, had a diameter of 14 in and a length of 18 ft 9 in, and was fitted with laser-homing head and nose fins. One of the bombs hit the bunker squarely and detonated, causing a small puff of smoke to blow out of one of the entrances. A few seconds later there was a large secondary explosion at the site.

During the afternoon, an F-16 of the 363rd TFW was shot down by ground fire. Captain William Andrews ejected and came down in Iraqi-held territory. Two helicopters of the 101st Airborne Division moved in to rescue him but one UH-60 was also shot down (five of the crew were killed, three were taken prisoner with injuries, including US Army doctor Major Rhonda Cornum). Other coalition combat losses during the day: one USAF OA-10 (pilot killed), one US Marine Corps AV-8B of VMA-331 (pilot killed).

28 February, Thursday President Bush declared a cease-fire, to run from midnight Washington time, 8:00 a.m. Baghdad time, exactly 100 hours after the beginning of the land offensive. On hearing of the declaration, the Iraqi government issued a statement claiming victory, but saying that its forces would observe the cease-fire.

Coalition combat losses during the day: US Army, one UH-60 (nine killed) and one UH-1 (three killed). One OV-1 Mohawk aircraft lost in a non-combat-related incident.

The war was over. It had taken just six weeks. For the first time in history, air power had lived up to the claims of its advocates. A 39-day air assault had smashed Iraq's air defenses, flattened any capability the country had to build weapons of mass destruction, and ruined Iraq's economy.

Coalition fighters shot down 35 Iraqi aircraft without loss in combat. The only reason it was not more was that the Iraqis did not come up to fight, being completely overwhelmed by the superiority of allied fighters. Allied aircraft flew more than 110,000 sorties, and dropped 88,500 tons of ordnance. Seven thousand tons were precision-guided weapons, used to devastating effect.

The air campaign was followed by a lightning ground war against an already shell-shocked Iraqi army. It was an attack which took only 100 hours to achieve the coalition aim of liberating Kuwait. Allied casualties were astonishingly low; less than 500 killed. On the other side, as many as 100,000 Iraqis were killed, with similar numbers captured or deserted. It had been one of the most one-sided wars in history.

Above: An A-10 tank buster returns to refuel and reload after a mission over the retreating Iraqi army. Iraqis had no answer to the attacks, and the carnage inflicted on the invaders was of awesome proportions.

Right: This image from the moving target indicator equipment aboard an E-8 J-STARS aircraft shows the Iraqis fleeing from Kuwait to Basra. Each sparkle indicates a moving vehicle and the strings show the massive exodus along the roads north. Attacking allied vehicles can be seen moving en masse from the left flank.

Below: Smashed Iraqi military vehicles, together with the wrecks of looted buses, commercial vehicles and private cars, litter the main highway from Kuwait to Basra. Tank busters such as Jaguars, Hornets, F-16s, A-10s and AH-64s attacked to particularly devastating effect.

Right: British troopers rappel from an RAF Chinook as they come to retake possession of and to clear the British embassy in Kuwait City.

Right: General H. Norman Schwarzkopf grins at the success of the huge force under his command. He was able to use the coalition's enormous technological and qualitative advantage over the Iraqis, especially in the air, to fight and win a campaign with miraculously few allied losses.

Below: Kuwait's joyous liberation (inset) was tempered by the knowledge that the war would have personal, political, economic and environmental consequences for many years to come. Not the least of the problems of the peace was what to do with hundreds of blazing oil wells, cynically destroyed by the Iraqis.

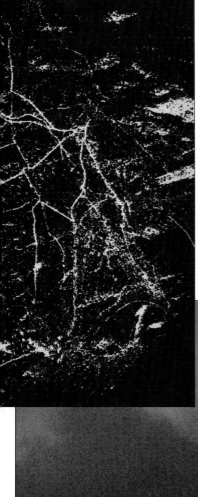

Air Order of Battle in the Gulf

US Air Force

Directly Assigned:

Air Force Systems Command

4411th J-STARS Sqn		E-8A	(Melbourne, FL) Riyadh/Mil City Apt (Jan/Mar)

Military Airlift Command

314th TAW	50th TAS	C-130E	(Little Rock AFB, AR) Bateen/Abu Dhabi Intl (Feb/Mar)
	61st TAS	C-130E	Incirlik AB, Turkey
317th TAW	??th TAS	C-130E	(Pope AFB, NC) Masirah & Thumrait, later forward deployed to Damman/King Fahd Apt
374th TAW	21st TAS	C-130E	(Clark AB, Philippines) Thumrait (Feb/Mar)
	345th TAS	C-130E	(Yokota AB, Japan) Thumrait (Feb/Mar)
435th TAW	37th TAS	C-130E	(Rhein Main AB, Germany) Al Ain, UAE (Aug/Mar)
463rd TAW	772nd TAS	C-130H	(Dyess AFB, TX) Al Kharj AB
	773rd TAS	C-130H	Al Kharj AB (Dec)
375th TAW	1401st MAS det 3	C-21A	(Barksdale AFB, LA) Riyadh/Mil City Apt (Aug & Feb/Mar)
	1401st MAS det 4	C-21A	(Peterson AFB, CO) Riyadh/Mil City Apt (Mar)
	1402nd MAS det 1	C-21A	(Langley AFB, VA) Riyadh/Mil City Apt (Jan/Mar)
	1402nd MAS det 3	C-21A	(Maxwell AFB, AL) Riyadh/Mil City Apt (Sep & Feb)
	1402nd MAS det 4	C-21A	(Eglin AFB, FL) Riyadh/Mil City Apt (Jan)

Special Operations Command

1st SOW	8th SOS	MC-130E	(Hurlburt Field, FL) Damman/King Fahd Apt (Aug/Mar)
	9th SOS	HC-130N/P	(Eglin AFB, FL) Damman/King Fahd Apt (Aug/Mar)
	16th SOS	AC-130H	(Hurlburt Field, FL) Location unknown (Sep/Mar)
	20th SOS	MH-53J	(Hurlburt Field, FL) Location unknown (Nov/Mar)
	55th SOS	MH-60G	(Eglin AFB, FL) Location unknown (Nov/Mar)
39th SOW	21st SOS	MH-53J	(RAF Woodbridge, UK) Incirlik & Batman AB, Turkey (Jan/Mar)
	67th SOS	HC-130N/P	(RAF Woodbridge, UK) Incirlik & Batman AB, Turkey (Jan/Mar)

Strategic Air Command (Recon & Bomber)

9th SRW	99th SRS	TR-1A/U-2R	(Beale AFB, CA) Taif (Aug/Mar)
	det 3	TR-1A/U-2R	RAF Akrotiri (Aug/Mar)
17th RW	95th RS	TR-1A	(RAF Alconbury, UK) Taif (Aug/Mar)
55th SRW	343rd SRS	RC-135U/V/W	(Offutt AFB, NE) Riyadh/Mil City Apt (Aug/Mar)
2nd BW	62nd & 596th BS	B-52G	(Barksdale AFB, LA) RAF Fairford, UK (Feb/Mar), Jeddah/King Abdul Aziz Intl Apt (Jan/Mar)
42nd BW	69th BS	B-52G	(Loring AFB, ME) Diego Garcia (Aug/Mar), Jeddah/King Abdul Aziz Intl Apt (Jan/Mar)
93rd BW	328th BTS	B-52G	(Castle AFB, CA) Diego Garcia (Aug), Jeddah/King Abdul Aziz Intl Apt (Jan/Mar), RAF Fairford (Feb/Mar)
97th BW	340th BS	B-52G	(Eaker AFB, AR) Diego Garcia (Jan/Mar)
379th BW	524th BS	B-52G	(Wurtsmith AFB, MI) Jeddah/King Abdul Aziz Intl Apt (Jan/Mar), RAF Fairford (Feb/Mar), Moron AB Spain (Feb)
416th BW	668th BS	B-52G	(Griffiss AFB, NY) Jeddah/King Abdul Aziz Intl Apt (Jan/Mar), RAF Fairford (Feb/Mar), Moron AB Spain (Feb/Mar)

Strategic Air Command (Tanker)

2nd BW	32nd ARS	KC-10A	(Barksdale AFB, LA) Milan-Malpensa Apt Italy & Zaragoza AB Spain (Jan/Mar)
	71st ARS	KC-135A	(Barksdale AFB, LA) Location unknown
5th BW	906th ARS	KC-135A	(Minot AFB, ND) Location unknown
7th BW	7th ARS	KC-135A	(Carswell AFB, TX) Location unknown
9th SRW	349th & 350th ARS	KC-135Q	(Beale AFB, CA) Riyadh/Mil City Apt (Aug/Mar)
19th ARW	99th & 912th ARS	KC-135R	(Robins AFB, GA) Mont-de-Marsan AB France (Feb/Mar), Muscat-Seeb (Aug), Riyadh/King Khalid Intl Apt (Jan)
22nd ARW	6th & 9th ARS	KC-10A	(March AFB, CA) Jeddah/King Abdul Aziz Intl Apt (Jan/Mar)
28th BW	28th ARS	KC-135R	(Ellsworth AFB, SD) Al Dhafra UAE (Aug), Muscat-Seeb (Aug)
42nd BW	42nd & 407th ARS	KC-135R	(Loring AFB, ME) Location unknown (Feb)
68th ARW	344th & 911th ARS	KC-10A	(Seymour Johnson AFB, NC) Jeddah/King Abdul Aziz Intl Apt (Jan/Mar)
92nd BW	43rd & 92nd ARS	KC-135A/R	(Fairchild AFB, WA) Location unknown
93rd BW	93rd & 924th ARS	KC-135A/R	(Castle AFB, CA) Location unknown
96th BW	917th ARS	KC-135A	(Dyess AFB, TX) Location unknown (Aug), Incirlik AB Turkey (Jan/Mar)
97th BW	97th ARS	KC-135A	(Eaker AFB, AR) Jeddah/King Abdul Aziz Intl Apt
301st ARW	??th ARS	KC-135R	(Malmstrom AFB, MT) Masirah (Dec), Muscat-Seeb (Aug)
305th ARW	70th & 305th ARS	KC-135R	(Grissom AFB, IN) Al Dhafra UAE (Sep), Riyadh/King Khalid Intl Apt (Jan)
		EC-135L	Riyadh/King Khalid Intl Apt (Jan/Mar)
319th BW	905th ARS	KC-135R	(Grand Forks AFB, ND) Al Dhafra UAE (Aug), Muscat-Seeb (Aug), Riyadh/King Khalid Intl Apt
340th ARW	11th & 306th ARS	KC-135R	(Altus AFB, OK) Al Dhafra UAE
376th SW	909th ARS	KC-135A	(Kadena AB, Okinawa) Riyadh/King Khalid Intl Apt (Jan)
379th BW	920th ARS	KC-135A	(Wurtsmith AFB, MI) Location unknown (Aug)
380th BW	310th & 380th ARS	KC-135A/Q	(Plattsburgh AFB, NY) Riyadh/King Khalid Intl Apt (Oct/Mar)
384th ARW	384th ARS	KC-135R	(McConnell AFB, KS) Al Dhafra UAE (Aug), Masirah (Dec)
410th BW	46th & 307th ARS	KC-135A	(K.I. Sawyer AFB, MI) Location unknown (Aug)
416th BW	41st ARS	KC-135R	(Griffiss AFB, NY) Al Dhafra UAE (Aug)

Pacific Air Forces

3rd TFW	3rd TFS	F-4E	(Clark AB, Philippines) Incirlik AB, Turkey

Tactical Air Command

1st TFW	27th & 71st TFS	F-15C/D	(Langley AFB, VA) Dhahran Intl Apt (Aug/Mar)
4th TFW	335th & 336th TFS	F-15E	(Seymour Johnson AFB, NC) Al Kharj (Dec/Mar), Thumrait (Aug), Al Kharj (by Jan/Mar)
23rd TFW	74th & 76th TFS	A-10A	(England AFB, LA) Damman/King Fahd Apt (Aug/Mar)
33rd TFW	58th TFS	F-15C/D	(Eglin AFB, FL) Tabuk/King Faisal AB (Sep/Mar)
35th TFW	561st TFS	F-4G	(George AFB, CA) Sheikh Isa Bahrain (Aug/Mar)
37th TFW	415th & 416th TFS	F-117A	(Tonopah TR, NV) Khamis Mushait AB (Aug/Mar)
67th TRW	12th TRS	RF-4C	(Bergstrom AFB, TX) Sheikh Isa Bahrain (Jan/Mar)
347th TFW	69th TFS	F-16C/D	(Moody AFB, GA) Al Minhad UAE (Jan/Mar)
354th TFW	353rd & 355th TFS	A-10A	(Myrtle Beach AFB, SC) Damman/King Fahd Apt (Aug/Mar)
363rd TFW	17th & 33rd TFS	F-16C/D	(Shaw AFB, SC) Al Dhafra UAE (Aug/Mar)
366th TFW	390th ECS	EF-111A	(Mountain Home AFB, ID) Taif (Aug/Mar)
388th TFW	4th & 421st TFS	F-16C/D	(Hill AFB, UT) Al Minhad UAE (Jan/Mar)
507th TACW	nil	nil	(Shaw AFB, SC) Riyadh (Aug/Mar)
552nd AW&CW	963rd, 964th & 965th AW&CS	E-3B/C	(Tinker AFB, OK) Riyadh/Military City Apt (Aug/Mar)
	7th ACCS	EC-130E	(Keesler AFB, MS) Riyadh/Military City Apt (Jan/Mar)
	41st ECS	EC-130H	(Davis Monthan AFB, AZ) Riyadh/Military City Apt (Jan/Mar)
602nd TACW	23rd TASS	OA-10A	(Davis Monthan AFB, AZ) Damman/King Fahd Apt (Nov/Mar)

United States Air Forces in Europe

10th TFW	511th TFS	A-10A	(RAF Alconbury, UK) Damman/King Fahd Apt (Dec/Mar)
20th TFW	79th TFS	F-111E	(RAF Upper Heyford, UK) Incirlik AB Turkey (Aug/Mar) also 55th & 77th TFS rotated to Incirlik, but 79th TFS was main unit during combat period
26th TRW	38th TRS	RF-4C	(Zweibrucken AB, Germany) Incirlik AB Turkey (Mar)
36th TFW	53rd TFS	F-15C/D	(Bitburg AB, Germany) Al Kharj (Jan/Mar)
	525th TFS	F-15C/D	(Bitburg AB, Germany) Incirlik AB Turkey (Dec/Mar)
48th TFW	492nd, 493rd & 494th TFS	F-111F	(RAF Lakenheath, UK) Taif (Aug/Mar)
50th TFW	10th TFS	F-16C/D	(Hahn AB, Germany) Al Dhafra UAE (Nov/Mar)
52nd TFW	23rd TFS	F-4G, F-16C/D	(Spangdahlem AB, Germany) Incirlik AB Turkey (Jan/Mar)
	81st TFS	F-4G	(Spangdahlem AB, Germany) Sheikh Isa Bahrain (Sep/Mar)
66th ECW	42nd ECS	EF-111A	(RAF Upper Heyford, UK) Incirlik AB Turkey (Dec/Mar)
	43rd ECS	EC-130H	(Sembach AB, Germany) Incirlik AB Turkey (Jan/Mar)
401st TFW	612th TFS	F-16C/D	(Torrejon AB, Spain) Incirlik AB Turkey (Jan/Mar)
	614th TFS	F-16C/D	(Torrejon AB, Spain) Doha Qatar (Aug/Mar)
32rd TFG	32nd TFS	F-15C/D	(Soesterberg AB, Netherlands) (Jan/Mar)

Air Force Reserve

403rd TAW	815st TAS	C-130H	(Keesler AFB, MS) Location unknown
434th ARW	72nd ARS	KC-135E	(Grissom AFB, IN) Jeddah/King Abdul Aziz Intl Apt (Aug/Mar)
452nd ARW	336th ARS	KC-135E	(March AFB, CA) Jeddah/King Abdul Aziz Intl Apt (Aug/Mar)
907th TAG	356th TAS	C-130E	(Rickenbacker ANGB, OH) (Oct/Mar)
913th TAG	327th TAS	C-130E	(NAS Willow Grove, PA) Thumrait
914th TAG	328th TAS	C-130E	(Niagara Falls IAP, NY) Sharjah
926th TFG	706th TFS	A-10A	(NAS New Orleans, LA) Damman/King Fahd Apt (Dec/Mar)
927th TAG	63rd TAS	C-130E	(Selfridge ANGB, MI) Sharjah (Oct/Mar)
939th ARW	71st SOS	HH-3E	(Davis Monthan AFB, AZ) Location unknown
940th ARG	314th ARS	KC-135E	(Mather AFB, CA) Jeddah/King Abdul Aziz Intl Apt

Air National Guard

117th TRW	106th TRS	RF-4C	(Birmingham MAP, AL) Sheikh Isa Bahrain (Aug/Mar)
126th ARW	108th ARS	KC-135E	(Chicago-O'Hare IAP, IL) Jeddah/King Abdul Aziz Intl Apt (Sep/Mar)
141st ARW	116th ARS	KC-135E	(Fairchild AFB, WA) Cairo West
190th ARG	117th ARS	KC-135E	(Forbes Field, KS) Jeddah/King Abdul Aziz Intl Apt (Aug/Mar)
128th ARG	126th ARS	KC-135E	(General Mitchell IAP, WI) Cairo West (Sep)
130th TAG	130th TAS	C-130H	(Yeager Airport Charleston, WV) Al Ain UAE later to Damman/King Fahd Apt (Oct/Mar)
101st ARW	132nd ARS	KC-135E	(Bangor IAP, ME) Jeddah/King Abdul Aziz Intl Apt
157th ARG	133rd ARS	KC-135E	(Pease ANG, NH) Jeddah/King Abdul Aziz Intl Apt
174th TFW	138th TFS	F-16A/B	(Hancock Field Syracuse, NY) Al Kharj (Dec/Mar)
166th TAG	142nd TAS	C-130H	(Gtr Wilmington Apt, DE) Al Ain UAE later to Al Kharj (Oct/Mar)
160th ARG	145th ARS	KC-135E	(Rickenbacker ANGB, OH) Jeddah/King Abdul Aziz Intl Apt (Jan/Mar), Dubai Intl Apt (Feb/Mar)
171st ARW	147th ARS	KC-135E	(Gtr Pittsburgh IAP, PA) Jeddah/King Abdul Aziz Intl Apt (Jan/Mar), Dubai Intl Apt (Jan/Mar)
170th ARG	150th ARS	KC-135E	(McGuire ANGB, NJ) Location unknown (Sep)
134th ARG	151st ARS	KC-135E	(McGhee Tyson Apt Knoxville, TN) Jeddah/King Abdul Aziz Intl Apt (Aug/Mar), Dubai Intl Apt (Feb/Mar)
169th TFG	157th TFS	F-16A/B	(McEntire ANGB, SC) Al Kharj (Dec/Mar)
168th ARG	168th ARS	KC-135E	(Eielson AFB, AK) Jeddah/King Abdul Aziz Intl Apt (Aug/Mar)
139th TAG	180th TAS	C-130H	(Rosecrans MAP, MO) Al Ain UAE (Sep/Mar)
136th TAW	181st ARS	KC-135E	(NAS Dallas, TX) Al Ain UAE later to Damman/King Fahd Apt (Sep/Mar)
151st ARG	191st ARS	KC-135E	(Salt Lake City IAP, UT) Jeddah/King Abdul Aziz Intl Apt (Aug/Mar)
152nd TRG	192nd TRS	RF-4C	(Reno-Cannon IAP, NV) Sheikh Isa Bahrain (Dec/Mar)
193rd SOG	193rd SOS	EC-130E	(Harrisburg IAP, PA) Riyadh/Mil City Apt & Bateen (Bateen/Abu Dhabi Intl ?) (Aug/Mar)
161st ARG	197th ARS	KC-135E	(Phoenix/Sk Harbor IAP, AZ) Location unknown (Sep)

Air Order of Battle in the Gulf

Regular Support:

Military Airlift Command

60th MAW	7th & 44th MAS	C-141B	*(Travis AFB, CA)*
	22nd & 75th MAS	C-5A/B	*(Travis AFB, CA)*
62nd MAW	4th & 8th MAS	C-141B	*(McChord AFB, WA)*
63rd MAW	14th, 15th & 53rd MAS	C-141B	*(Norton AFB, CA)*
436th MAW	9th & 20th MAS	C-5A/B	*(Dover AFB, DE)*
437th MAW	3rd, 17th, 41st & 76th MAS	C-141B	*(Charleston AFB, SC)*
438th MAW	6th, 18th & 30th MAS	C-141B	*(McGuire AFB, NJ)*
443rd MAW	56th MATS	C-5B	*(Altus AFB, OK)*
	57th MATS	C-141B	

Air Force Reserve

94th TAW	700th TAS	C-130H	*(Dobbins AFB, GA)* (Aug/Oct)
302nd TAW	731st TAS	C-130B	*(Peterson AFB, CO)* (to UK Aug/Mar)
433rd MAW	68th MAS	C-5A	*(Kelly AFB, TX)* (Aug/Mar)
439th MAW	337th MAS	C-5A	*(Westover AFB, MA)* (Aug/Mar)
440th TAW	95th TAS	C-130H	*(General Mitchell IAP, WI)* (Aug/Oct)
459th MAW	756th MAS	C-141B	*(Andrews AFB, MD)* (Aug/Mar)
908th TAG	357th TAS	C-130H	*(Maxwell AFB, AL)* (Aug)
910th TAG	757th TAS	C-130B	*(Youngstown MAP, OH)* Details of participation unknown
911th TAG	758th TAS	C-130H	*(Gtr Pittsburgh IAP, PA)* (Aug)
928th TAG	64th TAS	C-130H	*(Chicago O'Hare IAP, IL)* (Aug)
934th TAG	96th TAS	C-130E	*(Minneapolis St Paul IAP, MN)* (to UK Aug/Sept & Oct)
943rd TAG	303rd TAS	C-130B	*(March AFB, CA)* (to UK Sep/Mar)

The following AFRes associate units regularly provided crews to augment front-line personnel flying C-5s and C-141s from MAC wings:

315th MAW(A)	300th, 701st & 707th MAS(A)	C-141B	*(Charleston AFB, SC)*
349th MAW(A)	301st & 312th MAS(A)	C-5A/B	*(Travis AFB, CA)*
	708th & 710th MAS(A)	C-141B	*(Travis AFB, CA)*
445th MAW(A)	728th, 729th & 730th MAS(A)	C-141B	*(Norton AFB, CA)*
446th MAW(A)	97th & 313th MAS(A)	C-141B	*(McChord AFB, WA)*
512th MAW(A)	326th & 709th MAS(A)	C-5A/B	*(Dover AFB, DE)*
514th MAW(A)	335th, 702nd & 732nd MAS(A)	C-141B	*(McGuire AFB, NJ)*

Air National Guard

118th TAW	105th TAS	C-130H	*(Nashville Metro Apt, TN)* Details of participation unknown
133rd TAW	109th TAS	C-130E	*(Minneapolis St Paul IAP, MN)* (to Germany Oct/Nov & UK Jan/Mar)
146th TAW	115th TAS	C-130E	*(NAS Point Mugu, CA)* (to Germany Nov/Dec & UK Dec/Mar)
105th MAG	137th MAS	C-5A	*(Stewart ANGB, NY)* (Aug/Mar)
143rd TAG	143rd TAS	C-130E	*(Quonset Point Apt Providence, RI)* (to Germany Sep & UK Jan/Mar)
176th CG	144th TAS	C-130H	*(Anchorage IAP, AK)* Details of participation unknown
189th TAG	154th TAS	C-130E	*(Little Rock AFB, AR)* Details of participation unknown
145th TAG	156th TAS	C-130B	*(Charlotte-Douglas IAP, NC)* Details of participation unknown
165th TAG	158th TAS	C-130H	*(Savannah IAP, GA)* Details of participation unknown
179th TAG	164th TAS	C-130B	*(Mansfield Lahm Apt, OH)* Details of participation unknown
123rd TAW	165th TAS	C-130B	*(Standiford Fd Louisville, KY)* Details of participation unknown
167th TAG	167th TAS	C-130E	*(Martisburgh Apt, WV)* (to Germany Aug/Sep & UK Jan/Mar)
172nd MAG	183rd MAS	C-141B	*(Allen C Thompson Fd Jackson, MS)* (Aug/Mar)
137th TAW	185th TAS	C-130H	*(Will Rogers World Apt Oklahoma City, OK)* Details of participation unknown
153rd TAG	187th TAS	C-130B	*(Cheyenne MAP, WY)* Details of participation unknown

(Note: some Air Force Reserve Air National Guard C-130 units shown here as regular support had aircraft directly assigned.)

US Navy

Ships in Desert Storm 17 January to 28 February 1991:

CV-41/USS *Midway* CVW-5 'NF' (Sailed 2 Oct)

VFA-151	F/A-18A	VA-185	A-6E/KA-6D
VFA-192	F/A-18A	VAW-115	E-2C
VFA-195	F/A-18A	VAQ-136	EA-6B
VA-115	A-6E	HS-12	SH-3H

CV-60/USS *Saratoga* CVW-17 'AA' (Sailed 7 Aug)

VF-74	F-14A+	VAW-125	E-2C
VF-103	F-14A+	VAQ-132	EA-6B
VFA-81	F/A-18C	VS-30	S-3B
VFA-83	F/A-18C	HS-3	SH-3H
VA-35	A-6E/KA-6D		

CV-61/USS *Ranger* CVW-2 'NE' (Sailed 8 Dec)

VF-1	F-14A	VAW-116	E-2C
VF-2	F-14A	VAQ-131	EA-6B
VA-145	A-6E/KA-6D	VS-38	S-3A
VA-155	A-6E	HS-14	SH-3H

CV-66/USS *America* CVW-1 'AB' (Sailed 28 Dec)

VF-33	F-14A	VAW-123	E-2C
VF-102	F-14A	VAQ-137	EA-6B
VFA-82	F/A-18C	VS-32	S-3B
VFA-86	F/A-18C	HS-11	SH-3H
VA-85	A-6E/KA-6D		

CV-67/USS *John F. Kennedy* CVW-3 'AC' (Sailed 15 Aug)

VF-14	F-14A	VAW-126	E-2C
VF-32	F-14A	VAQ-130	EA-6B
VA-46	A-7E	VS-22	S-3B
VA-72	A-7E	HS-7	SH-3H
VA-75	A-6E/KA-6D		

CVN-71/USS *Theodore Roosevelt* CVW-8 'AJ' (Sailed 28 Dec)

VF-41	F-14A	VA-65	A-6E/KA-6D
VF-84	F-14A	VAW-124	E-2C
VFA-15	F/A-18A	VAQ-141	EA-6B
VFA-87	F/A-18A	VS-24	S-3A
VA-36	A-6E	HS-9	SH-3H

Ships which were on duty for Desert Shield only:

CV-62/USS *Independence* CVW-14 'NK' (Sailed 23 June to Dec)

VF-21	F-14A	VAW-113	E-2C
VF-154	F-14A	VAQ-139	EA-6B
VFA-25	F/A-18C	VS-37	S-3A
VFA-113	F/A-18C	HS-8	SH-3H
VA-196	A-6E/(no KA-6D assigned)		

CVN-69/USS *Dwight D. Eisenhower* CVW-7 'AG' (Sailed 8 March to 12 Sept)

VF-142	F-14A+	VAW-121	E-2C
VF-143	F-14A+	VAQ-140	EA-6B
VFA-131	F/A-18A	VS-31	S-3B
VFA-136	F/A-18A	HS-5	SH-3H
VA-34	A-6E/KA-6D		

Squadron/Aircraft Types & Carrier Air Wing Assignments

VF-1	F-14A	CVW-2	USS *Ranger* (NAS Miramar, CA)
VF-2	F-14A	CVW-2	USS *Ranger* (NAS Miramar, CA)
VF-14	F-14A	CVW-3	USS *John F. Kennedy* (NAS Oceana, VA)
VF-32	F-14A	CVW-3	USS *John F. Kennedy* (NAS Oceana, VA)
VF-33	F-14A	CVW-1	USS *America* (NAS Oceana, VA)
VF-41	F-14A	CVW-8	USS *Theodore Roosevelt* (NAS Oceana, VA)
VF-74	F-14A+	CVW-17	USS *Saratoga* (NAS Oceana, VA)
VF-84	F-14A	CVW-8	USS *Theodore Roosevelt* (NAS Oceana, VA)
VF-102	F-14A	CVW-1	USS *America* (NAS Oceana, VA)
VF-103	F-14A+	CVW-17	USS *Saratoga* (NAS Oceana, VA)
VA-46	A-7E	CVW-3	USS *John F. Kennedy* (NAS Cecil Field, FL)
VA-72	A-7E	CVW-3	USS *John F. Kennedy* (NAS Cecil Field, FL)
VFA-15	F/A-18A	CVW-8	USS *Theodore Roosevelt* (NAS Cecil Field, FL)
VFA-81	F/A-18C	CVW-17	USS *Saratoga* (NAS Cecil Field, FL)
VFA-82	F/A-18C	CVW-1	USS *America* (NAS Cecil Field, FL)
VFA-83	F/A-18C	CVW-17	USS *Saratoga* (NAS Cecil Field, FL)
VFA-86	F/A-18C	CVW-1	USS *America* (NAS Cecil Field, FL)
VFA-87	F/A-18A	CVW-8	USS *Theodore Roosevelt* (NAS Cecil Field, FL)
VFA-151	F/A-18A	CVW-5	USS *Midway* (NAS Atsugi, Japan)
VFA-192	F/A-18A	CVW-5	USS *Midway* (NAS Atsugi, Japan)
VFA-195	F/A-18A	CVW-5	USS *Midway* (NAS Atsugi, Japan)
VA-35	A-6E/KA-6D	CVW-17	USS *Saratoga* (NAS Oceana, VA)
VA-36	A-6E	CVW-8	USS *Theodore Roosevelt* (NAS Oceana, VA)
VA-65	A-6E/KA-6D	CVW-8	USS *Theodore Roosevelt* (NAS Oceana, VA)
VA-75	A-6E/KA-6D	CVW-3	USS *John F. Kennedy* (NAS Oceana, VA)
VA-85	A-6E/KA-6D	CVW-1	USS *America* (NAS Oceana, VA)
VA-115	A-6E	CVW-5	USS *Midway* (NAS Atsugi, Japan)
VA-145	A-6E/KA-6D	CVW-2	USS *Ranger* (NAS Whidbey Island, WA)
VA-155	A-6E	CVW-2	USS *Ranger* (NAS Whidbey Island, WA)
VA-185	A-6E/KA-6D	CVW-5	USS *Midway* (NAS Atsugi, Japan)
VAW-115	E-2C	CVW-5	USS *Midway* (NAS Atsugi, Japan)
VAW-116	E-2C	CVW-2	USS *Ranger* (NAS Miramar, CA)

Air Order of Battle in the Gulf

VAW-123	E-2C	CVW-1	USS *America (NAS Norfolk, VA)*
VAW-124	E-2C	CVW-8	USS *Theodore Roosevelt (NAS Norfolk, VA)*
VAW-125	E-2C	CVW-17	USS *Saratoga (NAS Norfolk, VA)*
VAW-126	E-2C	CVW-3	USS *John F. Kennedy (NAS Norfolk, VA)*
VAQ-130	EA-6B	CVW-3	USS *John F. Kennedy (NAS Whidbey Island, WA)*
VAQ-131	EA-6B	CVW-2	USS *Ranger (NAS Whidbey Island, WA)*
VAQ-132	EA-6B	CVW-17	USS *Saratoga (NAS Whidbey Island, WA)*
VAQ-136	EA-6B	CVW-5	USS *Midway (NAS Atsugi, Japan)*
VAQ-137	EA-6B	CVW-1	USS *America (NAS Whidbey Island, WA)*
VAQ-141	EA-6B	CVW-8	USS *Theodore Roosevelt (NAS Whidbey Island, WA)*
VS-22	S-3B	CVW-3	USS *John F. Kennedy (NAS Cecil Field, FL)*
VS-24	S-3A	CVW-8	USS *Theodore Roosevelt (NAS Cecil Field, FL)*
VS-30	S-3B	CVW-17	USS *Saratoga (NAS Cecil Field, FL)*
VS-32	S-3B	CVW-1	USS *America (NAS Cecil Field, FL)*
VS-38	S-3A	CVW-2	USS *Ranger (NAS North Island, CA)*
HS-3	SH-3H	CVW-17	USS *Saratoga (NAS Jacksonville, FL)*
HS-7	SH-3H	CVW-3	USS *John F. Kennedy (NAS Jacksonville, FL)*
HS-9	SH-3H	CVW-8	USS *Theodore Roosevelt (NAS Jacksonville, FL)*
HS-11	SH-3H	CVW-1	USS *America (NAS Jacksonville, FL)*
HS-12	SH-3H	CVW-5	USS *Midway (NAS Atsugi, Japan)*
HS-14	SH-3H	CVW-2	USS *Ranger (NAS North Island, CA)*

Other US Navy Units

HC-1	SH-3G	Bahrain	*(NAS North Island, CA)*
HC-2	CH-53E		
det 5		LPD-12/*Shreveport*	
HC-4	CH-53E	unknown	*(NAS Sigonella, Sicily)* (Mar)
HC-5	CH/UH-46D	seaborne	*(NAS Agana, Guam)* (Aug)
HC-6	CH/UH-46D	seaborne	*(NAS Norfolk, VA)*
det 1		AE-28/*Santa Barbara*	
det 4		AFS-2/USS *Sylvania*	
det 5		AOR-6/*Kalamazoo*	
HC-8	CH/UH-46D	seaborne	*(NAS Norfolk, VA)*
HC-11	CH/UH-46D	seaborne	*(NAS North Island, CA)*
det 3		AOR-3/USS *Kansas City*	
det 7		AE-33/USS *Shasta*	

(Note: 18 detachments operated aboard supply ships and support vessels.)

HCS-4	HH-60H	Tabuk	*(NAS Norfolk, VA)* (Dec/Mar)
HCS-5	HH-60H	Tabuk	*(NAS Point Mugu, CA)* (Dec/Mar)
HM-14	MH-53E	Dhahran ?	*(NAS Norfolk, VA)*
HM-15	MH-53E	Dhahran ?	*(NAS North Island, CA)*
HS-75 det A	SH-3H	Diego Garcia	*(NAS Jacksonville, FL)*
HSL-32	SH-2F	seaborne	*(NAS Norfolk, VA)*
HSL-33	SH-2F	seaborne	*(NAS North Island, CA)*
det 1		??-???/USS ???	
det 7		FFG-30/USS *Reid*	
HSL-34	SH-2F	seaborne	*(NAS Norfolk, VA)*
HSL-35	SH-2F	seaborne	*(NAS North Island, CA)*
det 3		CG-30/USS *Horne*	
det 7		??-??/USS ???	
det 9		FF-1088/USS *Barbey*	
det 10		??-???/USS ???	
HSL-36	SH-2F	seaborne	*(NAS Mayport, FL)*
det 8		FF-1068/USS *Vreeland*	
HSL-37	SH-2F	seaborne	*(NAS Barbers Point, HI)*
HSL-42	SH-60B	seaborne	*(NAS Mayport, FL)*
det 1		CG-56/USS *San Jacinto*	
det 3		CG-55/USS *Leyte Gulf*	
det 6		DD-980/USS *Moosbrugger*	
det 7		FFG-49/USS *Robert Bradley*	
det 9		FFG-50/USS *Taylor*	
det ?		FFG-8/USS *McInerney*	
HSL-43	SH-60B	seaborne	*(NAS North Island, CA)*
det 8		FFG-48/USS *Vandergrift*	
det 11		DD-971/USS *David R. Ray*	
HSL-44	SH-60B	seaborne	*(NAS Mayport, FL)*
det 5		FG-58/*Samuel B. Roberts*	
det 6		??-???/USS ???	
det 7		??-???/USS ???	
det 8		FFG-47/USS *Nicholas*	
det 9		CG-51/USS *Thomas S. Gates*	
HSL-45	SH-60B	seaborne	*(NAS North Island, CA)*
det ?		FFG-33/USS *Jarrett*	
HSL-46	SH-60B	seaborne	*(NAS Mayport, FL)*
det 7		CG-58/USS *Philippine Sea*	
HSL-47	SH-60B	seaborne	*(NAS North Island, CA)*
det 1		CG-52/USS *Bunker Hill*	
det 2		??-???/USS ???	
det 8		??-???/USS ???	
HSL-48	SH-60B	seaborne	*(NAS Mayport, FL)*
det 1		DD-963/USS *Spruance*	
HSL-49	SH-60B	seaborne	*(NAS North Island, CA)*
det 1		FFG-54/USS *Ford*	

(Note: these detachments operated aboard cruisers, destroyers and frigates.)

VP-1	P-3C	Jeddah, Bahrain, Masirah	*(NAS Barbers Point, HI)* (Nov)
VP-4	P-3C	Jeddah, Bahrain, Masirah	*(NAS Barbers Point, HI)*
VP-5	P-3C	Jeddah, Bahrain, Masirah	*(NAS Jacksonville, FL)*
VP-8	P-3C	Jeddah, Bahrain, Masirah	*(NAS Brunswick, ME)*
VP-11	P-3C	Jeddah, Bahrain, Masirah	*(NAS Brunswick, ME)*
VP-19	P-3C	Jeddah, Bahrain, Masirah	*(NAS Moffett Field, CA)*
VP-23	P-3C	Jeddah, Bahrain, Masirah	*(NAS Brunswick, ME)*
VP-40	P-3C	Jeddah, Bahrain, Masirah	*(NAS Moffett Field, CA)*
VP-46	P-3C	Jeddah, Bahrain, Masirah	*(NAS Moffett Field, CA)*
VP-91	P-3C	Jeddah, Bahrain, Masirah	*(NAS Moffett Field, CA)* (Feb/Mar)
VP-MAU	P-3C	Jeddah, Bahrain, Masirah	*(NAS Moffett Field, CA)*

VPU-1	P-3B	Jeddah, Bahrain, Masirah	*(NAS Brunswick, ME)*
VPU-2	P-3B	Jeddah, Bahrain, Masirah	*(NAS Barbers Point, HI)*

(Note: these P-3s were operated at Jeddah, Bahrain and Masirah, although details of squadron/base assignments are unknown; not all three bases had all 13 squadrons.)

VQ-1 det	EP-3E	Bahrain	*(NAS Agana, Guam)* (Jan/Mar)
VQ-2 det	EA-3B/EP-3E	Bahrain	(Jan/Mar)
det	EA-3B	Jeddah	*(NAS Rota, Spain)* (Jan/Mar)
det	EA-3B	Souda Bay, Crete	(Dec/Mar)
VQ-4	EC-130Q	unknown	*(NAS Patuxent River, MD)*
VR-22	C-130F	unknown	*(NAS Rota, Spain)* (Nov)
VR-24	C-2A	unknown	*(NAS Sigonella, Sicily)*
VR-55	C-9B	Naples, Bitburg & Sembach	*(NAS Alameda, CA)*
VR-57	C-9B	Naples, Bitburg & Sembach	*(NAS North Island, CA)*
VR-58	C-9B	Naples, Bitburg & Sembach	*(NAS Jacksonville, FL)*
VR-59	C-9B	Naples, Bitburg & Sembach	*(NAS Dallas, TX)*
VRC-30	C-2A	unknown	*(NAS North Island, CA)*
VRC-40	C-2A	unknown	*(NAS Norfolk, VA)*
VRC-50	C-2A/US-3A	Bahrain, Diego Garcia	*(NAS Cubi Point, Philippines)*
NARU Willow Grove	UC-12B	Bahrain	*(NAS Willow Grove, PA)* (Aug)

US Marine Corps

1st Marine Expeditionary Force/ 3rd Marine Air Wing

MAG-11

VMFA(AW)-121	VK F/A-18D	Sheikh Isa	*(MCAS El Toro, CA)* (Jan/Mar)
VMFA-212	WD F/A-18C	Sheikh Isa	*(MCAS Kaneohe Bay, HI)* (Dec/Mar)
VMFA-232	WT F/A-18C	Sheikh Isa	*(MCAS Kaneohe Bay, HI)* (Dec/Mar)
VMFA-235	DB F/A-18C	Sheikh Isa	*(MCAS Kaneohe Bay, HI)* (Aug/Mar)
VMFA-314	VW F/A-18A	Sheikh Isa	*(MCAS Beaufort, SC)* (Aug/Mar)
VMFA-333	DN F/A-18A	Sheikh Isa	*(MCAS Beaufort, SC)* (Aug/Mar)
VMFA-451	VM F/A-18A	Sheikh Isa	*(MCAS Beaufort, SC)* (Aug/Mar)
VMA(AW)-224	WK A-6E	Sheikh Isa	*(MCAS Cherry Point, NC)* (Aug/Mar)
VMA(AW)-533	ED A-6E	Sheikh Isa	*(MCAS Cherry Point, NC)* (Dec/Mar)
VMAQ-2	CY EA-6B	Sheikh Isa	*(MCAS Cherry Point, NC)* (Aug/Mar)
VMGR-234	QH KC-130T	Bahrain	*(NAS Glenview, IL)* (Sep/Mar)
VMGR-252	BH KC-130F/R	Bahrain	*(MCAS Cherry Point, NC)* (Nov/Mar)
VMGR-352	QB KC-130F/R	Bahrain	*(MCAS El Toro, CA)* (Nov/Mar)
VMGR-452	NY KC-130T	Bahrain/Jubail/ Sheikh Isa	*(Stewart ANGB, NY)* (Sep/Mar)
MCAS El Toro	5T UC-12B	Bahrain	*(MCAS El Toro, CA)* (Aug/Mar)
MCAS Yuma	5Y UC-12B	Bahrain	*(MCAS Yuma, AZ)* (Feb/Mar)

MAG-13

VMA-231	CG AV-8B	Al Jubail AB	*(MCAS Cherry Point, NC)* (Dec/Mar)
VMA-311	WL AV-8B	Al Jubail AB	*(MCAS Yuma, AZ)* (Dec/Mar)
VMA-542	WH AV-8B	Al Jubail AB	*(MCAS Cherry Point, NC)* (Dec/Mar)
VMA-513 det B	WF AV-8B	Al Jubail AB	*(MCAS Yuma, AZ)* (Dec/Mar)
VMO-1	ER OV-10A/D	Al Jubail AB	*(MCAS New River, NC)* (Sep/Mar)
VMO-2	UU OV-10A/D	Al Jubail AB	*(MCAS Camp Pendleton, CA)* (Sep/Mar)

(Note: the AV-8Bs initially deployed to Sheikh Isa in Aug/Sep but moved to Abdul Aziz in Dec when the facility was upgraded to accept V/STOL operations. The AV-8Bs operated from a number of forward positions including Kabrit and Tanajib.)

MAG-16

HMM-161	YR CH-46E	Abdul Aziz	*(MCAS Tustin, CA)* (Nov/Mar)
HMM-165	YW CH-46E	unknown	*(MCAS Kaneohe Bay, HI)*
HMLA-367	VT AH-1W/UH-1N	Abdul Aziz	*(MCAS Futenma, Okinawa)* (Sep/Mar)
HMLA-369	SM AH-1W/UH-1N	Abdul Aziz	*(MCAS Camp Pendleton, CA)* (Sep/Mar)
HMH-462	YF CH-53D	Abdul Aziz	*(MCAS Tustin, CA)* (Nov/Mar)
HMH-463	YH CH-53D	Abdul Aziz	*(MCAS Kaneohe Bay, HI)*
HMH-465	YJ CH-53E	Abdul Aziz to Ras Al Gar	*(MCAS Tustin, CA)* (Feb/Mar)
HMH-466	YK CH-53E	Ras Al Gar	*(MCAS Tustin, CA)* (Feb/Mar)

(Note: the helicopters of MAG-16 and MAG-26 were operated from an airfield within the King Abdul Aziz Naval Base which was a separate facility from that where the AV-8Bs and OV-10s were based.)

MAG-26

HMM-261	EM CH-46E	Abdul Aziz	*(MCAS New River, NC)*
HMM-266	ES CH-46E	Abdul Aziz	*(MCAS New River, NC)*
HMM-774	MQ CH-46E	unknown	*(NAS Norfolk, VA)* (Dec/Mar)
HMH-362	YL CH-53D	unknown	*(MCAS New River, NC)*
HMH-464	EN CH-53E	Ras Al Gar	*(MCAS New River, NC)* (Feb/Mar)
HMH-772	MS RH-53D	Abdul Aziz	*(NAS Alameda, CA)* (Dec/Mar)
HMA-775	WR AH-1J	Abdul Aziz	*(MCAS Camp Pendleton, CA)* (Dec/Mar)
HML-767	MM UH-1N	Abdul Aziz	*(NAS New Orleans, LA)* (Dec/Mar)

4th Marine Expeditionary Brigade

MAG-40

VMA-331	VL AV-8B	LHA-4/USS *Nassau*	*(MCAS Cherry Point, NC)* (Nov/Mar)
HMM-263	EG CH-46E	see note 1	*(MCAS New River, NC)*

Air Order of Battle in the Gulf

HMM-365	YM CH-46E	see note 1	*(MCAS New River, NC)*
HMH-461	CJ CH-53E	see note 1	*(MCAS New River, NC)*
HMLA-269	HF AH-1W/UH-1N	see note 2	*(MCAS New River, NC)*

(Note 1: the helicopter squadrons were divided between LPH-2/USS Iwo Jima and LPH-9/USS Guam, which along with the Gunston Hall, La Moure County, Manitowoc, Pensacola, Portland, Raleigh, Saginaw, Shreveport, Spartanburg County and Trenton made up Amphibious Group Two.)

(Note 2: land-based at Dhahran during Desert Shield, but embarked for Desert Storm.)

5th Marine Expeditionary Brigade
MAG-50

HMM-265	EP CH-46E	see note	*(MCAS Kaneohe Bay, HI)*
HMM-268	YQ CH-46E	see note	*(MCAS Tustin, CA)*
HMH-466 det	YK CH-53E	see note	*(MCAS Tustin, CA) (Nov)*
HMLA-169	SN AH-1W/UH-1N	see note	*(MCAS Camp Pendleton, CA) (Jan/Mar)*
HMA-773	MP AH-1J	see note	*(NAS Atlanta, GA) (Jan/Mar)*

(Note: helicopter squadrons were flown aboard LHA-1/USS Tarawa and LPH-11/USS New Orleans as part of Amphibious Group Three along with the Barbour County, Denver, Frederick, Germantown, Juneau, Mobile, Mount Vernon, Peoria and Vancouver. The Group was later joined by LPH-10/USS Tripoli with MH-53Es embarked for mine clearance duties in the northern Persian Gulf.)

13th Marine Expeditionary Unit

HMM-164	YT CH-46E	see note	*(MCAS Tustin, CA)*

(Note: the squadron was embarked aboard LPH-3/USS Okinawa which together with the Cayuga, Durham, Fort McHenry and Ogden formed Amphibious Group Alpha.)

Force Structure for Desert Spear on 24 February:

I Marine Expeditionary Force
1st Marine Expeditionary Brigade
5th Marine Expeditionary Brigade (embarked aboard assault ships)
7th Marine Expeditionary Brigade
1st Marine Division
1st Marine Air Wing

II Marine Expeditionary Force
4th Marine Expeditionary Brigade
13th Marine Expeditionary Unit (embarked aboard assault ships)
26th Marine Expeditionary Unit (embarked aboard assault ships)
2nd Marine Division
2nd Marine Air Wing

US Coast Guard

Nil	HU-25B	Bahrain	*(CGAS Cape Cod, MA) (Feb/Mar)*

US Army

82nd Airborne Division	OH-58A/D, UH-60A, AH-64A	*(Fort Bragg, NC) (Aug/Mar)*
101st Airborne Division	CH-47D, OH-58A/D, UH-60A, AH-64A	*(Fort Rucker, AL) (Aug/Mar)*
501st Bat/1st Armored Div	UH-1H, UH-60A, AH-64A	*(Jan/Mar)*
502nd Bat/2nd Armored Div	UH-1H, AH-64A	*(Jan/Mar)*
503rd Bat/3rd Armored Div	UH-1H, UH-60A, AH-1S	*(Jan/Mar)*
1st Bat/1st Aviation Reg	UH-1H	*(Ansbach, Germany) (Jan/Mar)*
2nd Bat/1st Aviation Reg	OH-58C, UH-60A, AH-64A	*(Ansbach, Germany) (Jan/Mar)*
3rd Bat/1st Aviation Reg	OH-58C, UH-60A, AH-64A	*(Ansbach, Germany) (Jan/Mar)*
5th Bat/158th Aviation Reg	OH-58D	*(Bonames, Germany) (Jan/Mar)*
6th Bat/158th Aviation Reg	UH-60A	*(Wiesbaden, Germany) (Jan/Mar)*
4th Bat/159th Aviation Reg	UH-1H, OH-58D	*(Stuttgart, Germany) (Jan/Mar)*
5th Bat/159th Aviation Reg	UH-1H, CH-47D	*(Schwabisch-Hall, Germany) (Jan/Mar)*
6th Bat/159th Aviation Reg	UH-1H, CH-47D, UH-60A	*(Schwabisch-Hall, Germany) (Jan/Mar)*
7th Bat/159th Aviation Reg	UH-1H, CH-47D	*(Nellingen, Germany) (Jan/Mar)*
2nd Bat/227th Aviation Reg	AH-64A	*(Hanau, Germany) (Jan/Mar)*
3rd Bat/227th Aviation Reg	AH-64A	*(Hanau, Germany) (Jan/Mar)*
2nd Bat/229th Aviation Reg	AH-64A	*(Illesheim, Germany) (Jan/Mar)*
4th Bat/229th Aviation Reg	OH-58C, UH-60A, AH-64A	*(Illesheim, Germany) (Jan/Mar)*
2nd Bat/6th Cavalry Reg	OH-58C, UH-60A, AH-64A	*(Illesheim, Germany) (Jan/Mar)*
3rd Bat/6th Cavalry Reg	OH-58C, UH-60A, AH-64A	*(Wiesbaden, Germany) (Jan/Mar)*
5th Bat/6th Cavalry Reg	AH-64A	*(Wiesbaden, Germany) (Jan/Mar)*
70th Transport Bat	UH-1H	*(Jan/Mar)*
Task Force Phoenix	OH-58D, UH-60A, EH-60C	*(Bad Kreuznach & Mainz-Finthen, Germany) (Jan/Mar)*
Task Force Skyhawk	OH-58D	*(Ansbach, Germany)(Jan/Mar)*
Task Force Viper	OH-58C, EH-60C	*(Hanau, Germany) (Jan/Mar)*
1st Cavalry Division	UH-1H, AH-64A	*(Jan/Mar)*
6th Cavalry Division	OH-58C, UH-60A, AH-64A	*(Jan/Mar)*
1st Infantry Division	UH-1H, AH-1S, UH-60A	*(Jan/Mar)*
24th Infantry Division	UH-1H, AH-1S, UH-60A	*(Jan/Mar)*
236th Medical Company	UH-60A	*(Landstuhl, Germany) (Jan/Mar)*
1st Mil Intel Bat	RC-12D	*(Wiesbaden, Germany) (Jan/Mar)*
2nd Mil Intel Bat	RC-12D, OV/RV-1D	*(Stuttgart, Germany) Al Qaysumah (Jan/Mar)*
224th Mil Intel Bat	RU-21H, OV/RV-1D	*(Sep)*

Ground Force Structure for Desert Spear on 24 February:
XVIII Airborne Corps
XVIII Corps Artillery
111 Corps Artillery
24th Infantry Division (Mechanized) including 197th Infantry Brigade
82nd Airborne Division
101st Airborne Division (Air Assault)
1st Cavalry Division including one regiment from 2nd Armored Division
3rd Armored Cavalry Regiment

VII Corps
1st Infantry Division (Mechanized) including one brigade from 2nd Armored Division
1st Armored Division
3rd Armored Division
2nd Armored Cavalry Regiment
11th Combat Aviation Brigade
VII Corps Artillery

Provisional Units

8th Air Division

801st BW(P)	B-52G	Moron AB, Spain	2nd BW, 416th BW
802nd ARW(P)	KC-10A	Milan-Malpensa, Italy	2nd BW
803rd	no details		
804th	no details		
805th	no details		
806th BW(P)	B-52G	RAF Fairford, UK	2nd, 93rd, 379th & 416th BW
807th ARW(P)	KC-135R	Mont-de-Marsan AB, France	19th ARW

(Note: other provisional units were established at Lajes with KC-10/KC-135s and possibly at Cairo West for B-52Gs.)

16th Air Division (Provisional) MAC

1620th TAW(P)	C-130	Abu Dhabi/Bateen	314th TAS
1630th TAW(P)	C-130E/H	Al Ain UAE	
1630th TAS(P)			130th TAS/WV ANG & 181st TAS/TX ANG
1631st TAS(P)			435th TAW
1632nd TAS(P)			142nd TAS/DE ANG & 180th TAS/MO ANG
1640th TAW(P)	C-130E/H	Masirah	including 317th TAW
1650th TAW(P)	C-130E/H	Sharjah	including 63rd TAS & 328th TAS AFRes
1660th TAW(P)	C-130E/H	Thumrait	including 327th TAS AFRes
1676th TAS(P)			21st TAS & 345th TAS of 374th TAW

17th Air Division (Provisional) SAC

1700th RW(P)	U-2R/TR-1A	Taif	9th SRW & 17th RW
1704th RS(P)			redesignated to 1701st
1701st ARW(P)	U-2R/TR-1A	Jeddah/King Abdul Aziz Intl Apt	SW(P) on 1 Jan to control 1708th BW(P) & 1709th ARW(P)
1702nd ARW(P)	KC-135R	Muscat-Seeb	including 28th BW & 319th BW
1703rd ARW(P)	KC-135A/R	Riyadh/King Khalid Intl Apt	376th SW
	KC-135R		including 19th ARW, 305th ARW, 319th BW
	EC-135L		305th ARW
1704th	no details		
1705th	no details		
1706th ARW(P)	KC-135E	Cairo West Apt, Egypt	WA & WI ANG
1707th ARW(P)	KC-135R	Masirah	
1708th BW(P)	B-52G	Jeddah/King Abdul Aziz Intl Apt	2nd, 42nd, 93rd, 379th & 416th BWs
1709th ARW(P)	KC-10A	Jeddah/King Abdul Aziz Intl Apt	22nd & 68th ARW
	KC-135E		AK, IL, KS, ME, NH, OH, TN ANGs & AFRes 72nd, 314th & 336th ARSs
1710th	KC-135A		97th BW
1710th	no details		
1711th ARW(P)	KC-135Q	Riyadh Mil City Apt	including 9th SRW & 380th BW
1712th ARW(P)	KC-135E	Abu Dhabi Intl Apt	including OH ANG
	KC-135R		42nd BW, 340th ARW & 416th BW
1713th ARW(P)	KC-135E	Dubai Intl Apt	OH, PA, TN ANGs
4300th BW(P)	B-52G	Diego Garcia	42nd & 97th BW
4409th OSW(P)	E-3B/C	Riyadh Mil City Apt	552nd AW & CW
1st TFW(P)	F-15C/D	Dhahran	1st & 36th TFW
4th TFW(P)	F-15E	Al Kharj	4th TFW & ANG F-16
	F-16A/B		Sqn
35th TFW(P)	F-4G	Sheikh Isa	35th & 52nd TFW
	RF-4C		67th TRW & ANG RF4 Sqn
48th TFW(P)	F-111F	Taif	48th TFW
	EF-111A		66th ECW

Air Order of Battle in the Gulf

354th TFW(P)	A-10A	Damman/King Fahd	10th, 23rd, 354th TFW & AFRes
	OA-10A		602nd TACW
363rd TFW(P)	F-16C/D	Al Dhafra	50th & 363rd TFW
388th TFW(P)	F-16C/D	Al Minhad	347th & 388th TFW

Operation Proven Force, Turkey
7440th Provisional Wing

38th TRS/26th TRW	RF-4C	(Zweibrucken AB, Germany) Incirlik AB, Turkey
32nd TFS/32nd TFG	F-15C/D	(Soesterberg AB, Netherlands) Incirlik AB, Turkey
525th TFS/36th TFW	F-15C/D	(Bitburg AB, Germany) Incirlik AB, Turkey
23rd TFS/52nd TFW	F-4G/F-16C	(Spangdahlem AB, Germany) Incirlik AB, Turkey
612th TFS/401st TFW	F-16C/D	(Torrejon AB, Spain) Incirlik AB, Turkey
42nd ECS/66th ECW	EF-111A	(RAF Upper Heyford, UK) Incirlik AB, Turkey
43rd ECS/66th ECW	EC-130H	(Sembach AB, Germany) Incirlik AB, Turkey
79th TFS/20th TFW	F-111E	(RAF Upper Heyford, UK) Incirlik AB, Turkey
3rd TFS/3rd TFW	F-4E	(Clark AB, Philippines) Incirlik AB, Turkey
various/552nd AW&CW	E-3B/C	(Tinker AFB, OK) Incirlik AB, Turkey
917th ARS/96th BW	KC-135A	(Dyess AFB, TX) Incirlik AB, Turkey (including aircraft from other units)
various	C-130B/E	(small numbers deployed from the 'Bravo Rotation' at RAF Mildenhall)
21st SOS/39th SOW	MH-53J	Batman AB, Turkey
67th SOS/39th SOW	HC-130N/P	Batman AB, Turkey
711th SOS/919th SOG	AC-130A	Location unknown

Desert Storm — US Total of Aircraft Assigned
(not including 'Proven Force' in Turkey)
Total=3614

USAF		USN		USMC		US Army	
210	F-16	89	F/A-18	78	F/A-18	237	AH-64
96	F-15	95	A-6E	20	A-6E	131	AH-1
48	F-15E	24	A-7E	12	EA-6B	299	UH-60
48	F-4G	92	F-14	60	AV-8B	64	UH-60V
42	F-117	17	F-14TRP	13	OV-10	24	EH-60
64	F-111	27	EA-6B	15	KC-130	295	OH-58C
18	EF-111A	29	E-2C	40	AH-1	92	OH-58D
86	B-52	48	S-3	40	CH-53	193	UH-1
194	KC-135	??	P-3	60	CH-46	121	UH-1V
2	EC-135L	??	EP-3E	30	UH-1	127	CH-47
30	KC-10					4	MH-47
194	A-10A						
132	C-130						
11	E-3						
2	E-8						
18	RF-4C						
9	EC-130						
4	HC-130						
4	MC-130						
4	AC-130						
22	HH-3/MH-53						
1238		421		368		1587	

Types Missing from List

C-21	EA-3B	RC-12
RC-135	SH-3H	C-12
U-2/TR-1		C-23
		RV/OV-1
		RU-21
		AH/MH-6

A USAF fact sheet gives certain quantities which in certain cases conflict with the above:

145	C-130	48	F-4G
256	KC-135	249	F-16
46	KC-10	144	A-10A
120	F-15C/D	18	EF-111A
48	F-15E		

Non-US Coalition Forces

United Kingdom (Operation Granby)

Al Jubail, Saudi Arabia
Support Helicopter Force Middle East (moved on 22 January to Riyadh/King Khalid Military City, then Iraq)

Chinook HC.Mk 1	7 Sqn lead with 18 Sqn & 240 OCU (RAF Gütersloh & Odiham)
Puma HC.Mk 1	230 Sqn lead with 33 Sqn (RAF Gütersloh & Odiham)
Sea King HAS.Mk 5	C Flt 826 Sqn (embarked aboard RFA Olna & RFA Sir Galahad plus other ships)
Sea King HC.Mk 4	845 Sqn, 848 Sqn & 846 Sqn (last embarked aboard RFA Fort Grange & RFA Argus)
Lynx HAS.Mk 3GM	815 Sqn (embarked aboard HMS Cardiff, Gloucester, London & Manchester); 829 Sqn (embarked aboard HMS Brazen)

Located at Al Jubail but distributed to various desert sites to support 1st (British) Armored Division

654 Sqn	Gazelle AH.1, Lynx AH.7	
659 Sqn	Gazelle AH.1, Lynx AH.7	
661 Sqn	Gazelle AH.1, Lynx AH.7	

Dhahran, Saudi Arabia

| Tornado det | Tornado GR.Mk 1/GR.Mk 1A | 31 Sqn lead with elements of 2, 9, 13, 14 & 17 Sqn (RAF Bruggen, Honington, Laarbruch & Marham) |
| Tornado ADV det | Tornado F.Mk 3 | 43 Sqn lead with 29 Sqn (RAF Leuchars & Coningsby) |

Muharraq, Bahrain

Buccaneer det	Buccaneer S.Mk 2B	208 Sqn lead with 12 Sqn & 237 OCU (RAF Lossiemouth)
Jaguar det	Jaguar GR.Mk 1A	41 Sqn lead with elements of 6 & 54 Sqn (RAF Coltishall)
Tornado det	Tornado GR.Mk 1	15 Sqn lead with elements of 9, 17, 27, 31 & 617 Sqn (RAF Brüggen, Laarbruch & Marham)
Victor det	Victor K.Mk 2	55 Sqn (RAF Marham)

Riyadh/King Khalid Intl Apt
RAF Air Transport det

	Hercules C.Mk 1P/C.Mk 3P	242 OCU lead with elements of 24, 30, 47 & 70 Sqn (RAF Lyneham), and No. 40 Sqn RNZAF
	VC10 K.Mk 2/K.Mk 3	101 Sqn (RAF Brize Norton)
	TriStar K.Mk 1	216 Sqn (RAF Brize Norton)
	BAe.125 CC.2/3	32 Sqn (RAF Northolt)

Support Helicopter Force Middle East (moved from Al Jubail on 22 January)

| Chinook HC.Mk 1 | 7 Sqn lead with 18 Sqn & 240 OCU (RAF Gütersloh & Odiham) |
| Puma HC.Mk 1 | 230 Sqn lead with 33 Sqn (RAF Gütersloh & Odiham) |

Tabuk, Saudi Arabia

| Tornado det | Tornado GR.Mk 1 | 16 Sqn lead with elements of 2, 9, 13, 14, 20 & 617 Sqn (RAF Brüggen, Honington, Laarbruch & Marham) |

Seeb, Oman

| Nimrod MR det | Nimrod MR.Mk 2P | 120 Sqn lead with 42 & 206 Sqn (RAF Kinloss & St Mawgan) |

Unconfirmed location

| Nimrod R det | Nimrod R.Mk 1P | 51 Sqn (RAF Wyton) |

Canada (Operation Friction)

Doha, Qatar

409 Squadron	CF-18A	(CFB Soellingen, Germany)
437 Squadron	CC-137	(CFB Trenton)
439 Squadron	CF-18	(CFB Soellingen, Germany)
441 Squadron	CF-18A	(CFB Cold Lake)

At sea, HMCS Athabascan and Protecteur

| 423 Squadron | Sea King CH.124A | (CFB Halifax/CFB Shearwater) |

France (Operation Daguet)

Riyadh/King Khalid Intl Apt

ET 60	DC-8F	ET 3/60 (Paris/Charles de Gaulle)
ET 61	C.160F, C-130H-30	ET 1/61, ET 2/61 & ET 3/61 (Orleans/Bricy)
ET 64	C.160NG	ET 1/64 (Evereux/Fauville)
ET 65	Nord 262 Mystère XX	ET 1/65 (Villa Coublay)
ERV 93	C-135F(R)	ERV 1/93, ERV 2/93, ERV 3/93 (Avord, Istres/Le Tubé & Mont-de-Marsan)

King Khalid Military City (later Rafha, then As Salman, Iraq)

| RHC 'Daguet' | Gazelle, Puma | 1ier RHC (Phalsbourg), 3ième RHC (Etain/Rouvres) |

Al Ahsa, Saudi Arabia

| EC 5 | Mirage 2000C | EC 1/5, EC 2/5, EC 3/5 (Orange/Caritat) |

Air Order of Battle in the Gulf

EC 11	Jaguar A	EC 1/11, EC 2/11, EC 3/11 *(Toul-Rosières)*, EC 4/11 *(Bordeaux-Mérignac)*
ER 33	Mirage F1CR	ER 1/33, ER 2/33, ER 3/33 *(Strasbourg/ Entzheim)*
EE 54	C.160 Gabriel	EE 1/54 *(Evreux/Fauville)*
EH 67	SA 330B Puma	EH 1/67 *(Cazaux)*

Doha, Qatar (Operation *Meteil*)

EC 12	Mirage F1C	EC 1/12, EC 2/12, EC 3/12 *(Cambrai/Epinoy)*

Italy (Operation *Locusta*)

Al Dhafra (Maqatra), Abu Dhabi

6° Stormo	Tornado	154° Gruppo *(Ghedi)*
36° Stormo	Tornado	156° Gruppo *(Gioia del Colle)*
50° Stormo	Tornado	155° Gruppo *(Piacenza/San Damiano)*

Bahrain

Sheikh Isa

Fighter Squadron	F-5E
Fighter Squadron	F-16C/D

Kuwait (Free Kuwait Air Force in exile)

Dhahran

9 & 25 Squadron	A-4KU, TA-4KU
18 & 61 Squadron	Mirage F1CK
?	Gazelle

King Khalid Military City

?	SA 330 Puma
?	AS 532C Cougar

New Zealand

Riyadh/King Khalid Intl Apt

40 Squadron	C-130H	assigned to RAF Air Transport Detachment *(Whenuapai)*

Qatar

Doha

7 Squadron	Mirage F1EDA

Australia

Unconfirmed location

37 Squadron	C-130E	*(Richmond AB, NSW)* – squadron provided resupply of naval presence in Gulf

Saudi Arabia

Dhahran

7 Squadron	Tornado IDS
13 Squadron	F-15C/D
21 Squadron	Hawk
29 Squadron	Tornado ADV
34 Squadron	Tornado ADV
37 Squadron	Hawk
42 Squadron	F-15C/D
66 Squadron	Tornado IDS (Forming)

Jeddah/King Abdul Aziz Airport

4 Squadron	C-130E/H, KC-130H

Khamis Mushait

6 Squadron	type unknown
15 Squadron	F-5E/F

Riyadh/Military City Airport

16 Squadron	C-130E/H, KC-130H
18 Squadron	E-3A, KE-3A

Tabuk

17 Squadron	F-5E/F, RF-5E, F-5B

Taif

3 Squadron	F-5E/F
5 Squadron	F-15C/D
10 Squadron	F-5E/F

Saudi Navy

?? Squadron	AS 565SA Panther	*Ras Al Jubail*

South Korea

Al Ain, UAE

?? Squadron	C-130H	*(Pusan ?)*

United Arab Emirates

Al Dhafra (Maqatra), Abu Dhabi

?? Squadron	Mirage 2000EAD

Aircraft of the Gulf War

UNITED STATES AIR FORCE

A-10A Thunderbolt II

Deployment

10th Tactical Fighter Wing 'AR' (RAF Alconbury, UK) – King Fahd Airport, Saudi Arabia A-10A

23rd Tactical Fighter Wing 'EL' (England AFB, LA) – King Fahd Airport, Saudi Arabia A-10A

354th Tactical Fighter Wing 'MB' (Myrtle Beach AFB, SC) – King Fahd Airport, Saudi Arabia A-10A

706th Tactical Fighter Squadron/926th Tactical Fighter Group 'NO' (NAS New Orleans, LA) – King Fahd Airport, Saudi Arabia A-10A

23rd Tactical Air Support Squadron/602nd Tactical Air Control Wing 'NF' (Davis Monthan AFB, LA) – King Fahd Airport, Saudi Arabia OA-10A

Mission

The A-10 was designed for anti-tank operations and was used in this primary mission against Iraqi armor in occupied Kuwait and eastern Iraq. A-10s also attacked other targets, including 'Scud-B' missile sites. OA-10s of the 23rd TASS, which have no specialized mission equipment, were used for Fast FAC (Forward Air Control) missions.

Service

A-10s were deployed to Saudi Arabia at the beginning of Operation Desert Shield and were used throughout the war. A pair of A-10s performed RESCAP support for a Navy F-14 pilot who ejected on 21 January. Two A-10 pilots from 76th TFS/23rd TFW destroyed a record 23 tanks on 25 February.

511th TFS/10th TFW 'AR':

79-0220 *"Yankee Express"*. **79-0224** *"Have Gun Will Travel"*. **80-0144** *"Poo!"*. **80-0157** *"Fightin' Irish"*. **80-0170** *"Lakanuki"*. **80-0172** *"Jennie Mei"*. **80-**

0194 *"Freedom Warthog – To Fly Fight Believe"*. **80-0208** *"Annabelle II"*. **80-0229** *"Memphis Belle III"*. **80-0277** *"Desert Dream"*. **81-0939** *"Rocky"*. **81-0947** *"Desert Belle"*. **81-0948** (hog in space artwork). **81-0953** *"Give 'Em Hell"*. **81-0964** *"Steal Your Face"* credited with helicopter kill on 15 February. **81-0967** *"Brothers in Arms"*. **81-0987** *"Just a Thumpin"*. **82-0657** *"Hog's Breath Saloon"*. plus **79-0218** loaned from 92nd TFS/81st TFW 'WR'.

74th TFS/23rd TFW 'EL':

79-0133. **79-0137**. **79-0166**. **79-0188**. **79-0189** *"Tiger Fifteen"*. **79-0190**. **79-0195**. **79-0196** *"Tiger III"*. **79-0201** *"Kansas"*. **79-0204**. **79-0207**. **79-0209** *"Burger's Queen"*. **79-0210** *"When Pigs Fly"*. **80-0173**. **80-0197**. **80-0210**. **80-0212**. **80-0224** *"Hog Heaven"*. **80-0246**. **82-0663**.

75th TFS/23rd TFW 'EL':

79-0186. **79-0213** *"The Heartbeat of America"*. **80-0151**. **80-0152**. **80-0187**. **80-0250**. **82-0662**. (Latter two transferred to 354th TFW.) Squadron not deployed to Gulf.

76th TFS/23rd TFW 'EL':

80-0181 destroyed at Forward Operating Location. **80-0188**. **80-0223**.

353rd TFS/354th TFW 'MB' 'Panthers':

78-0587 62 missions. **78-0593** *"The Fortune Teller"* 86 missions. **78-0594** *"Panther Princess"* 83 missions. **78-0595** *"Ripin Tear"* 55 missions. **78-0606** 44 missions. **78-0660** 72 missions. **78-0667** *"Indian Maiden"* 35 missions. **78-0675** 58 missions. **78-0677** *"Kiss of Death"* 55 missions. **78-0680** *"A View to a Kill"* 70 missions. **78-0681** *"Playtime"* 57 missions. **78-0699** 64 missions. **78-0715** *"Panther*

One" 68 missions. **78-0722** Lost in combat on 14 February (pilot Capt Phillis or 1Lt Sweet). **78-0725** 32 missions. **79-0096** *"Honey Buns"* left and *"Wicked Sensation"* right; 61 missions. **79-0124** 67 missions. **79-0126** *"Tawakyna Dude"* 59 missions. **79-0127** 73 missions. **79-0128** 72 missions. **79-0130** Lost in combat on 14 February (pilot Capt Phillis or 1Lt Sweet). **80-0250** 43 missions. **82-0661** 59 missions. **82-0662** 30 missions. **82-0664** 22 missions.

355th TFS/354th TFW 'MB' 'Falcons':

78-0591 *"Kelly Marie's Secrit Weapin"*. **78-0592** *"Bullet Express"*. **78-0599** *"Bird of Prey"*. **78-0603** *"Kimberly Anne"*. **78-0622** *"Fear No Evil"*. **78-0654** *"King of Pain"*. **78-0662** *"Eat This Saddam"*. **78-0664** *"Val's Avenger"*. **78-0665** *"Grim Reaper"*. **78-0678** *"Midnight Express"*. **78-0686** *"Night Penetrator"*. **78-0710** *"Darin Dawnie"*. **78-0713** *"Race Against the Night"*. **78-0714** *"Louisville Slugger"*. **78-0724** *"Leslie the Seminole Warrior"*. **79-0097** *"Dawg Hawg"*. **79-0099** *"Fang"*. **79-0100** *"Georgia Girl"*. **79-0112** *"Here Comes the Judge"*. **79-0115** *"Mud, Blood and No Beer"*. **79-0158** *"Falcon One"*. **79-0160** *"Dobber's Sting"*. **79-0163** *"Sharper Than Any Two-Edged Sword"*. **79-0173** *"The Full Armor of God"*.

706th TFS/926th TFG 'NO':

706th TFS A-10As were the most decorated to emerge from Desert Storm and were credited with the most kills per aircraft. **76-0531**. **76-0540** tail section damaged by anti-aircraft fire and repaired with entire section replaced. **76-0544**. **77-0205** *"Chopper One"* with one helicopter kill, although **77-0275** has been credited with the kill on 6 February. Aircraft achieved most tank kills in squadron with 27. **77-0240**. **77-0252**. **77-0255**. **77-0256**. **77-0260**. **77-0266**. **77-0268**. **77-0269**. **77-0271**. **77-0272**. **77-0273**. **77-0274**. **77-0275** credited with helicopter kill on 6 February. Only aircraft with white fin tip, all other in squadron were red. **77-0277**. **78-0582** on loan from 46th TFTS Barksdale AFB, LA, 18 tank kills.

23rd TASS/602nd TACW 'NF':

76-0529 1 nail (mission symbol). **76-0537** 21 nails. **76-0543** callsign *NAIL 53* shot down 19 February. **76-0547** 22 nails, plus 8 tanks, 4 armored personnel carriers, 23 anti-aircraft guns, 4 missile launchers, and 14 trucks destroyed while operating as a conventional A-10. **77-0183** 17 nails. **77-0185**. **77-0186** 18 nails. **77-0188**. **77-0190** 18 nails. **77-0197**. **77-0200** 22 nails. **77-0201** 19 nails. **77-0209** 4 nails. **77-0218** 22 nails. **77-0265** 10 nails. **77-0270** 16 nails.

B-52G Stratofortress

Deployment

801st Bombardment Wing (Provisional) – Moron, Spain B-52G

806th Bombardment Wing (Provisional) – RAF Fairford, England B-52G

1708th Bombardment Wing (Provisional) – Jeddah/King Abdul Aziz Int Apt, Saudi Arabia B-52G

4300th Bombardment Wing (Provisional) – Diego Garcia B-52G

2nd Bombardment Wing (Barksdale AFB, LA) B-52G

42nd Bombardment Wing (Loring AFB, ME) B-52G

93rd Bombardment Wing (Castle AFB, CA) B-52G

379th Bombardment Wing (Wurtsmith AFB, MI) B-52G

416th Bombardment Wing (Griffiss AFB, NY) B-52G

Mission

The B-52G was assigned a conventional bombing mission in Operation Desert Storm.

Service

Early in the war, B-52Gs bombed strategic targets, such as power-generating stations, in northern Iraq. Most B-52 operations were carried out against dug-in Iraqi ground forces, particularly Republican Guard units in northwest Kuwait. According to crews, mission marker silhouettes (in the shape of a bomb) painted on aircraft were color-coded as follows: black, missions from Moron; red, missions from Fairford; white, missions from Jeddah New. The eight B-52Gs operating from Fairford totalled 975.5 combat hours. The 806th BMW(P) was in existence exactly one month and ended its presence at Fairford on 9 March.

801st BW(P):

57-6501 (416th BW) *"Ragin' Red"*. **57-6503** (2nd BW) *"Superstitious Aloysius"*. **57-6509** (2nd BW) *"Nine O Nine"*. **57-6515** (416th BW) *"Mohawk Warrior"*. **58-0159** (379th BW) *"Alley Oop's Bold Assault"*.

806th BW(P):

57-6498 (416th BW) *"Ace in the Hole"* 11 missions. **58-0168** (379th BW) 2 missions.

1708th BW(P):

57-6492 (379th BW) *"Old Crow"*. **57-6504** (2nd BW). **57-6508** (2nd BW). **58-**

58-0182 (379th BW) *"What's Up Doc ?"* 5 missions. **58-0204** (379th BW) *"Special Delivery"* 6 missions.

0159 (379th BW) *"Alley Oop's Bold Assault"*. **58-0164** (416th BW) *"SAC Time"*. **58-0173** (379th BW).

4300th BW(P):

58-0195 (42nd BW) *"The Moose is Loose"* 46 missions.

C-5 Galaxy

Deployment

60th Military Airlift Wing (Travis AFB, CA) C-5A/B

436th Military Airlift Wing (Dover AFB, DE) C-5A/B

443rd Military Airlift Wing (Altus AFB, OK) C-5B

137th Military Airlift Squadron/105th Military Airlift Group (Stewart ANGB, NY)** C-5A

68th Military Airlift Squadron/433rd Military Airlift Wing (Kelly AFB, TX)* C-5A

337th Military Airlift Squadron/439th Military Airlift Wing (Westover AFB, MA)* C-5A

** Air National Guard units and *Air Force Reserve units mobilized for active duty with MAC.

Mission

The C-5A/B Galaxy shares with the C-141B StarLifter the role of strategic airlift for Military Airlift Command. Virtually all C-5s participated in the massive airlift between the USA and the Gulf region during Desert Shield and Desert Storm.

Service

C-5s topped the tonnage of the entire Berlin airlift in the first 21 days of Desert Shield and continued, thereafter, to break records for tons of matériel and numbers of people transported from the US to the Persian Gulf. C-5A 68-0228 of the 60th MAW (Travis AFB, CA) crewed by Reservists of the 433rd MAW (Kelly AFB, TX) crashed at Ramstein 29 August 1990 during a Desert Shield airlift

mission carrying maintenance equipment and medical supplies in Desert Shield. The crash was attributed to a faulty thrust reverser. Thirteen were killed.

All 80 front-line and 46 Reserve C-5s were extensively involved in Operations Desert Shield and Desert Storm.

KC-10A Extender

Deployment

802nd Air Refueling Wing (Provisional) – Milan/Malpensa Apt Italy KC-10A
2nd Bombardment Wing (Barksdale AFB, LA) KC-10A
22nd Air Refueling Wing (March AFB, CA) KC-10A
68th Air Refueling Wing (Seymour Johnson AFB, NC) KC-10A

Mission

The KC-10, derived from the DC-10 airliner, was developed as an ATCA (Advanced Tanker/Cargo Aircraft) with the dual role of airlifting and air refueling aircraft for long deployments, as during the Desert Shield/Desert Storm airlift.

Service

KC-10s handled much of the supporting work in deploying fighter wings and other units from the United States during desert Shield. In the conflict, KC-10s refueled both Air Force and Navy aircraft on combat missions against Kuwait and Iraq. One KC-10 made a dramatic save of an F-111F in the early hours of 17 January when the latter's air base at Taif was fogged in.

At least half of the fleet of 59 KC-10As were directly assigned to Desert Storm with the remainder conducting numerous resupply sorties between the USA and the Gulf.

A KC-10A Extender refuels a Navy EA-6B. The KC-10 has an integral hose drum unit (HDU) for Navy aircraft as well as the flying boom for USAF refueling.

C-12A/F Huron

Deployment

United States Embassy Riyadh C-12A
US Military Training Mission (Dhahran International Airport) C-12A
58th Military Airlift Squadron/608th Military Airlift Group (Ramstein AB, Germany) C-12F

Mission

The C-12A/F was assigned the intra-theater airlift to transport senior officers between locations in the Gulf region.

Service

C-12s operating from Riyadh and Dhahran were frequent visitors at installations across the Middle East, while those of the 58th MAS supported the US presence in Turkey.

C-20A Gulfstream III

Deployment

58th Military Airlift Squadron/608th Military Airlift Group (Ramstein AB, Germany) C-20A

Mission

C-20 Gulfstream aircraft provide both long-distance and intra-theater airlift for personnel.

Service

C-20s were employed to transport senior officers and government officials throughout the Gulf region. One aircraft was specifically assigned to General Norman Schwarzkopf for his exclusive use during the campaign. Other Stateside-based Gulfstreams visited the Middle East during the eight-month build-up and combat period.

58th MAS/610th MAG: 83-0500. 83-0501. 83-0502.

C-21A Learjet

Deployment

detachment 3/1401st Military Airlift Squadron (Barksdale AFB, LA) C-21A
detachment 4/1401st Military Airlift Squadron (Peterson AFB, CO) C-21A
detachment 1/1402nd Military Airlift Squadron (Langley AFB, VA) C-21A
detachment 3/1402nd Military Airlift Squadron (Maxwell AFB, AL) C-21A
detachment 4/1402nd Military Airlift Squadron (Eglin AFB, FL) C-21A
Based at Riyadh Military City Airport, Saudi Arabia

Mission

The C-12A (Learjet) was acquired by the US Air Force for the OSA (Operational Support Airlift) mission, transporting personnel and small, high-value items of equipment within a theater. C-21As deployed to the Persian Gulf region were to link other bases with CENTAF headquarters in Riyadh.

Service

Duties were to transport high-ranking personnel within the theater, to carry back-up copies of the daily ATO (Air Tasking Order) from Riyadh to bases operating tactical aircraft, and to carry imagery from RF-4C reconnaissance missions from Bahrain to Riyadh.

84-0108. 84-0110. 84-0111. 84-0112 (det 3/1401st MAS). **84-0115. 84-0117** (det 1/1402nd MAS). **84-0123. 84-0125** (det 3/1402nd MAS). **84-0140** (det 4/1402nd MAS).

C-29A

Deployment

1467th Facility Checking Squadron (Scott AFB, Illinois) – various locations in the Persian Gulf region

Mission

The C-29A C-FIS (Combat Flight Inspection System) aircraft was obtained to inspect and validate the operation of flight navigation systems at fixed facilities.

Service

C-29As were deployed to the Middle East at regular intervals to evaluate new and existing navigation systems and airfield radars during Desert Shield and Desert Storm.

C-130E/H Hercules

Deployment

314th Tactical Airlift Wing (Little Rock AFB, AR) C-130E
317th Tactical Airlift Wing (Pope AFB, NC) C-130E
374th Tactical Airlift Wing (Yokota AB, Japan & Clark AB, Philippines) C-130E
435th Tactical Airlift Wing (Rhein Main AB, Germany) C-130E
463rd Tactical Airlift Wing (Dyess AFB, TX) C-130H
63rd Tactical Airlift Squadron/927th Tactical Airlift Group (Selfridge ANGB, MI) C-130E
327th Tactical Airlift Squadron/913th Tactical Airlift Group (NAS Willow Grove, PA) C-130E
328th Tactical Airlift Squadron/914th Tactical Airlift Group (Niagara Falls IAP, NY) C-130E
815th Tactical Airlift Squadron/403rd Tactical Airlift Wing (Keesler AFB, MS) C-130H
130th Tactical Airlift Squadron/130th Tactical Airlift Group (Charleston, WV) C-130H
142nd Tactical Airlift Squadron/166th Tactical Airlift Group (Wilmington, DE) C-130H
180th Tactical Airlift Squadron/139th Tactical Airlift Group (Rosecrans, MO) C-130H
181st Tactical Airlift Squadron/136th Tactical Airlift Wing (Dallas, TX) C-130H
Plus other Air Force Reserve and Air National Guard units on direct assignment and regular support.

Mission

The C-130E/H was the primary tactical airlifter employed to distribute personnel, equipment and munitions within the theater of operations. All Middle East-based C-130s were equipped with the Adverse Weather Aerial Delivery System (AWADS) for low-level, bad-weather operations.

Service

Prior to Desert Storm C-130E/Hs flew 11,799 sorties with a remarkable departure reliability rate of 97 per cent.

According to manufacturer's figures, 700 C-130E/Hs supported combat operations during Desert Storm, although this total seems to be vastly inflated as the US Air Force only possesses some 550 pure airlift

The Lockheed C-130 Hercules was the anti-Saddam coalition's primary tactical transport during the Gulf war. C-130s were also an important element on the air bridge between the USA, Europe and the Gulf.

versions of the Hercules, and this latter total includes the A and B models which were not deployed to the Gulf. Approximately 130 C-130E/H models were directly assigned to Desert Storm. C-130s participated in a number of the operations including the movement of troops and equipment of the 82nd Airborne Division from its garrison at Champion Main (Safwa, Saudi Arabia) to a Forward Operating Location close to the ground combat zone during Operation Desert Sabre. Resupply of ground forces frequently necessitated C-130s landing on improvised desert air strips and roads across northern Saudi Arabia. A small number of C-130Es directly supported AC-130Hs and MC-130Es performing special operations missions.

AC-130A/H Spectre Gunship

Deployment

16th Special Operations Squadron/1st Special Operations Wing (Hurlburt Field, FL) AC-130H
711th Special Operations Squadron/919th Special Operations Group (Duke Field, FL) AC-130A

Mission

The AC-130A was fitted with two 40-mm cannons, two 20-mm Vulcan cannons, and two 7.62-mm miniguns; the AC-130H had similar weaponry except that one 40-mm cannon was replaced by a 105-mm howitzer and the miniguns were deleted. Both models were equipped with sensors and target-acquisition systems including forward-looking infra-red and low light television.

Service

The five AC-130Hs were deployed during September to conduct night operations against ground targets often close to friendly forces, although they were restricted to areas with a low air-defense threat. Despite this, one AC-130H was lost in combat off the Kuwait coast on 31 January while engaging a 'FROG-7' (Free Rocket Over Ground) site which was threatening some US Marines. The aircraft crashed off shore, killing all 14 on board. Six AFRes AC-130As were deployed eastwards during February although the squadron has denied they were located in Saudi Arabia. Air Force statistics of aircraft deployed show only the AC-130H employed in Desert Storm, so it is quite likely the A models, which returned home with mission symbols on the nose, were in Turkey for Operation Proven Force.

AC-130H: **69-6567. 69-6569. 69-6570. 69-6572. 69-6576.**
AC-130A: **54-1623. 54-1630** *"Azrael – Angel of Death"* 3 missions. **55-0011. 55-0014** *"Jaws of Death"* 20 missions. **55-0029. 56-0509.**

Aircraft of the Gulf War

EC-130E/H Hercules

Deployment
41st Electronic Combat Squadron/28th Air Division (Davis Monthan AFB, AZ) EC-130H Compass Call
43rd Electronic Combat Squadron/66th Electronic Combat Wing 'SB' (Sembach AB, Germany) EC-130H Compass Call
193rd Special Operations Squadron/193rd Special Operations Group PA ANG (Harrisburgh, PA) EC-130E(CL) Comfy Levi & EC-130E(RR) Rivet Rider
7th Airborne Command & Control Squadron/28th Air Division (Keesler AFB, MS) EC-130E

Mission
The four different versions of the EC-130 perform a variety of electronic intelligence, airborne battlefield command and control, and psychological warfare duties.

Service
The EC-130Es of the 7th ACCS house an Airborne Battlefield Command and Control Centre (ABCCC) in capsule form which can be airlifted to various locations. Two versions were employed, consisting of the ABCCC II capsule with manual plotting boards and grease pencils, and the advanced ABCCC III which uses computer generated text and graphics and a digital switching system to detect Iraqi armored forces and provide target data for airborne attack.

Two variants of the EC-130E (CL and RR) 'Volant Solo II' were employed to conduct Elint (electronic intelligence) and Comint (communications intelligence) operations, including psychological warfare operations broadcasting messages encouraging enemy forces to surrender.

The Compass Call EC-130H conducted communications jamming of enemy radars during combat missions by strike packages. EC-130s were stationed in Saudi Arabia at Riyadh King Khalid International Airport (which later became Riyadh Military City Airport) although these specialist aircraft

were probably forward located during Desert Storm. A small number of 43rd ECS

EC-130Hs operated at Incirlik, Turkey, during Operation Proven Force.

MC-130E Combat Talon I Hercules

Deployment
7th Special Operations Squadron/1st Special Operations Wing (Rhein Main AB, Germany) MC-130E
8th Special Operations Squadron/1st Special Operations Wing (Hurlburt Field, FL) MC-130E

Mission
The MC-130E Combat Talon is employed by special operations forces (USAF Special Operations Command) to insert and retrieve personnel behind enemy lines and to support other actions by Army Green Berets, Navy SEALs, and the joint-service Delta Force.

Service
MC-130Es supported special operations ground forces inside Iraq. Early in the war MC-130Es dropped BLU-82/B 'Big Blue' bombs each weighing 15,000 lb and filled with fuel-air explosives to clear mine fields. The 'mother of all bombs' was palletized for carriage aboard the MC-130E and was simply rolled out of the rear cargo door by Special Forces teams. 1st SOW C-130E 63-7898 supported the special operations deployment to the Middle East.

7th SOS:
64-0523. 64-0561.

8th SOS:
64-0551. 64-0559. 64-0562. 64-0568.

HC-130N/P Hercules

Deployment
9th Special Operations Squadron/1st Special Operations Wing (Eglin AFB, FL) HC-130N/P
67th Special Operations Squadron/39th Special Operations Wing (RAF Woodbridge, UK) HC-130N/P

Mission
Although initially obtained to conduct military and civilian rescue missions, the HC-130 has been developed to extend the range of rescue helicopters by inflight refueling. The increasing importance of special operations and combat rescue has been reflected in the usage of night vision goggles by the crew and the implementation of special ops tactics.

Service
Four HC-130N and Ps were flown to the Middle East during August from the 1st SOW at Eglin AFB, while the 67th SOS aircraft deployed to Incirlik and Batman, Turkey, for Operation Proven Force.

9th SOS:
69-5819. 69-5828. 65-0993. 66-0215.

67th SOS:
69-5823. 65-0973. 66-0223.

EC-135L

Deployment
1703rd Air Refueling Wing (Provisional) – King Khalid International Airport, Riyadh
305th Air Refueling Wing (Grissom AFB, Indiana)

Mission
EC-135Ls were modified to perform airborne relay of coded communications for the launch and control of Minuteman missiles for SAC.

Service
The two EC-135Ls were deployed to the Middle East to perform communications relay between satellites and ground stations to speed up the transmission of 'Scud' missile detection information. The two aircraft retured to Grissom AFB on 7 March suitably adorned with 'Scud' missile symbols on the nose.

KC-135A/E/Q/R Stratotanker

Deployment
807th Air Refueling Wing (Provisional) (Mont-de-Marsan AB, France) KC-135R

1702nd Air Refueling Wing (Provisional) (Muscat-Seeb) KC-135R
1703rd Air Refueling Wing (Provisional) (Riyadh/King Khalid Intl Airport) KC-135A/R
1706th Air Refueling Wing (Provisional) (Cairo West Airport, Egypt) KC-135E
1707th Air Refueling Wing (Provisional) (Masirah) KC-135R
1708th Air Refueling Wing (Provisional) (Jeddah/King Abdul Aziz Intl Airport) KC-135A/E
1711th Air Refueling Wing (Provisional) (Riyadh Military City Airport) KC-135A/Q
1712th Air Refueling Wing (Provisional) (Abu Dhabi Intl Airport) KC-135E/R
1713th Air Refueling Wing (Provisional) (Dubai Intl Airport) KC-135E

Mission
The KC-135A/E/Q/R series is the US Air Force's standard tanker for air refueling operations.

Service
During Operation Desert Shield KC-135s refueled deploying aircraft from the USA and Europe to the Persian Gulf before switching to the delivery of personnel and equipment to assist MAC airlifters with this task. Approximately 200 KC-135s were directly assigned to the theater, being operated by provisional air refueling wings, while several hundred other tankers regularly operated between the USA and the Gulf region. During Desert Storm KC-135s flew

thousands of missions to support Air Force, Navy, Marine Corps and coalition fighter aircraft on combat missions. Although restricted to designated refueling tracks in the airspace above northern Saudi Arabia, KC-135s ventured across the Iraq border to provide fuel to warplanes which were below the safe minimum.

Virtually every one of the 630 plus KC-135A, E, Q and R models in the SAC, Air Force Reserve and Air National Guard inventory were either stationed in the Middle East or provided direct support of the operation.

RC-135U/V/W

Deployment
detachment of the 55th Strategic Reconnaissance Wing at Riyadh Military Airport
55th SRW also launched missions from regular detachment at Hellenikon AB, Greece

Mission
The RC-135U/V/W 'Rivet Joint' aircraft were designed to gather signals intelligence from the safety of friendly or international airspace. With an array of specialized radars and sensors, the RC-135s obtain electronic intelligence to identify enemy radars, communications intelligence and many other forms of strategic data.

Service
RC-135s were among the first Air Force aircraft to deploy to the Middle East, with one aircraft staging to the region on 4 August, which was just two days after the Iraq invasion of Kuwait. The RC-135s conducted numerous missions along the Iraqi border to gather intelligence during the build-up and the war itself. Several RC-135s spent many months in the region, as epitomized by 62-4135 which was inscribed with 83 mission symbols on the nose. The 55th SRW has a number of support and trainer aircraft which flew dozens of sorties between the USA and Riyadh.

Aircraft of the Gulf War

C-141B StarLifter

Deployment
60th Military Airlift Wing (Travis AFB, CA) C-141B
62nd Military Airlift Wing (McChord AFB, WA) C-141B
63rd Military Airlift Wing (Norton AFB, CA) C-141B
437th Military Airlift Wing (Charleston AFB, SC) C-141B
438th Military Airlift Wing (McGuire AFB, NJ) C-141B
443rd Military Airlift Wing (Altus AFB, OK) C-141B
756th Military Airlift Squadron/459th Military Airlift Wing* (Andrews AFB, MD) C-141B
183rd Military Airlift Squadron/172nd Military

Airlift Group** (Jackson, MS) C-141B
* Air Force Reserve and ** Air National Guard units mobilized for assignment with MAC.

Mission
The C-141B StarLifter shares with the C-5A/B Galaxy the role of strategic airlift for the US Military Airlift Command. Some 265 C-141Bs participated in the massive airlift between the United States and the Desert Shield/Desert Storm region.

Service
C-141B StarLifters joined with C-5A/Bs in bearing the brunt of the strategic airlift during Desert Shield and Desert Storm.

E-3B/C Sentry

Deployment
Based at Riyadh/King Khalid International Airport (later renamed Riyadh Military City Airport) and Incirlik AB, Turkey

Mission
The E-3B/C Sentry AWACS (Airborne Warning And Control System) is employed for management of air assets, to provide threat warning and to control the assets assigned to cope with the threat. The E-3C version is an upgrade with 14 operator consoles replacing the nine on earlier versions, and other minor improvements.

Service
E-3B/C Sentry AWACS aircraft have operated on a rotational basis in Saudi Arabia for years. When they were needed in larger numbers to support Operation Desert Shield and Operation Desert Storm, the 522nd AWAC Wing had a trained cadre of personnel who – unlike most others who participated – had extensive experience operating in the Persian Gulf region.

E-3B: **71-1407. 71-1408. 73-1675. 75-0556. 75-0557. 76-1605. 77-0351. 77-0352. 77-0354. 77-0355. 78-0577. 78-0578. 79-0001.** E-3C: **80-0137. 80-0138. 80-0139. 81-0004. 82-0006. 82-0007. 83-0008.**

AWACS radar and control aircraft gave allied commanders complete control over the air battle.

E-8 J-STARS

Deployment
4411th Joint STARS Squadron

Mission
The E-8A Joint STARS (Surveillance Target Attack Radar System) aircraft, operated by US Air Force crews and linked to US Army battlefield forces, uses airborne radars to peer over 100 miles (161 km) into enemy territory to spot armored weapons and other military assets.

Service
Although still in developmental stage, the two prototype aircraft were flown to Riyadh in early January 1991 to provide US Central Command (CENTCOM) with a real-time method of tracking armor and other military vehicles. The two aircraft flew 54 missions and logged 600 combat hours before they returned to the Grumman Melbourne, Florida, plant on 6 March.

86-0416/N770JS. 86-0417/N8411.

RF-4C Phantom

Deployment
35th Tactical Fighter Wing (Provisional) – Sheikh Isa Air Base, Bahrain
106th Tactical Reconnaissance Squadron (AL ANG) 'BH' (Birmingham, Alabama) (August-December 1990) – Air National Guard unit when not, as in Desert Storm, called to active duty
192nd Tactical Reconnaissance Squadron (NV ANG) (Reno, Nevada) using 'BH' (flying Alabama aircraft) – never called to active duty
67th Tactical Reconnaissance Wing 'BA' (Bergstrom AFB, TX)
7440th Composite Wing – Incirlik AB, Turkey
26th Tactical Reconnaissance Wing 'ZR' (Zweibrucken AB, Germany)

Mission
The RF-4C is a dedicated photo-reconnaissance platform used to gather tactical photography and intelligence.

Service
At the start of Operation Desert Shield in August 1990, the Alabama Air National Guard was deployed on a voluntary basis with six aircraft as the only RF-4C unit with LOROP (LOng-Range Oblique Photography), i.e., KS-127 66-in focal length cameras. These participated in cross-border reconnaissance from distances up to 50 miles (80 km) during the military build-up. One RF-4C was lost during Operation Desert Shield. As attrition replacements, one aircraft was deployed from the Mississippi Air National Guard and one from the Nevada Air National Guard. During Operation Desert Storm, RF-4Cs carried out daytime (only) tactical reconnaissance, including searching for facilities associated with mobile 'Scud' missile launchers. RF-4Cs operating from

Turkey covered targets near the border of western Iraq. The Incirlik aircraft deployed on 3 February; flew their first mission on 5 February; completed 103 combat sorties; and returned to Zweibrucken on 11 March. A second Alabama RF-4C was lost after the conclusion of Operation Desert Storm.

Sheikh Isa:
106th TRS 'BH':
64-1033. 64-1034. 64-1044 lost 8 October 1990 during Desert Shield; crew killed. **65-1047** flew in every one of the unit's Desert Storm missions. **64-1056** lost 31 March 1991; crew ejected safely. **65-0833. 65-0834** *"Recce Rebels Birmingham"* sharksmouth – deployed from unit as attrition replacement for **64-1044**. **65-0893** sharksmouth. **65-0886.**

Incirlik:
26th TRW 'ZR':
68-0554. 68-0555. 68-0557. 69-0370.

Long in the tooth but still effective, the RF-4C was the USAF's only tac recon asset.

F-4E Phantom

Deployment
3rd Tactical Fighter Squadron/3rd Tactical Fighter Wing 'PN' (Clark AB, Philippines) F-4E
7440th Composite Wing Incirlik AB, Turkey F-4E

Mission
The F-4E still serves in a few units as a ground attack and multi-role fighter aircraft.

Service
Six F-4Es from Clark Field, Philippines, were deployed to Incirlik during the build-up preceding Operation Desert Storm. It appears that they may not have been used in combat operations.

F-4G Phantom

Deployment
35th Tactical Fighter Wing (Provisional) – Sheikh Isa Air Base, Bahrain
81st TFS/52nd TFW 'SP' (Spangdahlem AB, Germany)
561st TFS/35th TFW 'WW' (George AFB, CA)
7440th Composite Wing Incirlik AB, Turkey
23rd TFS/52nd TFW (Spangdahlem AB, Germany)

Mission
The F-4G 'Wild Weasel' is an electronic warfare aircraft assigned the lethal SEAD (Suppression of Enemy Air Defenses) mission, using AGM-88 HARM (High-speed Anti-Radiation Missiles) to attack air-defense radar sites.

Service
F-4G 'Wild Weasels' were among the busiest aircraft of the war. In one day, 3 February, two-squadrons – the 561st (George AFB, CA) and 81st (Spangdahlem AB, Germany) flew 86 combat sorties. F-4Gs flew 2,331 combat sorties and 8,587 combat hours against Iraqi air-defense radars, including some located near Baghdad, without loss.

23rd TFS/52nd TFW 'SP':
69-0244. 69-0247. 69-0260. 69-0269. 69-0274. 69-0285. 69-7209. 69-7228. 69-7291. 69-7546. 69-7566. 69-7582.

81st TFS/52nd TFW 'SP':
69-0242 borrowed from 23rd TFS, SAM silhouettes on port splitter. **69-0245** borrowed from 23rd TFS, SAM silhouettes on port splitter. **69-0251. 69-0253** borrowed from 480th TFS, SAM silhouettes on port splitter. **69-0270. 69-0278** borrowed from 23rd TFS, SAM silhouettes on port splitter. **69-0286** SAM silhouettes on port splitter. **69-7210. 69-7212** borrowed from 23rd TFS, 5 SAM silhouettes on port splitter. **69-7234. 69-7267** SAM silhouettes on port splitter. **69-7268** SAM silhouettes on port splitter. **69-7286. 69-7293. 69-7556. 69-7558. 69-7579.**

561st TFS/35th TFW 'WW':
69-7263 *"SAM Slayer".*

Aircraft of the Gulf War

F-15C/D Eagle

Deployment

1st Tactical Fighter Wing 'FF' (Langley AFB, VA) Dhahran, Saudi Arabia
4th Tactical Fighter Wing (Provisional) Al Kharj Air Base, Saudi Arabia
33rd Tactical Fighter Wing (58th TFS) (Eglin AFB, FL) Tabuk, Saudi Arabia
53rd Tactical Fighter Squadron 'BT' (Bitburg, Germany)
525th Tactical Fighter Squadron (Bitburg, Germany) Incirlik, Turkey
32nd Tactical Fighter Squadron/32nd Tactical Fighter Group 'CR' (Soesterberg AB, Netherlands) F-15C Incirlik, Turkey

Mission

The F-15C is the US Air Force's premier air-to-air combat fighter and is charged with gaining and holding air supremacy.

Service

F-15Cs (plus one or two F-15Ds assigned to Dhahran) flew combat air patrols during Desert Shield and escorted other aircraft on combat missions during Desert Storm. Most air-to-air engagements were fought by F-15Cs, and most of these were by the 58th TFS.

27th TFS/1st TFW:
82-0008. 82-0010. 82-0022. 82-0023. 82-0029. 82-0037. 83-0011. 83-0019. 83-0027. 83-0028. 83-0029. 83-0030. 83-0031. 83-0032. 83-0033. 83-0034. 83-0035. 83-0039. 83-0040. 83-0041. 83-0042. 83-0043. 82-0046 (F-15D). 82-0047 (F-15D). 83-0050 (F-15D).

71st TFS/1st TFW:
81-0025. 81-0030. 81-0031. 81-0033. 81-0035. 82-0009. 82-0012. 82-0014. 82-0017. 82-0018. 82-0019. 82-0021. 82-0036. 83-0010. 83-0012. 83-0013. 83-0014. 83-0017. 83-0018. 83-0021. 83-0022. 83-0025. 83-0026. 83-0037. 83-0047 (F-15D). 83-0048 (F-15D). 83-0049 (F-15D).

58th TFS/33rd TFW 'EG':
85-0094. 85-0096. 85-0098. 85-0099 one kill. 85-0100. 85-0101 one kill. 85-0102 "Gulf Spirit" three kills. 85-0103. 85-0104 one kill. 85-0105 two kills. 85-0106. 85-0107 one kill. 85-0108 one kill. 85-0110. 85-0111. 85-0113. 85-0114 two kills. 85-0115. 85-0118. 85-0119 one kill. 85-0120. 85-0122 one kill. 85-0124

two kills. **85-0125** one kill.

53rd TFS/36th TFW 'BT':
79-0078 two kills. 84-0001. 84-0002. 84-0005. 84-0010 one postwar kill. 84-0013. 84-0014 one postwar kill. 84-0015 one postwar kill. 84-0016. 84-0019 two kills. 84-0021. 84-0022. 84-0023. 84-0025 two kills. 84-0027 two kills.

525th TFS/36th TFW 'BT':
79-0025. 79-0036. 79-0037. 79-0048 one kill. 79-0057. 79-0058. 79-0064 borrowed from 22nd TFS. 79-0069 one kill. 79-0079. 80-0003 one kill. 80-0004 borrowed from 22nd TFS. 80-0005. 80-0010 borrowed from 32nd TFS. 80-0012 one kill. 80-0019. 80-0028. 80-0031. 81-0028.

32nd TFS/32nd TFG 'CR':
79-0021 two kills.

F-15E Strike Eagle

Deployment

4th Tactical Fighter Wing (Provisional) – Al Kharj Air Base, Saudi Arabia

Mission

The F-15E Strike Eagle is a dual role tactical aircraft with air-to-air and air-to-ground capability. During Desert Storm, F-15Es were assigned strike missions against a variety of targets, including 'Scud' missile launch sites.

Service

Though targetting pods intended for use on the F-15E were not available at the beginning of the war, hindering the capability of the aircraft to drop precision

ordnance, F-15Es from two Stateside squadrons (335th TFS 'Chiefs' and 336th TFS 'Rocketeers', both part of the 4th TFW 'SJ' at Seymour Johnson AFB, NC) flew hundreds of combat missions beginning in the early hours of the war. Two F-15Es were lost in combat.

335th TFS/4th TFW 'SJ':
87-0198 45 missions. 87-0199. 87-0200 54 missions (most flown in squadron). 87-0204. 87-0208. 88-1670 20 missions. 88-1674. 88-1683 49 missions. 88-1686 52 missions; 335th TFS CO's a/c. 88-1688. 88-1694. 88-1698 43 missions. 88-1708 45 missions. 89-0476 42 missions. 89-0487 one helicopter kill. 89-0489 39 missions.

336th TFS/4th TFW 'SJ':
87-0196. 88-1675. 88-1691.

F-16A/B/C/D Fighting Falcon

Deployment

4th Tactical Fighter Wing (Provisional) F-16 Division – F-16A block 10 – Al Kharj Air Base, Saudi Arabia
157th TFS/169th TFG F-16A SC ANG** McEntire ANGB, SC 'SC'
138th TFS/174th TFW NY ANG** Hancock Field, Syracuse, NY 'NY'
363rd Tactical Fighter Wing (Provisional) – F-16C block 25 – Al Dafra Air Base, Sharjah, United Arab Emirates
17th TFS, 33rd TFS, Shaw AFB, SC 'SW'
10th TFS Hahn AB, Germany 'HR'
388th Tactical Fighter Wing (Provisional) – F-16C block 40 – Alminhad, United Arab Emirates
4th TFS/388th TFW, 421st TFS/388th TFW, Hill AFB, UT 'HL'
69th TFS/347th TFW, Moody AFB, GA (after 69th TFS was briefly at King Fahd) 'MY'
401st Tactical Fighter Wing 'TJ' (614th TFS, Torrejon AB, Spain) – F-16C block 30 – Qatar
7740th Composite Wing (Provisional) F-16 Division – F-16C block 30 – Incirlik, Turkey Det 1/401st TFW 'TJ', Torrejon AB, Spain 23rd TFS/52nd TFW.
**Air National Guard units when not, as during Desert Storm, called to USAF active duty

Mission

The F-16A/C was employed in the air-to-ground role primarily for BAI (Battlefield Area Interdiction) and was used against Iraqi troops, vehicles, and forward installations.

Service

F-16A/Cs were deployed from the beginning of Operation Desert Shield and used throughout the war. Five F-16s were lost in combat and two more in non-combat mishaps.

10th TFS/50th TFW 'HR':
84-1267. 84-1271. 84-1275. 84-1278. 84-1282. 84-1284. 84-1290. 84-1295. 84-1298. 84-1299. 84-1306. 84-1315. 84-1374. 84-1376. 84-1377. 84-1385. 84-1387. 84-1388. 85-1403. 85-1405. 85-1407. 85-1416. 85-1418.

69th TFS/347th TFW 'MY':
88-05516. 88-0522. 88-0546. 89-2024 79 missions (most flown in squadron).

17th TFS/363rd TFW 'Owls' 'SW':
83-1159 "Bat Man" 45 missions. 83-1165 "Here Hussein Surprise" 42 missions. 84-1213 "Tazmanian Devil" 47 missions. 84-1215 "Fosters Express" 46 missions. 84-1217 "Owl" 39 missions; Sqn CO's a/c. 84-1223 "Husseins Worst Nightmare" 44 missions. 84-1226 36 missions; 84-1236 46 missions. 84-1238 14 missions; DS tail code***. 84-1241 "Hooter Standards" 46 missions. 84-1243 51 missions. 84-1244 "Eat My Shorts Hussein" 56 missions. 84-1247 37 missions. 84-1251 58 missions. 84-1252 58 missions. 84-1254 38 missions. 84-1256 "Night Stalker". 84-1257 "Desert Storm" 49 missions. 84-1261 "Blood Storm" 40 missions. 84-1262 50 missions. 84-1287 6 missions. 84-1296 29 missions; DS tail code***. 84-1300 did not fly combat missions; DS tail code***. 84-1378 35 missions. 85-1419 "363 TFW Desert Shield" 57 missions; Wing CO's a/c.
***DS tail code reportedly indicates designated spares acquired from 10th TFS/50th TFW and retained by 17th TFS/363rd TFW.

33rd TFS/363rd TFW 'Falcons' 'SW':
83-1141. 83-1142 "Harmful FX". 83-3344. 83-1146. 83-1148. 83-1150 "Max

Thrust". 83-1152. 83-1153. 83-1157. 83-1158 "Sweet But Deadly". 83-1161. 83-1164. 84-1212 painted for one week in desert tan. Visual effects poor, wingman lost him just after take-off and turned sharply away to avoid a mid-air collision. 84-1219 "Hot Cock". 84-1226. 84-1234. 84-1240 "Wild Thang" plus bespectacled shark on nose wheel door. 84-1260. 84-1265 "Wild Child". 84-1268. 84-1281 "Hammer Time". 84-1381. 85-1520 "Code One Candy" (possibly not a Desert Storm participant).

138th TFS/174th TFW 'NY':
79-0289. 79-0351. 79-0352. 79-0382. 79-0388. 79-0391. 79-0401. 79-0403. 79-0404.

157th TFS/169th TFG:
79-0288. 79-0289. 79-0293. 79-0296.

79-0297. 79-0304. 79-0320. 79-0321.

23rd TFS/52nd TFW:
85-1552. 86-0224. 86-0227. 86-0232. 86-0237. 86-0242. 86-0244. 86-0246. 86-0248. 86-0260. 86-0287. 87-0270. 87-0336.

4th TFS/388th TFW:
88-457. 88-473. 88-474. 88-479. 88-482. 88-507. 88-513.

421st TFS/388th TFW:
87-355. 88-422. 88-424. 88-429. 88-450. 88-452. 88-470.

614th TFS/401st TFW:
86-288. 87-223. 87-230. 87-244. 87-242. 87-243. 87-249. 87-259.

Aircraft of the Gulf War

F-111E/F & EF-111A Raven

Deployment

20th Tactical Fighter Wing 'UH' (RAF Upper Heyford, UK) F-111E
48th Tactical Fighter Wing 'LN' (RAF Lakenheath, UK) F-111F
66th Electronic Combat Wing 'UH' (RAF Upper Heyford, UK) EF-111A
388th Tactical Fighter Wing 'MO' (Mountain Home AFB, ID) EF-111A
7440th Composite Wing Incirlik AB, Turkey

Mission

The EF-111A (converted F-111A) is an electronic warfare aircraft assigned the non-lethal SEAD (Suppression of Enemy Air Defenses) role to jam an enemy's radar and electronics.

The F-111E is a long-range, all-weather strike aircraft.

The F-111F is a long-range, all-weather strike aircraft equipped with the Pave Tack laser designator system and capable of designating its own targets for laser-guided bombs. The 493rd TFS is the only squadron capable of employing the GBU-15 imaging infra-red guided bomb.

Service

F-111Es operated from Turkey against targets in western Iraq.

F-111Fs were used initially to bomb hard targets such as aircraft shelters and later proved effective against Iraqi armored vehicles and main battle tanks. F-111Fs were employed to bomb a pair of manifolds at an Iraqi-sabotaged oil pumping facility off Kuwait that was spilling crude oil into the Persian Gulf. F-111Fs flew 2,500 sorties and were credited with 2,203 confirmed hits, destroying 920 tanks and armored vehicles, 245 hardened aircraft shelters, 113 bunkers and 160 bridges. In the final days of the war, F-111Fs used GBU-28 'bunker bombs' to attack the Iraqi command staff near Baghdad. No F-111Fs were lost in combat. Two sustained damage from Iraqi gunfire.

EF-111As were used to jam Iraqi radars. The first aerial victory of the war, yet to be officially credited by the US Air Force, occurred when an EF-111A outmaneuvered an Iraqi Mirage F1 fighter and forced it to collide with the ground. One EF-111A was lost in combat and the crew was killed.

492nd TFS/48th TFW 'LN':
70-2365. 70-2378. 70-2379. 70-2399. 70-2406. 70-2411. 70-2413. 71-0883. 71-0884. 72-1442. 72-1451. 74-0177. 74-0181. 74-0182.

493rd TFS/48th TFW 'LN':
70-2362. 70-2371. 70-2384. 70-2396. 70-2398. 70-2399. 70-2403. 70-2404. 70-2414. 70-2417. 71-0886. 71-0887. 71-0891. 74-0180. 74-0183 lost in accident on 9 October 1990.

494th TFS/48th TFW 'LN':
70-2364. 70-2390 ''Miss Liberty II'' 48th TFW CO's a/c. **70-2405. 70-2408. 70-2409. 71-0892. 72-1443. 72-1444. 72-1448. 73-0712. 73-0715. 74-0178** 494th TFS CO's a/c; 56 missions (most flown in wing).

495th TFS/48th TFW 'LN':
70-2378. 70-2406. 70-2411. 70-2414. 71-0883 (squadron not deployed, but aircraft borrowed by the three other squadrons).

390th ECS/366th TFW:
66-0014. 66-0041. 66-0030. 66-0016 destroyed Iraqi Mirage F1 17 January. **66-0023** EF-111A lost in combat 14 February (a former F-111A which had participated in the Combat Lancer deployment to Vietnam in 1968).

55th TFS/20th TFW:
67-0121. 68-0004. 68-0005. 68-0013. 68-0026. 68-0029. 68-0061. 68-0076.

77th TFS/20th TFW:
68-0015. 68-0017. 68-0039. 68-0040. 68-0046. 68-0050.

79th TFS/20th TFW:
67-0120. 68-0016. 68-0031. 68-0049. 68-0068. 68-0069. 68-0072. 68-0074.

42nd ECS/66th ECW:
66-0047. 66-0055. 67-0034. 67-0035. 67-0042.

The Pave Tack-equipped F-111Fs of the 48th TFW operated out of Taif, in Saudi Arabia.

F-117A Night Hawk

Deployment

37th Tactical Fighter Wing 'TR' (Tonopah, Nevada) – Khamis Mushait Air Base, Saudi Arabia

Mission

The F-117A employs low observable technology (stealth) to reduce the likelihood of detection on radar in time for defenses to be effective. The aircraft is intended for night and bad-weather operations against exceedingly high-value targets determined by the National Command Authority.

Service

F-117As operated against targets in Baghdad from the beginning of the war, using stealth and precision delivery to take out command facilities, control bunkers, bridges and other facilities, with minimal loss of civilian life in the immediate area.

791 ''Lazy Ace''. **808** ''Thor''. **810** ''Dark Angel''. **813** ''Toxic Avenger''. ''37 TFW'' 29 missions. **814** ''Final Verdict''. **816. 818. 825** ''Mad Max''. **828** ''37 TFW''. **829. 830** ''Black Assassin''. **842. 843.**

The Lockheed F-117A 'Stealth Fighter' operated from Khamis Mushait AB.

MH-53J

Deployment

20th Special Operations Squadron/1st Special Operations Wing (Hurlburt Field, FL) MH-53J
21st Special Operations Squadron/39th Special Operations Wing (RAF Woodbridge, UK) MH-53J

Mission

The MH-53J Pave Low is employed for special operations, including combat rescue, by the US Air Force's Special Operations Command.

Service

MH-53Js were employed on a variety of special operations missions in the Persian Gulf region.

20th SOS:
68-10356. 68-10367. 68-10369. 68-10930. 69-5789. 69-5795. 69-5797. 70-1630.

21st SOS:
68-8284. 695784. 69-5796.

The MH-53J can be used on clandestine operations by night.

MH-60G Pave Hawk

Deployment

55th Special Operations Squadron/1st Special Operations Wing (Eglin AFB, FL) MH-60G

Mission

The MH-60G was developed as a combat rescue version of the Army UH-60A for special operations with the fitment of an air refueling probe, .50-caliber machine guns, plus equipment and avionics required for special ops duties.

Service

Eight MH-60Gs were airlifted to the Middle East to conduct special operations duties within Saudi Arabia and probably inside Iraq.

88-26006. 88-26008. 88-26009. 88-26010. 88-26011. 88-26012. 88-26013. 88-26014.

The MH-60G was developed in the 1980s as a combat rescue and special operations machine.

Aircraft of the Gulf War

U-2R/TR-1A

Deployment
1700th Reconnaissance Wing (Provisional) Taif, Saudi Arabia U-2R/TR-1A
9th Strategic Reconnaissance Wing (Beale AFB, CA) U-2R/TR-1A
detachment 3, 9th Strategic Reconnaissance Wing (RAF Akrotiri, Cyprus) TR-1A
17th Reconnaissance Wing (RAF Alconbury, UK) TR-1A

Mission
Operating at high altitude, the U-2Rs and TR-1As provided stand-off reconnaissance using synthetic aperture radar, cameras and Sigint equipment. Real-time transfer of data via satellite was enhanced by the employment of the Senior Span system housed in an elongated oval dome mounted on the upper fuselage of U-2Rs.

Service
U-2Rs of the 9th SRW regularly monitor the Middle East from Cyprus, but operations stepped up as tensions grew. Before the war the aircraft gave coalition commanders excellent intelligence from deep in Iraq, a supply which continued throughout and after the war. Particular tasks involved monitoring Iraqi armor movements, and spotting 'Scuds' and ships for attack by strike aircraft.

95th RS/17th RW & 99th SRS/9th SRW:
TR-1A: **80-1074. 80-1081. 80-1085. 80-1088. 80-1092. 80-1099.**

99th SRS/9th SRW:
U-2R: **68-10331** (Senior Span). **68-10338** (Senior Span). **80-1070** (Senior Span). **80-1076. 80-1096. 80-1098.**

UNITED STATES ARMY

C-12C/D/J Huron

Deployment
207th Aviation Company (Heidelberg, Germany) Dhahran Intl Airport C-12C
Berlin Brigade (Berlin/Templehof, Germany) C-12C
Headquarters US Southern Command (MacDill AFB, FL) Dhahran Intl Airport C-12D

Mission
As with the Air Force, Navy and Marine Corps, senior Army officials were transported within the Gulf region by a number of C-12s borrowed from various Stateside and European units.

Service
At least 12 C-12s of three different versions were stationed in Saudi Arabia, with the majority being located at Dhahran and others based at Riyadh.

C-23B Sherpa

Deployment
One Stateside-based unit, designation unknown

Mission
The Army acquired a number of C-23s to distribute outsized cargoes, such as helicopter engines, to remote areas, relieving MAC of this duty and affording a degree of autonomy.

Service
Five Army Sherpas were delivered from the Sydenham, UK, factory direct to Saudi Arabia during February and March 1991. At the completion of their Gulf duty they returned to Sydenham during May.

88-1861. 88-1863. 88-1864. 88-1866. 88-1867.

UH-1H/V Iroquois

Deployment
Between 200 and 300 UH-1s were drawn from US Army units worldwide to support the build-up of forces in the Gulf

Mission
The UH-1, which was affectionately known as the 'Huey' in Vietnam, was the Army's principal utility and transport helicopter, although it has largely been replaced by the UH-60. Nevertheless, the type is still in widespread use, particularly for medical evacuation and general duties.

Service
UH-1Hs were employed transporting personnel and equipment between the large number of Army bases and desert strips. The UH-1V 'Dustoff' version performed medical evacuation with the movement of casualties. According to one official release, 193 UH-1Hs and 121 UH-1Vs were directly assigned to Desert Storm. One UH-1 was lost in combat, another in a non-combat accident, while a third crashed during a postwar sortie.

RC-12D Huron

Deployment
1st Military Intelligence Battalion (Wiesbaden, Germany) Al Qaysumah, Saudi Arabia RC-12D

AH-6/MH-6/OH-6 Cayuse

Deployment
Many US Army units

Mission
The OH-6 LOH (Light Observation Helicopter), or 'Loach', from the Vietnam era, remains in service in some units for artillery spotting and forward air control. Armed AH-6 and MH-6 versions are in inventory with special operations forces.

Service
It is believed that special operations forces, especially US Army Special Forces, employed AH-6 and MH-6 aircraft in operations behind Iraqi lines. No details have been released.

2nd Military Intelligence Batallion (Stuttgart, Germany).Al Qaysumah, Saudi Arabia RC-12D

Mission
The RC-12D Guard Rail aircraft is a communications intelligence and D/F (direction-finding) platform used for reconnaissance against enemy forces at the tactical level.

Service
RC-12Ds were employed to support US Army operations in the Persian Gulf. RC-12Ds and similar RU-12Hs are not considered survivable on the modern battlefield and operate some distance back from the forward line of troops. Some RC-12Ds returned to Wiesbaden on 4 April.

1st MIBtn:
78-23141. 78-23142. 78-23143. 80-23375 Lost in accident. **80-23377. 81-23542.**

2nd MIBtn:
78-23144. 80-23371. 80-23373. 80-23374. 80-23378.

CH-47 Chinook

Deployment
101st Airborne Division (Fort Campbell, KY) CH-47D
159th Aviation Regiment (Schwabisch-Hall, Germany) CH-47D
plus other units

Mission
The CH-47 Chinook is the US Army's heavy transportation helicopter, employed to move troops and heavy equipment.

Service
CH-47s carried equipment and personnel, brought back captured Iraqi prisoners of war, and spearheaded the ground offensive by the 101st Airborne Division (Air Assault). A CH-47 was lost on 1 March, just after the formal cease-fire.

Aircraft of the Gulf War

OH-58A/C/D Kiowa

Deployment
1st Infantry Division (Fort Riley, KS) – Saudi Arabia
82nd Airborne Division (Fort Bragg, NC) – Champion Main Safwa, Saudi Arabia
101st Airborne Division (Air Assault) (Fort Campbell, KY) – Saudi Arabia
Most major US Army units

Mission
The OH-58A/C Kiowa is the US Army's standard observation and light reconnaissance helicopter and is often used in direct support of battlefield helicopters such as the AH-64 Apache. The OH-58D Kiowa Warrior, developed under the US Army's AHIP (Armed Helicopter Improvements Program) employs mast-mounted sight and other improvements to support AH-64 operations. A small number of OH-58Ds were operated by US Army special operations personnel aboard US Navy vessels in the Persian Gulf.

Service
OH-58A/C Kiowas operated everywhere with the US Army during Operation Desert Storm. OH-58D AHIP special operations aircraft operating from the frigate USS Nicholas (FFG-47) and other vessels attacked Iraqi-held platforms in the Persian Gulf and assisted in the taking of numerous Iraqi prisoners of war.

1st InfDiv:
OH-58A/C: **68-16775. 68-16925. 68-16948. 68-16949. 69-16113. 69-16279. 69-16301. 70-15443. 70-15488. 70-15634. 71-20433. 71-20625. 71-20769. 71-20846. 72-21092. 71-20349. 71-21084.**

EH/UH-60 Black Hawk

Deployment
First Cavalry Division (Fort Hood, TX)
82nd Airborne Division (Fort Bragg, NC)
101st Airborne Division (Fort Campbell, KY)
Most major US Army units

Mission
The UH-60 Black Hawk is the US Army's principal utility and transport helicopter and is widely in service for general duties and for medical evacuation.

Service
UH-60A/L Black Hawks carried people and equipment throughout the theater during Desert Shield and Desert Storm. UH-60V 'Dustoff', or medical evacuation, helicopters assisted with the movement of some casualties. One UH-60 was lost in combat while attempting to rescue a downed F-16 pilot. Two were lost in non-combat mishaps. Twenty-four EH-60A 'Quick Fix' electronic intelligence versions were assigned to Desert Storm. Numerically the Black Hawk was the most prolific helicopter in the Gulf, with 299 UH-60As and 64 UH-60Vs.

The Sikorsky UH-60 Black Hawk has replaced the UH-1 as the US Army's primary assault helicopter. Nearly 300 of the type served in the Gulf, equipping the aviation battalions of all major US Army formations.

AH-64A Apache

Deployment
First Cavalry Division (Fort Hood, TX)
82nd Airborne Division (Fort Bragg, NC)
101st Airborne Division (Fort Campbell, KY)

Mission
The AH-64 Apache is a battlefield helicopter designed to employ AGM-114A Hellfire missiles against armor and other targets.

Service
Eight AH-64 Apaches of Task Force Normandy, formed from the 101st Airborne Division's 1st Battalion, 101st Aviation Regiment under Lieutenant Colonel Dick Cody, fired the first allied shots of the war at 2:38 a.m., 17 January, when they used Hellfire missiles, 2.75-in rockets, and 30-mm ammunition to destroy two key Iraqi air-defense radar bunkers, thereby creating a corridor to enable more than 100 strike aircraft to proceed undetected to Baghdad. This special operation entailed a four-day, 950-mile (1528-km) trip begun on 14 January and required Task Force Normandy to refuel at temporary locations. As the war progressed, the AH-64 Apache proved highly effective against a variety of Iraqi targets, including armor. A few friendly casualties were caused by fire from AH-64s. One AH-64 may have been lost in combat. One was also lost in a non-combat mishap.

The McDonnell Douglas AH-64 Apache was the first aircraft in action at the start of the war, and Apaches formed the spearhead of the 100-hour ground offensive that was to conclude the conflict.

RU-21A/B/C/D/H King Air

Deployment
224th Military Intelligence Battalion

Mission
The RU-21H Guard Rail aircraft is a communications intelligence and D/F (direction-finding) platform used for reconnaissance against enemy forces at the tactical level.

Service
RC-21Hs were employed to support US Army operations in the Persian Gulf. RU-21Hs and more recent RC-12Ds are not considered survivable on the modern battlefield and operate some distance back from the forward line of troops. Some RU-21Hs returned to the US in early April.

RU-21A, B and C aircraft came from Army Reserve units.

RU-21A: **67-18113** "Patriot". **67-18114** "From the US". **67-18115**.
RU-21B: **67-18077** "Great Balls of Fire". **67-18087** "Sportsman". **67-18093** "Catch 22".
RU-21C: **67-18085** "From Riches to Rags".
RU-21D: **67-18110** USAICS.
RU-21H: **70-15879. 70-15886. 70-15887. 70-15889. 70-15891. 70-15893. 70-15903.**

OV/RV-1 Mohawk

Deployment
1st Military Intelligence Battalion (Wiesbaden, Germany) Al Qaysumah, Saudi Arabia OV/RV-1D
2nd Military Intelligence Battalion (Stuttgart, Germany) Al Qaysumah, Saudi Arabia
224th Military Intelligence Battalion

Mission
The OV-1 Mohawk is a battlefield observation and utility aircraft employed for support duties for the US Army. Some OV-1D are equipped with SLAR (Side-Looking Airborne Radar) for battlefield support. The RV-1D is a battlefield Elint derivative.

Service
OV-1Ds and RV-1Ds were deployed to Saudi Arabia to support US Army ground operations during Operation Desert Storm. Many returned to the US in early April.

1st MIBtn:
OV-1D: **67-18910. 67-18919. 68-15943.**
RV-1D: **62-5897. 64-14273.**

2nd MIBtn:
OV-1D: **62-5876. 62-5902. 67-18908. 67-18910. 68-15950. 68-15953. 68-15956. 68-15962. 68-16996. 69-17004. 69- 17008.** RV-1D: **62-5891. 64-14244. 64-14246. 64-14247.**

224th MIBtn:
OV-1D: **67-18907. 67-18912. 67-18918. 67-18921. 67-18926. 68-15952. 68-15960. 68-15963. 69-17007. 69-17009. 69-17011.** RV-1D: **64-14243. 64-14252. 64-14255. 64-14261. 64-14265.**

Aircraft of the Gulf War

UNITED STATES NAVY
Aircraft carriers and their air wings

USS *Independence* (CV-62); CVW-14 (NK)
Independence returned to the US in December, having been involved in Desert Shield from the beginning. She also entered the Persian Gulf on 8 August, the first time an American carrier had been in that restricted area for some time.

USS *John F. Kennedy* (CV-67); CVW-3 (AC)
Kennedy left its homeport of Norfolk, Virginia, on 15 August having only the five previous days to prepare for departure. Working around-the-clock, *JFK*'s crew loaded their ship, took care of personal affairs, and sailed on Wednesday, 15 August. One of two carriers in the Gulf that did not operate F/A-18 Hornets, *Kennedy* took the two last A-7 squadrons on their last deployment and into their last war.
After wandering back and forth from the Mediterranean to its battle station in the Red Sea, *Kennedy* returned to Norfolk on 28 March 1991.

USS *America* (CV-66); CVW-1 (AB)
America left Norfolk, Virginia, along with *Roosevelt*, on 28 December 1990. She arrived on station in the Red Sea immediately after the outbreak of Desert Storm, and joined *Kennedy* and *Saratoga* as part of CTF-155. However, *America* departed the Red Sea in early February and entered the Persian Gulf to support the proposed amphibious operation planned as part of the impending ground war.
With the start of the ground war, however, the amphibious forces were held offshore Kuwait, serving as a feint to hold

the Iraqis' attention. *America* returned to Norfolk in early April 1991.

USS *Ranger* (CV-61); CVW-2 (NE)
One of four 'Forrestal'-class vessels, *Ranger* is one of the oldest carriers in service, and has seen a great deal of combat, including cruises to Southeast Asia. *Ranger* sailed on 8 December with virtually an all-Grumman air wing which included F-14s, A-6s and E-2s, and was only one of two carriers that did not operate F/A-18s.

USS *Theodore Roosevelt* (CVN-71); CVW-8 (AJ)
Roosevelt was the newest carrier on duty in the Persian Gulf, her Desert Storm deployment being only her second. *TR* left her homeport of Norfolk, Virginia, in the early afternoon of 28 December 1991.

USS *Dwight D. Eisenhower* (CVN-69); CVW-7 (AG)
Together with *Independence*, *Ike* was in the Mediterranean preparing to return home after a normal deployment when Iraq invaded Kuwait. On 7 August, *Eisenhower* transitted the Suez Canal into the Red Sea, where she maintained a roving patrol until ordered home. She returned to Norfolk, Virginia, on 12 September 1990. *Ike* carried two of only four F-14A(Plus) squadrons to serve in Desert Shield/Storm.

USS *Saratoga* (CV-60); CVW-17 (AA)
Saratoga was one of the least combat-experienced carriers in the Gulf, her service being limited to one cruise in Vietnam, and

quick-burst responses in 1986 against Libya. However, the ship was on station in Desert Shield, having left its homeport of Mayport, Florida, on 7 August 1990, and entered the Red Sea on 22 August. The 'Forrestal'-class carrier's CVW-17 included two of the four F-14A(Plus) squadrons to see service in the Gulf, and the only two A(Plus) squadrons to actually fly in the war.
Saratoga returned to Mayport on 28 March 1991, after an eight-month deployment.

USS *Midway* (CV-41); CVW-5 (NG)
The oldest carrier in operation in the US fleet, *Midway* is also the only CV homeported outside the US, and is forward-based at Yokosuka, Japan. The lead ship of

*USS **Saratoga** entered the Red Sea in August 1990.*

her three-ship class (including USS *Franklin D. Roosevelt* [CV-42] and USS *Coral Sea* [CV-31], long since decommissioned), *Midway* has been due for decommissioning several times, but she made one more deployment, to the Persian Gulf. She was the only carrier in the Gulf not flying the F-14.

Aircraft
Note: squadrons occasionally change individual aircraft side numbers, which accounts for one aircraft's bureau number (BuNo) appearing with two different three-digit side numbers, or the same side number appearing with two different BuNos.

EA-3B Skywarrior

Mission
The EA-3B was stationed in the Middle East in small numbers to provide pre- and post-strike reconnaissance to the Red Sea carrier battle groups.

Service
The elderly Skywarriors of VQ-2 operating from Jeddah were on station for each Red Sea carrier battle group strike into Iraq to gather valuable reconnaissance information. In particular the A-3s co-ordinated activities with E-2Cs and EA-6Bs for the targetting of HARM missiles. In addition A-3s operating from the detachment at Soudha Bay, Crete, supported USAF missions into northern Iraq.

EA-3B: **146452/002. 146454/004. 146455/005.** TA-3B: **144865/011** – allocated tail code 'JQ' but not carried.

A-6E/KA-6D Intruder

Mission
Long-range strike and interdiction, with surface-strike and SEAD, and aerial tanking as secondary roles.

Service
Having recently celebrated its 25th anniversary with the fleet, the Intruder is the most combat-experienced aircraft in the Navy and Marine Corps. While the Navy is desperately seeking a replacement for the ageing A-6, the Intruder carries on, having participated in every combat action since Vietnam.
In the Gulf war, Navy Intruders were among the first aircraft into Iraq and their crews experienced some of the most

intense flak concentrations seen throughout the war. A-6s operated in the Persian Gulf, destroying Iraqi ships and facilities.
Intruders also participated in their main secondary roles as airborne tankers, using the dedicated KA-6D.

USS *Independence*:
VA-196:
A-6E: **152905/NK-500. 155673/NK-501. 152902/NK-502. 155610/NK-503.**

USS *Eisenhower*:
VA-34:
A-6E: **155712/AG-501. 149949/AG-504. 155592/AG-505. 158042/AG-507.**

USS *Midway*:
VA-115:
A-6E only: **NF-400** series.

VA-185:
A-6E & KA-6D: **NF-500** series.

USS *John F. Kennedy*:
VA-75:
A-6E: **162190/AC-500** 45 missions. **162191/AC-501** 25 missions. **162192/AC-502** 25 missions. **162193/AC-503** 35 missions. **162194/AC-504** 34 missions. **162195/AC-505** 26 missions. **162196/AC-506** 29 missions. **162198/AC-507** 39 missions. **162199/AC-510** 30 missions.

USS *America*:
VA-85:
A-6E: **155678/AB-500. 161106/AB-501. 155664/AB-502. 155710/AB-503.**

USS *Saratoga*:
VA-35:
A-6E: **154135/AA-500. 155661/AA-501** 14 missions. **158539/AA-502** hit by SAMs.

USS *Ranger*:
VA-145:
A-6E: **162182/NE-501. 162201/NE-503 VA-155 A-6E 161670/NE-405.**

USS *Theodore Roosevelt*:
VA-36:
A-6E: **158051/AJ-530. 155716/AJ-532. 161667/AJ-533. 159176/AJ-534.**

EA-6B Prowler

Mission
Electronic countermeasures (ECM) and SEAD.

Service
Prowlers saw their first combat missions in Vietnam in 1972, and have been in constant use by carrier air wings. They have also supported other services, especially the Air Force, whose EF-111 Ravens are not considered to have the high-level ECM capability of the four-place EA-6Bs.
During the Gulf war, every one of the carriers participating in Desert Shield and

VA-65:
A-6E: **161675/AJ-500. 155718/AJ-501. 157001/AJ-502. 155620/AJ-503. 149957/AJ-504. 161659/AJ-505.**

Desert Storm had one Prowler squadron. The aircraft provided ECM coverage for nearly every coalition operation, usually including one to three HARM shoots per aircraft.
Although they normally stood off, away from the main strike in Vietnam, Prowlers drove in toward Iraqi targets, and were themselves occasional targets for AAA and SAM sites.

USS *Independence*:
VAQ-139:
160709/NK-604. 161247/NK-605. 158034/NK-606. 163045/NK-607.

Aircraft of the Gulf War

USS *Eisenhower*:
VAQ-140.

USS *Midway*:
VAQ-136:
63935/NF-605.

USS *John F. Kennedy*:
VAQ-130:
162224/AC-606. 163399/AC-621.
163402/AC-622. 163404/AC-624.
Squadron claims to be first Prowler unit to
fire HARMs in combat.

USS *America*:
VAQ-137:

159882/AB-607. 161348/AB-622 7
missions. **162938/AB-624** 7 missions.

USS *Saratoga*:
VAQ-132:
159912/AA-605. 162934/AA-606.
161245/AA-607.

USS *Ranger*:
VAQ-131:
159587/NE-605. 161885/NE-606.
163525/NE-???.

USS *Theodore Roosevelt*:
VAQ-141:
163527/AJ-621.

A-7E Corsair II

Mission
Light attack/interdiction and SEAD.

Service
Although only two A-7 squadrons
participated in the Gulf war, their
deployment was unique in several ways.
VA-72 and VA-46 were scheduled to
transition to the F/A-18 and had already sent
more than half of their aircraft and personnel
to other assignments. The hurried
deployment of their ship, *Kennedy*,
precluded the Navy's original plan to send
VA-37 and VA-105, the other remaining
Atlantic Fleet Corsair squadrons. Thus,
VA-37 and VA-105 were allowed to continue
their transition to the Hornet, and VA-46 and
VA-72 were quickly reassembled and sent to
the Gulf as part of CVW-3 in *Kennedy*.
The last two A-7 squadrons took their
aircraft out in the proverbial blaze of glory,
participating in the first strikes of Desert

Storm, and continuing through the entire
war with HARM and Walleye missions as
well as iron-bomb strikes against Iraqi
facilities.
The Navy's VA A-7 community's 24-year
career ended with the decommissioning of
VA-46 and VA-72 on 23 May 1991, at NAS
Cecil Field, Florida.

USS *John F. Kennedy*:
VA-46:
160714/AC-301. 160715/AC-302
159967/AC-305. 160613/AC- 306.
160713/AC-307. 158026/AC-314.

VA-72:
160552/AC-400 31 missions. **158842/
AC-402** and **AC-412. 159999/AC-403**
damaged on landing and ditched overboard
after removal of all usable parts. **159971/
AC-404. 159285/AC-405. 160873/
AC-414.**

C-2A Greyhound

Mission
Carrier onboard delivery (COD).

Service
The C-2s performed daily sorties between
shore stations and the carriers at sea,
delivering personnel, small cargoes and,
most importantly of all, mail.

VR-24:
**162176/JM-20. 162153/JM-21. 162159/
JM-22. 162172/JM-26. 162158/JM-27.**

VRC-30:
162170/RW-35.

VRC-40:
162168/AJ-046.

VRC-50:
162154/RG-425. 62173/RG-427.

C-9B Skytrain II

Mission
Provided long-range airlift for personnel and
high priority cargo in support of fleet and
Reserve operations.

Service
The Navy's dedicated transport squadrons
which operate the C-9B are all Reservist
units. Four were mobilized in late December
and assigned to Military Airlift Command for
duty in Desert Shield and Desert Storm.
They were stationed in Europe at Bitburg

and Sembach Air Bases, Germany, and at
Naples, Italy, to replace the front-line VR
assets which were relocated to the Gulf.

VR-55:
159113/RU. 159120/RU. 160051/RU.

VR-57:
159114/RX. 159115/RX. 159116/RX.

VR-58:
160048/JV. 160049/JV. 160050/JV.

VR-59:
161266/RY. 161529/RY. 161530/RY

UC-12B Huron

Mission
The UC-12B was employed in the Gulf
region for special logistics support.

Service
The single UC-12B operated from Bahrain by
the Commander Headquarters Middle East
Forces was bolstered by the addition of two

Navy and two Marine Corps examples from
the USA.

HQ CMEF **161205/8K** was joined by Navy
aircraft **161188/7W** from NAS Willow
Grove, PA, and **161505/F** from NAS
Pensacola, FL, together with the two Marine
Hurons **161196/5Y** and **161197/5T** from
MCAS Yuma, AZ, and MCAS El Toro, CA,
respectively.

C-130 Hercules

Mission
Two versions of the C-130 Hercules were
operated in the Middle East; the C-130F and
EC-130Q submarine communications
platform.

Service
VR-22 'JL' stationed at NAS Rota, Spain,
provided a number of C-130Fs to ferry stores
and equipment within the Middle East
region. EC-130Qs from VQ-4 were
operational in the Middle East, although
details of their participation are unknown.

Aircraft of the Gulf War

E-2C Hawkeye

Mission
Airborne early warning.

Service
The carrier AEW mission has had its proponents and detractors since the days of the piston-engined E-1. The E-2A proved wanting in Vietnam, and it was not until the current versions of the E-2C reached service that the aircraft established a more solid reputation within its air wings.

Basically a single-mission platform, the E-2 provides air control services, monitoring airborne targets – friend and foe – and watching for threats to friendly aircraft and ships.

In concert with the larger AWACS, E-2s played an important, but subdued, role in the Gulf war as they sorted out the huge numbers of aircraft in the air around specific targets. Several E-2 sorties resulted in the succesful outcome of a particular air-to-air engagement or air-to-ground mission, with the Hawkeye crew being credited with an 'assist'.

USS Independence:
VAW-113:
161096/NK-600. 159498/NK-601. 160703/NK-602. 161227/NK-603.

USS Eisenhower:
VAW-121.

USS Midway:
VAW-115.

USS John F. Kennedy:
VAW-126:
162616/AC-601 14 missions. **162617/AC-602** 7 missions. **162618/AC-603.**

USS America:
VAW-123:
162619/AB-600 8 missions. **162801/AB-601** 10 missions. **162797/AB-602** 4 missions. **162793/AB-603** 4 missions.

USS Saratoga:
VAW-125:
159107/AA-600 with marking for double kill on 17 January when crew vectored four VFA-81 F/A-18Cs to a pair of MiG-21s, resulting in two Hornets shooting down the MiGs for the Navy's only fixed-wing kills of the war. **158643/AA-601. 158638/AA-602. 160700/AA-603.**

USS Ranger:
VAW-116.

USS Theodore Roosevelt:
VAW-124.

F-14A Tomcat

Mission
Fleet air defense, air superiority, strike escort, photo reconnaissance.

Service
As the threat from the Iraqi air force quickly waned, Tomcat crews usually flew two types of missions during the war: strike escort and TARPS reconnaissance. Each carrier air wing has two fighter (VF) squadrons equipped with the F-14. One of these squadrons – usually the second unit with the 200-series – is the TARPS squadron and dedicates two or three of its aircraft to the dual mission. This dedication is important because it requires that the designated aircraft have their cockpits equipped with TARPS-specific instrumentation. After an initial uncertainty as to its importance in the war, TARPS quickly became a vital source of mission and target photography.

USS Independence:
VF-21:
161603/NK-200. 161607/NK-201. 161617/NK-202. 161619/NK-203.

USS John F. Kennedy:
VF-14:
162700/AC-100. 162691/AC-101. 159463/AC-102. 160386/AC-103.

VF-32:
162701/AC-200. 162694/AC-201. 160384/AC-202.

USS America:
VF-33:
162698/AB-200. 162705/AB-201.

VF-102:
162695/AB-100. 162704/AB-102.

USS Ranger:
VF-1:
162601/NE-102. 162611/NE-111.

USS Theodore Roosevelt:
VF-41:
162703/AJ-100. 162689/AJ-101.

VF-84:
162688/AJ-200. 162692/AJ-201.

F-14A(Plus) Tomcat

USS Eisenhower:
VF-142:
163220/AG-111.

VF-143:
162915/AG-204.

USS Saratoga:
VF-74:
162925/AA-100. 162919/AA-101. 161434/AA-102. 162923/AA-103. 162924/AA-104. 163221/AA-105.

VF-103:
162921/AA-200. 163219/AA-201. 161873/AA-202. 162920/AA-203.

F/A-18A/C Hornet

Mission
Light attack/interdiction, suppression of enemy air defenses (SEAD), and air superiority.

Service
Other than the 1986 operations against Libya, Desert Storm was the Hornet's first combat test. Fears about the aircraft's short range were realized to a large extent, and most missions – whether from Navy carriers or Marine Corps shore bases – were flown with two or three external fuel tanks. However, initial assessments of the F/A-18's contribution are favorable. Two VFA-81 F/A-18Cs also scored the only two fixed-wing kills by US Navy aircraft when they shot down two Iraqi MiG-21s on 17 January 1991.

USS Independence:
VFA-25:
163705/NK-400. 163754/NK-401. 163755/NK-402. 163757/NK-403.
163759/NK-404. 163748/NK-405. 163766/NK-406. 163764/NK- 407.

VFA-113:
163758/NK-300. 163756/NK-301. 163760/NK-302. 163761/NK-303. 163746/NK-304. 163765/NK-305. 163767/NK-306. 163762/NK-307.

USS Eisenhower:
VFA-131:
164215/AG-400. 164201/AG-401.

VFA-136:
162444/AG-302. 162430/AG-310.

USS Midway:
VFA-151. VFA-192. VFA-195.
USS America:
VFA-82:
163467/AB-300. 163448/AB-305.

VFA-86:
163443/AB-400. 163437/AB-401.

USS Saratoga:
VFA-81:
163508/AA-401. 163484/AA-403 shot down during first night raid 17 January, pilot KIA. **163491/AA-405. 163502/AA-410** one MiG-21 kill.

VFA-83:
163506/AA-301. 163503/AA-302.

USS Theodore Roosevelt:
VFA-15:
163101. 163113. 163121.

Aircraft of the Gulf War

SH-2F Sea Sprite

Mission
The SH-2F was operated in the light multi-purpose role aboard dozens of warships in the Persian Gulf and Red Sea. Apart from providing a vital connection between shore stations and the ship, the Sea Sprites performed SAR and had a limited offensive capability.

Service
SH-2Fs from six squadrons were operated by numerous single or two-plane detachments aboard vessels such as frigates and destroyers.

HSL-32: tail code HV
HSL-33: tail code TF
HSL-34: tail code HX
HSL-35: tail code TG
HSL-36: 162581/HY-332
HSL-37: tail code TH

SH-3G/H Sea King

Mission
The prime duty of the SH-3H was anti-submarine warfare as part of each carrier air wing, while the SH-3G performed a variety of ship-to-shore functions including medical support and rescue.

Service
The SH-3H operates close- to medium-range ASW protection as well as plane guard sorties during carrier operations. In addition the SH-3s also perform a limited carrier onboard delivery (COD) service. Six squadrons operated the type aboard the carriers in the Persian Gulf and Red Sea. HC-1 and HC-2 operated at least five SH-3Gs from Bahrain, while reserve squadron HS-75 from NAS Jacksonville, FL, was mobilized for Gulf duty, although at least one of their helicopters was based at Diego Garcia.

USS Independence:
HS-8:
149713/NK-610. 149719/NK-611.
149894/NK-612. 149897/NK- 613.
151549/NK-614. 151551/NK-615.

USS Midway:
HS-12.

USS John F. Kennedy:
HS-7.

USS America:
HS-11.

USS Saratoga:
HS-3:
149988/AA-610.

USS Ranger:
HS-14.

USS Theodore Roosevelt:
HS-9:
149725/AJ-610. 149735/AJ-611.

HC-1:
151536/UP-01.

HC-2:
148970/HU-740 "Desert Duck". 151539/HU-742 "Stealth Duck". 148047/HU-744 "Wild Duck". 149733/HU-746.

HS-75:
148035/NW-610. 149923/NW-615.

The Boeing Helicopters CH-46 Sea Knight is used by the US Navy for transport duties, in particular in the vertrep (vertical replenishment, or replenishing vessels by air) role.

CH-53E Super Stallion

Mission
The CH-53E has the primary duty of airlifting heavy cargoes between shore and Fleet ships at sea.

Service
HC-4 from NAS Sigonella, Sicily, relocated the majority of its complement to the Gulf.

MH-53E Sea Dragon

Mission
The MH-53E was designed as a dedicated mine countermeasures version of the Marines CH-53E.

Service
Both MH-53E squadrons were deployed to Dhahran to conduct mine clearance of the northern Persain Gulf to enable warships to transit this area safely. HM-14 helicopters were deployed aboard LPH-10/USS Tripoli until the ship was damaged by a mine on 18 February. The helicopters were temporarily operated aboard the LPH-11/USS New Orleans and AGF-3/USS La Salle while the Tripoli received repairs.

CH/UH-46D Sea Knight

Mission
Two varieties of H-46 Sea Knights were employed aboard logistics vessels for vertical replenishment.

Service
Four squadrons operated the CH- and UH-46D within 18 detachments. Apart from supporting US Navy ships, the H-46s flew supplies to English, French, Greek, Portuguese, Spanish and Saudi vessels.

HC-5 det 3:
CH-46D: **151926/RB-03.**

HC-6:
CH-46D: **151953/HW-06. 154032/HW.**

HC-8:
CH-46D: **153405/BR-43.**

HC-11 det 9:
UH-46D: **153314/VR-52. 151905/VR-64.**

SH-60B Seahawk

Mission
Anti-submarine warfare, LAMPS III (SH-60B) and general rescue duties.

Service
HSL squadrons provided one- or two-plane detachments for various ships in a battlegroup, as well as a secondary, but important, SAR capability.
In the Gulf, HSL helicopters also provided aerial cover to the boarding parties that enforced the maritime blockade of Iraq. They also were involved in several short firefights between coalition forces and Iraqi offshore facilities.

HSL-42: tail code HN
HSL-43: tail code TT
HSL-44: tail code HP
HSL-45: 162338/TZ-43
HSL-46: tail code HQ
HSL-47: tail code TY
HSL-48: tail code HR
HSL-49: tail code TX ?

Aircraft of the Gulf War

HH-60H Rescue Hawk

Mission
Combat search and rescue (SAR) and anti-terrorist support.

Service
With a specialized version of the H-60, and newly arrived in service, these two squadrons were Naval Air Reserve units that were mobilized with two 50-man, two-plane detachments forming one unit based at Al Jouf, Saudi Arabia, and known by their callsign, "Spike". The other unit was at Tabuk, Saudi Arabia.

P-3C Orion

Mission
Long-range anti-submarine warfare. With no threat from Iraqi submarines, P-3s flew surveillance and targetting missions in the northern Persian Gulf.

Service
Following a request in October 1990 to provide Reserve crews for fleet VP units involved in Desert Shield, 19 men from VP-91 and 17 men from VP-MAU took two VP-91 P-3Cs to the Persian Gulf in February 1991. For the next 30 days, these Naval Air Reservists flew around-the-clock missions in support of Desert Storm, including surface surveillance and forward reconnaissance for targetting and BDA. The tasking was in conjunction with strike aircraft; the P-3 crews fingered the targets and the strike aircraft attacked them.

Squadrons operational in the Middle East were VP-1 'YB', VP-4 'YD', VP-5 'LA', VP-8 'LC', VP-11 'LE', VP-19 'PE', VP-23 'LJ', VP-40 'QE', VP-46 'RC', VP-91 'PM', VP-MAU 'LB', VPU-1 nil and VPU-2 nil. Although the majority of squadrons have a tail code assigned, none was carried during Desert Storm.

EP-3E Aries Orion

Mission
Electronic surveillance in support of operations.

Service
Flew in-theater reconnaissance support missions.

VQ-1:
148887/33. 150498. 150501 – allocated tail code 'PR' but not carried.

VQ-2:
149668/21. 150505/24 – allocated tail code 'JQ' but not carried.

S-3A/B & US-3A Viking

Mission
Long-range anti-submarine warfare, aerial tanking.

Service
With the threat of attack from Iraqi submarines virtually non-existent, the S-3s

of Desert Storm were without a primary mission. Several squadrons were occasionally left 'on the beach' to allow more room on their ships. A few aircraft provided shuttle service for people and supplies, augmenting the dedicated COD squadrons.

As the war progressed, the S-3 found a more low-key role as a long-range surface surveillance platform, and occasionally, as a strike aircraft against surface targets. The Viking has always had the capability of carrying bombs and missiles, and a few squadrons got the chance to fly strikes.

USS *Independence*:
VS-37:
160572/NK-700. 160596/NK-701.

USS *Eisenhower*:
VS-31:
160604/AG-702. 159387/AG-704. 159769/AG-707.

USS *John F. Kennedy*:
VS-22:
160600/AC-700. 159418/AC-701.

USS *America*:
VS-32:
159751/AB-701. 159766/AB-702.

USS *Saratoga*:
VS-30:
159740/AA-700. 160605/AA-704. 159390/AA-710.

USS *Ranger*:
VS-28.

USS *Theodore Roosevelt*:
VS-24:
159753/AJ-707.

VRC-50:
157998/RG-712 "Miss Piggy".

UNITED STATES MARINE CORPS

A-6E Intruder

Mission
The A-6 served the Marine Corps in the medium all-weather attack role in support of ground forces.

Service
A-6s were among the first Marine Corps aircraft to relocate to the Middle East with VMA(AW)-224 arriving in Bahrain in August

followed four months later by VMA(AW)-533.

VMA(AW)-224:
155673/WK-500. 152641/WK-501. 155684/WK-502. 161090/WK-504. 157017/WK-506. 154167/WK-507.

VMA(AW)-533:
161663/ED-401. 161689/ED-403. 160431/ED-404. 154158/ED-410. 161111/ED-411.

KC-130F/R/T Hercules

Mission
The KC-130 tanker was employed primarily to support deploying Marine Corps fighter and attack aircraft, and once in-theater to provide air refueling of strike packages.

Service
A composite squadron of VMGR-252 and -352 deployed to Bahrain in August with 8 KC-130s under command of the latter unit's CO. These were followed by VMGR-452 which deployed to Al Jubail with 7 KC-130Ts. VMGR-234 KC-130s were also involved.

EA-6B Prowler

Mission
The EA-6B was the Marine Corps' only dedicated electronic warfare aircraft.

Service
Twelve Prowlers deployed to Sheikh Isa during August as part of the overall Marine Corps combat package. During the Desert Shield period EA-6Bs helped develop the overall intelligence picture of Iraqi defenses.

VMAQ-2:
158040/CY-04. 158540/CY-05. 159907/CY-06. 160435/CY-10. 160788/CY-13. 162939/CY-16 38 missions. 158031/CY-17. 163035/CY-52 31 missions. 158035/CY-??.

AV-8B Harrier II

Mission
The AV-8 was engaged in close air support duties.

Service
Four complete squadrons and one six-plane detachment were in-theater for Desert Storm. The first squadrons to arrive in August were stationed at Sheikh Isa although they relocated to Al Jubail/King Abdul Aziz Naval Base once the latter facility had been upgraded to accept vertical take off/landing aircraft.

VMA-231:
163514/CG-00. 163662/CG-01. 163665/CG-02. 163673/CG-03.

VMA-311:
163660/WL-04. 163661/WL-05. 163664/WL-06. 163690/WL-07.

VMA-331:
tail code VL.

VMA-513 det B:
163192/WF-41. 163193/WF-42. 163203/WF-43. 163204/WF-44.

Aircraft of the Gulf War

F/A-18A/C Hornet

Mission
Fighter-attack. Much the same as the Navy's VFA squadrons, but more closely allied with ground operations in the marine aviation role of close air support (CAS).

Service
All USMC tactical jet squadrons – except the Harrier-equipped VMAs – were based at Sheikh Isa AB, Bahrain. The aircraft flew CAS, SEAD and strike missions in the Kuwait theater of operations.

VMFA-212:
F/A-18C: **163728/WD.**

VMFA-232:
F/A-18C: **163735/WT-00. 163738/WT-03. 163751/WT-11.**

VMFA-235:
F/A-18C: **163782/DB-12.**

VMFA-314:
F/A-18A: **162475/VW. 163144/VW.**

VMFA-333:
F/A-18A: **161976/DN-07. 161985/DN-11.**

VMFA-451:
F/A-18A: **163118/VM-00. 163132/VM-01. 163147/VM-12.**

F/A-18D Hornet

Mission
The two-seat F/A-18D was assigned as the fast forward air controller working with other US and coalition aircraft.

Service
The Marine Corps' sole F/A-18D all-weather fighter/attack squadron was deployed by January and saw action in continuous 'all Marine strikes' composed of between 40 and 60 aircraft.

VMFA(AW)-121:
164040/VK.

AH-1J Sea Cobra

Mission
Close air support attack helicopter employed solely by the Reserves.

Service
Two Marine Reserve units deployed to the Middle East (HMA-773 and HMA-775).

UH-1N Iroquois

Mission
The UH-1N was employed primarily in the scout role to directly support the AH-1s.

HML-767: tail code MM.
HMLA-169: tail code SN.
HMLA-269: tail code HF.
HMLA-367: tail code VT.
HMLA-369: tail code SM.

CH-46E Sea Knight

Mission
The versatile CH-46E was employed in large numbers to transport assault forces between various desert locations and to land Marines ashore from vessels in the Persian Gulf.

Service
Ten CH-46E squadrons were active during Desert Storm, performing a variety of duties ranging from the movement of troops to resupply and medevac. Units deployed were HMM-161, 164, 165, 261, 263, 265, 266, 268, 365 and 774.

OV-10A/D Bronco

Mission
The Bronco was to perform aerial observation and orchestrate close air support strikes against ground targets.

VMO-1: tail code ER.
VMO-2: tail code UU.

CH-53A/D Sea Stallion & CH-53E Super Stallion

Mission
The large CH-53 was also engaged in the movement of ground forces, but had the added capability of ferrying artillery pieces and light armor suspended beneath the fuselage.

Service
Three CH-53D and four CH-53E units were flown on land and sea. CH-53 and CH-46s flew teams to forward remote locations to establish arming and refueling points for advancing Marine units.

HMH-462: CH-53D.
HMH-362: CH-53D: tail code YL.
HMH-461: CH-53E: tail code CJ.
HMH-463: CH-53D: tail code YH.
MH-464: CH-53E: tail code EN.
HMH-465: CH-53E: tail code YK.

RH-53D

Mission
Like their Naval counterparts the primary role of the RH-53D is mine countermeasures.

Service
Marine Reserve squadron HMH-772 detachment A from NAS Alameda, CA, was operated at Al Jubail with six RH-53Ds.

AH-1W Sea Cobra

Mission
Advanced version of the attack helicopter operated by front-line Marine Corps squadrons.

Service
Four light attack squadrons were active throughout Desert Storm with HMLA-367 and 369 being shore based while HMLA-169 and 269 were embarked.

HMLA-169: tail code SN.
HMLA-269: tail code HF.
HMLA-367: tail code VT.
HMLA-369: tail code SM.

In addition, seven **HMLA-267** helicopters were loaned (tail code UV).

Aircraft of the Gulf War

UNITED KINGDOM

Puma and Aérospatiale Cougar

Deployment
A composite RAF Puma squadron was assembled from No. 33 Squadron at Odiham and No. 230 Squadron from Gütersloh, Germany, using aircraft mainly from Odiham. These Westland Puma HC.Mk 1s were air-freighted from Brize Norton in USAF Lockheed C-5s, beginning on 1 November 1990, and initially operated from Ras al Ghar.

The French Army Light Aviation (ALAT) advanced party arrived at Yanbu, Saudi Arabia, on 9 September, including two Aérospatiale SA 330B Pumas of the 3ième Régiment d'hélicoptères de combat as air freight. A further dozen of 5ième RHC arrived on the carrier *Clemenceau* and all transferred to King Khalid Military City on 26 September, there to be joined by four more from 4ième RHC on 31 October. The SA 330B Puma force then formed 7ième and 8ième Escadrilles of the 5ième RHC, relieved in December by 3ième RHC. Further helicopters of 1ier RHC left Toulon by sea on 31 December, increasing the ALAT Puma strength to 38. Two French air force SA 330Ba Pumas were used for communications.

Kuwaiti helicopters which escaped to Saudi Arabia included six SA 330H Pumas and four AS 532SC Cougars (previously known as AS 532F Super Pumas).

Mission
Army support is the prime duty of the Puma, involving carriage of up to 16 troops or 2.5 tonnes of underslung load such as ammunition. The French contingent included the prototype Orchidée Puma with underslung radar for battlefield surveillance.

Service
Nineteen RAF Pumas accompanied the ground forces throughout the campaign, operating from several improvised airstrips. Returns to the UK began by C-5 on 17 March. French support Pumas operated on the flank of the coalition spearhead nearest to Baghdad. The surveillance Puma carried a simplified version of the Orchidée system and flew 24 sorties between 3 and 27 February, including some in support of US Army AH-64 Apaches.

Royal Air Force:
XW200 A. XW201 B. XW204 C. XW206 D. XW207 E. XW216 F. XW217 G. XW220 H. XW222 J. XW225 K. ZA934 L. ZA935 M. ZA936 N. ZA937 O. ZA939 P. XW214 R. XW224 S. XW226 T. XW231 U.

Aviation légère de l'armée de terre:
1052 BSV (Orchidée radar). 1067 ADD *"203"*. 1128 BUU *"162"*. 1192 ADE *"164"*. 1130 ARB *"155"*. 1192 ADE *"164"*. 1228 CLO *"16"*. 1269 BZD *"202"*. 1438 ARF *"14"*. AUD. AUH. BUQ. CZL. CZV. 1455 ARA *"201"*. 5682 ADK *"211"*, and others.

Armée de l'air:
1311 67-DC. 1321 67-GB.

Kuwait Air Force:
1281 554. 1284 555. 1286 556. 1298 558. 1315 561. 1317 562. 2117 544 – Cougar. 2126 546 – Cougar. 2133 542 – Cougar. 2134 543 – Cougar.

The Puma family was used by the Royal Air Force (right above), the French army and air force, and by Free Kuwait forces (right).

BAe VC10 K.Mk 2 and K.Mk 3

Deployment
No. 101 Squadron dispatched two VC10s to Seeb, Oman, on 11 August 1990 to support Jaguars and Nimrods. Further detachments were installed at Muharraq, Bahrain, and King Khalid IAP, Riyadh, Saudi Arabia. The Muharraq detachment of K.Mk 2s was temporarily withdrawn between mid-December and mid-January. All nine VC10s were eventually deployed.

Mission
VC10s supported mainly RAF attack missions, each refueling a flight of four Tornados or Jaguars.

Service
Essential to the UK war effort, VC10s were responsible for ensuring attack missions were fully refueled and able to begin the penetration phase of their raids at precisely the time required in their operational orders. Heavily-loaded Tornados needed two refuelings inbound and one on return, requiring the tanker to orbit close to, or within, Iraqi territory for up to an hour. VC10s flew 381 sorties (1,350 hours) during hostilities, dispensing 6,800 tonnes of fuel. The squadron returned to base on 13 March.

ZA140 A. ZA141 B *"The Empire Strikes Back"*. ZA142 C *"The Empire Strikes Back"*. ZA143 D. ZA144 E. ZA147 F. ZA148 G. ZA149 H. ZA150 J.
(No mission markings carried; A-E are Mk 2s, F-J are Mk 3s.)

A VC10 tanker refuels a Prowler and a Tomcat of the US Navy. British and US Navy aircraft used the same probe-and-drogue refueling system.

Boeing Vertol Chinook HC.Mk 1

Deployment
Three Chinooks were flown from Mildenhall to Saudi Arabia by USAF Lockheed C-5s on the night of 24/25 November 1990. A further eight arrived by sea at Al Jubail on 6 January and four more were airfreighted during January. Aircraft and personnel were drawn from No. 7 Squadron at Odiham and No. 18 Squadron at Gütersloh, Germany, to form Chinook Squadron Middle East, which operated 15 helicopters.

Mission
Chinooks were responsible for transporting army personnel and equipment – up to 12 tonnes in one lift – prior to and during the land war. Some undertook night missions, for which a disruptive black camouflage was oversprayed.

Service
Initially at Ras al Ghar, the RAF Support Helicopter force moved with the army to several desert locations, assisting the secret redeployment to the west for the outflanking movement launched on 24 February. With the start of the land battle, Chinooks ferried 3,500 POWs to rear camps, 85 at a time. Chinook Squadron Middle East flew 1,000 hours and lifted over 1,000,000 kg of freight in the first seven weeks of operations – 84 per cent of the total carried by all UK support helicopters, including RN Sea Kings. Two Chinooks were returned to Odiham by C-5 on 15 March, but the sea journey by 12 more was interrupted when they were diverted to Turkey for relief deliveries to Kurdish refugees in northern Iraq.

ZA671 O night camouflage. ZA675 B. ZA677 U night camouflage. ZA679 Z. ZA682 N. ZA683 W. ZA684 L. ZA707 V night camouflage. ZA712 R night camouflage. ZA720 P night camouflage. ZD575 H. ZD576 G. ZD980 J. ZD981 D night camouflage. ZD982 I.

The RAF is one of the largest users of the Boeing Helicopters CH-47 Chinook, which in British service have the designation HC.Mk 1. About a dozen RAF Chinooks were deployed to Saudi Arabia for the Gulf war.

BAe Buccaneer S.Mk 2B

Deployment
Twelve aircraft from Lossiemouth Wing, plus personnel of Nos 12 and 208 Squadrons and No. 237 OCU. First two arrived at Muharraq, Bahrain, on 26 January 1991, and detachment was at full strength on 8 February.

Mission
Laser designation for Tornados based at Muharraq and Dhahran. Later dropped own bombs.

Service
First mission 2 February. Used AN/AVQ-23E Pave Spike laser pod. Bridge targets initially, progressing to hardened aircraft shelters and airfield paved surfaces. Additionally, dropped own 1,000-lb (454-kg) LGBs during Tornado raids from 21 February. Total of 216 sorties flown, and 48 bombs dropped. Returned to Lossiemouth early in March.

(Named for brands of Scottish whisky)
XV352 U *TAMDHU* (10 mission symbols).
XV863 S *TAMNAVOULIN "Debbie, Sea Witch"* (six mission symbols). **XW530 E** *GLENMORANGIE* (12 mission symbols). **XW533 A** *GLENFARCLAS "Fiona, Miss Jolly Roger"* (11 mission symbols). **XW547 R** *THE MACALLAN "Pauline, Guinness Girl"* (11 mission symbols). **XX885 L** *FAMOUS GROUSE "Caroline, Hello Sailor"* (seven missions, one Antonov An-12). **XX889 T** *LONGMOM* (14 mission symbols). **XX892 I** *GLEN LOSSIE* (eight mission symbols). **XX894 O** *ABERLOUR* (seven mission symbols). **XX895 G** *GLENFIDDICH "Lynn, Jaws"* (five mission symbols). **XX899 P** *LINKWOOD*

"Laura, Laser Lips". **XX901 N** *GLEN ELGIN "Kathryn, The Flying Mermaid"* (nine missions, one Antonov An-12).

Old but still potent, the Buccaneer was sent to the Gulf to provide laser designation for RAF Tornados.

Handley Page Victor K.Mk 2

Deployment
No. 55 Squadron began deploying from Marham to Muharraq, Bahrain, on 14 December 1990, initially with four aircraft, increasing to six by 16 January and eight on 19 January.

Mission
Victors were used in the aerial tanking role throughout Desert Storm, delivering fuel to RAF Tornados and Jaguars, as well as to carrier-based aircraft of the US Navy.

Service
The first Victor mission launched at 2250 GMT on 16 January. Six aircraft returned to Marham on 17 and 18 March, while two others remained in Bahrain to support the Tornado squadron retained there. Victors flew 299 combat-support sorties totalling 870 hours.

XH671 *SLINKY SUE* later *SWEET SUE* (41 mission symbols).
XH672 *MAID MARION* (52 mission symbols). **XL161** no name (44 mission symbols). **XL164** *SAUCY SAL* (41 mission symbols). **XL190** no name (20 mission symbols). **XL231** *LUSTY LINDY* (16 mission symbols). **XM715** *TEASIN' TINA* (38 mission symbols). **XM717** *LUCKY LOU* (42 mission symbols).

Still one of the most dramatic-looking aircraft in service, the Handley Page Victor was a highly capable bomber, most examples of which were converted into equally capable tankers in the 1960s and 1970s.

Lockheed Hercules C.Mk 1 and C.Mk 3

Deployment
RAF Hercules of the Lyneham Transport Wing (Nos 24, 30, 47 and 70 Squadrons, plus No. 242 OCU) were involved in moving men and supplies as soon as the UK announced on 9 August 1990 its intention of deploying forces to the Gulf in response to Iraq's invasion. From 1 November onwards, an Air Transport Detachment (ATD) of RAF Hercules was maintained at King Khalid International Airport, Riyadh, for internal freight distribution. The ATD began with three RAF aircraft and built up to seven on 14 January, plus two New Zealand C-130H Hercules added on 23 December.

Mission
Hercules based in Saudi Arabia were used for tactical transport, including air delivery to forward airstrips. For the latter duty, they wore a black protective coating on the fuselage undersides. A further six RAF Hercules – two of them painted desert pink – were operated from the United Arab Emirates, crewed by No. 47 Squadron. Roles included carrying fuel for covert helicopter operations.

Service
Hercules were heavily employed before, during and after Desert Storm, the ATD comprising mostly short-fuselage C.Mk 1s, plus the similar New Zealand C-130Hs. Between 16 January and 27 February, the ATD flew 1,275 sorties (1,643 hours), carrying 13,912 passengers and 7.4 million lb (3356 tonnes) of freight. On 28 February, three Hercules were the first coalition fixed-wing aircraft to land at Kuwait City Airport after its liberation. RNZAF Hercules returned home early in April, and the RAF contingent reduced to a C.Mk 1 and a C.Mk 3 which transferred to Muharraq, Bahrain, on 13/14 April for continued service.

Royal Air Force:
Most RAF Hercules were involved with Desert Shield/Desert Storm, including:
XV205. XV206.

Royal New Zealand Air Force:
NZ7001. NZ7002. NZ7004.

The Lockheed C-130 Hercules, given the designation C.Mk 1 and C.Mk 3 in British service, is an indispensable part of any modern military operation.

Lockheed TriStar K.Mk 1

Deployment
No. 216 Squadron's fleet of three TriStar KC.Mk 1s, three Tristar K.Mk 1s and two TriStar C.Mk 2s operated from Brize Norton, but two of the K.Mk 1 tankers were intermittently used from Muharraq, Bahrain, in combat-support roles.

Mission
Tanker-transport TriStar KC.Mk 1s were involved in deploying combat aircraft to the Gulf theater before, during and after Desert Storm, being able to carry heavy equipment as well as to refuel aircraft in flight.

Service
Pink desert camouflage was applied to two K.Mk 1 tankers on 18 and 23 January, preparing them for missions flown from Bahrain in support of RAF attack aircraft. These were interspersed with regular sorties to the UK, carrying freight and escorting replacement combat aircraft. The two delivered approximately 1,000 tonnes of fuel during the conflict.

Individual aircraft
ZD949 Pink camouflage *"Pinky"*.
ZD951 Pink camouflage *"Perky"*.

Like the American KC-10, the TriStar has a significant cargo capacity, as well as refueling capability.

Panavia Tornado GR.Mk 1

Deployment
Attack-tasked Tornados of the RAF were installed at Muharraq, Bahrain, from 29 August 1990; Tabuk, Saudi Arabia, from 8 October; and Dhahran, Saudi Arabia, from 3 January 1991. Detachments each comprised approximately 24 crews from several squadrons, plus 15 aircraft provided by Brüggen and Laarbruch, RAF Germany. Personnel included crews from Nos XV (lead), IX, 17, 27, 31 and 617 Squadrons at Muharraq; Nos 16 (lead), 2, IX, 14 and 20 Squadrons at Tabuk; and Nos 31 (lead), IX, 14 and 17 Squadrons at Dhahran. There was a reconnaissance detachment of six GR.Mk 1As at Dhahran from 14 January 1991, with crews from Nos II and 13 Squadrons. A TIALD laser-designator flight of five aircraft was at Tabuk from 6 February, with crews from Nos II, 13, 14, 16 and 617 Squadrons.

Mission
GR.Mk 1s undertook counter-air attacks with JP 233 anti-runway weapons during the first three nights of conflict, then adopted free-

Aircraft of the Gulf War

fall bombing against airfields and other strategic targets, followed by laser-guided bombing from early February. Some Tabuk aircraft were assigned to defense-suppression with BAe ALARM anti-radar missiles.

Service

Bombing and ALARM Tornados were employed from the night of 16/17 January, recce aircraft from 18/19 January. Laser-guided bombing was introduced at Muharraq on 2 February and at Dhahran from 5 February, using Buccaneer designators. TIALD Tornado designators were operational from 10 February for Tabuk-based bombers. Precision weapons were used against bridges and airfields. Tornados flew 135 recce, 95 TIALD, 52 ALARM and over 1,500 bombing sorties, dropping over 100 JP 233s, 4,200 free-fall bombs and 950 laser-guided bombs, and firing 123 ALARMs. Withdrawal began from Tabuk on 11 March, followed by Dhahran; 12 aircraft were retained at Muharraq for several months.

Based at Muharraq:

ZA392 EK Flew into ground shortly after JP 233 attack, Shaibah air base, 18 January; crew killed. **ZA396 GE** Hit by Roland SAM during loft bombing at Tallil air base, 20 January; crew ejected. **ZA399 GA** Nose art: Old woman with Zimmer frame *"Hello Kuwait G'bye Iraq"*. **ZA455 EJ** *"Triffid Airways"* (25 mission symbols). **ZA456 M** *MEL "Hello Kuwait G'bye Iraq"*. **ZA459 EL. ZA463 Q** *FLYING HIGH* (Garfield nose art). **ZA469 I. ZA471 E** *EMMA "Snoopy Airways"* (32 mission symbols). **ZA472 EE** Replacement aircraft; no missions. **ZA475 P** *"Triffid Airways"* (22 mission symbols). **ZA491 N** *NIKKI "Snoopy Airways"* (29 mission symbols). **ZA492 FE** (29 mission symbols). **ZD717 C** *"Hello Kuwait G'bye Iraq"*; Shot down by two SA-2 SAMs 12 miles west of Fallujah 14 February; navigator killed; Brüggen for repairs. **ZD790 D** *DEBBIE "Snoopy Airways"* (38 mission symbols). **ZD791 BG** Shot down by flak while bombing Shaibah air base on 17 January; crew ejected. **ZD792 CF** *NURSIE* (36 mission symbols). **ZD809 BA** *AWESOME ANNIE "Hello Kuwait G'bye Iraq"* (33 mission symbols). **ZD890 O** *"Hello Kuwait G'bye Iraq"*; nose art: reclining nude (28 mission symbols). **ZD892 H** *HELEN "Snoopy Airways"* (31 mission symbols).

Based at Tabuk:

*ALARM-capable (but also performed bombing missions)
ZA393 CQ *SIR GALAHAD* (seven TIALD mission symbols). **ZA406 DN** (10 TIALD mission symbols). **ZA446 EF** (21 mission symbols). **ZA447 EA** *MIG EATER* (40 mission symbols). **ZA452 GK** *GULF KILLER* (32 mission symbols). **ZA460 FD** *FIRE DANCER.* **ZA465 FK** *FOXY KILLER* (44 mission symbols). **ZA467 FF** Shot down while bombing Ar Rutbah radar site on 22 January; crew killed. **ZA473 FM** *FOXY MAMA.* **ZA492 FE. ZD719 AD*** Later to Dhahran. **ZD739 AC** *ARMOURED CHARMER* (36 TIALD mission symbols). **ZD744 BD** *BUDDHA* (ex Muharraq). **ZD746 AB*** *ALARM BELLE* (36 mission symbols). **ZD747 AL*** *ANNA LOUISE* (29 missions). **ZD748 AK*** *ANOLA KAY!* (17 missions). **ZD810 AA*** (28 missions, eight ALARM sorties). **ZD844 DE** *DONNA EWIN* (20 TIALD mission symbols). **ZD845 AF*** *ANGEL FACE* (20 mission symbols). **ZD848 BC** Nose art: kneeling girl (19 TIALD mission symbols). **ZD850 CL*** *CHERRY LIPS* (18 mission symbols). **ZD851 AJ*** *AMANDA JANE* (35 mission symbols). **ZD893 AG*** Abandoned near base due to control restriction on 20 January, crew ejected.

Based at Dhahran:

ZA370 A Reconnaissance. **ZA371 C** Reconnaissance. **ZA372 E** *SALLY T* Reconnaissance. **ZA373 H** Reconnaissance (22 missions). **ZA374 CN** *MISS BEHAVIN'* (33 mission symbols). **ZA376 –** *MRS MIGGINS* (31 mission symbols). **ZA397 O** Reconnaissance. **ZA400 T** Reconnaissance. **ZA403 CO** Destroyed on 23 January when bomb exploded on release over target; crew ejected. **ZA457 CE** *BOB* (39 mission symbols). **ZA461 DK. ZA490 GG** *GIGI* (eight mission symbols). **ZD707 BK. ZD715 DB** *LUSCIOUS LIZZIE.* **ZD719 AD** *CHECK SIX* (ex Tabuk) (five mission symbols). **ZD740 DA** *DHAHRAN ANNIE* (27 mission symbols). **ZD745 BM** *BLACK MAGIC* (38 mission symbols). **ZD792 CF** *NURSIE* (36 mission symbols). **ZD843 DH** Damaged by ZA403's bombs on 23 January. To Brüggen for repair. **ZD847 CH** *WHERE DO YOU WANT IT?*. **ZD895 BF.**

RAF Tornados, armed with AIM-9L Sidewinder missiles for self-defense, fly in formation over the Saudi desert during the long, slow build-up to war. British Tornados were based at Dhahran along with the Saudi Tornado force, at Tabuk in western Saudi Arabia, and at Muharraq, Bahrain.

Panavia Tornado F.Mk 3

Deployment

Twelve Tornado F.Mk 3 interceptors of Nos 5 and 29 Squadrons, temporarily at Akrotiri, Cyprus, for training, were deployed to Dhahran, Saudi Arabia, on 11 August 1990, but were replaced by 18 aircraft from Leeming (Nos 11, 23 and 25 Squadrons) from 30 August. Personnel from Nos 43 and 29 Squadrons (Leuchars and Coningsby, respectively) took over from early December onwards.

Mission

Tornado F.Mk 3s shared, with Saudi Tornado ADVs and Saudi/USAF F-15 Eagles, the task of mounting four-hour combat air patrols over northern Saudi Arabia. These were maintained 24 hours per day from August 1990 and throughout Desert Storm.

Service

Tornado F.Mk 3s saw no action during Desert Storm, despite long hours of patrols. On 18 January, an attempt to intercept Iraqi Mirage F1s ended when the latter used their superior speed at medium altitude to outrun the interceptors. The force flew its last mission on 8 March 1991 and began returning to the UK on 13 March.

ZE158 D. ZE159 O. ZE161 R. ZE164 G. ZE165 U. ZE200 L. ZE200 A. ZE204 B. ZE206 C. ZE887 E. ZE907 K. ZE908 X. ZE934 Q. ZE936 F. ZE961 H. ZE968 J. ZE969 L. ZE982 P.

The first RAF aircraft sent to the Gulf to defend the Saudi oilfields were Tornado F.Mk 3 interceptors, which had been on a training deployment in Cyprus as the Iraqis invaded Kuwait.

SEPECAT Jaguar GR.Mk 1A

Deployment

Twelve Jaguars of the Coltishall Wing (Nos 6, 41 and 54 Squadrons), plus personnel from Coltishall and No. 226 OCU at Lossiemouth. Left UK 11 August 1990 for Thumrait, Oman, and for Muharraq, Bahrain, in October 1990.

Mission

Assigned to daylight Battlefield Air Interdiction (BAI) attacks on tactical targets, mainly in Kuwait. Used 1,000-lb (454-kg) bombs, CBU-87 cluster-bombs and CRV-7 rockets against SAM and coastal-defense missile sites, artillery, armored concentrations, barracks, POL storage and naval vessels.

Service

In action from 17 January. Flew 618 sorties, including 31 reconnaissance with centerline pod for own mission planning; dropped 750 bombs and 393 cluster-bombs; fired 608 rockets and 9,600 rounds of 30-mm ammunition. Returned to Coltishall on 12 and 13 March 1991.

XX725 T *JOHNNY FARTPANTS* (47 mission symbols). **XX733 R** un-named; Nose art: fighter pilot (39 mission symbols). **XX748 U** un-named (36 mission symbols). **XX962 X** *FAT SLAGS* (37 mission symbols). **XZ106 O** un-named; Nose art: girl with Union Jack (35 mission symbols). **XZ118 Y** *BUSTER GONAD* (38 mission symbols). **XZ119 Z** *KATRINA JANE* (40 mission symbols). **XZ356 N** *MARY ROSE* (33 mission symbols). **XZ358 W** *DIPLOMATIC SERVICE* (14 mission symbols). **XZ364 Q.** **XZ367 P** *DEBBIE*; Nose art: changed to white rose (40 mission symbols). **XZ375 S** *GUARDIAN READER* (17 mission symbols).

Jaguars from the Coltishall wing were among the first British forces deployed to the Middle East. Like most coalition aircraft, the Jaguars were fitted with AIM-9 Sidewinders for self-defense.

Westland Lynx HAS.Mk 3

Deployment

Royal Navy Lynx of No. 815 Squadron, Portland, were part of the Armilla Patrol in Gulf waters on the day on which Iraq invaded Kuwait. Eventually, 10 Lynx were employed during Desert Storm.

Mission

Lynx enforced the naval blockade of Iraq prior to hostilities and were active in attacks on the Iraqi navy, using BAe Sea Skua anti-ship missiles. Whittaker AN/ALQ-167 'Yellow Veil' jamming pods were fitted to decoy Aérospatiale Exocet anti-ship missiles, but were not required.

Service

Assistance was provided by Lynx in storming occupied oil platforms and spotting Iraqi vessels for later attack. Fifteen Sea Skuas were launched by Lynx from HMS *Cardiff* and HMS *Gloucester*, of which 14 struck their targets. Iraqi vessels hit comprised five TNC 45 patrol boats, two assault craft, two TNC 43 minelayer/sweepers and two Zhuk patrol craft. Each Lynx flew over 100 hours on operations.

XZ227 **405** HMS *London*.
XZ228 **443** HMS *Jupiter*.
XZ230 **335** HMS *Cardiff*.
XZ239 **343** HMS *Brilliant*.
XZ253 **342** HMS *Brilliant*.
XZ256 **330** HMS *Brazen*.
XZ720 **410** HMS *Gloucester*.

Below: HMS Brazen's Lynx HAS.Mk 3 frames the destroyer HMS Gloucester. Navy Lynx were very successful, particularly when using Sea Skua missiles to destroy or damage a large part of Iraq's force of fast naval attack craft.

Westland Sea King HC.Mk 4

Deployment
Two Sea King HC.Mk 4s (all of which are based at Yeovilton) were deployed with 'B' Flight of No. 846 Squadron, Fleet Air Arm, to Gulf waters aboard RFA *Fort Grange* on 22 August 1990, while four more of 'C' and 'D' Flights of the same unit sailed from the UK with RFA *Argus* on 31 October. Six from No. 845 Squadron and six from No. 848 Squadron (commissioned for Gulf operations on 6 December) arrived at Al Jubail, Saudi Arabia, by sea on 6 January. Two more were airfreighted by USAF C-5A from Yeovilton to Dhahran on 21 February for Nos 846 and 848 Squadrons.

Mission
Sea Kings from *Fort Grange* were assigned to the Helicopter Delivery Service to Royal Navy ships, transferring base to RFA *Fort Austin* during the conflict, and those of *Argus* to medical evacuation. Mine-hunting was also conducted. The others were used for Army support.

Service
Medical evacuation helicopters were used principally for accidents and illness. Transport Sea Kings moved with the army, operating from desert strips, complementing the RAF's Chinooks and Pumas as part of the combined-services Support Helicopter Force Middle East. Operating initially from

King Khalid Military City, they transferred westwards then accompanied the advance 50 miles (80 km) inside Iraq, ending their war tour at a forward base 10 miles (16 km) northwest of Kuwait City. Typically, No. 846 Squadron flew 500 sorties in 1,000 hours during hostilities. Duties included transport of Iraqi POWs. Fifteen Sea Kings arrived back in the UK early in April, but three were retained until later in 1991.

845 Squadron:
ZA312 B. ZA313 E. ZD477 A. ZD480 C. ZE425. ZF117 D. ZG820 F.

846 Squadron:
ZA291 –. ZA293 VP. ZA296 VK. ZD478 VM. ZD479 VJ. ZE425 –. ZF118 VL. ZF119 VO.

848 Squadron:
ZA298 WA later WJ. ZA314 WD later WM. ZE427 WB later WK. ZE428 WC later WL. ZG821 WE later WN. ZG822 WF later WO.

Royal Navy Sea King were employed on a variety of tactical transport tasks. Most arrived in-theater aboard Royal Fleet Auxiliary vessels.

Westland Lynx AH.Mk 7

Deployment
1 (British) Corps in Germany provided 24 Lynx for Gulf operations, these being shipped from Bremerhafen or flown out from Ramstein by USAF transport aircraft early in December. Contributing units included Nos 654 and 669 Squadrons of No. 4 Regiment at Detmold and No. 661 Squadron of No. 1 Regiment at Hildesheim.

Mission
Lynx were assigned to anti-armor missions with TOW missiles in support of 1 (British) Armoured Division in the Gulf theater. Additional roles were armed escort, forward reconnaissance, utility transport and casualty evacuation. Scouting for targets was undertaken by Westland-Aérospatiale Gazelles from the same units.

Service
Despite advancing into Iraq with the British component of land forces, the anti-armor helicopter force failed to encounter the

resistance anticipated, although many vehicles were destroyed. Most Lynx were shipped back to Germany during March 1991.

XZ209 M. XZ217 G. XZ219 H. XZ651 U. XZ654 W.

Below: Army Lynx saw some action, although the speed of the allied advance and the Iraqi collapse meant that there were few anti-armor missions flown in the Gulf.

CANADA

Boeing CC-137

Deployment
One of No. 437 Squadron's two tanker-capable CC-137s from Trenton redeployed to Doha, Qatar.

Mission
Inflight refueling of CF-18 Hornets.

Service
The CC-137 replenished CF-18s throughout the conflict.

13704. 13705.
(No more than one at any time.)

McDonnell Douglas CF-18 Hornet

Deployment
Eighteen Hornets of No. 409 Squadron from Söllingen, Germany, were dispatched to

Doha, Qatar, on 6/7 October 1990 as the key element of Canadian Air Task Group Middle East. Personnel of No. 439 Squadron, including 22 pilots, adopted the detachment in mid-December, with support from No. 416 Squadron (15 pilots) from Cold Lake. A further six aircraft were added on 12 January and two more soon afterwards.

Mission
Hornets were initially tasked with protecting coalition warships in the Gulf from Iraqi attacks (particularly with Exocet missiles), this Combat Air Patrol (CAP) duty starting prior to hostilities. The Hornet force was cleared by Ottawa for 'sweep and escort' missions on 16 January, the first successful raid taking place on 24 January, after a weather-abort on 21 January. They participated in overland close air support missions from 25 February onwards. Final personnel returned to Germany on 20 April.

Service
CF-18s generated 5,730 hours between October 1990 and 28 February 1991, flying 770 CAP sorties, 168 fighter-sweep and escort sorties and 56 close air support sorties.

34 aircraft – maximum of 26 at any one

time, including:
188743. 188748. 188751. 188753. 188754. 188758. 188769. 188780. 188782.

Canadian CF-18 Hornets were originally tasked with air defense of allied shipping in the Gulf.

Aircraft of the Gulf War

Sikorsky Sea King

Deployment
Frigate HMCS *Athabaskan* and supply ship *Protecteur* sailed from Halifax on 24 August, each with two CH-124 Sea Kings of No. 423 Squadron, Shearwater, and arrived in the Gulf on 27 September. Two more helicopters arrived later. UK supply ship RFA *Olna* embarked two Westland Sea King HAS.Mk 5s of No. 826 Squadron, Culdrose, on 18 August, these later transferring to the Netherlands oiler, HrMs *Zuijderkruis*.

Mission
Sea Kings were tasked with assisting the interception of vessels suspected of breaking the UN trade embargo with Iraq.

Service
The first intercept of a cargo vessel by Canadian Forces occurred on 2 October 1990. CF Sea Kings then undertook over a quarter of subsequent missions and had boarded 30 ships before the outbreak of fighting.

Canadian Forces:
12404. 12426.

Royal Navy:
ZA137 137. XZ577 138.

Below: Canadian Sea Kings were assembled by United Aircraft of Canada, with the designation CH-124. Equivalent to the US Navy's SH-3A, the CH-124 force has been updated several times over the years.

Above: The two CH-124s deployed to the Middle East aboard a destroyer and a replenishment ship were used to patrol the Gulf in support of the UN blockade of Iraqi trade.

FRANCE

Aérospatiale Gazelle

Deployment
France's Aviation légère de l'armée de terre (ALAT) deployed four Gazelles of 3ième RHC as air freight, these arriving at Yanbu, Saudi Arabia, on 9 September. A further 30 Gazelles of 5ième RHC arrived at Yanbu on 22 September by sea, and all transferred to King Khalid Military City on 26 September. A further 20 Gazelles of 1ier and 5ième RHCs arrived on 31 October, and further reinforcements from 1ier RHC sailed from Toulon on 31 December. Total French Gazelle deployment was 88. 3ième RHC replaced 5ième RHC in December. The UK's Army Air Corps sent 24 Gazelle AH.Mk 1s to Saudi Arabia during December, from Nos 654, 659 and 661 Squadrons in Germany. Fifteen Kuwaiti SA 342L versions escaped to Saudi Arabia on 2/3 August 1990.

Mission
The French contingent comprised 14 SA 341F versions for liaison and communications; 14 SA 341F/Canon for armed reconnaissance and escort; and 60 SA 342Ms armed with Euromissile HOT anti-tank missiles. Kuwaiti SA 342Ls were also HOT-equipped, while UK Gazelle AH.Mk 1s were assigned to unarmed scouting as well as liaison.

Service
Gazelles accompanied their respective armies on the advance into Iraqi territory from 24 February. Earlier action was seen by KAF Gazelles during the battle of Khafji on 30/31 January, when at least one Iraqi tank was destroyed. ALAT Gazelles fired 187 HOTs against Iraqi targets.

ALAT:
1296 BOT (SA 341F). (SA 342M). 4039 BPF. 4066 BOJ. 4084 BPG *"81"*. 4171 BPT, also AEH, ATL *"142"*, ATP, BPA. 4146 BQD. 4189 BYG *"67"*. 4200. 4219 BWF. 4227 BOH *"33"*. 4227 BYH *"64"*.

Army Air Corps:
XW909. XX416. XX437 C. XX437. XX453. XX454 K. XX455. XZ292. XZ298. XZ337.

Kuwaiti Air Force:
1126 504. 1322 507. 1331 511. 1339 512. 1341 514. 1342 515. 1349 517. 1352 519.

The HOT missile-armed Gazelle is France's primary anti-armor helicopter.

Boeing C-135FR

Deployment
The 93ième Escadre de ravitaillement en vol maintained a refueling detachment of 10 aircraft at King Khalid IAP, Riyadh, Saudi Arabia, during hostilities. An initial two aircraft were based there after 15 October 1990, six being present from 15 January. Crews were provided by ERV 1/93 Aunis from Istres; ERV 2/93 Sologne from Avord, and ERV 3/93 Landes from Mont-de-Marsan.

Mission
Although capable of transport, the French C-135s were used primarily as air refuelers during hostilities. They are fitted with a drogue and short length of hose at the end of their USAF-style tailbooms.

Service
By 28 February, French tankers had flown 327 sorties since arrival, of which 220 (totalling 913 hours) were mounted after 15 January. They refueled 185 Jaguars, 437 Mirage 2000s, 65 Mirage F1CRs, eight USN F-14 Tomcats and a single USN EA-6B Prowler, for a total of 1,693 tonnes of fuel. Returns to France began on 4 March.

38470 93-CA. 38471 93-CB. 38472 93-CC. 38474 93-CE. 38475 93-CF. 12735 93-CG. 12736 93-CH. 12737 93-CI. 12738 93-CJ. 12739 93-CK. 12740 93-CL.

Normally used to support France's force of Mirage IV nuclear bombers, the Boeing C-135FR tankers of the French air force were deployed to the Gulf to support French fighters and strike aircraft.

Dassault Mirage F1

Deployment
The 12ième Escadre de chasse at Cambrai dispatched the first of eight Mirage F1Cs to Doha, Qatar, on 17 October 1990. Personnel came from EC 1/12 'Cambresis', EC 2/12 'Picardie' and EC 3/12 'Cornouaille'. Kuwait was able to fly 15 Mirage F1CKs of Nos 18 and 61 Squadrons out of Ali al Salem Air Base on 2/3 August.

Mission
EC 12's aircraft were assigned to boost the air defense of Qatar, complementing the local air arm's Mirage F1s.

Service
No Iraqi air attacks were made on Qatar and the French F1 detachment was not called into action. The detachment flew 150 sorties (130 hours) in Desert Storm. The Kuwaiti aircraft regrouped at Taif, Saudi Arabia, but transferred to Dhahran during January.

France:
231 12-YH. 236 12-KB. 248 –. 255 –. 257 12-YI. 272 12-YH. 274 –. 280 12-KM.

Kuwait:
701. 703. 706. 708. 710. 715. 717. 719. 722. 723. 724. 727.

The Dassault Mirage F1 was the only fighter to be used by both sides in the conflict. The Kuwaiti aircraft were flown to Saudi Arabia from their bases just before they were overrun by Iraqi troops.

Dassault Mirage F1CR

Deployment
Mirage F1CRs of the 33ième Escadre de reconnaissance left Strasbourg on 3 October 1990 for Al Ahsa, Saudi Arabia. Eight were initially deployed, of which six were employed during hostilities.

Mission
The primary reconnaissance capability of the F1CR was used prior to the war for surveillance of the Iraqi fortifications on the border with Saudi Arabia. The attack capability was employed in joint bombing missions with Jaguars.

Service
Mirage F1s were grounded during the opening phases of Desert Storm for fear of confusion with similar Iraqi aircraft. The first of several Mirage-Jaguar missions was then flown on 26 January, the F1CR using its superior, radar-assisted navigation suite to lead the raid. Aircraft flew 114 sorties (264 hours) during Desert Storm. The aircraft returned to France early in March.

604 33-CE. 622 33-CR. 623 33-CM. 624 33-NE. 627 33-NI. 629 33-CG. 632 33-TM. 634 33-CK. 635 33-TH. 641 33-NT.

Right; The advanced side-looking radar reconnaissance system of the Mirage F1CR made it one of the coalition's more important reconnaissance-gathering tools, particularly in the weeks leading up to the start of the war.

Dassault Mirage 2000C

Deployment
The first four of an eventual 14 Mirage 2000Cs left the 5ième Escadre de chasse base at Orange on 3 October 1990 for Al Ahsa, Saudi Arabia.

Mission
Mirage 2000Cs were assigned to combat air patrols in support of Jaguar missions, carrying MATRA Super 530 and Magic 2 AAMs. (Air-defense missions within Saudi air-space had begun on 12 December 1990.)

Service
France's air-defense force was only brought into the coalition order of battle on 6 February 1991, and it was involved in no air fighting. Desert Storm sorties totalled 508 (1,416 hours). First aircraft returned home on 18 March.

39 5-NB. 40 5-OI. 47 5-NC. 45 5-OM. 51 5-OG. 57 5-AJ. 58 5-AK. 59 5-OB. 61 5-OD. 62 5-AL. 63 5-OK. 65 5-NH. 66 5-ON. 70 5-AO. 72 5-NI. 73 5-NM. 74 5-AF.

The Dassault Mirage 2000 is France's front-line air-defense fighter, but like all such aircraft deployed to the Gulf, with the notable exception of the American F-15, it saw little or no combat.

SEPECAT Jaguar A

Deployment
The 11ième Escadre de chasse, at Toul, was put on alert on 16 September 1990 and dispatched its initial batch of aircraft to Al Ahsa, Saudi Arabia, on 15 October. The wing's four squadrons are EC 1/11 'Roussillon', EC 2/11 'Vosges', EC 3/11 'Corse' and EC 4/11 Jura – the last detached to Bordeaux. In total, 28 Jaguars were deployed, personnel including pilots from 7ième Escadre at St Dizier.

Mission
As with RAF Jaguars, the aircraft were tasked with battlefield air interdiction, attacking tactical targets in Kuwait. Missions into Iraq were authorized from 24 January onwards and some strategic targets (bridges) were also attacked.

Service
French Jaguars mounted their first mission on 17 January 1991 and were active until 27 February, supported by Mirage F1CRs and tanker C-135FRs. They flew 615 sorties (1,088 hours) in Desert Storm and made 185 contacts with C-135FRs. Returns to France began on 5 March. None was lost, but one was seriously damaged by a SAM and had to be airfreighted home.

A1 11-RW. A58 11-RH. A87 11-RX. A89 11-MM. A90 11-MB. A91 11-YG. A94 11-ES. A97 11-RG. A99 11-EI. A100 11-ER. A101 11-ED. A103 11-MA. A104 11-EK. A107 11-MV. A108 11-MP. A112 11-MO. A115 11-RL. A117 11-MH. A122 11-EQ. A123 11-YN. A133 11-EF. A135 11-RJ. A137 11-EJ. A139 11-EV. A140 11-EL. A148 11-YD. A150 11-YK. A153 11-RB. A157 11-YK. A158 11-RM. A159 11-RV.

French Jaguars have been deployed to the desert before, most notably in Chad in the late 1980s. They were the most active of all French combat aircraft in the Gulf.

ITALY

Panavia Tornado IDS

Deployment
Eight Tornados from 154°, 155° and 156° Gruppi were stationed at Al Dhafra (Maqatra) in Abu Dhabi from 2 October 1990, being declared operational on 6 October. Two more were added later from a pool of 12 aircraft with Gulf modifications and camouflage.

Mission
In common with their RAF counterpart, the GR.Mk 1, the aircraft were assigned to counter-air attacks on Iraqi airfields.

Service
The first mission was flown on the night of 17/18 January, but unfamiliarity with the use of a drogue attached to a USAF KC-135 resulted in only one aircraft being able to refuel and undertake the assigned mission – from which it failed to return. Thereafter, four Tornados were configured as 'buddy' tankers, reducing the bombing force to four. By the end of hostilities, the aircraft had flown 226 sorties in 32 missions and dropped 565 1,000-lb (454-kg) Mk 83 bombs.

MM7019 19. MM7035 35. MM7050 50. MM7061 61. MM7067 67. MM7070 70. MM7073 73. MM7074 74. MM7075 75. MM7076 76. MM7086 86. MM7088 88.

Italian Tornados based in Abu Dhabi were assigned targets similar to their British and Saudi counterparts. The most dangerous of these were the low-level counter-air missions against the huge, well-defended Iraqi airfields.

Aircraft of the Gulf War

KUWAIT
McDonnell Douglas A-4KU Skyhawk

Deployment
Twenty Skyhawks of Nos 9 and 25 Squadrons escaped from their base at Ahmed al Jaber on 2/3 August and sought refuge at Bahrain before regrouping at Dhahran, Saudi Arabia.

Mission
Skyhawks were tasked with daylight attack missions in the area of Kuwait.

Service
Operations began on 17 January – initially disastrously, when 11 out of a flight of 12

dropped their bombs on Saudi territory. The one A-4 loss was sustained on this mission.

801. 802. 807. 809. 811. 813. 814. 816. 817. 818. 819. 820. 822. 824. 825. 827. 828. 829. 884. 886.

The A-4 Skyhawk was not the most advanced aircraft in the region, but in the hands of refugee Kuwaiti pilots it was not to be ignored.

SAUDI ARABIA

Aérospatiale AS 565SA Panther

Deployment
Twenty Panthers (previously known as SA 365 Dauphin 2s) were based at Al Jubail Naval Airport in August 1990.

Mission
Primary role of the Panther is anti-shipping attack with Aérospatiale AS 15TT missiles, operating from the stern platforms of frigates.

Service
Regular patrols of Saudi waters were flown by Panthers (and Aérospatiale AS 532 Cougars of the same service). A Panther sank two Iraqi patrol boats with AS 15s near Maradim Island on 30 January and the same helicopter destroyed a further three in the same area on 3 February.

Individual aircraft
6173. 6176. 6199. 6200. 6201.

BAe Hawk Mk 65

Deployment
Two Squadrons of Hawks (Nos 21 and 37) were stationed at Dhahran in August 1990. Six Kuwaiti Hawk Mk 64s escaped to Bahrain on 2/3 August and were placed under control of the RSAF.

Mission
Hawks were assigned to light attack missions in Desert Storm, having had the peacetime role of weapons training.

Service
Hawks are reported to have undertaken a small number of light attack missions into Kuwait.

Royal Saudi Air Force:
2110-2121. 3751-3768.
Kuwait Air Force:
None identified.

The British Aerospace Hawk is a combat-capable advanced trainer which can be used for air defense or for light attack missions. Saudi Hawks are reported to have flown some attack missions into Kuwait.

McDonnell Douglas F-15C Eagle

Deployment
RSAF units operational in August 1990 were No. 5 at Taif, No. 6 at Khamis Mushait and No. 13 at Dhahran. Emergency supply during the same month of 24 ex-USAF Eagles allowed No. 42 Squadron to form at Dhahran.

Mission
F-15s from Dhahran took turns with their USAF counterparts, plus Tornado F.Mk 3s of the RAF and RSAF, to mount continuous four-hour CAPs from August onwards.

Service
CAPs continued to be flown after 17 January. On 24 January an Eagle shot down two Iraqi aircraft – apparently both Mirage F1s – the RSAF's sole air-to-air claims for Desert Storm. One aircraft of No. 6 Squadron was lost in a training accident on 13 February.

No. 13 Squadron:
619 (F-15D). 1305. 1307. 1309. 1310. 1311. 1312. 1314. 1321 (F-15D). 1322 (F-15D).

No. 42 Squadron:
4201-4222, plus F-15Ds 4223-4224.

Northrop F-5

Deployment
RSAF F-5Es were operating with Nos 3 and 10 Squadrons at Taif, No. 15 Squadron at Khamis Mushait, and No. 17 Squadron at Tabuk in August 1990.

Mission
Only Tabuk-based aircraft were used during Desert Storm. Missions comprised light attack by F-5E Tiger IIs and reconnaissance by RF-5E Tigereyes.

Service
Missions were flown throughout hostilities. One F-5E was lost in action on 13 February.

RF-5E: 1709. 1710. 1717. 1719.

Panavia Tornado ADV

Deployment
In August 1990, No. 29 Squadron was operating at Dhahran, including the nucleus of No. 34 Squadron.

Mission
CAPs were flown in conjunction with USAF and RSAF F-15 Eagles and RAF Tornado F.Mk 3s.

Service
No air-to-air claims were made during hostilities.

2901-2912. 3451-3462.

Above: Undoubtedly the most effective and successful air superiority fighter of the war, the McDonnell Douglas F-15 Eagle equipped four Saudi fighter squadrons. It was a Saudi F-15 pilot who made the only non-American kills of the war.

Right: Air Defence Variant Tornados of the Royal Saudi Air Force were integrated into Saudi Arabia's multinational air-defense network, but like their British equivalents they achieved no successes, never finding the Iraqi air force in the air.

Panavia Tornado IDS

Deployment
No. 7 Squadron at Dhahran was operational in August 1990 and No. 66 Squadron was in process of formation at the same base.

Mission
RSAF Tornado IDS were allocated to interdiction and counter-air missions.

Service
The first mission was flown against Iraqi airfields on the night of 17/18 January. One aircraft was lost on the following night.

701-705. 757-768. 770-774. 6601-6603.

The Interdictor Strike variant of the Tornado was more successful than the fighters, being used along with British Tornados to attack strategic targets deep within Iraq.

BAHRAIN

Northrop F-5E Tiger II/GD F-16 Fighting Falcon

Aircraft of the Bahrain Emiri Air Force – Northrop F-5E Tiger IIs and/or General Dynamics F-16A Fighting Falcons – flew their first defensive mission from Sheikh Isa AB on 25 January and began offensive operations on the following day.

QATAR

Dassault Mirage F1EDA

The Qatar Emiri Air Force used Dassault Mirage F1EDAs of No 7 Squadron at Doha from 22 January onwards. These undertook local air defense missions but may also have attacked targets in Kuwait.

UNITED ARAB EMIRATES

Dassault Mirage 2000EAD

UAE Dassault Mirage 2000EADs from Maqatra, Abu Dhabi, began air operations on 19 February, apparently for local air defense. Technical support was provided by the French air force.

Right: Aircraft from the air forces of other Gulf Co-operation Council members played small parts in the war, most, like this UAE Mirage 2000, being used to defend their own home territories.

The anti-Saddam coalition was a multinational effort, with countries like Korea making a token gesture of sending a C-130 Hercules to assist in operations and for medical and humanitarian transport.

Argentina was also a coalition partner, sending a destroyer to serve in the Gulf to help enforce the United Nations blockade of Iraq. This Fokker F28 of the Argentine air force was also sent to the region.

Gulf Aircraft Weapons

General Purpose (**GP**) bombs included the 500-lb **Mk 82**, 1,000-lb **Mk 83** and 2,000-lb **Mk 84**. These bombs were all roughly one-half casing and one-half explosive, with an ablative coating to inhibit them from exploding during shipboard fires. The USAF didn't use any version of the Mk 83. A number of different fins could be fitted to these bombs, the most common being the conical-finned, Low-Drag, General Purpose (**LDGP**) fin. High-drag fins included the Vietnam-era **Snakeye** (**SE**) favored by the USN and USMC. (The 'eye' suffix identified a weapon developed by the Naval Weapons Center at China Lake, California). The USAF preferred the newer Air-Inflatable Retard (**AIR**) bomb because it could be released at higher airspeeds. AIRs were only fitted to Mk 82s and 84s and were often referred to by their canister designations, Bomb Stabilizing and retarding Unit (**BSU**), **-49** and 50.

Different fuzes were used with the Mk 80-series bombs to produce the desired damage to a given target. The M904 and munitions fuze unit (**FMU**) **-54** were the most common impact fuzes. Delay fuzes included the FMU-26, -72 and -139. The FMU-113 was used for proximity detonation, making the bomb explode before it hit the ground, thus maximizing its blast effect. A poor man's way to get a similar effect was to stick an M904 on the end of a pipe, a method dating from Vietnam, known by the name 'daisy-cutter'. Despite extensive media use of this term to refer to the Bomb Live Unit (**BLU**) -82 dropped by MC-130s, the term actually referred to the fuze extender, not a particular bomb.

The Mk 7 dispenser was used to form a variety of Cluster-Bomb Units (**CBU**s). The **Mk 20 Rockeye II** consisted of a Mk 7 filled with 247 Mk 118 anti-tank bomblets. The Mk 20 was the only version of the Mk 7 family used by the USAF. The **CBU-59/B** Anti-Personnel, Anti-Material (**APAM**) was a Mk 7 Mod 4 filled with 717 BLU-77/B bomblets. The **CBU-78/B** was a Mk 7 filled with 26 BLU-91/B anti-personnel mines and 38 BLU-92/B **Gator** anti-tank mines. The standard Mk 7 fuze was the Mk 339. The term BLU was used to refer to any modern warhead.

A-4KU (Douglas Skyhawk)

Free Kuwaiti A-4s had a standard load of 450-gal inboard fuel tanks along with either five Mk 7 dispensers or Mk 82s, including LDGPs, LDGPs with daisy-cutter fuze extenders and SEs. These bombs were mounted on the outboard pylons and centerline Triple Ejector Rack (**TER**).

Above: A Kuwaiti A-4KU with two fuel tanks and five Mk 82 SE bombs. The cluster-bomb dispensers were effective against area targets such as troop or vehicle concentrations. The fuze extenders ensured the bombs exploded above ground, creating maximum blast effect.

A-6E (Grumman Intruder)

A 300-gal centerline fuel tank appears to have been standard on all A-6Es. They were seen with loads of 10 Mk 82 LDGP or SE bombs mounted on inboard Multiple Ejector Racks (**MER**s), with the front-inboard shoulder stations empty, together with 12 Mk 7s on the outboard MERs. Other loads included four pylon-mounted Mk 83 1,000-lb LDGP bombs or outboard MERs loaded with 12 Mk 82 LDGPs.

Virtually all USN/USMC Precision-Guided Munitions (**PGM**s) were employed. These included Paveway II Guided Bomb Units (**GBU**s). The 2,000-lb **GBU-10E/B**, 500-lb **GBU-12D/B** and 1,000-lb **GBU-16B/B**

A-6E (continued)
Laser-Guided Bombs (**LGB**s) were all used. **Paveway II** bombs were externally distinguishable from Paveway I bombs by their 'pop-out' wings which made handling and carriage easier. Both bombs had 'bang-bang' guidance systems, which used full control deflection to alter the bomb's path, thus shortening their range.

Sometimes bomb loads were mixed. For example, a *Saratoga* A-6E was seen with Mk 83 LDGPs on the front-shoulder and aft-bottom MER stations on the outboard pylons, along with a single GBU-12D/B LGB loaded on each inboard pylon.

Other A-6E ordnance reportedly included Air-to-Ground Missiles (**AGM**) -45s, -62s and -123s. The **AGM-45 Shrike** was a Vietnam-era anti-radiation missile. A total of 124 **AGM-62** Extended-Range/Data-Link (**ER/DL**) **Walleye II** (Mk 13 Mod 0) unpowered PGMs was expended. The **AGM-123A Skipper II** rocket-powered LGB consisted of a Mk 83 1,000-lb bomb, a Paveway II seeker head and a new tail section incorporating the Mk 78 rocket motor, also used by the Shrike missile.

Virtually all Navy attack aircraft employed the Tactical, Air-Launched Decoy (**TALD**) during the opening stages of Desert Storm. These unpowered decoys displayed radar signatures which were difficult to distinguish from an actual aircraft, and thereby attracted a lot of attention from Surface-to-Air Missiles (**SAM**s). A powered Improved-TALD (**ITALD**) was under development, but not used.

An A-6E from the USS *Kennedy* made the first of seven combat launches of the Stand-Off, Land-Attack Missile (**SLAM**) **AGM-84E Harpoon**, four of which hit their targets. SLAM used an AGM-65D Infra-Red (**IR**) seeker and an AGM-62 video data link mated to the standard AGM-84A 500-lb warhead.

A-6Es were reported to have carried the **Mk 77** 500-lb class napalm bombs, as well as 2.75-in and 5.0-in Folding Fin Aircraft Rocket (**FFAR**) pods. There were a number of very similar 2.75-in FFAR pods which had either seven or 19 tubes. Seven-tube pods included the USN/USAF **M260** LAuncher Unit (**LAU**) -68 and USAF **M261**. Nineteen-tube pods included the USN **LAU-69** and USAF **M200**. The primary 5.0-in FFAR pod was the four-tube **LAU-97**, which was only used by the USN/USMC.

Below: Mk 7 dispensers in front of an A-6E loaded with 12 Mk 82 LDGPs. Mk 7s were used for several US Navy cluster-bombs. The two yellow bands denote a fire-resistant bomb.

Precision-Guided Munitions

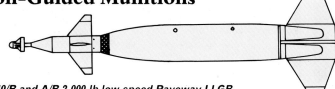

Above: GBU-10/B and A/B 2,000-lb low-speed Paveway I LGB.

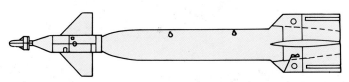

Above: GBU-10I 2,000-lb Paveway II Penetrator LGB (wings stowed)

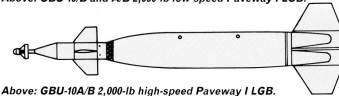

Above: GBU-10A/B 2,000-lb high-speed Paveway I LGB.

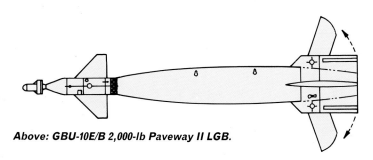

Above: GBU-10E/B 2,000-lb Paveway II LGB.

An ordnance specialist makes final checks on three CPU-123/B 1,000-lb British LGBs destined to destroy an Iraqi bridge. Tornados used three LGBs for bridges, but only needed two for hardened aircraft shelters.

Gulf Aircraft Weapons

EA-6B (Grumman Prowler)

Several EA-6B configurations were observed during Desert Storm. One had airborne countermeasures, special type (**ALQ**) **-99** Electronic CounterMeasures (**ECM**) pods on the centerline, left outboard and right inboard pylons. A fuel tank was carried on the left inboard pylon while an **AGM-88** High-Speed, Anti-Radiation Missile (**HARM**)

was carried on the right outboard. Another configuration was centerline and right outboard ALQ-99s, right inboard and left outboard AGM-88s and a left inboard fuel tank. A third configuration had the ALQ-99s on the outboard pylons, an AGM-88 on the left inboard, and a fuel tank on the right (and probably the centerline as well.)

A-7E (Vought Corsair II)

This was the last war for the A-7, and the units which flew them had been in the early stages of transition to the F/A-18 when Desert Shield began. They quickly reclaimed their A-7Es and deployed.

Air Intercept Missile (**AIM**) **-9L/M** Sidewinders were often carried on day missions. Inboard pylon fuel tanks appeared to have been standard.

A photo of VA-72 'Blue Hawks' aircraft from the *Kennedy* (in the Red Sea), taken on the first night of the air war, showed the middle wing pylon removed from all aircraft. While some carried AGM-88s, others carried single Mk 7s on the outboard pylons. They also were seen later in the war carrying AGM-62s on the left center pylon, with an empty right center pylon and AIM-9 rails – all other pylons were removed.

Apparently, aircraft based in the Persian Gulf in the early days of the war only carried one inboard tank to allow carriage of three AGM-88s on the other inboard and middle wing pylons. Up to four Mk 83 LDGP bombs with no fuel tanks were also seen there. (Although usually mounted to the outboard pylons, one aircraft was seen with the bombs mounted on the outboard two sta-

tions on the left wing and the inboard and outboard stations on the right – probably to circumvent a pylon malfunction.)

An A-7E used an airborne armament remote control (AWW)-9 Walleye data-link pod to guide the A-6-launched SLAM described in the A-6E section.

Above: An A-7E with an AIM-9L/M and six TER-mounted Mk 7 dispensers.

A-10A (Fairchild Thunderbolt II)

One-hundred-and-forty-four A-10As flew over 8,500 sorties and dropped 23,927 bombs during Desert Storm. In its primary role it killed more than 1,000 tanks, 1,200 artillery pieces and 2,000 military vehicles ('Warthogs'); trolled for Scuds in western Iraq ('Scud Hogs'); attacked SAM, Anti-Aircraft-Artillery (**AAA**) and radar sites ('Wart Weasels'); and even bagged a pair of helicopters, scoring the only gun kills of the war (yes, 'Wart Eagles'!).

A-10As had a total of 11 weapons pylons, numbered starting on the left outboard with station 1. Station 6, the centerline pylon, seems to have been seldom, if ever, used throughout the war. Many times the middle wing (stations 2 and 10) and outboard fuselage (stations 5 and 6) pylons were removed, especially early in the war.

Usually, two AIM-9L/Ms were mounted on station 1. The missile rails were mounted

Above: This A-10A carries a 'flat-two' load of four Mk 82 LDGPs inboard of the landing gear, AGM-65 Mavericks on LAU-117 single rail launchers outboard, two AIM-9L/Ms on the left outboard pylon and a long ALQ-119 on the right (indicating a US-based unit).

on either side of a 14-in×54-in spacer plate suspended from the 14-in lugs of the pylon. The back edge of the plate was about 14 in from the trailing edge of the pylon. The 91-in-long missile rails were mounted with the front tips 28 in from leading edge of the plate.

ALQ-119 long (US-based units) or **ALQ-131** shallow (Europe-based units) ECM pods were carried on the right outboard pylon, station 11.

AV-8B (McDonnell Douglas/British Aerospace Harrier II)

The 88-strong Harrier II component of Desert Storm contributed 3,380 sorties while dropping 5.95 million lb of ordnance. Average mission length was just over an hour and forward basing allowed delivery of bombs within 10 minutes of take-off. Medium-altitude attacks were used until the start of the ground war when low-altitude attacks were also used. On the down side, the AV-8B showed a low tolerance for battle damage – whenever one was hit by a SAM, it crashed.

AIM-9L/Ms were mounted on the left outboard pylon only – the right pylon had the launcher rail fitted but no missile was carried. Fuselage gun pod installation was standard, although a couple of aircraft were

seen with the alternate ventral strakes.

Four Mk 7 dispensers, Mk 82 LDGP or SE, or Mk 83 LDGP bombs, were carried on the inboard pylons. These were delivered from dive angles in excess of 30°.

In preparation for the ground campaign, Mk 77s were employed to ignite and burn off oil in Iraqi defensive trenches. Also used were Fuel-Air Explosives (**FAE**) to detonate Iraqi minefields. These included **CBU-55** and -72 500-lb class bombs. Both consisted of the Suspension Underwing Unit (**SUU**) **-49** dispenser and three BLU-73 bomblets, which exploded with a force of about 10 atmospheric pressures. The **CBU-72** was a modification of the earlier CBU-55 for use on high performance aircraft. This type of bomb

was only used by Marine aircraft.

Early in the war, a gray-painted centerline store similar in shape to the BAe reconnaissance pod was carried on several AV-8Bs. This was the only centerline store noted on Harriers throughout the war.

Only a very few of the laser-guided **AGM-65E** Maverick missiles were expended by AV-8Bs. These were mounted on single-rail LAU-117s and utilized ground-based laser designation.

Other weapons reportedly carried by Harriers included GBU-12D/B and GBU-16B/B LGBs, as well as 2.75-in and 5.0-in FFAR pods.

Above: Four fire-resistant Mk 83 LDGPs are mounted on this AV-8B's inboard pylons, with at least one AIM-9L/M on the outboard.

Below: GBU-12D/B 500-lb Paveway II LGB.

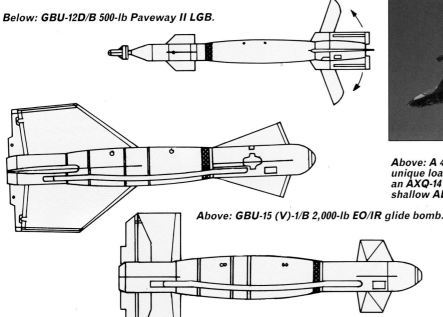

Above: GBU-15 (V)-1/B 2,000-lb EO/IR glide bomb.

Above: GBU-15 (V)-2/B 2,000-lb EO/IR glide bomb.

Above: A 493th TFS F-111F with its unique load of two GBU-15(V)-1/Bs, an AXQ-14 data-link pod and a shallow ALQ-131.

Above: A GBU-16B/B is prepared for its one-way mission. Fins were not attached until after the bomb was on the aircraft.

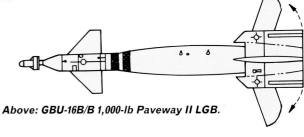

Above: GBU-16B/B 1,000-lb Paveway II LGB.

Gulf Aircraft Weapons

A-10A (continued)

A total of about 5,500 **AGM-65 Mavericks** (each costing about $70,000) were expended, 5,013 by A-10As. For the first month of the air war, when Mavericks were carried, they were on LAU-117s mounted on stations 3 and 9, just outboard of the landing gear. Generally, loads were half AGM-65A or B Electro-Optical (**EO**) and half AGM-65D IR versions. The EO missiles' seeker domes were clear, while live IR domes had a silverish appearance; training IR heads were a yellowish-orange color.

Some aircraft, probably OA-10As, appeared with, in addition to the above, LAU-68s mounted on stations 2 and 10 along with single, pylon-mounted Mk 82 LDGP bombs on stations 4 and 8, just inboard of the landing gear.

The action to regain Khafji was the first time stations 4 and 8 were seen equipped with TERs. These were the only stations so loaded. They had 'slant-two' loads of Mk 20s or three Mk 82 LDGPs in addition to the AGM-65s, ECM pods and AIM-9s. **'Slant-two'** means two weapons were loaded on the TER's bottom and outboard stations. Slightly later in the war, TER loadings seemed to switch to **'flat-twos'** where the bombs were loaded on the two shoulder stations only. Mk 20, Mk 82 LDGP and SUU-30H/Bs were loaded this way.

The **CBU-52** was an SUU-30H/B dispenser with 217 BLU-61 grapefruit-sized fragmentation bomblets. **CBU-58** was an SUU-30H/B with 650 orange-sized BLU-63 fragmentation bomblets. **CBU-71** was an SUU-30H/B with 650 BLU-86 fragmentation bomblets. **CBU-71A** was an SUU-30H/B with 650 BLU-68 fragmentation bomblets. SUU-30s could employ the FMU-26, M907 or Mk 339 time-delay airburst and FMU-56 or -110 proximity fuzes.

Once the focus of the aerial campaign turned to softening up the Iraqi positions in Kuwait, as many as six Mk 20s or SUU-30H/Bs were seen, pylon-mounted on stations 3, 4, 5, 7, 8 and 9. Also noted at the same time was the removal of some AIM-9 installations from station 1; Mk 20s on stations 2, 4, 8 and 10; and AGM-65s on stations 3 and 9. At least one aircraft had its ALQ-119 moved from station 11 to station 1, probably to overcome a pylon electrical malfunction.

Just prior to the ground war, 23rd TFW aircraft were seen with the standard AIM-9/ ALQ-119 installation; empty pylons on stations 2, 6 and 10; pylon-mounted Mk 82 LDGP bombs on stations 4, 5, 7 and 8; and triple-rail LAU-88 launchers with AGM-65Ds mounted on the bottom and outboard rails. The day before the ground war started A-10As used AGM-65s to destroy the valves used to feed oil into the Iraqi fire trenches.

The M117 (not Mk 117) GP bomb was a Korean war vintage weapon, directly descended from World War II-era bombs. While it had a US Army Air Force designation, the later Mk 80-series bombs had a US Navy designation. (The M117R had 'Snakeye' type fins).

Both the CBU-87 and CBU-89 used the Tactical Munition Dispenser (**TMD**). The **CBU-87** was an SUU-65 dispenser with 214 BLU-97 Combined Effects Munition (**CEM**) bomblets, while the **CBU-89** was an SUU-64 dispenser with a combination of 72 BLU-91 anti-personnel and 24 BLU-92 **Gator** anti-tank mines. Visually similar, the SUU-65's pop-out fins canted after it was dropped to spin the weapon for greater bomblet dispersion.

A proposal was made, but never implemented, for B-52-dropped GBU-12s to be guided against Iraqi tanks by F-111Fs or F-15Es. Also, no **AGM-142 'Have Nap'** (the Israeli 'Popeye') glide bombs were used. While there were reports of M129 leaflet bombs and CBU-72 FAE being dropped, it's extremely unlikely these weapons were actually employed by B-52s.

MC-130E (Lockheed Hercules)

These special operations aircraft reportedly dropped a total of 11 **BLU-82** 15,000-lb bombs, the blast effect of each bomb killing virtually everything within a 3-4-mile radius. The BLU-82s were High Capacity, Light-Case (**HCLC**) bombs, with an explosive content of over 80 per cent to maximize damage. The MC-130s were also responsible for dropping a majority of the psychological warfare leaflets.

F-111E (General Dynamics)

Although externally similar to the F-111F, without a PGM guidance capability the F-111E was of limited effectiveness in this medium-altitude war. Flying from Incirlik, Turkey, the 18 E-models from RAF Upper Heyford, UK, attacked area targets in the northern half of Iraq. None of the Avionics Modernization Program (**AMP**) aircraft participated in combat.

F-111Es primarily employed four pylon-mounted CBU-87 or -89 cluster-bombs. They could also carry four pylon-mounted Mk 84 LDGP or eight Mk 82 LDGP bombs mounted on Bomb Release Unit (**BRU**) -3/A bomb racks (a streamlined version of MERs used by other aircraft) carried on the outboard pylons. Carriage of BRUs was usually by a **'slant-four'** configuration on the outboard and bottom BRU stations, although **'flat-four'** loads, using only the shoulder stations, could have been used as well. F-111Es carried their ALQ-131 shallow ECM pods on the aft fuselage station.

F-111F (General Dynamics)

One of the biggest heroes of the air war was the F-111F with its ability to deliver a wide variety of PGMs. They were flown out of Taif, Saudi Arabia, by the 48th TFW from RAF Lakenheath, England. The 'Statue of Liberty' wing used a 'rainbow' maintenance operation, reforming its peacetime structure into wartime teams. The 492nd TFS (blue) became 'Justice', the 493rd TFS (yellow) 'Freedom', the 494th TFS (red) 'Liberty', and the 495th TFTS (green) 'Independence', which was shortened to 'Indy'. Like the proverbial 'bad girls', they went everywhere – including Baghdad – to destroy bridges, airfields, tanks, artillery, pumping stations, communications facilities and anything else that would hold still long enough to have a bomb put on it. Behind closed doors one very senior commander said, ''I want this target hit – give it to the F-111s.''

In 2,500 sorties, the 66 deployed F-111Fs (out of a total of 84) destroyed 2,203 targets, including confirmed direct hits on 920 tanks (although the total number destroyed may be closer to 1,500), 252 artillery pieces, 245 Hardened Aircraft Shelters (**HAS**s), 13 runways and 12 bridges (with another 52 seriously damaged). It's significant to note that no other US unit has given such a detailed accounting of its successes (or lack thereof) backed up by videotaped proof. The

B-52G (Boeing Stratofortress)

B-52s flew 1,624 missions, dropping 25,700 tons of bombs – 29 per cent of the total tonnage delivered during the war. Whatever else these raids accomplished, they had a devastating effect on Iraqi morale. The venerable Big Ugly Fat F***ers (**BUFF**s) operated from Jeddah, Saudi Arabia; Moron, Spain; Fairford, England; and Diego Garcia. They attacked the area targets such as troop

A B-52G launches with nine M117 GP bombs on each of its Heavy Stores Adapter Beams (HSABs), and another 27 in the bomb bay.

concentrations, airfields, factories, oil refineries, munitions storage areas, rail yards and minefields.

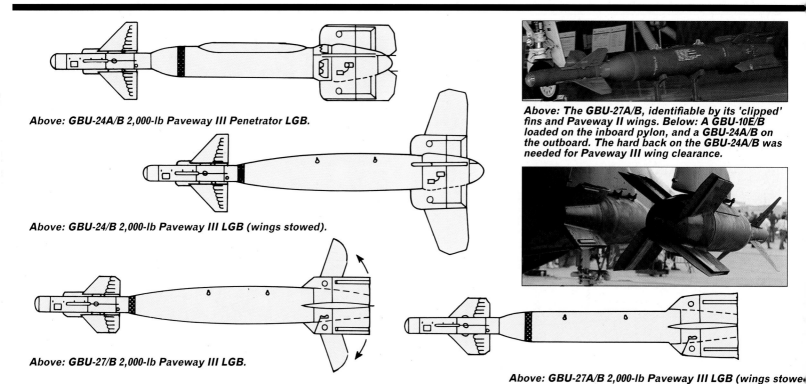

Above: GBU-24A/B 2,000-lb Paveway III Penetrator LGB.

Above: GBU-24/B 2,000-lb Paveway III LGB (wings stowed).

Above: GBU-27/B 2,000-lb Paveway III LGB.

Above: The GBU-27A/B, identifiable by its 'clipped' fins and Paveway II wings. Below: A GBU-10E/B loaded on the inboard pylon, and a GBU-24A/B on the outboard. The hard back on the GBU-24A/B was needed for Paveway III wing clearance.

Above: GBU-27A/B 2,000-lb Paveway III LGB (wings stowe~~

Gulf Aircraft Weapons

F-111F (continued)

48th TFW dropped 5,500 bombs weighing 3,650 tons and costing $93 million. Of more than 8,000 PGMs delivered by the USAF, 4,660 were delivered by F-111Fs.

Because of clearance problems with AIM-9L/Ms, F-111s could only carry **AIM-9P**s (with their smaller tail wings) on the wing pylon shoulder stations. AIM-9Ps were only carried on a few aircraft, and only on the first night of Desert Storm. Pool video showed loads of either two GBU-24s or GBU-15s mounted on outboard pylons with AIM-9Ps on the inboard pylons. Another photo showed four pylon-mounted TMDs with AIM-9Ps on the outboard pylon shoulder stations. Although modifications to allow employment of AIM-9L/Ms were under study, none had been completed by Desert Storm.

Apparently the only use of BRUs by an F-111F occurred early in the war when a 'Freedom' airplane delivered 12 Mk 82s (probably AIRs). These were probably carried on BRUs loaded on the outboard pylons. Consideration was also given to using them with previously untried loads of 12 GBU-12s or 'flat-eight' TMDs.

Loads of four pylon-mounted TMDs were employed throughout the war on over 100 sorties. However, CBU-89s were only used for about the first week of the air war on about 50 sorties, and then conserved in case of a prolonged ground war.

Virtually the only time during Desert Storm the F-111F was singled out for special attention was when it used two **GBU-15(V)-1/B** stand-off weapons to destroy the Iraqis were using to create history's largest oil slick in the Persian Gulf. Aside from the Clark AB-based F-4Es, the F-111F was the only Desert Storm aircraft qualified to deliver the GBU-15. This PGM existed in two basic versions: EO- and IR-guided. However, since virtually all F-111 attacks were at night (with the exception of one daytime mission) only the IR version was employed. The seeker heads were the same as those used on AGM-65s. Only about 75 GBU-15(V)-1/Bs were employed.

F-111F 72-1448 with a load of four GBU-12D/Bs. The gondola of the aft-mounted, shallow ALQ-131 is just visible below the ventral fin.

Apparently neither the **AGM-130** (rocket-powered GBU-15) or GBU-15(V)-2/Bs (using the AGM-130 airfoil groups) was used. Also, GBU-15Is, using the BLU-109 warhead, weren't ready for use during Desert Storm. For the GBU-15 mission, the airborne television, special-type (**AXQ**) **-14** data link pod was mounted on the aft fuselage station and the ALQ-131 shallow configuration ECM pod on the forward fuselage station (on the Pave Tack pod cradle). When LGBs were employed no data link pod was needed, so the ECM pod was mounted at its normal location on the aft fuselage station, thus allowing the airborne-visual, special-type (**AVQ**) **-26 Pave Tack** infra-red laser-designator pod to rotate out and assist in weapons delivery. The aircraft carrying the AXQ-14 pod controlled the bomb, which could be launched from another aircraft. Only one or two bombs would be carried per aircraft, always mounted on the outboard pylons.

The primary weapons of the F-111F were LGBs and, depending on the mission, it carried up to four pylon-mounted GBU-10s, -12s or -24s. (If only two bombs were carried, they would be on the outboard pylons.) About 500 GBU-10C/Bs, 400 GBU-10Is, 150 GBU-24/Bs and nearly 1,000 GBU-24A/Bs were used against bunkers, bridges, and HASs. The **GBU-10I** was a GBU-10 nose and tail section mounted to a BLU-109. It was probably used to conserve the much more expensive Paveway III guidance kits. The **GBU-24/B** was a Mk 84 warhead mounted to a Paveway III guidance kit, while the **GBU-24A/B** mated the BLU-109 'I-2000' penetrator warhead to the same basic kit. The **Paveway III** bombs used a proportional guidance system which increased bomb range and accuracy. The Paveway III weapons were also known as Low-Level, Laser-Guided bombs (**LLLGB**s)

even though that aspect of their performance was seldom exercised during Desert Storm.

During periods of bad weather, a mixed load of either two GBU-10s or -24s was carried on outboard pylons along with two Mk 84s on the inboard pylons. If the weather were good, the GBUs would be dropped on pinpoint targets; if it were bad the Mk 84s would be employed for area bombing. (About 100 Mk 84s were delivered by F-111Fs throughout the war.) Apparently using the same logic, some aircraft used mixed loads of GBU-10s on the inboard pylons and -24s on the outboards.

About 2,500 GBU-12B/Bs were used to dramatically decrease the size of Iraq's tank and artillery inventory prior to the start of the ground war during 'tank plinking' operations, including one raid where 20 aircraft carrying 80 bombs destroyed 77 tanks. When it was discovered that the F-111Fs had destroyed

10 times more tanks than the F-16s, the F-16s were directed to cease attacks by mid-afternoon each day to allow the dust to settle before the 'Aardvarks' went to work at night! The F-111F was the 'improved tactics' military briefers very coyly avoided talking about.

On 27 February, the final night of the war, two F-111Fs each delivered from their left outboard pylon a single 4,700-lb **GBU-28/B 'Deep Throat'** bomb capable of penetrating deep into the earth before exploding. (The venerable 'Aardvark' won the honor of dropping these weapons in a fly-off against the F-15E, which revealed temporary shortcomings in F-15E's delivery capabilities.) They were dropped on the bunkers at the Al Taji AB, just north of Baghdad. Much like the atomic bombs which ended World War II, these bombs sent a clear message to the Iraqi leadership that they were personally at risk.

F-117A (Lockheed)

The 44 'Black Jets' deployed to the Gulf owned the night skies over Baghdad from the beginning of the air war. The Iraqis called it 'the Ghost' in their communications. All of its 1,271 combat sorties were flown at night from Khamis Mushait, Saudi Arabia, by the 37th TFW from Tonopah AB, Nevada. First to deploy was the 415th TFS in August, followed by the 416th TFS in December and a portion of the 417th TFTS in late January.

Throughout the war, the F-117As carried two each of the GBU-10E/B, GBU-10I and

An F-117A with its center-hinged weapons bay open. The weapon trapeze can be seen protruding from the right bay.

GBU-12D/B Paveway II or GBU-27 Paveway III LGBs. The **GBU-27/B** and **GBU-27A/B** were similar to their GBU-24 counterparts except that they had slightly shorter adapter collars and 'clipped' nose fins to allow the bombs to fit in the F-117A's weapons bay.

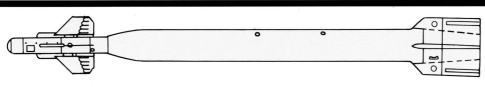

Left: GBU-28/B 4,700-lb 'Deep Throat' LGB.

Free-Fall Weapons

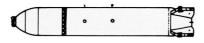

Above and below: The Mk 7 dispenser was configured with several kinds of bomblets to form the Mk 20 Rockeye II, CBU-59 APAM or CBU-78 Gator cluster-bombs. The USAF only used the Mk 20 variant. Two Mk 7s have been preloaded on this HER and await their ride on a F/A-18.

Above and below: The CPU-123/B was a Paveway II guidance kit mated to a British Royal Ordnance Mk 13 or Mk 18 1,000-lb bomb. This was the only LGB employed by British aircraft during Desert Storm.

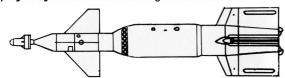

Gulf Aircraft Weapons

F-117A (continued)

The final figures on PGMs are something like this: The USAF dropped 64 per cent of the 88,500 total tons and about 90 per cent of the 7,400 tons of PGMs dropped by US forces (this figure apparently included only bombs, and excluded other types of PGMs, such as Maverick and Hellfire missiles). A reasonable guess would be that of this amount, 2,900 tons were delivered by F-111Fs, 2,000 by F-117As and about 1,000 by F-15Es. Despite claims that would lead one to believe otherwise, all aircraft delivering LGBs – by far the most common type of PGM – enjoyed an 80-90 per cent success rate with them; while dumb bombs only hit their targets about 5-25 per cent of the time (depending on the target type). Writing off the other 81,100 tons as harassment bombing, it probably cost less than $200 million in PGMs to put Iraq back into the pre-industrial age. (Paveway II LGBs cost about $10,000 each, Paveway IIIs about $40,000, and GBU-15s about $150,000).

F-4E (McDonnell Douglas Phantom II)

Six F-4Es from Clark AB, Philippines, deployed to Incirlik AB, Turkey, during Desert Storm. It is most probable that they were brought in for their PGM capability, which includes both the GBU-15 TV/EO glide bomb and the AVQ-26 Pave Tack pod, both also used by the F-111F. In any event, the centerline-carried Pave Tack pods didn't show up until after the war had ended, and it is unclear if the F-4Es saw any combat.

F-4G (McDonnell Douglas Phantom II)

Forty-eight F-4G 'Wild Weasels' flew more than 2,800 sorties during Desert Storm using callsigns taken from popular American beer names. Aircraft were drawn from both George AFB, California, and Spangdahlem AB, Germany, to form an all-F-4G force based at Sheikh Isa, Bahrain. At least some of

F-4Gs refueling. In addition to wall-to-wall AGM-88 HARMs, they carry AIM-7F Sparrows on the aft fuselage stations and the same centerline fuel tank used by the F-15.

F-4G (continued)

the George aircraft were equipped with the single-piece front windscreen. There is an additional mixed F-16C/F-4G unit made up for Spangdahlem assets based at Incirlik AB, Turkey. It's unclear if the stated total of 48 F-4Gs included the Incirlik aircraft. Unofficial reports indicate the actual number of F-4Gs involved may have been closer to 70.

The right-forward Sparrow well was always vacant, but the left-forward one carried an ECM pod. For aircraft from George this was the **ALQ-184** ECM pod (similar to an ALQ-119 in outward appearance, but with a longer gondola), while the Spangdahlem aircraft used the deep ALQ-131 pod. Also standard were aft-fuselage-mounted AIM-7F Sparrow medium-range AAMs. The centerline fuel tanks were the same as those used on F-15s. Up to four AGM-88 HARMs were carried on the wing pylons. The more normal load was two HARMs on the inboard wing pylons and two outboard fuel tanks. Bahrain was the focal point for receipt and distribution of all AGM-88s. A total of more than 1,000 HARMS was fired during the war, about 400 by F-4Gs (although unofficial reports indicate the actual numbers may be substantially higher).

During a three-to-four day period AGM-45 Shrikes were substituted for HARMs. This stopped once units in the field were able to educate higher headquarters about HARM capabilities, convincing them the missiles weren't being wasted.

The Incirlik-based 23rd TFS operated mixed F-4G/F-16C formations. The F-16Cs were totally dependent on information from, and basically served as an extra set of pylons for, the F-4Gs. They flew three four-ship formations for daytime strikes and two for night. Compositions of these formations varied, but the first two were a mix of the two types of aircraft, while the third was all F-16.

F-14A/A+ (Grumman Tomcat)

The Tomcat's standard load was two AIM-7F/M Sparrow missiles and two AIM-9L/M Sidewinder missiles on the wing glove pylons, two AIM-7F/Ms on the aft fuselage stations, two **AIM-54C Phoenix** missiles on the forward fuselage stations and external fuel tanks. (The differences between the AIM-7F and M models and AIM-9L and M models are not externally apparent.) One unconfirmed (and probably incorrect) report stated that until it became apparent that the air threat would be minimal, they carried four AIM-54Cs. Tomcats also utilized the Tactical Air Reconnaissance Pod System (**TARPS**) often carrying **ALQ-167** jamming pods.

F-15C (McDonnell Douglas Eagle)

A total of 120 USAF F-15Cs and Ds participated in Desert Storm (it is unclear if this number includes the 28 aircraft which flew from Incirlik, Turkey). Their standard armament was four each of AIM-7F/Ms and AIM-9L/Ms, plus three 600-gal fuel tanks. Despite their spotty reliability, AIM-7s scored the vast majority of kills. Some **AIM-120A** Advanced, Medium-Range, Air-to-Air Missiles (**AMRAAM**s) were carried late in the war by the 33rd TFW, but not used. When loaded, they replaced the AIM-9s on the inboard pylon stations.

The only Saudi kills were registered when a No. 13 Squadron F-15C scored a double kill on Iraqi F1EQ-5s carrying Exocet missiles. Although normally configured like the American Eagles, midway through the air war a Saudi F-15C was shown during a television report with conformal fuel tanks, a full load of missiles and three pylon-mounted Mk 84 LDGP bombs on wing and centerline stations.

An F-15C reveals its three fuel tanks, fuselage-mounted AIM-7Ms and wing-mounted AIM-9Ms.

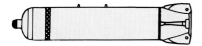

Above: SUU-30H/B with FMU-56 fuze.

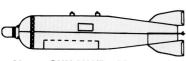

Above: CBU-87/B CEM with FZU-39/B fuze.

Above: CBU-89/B Gator with FZU-39/B fuze.

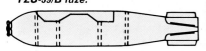

Above: BL755 cluster-bomb.

Above: An F-16C carrying a TMD, used to form both CEM and Gator cluster-bombs.

Above left: A Jaguar GR.Mk 1 with four BL755 cluster-bombs loaded on tandem beams.

Left: Cluster-bombs in action! Four SUU-30H/B dispensers at various stages of function.

Gulf Aircraft Weapons

F-15E (McDonnell Douglas Eagle)

Forty-eight F-15Es from both the 335th and 336th TFSs of the 4th TFW from Seymour Johnson AFB participated in Desert Storm. Based at Al Kharj, Saudi Arabia, each squadron flew about 1,100 missions. Using sports-car-name call signs, the 'Mud Hens' employed up to 12 bombs on Conformal Fuselage Tank (**CFT**) pylons. These included Mk 82 LDGP bombs, Mk 20, SUU-30H/B or TMD cluster-bombs.

At first, four AIM-9L/M missiles were carried, along with three 600-gal fuel tanks. (Sometimes, these tanks were borrowed from the light-gray, air-to-air F-15s.) As it became apparent that the Iraqi air force wouldn't play, the number of AIM-9s dwindled to as few as two, carried on the outboard shoulder stations. Some aircraft were seen on the ground loaded with bombs and a centerline tank, but no wing tanks. One of the most unusual loads seen (probably from early in the conflict) was three fuel tanks, outboard AIM-9L/Ms, a LANTIRN nav pod, six Mk 20s on the right

CFT and two AIM-7F/Ms on the left one! At least one aircraft was photographed with four AIM-7F/Ms loaded on its CFT.

All F-15Es were equipped with Low-Altitude, Navigation and Targetting, Infra-Red, for Night (**LANTIRN**) navigation pods mounted on the right inlet station. A very limited number of the still-developmental targetting pods (which were left-inlet mounted) deployed with the 335th TFS in December 1990 and then divided between the two squadrons.

For much of the war, large numbers of F-15Es were assigned to 'Scud' hunting, a duty they were better able to perform than anyone else because of their Synthetic Aperture Radar (**SAR**). For these missions, a two-ship formation would be launched. The leader carried four GBU-10C/Bs mounted on the front and rear 'bottom' CFT pylons, two 600-gal fuel tanks on the wing pylons, an empty centerline pylon and both types of LANTIRN pods. The `` wingman was configured similarly, but

without the targetting pod, and carried either six CBU-87/B CEM or 12 Mk 82 LDGP bombs.

The anti-armor missions conducted just prior to the beginning of the ground war also used the same basic two-ship tactics. These aircraft were seen with wing (but without centerline) fuel tanks carrying four GBU-12B/B Paveway II LGBs mounted on the front and back 'top' CFT pylons. Up to eight GBU-12s were carried, using both the

A night take-off of a F-15E carrying only a LANTIRN navigation pod.

'top' and 'bottom' CFT pylons for these 'tank plinking' operations. The wing aircraft, which weren't equipped with the targetting pods, had their GBU-12s 'buddy lased' from the lead F-15E.

F-16A/C (General Dynamics Fighting Falcon)

The F-16 community sent 249 aircraft to the Gulf, flying nearly 13,500 sorties (it is unclear if this includes the 24 normal plus additional 'Wild Weasel' F-16s deployed to Turkey). They were used from high altitude for road and rail reconnaissance, and bombing area targets such as barracks, factories, oil refineries and power plants, as well as daylight harassment bombing of the Iraqi army. While extensive, F-16 operations did relatively little damage when compared with A-10As or PGM-capable aircraft. This was because their bombing system, designed for low-altitude attacks, wasn't accurate enough for hitting tank-sized targets from the 10,000-ft-plus altitudes at which they were forced to fly because of the AAA threat. (During the last three weeks of the war, the weather was so bad that this had to be dropped to 7,000 ft.)

AIM-9L/Ms were carried on the wingtip stations and (rarely) on the outboard wing stations. Inboard wing tanks and a centerline ALQ-131 deep or ALQ-119 long ECM pod were standard. Although pods were predominantly 36375 gray, both olive drab and partially olive-drab/partially gray pods were seen as well. Mk 84 AIR, SUU-30H/B,

TMDs or AGM-65 Mavericks (on LAU-117s) were carried on the center wing pylons.

As operations moved into Kuwait, higher drag loads such as TERs with six Mk 82 LDGPs or 'slant-two' loads of SUU-30H/Bs or TMDs became possible. Also seen at this time were aircraft with no wing tanks carrying four pylon-mounted Mk 84 AIRs or Mk 84 LDGPs. (Although Mk 84 AIRs were normally equipped with a nose plug and tail fuze, they were sometimes seen with what appeared to be FMU-113 proximity fuzes when carried by F-16s.) It's possible, but unlikely, that M129 leaflet bombs were also employed.

As noted in the F-4G section, F-16Cs of the 23rd TFS carried a variety of weapon loads. Their basic configuration had both wingtip and outer wing AIM-9L/Ms, inboard fuel tanks and a centerline ALQ-131 deep ECM pod. Center wing stations carried AGM-45 or -88 anti-radiation missiles, Mk 82 or 84 LDGP bombs, and CBU-5BH/B or CBU-87 cluster bombs. They didn't carry any AGM-65 Mavericks. They would have carried LGBs, to be designated by F-4Es, had the war lasted longer.

F-16As of the 174th TFW (NY ANG's 'The Boys from Syracuse') were specially equipped for the Close Air Support (**CAS**) role and equipped with the Gun Pod Unit (**GPU**) -5 30-mm gun. Because software limitations prevented accurate aiming of the

In addition to two fuel tanks and four AIM-9L/Ms, this F-16C carries an ALQ-131 ECM pod and an MXU-648 baggage pod.

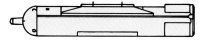

Above: CBU-55/72 Fuel-Air Explosive (FAE).

Below: Mk 77 napalm bomb.

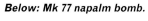
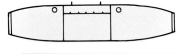

Above: Mk 77 napalm bomb loaded on an A-6E.

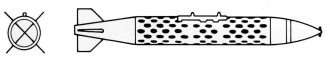
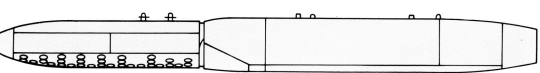

Left: BLG-66 Belouga cluster-bomb.

Above and below: Used only by RAF and RSAF Tornados, these massive JP 233 dispensers ejected runway-cratering bomblets from the rear section, and anti-personnel mines from the front (to discourage runway repair).

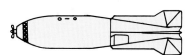

M117 GP 750-lb bomb with M904 fuze (above), and M117R 750-lb bomb with nose plug (below).

Below: M129 leaflet bomb with M904 fuze.

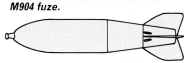

Gulf Aircraft Weapons

F-16A/C (continued)

guns, they were only used for one day. When used, the aircraft carried the GPU-5 on the centerline, two inboard fuel tanks, an AGM-65D on the right center wing pylon and an ALQ-119 long ECM pod on the left. Although the 174th fired 73 Mavericks during the war, they found it to be very workload-intensive for use on a fast, single-seat aircraft. The standard formation used by this unit was four aircraft, two carrying six Mk 82 LDGPs and the other two carrying six Mk 20s. (If only four bombs were carried, they were loaded as 'slant-twos'.) While they employed the CBU-87, without computer ballistics their F-16As weren't able to accurately deliver it.

The 72 Block-42 F-16Cs of the 388th TFW from Hill AFB, Utah, were equipped with LANTIRN pods mounted on the left chin station. No targetting pods (which would have been mounted on the right chin station) were used. (LANTIRN pods were mounted on the opposite sides of F-15s and -16s.) They did some 'Scud' hunting with a navigation pod, two wing tanks, a 'slant-two' load of CBU-87 CEM on center wing TERs, wingtip-mounted AIM-9Ms, and a centerline ALQ-131 ECM pod. A senior pilot stated that these aircraft didn't do "well on the battlefield" because they were forced to fly too high for LANTIRN to work well. They also flew some daytime missions with the same configuration except for pylon-mounted Mk 84 AIRs and no LANTIRN pod.

Towards the end of hostilities the newer, Global Positioning System (**GPS**)-equipped F-16Cs were finding targets, and determining accurate co-ordinates and passing them on to other F-16s. This system, known an **'Killer Scouts'**, was designed to maximize the effectiveness of the F-16s, despite their very short range. Consideration was given to having F-16s drop GBU-12s to be guided against Iraqi tanks by F-111Fs.

F/A-18A/C (McDonnell Douglas Hornet)

A centerline fuel tank appears to have been standard, as were wingtip-mounted AIM-9L/M missiles. For short-range missions, up to four pylon-mounted AGM-88 HARMs, Mk 83 or Mk 84 LDGP bombs were carried. Another option was Horizontal Ejector Rocks (HERs) on the inboard pylons loaded with Mk 82 LDGPs, with an additional Mk 82 LDGP on each outboard pylon. A very common configuration was inboard Mk 84 LDGPs and outboard AGM-88s. A third configuration was a fuel tank on the right inboard pylon and AGM-88s on the other wing pylons. For longer-range missions, fuel tanks were mounted on both inboard pylons, and the outboard pylons were loaded with either AGM-88s or dual bomb racks loaded with either four Mk 82 LDGPs or Mk 7 dispensers.

AIM-7F/M Sparrows were usually seen on F/A-18 fuselage stations (day missions), but ground-attack FLIR pods were also seen (night missions). One interesting configuration was tip AIM-9s, inboard fuel tanks, three pylon-mounted Mk 20s on the centerline and outboards, a left AIM-7, and right Laser Spot Tracker/Strike Camera (**LST/SCAM**) pod. Relatively poor performance of the LST/SCAM generated Navy interest in a LANTIRN-based system.

Some night-fighter F/A-18Ds were used as Fast Forward Air Controllers (**Fast FAC**s) with a right fuselage AIM-7 (but no AIM-9s),

An F/A-18 with tip-mounted AIM-9L/Ms, a centerline fuel tank and six Mk 82 LDGP bombs.

a left fuselage LST/SCAM, wing tanks, and two LAU-97 FFAR pods mounted on the outboard of dual bomb racks. One of these aircraft was the first to spot the massive retreat of the Iraqi army from Kuwait City. Three of the Fast FACs then co-ordinated the destruction of the convoy by other aircraft at the rate of eight aircraft every 15 minutes for several hours. It was reported that the Marines used CBU-78 Gator mines to block the highway, but it's unclear if the F/A-18D dropped them or directed another aircraft to.

Other weapons reportedly used by F/A-18s included AGM-45 Shrikes, AGM-62 Walleyes, AGM-65D Mavericks, AGM-123 Skipper IIs, ADM-141 TALDs, GBU-10E/B, -12D/B and -16B/B LGBs, Mk 77 napalm and CBU-72 FAE.

AH-1W (Bell Sea Cobra)

Sea Cobras primarily carried inboard LAU-68s and outboard sets of four multiple launchers to ground (**BGM**)-71 Tube-launched, Optically-tracked, Wire-guided (**TOW**) missiles. They also reportedly carried CBU-55 FAE, **AGM-114 Hellfire** anti-tank missiles and **AGM-122A Sidearm** anti-radiation missiles. The Sidearm was a modification of the AIM-9C Semi-Active Radar Homing (**SARH**) version of the Sidewinder family. It looked very much like an AIM-9D/G/H.

AH-64A (McDonnell Douglas Apache)

Apaches, led to their targets by Air Force MH-53J Pave Low IIIs, started the air war with attacks on Iraqi early warning radar sites. They also destroyed more than 500 tanks, 120 Armored Personnel Carriers (**APC**s), 120 artillery pieces, 30 AAA sites, 10 helicopters and 10 aircraft, and helped capture 4,500 Iraqi troops.

The standard Apache ordnance load was two sets of four AGM-114 Hellfire missiles mounted on its inboard pylons along with two 19-tube, 2.75-in FFAR pods (similar to the LAU-69, probably the M261) on the outboard pylons, although the positions were sometimes reversed. There were also reports of loads of 16 Hellfires being employed, but this appears to have been much less frequent.

An AH-64 over the desert. The M261 19-tube rocket pods are mounted outboard, with empty Hellfire launchers inboard.

OV-10D (Rockwell Bronco)

An AIM-9 launcher rail was seen mounted on either the left or right wing pylon (probably for carriage of AGM-122 Sidearms), with a 150-gal centerline fuel tank and two LAU-97 FFAR pods on the outboard sponsons. OV-10s also were reported to

A prewar photo of OV-10Ds loaded with LAU-97 rocket pods and three fuel tanks.

have carried LAU-68 and -69 FFAR pods, CBU-55 FAE, and CBU-78 Gator.

Left: Mk 82 LDGP 500-lb bomb with M904 fuze.

Below: Mk 82 AIR 500-lb bomb with nose plug and (below right) drawing of deployed ballute.

Left: Mk 82 LDGP 500-lb bomb with M904 on fuze extender.

Below: Mk 82 SE 500-lb bomb with M904 fuze.

Below: Three TER-mounted Mk 82 SE (Snakeyes) with M904 fuzes loaded on the centerline of a Kuwaiti A-4KU.

Combat bomb dumps aren't tidy affairs. M117s await fins (below), and (right) Mk 84s minus their fuzes.

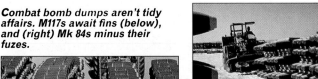

S-3B (Lockheed Viking)

VS-24 from the *Roosevelt* used one of its S-3Bs to attack an AAA site near Kuwait City, using six Mk 82 LDGPs dropped from TERs carried on its outboard pylons.

Buccaneer S.Mk 2 (British Aerospace)

Mobilized and deployed into combat in just 10 days, Buccaneers were used beginning on 2 February as a 'buddy lase' platform in support of Tornados. Using the US-developed **AVQ-23E Pave Spike** daytime-only laser-designator pod, these 12 Bahrain-based aircraft enabled Tornados to accurately deliver LGBs from medium altitudes.

The standard configuration was an **ALQ-101(V)-10** ECM pod on the right outboard, and the Pave Spike on the left inboard station. Despite the capability of carrying a slipper tank on the right inboard station, this does not appear to have been done; only pylons were seen to be fitted. However, AIM-9L/Ms were carried initially on the left outboard station.

Lasing for Tornados was done from level

Buccanneer S.Mk 2 with an AVQ-23E Pave Spike pod on the inboard pylon and an AIM-9L on the outboard pylon.

flight. Just prior to the beginning of the ground war, Buccaneers also began to drop their own Portsmouth Aviation CPU-123/B 1,000-lb Paveway II LGBs. This was done from a dive after the Tornados had dropped their bombs. The bombs were seen carried on both the right inboard and left outboard stations, but it's unclear if more than one at a time was carried.

The Buccaneers flew 218 sorties, guiding a total of 169 LGBs, including 48 of their own, while attacking 24 bridges and 15 airfields.

Hawk Mk 60 (British Aerospace)

Three Mk 83 LDGP bombs on the centreline and inboard pylons along with two AIM-9Ls on the outboard pylons were reported prior to the war as the standard combat load. However, it isn't clear that any Hawks saw combat.

Jaguar A (SEPECAT)

The French air force was based at Al Ahsa airfield with 27 Jaguars, 12 Mirage 2000s, four Mirage F1CRs and two Puma helicopters. A total of about 1,200 combat sorties was flown by these aircraft.

The standard Jaguar A load included the **Barem** ECM pod on the left outboard pylon and the **Phimat** chaff pod on the right. Very soon after the beginning of hostilities the Phimat pod was replaced with a Magic 2 air-

Jaguar A (continued)

to-air missile on at least some aircraft.

Two basic ordnance configurations were employed. One used a 264-gal centreline fuel tank and side-by-side bomb racks mounted on inboard wing pylons, each loaded with two of either **250-kg LDGP** or **Belouga** cluster-bombs. (The Belougas required low-altitude delivery tactics and for this reason saw very limited use.) The other used a fuel tank mounted on the left wing, an **AS 30L** laser-guided missile on the right, and a centreline Automatic Tracking Laser Illumination System (**ATLIS**) designator pod. About 60 AS 30Ls were fired during the war with approximately 80 per cent hitting their targets.

Reports indicated that 100-mm rockets were also employed.

Jaguar A launching on another mission. Visible are the 264-gal centreline fuel tank and Barem ECM pod.

Jaguar GR.Mk 1 (SEPECAT)

Twelve Jaguars from RAF Coltishall, UK, were based at Bahrain and flew 617 sorties during Desert Storm. Prior to the ground war they flew missions primarily in southern Kuwait. Once the ground war started they attacked the Republican Guard in northern Kuwait. Targets included SAM, AAA, Silkworm Surface-to-Surface Missiles (**SSM**), artillery, multiple rocket launchers, armor, barracks, storage areas and airfields.

The standard configuration included an ALQ-101 ECM pod on the left and a Matra Phimat chaff pod on the right outboard pylon. Additionally, airborne countermeasures ejection (**ALE**) -40 countermeasure dispensers were mounted beneath the engines. Overwing AIM-9L missiles were carried during the initial phases of the war.

During the first few days, two 264-gal tanks were carried on the inboard wing stations. However, that limited weapons carriage to two **British 1,000-lb bombs** on the centreline. To increase the weapons load, the configuration was changed to a

British Jaguar GR.Mk 1 with two overwing AIM-9Ls, Phimat chaff pod, finned-fuel tank and a BAe reconnaissance pod.

centreline fuel tank, with weapons carried on the inboard pylons. Four of the 1,000-lb bombs or improved **BL755** cluster-bombs could be mounted front and back on inboard pylons. While 750 1,000-lb bombs were dropped, only eight of the low-altitude-only BL755s were expended. CBU-87 CEM was rushed into service and 385 of them were dropped directly from the inboard pylons. Finally, 32 **LAU-5003** 19-tube pods of **CVR-7** 2.75-in FFARs were fired. No LGBs were delivered by Jaguars.

Beginning about 11 February, two aircraft were used for reconnaissance missions. One would use the standard BAe pod while the other used a LOng-Range, Oblique Photography (**LOROP**) pod. Both pods were centreline mounted, in addition to inboard pylon-mounted fuel tanks and the normal ECM pods.

Above: A B-52G fitted with an AGM-28 'Hound Dog' pylon, rack adapter beam and two MERs holding M117 GP bombs.

Above: FMU-113 proximity fuzes – the modern 'daisy-cutter'.

Below: Mk 83 LDGP 1,000-lb bomb with M904 fuze.

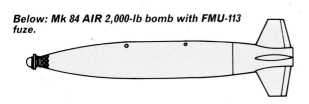

Below: Mk 84 AIR 2,000-lb bomb with FMU-113 fuze.

Above: An F-16C (deep ALQ-131 ECM pod on centreline) takes off with fuel tanks, AIM-9L/Ms and Mk 84 LDGPs. Below: An A-6E with GBU-12D/B, three Mk 83 LDGPs and centreline fuel tank.

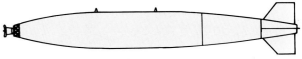

Above and left: Mk 84 LDGP with M904 fuze, and drawing of deployed ballute.

Gulf Aircraft Weapons

Mirage F1 (Dassault-Breguet)

French F1CRs carried **Raphael** Side-Looking Airborne Radar (**SLAR**) on their centerline, two 1200-liter underwing fuel tanks on the inboard pylons; a **Barem** ECM pod on the left and a **DB3163 Remora** ECM pod on the right outboard pylons; and two Magic 2 missiles on the wingtips. These aircraft were used prior to hostilities for border surveillance missions, but once war broke out were initially withheld to prevent confusion between good and bad F1s. Both the French F1CRs and Kuwaiti F1CK-2s also sometimes carried four 500-lb bombs (on the centerline) or two each R530Ds (on the inboard pylons with a 1200-liter fuel tank on the centerline).

Below: French Mirage F1CR and Jaguar A in formation, fitted with Barem ECM pods on the left outboard pylon.

Mirage 2000 (Dassault-Breguet)

Standard fit was a 1200-liter centerline fuel tank, two Matra **Super R530D** and two **Magic 2** air-to-air missiles. The Mirage 2000's lack of fuel capacity ensured that its pilots became very proficient at air-to-air refueling.

This Mirage 2000 sports two 1700-liter fuel tanks and Magic 2 AAMs with a clean centerline; a good deployment configuration.

Tornado F.Mk 3 (Panavia)

Based at Dhahran, Saudi Arabia, the 12 F.Mk 3s carried a standard load of four each of **Skyflash** (an AIM-7E-2 look-alike) and AIM-9L/Ms, as well as two fuel tanks. The four-finned, 495-gal fuel tanks were usually swapped with the GR.Mk 1s for their two-finned, 330-gal ones. Two Tracor ALE-40 chaff and flare dispensers were fitted beneath the engine bays, and Phimat dispenser pods were fitted to the right outboard AIM-9 rail.

Tornado F.Mk 3 with 'Hindenberger' fuel tanks, four belly-mounted Skyflashes, three AIM-9Ls and a chaff dispenser.

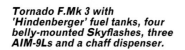

Tornado GR.Mk 1 (Panavia)

Three squadrons, each with 15 Tornado GR.Mk 1s, were based in the east at Bahrain (home of Snoopy and Triffid Airways) and Dhahran (with palm tree mission markings), while to the west were the shark-mouths of Tabuk (including nine ALARM and, eventually, five TIALD aircraft). An additional six GR.Mk 1A reconnaissance aircraft were also based at Dhahran. Because they had more powerful engines, all deployed aircraft were from RAF Germany, and (due to rotations) 61 actually saw combat.

The standard GR.Mk 1 configuration included AIM-9L/M missiles carried on the external shoulder stations of the inboard pylons. These pylons also mounted the external fuel tanks, which had the 330-gal GR.Mk 1 fuel tanks replaced by the 495-gal tanks of the F.Mk 3. A **SkyShadow** ECM pod was carried on the left outboard station, along with a **BOZ-107** countermeasurers dispenser pod on the right. The GR.Mk 1As flew 128 sorties and were configured like the GR.Mk 1s except they also carried two 330-gal fuel tanks under the fuselage. Unlike the F.Mk 3s, no ALE-40s were fitted to the GR.Mk 1s or GR.Mk 1As.

A total of about 100 JP 233 runway denial weapons (carried two at a time) was expended during the first few days of the air war. With the switch to medium-altitude tactics, loads of (at first) eight and (later) five British 1,000-lb bombs were employed. A total of about 4,200 of these bombs was dropped.

When teamed with Buccaneers for 'buddy lase' missions to deliver British 1,000-lb Paveway II LGBs, they carried up to three bombs on the two forward and centerline stations. About 990 of these bombs were delivered by Tornados. Beginning on

Tornado GR.Mk 1 with 'Hindenberger' fuel tanks, a BOZ-107 dispenser pod and CPU-123/B LGBs.

10 February, two pods which gave the Tornados a self-designation capability were introduced into combat. Known as Thermal Imaging And Laser Designator (**TIALD**), they were carried on the front left pylon. A total of 95 TIALD sorties was flown from Tabuk, permitting Red Sea-based Tornados to employ LGBs. Although TIALD aircraft were capable of delivering their own LGBs, in practice they carried an extra 330-gal fuel tank on the right fuselage.

Air-Launched, Anti-Radiation Missiles (**ALARM**s) could initially only be carried on the wing pylons, with two 330-gal fuel tanks on the fuselage pylons and one ALARM on each inboard wing pylon (ECM pods and AIM-9Ls were standard). However, by the beginning of hostilities, the standard configuration was 495-gal fuel tanks on the wing pylons with three ALARMs on the fuselage pylons. About 120 ALARMs were fired.

The war ended before the Tornados could begin the planned use of both CBU-87 CEM and GBU-10D/B LGBs.

Italian Tornados flew with the same basic configuration as the British ones, but their primary weapon was Mk 83 LDGPs dropped using level deliveries from medium altitude. They also refueled each other using a buddy refueling store similar to the US Navy D-704.

Saudi Tornado IDSs also employed JP 233 as well as British and US parachute-retarded bombs. Video appeared to show them with two Mk 84 LDGPs on outboard forward fuselage stations.

Above: SAMP Type 25 250-kg bomb.

Below and right: British 1,000-lb bomb; there are two types of low drag fins for these bombs, both with 23-in spans.

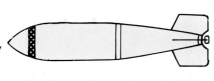

Above and below: BLU-82 15,000-lb blast bomb with M904 fuze on extender. Note elaborate tie-down to a standard cargo pallet – the whole lot was shoved out the back of an MC-130E!

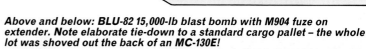

Powered Air-to-Ground Weapons

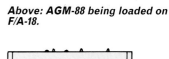

Above and above left: *An AS 30L is prepared for loading on a Jaguar A. Most fins are attached once the missile is actually mounted.*

Above: AGM-65 Maverick.

Above: *AGM-65D Maverick being prepared for loading. The silvery seeker head denotes a live IR round.*

Below: *F-4Gs (deep ALQ-131 ECM pod on left-front Sparrow well) with four AGM-88 HARMs and F-15 centerline fuel tank, but no AIM-7Fs.*

Above: AGM-84A-D Harpoon.

Above: AGM-84E SLAM.

Above: *AGM-88 being loaded on F/A-18.*

Above: 19 tube 2.75-in FFAR pod.

Above: AGM-88 HARM.

Below and bottom: *LAU-97 5.0-in FFAR pod.*

Above: AGM-45 Shrike.

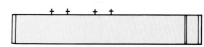

Air-to-Air Missiles

Right: *AIM-9P-3 Sidewinder.*

Left: *AIM-9L/M Sidewinder.*

Left: *Magic 2.*

Above: *Typical Mirage 2000 combat load of Magic 2 short-range AAM (left) and Super R530D (right).*

Above: *AIM-9L/M being carried to a fighter.*

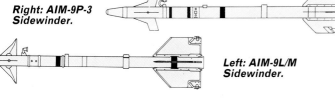

Above: Super R530D.

Above: Skyflash.

Above and below: *AIM-54C Phoenix. F-14 with a typical combat load of AIM-9M Sidewinders, AIM-7M Sparrows, a single AIM-54C Phoenix and fuel tanks.*

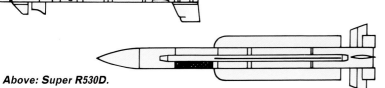

Above: AIM-7F/M Sparrow.

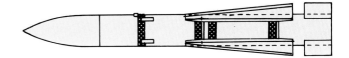

Below: *AIM-120A AMRAAM.*

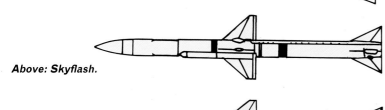

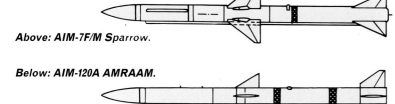

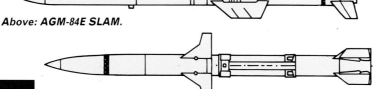

Royal Air Force Nose Art

Whereas most US nose art appeared after the war, and was relatively uncommon, virtually all RAF types in-theater received nose art during the conflict.

Buccaneer XX901/N 'The Flying Mermaid/Glen Elgin' (starboard)

Buccaneer XV863/S 'Sea Witch/Tamnavoulin' (starboard)

Buccaneer XX885/L 'Hello Sailor/Famous Grouse' (starboard)

Buccaneer XX899/P 'Laser Lips Laura/Linkwood'

Buccaneer XX895/G 'Jaws/Glenfiddich' (starboard)

Buccaneer XX895/G 'Jaws/Glenfiddich' (starboard)

Buccaneer XX901/N 'The Flying Mermaid/Glen Elgin'

Buccaneer XW533/A 'Miss Jolly Roger/Glenfarclas'

Buccaneer XW547/R 'Guinness Girl/The Macallan' (starboard)

Buccaneer XX885/L 'Hello Sailor/Famous Grouse'

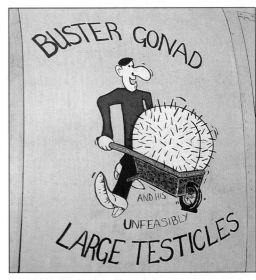

Jaguar GR.Mk 1 XZ118 'Buster Gonad . . .'

Buccaneer XW530/E 'Glenmorangie'

Jaguar GR.Mk 1A XZ356/N 'Mary Rose'

Jaguar GR.Mk 1 XZ364/ 'Sadman'

Jaguar GR.Mk 1 XZ375/ 'The avid Guardian reader'

Jaguar GR.Mk 1 XZ119/ 'Katrina Jane'

Jaguar GR.Mk 1 XX962/ 'Fat Slags'

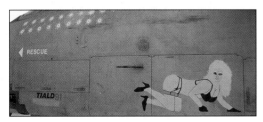

Tornado GR.Mk 1 (TIALD) ZA406/BC

Tornado GR.Mk 1 ZA456/M 'Hello Kuwait, G'bye Iraq'

Tornado GR.Mk 1 (TIALD) ZD739/AC 'Armoured Charmer'

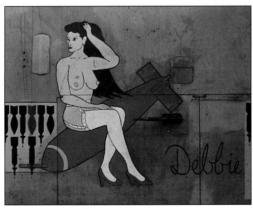

Tornado GR.Mk 1 ZD790/D 'Debbie'

Tornado GR.Mk 1 ZD740/DA 'Dhahran Annie'

Tornado GR.Mk 1 ZD744/BD 'Buddha'

Tornado GR.Mk 1 ZA491/N 'Nikki'

Tornado GR.Mk 1 ZD746/AB 'Alarm Belle' (ex 'Arse Bandeet')

Tornado GR.Mk 1 ZA471/E 'Emma'

Royal Air Force Nose Art

Tornado GR.Mk 1 (ALARM) ZD719/AD 'Check Six'

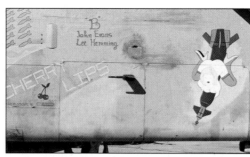

Tornado GR.Mk 1 ZD850/CL 'Cherry Lips'

Tornado GR.Mk 1 ZA374/CN 'Miss Behavin' '

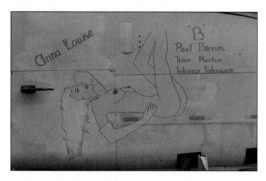

Tornado GR.Mk 1 ZD715/AL 'Anna Louise' (starboard)

Tornado GR.Mk 1 ZD715/AL 'Anna Louise'

Tornado GR.Mk 1 ZD890/O 'Hullo Kuwait, G'bye Iraq'

Tornado GR.Mk 1 ZD809/BA 'Awesome Annie'

Tornado GR.Mk 1 (ALARM) ZD748/AK 'Anola Kay'

Tornado GR.Mk 1 ZD715/DB 'Luscious Lizzie'

Tornado GR.Mk 1 ZA447/EA 'MiG Eater'

Tornado GR.Mk 1 ZA452/GK 'Gulf Killer'

Tornado GR.Mk 1 ZA465/FK 'Foxy Killer'

Victor K.Mk 2 XH672 'Maid Marian'

Royal Air Force Nose Art

Tornado GR.Mk 1 ZA463/Q 'Flying High' (starboard)

Victor K.Mk 2 XH671 'Sweet Sue' (ex 'Slinky Sue')

Hercules C.Mk 1P XV190 'Betty Boob'

Victor K.Mk 2 XL231 'Lusty Lindy'

Victor K.Mk 2 XL164 'Saucy Sal'

Hercules C.Mk 1P XV192 'The Silver Tounged Cavalier'

Victor K.Mk 2 XM717 'Lucky Lou'

Hercules C.Mk 1P XV297 'Where's the beach?'

Victor K.Mk 2 XM715 'Teasin' Tina'

Hercules C.Mk 1P XV306 'The Baron'

Hercules C.Mk 1P XV292 'Dennis the Menace'

Kills and Losses

AERIAL VICTORIES

(Kills on same date are not listed in time sequence.)

Kill No. 1
17 January 1991:
MiG-29 by F-15C 85-0125, 58th TFS/33rd TFW, Eglin (Tabuk) using AIM-7M. Captain Jon K. Kelk. Credited as first kill of the war.

Kills Nos 2 and 3
17 January 1991:
Two Mirage F1EQs by F-15C 85-0105, 58th TFS/33rd TFW, Eglin (Tabuk) using AIM-7M. Captain Robert E. Graeter.

Kill No. 4
17 January 1991:
Mirage F1EQ by EF-111A 66-0016, 42nd ECS/66th ECW, Upper Heyford (Taif). Captain James Denton (pilot) and Captain Brent Brandon (EWO). MiG gave chase to EF-111A over western Iraq and fired missile. EF-111 pilot dived to low altitude, ejected chaff and flares and banked hard right, causing MiG to crash. Not on official list.

Kill No. 5
17 January 1991:
Mirage F1EQ by F-15C 83-0017, 71st TFS/1st TFW, Langley (Dhahran), using AIM-7M. Captain Steven W. 'Tater' Tate. West of Baghdad.

Kills Nos 6 and 7
17 January 1991:
F-7A (MiG-21) by F/A-18C 163508, VFA-81 'Sunliners'/CVW-17, USS *Saratoga*, using AIM-9M. Lieutenant Commander Mark I. 'MRT' Fox.
F-7A (MiG-21M) by F/A-18C 163502, VFA-81 'Sunliners'/CVW-17, USS *Saratoga*, using AIM-7M. Lieutenant Nicholas 'Mongo' Mongillo. Four VFA-81 Hornets were en route to a ground target when attacked by MiGs. E-2 Hawkeye from VAW-125 vectored two Hornets to shoot down the MiGs.

Kills Nos 8 and 9
17 January 1991:
MiG-29 by F-15C 85-0107, 58th TFS/33rd TFW, Eglin (Tabuk), using AIM-7M. Captain Charles J. 'Sly' Magill, USMC. Captain Magill on exchange to 58th TFS at the time of Desert Storm.
MiG-29 by F-15C 85-0108, 58th TFS/33rd TFW, Eglin (Tabuk), using AIM-7M. Captain Rhory R. 'Hoser' Draeger.
Two MiGs on CAP south of Al Taqaddum airfield.

Kills Nos 10 and 11
19 January 1991:
MiG-25 by F-15C 85-0099, 58th TFS/33rd TFW, Eglin (Tabuk), using AIM-7M. Captain Lawrence E. 'Cherry' Pitts.
MiG-25 by F-15C 85-0101, 58th TFS/33rd TFW, Eglin (Tabuk), using AIM-7M. Captain Richard C. Tollini.

Kill No. 12
19 January 1991:
MiG-29 by F-15C 85-0114, 58th TFS/33rd TFW, Eglin (Tabuk), maneuver kill. Captain Cesar A. 'Rico' Rodriguez. MiG attempting to evade F-15 attack, misjudged pull-out and flew into ground.

Kill No. 13
19 January 1991:
MiG-19 by F-15C 85-0122, 58th TFS/33rd TFW, Eglin (Tabuk), using AIM-7M. Captain Craig W. Underhill.

Kill No. 14
19 January 1991:
Mirage F1EQ by F-15C 79-0069, 525th TFS/36th TFW, Bitburg (Incirlik), using AIM-7M. Captain David S. Prather.

Kill No. 15
19 January 1991:
Mirage F1EQ by F-15C 79-0021, 32nd TFS/32nd TFG, Soesterberg (Incirlik), using AIM-7M. Lieutenant David G. Sveden.

Kills Nos 16 and 17
24 January 1991:
Two Mirage F1EQs by F-15C, No. 13 Squadron, Royal Saudi Air Force, Dhahran, using AIM-9Ps. Captain Ayehid Salah al-Shamrani. Mirages escorting at least one other Mirage which was carrying Exocet anti-ship missile.

Kills Nos 18, 19 and 20
26 January 1991:
MiG-23 by F-15C 85-0119, 58th TFS/33rd TFW, Eglin (Tabuk), using AIM-7M. Captain Rhory R. 'Hoser' Draeger (second kill).
MiG-23 by F-15C 85-0104, 58th TFS/33rd TFW, Eglin (Tabuk), using AIM-7M. Captain Anthony E. 'Kimo' Schiavi.
MiG-23 by F-15C 85-0114, 58th TFS/33rd TFW, Eglin (Tabuk), using AIM-7M. Captain Cesar A. 'Rico' Rodriguez (second kill).
Four F-15s were vectored towards four Iraqi jets leaving H2 airfield when four more MiG-23s took off. One MiG turned back and landed, but other three engaged and destroyed.

Kills Nos 21, 22, 23 and 24
27 January 1991:
Two MiG-23s by F-15C 84-0025, 53rd TFS/36th TFW, Bitburg (Al Kharj), using AIM-9M. Captain Jay T. Denney.
MiG-23 and Mirage F1EQ by F-15C 84-0027, 53rd TFS/36th TFW, Bitburg (Al Kharj), using AIM-7M. Captain Benjamin D. Powell. South of Baghdad.

Kill No. 25
29 January 1991:
MiG-23 by F-15C 79-0022, 53rd TFS/36th TFW, Bitburg (Al Kharj), using AIM-7M. Captain Donald S. Watrous. MiG attempting to flee to Iran.

Kill No. 26
29 January 1991:
MiG-23 by F-15C 85-0102, 58th TFS/33rd TFW, Eglin (Tabuk), using AIM-7M. Captain David G. Rose. MiG attempting to flee to Iran.

Kill No. 27
2 February 1991:
Il-76 by F-15C 79-0074, 525th TFS/36th TFW, Bitburg (Incirlik), using AIM-7M. Captain Gregory P. 'Dutch' Masters.

Kills Nos 28, 29, 30 and 31
6 February 1991:
Two MiG-21s by F-15C 79-0078, 53rd TFS/36th TFW, Bitburg (Al Kharj), using AIM-9M. Captain Thomas N. 'Vegas' Dietz.
Two Su-25s by F-15C 84-0019, 53rd TFS/36th TFW, Bitburg (Al Kharj), using AIM-9M. Lieutenant Robert W. 'Digs' Hehemann.
Four aircraft caught attempting to escape to Iran.

Kill No. 32
6 February 1991:
Mi-8 by F-14A 162603, VF-1, 'Wolf Pack'/CVW-2, USS *Ranger*, using AIM-9M. Lieutenant Donald S. Broce (pilot) and Commander Ron D. McElraft (RIO).

Kill No. 33
6 February 1991:
BO 105 by A-10 77-0205, 706th TFS/926th TFG (AFres), New Orleans (King Fahd), using GAU-8. Captain Robert R. Swain, Jr. First ever kill for A-10. Two gun passes following anti-armor mission.

Kills Nos 34, 35 and 36
7 February 1991:
Two Su-20/22s by F-15C 85-0102, 58th TFS/33rd TFW, Eglin (Tabuk), using AIM-7M. Captain Anthony R. Murphy.
Su-20/22 by F-15C 85-0124, 58th TFS/33rd TFW, Eglin (Tabuk), using AIM-7M. Colonel Rick N. Parsons. 'Fitters' heading for sanctuary in Iran.

Kill No. 37
7 February 1991:
Helicopter by F-15C 80-0003. 525th TFS/36th TFW, Bitburg (Incirlik), using AIM-7M. Major Randy W. May. Thought to be Mil Mi-8 'Hip'.

Kill No. 38
11 February 1991:
Helicopter by F-15C 79-0048, 525th TFS/36th TFW, Bitburg (Incirlik), using AIM-7M. Captain Steven B. Dingee. Thought to be Puma.

Kill No. 39
11 February 1991:
Helicopter by F-15C 80-0012, 525th TFS/36th TFW, Bitburg (Incirlik), using AIM-7M. Captain Mark McKenzie. Thought to be Mi-8.

Kill No. 40
14 February 1991:
Helicopter by F-15E 89-0487, 335th TFS/4th TFW, Seymour Johnson (Al Kharj), using GBU-10. Captain Richard T. Bennett (pilot) and Captain Daniel B. Bakke (WSO). Thought to be Hughes 500. Destroyed by 2,000-lb laser-guided bomb which struck it in the hover. Near Al Quain while F-15E on 'Scud' patrol.

Kill No. 41
15 February 1991:
Helicopter by A-10A 81-0964, 511th TFS/10th TFW, Alconbury (King Fahd), using GAU-8. Captain Todd K. Sheehy. Thought to be Mil Mi-8 'Hip' or possibly Puma. First firing pass 300 rounds, second 200 rounds.

Post-war Kill No. 1
20 March 1991:
Su-22 by F-15C 84-0014, 53rd TFS/Bitburg (Al Kharj), using AIM-9M. Captain John T. Doneski.
Ceasefire conditions restricted Iraq to helicopter flights only.

Post-war Kill No. 2
22 March 1991:
Su-22 by F-15C 84-0010, 53rd TFS/36th TFW, Bitburg (Al Kharj), using AIM-9M. Captain Thomas N. 'Vegas' Dietz (third kill).

Post-war Kill No. 3
22 March 1991:
Pilatus PC-9 by F-15C 84-0015, 53rd TFS/36th TFW, Bitburg (Al Kharj), maneuver kill. Lieutenant Robert W. 'Digs' Hehemann (third kill).
PC-9 was accompanying Su-22 when both were attacked. No missile fired at PC-9 but pilot bailed out when intercepted.

US COMBAT LOSSES

17 January 1991, Combat Loss # 1:
F/A-18C 163484 (AA 403), VFA-81, USS *Saratoga* (CV-60). Lieutenant Commander Michael Scott 'Spike' Speicher, 33, Jacksonville, Florida, killed. Downed by SA-6.

17 January 1991, Combat Loss # 2:
A-6E 161668 (AA 510), callsign RAYGUN 510, VA-35 'Black Panthers', USS *Saratoga* (CV-60). Pilot Lieutenant Robert Wetzel, 30, New Jersey Institute of Technology (1985), POW, released 4 March 1991. Bombardier/navigator Lieutenant Jeffrey N. Zaun, 28, Cherry Hill, NJ, POW, US Naval Academy (1984), released 4 March 1991.

17 January 1991, Combat Loss # 3:
A-6E 158539 (AA 502), VA-35, CV-60. Returned safely but damaged beyond economical repair. Crew okay.

18 January 1991, Combat Loss # 4:
A-6E 152928, VA-155, CV-61. Lieutenant William T. Costen, 27, of St Louis, pilot, killed. Lieutenant Charles J. Turner, 29, of Richfield, Minnesota, bombardier/navigator, killed. Remains were turned over to Red Cross by Iraqis. Four A-6Es were *en route* to target flying 30-second separation in trail at 500 ft, 365 nm from *Ranger* in bad weather, when engaged by ground fire. The number two in the strike package was hit, apparently from the three-o'clock position. The crew apparently did not eject.

18 January 1991, Combat Loss # 5:
F-15E, 4th TFW(P)/4th TFW. Majors Thomas F. Koritz, 39, of Rochelle, Illinois, pilot, and Donnie R. Holland, 42, of Bastrop, Louisiana, WSO, killed. Remains returned to US in mid-March.

18 January 1991, Combat Loss # 6:
OV-10A 155435, VMO-2. Lieutenant Colonel Clifford M. Acree, 39, of Oceanside, California, pilot, POW; Chief Warrant Officer Guy L. Hunter, 46, of Camp Pendleton, California, POW.

19 January 1991, Combat Loss # 7:
F-4G 69-7571, 81st TFS/52nd TFW, Bahrain. Pilot Captain Tim Burke. Crew okay. Copyrighted story from *Inside the Pentagon* 31 January: "An investigation has revealed that enemy fire, not mechanical failure, caused the 19 January crash of a USAF F-4G 'Wild Weasel', according to DoD officials. The revelation comes as F-4G supporters in the Air Force, claiming that the 'Wild Weasels' have 'proved invaluable in Operation Desert Storm', move to save some of the ageing F-4G fleet from an imminent retirement.

"Air Force sources last week said that the F-4G had run out of gas while trying to land and the Defense Department classified the cause of the crash as a mechanical failure. DoD spokesman Jan Walker said this week that the crash was reclassified as a 'hostile loss' on 28 January after the investigation revealed that a bullet had pierced the aircraft's fuel tank. The puncture caused 'a loss of fuel pressure' and the eventual downing of the 'Wild Weasel', said Walker. Both crew members successfully ejected before it hit Saudi Arabian soil.

"Returning from the mission, the 'running on empty' 'Wild Weasel' had sought aerial refueling, said a source. A dense fog scuttled the refueling and the F-4G was quickly directed towards a friendly Saudi airstrip by a USAF Airborne Warning & Control System (AWACS) aircraft.

"The airstrip was equipped with runway lights, but no approach lights, requiring the use of precision approach radar, he said. The first four landing attempts were unsuccessful. During the fifth pass the aircraft ran out of fuel. Its engine seized and both crew members used their ejection seats to 'punch out' of the aircraft, said the source."

20 January 1991, Combat Loss # 8:
F-16C 87-0257, 614th TFS/401st TFW(TJ), Qatar. Captain Harry M. ('Mike') Roberts, 30, of Savannah, Georgia, POW.

20 January 1991, Combat Loss # 9:
F-15E 88-1692, 4th TFW(P). Colonel David W. Eberly, 43, of Goldsboro, NC, POW; Major Thomas E. Griffith, Jr, 34, of Sparta, NJ, POW, released 4 March 1991. F-15E disappeared on a night mission. POWs arrived at Andrews AFB 10 March 1991. Eberly's name was painted on F-15E-48-MC 89-0491, 334th TFS/4th TFW (not a Desert Storm participant), seen at Langley AFB 8 March 1991.

20 January 1991, Combat Loss # 10:
F-16. Major Jeffrey Scott Tice, 35, of Sellersville, PA.

21 January 1991, Combat Loss # 11:
F-14A(Plus) 161430 (AA 212), VF-103, CV-60, callsign CLUBLEAF 212. Pilot Lieutenant Devon Jones rescued by two AF A-10 Thunderbolts and Special Ops helicopter; RIO Lieutenant Lawrence Randolph ('Rat') Slade, 26, of Wayland, Massachusetts, POW. A TARPS bird downed by derivative of the SA-2 developed by the Iraqis with a ground-guided optical tracker.

Kills and Losses

US COMBAT LOSSES (continued)

24 January 1991, Combat Loss # 12: **F-16**. Pilot rescued in Persian Gulf by SH-60B of HSL-44 Detachment 8 from guided missile frigate *Nicholas* (FFG-47).

28 January 1991, Combat Loss # 13: **AV-8B** 163518, VMA-311, Cherry Point (King Abdul Aziz Airfield). Captain Michael C. Berryman, 28, of Cleveland, Oklahoma, POW. Released 5 March 1991.

31 January 1991, Combat Loss # 14: **AC-130H** 69-6567. Fourteen crew members killed, originally listed as missing. Remained after daylight to assist Marines threatened by a 'Frog'-7 site. Apparently was shot down in a 'lucky shot' by a hand-held missile. Divers found the undersea wreckage on 6 March 1991. Crew: First Lieutenant Thomas Clifford Bland, 26, of Gaithersburg, Maryland; Staff Sergeant John P. Blessinger, 33; Master Sergeant Paul G. Buegge, 43; Sergeant Barry M. Clark, 26; Captain Arthur Galvan, 33; Captain William D. Grimm, 28; Staff Sergeant Timothy R. Harrison, 31; Technical Sergeant Robert K. Hodges, 28; Sergeant Damon V. Kanuha, 28; Master Sergeant James B. May, 30; Staff Sergeant John L. Oelschlager, 28; Staff Sergeant Mark J. Schmauss, 30; Captain Dixon L. Walters, 29; Major Paul J. Weaver, 34.

2 February 1991, Combat Loss # 15: **A-6E** 155632 (AJ 531), VA-36 'Road Runners', CVN-71. Lieutenant Patrick K. Connor, 25, and Lieutenant Commander Barry T. Cooke, 35, missing in action, were based on the USS *Theodore Roosevelt*. By 'optical AAA'.

2 February 1991, Combat Loss # 16: **A-10**. Captain Richard D. Storr, 29, of Spokane, Washington, POW. By 'optical AAA'.

5 February 1991, Combat Loss # 17: **F/A-18A**, VFA-87. Lieutenant Robert J. Dwyer, 32, of Worthington, Ohio, killed.

9 February 1991, Combat Loss # 18: **AV-8B** 162081 (CG-09), callsign JUMP 57 (usual callsign SHANK), VMA-231/MAG-13. Over Kuwait. Captain Russell A. C. ('Bart') Sanborn, 27, of Deland, Florida, POW.

14 February 1991, Combat Loss # 19: **EF-111A** 66-0023 (ex-Combat Lancer aircraft), 42nd ECS/66th ECW, Incirlik (Upper Heyford). Crashed just over border in Saudi Arabia. Captain Douglas L. Bradt, 29, pilot, of Houston, killed; Captain Paul R. Eichenlaub II, EWO, 29, of Bentonville, Arkansas, killed. Apparently shot while over Iraq or Kuwait, whether by missile or AAA is not yet known. No doubt fearful that some of the plane's supersecret gear would fall into enemy hands, the pilot managed to nurse his aircraft back across the border, into Saudi airspace, before ejecting. He and his electronics operator were both found dead later, but American ground troops reached the plane's wreckage and posted guards.

14 February 1991, Combat Loss # 20: **A-10A**, 353rd TFS/354th TFW, Myrtle Beach (see next entry). First Lieutenant Robert James Sweet, 24, of Washington, Pennsylvania, USAF Academy (1988), POW, captured 15 February 1991. Released 5 March.

14 February 1991, Combat Loss # 21: **A-10A**, 353rd TFS/354th TFW, Myrtle Beach. Two A-10s shot down while attacking Iraqi Republican Guard tanks in northwestern Kuwait. Captain Steven Richard Phillis, 30, of Rock Island, Ill, killed. Remains recovered and identified and funeral held 17 April 1991. Phillis' name appeared on aircraft 78-0699, which survived the war. The two losses on 14 February apparently were 78-0722 and 79-0130.

17 February 1991, Combat Loss # 22: **F-16C** block 25 84-1218, 17th TFS/363rd TFW(P). Captain Scott ('Spike') Thomas, 27, of Texas, had engine fire coming off target. Down 40 miles in enemy territory; pilot rescued by helicopter. Fellow pilot First Lieutenant Eric ('Neck') Dodson aided rescue.

19 February 1991, Combat Loss # 23: **OA-10A** 76-0543, 23rd TASS/602nd TACW, callsign NAIL 53. Lieutenant Colonel Jeffrey D. Fox, 40, of Fall River, Massachusetts, operations officer, POW.

20 February 1991, Combat Loss # 24: **OH-58**. CWO Hal H. Reichely, 27, of Marietta, Georgia; SPC Michael D. Daniels, 20, of Fort Leavenworth, Kansas, both killed. Crashed on night mission.

21 February 1991, Combat Loss # 25: **MH-60** special ops helo. Seven killed; cover story said crashed in Saudi Arabia but actually in Iraq.
Note: Army is not believed to have any MH-60 other than MH-60K in test status in US. Air Force has some MH-60s. This incident does not appear on any official documents and may be a 'garble' for the non-combat loss of a UH-60 on the same date.

23 February 1991, Combat Loss # 26: **AV-8B** 161573, VMA-542, Cherry Point (King Abdul Aziz Airfield). Captain James N. Wilbourne, killed.

25 February 1991, Combat Loss # 27: **AV-8B** 163190, VMA-542, Cherry Point (King Abdul Aziz Airfield). Pilot, Captain Scott Walsh, rescued, possibly by SH-60.

25 February 1991, Combat Loss # 28: **OH-58**. Listed in DoD working document as an AH-64. Crashed in fog. Crew okay.

25 February 1991, Combat Loss # 29: **OV-10A** 155424 ER-15, VMO-1/MAG 13. Major Joseph J. Small, 39, of Racine, Wisconsin, pilot, POW. Observer Captain David M. Spellacy, 28, of Columbus, Ohio, killed. Shoulder-mounted missile.

27 February 1991, Combat Loss # 30: **F-16C** block 25 84-1390, 10th TFS (Hahn)/363rd TFW(P), UAE. Captain William F. Andrews, 32, of Waterloo, New York, instructor pilot, POW. USAF Academy (1980). Reported by one source to have been flying too low and hit by SA-16. Awarded the Air Force Cross for preventing missile shooters from getting a wingman.

27 February 1991, Combat Loss # 31: **UH-60**, 101st Airborne Division. Shot down in southern Iraq trying to rescue F-16 pilot Andrews. Major (Dr) Rhonda L. Cornum, 36 (flight surgeon for the 2nd Attack Helicopter Battalion), of Freeville, NY, POW; SPC Troy A. Dunlap, 20, of Massac, Illinois, POW; Staff Sergeant Daniel J. Stamaris, Jr, 31, of Boise, Idaho, POW. Captain Reginald C. Underwood, 27, of Lexington, Kentucky; CWO Robert G. Godfrey, 32, of Phoenix, Alabama; Staff Sergeant William T. Butts, 30, of Waterford, Connecticut; CWO Philip M. Garvey, 39, of Pensacola, Florida; Sergeant Patbouvier E. Ortiz, 27, of Ridgewood, New York, all killed.

27 February 1991, Combat Loss # 32: **AV-8B** 162740, VMA-331, USS *Nassau* (LHA-4). Captain Reginald C. Underwood, 27, of Lexington, Kentucky, killed.

27 February 1991, Combat Loss # 33: **OA-10A** 77-0197, 23rd TASS/602nd TAW, callsign NAIL 51. First Lieutenant Patrick B. Olson, 26, of Washington, NC, killed. Bad weather. Hit, attempted to recover at FOL, aircraft flipped over, killing pilot. The aircraft was buried at the FOL.

28 February 1991, Combat Loss # 34: **UH-60**, 1st Aviation Regiment, Fort Riley, Kansas. Crew killed: First Lieutenant Donaldson P. Tillar III, 25, of Miller School, Virginia; WO1 David G. Pleach, 23, of Portsmouth, New Hampshire; WO George R. Swartzendruber, 35, of San Diego, California; WO John K. Morgan, 28, of Bellevue, Washington; Staff Sergeant Johnathan H. Kamm, 25, of Mason, Ohio; SFC Gary E. Streeter, 39, of Manhattan, Kansas; Sergeant Cheryl L. O'Brien, of Long Beach, California; Sergeant Jason C. Carr, 24, of Halifax, Virginia; Sergeant Lee A. Belas, 22, of Port Orchard, Washington.

28 February 1991, Combat Loss # 35: **UH-1**, US Army. Crew killed: First Lieutenant Daniel H. Graybeal, 25, of Johnson City, Tennessee; WO1 Kerry O. Hein, 28, of Sound Beach, New York; Staff Sergeant Michael R. Robson, 30, of Seminola, Florida.

COALITION AIR LOSSES

PREWAR LOSSES

18 October 1990, British Prewar Loss # 1: **Tornado GR.Mk 1** ZA466/FH, No. 16 Squadron, Tabuk. Arrester barrier was incorrectly raised at the approach end of the runway and caught the main undercarriage, forcing the aircraft sharply down on the runway. Squadron Leaders Ivor Walker and Bobby Anderson ejected, minor injuries. Was replaced at Tabuk by ZA460 (FD). Thought to have suffered Category 4 damage and shipped back to UK for repairs. Arrived at Abingdon by road transport 23 November 1990. Had deployed on 9 October 1990 to Akrotiri and then to Tabuk. Spine broken, fire in refueling probe assembly. In store at Wroughton, repair unlikely.

13 November 1990, British Prewar Loss # 2: **Jaguar GR.Mk 1A** XX754, No. 54 Squadron. Flight Lieutenant Keith Collister killed. Crashed while on a low-level flight over Qatar. Had deployed 2 November 1990 from Coltishall via a night stop at Akrotiri to Bahrain.

13 January 1991, British Prewar Loss # 3: **Tornado GR.Mk 1** ZD718/BH, No. 14 Squadron. Crashed on a low-level training mission. Flight Lieutenants Kieran Duffy and Norman Dent killed. Had deployed to Saudi Arabia from Brüggen, and was in place by 4 January 1991.

COMBAT LOSSES

17 January 1991, British Combat Loss # 1: **Tornado GR.Mk 1** ZD791/BG, No. XV Squadron, Muharraq. Flight Lieutenant John Peters, 28, POW, released 4 March 1991; Flight Lieutenant Adrian ('John') Nichol, 27, POW, released 5 March 1991. Lost Thursday early morning; second wave attack on Shaibah airbase with 1,000-lb bombs. Reports suggested that injuries to the crew were the result of a bird strike which caused the loss of this jet and the crew's ejection. Nichol: "Parachute drill went out of the window. We landed on our backsides."

Early reports were that the aircraft crashed in Iraq as a result of a technical problem rather than combat damage. One report claimed they hit a buzzard which went down an engine intake. The crew reported an engine fire before ejecting. There were reports of an attempted rescue. Current reports suggest that flak hit the Sidewinder missile, which exploded and 'took out' the engine.

18 January 1991 (17 January GMT), British Combat Loss # 2: **Tornado GR.Mk 1** ZA392/EK, No. XV Squadron, Muharraq (CO No. 27 Squadron). Crew killed: Wing Commander Nigel Elsdon, 39, pilot; Flight Lieutenant Robert ('Max') Collier, 42. Both men home-based at Marham. Elsdon was the most senior allied officer killed in the campaign. Crashed three minutes after JP 233 attack on Shaibah, possibly hit by SAM. Bodies arrived in UK 19 March 1991.

20 January 1991, British Combat Loss # 3: **Tornado GR.Mk 1** ZA396, Muharraq, No. 27 Squadron. Flight Lieutenant David Waddington, 24, pilot, POW; Flight Lieutenant Robert Stewart, 44, navigator, POW, both released 5 March 1991. Lost on an attack mission on Tallil airfield in southern Iraq, possibly hit by Roland SAM. Stewart reportedly captured by Iraqi civilians on 23 January 1991 and handed to military authorities in return for payment of $20,000.

22 January 1991, British Combat Loss # 4: **Tornado GR.Mk 1** ZA467/FF, No. 16 Squadron, Tabuk. Squadron Leader Gary Lennox, 34, pilot, and Squadron Leader Kevin Weeks, 37, both killed. Both from Laarbruch. During attack on Ar Rutbah radar station using 1,000-lb bombs.

23 January 1991, British Combat Loss # 5: **Tornado GR.Mk 1** ZA403/CO, No. 17 Squadron, Dhahran. Flying Officer Simon Burges, 23, pilot, POW; Squadron Leader Robert Ankerson, 40, navigator, POW, both released 5 March 1991. Initially reported as lost on a combat mission that was not against an Iraqi airfield, this due to a change of tactics. Bomb exploded on release, detonating others.

14 February 1991, British Combat Loss # 6: **Tornado GR.Mk 1** ZD717, No. XV Squadron, Muharraq. Flight Lieutenant Rupert Clark, 31, pilot, POW, released 6 March 1991; Flight Lieutenant Stephen Hicks, 26, navigator, killed. Both from Laarbruch. Hit by two SA-2s on LGB attack over Al Taqaddum airfield. General radio chat drowned out warnings. Aircraft last in eight-Tornado, four-Buccaneer package. This was the only such raid, RAF reverting to two Buccaneers with four Tornados.

17 January 1991, Italian Combat Loss # 1: **Tornado** MM7074, 50° Stormo/155° Gruppo. Eight Italian Tornados took off on a mission which required air refueling *en route*. One aborted before the refueling rendezvous with mechanical problems. Of the remaining seven, six were unable to accomplish the refueling transfer with an American KC-135 because of pilot skill/training, and had to return to base still carrying ordnance. One Tornado refueled successfully, flew the mission, and was shot down in combat. Flight Captain Mario Bichirloni, POW.

17 January 1991, Kuwaiti Combat Loss # 1: **A-4KU**.

NON-COMBAT LOSSES

19 January 1991, Saudi Non-Combat Loss # 1: **Tornado**. Crew okay.

20 January 1991, British Non-Combat Loss # 1: **Tornado GR.Mk 1** ZD893/AG, No. 20 Squadron. Squadron Leader Peter Batson, pilot, Wing Commander Mike Heath, navigator, ejected safely suffering minor injuries, were airlifted home 24 January 1991. Suffered control restriction after take-off. Pilot flew around for 1 hr 20 min burning off fuel, jettisoned eight 1,000-lb and made two landing attempts. Crew then ejected.

13 February 1991, Saudi Non-Combat Loss # 2: **F-15C**, No. 6 Squadron, Khamis Mushait.

13 February 1991, Saudi Combat Loss # 1: **F-5E**, No. 17 Squadron, Tabuk. Pilot okay.

Kills and Losses

US PREWAR LOSSES

29 August 1990:
C-5A 68-0228, 60th MAW Ramstein AB, Germany. Thirteen killed, four survivors.

3 September 1990:
F-16C block 25 83-1151, 33rd TFS/363rd TFW(P), Sharjah, UAE. Captain Richard Setzer ejected safely. Fire coming from engine had been observed by wingman.

30 September 1990:
F-15E 87-0203, 336th TFS/4th TFW. Major Peter S. Hook and Captain James B. Poulet killed.

8 October 1990:
RF-4C 64-1044, 106th TRS/117th TRW (AL ANG). Major Barry K. Henderson and Major Stephen G. Schramm killed.
UH-1N 160178 and **UH-1N** 160622, HMLA-267. Eight killed.

11 October 1990:
F-111F 74-0183, 45th TFS/48th TFW. Captain Thomas R. Caldwell and Captain Frederick A. Reid killed.

24 November 1990:
CH-53E 161393, HMH-465.

US NON-COMBAT LOSSES

20 January 1991, Non-Combat Loss # 1:
UH-60. One crew killed, Staff Sergeant Galand V. Haily, 37, of Baltimore, Maryland.

20 January 1991, Non-Combat Loss # 2:
AH-64A. Crew okay.

22 January 1991, Non-Combat Loss # 3:
AV-8B. First Lieutenant Manuel Rivera, Jr, 31, of Bronx, NY, killed.

22 January 1991, Non-Combat Loss # 4:
AH-1. Crew recovered safely.

24 January 1991, Non-Combat Loss # 5:
F/A-18, USS *Theodore Roosevelt* (CVN-71). Pilot okay.

26 January 1991, Non-Combat Loss # 6:
A-7E 158830, VA-72, took barricade; stripped it and shoved it over the side.

29 January 1991, Non-Combat Loss # 7:
OH-58. Crew okay.

2 February 1991, Non-Combat Loss # 8:
AH-1J, HMA-775. Non-combat escort mission in Saudi Arabia, crew of two killed. (Marine Corps) Major Eugene T. McCarthy, 35, of Brooklyn, NY, a graduate of Annapolis, a Reservist and helicopter pilot. Captain Johnathan R. Edwards, 34, of Terrace Park, Ohio.

3 February 1991, Non-Combat Loss # 9:
B-52G, 4300th PBW, Diego Garcia (42nd BMW Loring). Lost to mechanical causes in the Indian Ocean returning from a mission. Three rescued, one confirmed dead, two missing. Massive electrical failure during landing approach at Diego Garcia.

3 February 1991, Non-Combat Loss # 10:
UH-1, HMLA-369. Crew killed: Captain James K. Thorp, 30, of Valley Station, Kentucky; Captain David R. Herr, Jr, 28, of Fort Worth, Texas; Corporal Albert G. Haddad, Jr, 22, of Denton, Texas; Corporal Kurt A. Benz, 22, of Garden City, Michigan.

6/7 February 1991, Non-Combat Loss # 11:
UH-1. One killed, four injured. Army.

7 February 1991, Non-Combat Loss # 12:
F-18. Carrier-based, lost in Persian Gulf while returning to carrier.

15 February 1991, Non-Combat Loss # 13:
A-6E, 155602. Cracked up on deck of USS *America* (CV-66). Pushed over side after hydraulic failure. Crew ejected and aircraft was hanging over side. Crew safe.

16 February 1991, Non-Combat Loss # 14:
F-16C block 25 84-1379, 17th TFS. Captain Dale Thomas Cormier, 30, of Crystal Lake, Illinois, killed.

20 February 1991, Non-Combat Loss # 15:
CH-46E.

US NON-COMBAT LOSSES (continued)

20 February 1991, Non-Combat Loss # 16:
UH-60. Crew killed: Captain Charles W. Cooper, 33, of St Charles, Illinois; CWO Michael F. Anderson, 36, of Frankfurt, Indiana; Sergeant Major Patrick R. Hurley, 37, of New Douglas, Illinois; Master Sergeant Elroy A. Rodrigues, 34, of Key West, Florida; Master Sergeant Otto F. Clark, 35, of Corinth, NY; Sergeant Christopher J. Chapman, 25, of Charlotte, NC; Sergeant Mario Vega Velasquez, 35, of Ponce, Puerto Rico.

21 February 1991, Non-Combat Loss # 17:
F-16. Flamed out during refueling; pilot ejected and was rescued.

21 February 1991, Non-Combat Loss # 18:
CH-46E. Crash landed and burned.

22 February 1991, Non-Combat Loss # 19:
SH-60B.

22 February 1991, Non-Combat Loss # 20:
UH-46D, HC-8 Det 3. Ditched in Persian Gulf. PO3C James F. Crockford, 30, of Venice, California, killed.

25 February 1991, Non-Combat Loss # 21:
CH-46E 154845, HMM-161.

[25 February 1991?] Non-Combat Loss # 22:
OV-10. Crew okay.

US POSTWAR LOSSES

1 March 1991, Postwar Loss # 1:
CH-47, 159th Aviation Battalion, 24th Infantry Division. Crew killed: Major Marie Rossi, 32, of Oradell, NJ, pilot; CWO Robert Hughes, 35, of Vernon, CT, copilot; SPC William C. Brace, 24, of Fountain Hill, PA; Staff Sergeant Mike A. Garrett, 31, of Laurel, Mississippi. Flew into microwave tower. Two days earlier, Rossi had been the subject of TV film footage as one of many helicopter pilots supporting the 101st Airborne Division drive into Iraq. She was the highest-ranking American killed in action.

2 March 1991, Postwar Loss # 2:
UH-1. Army; four injured.

6 March 1991, Postwar Loss # 3:
AH-1J, HMA-775. Two injured.

8 March 1991, Postwar Losses # 4 and # 5:
F/A-18C. F/A-18C midair. Marine Corps non-combat midair collision. Both pilots rescued.

13 March 1991, Postwar Loss # 6:
F-16. Pilot rescued.

13 March 1991, Postwar Loss # 7:
UH-60. US Army. Six killed.

19 March 1991, Postwar Loss # 8:
AV-8B, VMA-331, USS *Nassau* (LHA-4). Crashed in Red Sea; pilot ejected and was rescued.

31 March 1991, Postwar Loss # 9:
RF-4C 64-1056, Alabama ANG aircraft with Reno ANG crew. [RF-4Cs moved from UAE to Bahrain 19 December 1990, when Reno relieved Birmingham.] Captain John Norman, pilot, Captain Jeff Kregel, WSO, ejected safely. Quote from Colonel James F. Brown, 117th TRW commander: "64-1056 went into the Gulf [on 31 March 1991]. They had a [bleed air] duct failure and a catastrophic engine failure right after take-off [from Bahrain?]. Six minutes after take-off they punched out of it. Good choice – they stayed in it about four minutes too long. It's resting in 10 to 60 ft of water and they're not going to recover it."

Glossary

AAA	Anti-Aircraft Artillery	**CBU**	Cluster-Bomb Unit	
AAM	Anti-Aircraft Missile	**CENTAF**	CENTral Air Force	
AB	Air Base	**Comint**	Communications intelligence	
ACM	Air Combat Maneuvering	**CRAF**	Civilian Reserve Air Fleet	
AGM	Air-to-Ground Missile	**DoD**	Department of Defense	
AIM	Air Intercept Missile	**ECM**	Electronic CounterMeasures	
ALARM	Air-Launched Anti-Radiation Missile	**Elint**	Electronic intelligence	
AMRAAM	Advanced Medium-Range Air-to-Air Missile	**EMCON**	EMission CONtrol	
AOC-in-C	Air Operations Commander-in-Chief	**ESM**	Electronic Support Measures	
APC	Armored Personnel Carrier	**EW**	Electronic Warfare	
ASARS	Advanced Synthetic Aperture Radar System	**FAC**	Forward Air Control	
ATO	Air Tasking Order	**FARP**	Forward Air-Refueling Point	
AVM	Air Vice Marshal	**FOL**	Forward Operating Location	
AWACS	Airborne Warning And Control System	**GBU**	Guided Bomb Unit	
BDA	Bomb Damage Assessment	**GPS**	Global Positioning System	
BLU	Bomb Live Unit	**HARM**	High-speed Anti-Radiation Missile	
BN	Bomber/Navigator	**HAS**	Hardened Aircraft Shelter	
CAG	Carrier Air Group commander	**HAV**	High Asset Value	
CAP	Combat Air Patrol	**HAVCAP**	High Asset Value Combat Air Patrol	
CAS	Close Air Support	**HOT**	Haut subsonique Optiquement téléguide tiré d'un Tube	
		HUD	Head-Up Display	
		IFF	Identification Friend or Foe	
		INS	Inertial Navigation System	
		IP	Initial Point	
		IS	Intelligence Specialist	
		J-STARS	Joint Surveillance Target Attack Radar System	

KAF	Kuwait Air Force	**SLAR**	Side-Looking Airborne Radar
LANTIRN	Low-Altitude, Navigation and Targetting, Infra-Red, for Night	**SSM**	Surface-to-Surface Missile
		STOL	Short Take-Off and Landing
LGB	Laser-Guided Bomb	**TAC**	Tactical Air Command
LOROP	LOng-Range Oblique Photography	**TALD**	Tactical Air-Launched Decoy
MAC	Military Airlift Command	**TARPS**	Tactical Air Reconnaissance Pod System
MAG	Military Air Group		
MAW	Military Air Wing	**TENCAP**	Tactical Exploitation of National CAPabilities
MEB	Marine Expeditionary Brigade		
MEF	Marine Expeditionary Force	**TFR**	Terrain-Following Radar
MoD	Ministry of Defence	**TIALD**	Thermal Imaging And Laser Designation
MRE	Meals, Ready to Eat		
NBC	Nuclear, Biological, Chemical	**TID**	Tactical Information Display
PGB	Precision-Guided Bomb	**TOT**	Time on Target
POL	Petrol-Oil-Lubricant	**TOW**	Tube-launched, Optically-sighted, Wire-guided
RAF	Royal Air Force		
RHAW	Radar Homing And Warning	**TRAM**	Target Recognition and Attack, Multisensor
RHWR	Radar Homing Warning Receiver		
RIO	Radar Intercept Officer	**UAE**	United Arab Emirates
RSAF	Royal Saudi Air Force	**USAF**	United States Air Force
RWR	Radar Warning Receiver	**USAFE**	United States Air Forces in Europe
SAC	Strategic Air Command	**USMC**	United States Marine Corps
SAM	Surface-to-Air Missile	**USN**	United States Navy
SAR	Search and Rescue	**V/STOL**	Vertical/Short Take-Off and Landing
SAR	Synthetic Aperture Radar	**WSO**	Weapons Systems Officer
SEAD	Suppression of Enemy Air Defenses		
Sigint	Signals intelligence		
SLAM	Stand-off Land Attack Missile		

INDEX

Picture credits

The publishers would like to thank the following for their help in supplying photographs.

The following individuals and organisations are abbreviated as follows:

Associated Press: AP
Yves Debay: YD
Robert F. Dorr: RFD
Peter B. Mersky: PBM
William J. Mondy: WJM

Press Association: PA
SIPA Press: SIPA
Frank Spooner Pictures: Spooner
US Department of Defense: DoD

Front cover: PH3 Chester O. Falkenhainer USN via PBM; PBM. **6:** AP, SIPA (two). **7:** Bob Archer, SIPA. **8:** Spooner, SIPA (two). **10:** Rex Features, AP. **11:** AP (two), Steven Cooper, Mark Hasara via RFD. **12:** Sqn Ldr Tony Paxton, Steven Cooper, AP. **13:** PBM (three). **14:** MoD. **15:** Sqn Ldr Tony Paxton, MoD (two), PBM. **16:** MoD, AP, DoD, RFD. **17:** DoD (two). **18-19:** PBM. **20:** PBM, Lt Cdr Dave Parsons via PBM, PBM. **21:** PBM (three). **22:** WJM, R.L. Ward, YD, Anderson (two). **23:** YD (two), DoD. **24:** WJM, David Donald, Sqn Ldr Tony Paxton (two), YD. **25:** Spooner. **26:** PBM, YD. **27:** DoD, WJM, Sqn Ldr Tony Paxton (three), DoD. **28:** via RFD, Capt. Andrew Hall USMC, via PBM. **29:** Lt Col. Leif Larsen (two), Carl E. Jones, DoD, YD. **30:** Tim Ripley, YD. **31:** YD, Sygma, YD (two), AP. **32:** Sygma (two), Dassault. **33:** YD (three), Sygma, Spooner. **34:** Dassault, YD. **35:** YD. **36:** Marco Amatimaggio. **37:** WJM, DoD, SIRPA, Bob Archer. **38:** DoD, YD, via Tim Ripley. **39:** YD (two), DoD (three), AP. **40:** AP, DoD, David Donald. **41:** via Tim Ripley, David Donald, Bob Archer. **42:** MoD, DoD (two), AP. **43:** AP (two), DoD. **44:** YD, RAF News, DoD via RFD, DoD. **45:** Marco Amatimaggio, PBM, J.R. Lowe, YD. **46:** Bob Archer, DoD, Mark Hasara via RFD, PBM. **48:** Pacemaker Press. **49:** Popperfoto, DoD (three), AP. **50:** Flt Lt Mike Lumb, AP, DoD (two). **51:** DoD (two), PBM. **52- 53:** DoD. **54:** RJF, DoD. **56:** Pacemaker Press, PA. **57:** Flt Lt Mike Lumb, Wg Cdr Mike Heath. **58-61:** PBM. **62:** PBM. **63:** PBM, DoD. **64:** DoD (two). **65:** DoD, 48th TFW, MSgt Lee Hincher via Bob Archer. **66:** DoD, Capt. Bob Thompson via Bob Archer. **68:** DoD (two), via RFD, Flt Lt Ian Price via Bob Archer. **69:** David Donald (three). **70-71:** PBM. **72:** Wg Cdr Mike Heath, Tim Ripley, DoD, PBM. **73:** RAF News, RDD, Steven Cooper, PBM. **74:** DoD (11), René J. Francillon (two), Tim Ripley. **75:** Michael M. Anselmo. **76-77:** PBM. **78:** DoD, AP. **79:** PBM, DoD (two). **80:** Gary Frederick via RFD, Richard Mullen. **81:** Richard Mullen, PBM. **82:** via RFD (two), Lt Col. Leif Larsen. **83:** PBM, Anderson (three), via Lt Col. Leif Larsen. **84:** DoD, Spooner. **85:** Sygma, AP (two), DoD (two). **86:** DoD, Anderson. **87:** Anderson, DoD. **88:** YD, Spooner. **89:** YD, DoD. **90:** PBM, Debra Millett via RFD. **91:** DoD (two), RFD. **92:** DoD (three), Pacemaker Press. **93:** DoD. **94:** RFD, SIPA. **95:** SIPA. **96-97:** PBM. **98:** PBM. **99:** Becky Colan via PBM. **100:** John Leenhouts via RFD, PBM. **102:** PBM, DoD. **103:** PBM (two). **104:** DoD, Gamma, PBM, Jeff Stout via RFD, Mark Hasara via RFD. **105:** Tim Ripley (two), Wg Cdr Mike Heath. **106:** DoD via Tim Ripley, AP. **107:** DoD (two). **108:** DoD. **109:** Bob Archer, PBM, DoD. **110:** Sygma, SIRPA, Spooner. **111:** Dassault, Aerospace, YD. **112:** SIRPA (two), Steve Hampson via Tom Ross, Spooner. **113:** Spooner, Bob Archer (two), SIRPA (two). **114-115:** Canadian Department of National Defense via Jeff Rankin-Lowe. **117:** DoD via Aerospace (four), Mark Hasara via Jim Rotramel. **118-119:** Tim Ripley. **120:** David Donald, Dave Fry. **121:** Dave Fry (two), Bob Archer, Terry Senior via Jon Lake, YD. **122:** Spooner, RFD, David Donald. **123:** Gamma/Spooner. **124:** DoD (three), South Carolina ANG (two). **125:** DoD (two). **126:** DoD (four), RFD, Werner Münzenmaier (two). **127:** RFD (two), Werner Münzenmaier (two). **128:** DoD via RFD, Lewis (three). **129:** Lewis, David Donald, Tom Ross, AP. **130:** PA, Popperfoto/Reuter. **131:** Sqn Ldr Mike Rondot (two), Gamma/Spooner, PA. **132-3:** Sqn Ldr Mike Rondot. **134:** Dave Parsons via PBM, PH2 Todd P. Chichonowitz via PBM, PBM. **135:** PH2 William Lipski via PBM. **136:** Dave Parsons via PBM (two), John Leenhouts via PBM. **137:** via PBM, John Leenhouts via PBM. **138:** DoD (two), Sygma, Michael M. Anselmo. **139:** Sqn Ldr Mike Rondot, MoD. **140:** Patrick H.F. Allen. **141:** Patrick H.F. Allen (four), PBM. **142-143:** Mike Menth via PBM. **144:** Sqn Ldr Mike Rondot, PA (two). **146:** via RFD, John Leenhouts via RFD. **147:** John Leenhouts via RFD (two), DoD, Werner Münzenmaier (two). **149:** MSgt Kit Thompson, Popperfoto. **150:** Popperfoto/Reuter. **151:** Gamma/Spooner (two), SIRPA, Aérospatiale. **152:** PA. **153:** Wg Cdr Mike Heath, PA, Pacemaker Press. **154:** Wg Cdr Mike Heath. **155:** R.L. Ward (two). **156:** R.L. Ward, Flt Lt Mike Lumb. **157:** Wg Cdr Mike Heath, Steve Hampson via Tom Ross, Sqn Ldr Mike Rondot. **158:** Military Scene, AP, Sygma. **159:** PA, Sygma (two), YD. **160:** DoD (two). **161:** Lt Col William Bryan (two), YD. **162:** Capt. Andrew Hall USMC, Richard Mullen. **163:** Bill Delaney via RFD (four), Capt. Andrew Hall USMC. **164:** Capt. Andrew Hall USMC (two), Bill Delaney via RFD. **165:** Carl E. Jones III. **166:** via Tim Ripley (two), DoD. **167:** YD (two), DoD (five), Sqn Ldr Tony Paxton, WJM (two), Paul Jackson. **168:** Richard Mullen (two), Tim Ripley. **169:** DoD (two), Richard Mullen, Tim Ripley. **170-1:** DoD. **172:** US Coast Guard via RFD, Dan Holzrichter (two). **173:** DoD, Capt. Andrew Hall USMC, YD, Dan Holzrichter. **174-5:** DoD. **176:** DoD, Wallace T. van Winkle, DoD via Tim Ripley, PBM. **177:** DoD, Sygma, YD. **178:** DoD, Werner Münzenmaier. **179:** Tim Ripley, DoD, Jim Dunn (two). **180:** DoD (two), via RFD. **181:** AP, YD (two). **182:** DoD, Grumman. **183:** AP (two), PBM, Sygma. **190:** WJM, Stuart Lewis. **191:** PBM, DoD. **192:** DoD (two), L.B. Sides, Bob Archer. **193:** David Donald, Bob Archer (two), DoD. **194:** AP, DoD (two). **195:** DoD (two), Richard Mullen (two). **196:** Bob Archer, David Donald, DoD, WJM. **197:** YD, AP, Sqn Ldr Tony Paxton. **198:** DoD, PBM. **199:** PBM, John Leenhouts via RFD, Bob Archer, Stuart Lewis, David Donald. **200:** DoD (three), PBM. **201:** Michael M. Anselmo, DoD (three), Richard Mullen (two). **202:** PBM, D. McMullen via Lt Col. Leif Larsen, David Donald, Capt. Andrew Hall USMC. **203:** DoD, PBM, Jim Dunn, Richard Mullen (two), YD. **204:** MoD, Paul Jackson, Dave Parsons via PBM, Phil Williams. **205:** Bob Archer, David Donald, Dave Fry, Steven Cooper. **206:** MoD (two), Sqn Ldr Mike Rondot. **207:** DoD (two), Phil Williams, Canadian Department of National Defense via Jeff Rankin-Lowe. **208:** Andrew H. Cline, Jeff Rankin-Lowe, Spooner, Paul Jackson, WJM. **209:** SIRPA (two), Sygma, Popperfoto. **210:** Steven Cooper, Paul Jackson (two), Sqn Ldr Tony Paxton. **211:** DoD, WJM, Wg Cdr Mike Heath. **212:** WJM, PBM, Spooner. **213:** DoD (two), Capt Carl E. Jones, Jim Rotramel, PBM. **214:** Lewis, William B. Folsom, David Donald. **215:** DoD (two), R.L. Ward, PBM. **216:** DoD (three), Sqn Ldr Mike Rondot, Jim Rotramel. **217:** DoD (two), D. McMullen via Lt Col. Leif Larsen, Flt Lt Mike Lumb. **218:** DoD (three), YD, Dan Holzrichter, WJM. **219:** Denis J. Calvert, Paul Jackson, Sqn Ldr Mike Rondot, Stuart Lewis, DoD, Jeff Stout via RFD. **220:** Dassault, R.L. Ward, DoD, MoD, RDD, Jeff Rankin-Lowe. **221:** DoD, DoD via Tim Ripley, SIRPA, Tim Ripley, Anderson, YD, DoD via PBM. **222:** Wg Cdr Mike Heath (three), R.L. Ward (eight), Jon Lake (two). **223:** Jon Lake (five), Wg Cdr Mike Heath (three), PBM, R.L. Ward, David Donald (three). **224:** Flt Lt Mike Lumb (two), R.L. Ward (four), Wg Cdr Mike Heath (four), David Donald (two). **225:** David Donald, Jon Lake (four), Flt Lt Mike Lumb, Lindsay Peacock (five). **Back cover:** PA, R.L. Ward, PH2 Todd P. Cichonowicz via PBM, DoD, DoD via RFD.